Windows 95 Power Toolkit

Cutting-Edge Tools & Techniques for Programmers

Windows 95 Power Toolkit

Cutting-Edge Tools & Techniques for Programmers

Richard Mansfield
Evangelos Petroutsos

VENTANA

Windows 95 Power Toolkit: Cutting-Edge Tools & Techniques for Programmers

Library of Congress Cataloging-in-Publication Data

Mansfield, Richard.
     Windows 95 power toolkit : cutting-edge tools & techniques for programmers / Richard Mansfield, Evangelos Petroutsos.
          p.   cm.
     Includes index.
     ISBN 1-56604-319-0
     1. Microsoft Windows (Computer file) 2. Operating systems (Computers)   I. Petroutsos, Evangelos. II. Title.
     QA76.76.063M3545 1996
     005.4'3—dc20   95-49559
                                                              CIP

First Edition 9 8 7 6 5 4 3 2 1
Printed in the United States of America

Ventana Communications Group, Inc.
P.O. Box 13964
Research Triangle Park, NC 27709-3964
919/544-9404
FAX 919/544-9472

Limits of Liability and Disclaimer of Warranty

Trademarks

About the Authors

Richard Mansfield's books have sold more than 400,000 copies worldwide. He was editor-in-chief of *Compute* magazine for seven years. His published work includes columns on computer topics, magazine articles, and several short stories. He is coauthor of *The Windows 95 Book* (Ventana). He is author of *Machine Language for Beginners* (Compute Press) and *The Visual Guide to Visual Basic for Windows* (Ventana), and 17 other computer books. He recently coauthored *The Visual Basic 4.0 Power Toolkit* (Ventana).

Evangelos Petroutsos received his master's degree in Computer Engineering from the University of California in 1982. He was a computer analyst at the California Institute of Technology for five years, before becoming an independent programming consultant for various companies including MCI and Infonet. He recently coauthored *The Visual Basic 4.0 Power Toolkit* (Ventana).

Acknowledgments

Our gratitude to the talented staff at Ventana Communications, particularly Neweleen Trebnik, Jessica Ryan, Marcia Webb, John Cotterman, Scott Hosa, Bradley King, and Pam Richardson. We would also like to thank Brian Little for his excellent technical review and Lisa Bucki for her helpful editing. We would like to thank Charles Brannon for his contribution of Chapter 6.

Dedication

Evangelos Petroutsos dedicates this book to Helen and Peter.
Richard Mansfield dedicates this book to Richard Earl Biggs.

Contents

Introduction

After the immense wave of books on Windows 95 hit the stores in August 1995, we noticed a strange gap. Something was clearly missing: there were no books covering advanced topics for the general reader.

Hundreds of titles covered Windows 95 for the beginner. A handful of highly technical books targeted programmers and technicians. But what about the average computer user who wants to go beyond the basics? What about people who already know how to use the Explorer, but want solid advice on using the dynamic System Monitor charts to optimize their hard drives? What about those who aren't computer scientists, but nevertheless want to understand and edit the new Windows 95 Registry? Of course some of the more elementary books touched on advanced topics. For example, some books mention the Registry briefly. However, in this book we devote two chapters to it.

In other words, we felt that there was a need for a book on sophisticated Windows 95 topics, written in clear, plain English so anyone could understand it—and use it to customize and optimize his or her computer.

We've taken pains to answer that need in this book. We avoid the techno-speak that all too often makes books on advanced computer subjects incomprehensible to the ordinary reader. We explore complex subjects and involved techniques, but by providing thorough explanations, numerous examples, and many step-by-step descriptions—we hope to ensure that even a beginner can follow along and achieve the desired results.

WHAT'S INSIDE

Chapter 1, "Windows 95: An Overview," begins with an exploration of the essential differences between Windows 3.1 and Windows 95: the new philosophy, the new techniques, and all the improvements. This chapter is designed for anyone who has just installed Windows 95 and wants to get up to speed quickly. We illustrate the new 3D look and explain its significance beyond its mere attractiveness; discuss in depth the new tools—special icons, the taskbar, Explorer, Shortcuts, Quick View, the right mouse button, and so on; explain docucentricity; and provide a complete table of operating system and application keyboard shortcuts.

Chapter 2, "The Registry," is an in-depth study of the Registry, which is a 600-page database that contains considerable information about the current state and history of the computer, and the user or users of that computer. The Registry is similar in function to Autoexec.bat, Config.sys, Win.ini, and System.ini, but far larger and far more useful. This is the first of the two chapters devoted to the Registry. It begins with an overview—a map of the main sections of the Registry. We explain how to manipulate your computing environment by understanding the zones and data within the Registry: how to change passwords, how to set icon preferences, and much more. We also illustrate how to work with Windows 95's Registry-management tools: Regedit and Poledit. Learn about the Registry and you're well on your way to mastery of your machine.

Chapter 3, "Extreme Customization," takes you deeper into the Registry, where you'll learn to customize your computer in ways that are not possible outside the Registry. You will find many practical examples, as well as discussions of the most important new features of the Windows 95 user interface, including shortcuts, shortcut menus, and file associations.

We also discuss the object-oriented nature of the Windows 95 user interface. As intuitive as the Windows 95 user interface is, a better understanding of the various objects you'll be working with will help you create an operating system that works your way. The Windows 95 user interface can be customized both cosmetically and functionally in ways that were not possible in earlier versions of Windows. We have attempted to cover all aspects of customization and, at the same time, provide a better understanding of the way Windows 95 works, by explaining the most important aspects of its object-oriented structure.

Chapter 4, "Tuning Up Windows," investigates all the ways you can fine-tune and optimize key peripherals under Windows 95. This includes time-savers that will increase your efficiency, along with various ways to maximize your system's performance. You'll learn how to install and cleanly uninstall applications; ways to keep your disk drives in good shape and running at top speed; and optimizing your swap file. You'll also learn about shortcut launching, printer management, disk compression, and more.

Chapter 5, "Communicating With the World," and Chapter 6, "It's a Wired World," deal with computer communications. Windows 95 was designed from the ground up to optimize communication. Chapter 5 covers the communications tools that come with Windows 95 and will show you how to use your computer to dial other computers and online services with your modem. We also show you how to connect to the Internet and how to build networks over the Internet, for the cost of a local phone call. This is known as *Internetworking* and we believe it will become quite popular in the near future.

Chapter 6 deals with networking—interconnecting computers to share files and printers, bringing together colleagues for enhanced communication and collaboration. Here you'll find all the information you need to attach your computer to a local area network. You'll find a thorough discussion of workgroup computing, the ideal way for teams and departments to work together more productively. You'll learn how to set up one or more workgroups within your company and how to manage those workgroups.

Because Windows workgroups aren't administered centrally, you should know how to share and how to protect your devices and disk(s) when you make them available to other users of the workgroup. Chapter 6 explores the Windows 95 tools for workgroup and remote computing, covers dial-up networking from a network's point of view, and provides an excellent starting point for those who want to set up a small network, or make the most of a network they may already be using.

Most major applications contain built-in *languages*—sets of commands that you can use to teach the application to behave in ways never imagined by its designers. In Chapter 7, "Customizing Applications," we'll explore numerous step-by-step examples to learn how to personalize your applications. We've also attempted to make the various examples useful in real-world situations, so you'll not only learn programming, but also can benefit from using the example programs in your everyday work. Clearly explained programming techniques will help you make the most of your Office 95 applications. Plus you'll find a brief introduction to OLE techniques that can make your applications work with each other the way you want. If you've ever been curious about computer programming, this chapter is a good place to start exploring.

Chapter 8, "Compound Documents & OLE," deals with inter-application communication. We'll show you how to make the Office 95 applications work together with a technique called Object Linking and Embedding (OLE). You'll also learn about embedding and in-place editing, a technique that lets you use the features of one application from within another one (using Excel's tools from within Word, for example). OLE also lets you link documents to other documents, so that every time one of them is edited, all linked documents are updated automatically.

In the second half of this chapter you'll find out how to program OLE operations to automate tasks that involve multiple documents, created in different applications. If you prepare Word reports based on Excel data, for example, you'll find out how to program Word and automatically create the reports from within Excel, without even opening Word. You'll also learn how to use SQL (Structured Query Language, pronounced "sequel") statements to extract the data you need from, for example, an Access database and move it into an Excel worksheet.

We hope that you'll enjoy the tips, techniques, and advanced topics covered in this book. We tried—through extended, clearly written tutorials—to demystify areas of Windows 95 that have traditionally been considered the domain of only people with advanced technical skills. Our goal was to make these useful techniques available to everyone. We wrote this book to allow anyone to take Windows 95 to the edge.

Richard Mansfield
Evangelos Petroutsos

Chapter 1

Windows 95: An Overview

It's been years since, in May 1990, Windows 3.0 took the computing world by storm. Windows is now by far the dominant way that people interact with computers. Estimates place its nearest rival, the Macintosh, at a 10 percent share of the personal computer market, with other operating systems such as UNIX and OS/2 in the single digits. Windows is the operating system on more than eight out of ten computers.

There are, of course, good reasons why Windows has been so overwhelmingly popular, but something good can always be improved. The programmers, designers, and artists at Microsoft haven't been idle for the past six years. They have made many enhancements to Windows, both visible and invisible.

In this chapter, we'll explore the essential differences between Windows 3.1 and Windows 95: the new philosophy, the new techniques, and all the improvements.

We'll assume that you know in general how a computer with a graphical user interface works, but that you're interested in an overview of Windows 95 in particular. This chapter should get you up and running under this exciting new operating system in short order.

THE NEW LOOK

The first thing most people notice is that Windows 95 is more attractive than earlier graphical user interfaces (GUI) such as Windows 3.1. The primary enhancement is added *depth*—a 3D, sculpted look has been added to virtually all the features and elements within Windows 95. Compare Figure 1-1 with Figure 1-2: Windows 3.1 is essentially two-dimensional, while Windows 95 appears etched, embossed, and otherwise three-dimensional—more like real objects.

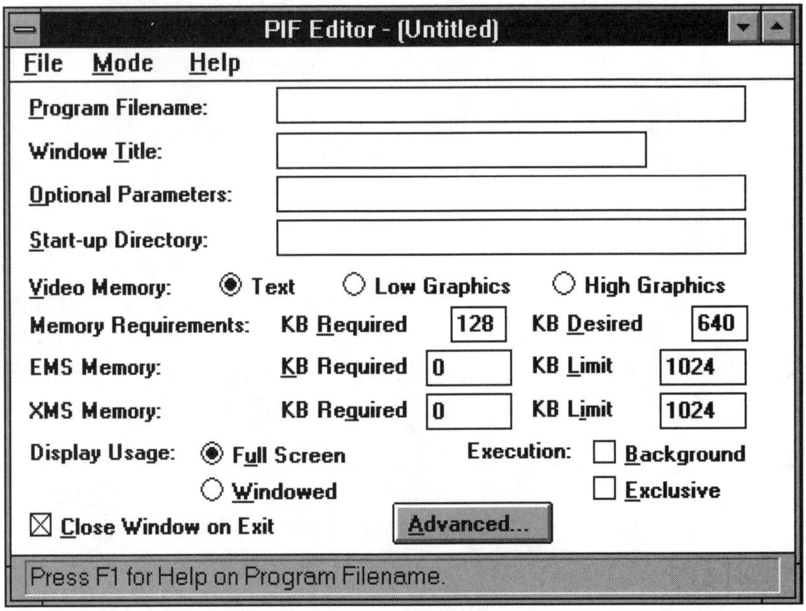

Figure 1-1: Windows 3.1 is essentially *flat* looking—there's little highlighting or shading.

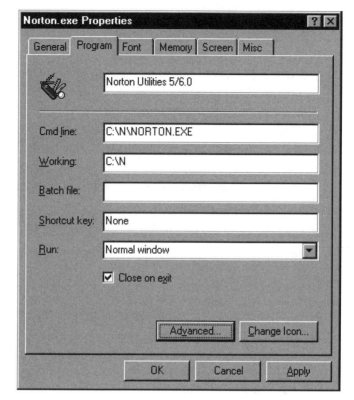

Windows 95 has a new look that's both attractive and, ultimately, more efficient for the user.

Figure 1-2: Windows 95 appears etched, embossed, and otherwise *dimensional*—more like objects in real life.

As you can see in the previous two figures, the Windows 3.1 look is fundamentally two-color; it's monochromatic like a simple text document. Windows 95, by contrast, has additional layers— superimposition and added visual cues. This new look is the result of considerable usability testing by Microsoft and of many interviews with focus groups. But there's more to the new appearance of the Windows 95 interface than just glamour, more than just its handsome appearance. People get important cues from dimension as well as from color.

Doubtless few choose to turn off the 3D effect.

Some applications designed to run under Windows 3.1 did have some 3D effects but offered an option that allowed you to turn off the 3D effects, though why you would ever want to is a mystery. Figure 1-3 shows Word for Windows 6.0 with the 3D Dialog and Display Effects option turned off. Figure 1-4 shows the default with Windows 95-style shading turned back on. This choice disappeared in Word 7.0, which was designed for Windows 95, so the word processor now always looks sculpted.

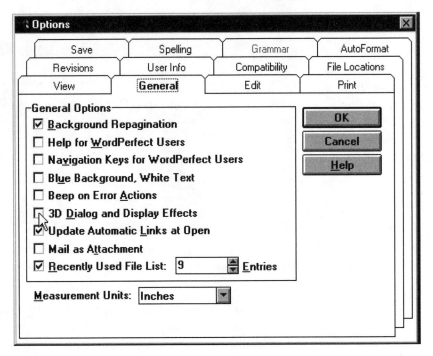

Figure 1-3: In some applications written for Windows 3.1, you can choose the option of turning off 3D shading. But why would you?

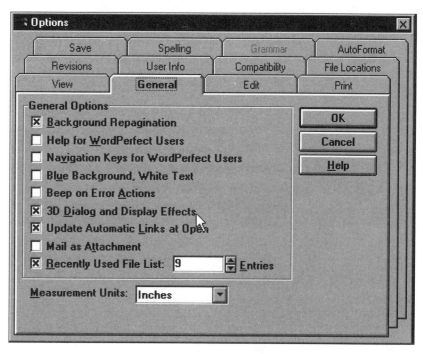

Figure 1-4: Three-dimensional shading is so much better looking (as well as more efficient) that nearly everyone will leave it on.

The User Interface

When you look at Windows 95, you're seeing a completely re-designed surface. Figure 1-5 illustrates many of the features that make Windows 95 both new and effective.

Windows 95 retains familiar features from Windows 3.1: the Desktop, icons, windows, and so on. If you're new to Windows 95, you won't be confused. You still launch programs by double-clicking on their icons, you can still drag things around, and all your familiar programs will still run.

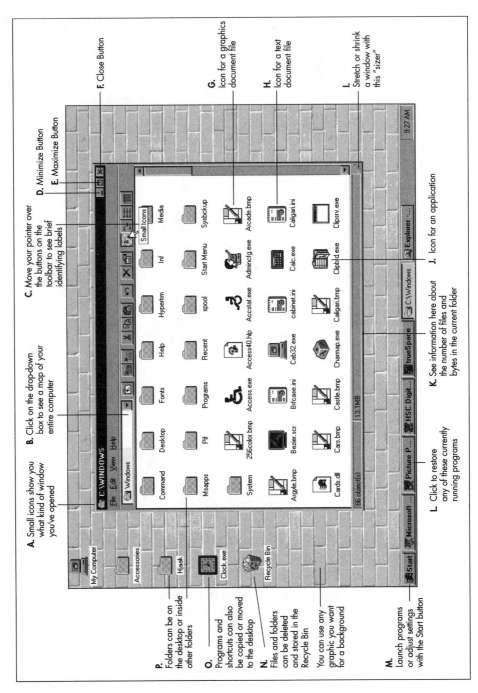

Figure 1-5: Many of the new interface features.

A. Small icons show you what kind of window you've opened

B. Click on the drop-down box to see a map of your entire computer

C. Move your pointer over the buttons on the toolbar to see brief identifying labels

D. Minimize Button

E. Maximize Button

F. Close Button

G. Icon for a graphics document file

H. Icon for a text document file

I. Stretch or shrink a window with this "size"

J. Icon for an application

K. See information here about the number of files and bytes in the current folder

L. Click to restore any of these currently running programs

M. Launch programs or adjust settings with the Start button

N. You can use any graphic you want for a background

Files and folders can be deleted and stored in the Recycle Bin

O. Programs and shortcuts can also be copied or moved to the desktop

P. Folders can be on the desktop or inside other folders

However, many new elements have been added. The My Computer icon provides a window to the highest overview of your system—the hard drive(s), Control Panel, printer(s), any network, the new Recycle Bin, and any folders (directories) that you've placed on the desktop. The Recycle Bin icon opens a folder on your hard drive where deleted files and folders are kept (until you empty the Bin). This provides a kind of file recovery should you change your mind about a deletion. The taskbar contains icons for all currently running programs (discussed in detail later). Directories are now called, as you may have noticed, *folders*. And there's the new Explorer, a replacement for the File Manager and Program Manager in previous versions of Windows. We'll devote a whole section below to this new feature. And there are many additional changes—some major, some minor—as we'll see throughout this chapter.

TIP

Windows 95 uses the term *folder* for what has been called a *directory* on DOS-based computers since the start of personal computing in the late '70s. A subdirectory is now called a *subfolder*. In this book we'll employ this new terminology.

Small Icons

As you can see in Figure 1-5, many new graphics techniques are at work in Windows 95. Here's an overview, starting from the top left of Figure 1-5 and moving clockwise. In several of its zones, Windows 95 uses small icons (25 percent as large as regular-size icons). The title bar of each opened Window contains a small icon, a reduced version of its regular-size icon in addition to the regular text title. In the case of a folder, the icon is a tiny folder. Likewise, you can select to view these small icons rather than the regular-size icons inside your folder or Explorer windows, thereby displaying more icons onscreen at one time. (To view small icons, click on the View menu, and then choose Small Icons.) And, there's even a secret trick in which you can make Windows 95 display a small thumbnail of each .BMP file as the icon, making it really easy to locate what you're looking for. This technique is explained in Chapter 3, "Extreme Customization."

The Toolbar

Toolbars are now pervasive in Windows applications as well as Windows 95 itself.

If you select Toolbar from the View menu (on any folder window or in the Explorer window), you'll see a set of quick-access buttons at the top of the current window, and a drop-down list showing your current general location. You can click on this drop-down list to see the major drives, the Control Panel window, Printer, and other primary elements of your machine. (This list is essentially identical to what you see when you double-click on the My Computer icon on the desktop.) If you want the current window to display the contents of one of these items, just click on its name in the drop-down list.

TIP

Some folder windows might not be wide enough on your screen to display all the icons. To see them, drag the frame of the window (or click on the Maximize button at the top right of the window) to enlarge it.

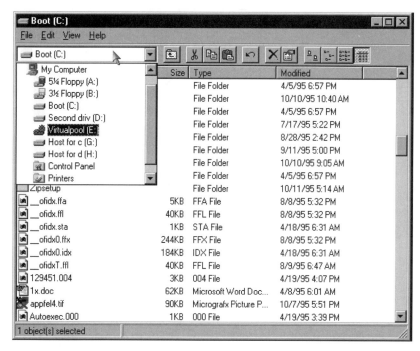

Figure 1-6: Click on the drop-down list on the toolbar and you'll see a map of your computer.

Hovering your mouse pointer (without clicking it) over a toolbar button displays a tool tip, a small label that describes what each button does. The buttons across the toolbar are, from left to right:

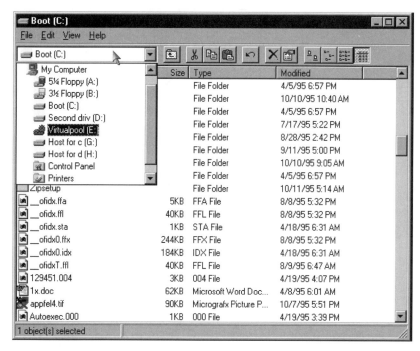 Up one level—takes you up one level in the hierarchy of folders. (Some folders can be inside other folders. For instance, you might have created a folder called "Art" and created two subfolders "Modern" and "Classical" within it.) If you are currently looking at the Modern folder, clicking on this Up one level button displays the "Art" folder contents. Similarly, if you're using the Microsoft Network (MSN), Up one level takes you from your current location to the next higher section in the Network's hierarchy. You can also move to the next level up by pressing the Backspace key.

Cut—allows you to *move* a folder or file from one folder to another. Click on this button, and the current file (the highlighted one) turns gray, indicating it's ready to be moved—that it's on the clipboard now, and no longer in the current folder. Then click on the folder where you want to move the cut file. Now click on the fourth button, Paste, to move the file. You can also move entire folders to new locations this same way. (Keyboard shortcuts for Cut and Paste, Ctrl+X, and Ctrl+V, also work this way.)

Copy—similar to Cut, described above. With Copy, however, when you Paste, the original file or folder stays in its original location, and a new copy is pasted into the target location.

Paste—moves or copies a file or folder to a new location. Puts the contents of the clipboard into the current location. See Cut, and Copy, above.

Undo—enables you to undo a mistake. If you decide that you made an error moving, copying, or deleting a file or folder, click on this button and the action you just took is now undone.

Delete—removes the selected file(s) or folder(s). However, the file or folder is merely moved to a special holding area called the Recycle Bin. If you decide you made a mistake deleting the file or folder, just click on the Undo button. Or, if you decide days or weeks later that you want to recover the file or folder, you can open the Recycle Bin by simply clicking on it and then moving or copying the item to its original location. Every so often you should clean out the Recycle Bin so it doesn't take up too much room on your disk drive. You do this by either moving the contents from the Bin to a floppy disk, for example, or by deleting the contents of the Bin forever by clicking on the Empty Recycle Bin option in the Recycle Bin's File menu.

TIP

You can fully delete something by holding down the Shift key while clicking the toolbar Delete button (the X symbol), or while pressing the Del key, or while dragging something to the Recycle Bin. When you delete while holding down the Shift key, the item is actually deleted, not merely moved to the Recycle Bin. If you right-click on the Recycle Bin icon, you can adjust its various properties. (See the next item.) The Bin size can be limited to a percentage of your hard drive, so it won't become huge should you forget to empty it. You can also choose to refuse to have files moved to the Bin. When you choose that option, files are immediately deleted as if you'd held down the Shift key as described above.

Properties—displays information about the currently selected item (the currently highlighted file or folder). You can display the same information by *right-clicking* (clicking on an item with the right mouse button) on an item, then selecting Properties from the drop-down menu that appears.

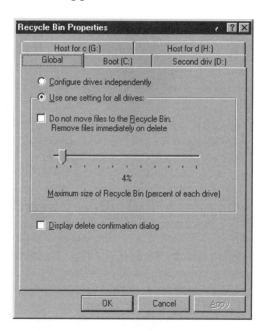

Figure 1-7: In its Properties window, you can adjust the Recycle Bin's behaviors.

Large Icons—displays each folder, program, or document as a regular-size icon.

Small Icons—displays each folder, program, or document as a small icon (25 percent as large as the large icon).

List—similar to the Small Icons option, except all items are displayed in columns, while small icons are displayed from left to right. Also, you cannot permanently rearrange the icons in List view, as you can with Small Icons view.

Look at file details when you need to make some room on your hard drive.

Details—adds descriptions of the size, type, and exact time of the most recent modification, to the small icons and titles displayed for each item.

There are several reasons to look at the details about files on your hard drive. For example, if your disk is getting full, you can see how large your various files are to decide which to remove from the hard drive and store on floppy disks or on a tape backup system, or even which to delete. In addition, you can look at "last modified" to find out which one of the two versions of the same document is the more current and delete the older one.

While in detail view, you can quickly sort the list by any detail header: Name, Type, Size, or Date. You can also select from among the same sorting options from the folder's View menu.

TIP

If you decide to view your files and folders in Details mode, try moving your pointer to the headings above the listed files and folders. When the pointer is near one of the vertical separator lines, it changes to a cross-arrow. If you drag the mouse horizontally (hold down the left button while moving the mouse), you can adjust the width of the various columns of information displayed by the Details option. Note the cursor in Figure 1-8, ready to drag a column. The easiest way to adjust this spacing so all the columns show up onscreen is to start by making enough space for the Name field. Then make enough space for the Size, Type, and Modified fields in that order. If you work from the right side (starting with the Modified field) or just randomly adjust the spacing, you'll find that doing so takes quite a bit longer than if you had started from the left side (where the Name field is located).

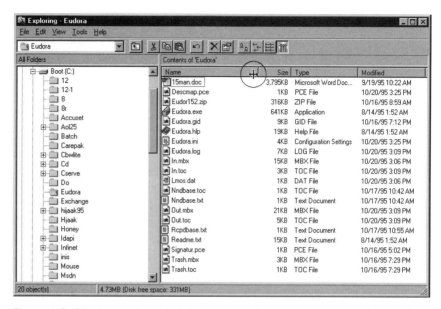

Figure 1-8: Clicking on the Details button reveals statistics about each item. The cursor (circled) changes to a double-arrow indicating you can drag to adjust the column sizes.

Three Important Buttons: The Minimize, Maximize & Close Buttons

The minimize, maximize, and close buttons aren't on the toolbar. Instead, you'll find them in the upper right corner of every window in Windows 95. The left (minimize) button shrinks the window to a small box on the taskbar, which is called *minimizing* the window. The program and whatever document you might be working on remain active: they are merely temporarily invisible. A minimized window is reduced to a button on the taskbar, and you can restore it by simply clicking its button on the taskbar. By minimizing windows, you can park programs that you plan to use again soon but don't want taking up space on the screen just now.

The maximize button (in the middle of these buttons) changes its appearance and function, depending on the current size of the window. In a normal window (one that's not filling the entire screen, but also isn't minimized), you'll notice that the icon is a box with a dark line at the top. Clicking on this icon will *maximize* the window, making it fill the screen. However, when maximized, this button changes to an image of two windows superimposed (see Figure 1-9, left). Click on it now and the window is reduced to the size it normally is—or to whatever size you last adjusted it. (When a window isn't filling the entire screen, you can adjust its size by dragging anywhere on the frame around the window. Move your mouse to the outer edge of the window until it changes to a two-sided arrow. Then press and hold the left mouse button as you move the mouse.)

Figure 1-9: The maximize button changes its appearance. When it looks like the example on the left, clicking it reduces the size of the window. Clicking the button shown on the right fills the screen with the window.

Clicking the close button, the rightmost button of the three that appear on every window (the one that looks like an X), shuts down the window. If the window is a running program, clicking the close button exits the program.

Dragging to Resize Windows

The resizing tab is a new feature now found on the lower right of many windows.

Using the rippled tab in the lower right of windows that are not filling the screen (not maximized) to stretch or shrink the window. (Not all applications have this sizer tab, but you can usually resize any window by dragging its borders or corners.) When you move your pointer onto the sizer, it turns into a diagonal double-arrow. You can drag a window two ways at once (horizontally and vertically at the same time). If a window doesn't have a sizer, you can still move your pointer to the lower right corner and resize it by dragging as if it did have a sizer. Also, a sizer won't appear on the various folder windows unless you've selected the Status Bar option on the View menu.

Status Bar

The *status bar* displays context-sensitive descriptions, messages, and such information as the time, the date, the current page, and so on. Along the bottom of some windows you'll see an area, usually just enough space to display a single line of helpful information. This area is the status bar. Aside from usually displaying a resizing tab, the status bar can contain descriptions of what's currently happening in an application or a window. For instance, in a word processor it can display the current page number, the total number of pages, the line and column, and so on. In a folder window similar to the one shown in Figure 1-10, this area contains descriptions of the purpose of the various menu items as you move your mouse pointer over each item.

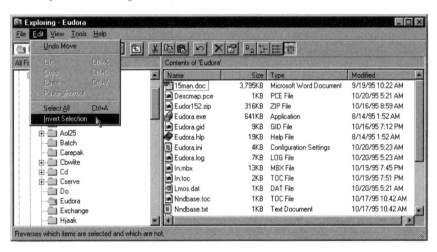

Figure 1-10: With the status bar visible, descriptions of menu items, such as "Reverses which items are selected and which are not" on the status bar in this figure, are displayed there as you move your mouse over each item.

The Taskbar

The taskbar displays buttons for all currently running programs. (You simply single-click an application's button and the application blows back up to visibility and usability.) Optionally, the status bar displays the time as well. (You might also see other icons, such as fax, volume control, and so on, along the right side of the taskbar.) Third-party software, including two of the shareware programs on this book's Companion CD-ROM, also locate little icons there. But perhaps most useful is the Start button, which launches programs and allows you to change settings. You can customize the Start button to suit your preferences and as a way to launch your favorite applications. Maybe best of all, all this can remain hidden until you move the mouse pointer down to the bottom of the screen, thereby revealing the taskbar and Start button. Click on Start, then Settings, and then Taskbar. Under Taskbar Options, choose Auto-hide.

The Start button pops up a set of options and nested menus. The Shut Down option offers the same orderly closing for Windows as does pressing Alt+F4 (after all applications have been closed). The Run option provides an alternative way to launch programs. It's particularly useful if you know the name and path of the application—just type it in and the program launches. You don't have to search through subdirectories to locate an icon. It's quick. The Help option is the standard Windows help feature, but the Find option is new. It's a good way to find files when you've forgotten their location on your hard drive. You can search by name, partial name (N*.DOC), size, date, or even by using a piece of text that you recall is located somewhere within the file.

The Settings option on the Start menu is a shortcut to the Printers folder or Control Panel. It also includes the properties sheet for the taskbar (as an alternative to right-clicking on the taskbar). The Documents option displays the 15 files you most recently worked on. These can be .DOC, .TXT, .GIF, .BMP, or other file types. The Programs option pops up an equivalent of Windows 3.1's Program Manager's Groups. Some applications insert themselves onto this menu during their setup. You'll also find some standard Windows 95 features here, such as the Explorer and Exchange. At the very top of this Programs menu is an item labeled Accessories that reveals Fax, Multimedia, System Tools (disk management), and other categories of utilities that you requested be installed during Windows setup.

Directly above the Start menu contents just mentioned is a place where you can put your own most frequently used applications. You can put Shortcuts or actual applications here, though Shortcuts make more sense since you don't waste disk space by using a pointer (a Shortcut) to the real location of an application on your hard drive. What's more, many applications expect to find auxiliary files like .DAT or .INI files in their home directory. For more about Shortcuts, see "Shortcuts" below. To add, remove, or otherwise manage the applications that appear on the Start menu, right-click on the taskbar, then choose Properties. Click on the "Start Menu Programs" icon.

GENERAL IMPROVEMENTS

Now let's look at some additional improvements to Windows: long filenames, docucentricity, in-place editing, and a new approach to DOS files.

Feel Free to Use Longer Filenames

The single most valuable improvement regarding files with Windows 95 is that you can give your files intelligible, *long* names. For over a decade, DOS and Windows users have struggled to overcome the limitation of 8.3 filenames: filenames are limited to eight characters plus a three-character extension. The extension is usually an identifier, which describes the type of file: text files have the extension .TXT, temporary files .TMP, backups .BAK, executable programs that *run* as opposed to documents that are loaded into those programs to be worked on are .EXE files. Word saves files with a .DOC extension and Paintbrush and other graphics programs added the .BMP extension for "bitmapped picture.")

These extensions are still added, but you can ignore them. Windows 95 uses them to identify the program that opens a document when you double-click on that document's icon or title in a folder. You won't even see the extensions unless you specifi-

Long, meaningful filenames are here at last.

cally deselect the option "Hide MS-DOS file extensions for files types that are registered" in any folder's (or the Explorer's) View-Options menu, on the View tab (see Figure 1-11). Because this option is selected by default when you first install Windows 95, you won't see filename extensions unless you specifically choose to.

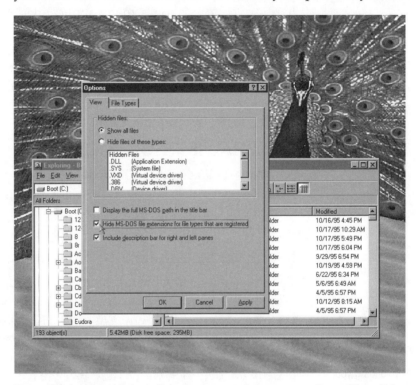

Figure 1-11: With this box clicked on, most of the names of your files will have no extensions. Note the option "Hide files of these types."

DOS users may well find the default "show no extensions" behavior disconcerting, but Microsoft is de-emphasizing filename extensions for a good reason. One of the original purposes of file extensions was that they allowed us to know which applications created which files. With Windows 95, there's no longer any need for the user to see that information. When you click on a .DOC file, Windows automatically launches the application you've associated with .DOC files. Also, because of the pre-Windows 95 eight-character filename limitation, many people were using the extension as part of the filename (as in SALES94.Q1, SALES94.Q2, and so on).With Windows 95, you can assign meaningful names to your files, such as "Sales figures for the 1st quarter of 1994" and leave extensions to the operating system. You can also use spaces in your filenames, but the following characters are still not permitted in a filename: \ / : * ? " < > or |. You can create a filename up to 256 characters long if you wish, but that might be overkill.

■ ■

TIP

Long filenames work best with programs that are updated for Windows 95. Older programs built for 3.11 won't work correctly with the new naming conventions. You'll still be restricted to 8.3 characters.

Technical note: A filename also includes its path, so you have to take into account a disk drive identifier (such as C:\) as well as any folder names (such as TODO). In other words, if your file is located in C:\TODO, the path is 7 characters long. The maximum path plus the filename length is 260 characters.

■ ■

DOCUCENTRICITY: A NATURAL WAY TO WORK

Before Windows 95, starting an application and then loading your work was a bit tedious.

Suppose you're working on building a birdhouse. Your tools, such as a saw and workbench, are probably in your workshop. So is the birdhouse. In the real world, tools are often right next to the object they are being used on. Knitting needles are stuck right into a sweater-in-progress.

Docucentricity means working directly with documents and letting Windows 95 provide the correct tools. Until Windows 95, however, this logical approach was seldom possible on a computer. Here's what you used to have to do to write a letter. In earlier versions of Windows, you would first double-click on a *program*. A program is a tool—it *does something to* raw material. A word processor, for instance, is a tool for doing something to words. Then, when that program was running in the computer, you could open a previously written letter (a *document* or the *data*, as it's called) that you wanted to work on.

This opening, or loading, of data involved clicking on the File menu inside the program, then clicking on the Open option. At this point, you were shown a list of disk drives, directories, subdirectories, and the documents (files) within them. You searched around until you found the document you were interested in working on, then double-clicked on its filename and, finally, you were ready to start working on your letter. Whew!

Now, though, with Windows 95, the approach to work shifts. You directly double-click on a *document,* not a program. Windows 95 looks at the extension. If it's a .DOC extension, Windows 95 knows that you want it loaded into your word processor and fires up the word processor with the document right there ready for you to start writing. So, when you're in any Explorer or folder window, just double-click on a document and you're off and running. Windows 95 automatically recognizes many more file types (filename extensions), and provisions are made (using View | Options menu on a folder or Explorer window) to easily manage the applications launched by the various extensions.

(Although Windows 3.1 also let you double-click on a document to start the program that edited it, you could do this only with the File Manager. In Windows 95, files are integrated into desktop folders, so it's much easier and more natural.)

In-place Editing

A second major feature of docucentricity is in-place editing. Let's look at an example using Microsoft Word for Windows.

Try clicking on the Insert menu to see what you can embed in a document.

If your word processor is a relatively recent version, it will have a way for you to insert objects such as graphics into text documents. In Word, click on the Insert menu, and then select Picture. Choose a file with a .BMP or .TIF extension or some other graphics file to embed within your document. (You can find sample .BMP files in your Windows folder.)

The picture is now in your text document. But you're in a word processor. What if you want to make some changes to this image? Word processors aren't much as graphics tools. There's no Fill with Color tool, no brush either. Why should you have to exit Word, load Paintbrush or some other graphics program, load in the picture, work on it, save the picture, close the graphics program, open Word, and then reinsert the picture?

Well, with Windows 95, you don't have to. (This particular feature foreshadowed Windows 95, appearing late in Windows 3.1 in a few applications.) As shown in Figure 1-12, you can simply double-click on the picture, and, temporarily, *Word itself changes*.

Figure 1-12: Adding a picture to a text document is easy in Windows 95. Best of all, you can edit this picture *without leaving Word*.

Notice in Figure 1-12 that an entire new row of buttons has been added along the bottom to Word, after we double-clicked on the picture. With these tools, borrowed from your photo-retouching program (or whatever you usually use to work with graphic files), you can add various kinds of captions, colors, and shapes.

While you're still "inside" Word—with all its specialized text-editing tools—you now also have a set of graphics tools appropriate for working on a picture. Click on the Close Picture button, and Word returns to its normal state—any changes you've made with the graphics tools are now part of the picture. This is one aspect of OLE, Object Linking and Embedding, which is an important set of features and techniques now being widely applied to applications and the Windows operating system itself.

With OLE we are witnessing a shift in the way computer users work. In the earlier days of computing, each program was a separate entity and there was no communication between them. A word processor could understand only its own documents. Later on, word processors could understand each other's files and open them. Then came the clipboard, a first step in inter-application communication. You could run two programs and move data back and forth between them via the clipboard. The weakness here was that both applications had to understand the same data formats. Then came a short-lived technique, DDE (dynamic data exchange), which ultimately lead to OLE and OLE Automation.

The day is coming when we can essentially ignore applications altogether.

The focus is shifting from applications to documents, and at some point, we probably won't be concerned with applications at all. We'll be working with documents, while applications shift around in the background, popping up as needed according to the type of information or document we're working on. This is similar to a smart caddie who hands you the right clubs, so you can keep your eye on the ball.

Open a Window Anywhere, Anytime

Windows 95 enables you to work more easily with the information stored on your computer. You don't have to run File Manager to display the contents of a particular drive. Here are a couple more docucentric features of Windows 95. You open folders by double-clicking on them. *Any* folder you open *anywhere* in Windows 95 becomes a window. The title of this window will be the same as the title of the folder.

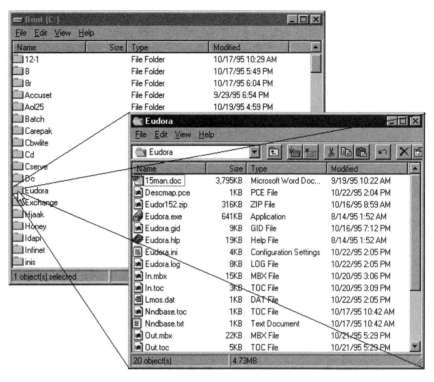

Figure 1-13: Double-click on any folder and a window opens up.

Making New Documents

Creating new documents is easy.

You can edit an existing document by double-clicking on it. But what if you want to create a new drawing, animation, text, music, or other kind of document? The easiest way is to simply right-click on the desktop. You'll see the menu, shown in Figure 1-14, that includes a New option. You can also get to this menu by right-clicking on any white space within a folder or the Explorer. The same menu is also available on the File menu of a folder or the Explorer.

Move your mouse pointer to New, and you'll see the various kinds of documents available on your system. What's listed is a catalog of the applications that you've installed (or those, such as WinPad, that come with Windows 95 itself). Each application *registers itself*, like a new guest in a hotel. This is how Windows 95 knows the kinds of documents you can create—and Windows 95 then opens the program with a blank window ready for you to start designing, writing, or composing. We'll have much more to say about the Registry in Chapter 2, "The Registry," and Chapter 3, "Extreme Customization."

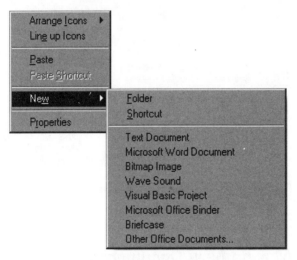

Figure 1-14: Right-clicking *between* documents or folders brings up a menu including the New option. Select New to create a new document.

If you already have an application running that will do what you're looking to do, you can click on its File menu and select the New option there. The opportunity to specify the nature of the new document will depend on the application. Graphics programs create graphics and can also create subcategories, such as color or grayscale. Figure 1-15 shows the response when you select File | New in Micrografx Picture Publisher.

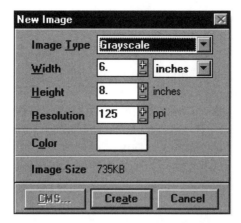

Figure 1-15: Select New from within a graphics application, and you'll see options like these.

No More PIF Editor

Figure 1-2 shows Windows 95's equivalent to Windows 3.1's PIF Editor (shown in Figure 1-1). In Windows 3.1, .PIF files enabled you to give Windows more information about how to run DOS-based applications. For example, you could specify the minimum amount of RAM the DOS application needed to run. In Windows 95, however, you right-click on any DOS file in a folder window or in the Explorer to access its properties. There is no separate, special PIF Editor anymore. Indeed, right-clicking is used extensively in Windows 95—almost any object reveals a useful menu when you right-click on it. Even a text document, when clicked on with the right mouse button, drops down such handy options as cut, copy, paste, font, and so on.

HELP FOUR WAYS

Help is now just a keypress away. When you press F1, you access a description of virtually any aspect of Windows 95, even down to the details of specific options within properties.

For example, if you right-click on the desktop and then select the properties of the desktop itself (which is actually the entire screen), you'll see options such as those shown in Figure 1-16. If you don't know the meaning of an option, click on it (to select it), and then press the F1 key. You'll see a box with a full explanation of the purpose of that option. If you right-click on an item, you'll see a small button asking "What's This?" Clicking on that button brings up the same help box.

Try right-clicking on some text in a dialog box then click What's This?

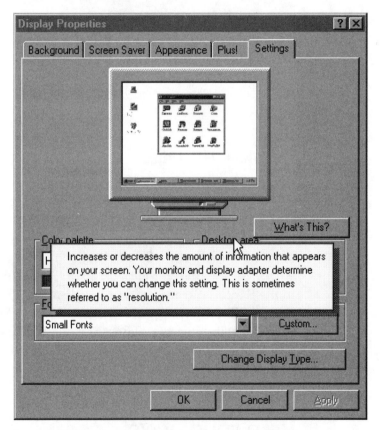

Figure 1-16: You can get helpful information virtually anywhere in Windows 95.

■ ■

TIP

The Help features in Windows 95 are structured differently than Help systems in previous versions. For one thing, you can find out general information by right-clicking on many objects, then selecting Properties. Also, some windows have a question mark symbol in the upper right corner (see Figure 1-16). Click on that symbol, and the icon becomes sticky and moves with your mouse pointer. Then click on some object or the title of an object (such as the Desktop area in Figure 1-16) to get Help.

But perhaps what's most interesting about Windows 95-style Help is that it's been fractured. Usability studies revealed that most people want Help to be brief and highly specific, and of those two qualities, brevity is by far the more desirable. Even if you request general Help by clicking on the Start button and then selecting Help, you get paragraph-long Help messages. No longer do you find those page-long dissertations characteristic of Windows 3.1 and DOS help. This doesn't mean that there's less Help, just that it's become more context-sensitive and been divided into smaller chunks. If you want to know everything on a particular topic, use the new Find option. (Click on Start|Help, and then click on the Find tab.) The Find option searches through *all* related Windows Help files (if you so choose) for occurrences of the word or phrase you're interested in.

■ ■

Of course, there's also the previously mentioned general Help and Index Help, which are available on the Start menu, by pressing F1 when something *isn't* selected, or on a window's Help menu. Those tiny pop-up boxes (called *tooltips*) appear when you move your mouse pointer across a button bar. We've also mentioned messages that appear in status bars when you move your mouse through menus. Then too, there are Wizards.

Wizards

In addition to all the other paths to Help in Windows 95, there are the new Wizards. Wizards are step-by-step, graphic instructions that ask you questions to guide you to the completion of a task. Most Microsoft applications have Wizards; some non-Microsoft

Wizards provide step-by-step help—they guide you through to the completion of a task.

applications have them; and Windows 95 itself uses them for some features. (The Add Printer in the Printer folder and the Find option in Help, are both Wizards.) Figure 1-17 shows one of the many Wizards in Word for Windows—this one creates calendars. (Applications from other vendors use other names for Wizards. Novell applications, for instance, call them *Coaches*.) This step-by-step guidance in a Q & A format is now part of the Windows environment and has become a popular way to solve multi-step problems.

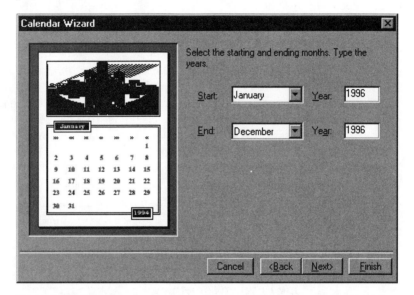

Figure 1-17: Word's calendar Wizard leads you through various styles of calendars you can print.

Networking

At last, networking is getting simpler.

The massive confusion and complexity of networking (linking computers together) is now yielding to a welcome simplicity. Windows 95 does a lot of the work for you. See Chapter 5, "Communicating With the World" to find out what's new for those wrestling with a network.

THE EXPLORER

The Program Manager and the File Manager, those two somewhat redundant and confusing file management features of Windows 3.1, are gone. In their places is the Explorer, a full-featured, integrated, sensible, and powerful system. Beginners may not want to use it, because its features can seem overwhelming at first.

You can start the Explorer several different ways. You can click on the Start button, then select Programs, and then Windows Explorer. Alternatively, if you have a Microsoft keyboard, press the Windows key plus E. If you prefer, locate the Explorer file in your Windows folder, and then drag it onto the desktop or the Start button for easy access. Yet another way to start the Explorer is to right-click on a folder (on your desktop or within any opened window). Then choose the Explore option. (Note: If you have a *file*, as opposed to a *folder*, selected, you may not see the Explore option. Try clicking on a folder, then look for Explore.) Finally, you can hold down the Shift key while double-clicking on any folder (or drive icon, for that matter). This, too, results in an Explorer view.

But what, precisely, *is* an Explorer view? To understand that, we'll begin by looking at an ordinary view—a typical window. Double-click on your My Computer icon, and then double-click your C: hard drive icon. What pops up is a typical disk drive window (see Figure 1-18).

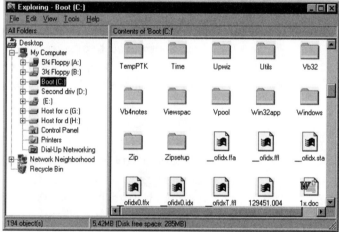

Figure 1-18: An ordinary window (top) has only one pane while the Explorer window always has two panes.

You can launch programs several different ways in Windows 95.

You can transform an ordinary window into an Explorer view by choosing Explore from its File menu, or from the menu that pops up when you right-click. The Explorer window is divided into two panes.

TIP

If you always want an Explorer view no matter what, click on the View menu in a folder or in the Explorer. Select Options, and then click on the File Types tab. Double-click in the list on Folder (not File Folder). Click on explore (see Figure 1-19), and then click on Set Default. From this point on, any time you double-click on a drive icon or a folder, you'll spawn the Explorer view.

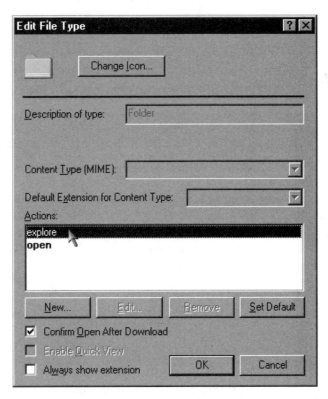

Figure 1-19: If you want to always use the Explorer view, click on this option. (You will not see the Content Type option if you aren't using the Internet.)

Another advantage to Explorer that bears mention is that it gives you more information about removable media than a regular file window. For example, Explorer tells you how much space is left on a floppy disk.

The purpose of the Explorer, and its primary virtue, is file management. The left pane is called the folders pane, and the right pane is called the files pane. It's easier with two panes to drag a file onto a folder, to copy it, or move it there. It's also easier to see the larger picture—the list of folders on the left, the list of folders, subfolders, or files on the right. However, many users prefer to work with *two* opened Explorers, dragging between them to rearrange the files. As mentioned earlier, an even simpler approach is to select a file by clicking on it and then pressing Ctrl+C (to copy it) or Ctrl+X (to cut it). Then open the folder you want to put the file in, and press Ctrl+V to paste it there.

TIP

Here's an exotic technique to move or copy a file. From a file folder or Explorer window, drag the file onto the desktop using the right mouse button. Choose Move Here or Copy Here from the Shortcut menu that appears. Then go to a different folder (click on it to select it), your target folder into which you plan to put the file, and right-drag the file there, this time choosing Move Here from the Shortcut menu.

Both file folder windows and Explorer windows have the same menus, and the same options on those menus, but the Explorer view has an additional menu: Tools. It contains the Windows search utility Find (discussed later in this chapter), network mapping if you're on a network, and a GoTo option that allows you to type in the name of a folder or path in order to move to that location. (Few people use this option.)

Some people prefer to use the ordinary file folder windows for launching programs and the Explorer for managing their files. However, with the many alternative file-launching techniques available in Windows 95, you might want to stick with the Explorer all the time. For example, you can launch files from the Start menu, from the Microsoft Office shortcut bar, or by assigning shortcut keys. (You assign a shortcut key by right-clicking on a DOS program's or a Windows program's *shortcut* icon and then choosing Properties. Click on the Program tab for DOS programs, or click on the Shortcut tab for Windows programs. Then click on the Shortcut Key text box and press the key you want to use.) Note that you can't create a shortcut key for the regular Windows program—you must make a shortcut first, as described later in this chapter.

■ ■

TIP

If you are among those who want to use ordinary file folder windows as well as the Explorer, here's a useful tip. Have you tried opening a folder and found that your preferences aren't being honored? Let's say that yesterday you opened a folder, clicked on the View menu, and choose to display the toolbar, and set the files display to Details because that's the way you like to look at your files. But today when you open another folder, the toolbar is not visible, and you're seeing the Large Icons files display.

You need to set default properties for all your folders. Here's how. Open a folder, and make any changes you want until you're seeing it the way you want to see it. Now press Ctrl, and click on the Close (*X*) icon to close the window. Click on Start, and then click on Shut Down to close Windows. From this point on, any new windows you open will conform to your preferences. Note, however, that folders you've *previously* opened retain the preferences you established when that window was last closed. Windows 95 keeps track of the settings for the 50 most recently opened folders. In addition, the Auto Arrange icons option doesn't remain in effect no matter what you do. The Windows default settings for an opened folder are: large icons, no toolbar, unsorted, and auto-arrange off.

■ ■

SHORTCUTS

It's the distinction between a mere pointer to a file and the actual file itself.

You can create a special kind of icon called a *shortcut* that launches any program or document—even a network folder or a disk drive. A shortcut isn't the same as the item itself—deleting a shortcut to a file doesn't delete the actual file from the disk. Moving the shortcut doesn't move the file to a different location on the disk, and so on. Instead, a shortcut is just a simple way of accessing items on your hard drive; it's a pointer, a representative of the item. You can create a shortcut by right-clicking on a regular icon.

To create a shortcut:

1. Open Explorer (or a folder window).
2. Locate the file (or Folder or drive icon or other item) that you want to create a shortcut for.
3. Right-click on the item's icon.
4. Click on "Shortcut" on the menu that pops up.

You can tell which icons are shortcuts, because they have tiny twisted arrows in their lower left corners. (You'll find much more about shortcuts in Chapter 3, including a way to change this arrow symbol to something else if you want.)

Figure 1-20: A shortcut icon is easy to recognize: a twisted arrow is in the corner, as shown in the icon on the right.

Windows 3.1 made a similar distinction between *the real file* and *a mere pointer to that file*. However, the two approaches were segregated into two entirely separate utilities (Program Manager and File Manager). In the File Manager in Windows 3.1, you could copy, delete, move, and otherwise *really* affect the files stored on your disk. However, the Program Manager's program group and program-item icons were only pointers, "shortcuts" similar to the shortcuts in Windows 95; you could delete or rearrange those icons without affecting the actual files on the disk drive. The purpose of the Program Manager was to provide a way of organizing and launching programs—regardless of their physical locations on the hard drive. Similarly, shortcuts in Windows 95 provide this same flexibility and more.

Shortcuts can make life easier in several ways:

❐ **Shortcuts are persistent.** That is, once you create a shortcut that points to a particular file, the shortcut remembers how to start that file even if the file is renamed. Obviously, this is quite useful in network environments in which other people have access to files that you, too, use. Once a shortcut is created, it continues to work no matter what somebody renames the disk file. If the original file is deleted, the shortcut becomes invalid. On the other hand, if the original file is moved to a different location on the same disk drive, Windows searches the hard drive for the new location of the shortcut and can usually repair the link.

❐ **Shortcuts simplify networked computing.** Instead of having to search the network for a particular item or program, you can reference a program or document on another computer as a shortcut icon, making it appear to be a local document on your own computer. You can also create a shortcut to a favorite network folder on your desktop that can be accessed quickly without having to take the trouble to re-establish the connection each time by accessing the network.

❐ **Shortcuts can be embedded.** For example, when you want to send a large file to someone else on your network, just drag the shortcut icon into the mail message. This technique has two benefits. First, since the shortcut is merely an address, a brief description of the real location

35

of the file, the shortcut uses much less room in the mail message than embedding the actual real file would. Second, when the mail recipient clicks on the shortcut icon to look at the file you've sent, he or she will be working with the original file. This avoids creating two copies of that file that will be floating around on the network. Using shortcuts in this manner eliminates a major problem that occurs when more than one person works on a document: which version of the document is the current one? With a shortcut, only one version of the document is in existence.

❏ **Shortcuts can store objects.** You can create a shortcut to some text in a Word document or a cell in a spreadsheet and use it as a convenient object in other documents. These types of shortcuts are also called *scraps*.

❏ **Shortcuts can point to currently nonexistent network resources on a dial-up network machine.** If the connection isn't already established, Windows dials the service provider for you, logs in, and then accesses the target of the shortcut.

❏ **Shortcuts can point to areas or services on the new Microsoft Network or to the Internet.** Click on the shortcut, and Windows 95 dials and maneuvers you to the target—all automatically. This way, you can create a folder and put shortcuts there for all your favorite e-mail targets, forums, Internet locations, and so on.

❏ **Shortcuts are versatile.** You can use them to point to disk drives, printers, folders, and so on. Also, you can create multiple shortcuts to the same target. If you want, put one on the desktop, another somewhere in your Explorer, another on the Start menu (just drag it onto the Start button, wherever you want.

WINDOWS 95 KEYBOARD SHORTCUTS

As you work with Windows 95, you might find yourself frequently using the mouse to do something better done via a keyboard shortcut. When you're typing text, moving your hand over to the mouse isn't efficient. Here's a list of all the keyboard shortcuts we've found in Windows 95, categorized by the context in which they are used. See if there's a shortcut here for a repetitive behavior that you've been using the mouse or menus to accomplish.

General Shortcuts

Here's a thorough list of keyboard shortcuts.

F1	Help
Alt+F4	Close an application or, if no applications are running, shut down Windows itself.
Any key	Cancels the application bar that shows when you press Alt+Tab. (Pressing Esc also does this, as does releasing the Alt+Tab keystroke.)
Shift+F10	Displays the same menu as right-clicking displays.
Ctrl+Esc	Pops up the Start menu (same as clicking on Start).
Alt+Tab	Cycles through running applications, starting with the most recently opened application. Can also be used to *toggle* between two applications (because the most recently used application is always the first one switched to when Alt+Tab is pressed).
Shift	While putting in a CD, pressing the Shift key suppresses the auto-play feature.

Menu Shortcuts

Alt+Underlined letter in menu	Drops down that menu.
Right or Left arrow	Moves across menu bar.
Down arrow	Drops down a highlighted menu.
F10 (or Esc)	Pops back up (closes) currently dropped menu.
Alt+Space	Drops down application's Control menu.

MDI Shortcuts

Some Windows applications permit a *multiple document interface* (MDI). For example, in Word for Windows, you can simultaneously edit two or more different files, and thus it is said that more than one document is open. In MDI situations, these keyboard shortcuts may be useful:

Alt+ -	If more than one document is open, pressing Alt+hyphen displays that *document's* Control menu. Otherwise, pressing Alt+hyphen results in the same action as pressing Alt+Space (it drops down an application's Control menu).
Ctrl+F4	If more than one document is open, it closes that document. If a single document is open, it exits the application.

Windows Key Shortcuts

The Microsoft Natural Keyboard features a pair of new, extra Windows keys—one on each side of the keyboard beside the Alt keys. Several useful shortcuts involve holding down a Windows key, while pressing a letter of the alphabet. We'll indicate the Windows key with the ⊞ symbol. Following are the keyboard shortcuts that take advantage of the Windows keys:

⊞	Pops up the Start menu (and reveals the taskbar, if hidden).
⊞+Tab	Cycles among the items on the taskbar.
⊞+Break	Accesses system properties (as if you'd clicked on Start I Settings I Control Panel I System or, alternatively, right-clicked on My Computer and then selected Properties).
⊞+E	Opens an Explorer window.
⊞+R	Runs a program (same as Start I Run. If you don't have a Microsoft Keyboard, press Ctrl+Esc to pop up the Start menu, then press R to choose Run).

⊞+F	Accesses the Find utility.
⊞+Ctrl+F	Find Computer (on a network).
⊞+M	Minimizes all open windows.
⊞+Shift+M	Restores all minimized windows.
⊞+F1	Opens Help with the Find engine active.

Property Sheets & Dialog Boxes

The Windows 3.1 dialog box has been largely abandoned in favor of the Windows 95-style property sheets. A single property sheet behaves much like a dialog box, but usually several property sheets are ganged together, and they are selected by clicking on their tabs. This is a visual metaphor of a card file. However, the following shortcut keystrokes work the same within both boxes and sheets.

Figure 1-21: The traditional Windows 3.1 dialog box.

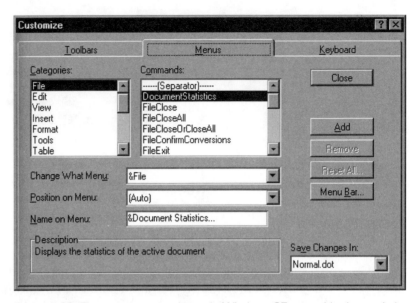

Figure 1-22: The new property sheets in Windows 95 resemble the cards in a card file.

Property Sheet & Dialog Box Shortcuts

Tab	Moves through text-entry areas or other interactive items on a dialog box.
Tab+Shift	Reverses the direction of movement through a dialog box.
Ctrl+Tab	Moves among the tabs in a property sheet.
Down or Up arrows	Move through the items in a list box (Figure 1-23).

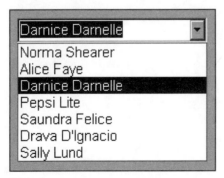

Figure 1-23: A list box contains items from which you can select one or more.

Alt+Down arrow	Drops down the list of a list box that is currently selected.
Home	Moves to the top of a list box.
End	Moves to the bottom of a list box.
Letter of the alphabet	Moves to the first item in a list box starting with that letter.
Space	Toggles the selection of a list box or check box.
Shift+Up arrow (or Down arrow)	Toggles the selection of a group of selected items in a list box.
Ctrl+Left arrow	Selects various items in a list box that aren't necessarily contiguous (same as Ctrl+Left mouse button).

Start Menu Shortcuts

▓	Pops up the Start menu (and reveals taskbar, if hidden).
Alt+S	If the desktop is currently the active zone (if no window has the focus), pops up the Start menu (and reveals taskbar, if hidden).
Ctrl+Esc	Pops up the Start menu (and reveals the taskbar, if hidden).

File Folder & Explorer Shortcuts

As you learned earlier in this chapter, file folder windows display a single group of icons, while Explorer windows are divided into two *panes*—the folders pane on the left and the files pane on the right. The following shortcuts help you work in both types of windows:

Letter of the alphabet	Jumps you to the folder or file that begins with that letter. Continue typing the name and eventually you'll highlight the folder or file you're looking for. Whether you jump to a folder or file depends on whether you're currently in the folders or files pane of the Explorer (sometimes referred to as "where the *focus* is," or the "currently selected" item).
Tab	Moves between the files pane, folders pane, and the primary drop-down menu.
Ctrl+G	Go to a particular folder (same as choosing Tools I Go To).
Ctrl+Z	Undoes last action.
Ctrl+A	Selects all files (and folders) in the files pane.
BackSpace	Goes one level higher in the Explorer or folder path.
F2	Allows you to rename a file or folder.
F3	Accesses Find.
F4	Drops down the list box.
F5	Refreshes (redraws) the listing (same as choosing View I Refresh).
F6	Moves between folders and files panes and main drop-down list (same as pressing the Tab key).
Ctrl+Shift while left-button-dragging a file or folder	Same as right-dragging. When you release the item, a menu pops up with the options: Move Here, Copy Here, Create Shortcut(s) Here, and Cancel.
Del	Sends the selected item to Recycle Bin.
Shift+Del	Fully deletes the selected item (it's not sent to the Recycle Bin).
Shift+drag item to Recycle Bin	Same as Shift+Del (full delete).
Ctrl+X	Cuts currently selected file or folder.
Ctrl+C	Copies currently selected file or folder.
Ctrl+V	Pastes currently cut or copied file or folder.

Alt+Enter	Allows you to see the properties of the currently selected drive, file, or folder. (If a DOS window is active at the time, this shortcut switches between full-screen and windowed DOS.)
Ctrl+drag file or folder with mouse	Copies the file or folder.
Ctrl+Shift+drag file or folder with mouse	Creates a shortcut.
+ (on numeric keypad)	Opens the currently selected item. For disk drives, this displays the drive's folder hierarchy. For folders, it displays a tree of subfolders.
- (on numeric keypad)	Closes the currently selected drive or folder.
* (on numeric keypad)	Expands the currently selected drive or folder's subfolders.
Right arrow	Reveals any subfolders within current folder (same as +) or, if subfolders have already been expanded, opens the first subfolder (displays its contents in the file pane). Right arrow has no effect if the file pane is the active pane.
Left arrow	Collapses the current folder. If it's already collapsed, moves one level higher in the Explorer or folder path (same as the Backspace key). Left arrow key has no effect if the file pane is the active pane.

Function Key Shortcuts

Here is a generalized list of the most common effects of pressing function keys, though behavior will often vary from application to application:

F1	Help.
F2	Varies according to the application you're in. When you're in the Explorer, pressing the F2 key allows you to rename a file or folder.

43

F3	Accesses Find Next. In the Explorer and most applications, pressing F3, accesses Find or Find Next. When Find is first invoked, you'll see the Find dialog box; after that, F3 triggers a search for the next instance of the target you've described. Pressing Ctrl+F usually displays the Find dialog box, regardless of whether a target has previously been described.
F4	Varies. +Ctrl: Close MDI* window. In Explorer: Drop down List Box. +Alt: Close currently active or selected window, application, or, if the desktop is active, close Windows itself.
F5	Varies. In the Explorer, pressing F5: refreshes (re-draws) the file list.
F6	Varies. In the Explorer: same as Tab, cycles between both panes and the drop-down list.
F7	Varies.
F8	Varies.
F9	Varies.
F10	Drops selected menu. +Shift, right mouse click.
F11	Rarely used.
F12	Rarely used.

Windows Application Shortcuts

Many Windows 95 applications have fallen in step with Word for Windows, the most popular word processor. It makes sense that you don't want to have to remember a different set of shortcut keys for each of your applications. Therefore, intelligent software manufacturers have largely adopted the Word keyboard shortcuts, a list of which follows:

F1	Help
Ctrl+F	Search
Alt+F4	Exit

Formatting

Shift+F3	Change capitalization (cycles through lowercase, initial caps, all caps)
Ctrl+Shift+>	Increases font size
Ctrl+Shift+<	Decreases font size
Ctrl+B	Toggles boldface
Ctrl+I	Toggles italics
Ctrl+E	Centers text
Ctrl+Z	Undoes last action

Editing

Shift+Arrow keys	Selects
F8+Arrow keys	Selects
Ctrl+left Mouse click in left margin	Selects entire document
Ctrl+A	Selects entire document
Shift+Ctrl+F8 and then arrow keys	Selects vertically
F8	Extends a selection
Esc	Cancels a selection made with F8
Any arrow key	Cancels a selection made with Shift+Arrow key or mouse
F8+ the character	Select from cursor to next instance of a particular character
Ctrl+C	Copies
Ctrl+V	Pastes
F2	Moves a selection

Navigating

Ctrl+Home	Goes to start of document
Ctrl+End	Goes to end of document
Ctrl+F6	Goes to next document window
Ctrl+Shift+F6	Goes to previous document window

The File Menu

Ctrl+N	Creates new document
Ctrl+O	Opens document
Ctrl+W	Closes document
Ctrl+S	Saves document
F12	Saves As
Ctrl+P	Prints document

The Edit Menu

Ctrl+Y or F4	Repeats last action
Ctrl+G	GoesTo

The View Menu

Alt+Ctrl+N	Normal
Alt+Ctrl+P	Page Layout

The Format Menu

Ctrl+D	Adjusts font

The Tools Menu

F7	Spelling
Shift+F7	Thesaurus

STICKY, FILTER & OTHER KEYS

The Accessibility Options window has some useful features.

Windows 95 has a built-in set of special features intended primarily for handicapped users, but some of these features might be of value to anyone. All are accessed by clicking on the Accessibility Options icon in the Control Panel. To open Control Panel, click on Start | Settings. One of the Accessibility Options features, Sticky Keys, allows you to press Shift, Ctrl, or Alt plus another key, without having to press the keys simultaneously. For example, to shut down a program, you can press Alt then release it, and then press F4 rather than pressing and holding Alt and then pressing F4.

The Filter Keys option ignores rapidly repeated keystrokes. A single Enter is recognized even when you hold down the Enter key or press it repeatedly and rapidly. Toggle Keys sounds a warning whenever you press the Caps Lock, Num Lock, or Scroll Lock keys. MouseKeys allows you to use the numeric keypad as a substitute mouse—moving the pointer around the screen and pressing substitute mouse buttons.

FIND ANYTHING

Even if you're not on a network, the new Windows 95 Find utility is useful. With hard disk drives now commonly ranging between 500 megabytes and a gigabyte, and growing larger, you can store thousands of different files on them. Keeping track of thousands of documents challenges even specialists—librarians attend graduate school to learn how to do it. However, with the Find utility you can have Windows 95 quickly search your entire hard drive for any particular folder or document.

Find is available on the Tools menu of the Explorer and also on the Start button menu. If you click on Find, then choose "On the Microsoft Network," you'll be able to locate forums, topics, and so on, on Microsoft's new online service. If you click on Find, then choose "Find Files or Folders," you'll discover a fast and extremely powerful searching tool—it can even look for specific text *within* files. You can also specify many qualities to narrow the search.

The new Find utility is easy to use, yet powerful. You can even use it to find material on a network or Microsoft's online service, The Microsoft Network.

Here's a brief example of how you can use the Find utility. Suppose that a couple of months ago you wrote some notes about your friend Jenny Paxton's application for a Rhodes scholarship, important notes that form the basis of an excellent character reference. Now you can't recall where you stored that file, or the name of the file either. However, you know that you wrote it in Notepad; you know the filename has a .TXT extension; and you know that you wrote the recommendation in 1996 and that the file contains the word "Rhodes." Easy. Just tell Find the details you do remember (Figure 1-24), and then click on the Find Now button. All files matching your criteria are displayed in a typical Windows 95 list. Double-click in that list on the file you want, and you've got it—ready to read, edit, or whatever you want to do with it. In fact, it would probably be sufficient to simply search for any file with the word "Rhodes" in it.

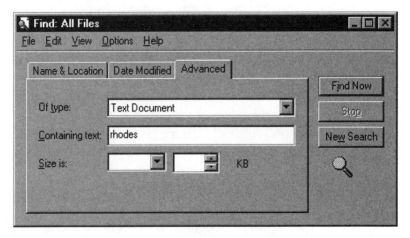

Figure 1-24: The Find utility quickly takes you to any location on your hard drive.

TIP

Press Ctrl+F to instantly bring up the Find utility (if a folder or the Explorer is currently active). If you have a new-style keyboard, such as the Microsoft Natural Keyboard, you can bring up the Find utility by holding down the Window key while pressing F.

EXTENDED DRAGGING

In earlier versions of Windows, you could rearrange icons *within* the Program Manager, but this was purely a visual reorganization (the file didn't actually move on the hard drive). You could also drag a file from the File Manager to the Printer icon. If the printer was activated (its minimized icon was on the desktop), you could print a document this way. Likewise, you could drag and drop a filename from the File Manager to a running application. (For instance, a text document file could be dragged and then dropped onto a running word processor.)

Dragging is fulfilling its potential in Windows 95. You can even drag text from a document to the desktop to create a "scrap."

However, this implementation of the drag and drop feature was a rather limited one. Windows 95 takes dragging into more useful territory. You can still do what you could do in Windows 3.1, but in Windows 95, you can drag and drop things all over the place. Drag a file from the Explorer or a folder window onto the desktop for quick access. Drag a document onto the Printer icon (which you can leave permanently on your desktop) to print the document. Even select text in a document (by dragging the mouse over it to highlight it), and then drag the selection onto the desktop to create a scrap.

Figures 1-25 and 1-26 demonstrate dragging a graphic file (Train.bmp) from one open folder to a graphics program, Picture Publisher (Pp50.exe). When you drop the graphic onto the Picture Publisher program's filename or icon, wham, Picture Publisher starts running and the train graphic is loaded and ready to work on. (In Windows 3.1, Picture Publisher would have to be already running—in which case loading the Train.bmp file could be just about as easy from the File | Load menu.)

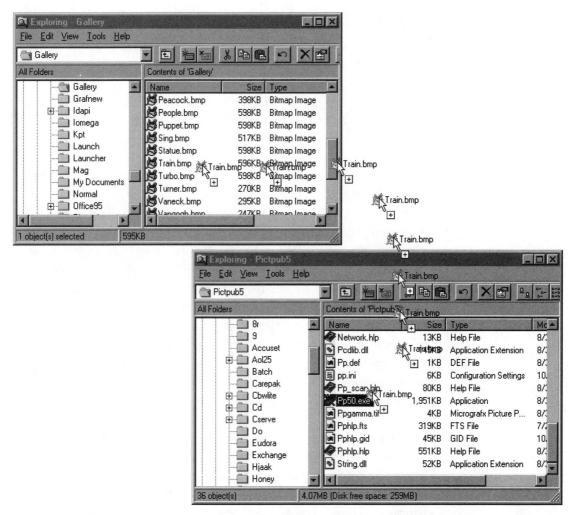

Figure 1-25: When you drag an icon, a ghostly gray version of it appears attached to your mouse pointer.

Figure 1-26: Dropping the dragged icon in Figure 1-25 opens the Picture Publisher application with the Train.bmp graphic loaded and ready to work on.

Right-Mouse Dragging

Move documents as often as you wish, but avoid moving *programs*.

If you drag an icon (for a file, folder, application, drive icon, or whatever) with the *right mouse button* pressed, you can choose between moving, copying, or creating a shortcut (a menu pops up when you drop the icon). (Ordinary dragging with the left button pressed always *moves* any item that's dropped on an empty space into a folder window, onto the desktop, or into the Explorer. Technically, ordinary dragging moves an item only if the target location is within the same disk drive or same volume on a Partitioned drive. When you're sending the item to a *different* drive, such as between the floppy drive A: and the hard drive, it is copied. Copying creates two instances of an item; moving, by contrast, transfers the item to a different location on the hard drive.

TIP

It's best to avoid moving *programs* around on your hard drive. You *could* copy programs, but why would you? They usually take up a lot of room. And you have a safety backup copy already in the box that the program came in when you bought it.

Word processors, fax programs, and most other programs create special subdirectories (subfolders) when you first install them. These subdirectories often contain essential support files that the program expects to find when you start it. Many programs simply look in the folder they are started in, and, if they don't find the support files (because you've moved the programs), they refuse to run. Moral: move or copy documents to your heart's content, but leave programs where they are.

QUICK VIEW

In the File menu of the Explorer or in a folder window, you might find an option called Quick View if you've selected a document's icon (single-clicked on the icon turning it darker). Note that if during Windows 95 setup, you chose not to include the Quick View option, you can install it later. Likewise, a system administrator of a network might also have chosen to set up your machine without the Quick View feature installed. In all those situations, you won't see the Quick View option on the File menu. If you want to install Quick View, double-click on the My Computer icon on the desktop, and then double-click on the Control Panel folder icon. Double-click the Add\Remove Programs icon. Select the Windows Setup tab, then click on Accessories, and then click Browse. Locate Quick View in the list, and click on it to place a check mark in the box next to it. Click OK, and follow the instructions to finish the installation.

With Quick View you don't even have to use an application to look at one of its files.

Quick View lets you see the contents of a document, even if you don't have the application that created the document installed on your computer. For example, you can view an Excel spreadsheet you got from a coworker, even if you don't have Excel installed on your machine. Of course, you can't edit the spreadsheet, but you can at least view it.

Quick View works because Windows 95 identifies the difference between executable programs such as WordPerfect and documents created by those programs. Recognizing this difference, Windows 95 quickly displays a selected document. (Remember that documents can be music, art, animations, etc.—as well as text.)

TIP

Right-click on any document icon, and then see it by clicking on Quick View in the shortcut menu.

WINDOW ANIMATION

Individual windows can be moved around and also resized on the desktop. Old hands understand this intuitively. But to make the idea of resizing (stretching, maximizing, minimizing, and normalizing) more easily grasped by beginners, a window's title bar (the top of the window) is always visible when a window is resized: fills the entire screen (maximizes), shrinks to an icon (minimizes), or opens to fill part of the screen (normalizes).

You can resize a window in several ways—clicking on one of the buttons at the top right of a window, clicking on the taskbar, double-clicking on an icon to open the window, and so on. When you open, close, or resize a window, Windows 95 shows you where the window came from by animating the explosion (or implosion) of the title bar to illustrate the window's new and previous positions (see Figure 1-27). This animation assists new users but most people will prefer this approach to the alternative—windows that simply *appear* in new locations as if they were slapped onscreen. An even more natural-looking animation feature is available if you install the Microsoft Plus! set of utilities. Right-click on the desktop, then select the "Plus!" tab. Click on the "Show window contents while dragging" option. With this feature, you'll see the entire insides of a window move when you drag it.

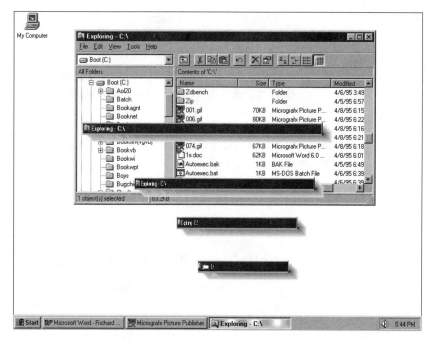

Figure 1-27: Animated title bars display a window being resized. We've clicked on the taskbar to explode an Explorer window.

THE MICROSOFT NETWORK

We've left one of the most interesting new features for last: the Microsoft Network (MSN). Deeply integrated into Windows 95 itself, the Microsoft Network has all the elements of a useful online service (forums, newsgroups, Internet, e-mail, etc.) as well as several significant and unique improvements. For one, the Microsoft Network is easy to use. The elements of Windows 95 that you already know how to use (the Find tool, the Explorer and its buttons, and the familiar menus) are identical in the Network. In a way, the Microsoft Network isn't really a separate program with a separate set of tools, as are all the other online services and telecommunication software. Instead, MSN is truly part of Windows 95.

With Windows 95, you can send messages as easily to the Microsoft Network as to the coworker at the next desk.

This integration has benefits for us, the users. It simplifies using the Microsoft Network; the e-mail system alone illustrates its ease of use. You can send messages to the Microsoft Network as easily as you can to a coworker on your local network. And the multimedia features of the Network are considerably more powerful than anywhere else. For example, you can use italics, boldface, color, and various typefaces in your e-mail messages. You can embed sounds or graphics. You can create shortcuts that take you directly to a particular part of the Network (or even the Internet) right from your desktop. The list goes on.

There's one drawback, though. Those gorgeous high-resolution graphics demand quite a bit of bandwidth on data transmission routes and on your machine. In a word, there's no free lunch. The Microsoft Network is slow when displaying graphics, and it almost always displays graphics. CD-ROM, computer video, and the Internet share these difficulties—their promise and ambitions outstrip the capabilities of current hardware and current phone connections. We are forced to wait and watch as graphics more or less slowly reveal themselves on our monitors. This situation, of course, will change over time. But for now MSN's comely surface, and its rich graphics exact a price, as beauty often does.

TECHNOLOGY UPDATE

Windows 95 is the fruit of years of usability testing and careful design. And the more you use it, the more you're likely to appreciate the care and thought that went into it. But not as easily visible are all the core technology improvements. There's the 32-bit flat memory model, which makes for efficient, fast, and reliable applications that you can *multitask*, allowing you to run many programs at the same time and even format a disk while simultaneously scrolling through a document. Windows 95 is also more dependable than earlier versions of Windows. It won't lock up or "freeze" the computer as often, if at all.

Graphics and multimedia have been accelerated. Windows 3.1 limitations, such as meager system resources, have been almost entirely eliminated. We've discussed long filenames, and there are numerous performance enhancements to the file system, which no longer relies directly on MS-DOS as did earlier versions of Windows. Don't worry if you don't yet appreciate what these enhancements mean for you. Throughout this book we'll examine various new technologies, and how they can make you more productive while making computing easier and more fun than ever before.

MOVING ON

Now that we've looked at the main novelties in Windows 95, it's time to get down to some useful details. In the next chapter, we'll see just what goes on in that 600-page document called the Registry. And we'll see what you can do to manipulate the state of your machine by understanding the zones and data within the Registry—how to change passwords, how to set icon preferences, how to use Regedit and Poledit, and much more. The Registry is a database that describes your machine state. Unless you're a beginner at computing, you'll want to find out about it. Learn about the Registry, and you're well on your way to a more complete command of your machine.

Chapter 2

The Registry

The Windows 95 Registry is a gateway. It's a huge database that contains all the information that was located in Windows 3.1's .INI files such as WIN.INI and SYSTEM.INI. The Registry also holds uninstall data; initialization conditions and preferences for applications; system-wide settings for networked computers; file extension registrations (associations); descriptions of all hardware components; the status of plug and play devices; and much more.

Why should you bother with the Registry? After all, the Control Panel and individual applications allow you to make many changes and adjustments to the way that your operating system and those individual programs behave. The answer is that there are changes you can't make without directly modifying the Registry itself, such as

- ❏ You can't rename the Recycle Bin.
- ❏ You can't remove the My Computer icon (and other icons) from your desktop.
- ❏ You can't turn off the taskbar animation or adjust the speed at which pop-out menus pop.

These and other features of your computer have been, for one reason or another, hidden from the ordinary user. In this chapter, we'll show you how to access these features and how to safely manipulate the Registry in other ways. You'll doubtless also find things you want to adjust yourself as you meander through the 600 plus pages within the Registry. Also, because the Registry is so fundamental to Windows 95, we'll point out other adjustments you can make to it throughout this book.

This chapter is an introduction to the Registry. In Chapter 3, "Extreme Customization," you'll find many tips on customizing your desktop, many of which require hacking the Registry.

But here let's look at the structure and organization of the Registry.

IF THERE'S TROUBLE

Throughout this chapter, Chapter 3, and the rest of this book, you'll find various things you can edit in the Registry to change the way your computer behaves. Before making any changes, however, we urge you to make a backup of your Registry. We describe how to do this later in this chapter in the section, "Backing Up & Restoring the Registry." Windows 95 itself maintains a safety backup, as described below, but redundancy in these matters is a virtue.

Note also that you can make two fundamental kinds of changes to the Registry: adjusting the value or data in a particular entry, or adding a new entry. You can usually reverse the effect of having changed a number or some text (of having adjusted a value) by merely typing the original value back in. If you've added a new entry, simply delete it to restore the machine to its original state.

REGISTRY DESIGN

The Registry is designed so the average user will leave it alone. For one thing, Registry settings are sometimes expressed in "hexadecimal" numbers or other exotic formats (see the "Computer Math" section later in this chapter). Most people will find those number systems baffling. Also, the Registry Editor, *Regedit,*

The Registry is deliberately hidden from most users.

doesn't appear along with the other Windows utilities on the Start menu. Another Registry editor, *Poledit*, isn't even copied onto your hard drive during Windows setup. Microsoft didn't intend for these tools to be used by end users. At least, this is how we interpret the nearly complete lack of documentation on the Registry, one of the most important mechanisms built into Windows 95.

In Windows 3.1, the .INI files that controlled many aspects of Windows operation were merely text files, easily edited by the casual user within Notepad. The .INI files were somewhat more sophisticated than their DOS predecessors AUTOEXEC.BAT and CONFIG.SYS—at least entries were grouped into logical sections. A typical WIN.INI file starts like this:

```
[windows]
load=
run=
NullPort=None
device=HP LaserJet III,HPPCL5MS,LPT1:

[Desktop]
Wallpaper=(None)
TileWallpaper=0
WallpaperStyle=2
Pattern=(None)
```

A user would quickly recognize that changing TileWallpaper=0 to TileWallpaper=1 turned on the tiling feature of Windows wallpaper. Computer magazines widely reported the existence of a utility called SYSEDIT, which was a text editor that automatically loaded the .INI files, CONFIG.SYS, and AUTOEXEC.BAT for editing. You could, though, just as easily have used Notepad.

The Registry isn't brand new, but the earlier Windows 3.1 version, REG.DAT, was rather generally ignored and rather tiny when compared to the Registry in Windows 95. In Windows 3.1, the Registry was used only by applications to hold some OLE (Object Linking and Embedding, see Chapter 7) information. The Windows 3.1x Registry-like files WIN.INI and SYSTEM.INI still appear in Windows 95 for compatibility with Windows 3.1 programs that expect to utilize them as storage and reference

There was a Registry in Windows 3.1x, but it was largely unused.

resources. However, programs written for Windows 95 are expected to store everything within the Registry.

The Windows 95 Registry is both extensive and well concealed. The data in the Registry is actually held in two *binary* (as opposed to text) files: USER.DAT and SYSTEM.DAT. If you load one of them into a text editor or word processor, you'll see a confusion of miscellaneous symbols with a few recognizable words here and there.

These .DAT files are most likely located in the Windows folder on your hard disk. Although that is the default location—these components of the Registry can be stored pretty much anywhere that's convenient. If you're on a network, USER.DAT is stored in the home directory of each user, and SYSTEM.DAT is stored on the computer from which it works. Some additional files whose filenames end in .POL (for policies), are located in a central but secure location within the network, if your computer is part of a network.

Separating the Registry into these files offers, among other advantages, greater flexibility. An individual user's preferences do not take over a particular computer. For instance, if you log onto a coworker's computer, *your* desktop setting preferences will appear as usual. It's your user ID that triggers the Registry to display your preferences on any machine you log onto on the network. This way, several people can share a workstation or log onto a network from any computer, and each will see his or her personal configuration— the wallpaper you've selected and so on. Also, administration of a network is simplified because the system-wide settings are all controlled by a Policy Editor (the *Poledit* program to which, presumably, only the administrator has access). The administrator can, by making changes to this single file, affect system-wide modifications. Note that policy settings override any settings in USER.DAT or SYSTEM.DAT that conflict with them. Beyond this, though, each individual computer also has a group of settings within the Registry (Does it have a modem? Is it attached to a printer?). So when you log on, the Registry provides a combination of your preferences and local machine settings. In this chapter, we'll focus on USER and SYSTEM, leaving the network aspects of policies for Chapter 5, "Communicating With the World." However, we'll take a look at Poledit at the end of this chapter.

Each Registry .DAT file is automatically backed up each time you successfully start Windows. Windows names these backup files USER.DA0 and SYSTEM.DA0. When you shut Windows down, USER.DAT and SYSTEM.DAT probably have changed, but the .DA0 files will be left undisturbed in case they're needed. What's more, USER.DAT, SYSTEM.DAT, and POLICIES.DAT (and the associated backup .DA0 files) are "hidden" files, meaning they don't show up in DOS DIR listings, nor do they, by default, appear in folder window or Explorer window listings. They are also created as system files—required by Windows to run—and read-only (meaning they can't be modified directly or accidentally deleted).

.INI Weaknesses

Why were the .INI files of earlier versions of Windows replaced by the Registry in Windows 95? Beyond poor security (anybody could edit them), the .INI approach had several additional weaknesses. For one, text data is less quickly searched than you can search through an optimized binary file. For another, there was an upper size limit on WIN.INI of 64KB, and after users engorged it with dozens of font descriptions and application initialization and configuration information, WIN.INI could burst. Some applications used their own private .INI files, but these files too were just as insecure—just as corruptible, deletable, and as easily edited by users. This proliferation of widely distributed .INI files caused headaches when a problem arose: Where do you look for information to help isolate the cause? Now in Windows 95 things are coalescing into a single, easily searched, and relatively secure, Registry.

The Windows 3.1 .INI files also proved cumbersome and in some ways inefficient. As users installed and removed applications on their hard disks, the various settings of these applications nonetheless remained in the .INI files. Windows 95 applications are supposed to use the Registry to store even their uninstall information. This way, when you remove a properly installed Windows 95 application, all traces of it should be gone from the Registry. In the next chapter we'll show you what each application is supposed to do with the Registry.

Lost & Corrupted

If disaster strikes and your USER.DAT or SYSTEM.DAT file is deleted, corrupted, or renamed, Windows 95 will nonetheless start running. If SYSTEM.DAT is missing, Windows complains, displaying the warning screen, shown in Figure 2-1, and starts in Safe Mode. In Safe Mode, Windows starts up with the bare minimum default settings (which includes settings for VGA graphics, no network, the Microsoft mouse driver, and only those device drivers essential to running Windows). Peripherals, such as your printer or CD-ROM unit, are unavailable.

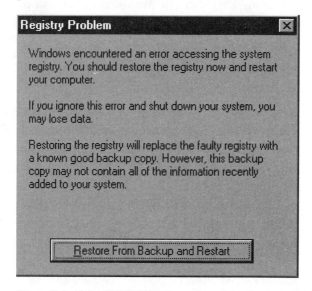

Figure 2-1: If the SYSTEM.DAT portion of the Registry is unavailable at startup, Windows displays this message.

As you can see in Figure 2-1, with a Registry file missing, Windows asks you to permit it to restore the backup file (SYSTEM or USER with a .DA0 extension). If it fails to find *that* file, it displays another message asking your permission to shut itself down until you can somehow restore the necessary file. However, if you refuse this request, Windows will nevertheless start after reminding you that you might "lose data" because it is currently operating with damage to its nervous system.

If the missing portion of the Registry is USER.DAT (and it's also missing USER.DA0), a similar startup pattern emerges. The ultimate result is that Windows runs fairly close to normal but without your personal preferences in effect. For example, if you've previously requested that the taskbar autohide itself, it won't. The desktop background is that dull loden green that you might remember from when you first installed Windows 95, before you changed it to a tolerable color. And the Tip-of-the-Day window appears, a little ceremony that you've probably requested long ago *not* to appear every time Windows starts.

If all four primary Registry files, SYSTEM.DAT, USER.DAT, and their backups, are somehow missing, Windows displays the message "Windows has detected a Registry/configuration error. Choose Safe Mode to start Windows with a minimal set of drivers." However, now even Safe Mode won't start. Instead, no matter what you do, Windows won't run. It repeatedly sends you back to the request for Safe Mode in that same DOS-like list that you get if you press F8 during Windows startup. In this situation you're requested to re-install Windows 95, which indeed you must do.

STARTING THE REGISTRY EDITOR

There's much of interest to the advanced Windows user in the Registry. There are many tricks you can try—tricks that aren't possible without adjusting the Registry.

Let's take a look at it. Click on the Start button and choose Run. In the Open text box of the Run dialog box, type **regedit**. Click OK to run the regedit application; the Registry Editor window opens (see Figure 2-2). Regedit (the Registry Editor) is a program located in your Windows directory that can search, and permit you to edit, your Registry. A similar editor, Poledit, is available to edit the network-related portion of the Registry and is discussed in Chapter 5 and at the end of this chapter.

The entries in the Registry are called *keys*. Each key in the registry can hold a number of subkeys and named values (data that relates to the key). Subkeys are similar to subdirectories, potentially holding other subkeys and additional named values.

63

Named values act like variables stored within a key: we "open" our key, provide a value (text or numerical data) to store in the key, and come up with a Name under which to store it. Later we can retrieve data stored in the key by opening the key and providing the variable name of the value we want.

This is similar to the way that you can locate a file in the Explorer, by providing first the path (the folder names and subfolder names) and then the specific filename. Note in Figure 2-2 that the key is "HKEY_CURRENT_CONFIG" and the subkeys are Display\Settings. Thus, the complete path (always shown in the status bar at the bottom of the Regedit window) is HKEY_CURRENT_CONFIG\Display\Settings. The name of the particular value that's currently selected is "BitsPerPixel" and the actual value, the data itself, is 16.

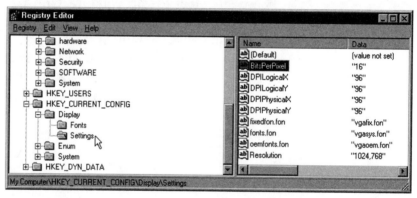

Figure 2-2: The Registry Editor, a utility for managing the Registry.

Notice in Figure 2-2 that the subkeys Display\Settings under the key HKEY_CURRENT_CONFIG contains 10 values: a default, and nine values that relate to the monitor's current settings: number of bits per pixel (8 bits per pixel correspond to 256 colors; 16 bits per pixel, as shown in Figure 2-2, means High Color), dots per inch, the resolution (1024 x 768), and the names of the system fonts. The first value of the Settings key is the default one, the second value is BitsPerPixel, and so on. So, to view or change the values controlling your display's characteristics, you must know under which subkey they are stored and the exact location of the subkey in the hierarchy of the Registry. However, if you don't know precisely where to look in the Registry, you can search it.

MAPPING THE REGISTRY

If you are unfamiliar with the Registry, the fact that it's about one megabyte large might, at first, seem alarming. However, there's structure to the Registry: and locating a given piece of information is not as formidable as it may initially appear. What's more, there are shortcuts to locating information. Let's start exploring the Registry from the outer levels by looking at the general structure and purpose of each of the primary keys listed in the left pane of the Registry Editor window. These are the keys you first see when you run the Registry Editor program, and the name of each of them begins with HKEY_. Each of the primary branches in the Registry holds a particular kind of information. They are listed below.

Don't be put off by the sheer size of the Registry; it's searchable.

HKEY_CLASSES_ROOT

This section of the Registry holds OLE (Object Linking and Embedding) or DDE (Dynamic Data Exchange) information about applications that have been installed or documents with particular filename extensions, such as . TXT. The keys listed under HKEY_CLASSES specify classes (types of objects or documents). If you, the user, double-click on a file with the extension .TXT, Windows can look in this list and discover that the "content type" of a .TXT object is, as the Registry calls it, a "txtfile," short for text file.

There are, in a sense, two lists here. In one, all the entries start with a dot, showing that they're filename extensions (.WAV, .REG, and so on). The other is an alphabetic listing, containing application and utility program names (FaxCover.Document, AudioCD, WordDocument, and so on). In the application listings you'll find three basic kinds of information: a description of the application, its icon, and the default behavior of the application when it is activated in an OLE or DDE activity. For instance, the entry for the AudioCD utility describes it as "AudioCD." In the DefaultIcon subkey for the AudioCD key, that application's default icon is described like this: C:\WINDOWS\SYSTEM\shell32.dll,40. This translates to: this icon is located in the user's WINDOWS\SYSTEM folder and is the fortieth icon in the library named SHELL32.DLL.

TIP

When you right-click on a shortcut on the Windows desktop or in a file window, and select Properties, you can click on the Shortcut tab and choose Change Icon. No matter what icon the item currently uses, you can Browse to C:\WINDOWS\SYSTEM\shell32.dll. It's a repository of 80 icons from which you can choose. Also take a look at the icons in COOL.DLL.

HKEY_CURRENT_USER

The keys in this area describe settings and configuration information about the particular user that is currently logged onto the computer. This way, no matter which machine on a network this user logs on to, his or her preferences and settings are activated. The subkeys within CURRENT_USER are:

❒ **AppEvents:** This subkey would better be named *SoundEvents*. This area lists the path and filename for .WAV files that are to be played when particular events in Windows occur (such as a critical error, a question, maximizing a window, and so on). Alternative sound schemes are available in the Microsoft Plus! Pack (a collection of utilities and extras you can buy to use with Windows 95) and you could assign any sound to a Windows event in the Control Panel as well. However, individual applications also register their sounds in this location, and you can change them by simply changing the .WAV filename and path pointed to by the data field of that key. For example, America Online inserts two filenames and paths here under the HKEY_CURRENT_USER key in the Schemes\Apps subkeys: one for its "Welcome" audio and another for "you've got mail." One amusing trick is to point to .WAV sound files of a toilet flushing or trash crashing in the Empty Recycle Bin entry.

❒ **Control Panel:** This subkey contains some of the data stored in the WIN.INI and SYSTEM.INI files of Windows 3.1. You'll find subkeys for most of the folders in the Control Panel: Accessibility, Appearance, Colors, Cursors, Desktop, and International.

❒ **InstallLocationsMRU:** Affects the drives from which the most recently installed applications were loaded. MRU means *most recently used.*

❒ **Keyboard layout:** Identifies the currently active keyboard layout (as set by the keyboard icon in the Control Panel).

❒ **Network:** Describes both permanent and temporary network connections.

❒ **RemoteAccess:** Describes various details about your dial-up connection. For example, if you use a particular Internet service, you'll find its PPP script path here along with your user name, your area code, the name of your Internet provider, and so on.

❒ **Software:** Setup and preferences settings for your applications (or the applications of the user currently logged onto the computer). You're likely to find only Microsoft products listed here until you've installed other manufacturers' applications that are Windows 95 sensitive and, therefore, presumably, avail themselves of the Registry as an alternative to WIN.INI, SYSTEM.INI, or .INI files created by the application itself.

HKEY_LOCAL_MACHINE

Recall that a particular computer can host more than a single user. When a user specifies a logon ID to logon to a particular machine, the settings described in CURRENT_USER take effect. However, other settings for drivers, hardware, and peripherals must remain the same for *any* user of this computer. So, for example, Plug and Play information goes here; device drivers (like scanner information) can be put here by applications; and the user affects this location when using Add New Hardware in the Control Panel. LOCAL_MACHINE is the repository for all the information that Windows 95 needs to know when it starts running, no matter who the current user is.

The subkeys within LOCAL_MACHINE are:

❐ **Config:** It's possible to have more than a single startup configuration for a computer. For instance, if you dock a portable into a network, that portable should be configured differently than when it's used alone on the road. The various configurations for a computer are listed as "hardware profiles" in the System option in the Control Panel. Each separate configuration (if, indeed, there are more than one) is given its own identifier and its own subkey under Config—0001, 0002, and so on. Config describes the essential display fonts, the screen resolution, bits per pixel, attached printers, and so on.

❐ **Enum:** Describes the hardware ID, manufacturer, drive letter, and so on, for various peripherals, including the disk drive, printer, and monitor.

❐ **Hardware:** Lists the available serial ports.

❐ **Network:** Identifies the network the current user is logged onto and the username.

❐ **Security:** Identifies the network security provider.

❐ **Software:** At this point, you're likely to find only Microsoft applications registered here. As time goes on and other software manufacturers make use of the Registry, their entries will appear in this zone along with the Microsoft programs. This is the location where applications are to store their configuration, startup, and prefer-

Few applications other than those from Microsoft currently use the Registry.

ences data, as opposed to the previous practice of storing them in WIN.INI, SYSTEM.INI, or the application's own private .INI file. Under Classes you'll find the same extension information (such as .TXT), followed by particular application OLE and other information that was described previously under HKEY_CLASSES_ROOT earlier in this section.

❒ **System:** Here you'll find most of the information Windows 95 needs when it first starts up—device drivers, network name, the file system, keyboard configuration, multimedia components, national language, performance statistics or "PerfStats," printer, and time zone information.

HKEY_USERS

This key describes the user profiles for all those who have logged onto the current computer. If only one person uses the machine, only the .Default subkey is listed. The information stored here includes Control Panel settings, such as the user's preferred sounds associated with various events. You'll find information duplicated here (both the keys [names] and the data stored under HKEY_CURRENT_USER described earlier in this section). The distinction is that HKEY_CURRENT_USER describes the preferences and settings of the person currently logged on.

HKEY_USERS on the other hand, includes a subkey for every user who has *ever* logged onto this machine. These preferences include application settings (if the application stores them in the Registry), screen colors, and so on.

HKEY_CURRENT_CONFIG

This key contains the fonts and printer information that you'll also find in HKEY_LOCAL_MACHINE.

HKEY_DYN_DATA

This key is the location of *dynamic* information—data that should be kept in the machine's random access memory because it has to be available to the operating system extremely rapidly. You'll find network statistics and the current system configuration—any information, such as a peripheral that has to be plugged in or pulled off the machine (plug and play or docking), information that the system will immediately require.

USING THE REGISTRY EDITOR

The Registry Editor looks remarkably like the Explorer, and, indeed, the two panes serve similar functions in both utilities. On the left side of the Registry Editor window, you see the path, a set of nested keys (like the Explorer path) that assist you in locating zones within the Registry and make it easy for Windows to quickly search for a particular piece of data. In the left pane, you click a plus beside a key to display its subkeys, and click a minus beside a key or subkey to collapse the view of the subkeys it contains. You click (select) a subkey on the left to see its contents—the Name(s) and Value(s) in the right pane.

In the right pane, you see the equivalent of a filename, the *name* of a particular piece of data (the *value*). In Figure 2-2, you can see that the path is: HKEY_CURRENT_CONFIG\Display\Settings. The Name of the particular value that's currently selected is "BitsPerPixel" and the actual value, the data itself, is 16.

This bifurcation between name and data is hardly limited to the Registry Editor. It appears throughout computer programming as the distinction between a variable name and the contents of that variable; or between a specific address in memory and the contents at that location. Indeed, a great deal of mental activity, both animal and human, can be described by the relationship and the distinction between the location of something, and that something itself. Huge bases of information are indexed in the brain with descriptive tags, the *names*, pointing to the whereabouts of information stored at the location identified by the tag. The Registry uses a set of keys, branches, and subkeys, which are functionally identical to the way a hard drive is organized by folders, subfolders, particular filenames, and, finally, the goal of all this organizing activity—the data within that particular file.

This arrangement of main and subordinate keys within the path of each particular datum in the Registry permits Windows 95 to quickly bounce along the branches down to the correct location to retrieve the information it's looking for. This database optimization technique is essential because the Registry is a truly huge database. In most computers, it hovers around 1MB, which translates into about 650 pages of text. Searches of the *entire* contents of the Registry, piece by piece, would seriously retard the performance of Windows 95. It would be as if you had to look for a file by reading through a long list of filenames without the benefit of folders and subfolders. Without some kind of organization, some *tree structure* or other method of categorization, data management is, to say the least, quite cumbersome.

Searching the Registry

The Registry is a hierarchical database. Information is organized so that applications or the operating system can rapidly locate information. The applications know where to look for specific information (in other words, they know the names of their keys), and they can get there more or less instantly. The Registry is also searchable by curious users: You can locate any entry with the Find and Find Next commands on the Registry Editor's Edit menu. Use them the same way that you would with any word processing application. Regedit's Find command is not instantaneous because it searches the entire Registry as if it were a huge text file. And recall that the Registry *is* a huge piece of work—it's not uncommon for the Registry to be 1MB. Anything can be searched for: keys, subkeys, names, data, or individual pieces of text or digits within the data. You have the option of narrowing the search to keys, names, or data, or any combination of them.

You can also choose "Match whole string only," which means that only an exact match will be displayed (searching for HKEY will not display HKEY_CURRENT_CONFIG, for instance). However the search is never case-sensitive, so capitalization doesn't matter.

If you know the location of the required information (the path to the desired Name), you can locate it faster that way than by using the Find command. Simply navigate through the keys and subkeys—just as you can locate a particular file in Explorer more quickly by opening successive folders, than by using the Explorer's Find command.

Navigating the subkeys is a faster way to locate information, if you know the path.

But, since the Registry is searchable, let's search it. When you first install Windows 95, it displays a Tip-of-the-Day window each time you start your computer, informing you of tricks and techniques that make using the operating system easier or more pleasant. These tips keep reappearing each time you run Windows until you tell Windows to stop displaying them. The first tip displayed is: "If you don't know how to do something, you can look it up in Help. Just click the Start button, and then click Help." There are 48 of these tips, and you can read them by searching the Registry for "If you don't know," which appears only within the tips list. Open Regedit's Edit menu and click Find (or press Ctrl+F), type **If you don't know how** in the Find What text box, click Find Next, and the Registry Editor takes you to the location displayed in Figure 2-3.

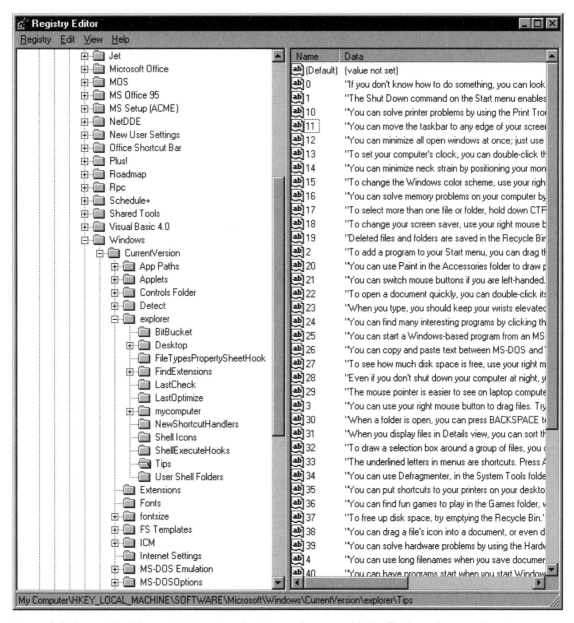

Figure 2-3: Search for "If you don't know how" to locate the area with the Registry that contains the Windows 95 tips.

You can learn several things from Figure 2-3. First, the path (technically the *key*) of this data is displayed in the status bar at the bottom of the screen: My Computer\HKEY_LOCAL_MACHINE\ SOFTWARE\Microsoft\Windows\CurrentVersion\explorer\Tips. The "ab" icons next to the value names identify the values as *text* data as opposed to numeric data. Figure 2-4 shows the two kinds of icons that can appear next to data.

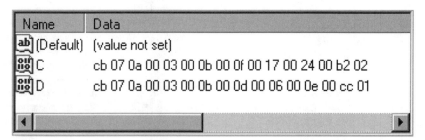

Figure 2-4: You'll find most data within the Registry is in ordinary text form and preceded by "ab" icons, symbolizing alphabetic data. However, some is numerical, and its icon contains "0-11 11 0" to indicate that the data is in hexadecimal format, or at least in some way numeric rather than text.

Now go back up to the beginning by clicking on the My Computer icon at the very top of the left pane. Search for "tips," and you also find this list. At this point, search again for "tips" by pressing F3 (the equivalent of the Find Next command on the Edit menu) repeatedly until you locate the triggers that determine whether the tips are even shown at startup and, if so, which tip appears. This setting says that the next tip to be shown will be tip #2, but since the Show value is zero (00 00 00 00), no tip is actually shown.

```
For:

HKEY_USERS\.Default\Software\Microsoft\Windows\CurrentVersion\
Explorer\Tips:
Name     Data
Next     02 00
Show     00 00 00 00
```

This setting displays the third tip:

Name	Data
Next	03 00
Show	01 00 00 00

Show has only two states (possible data contents for the value), 01 00 00 00 for true and 00 00 00 00 for false. You might be wondering what those paired sets of numbers represent. Why not just use 0 and 1? Before we continue, let's explain the meaning of binary and hexadecimal numbers. If you understand computer numeric systems, please skip to page 78. The Registry saves data (values) as either text ("string" values), binary numbers, or DWORD values (Double WORDs, which are sequences of bits, 32 to be exact, represented as eight hexadecimal numbers. If you are conversant in computer numeric systems, feel free to skip ahead to the section called "Useful Tricks," if not, keep on reading.

Computer Math: Understanding Binary & DWORD Values in the Registry

The computer doesn't count the way we do. Metaphorically speaking, it has little "light bulbs" for a memory—these light bulbs can only be on or off. So, the computer bases its counting on a two-state, or *binary*, method. We, on the other hand, use a decimal, or ten-state, approach. We do this because we started counting by using our fingers, of which we have ten. The number 3 always represents the same *idea* in any counting system, but how you *group* numbers determines how you'll manipulate them when dividing, counting change, and so on.

There are implications that arise from this distinction between humans and computers. For one thing, we naturally divide numbers into groups that are multiples of ten: 100, 1,000, and so on. Computers, by contrast, naturally create divisions based on the powers of 2 (a *power* is a number multiplied by itself): 2, 4, 8…1,024, and so on.

For example, computer memory is measured in kilobytes which should, by definition, mean 1,000 bytes since *kilo* means 1,000. But to the computer, a kilo of something is 1,024 because that's a natural boundary when you count by twos. 1,000 isn't. This is why computer equipment is sometimes quantified in what seems, to us, an arbitrary way. When you buy a 512 megabyte hard drive, you might wonder why it's not just rounded off to 500. The reason is that 512 is a power of two; 500 isn't.

Binary means two states, like a light bulb. A single *bit* is one of these binary objects—capable of either being on or off, true or false. However, for convenience, bits are often expressed as a group of eight bits called a *byte*.

It's interesting that the word *bit* is frequently explained as short for *BInary digiT*. It's technically true that information theorists defined it early in this century in this way. However, the word *bit* goes back several centuries. There was a Spanish silver coin that was soft enough to be cut with a knife into eight pieces—hence, *pieces of eight*. A single piece of this coin was called a bit and, as with computer memory, it meant that you couldn't slice it any further. The word *bit* survives even today as in the phrase *two bits* meaning 25 cents. If you divide a dollar into eight pieces and give somebody two of them, that's a quarter. The meaning of bit has persisted over the centuries.

Here's a list of our familiar decimal numbers and their hexadecimal and binary equivalents:

Decimal		Hex	Binary
0		00	00000000
1		01	00000001
2		02	00000010
3		03	00000011 (1 plus 2)
4		04	00000100
5		05	00000101 (4 plus 1)
6		06	00000110
7		07	00000111
8		08	00001000
9		09	00001001
10	Note digit "A"	0A	00001010
11		0B	00001011
12		0C	00001100
13		0D	00001101
14		0E	00001110
15		0F	00001111
16	Note new column	10	00010000
17		11	00010001

As you can see in the above list, column position matters when writing binary numbers. A 2 in the "singles" column in decimal means 2. But in the 10's column, it means 20. Similarly, in the list of hex (hexadecimal) numbers, 2 in the rightmost column means 2, but in the next column over it means *32*. Hex numbers are represented by 1's, then 16's. That's why they sometimes have A through F in them—you run out of the familiar 10 digits 0-9 and so A, B, C, D, E, and F are used to represent 10, 11, 12, 13, 14, and 15. Note that it's easiest to read binary numbers from right to left, starting with the least significant digits.

Notice too that where decimal numbers use 10 digits (numeric symbols) and hex numbers use 16 digits, binary numbers use only two: 0 and 1. Notice also that hex and binary are quite similar. If you divide the eight digits of a binary number into two zones, they directly relate to the two columns of the hex equivalent: hex 10 (which represents decimal 16) is quite clearly the same as binary 0001 0000.

Instead of the familiar decimal symbol 10, hex uses the letter *A* because 10 is where decimal numbers run out of digits (symbols) and start over again with a 1 and a 0. The difference is that, in hex, the 1 in the "tens" column is really a decimal 16. *The second column in a hex number is a "sixteens" column.* Eleven in hex means 17 in decimal. To figure out the real meaning of a hex number, just multiply the left column by 16, and add the right column to it. Thus, 1A would be 1 * 16 plus 10 or 26. And, by extension, when you have additional columns in a hex number, you should use the powers of 16 for each column.

For example, the hex number 1011 would be translated by remembering that the rightmost column is the 1s, the next column from the right is the 16s. Therefore, 11 is 17. However, the next two digits from the right, 10, are also translated first (into 16), then multiplied by 256 (16 times 16, or 16^2), resulting in 4113. Hex numbers are listed two ways in the Registry. One way is with spaces between pairs of numbers, like 10 11 1D 2A, and 2. With commas between pairs like 10, 12, 3B, 00. This latter format means that each number is separate—not meant to be seen or translated into a single, large number. Without the commas, the number is a single, large number.

USEFUL TRICKS

Now that we've looked at the overall map of the Registry and the various zones within it, let's get down and do some fiddling. But to be safe, we'll first make an extra backup so you can easily restore your computer should something go awry.

Backing Up & Restoring the Registry

Before going on, let's make a safety backup of your Registry. We're going to be adjusting several Registry settings, and, although there already is a set of backups—the .DA0 files we mentioned above—it won't hurt to be extra cautious. So start the Registry Editor (click the Start button, click Run, and type **regedit** in the Open text box, and click OK). When the Registry Editor is running, click to open the Registry menu, and then select Export Registry File. You'll see the dialog box shown in Figure 2-5.

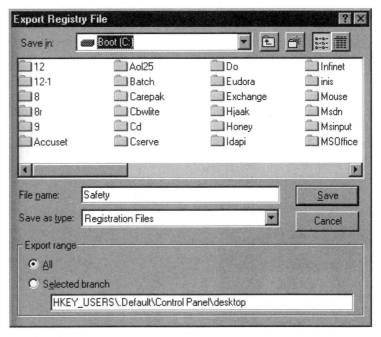

Figure 2-5: You can save the entire Registry as a text file (with the .REG extension) from this dialog box.

Be sure to click on the All button under Export Range. Then save your Registry with a name such as Safety, and specify the folder where you want to store it. The extension .REG is appended automatically when the file is saved. Note that this file differs from the three .DAT files discussed previously in this chapter. For one thing, it contains the entire Registry contents and, more importantly, it is in *text* format. So you can import it into your word processor and, if you wish, edit it there. If you resave it and intend to later import it back into the Registry, be sure to save it using the *text only* option in your word processor. (Click on Save As in the File menu, then choose Text Only as the file type in the Save As dialog box.)

Notice that there's also an option in the Export Registry File window to save only the currently selected "branch" within the Registry—in other words, the currently highlighted key and all the contents within it. This can save some time if you're only planning to edit a particular portion of the Registry. But for now, let's make a complete backup.

If you save the complete Registry, Windows 95 creates a text file that's likely to be around 1MB in size, or 600-700 pages of editable text. Our purpose for now, though, is merely to save the entire Registry in case something goes wrong and we need to restore the Registry to its current state. (We'll look at the Export Registry feature in more detail later in this chapter.)

If you encounter serious problems (Windows is very unstable), here are the steps to restore the Registry from within Windows 95. This procedure replaces the damaged .DAT files with the backup .DA0 files:

> If you have real problems, here's how to restore things back to normal.

1. Restart Windows 95 in MS-DOS mode by clicking the Start button, then Shut Down. Or turn off the power to your computer, then turn it back on and press F8. Choose Command Prompt Only from the menu that eventually appears.

2. Log onto the drive where Windows is installed, if needed. Type **cd windows** to get to the Windows directory.

3. Type the following, and press the Enter key after each line:
   attrib -h -r -s system.dat
   attrib -h -r -s system.da0
   copy system.da0 system.dat
   attrib -h -r -s user.dat
   attrib -h -r -s user.da0
   copy user.da0 user.dat

4. Turn your computer off, then back on.

Changing the Menu Delay Speed

That done, let's make a change to the Registry to modify the speed with which menus appear. This option isn't available from the Control Panel or, indeed, from anywhere other than by directly modifying the Registry as we're about to do. To observe the default menu speed, click on the Start button, then move your mouse pointer up to Programs. A second menu pops out. Move your pointer to Accessories on this second menu, and a third menu pops out. As shipped from the factory, Windows 95 inserts a 400 millisecond delay (about half second) before a submenu pops out. Do you want them to pop out instantly? Here's how to make that happen.

Start the Registry Editor running by typing **regedit** using the Start button's Run option. You can get to the correct location in the Registry in two ways. Your target is HKEY_CURRENT_USER\ Control Panel\desktop. The first approach is to work your way down the tree of keys just as you might locate a particular file by working your way down opening folders and subfolders in Explorer. So double-click on the HKEY_CURRENT_USER subkey. (Note the small + next to the key folder icon, indicating that subkeys are under it and aren't yet visible. Instead of double-clicking on the key's name, you can click on the plus beside it.) Then scroll down until you see the Control Panel subkey, and double-click on that. Then click on the desktop subkey, so its folder icon changes into an open folder.

In the right pane, you should see the settings for various Control Panel options shown in Figure 2-6. Note that your Control Panel might be differently configured and have more or fewer entries in it than the one you see in Figure 2-6. The second way to get to this location in the Registry is to use the Edit Find command (or press Ctrl+F), type one of the terms (such as CursorBlinkRate) into the Find What text box, and click Find Next.

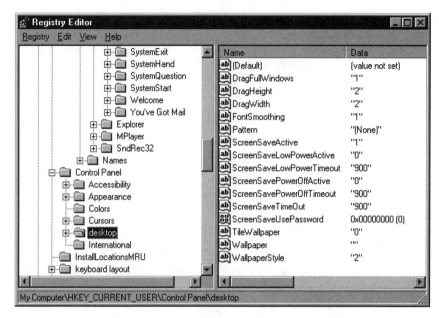

Figure 2-6: Here's where several Control Panel options are stored.

However you get here, you'll now want to add this new entry: MenuShowDelay. To add a new item "Name" and its associated data to the list of Names for the desktop subkey in the right pane, right-click on the desktop icon in the left pane so that it's highlighted (see Figure 2-6). A shortcut menu appears. Click New, then String Value as shown in Figure 2-7. (If you prefer not to right-click, you can open the Edit menu, click New, then click String Value from the submenu that appears.)

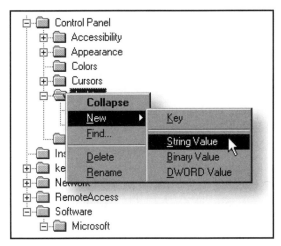

Figure 2-7: To add a new entry, choose New, then String Value from the menu that appears when you right-click on the desktop icon.

After choosing the New|String Value command, a highlighted new entry appears in the right pane, as shown in Figure 2-8.

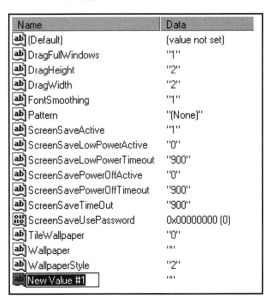

Figure 2-8: The Registry Editor prompts you to enter a new value Name in the right pane. (If you don't see FontSmoothing or some of the other options shown here, you don't have Microsoft Plus! installed.)

Type **MenuShowDelay** as the name of the item. Click on some other entry or on the blank background of the Registry to "set" the new item. This removes the focus from the new item (it's no longer highlighted). Now we want to give it a value (data). Select MenuShowDelay again by right-clicking on it to highlight it and to display a shortcut menu, then choose Modify (or simply double-click on the name). An Edit String dialog box appears. In the Value data text box of that dialog box, enter a number between 0 and 1,000—in other words, a delay of none or as much as a full second. (Don't use quote marks around your number. They'll automatically be inserted because you've stated that this is a *string value* by choosing the New String Value command—the word *string* is used in computerese to mean *text*. And text variables are always surrounded by quotes.)

Type **0** if you want the menus to really *pop* out instantly. Then click on the OK button to close the Edit String window. To see the effect of the change you just made, you can restart Windows or you can follow the instructions in the Tip below. You've told Windows 95 how quickly you want pop-out menus to appear, and any time you want to adjust this setting, go back into Regedit, right-click on MenuShowDelay, and then choose Modify.

TIP

You don't always have to close the Registry and restart your computer for changes you make to the Registry to take effect. Even with the Registry open, you can select (move the focus to) the desktop (just click on it) and press F5. Some changes to the Registry take effect immediately when you use this technique. Other changes require that you restart Windows.

Renaming the Recycle Bin

You can now rename the Recycle Bin.

For some reason, you are permitted to rename the Inbox, Network Neighborhood, and even the My Computer desktop icons. Just right-click on any one of these icons on the desktop, and then choose Rename and type the new name. However, you aren't allowed to rename the Recycle Bin. Perhaps the thinking was that you might give it an offensive name. Registry to the rescue.

To rename the Recycle Bin desktop icon:

1. Start Regedit running, if it isn't started. Make sure that the top item, My Computer, is selected.

2. Use the Edit Find command (or press Ctrl+F), type **Recycle Bin** in the Find what text box, and click Find Next. Your first hit on this target should be this path: HKEY_CLASSES_ROOT\CLSID\ followed by a long string of numbers. In the right pane, you should see (Default) in the Name column and "Recycle Bin" in the Data column.

3. Double-click on (Default).

4. Change the Value data text box entry in the Edit String window to a suitable (and refined) term of your choice, then click OK.

While we're at it, here's how to change the icons used to represent an empty and a full Recycle Bin. Search for "empty" until you locate something like this:

```
"empty" "C:\WINDOWS\SYSTEM\shell32.dll,31"
"full" "C:\WINDOWS\SYSTEM\shell32.dll,21"
```

Note, if you don't find these entries in your Registry, check to be sure that you've got the Keys, Values, and Data check boxes in the Find window checked. Also, uncheck the Match Whole String Only check box.

The tags *empty* and *full* describe the locations of the two Recycle Bin icons. In the preceding example, the icon for the empty Recycle Bin is the thirty-first icon in the file C:\WIN95\SYSTEM\ SHELL32.DLL (any .DLL or .EXE file can contain icons). To substitute a different icon, right-click on the word *empty* and choose Modify. Now type the pathname of any icon file, even a .BMP file (as long as it's dimensions are 32 x 32 pixels, so that it has the dimensions of a typical icon). If you are going to use a .BMP file whose dimensions are larger than the dimensions of an icon, Windows will resize it and the result may look unappealing. Also, this resizing slows things down.

Suppressing Animation

If you don't like the way Windows 95 blows up an application when you click on it in the taskbar, and visually reduces them back to the taskbar when you minimize a window, here's how to turn off this animation. Start the Regedit program running, then press Ctrl+F, and search for *MinAnimate*. This value will be set to the default 1 (on). Double-click on MinAnimate and change the 1 to a 0 (for off). You must restart Windows before this change takes effect.

Preventing CD AutoPlay

At first you might have liked the effect: you put a CD into your CD-ROM drive and a message screen automatically appears by default or a program on the CD starts running (see Figure 2-9). You don't have to double-click an icon or go to the Explorer or use a Start menu command to launch an application on the CD or to play an audio CD. This is Windows 95 *AutoPlay* and it must have seemed a good idea at the time.

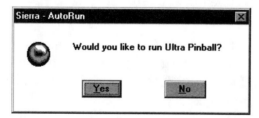

Figure 2-9: Since this CD has a program named AUTORUN.EXE on it, this message automatically appears whenever you load the CD into your CD-ROM drive.

In theory, this feature is rather plug-and-play-like, but after a while many people find that it's annoying in practice. What's more, some users have reported problems with applications— with Word 7 maximized, for example, AutoPlay can cause some machines to hang and require rebooting. If you want to *temporarily* bypass the AutoPlay feature, you can press the Shift key while inserting a CD. To permanently suppress AutoPlay, run Regedit, then search for *AutoInsertNotification* in the Registry. Double-click on this Name, and in the Edit window that pops up, change the 01 value data to 00.

Removing Permanent Icons

InBox, Network Neighborhood, the Microsoft Network, Recycle Bin—there they sit on your desktop. You can't delete them. (The Inbox for Microsoft Exchange, MSN, and Network Neighborhood are there only if you set up Windows 95 with them, but others are sitting there on *everyone's* desktop.)

Some people like a clean, blank desktop with no distractions. They don't like the way the titles under the icons mess up their wallpaper. Whatever your reason, here's how you can get rid of these icons, while still being able to launch the programs that the icons represent. Let's assume that you've created a shortcut key to launch MSN, or you've got it on your Start button menu, or on the Microsoft Office toolbar. Since you never use the Microsoft Network icon to launch MSN, so why should you have to stare at that useless icon?

To remove that icon, you want to locate this branch in the Registry:

```
HKEY_LOCAL_MACHINE\SOFTWARE\Microsoft\Windows\CurrentVersion\explorer\
Desktop\NameSpace
```

The quickest way to ferret out this Registry entry is to start Regedit running by clicking on Start|Run, and type **Regedit**. Then choose Find from the Edit menu (Ctrl+F), type **NameSpace** in the Find What text box, and click Find Next. Click the plus beside the NameSpace subkey folder icon to display the subkey folders it holds (Figure 2-10). These subkey folders represent the "permanent" icons on your desktop.

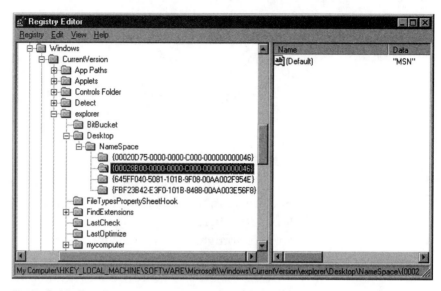

Figure 2-10: This list contains any persistent desktop icons on your machine.

Click on any of those folders under NameSpace to see the name of the icons it represents on your desktop.

At this point, you might want to save this particular branch of the Registry, so you can restore these icons later if you wish. Click on the NameSpace folder icon to highlight it. Click on the Registry menu, then choose Export Registry File. Click on the Selected Branch button so you don't save the entire Registry. Then continue as you would to save the full Registry File to save it to disk.

If you want to be permanently rid of one of the icons listed under NameSpace, right-click on its folder icon and select Delete from the shortcut menu. For many of the changes we're making to the Registry, you must restart Windows. However, in this case, you can simply click on the desktop (to make it the "active" element in Windows, the element with the "focus), then press F5 to refresh it. You'll see the effect immediately.

Reversing It

To restore one or more of the icons removed using this technique, start the Registry Editor and, from the Registry menu, choose Import Registry File. Load back in the .REG file you saved of this branch.

Eliminating My Computer

Unfortunately, the My Computer icon is not on the list of desktop icons just described because My Computer is more tenacious than anything in Windows 95 other than the Start button. You just cannot take My Computer away unless you use the method described in this section.

My Computer is the most adhesive of all icons—it just doesn't want to go away.

Removing *all* desktop icons is possible with this technique. Even My Computer goes away. You get a really clean screen (but, as you might expect, there's a slight penalty). For the absolute purist, here's how you can prevent everything from intruding on your desktop. You can move the Printer and other default desktop icons into a folder on Explorer. You can also dump some of them in the Recycle Bin. But My Computer is the outermost shell of the system. You can't move it to a folder. That would be as fantastic as trying to store your garage in your car.

To make My Computer disappear—so the desktop is entirely vacant—we'll add to the Registry a "NoDesktop" setting. (Note: There's an even easier way to do this with the Policy Editor—see "Poledit: For Parents & Others" below.) To make the change directly to the Registry, click on the Start button and choose Run. Then type **Regedit** and press Enter in the Run dialog box. When the Registry appears, start it running by double-clicking on its name.

At the top of the left pane, you'll see the key folders labeled HKEY_CLASSES_ROOT and so on. Navigate the series of folders until you get to HKEY_USERS\.Default\Software\Microsoft\Windows\CurrentVersion\Policies\Explorer. To get there, double-click on HKEY_USERS; then double-click on .Default, then Software, then Microsoft, and so on until you've finally double-clicked on Explorer. With the Explorer folder icon highlighted, click on the Edit menu, then New, then DWORD Value. When you see a new value entry in the right pane titled New Value #1, right-click on it and then select Rename. Enter the name **NoDesktop** and press the Enter key. Right-click on the new NoDesktop name, and select Modify. Type **1** (the digit 1) and click OK. Now shut down the Regedit program by selecting Exit from the Registry menu. You've done it now!

You'll have to shut down and restart the computer before this change takes effect. When Windows starts up again, it will check the Registry and find your change. Voilà, an empty desktop! You'll notice something else—you can no longer right-click on the desktop to change wallpaper, color schemes, and so on. However, it's easy enough to click on Start, select Settings, select Control Panel, and then double-click the Display icon to accomplish the same thing.

Reversing It

If you decide that you want to go back to the way things were, if you miss the My Computer icon, it's easy enough to reverse the process. Just start the Registry Editor again and follow the method described above to get down to your NoDesktop entry. Right-click on it to display a submenu then select Delete and close the Registry Editor program.

USING .REG FILES

We've seen how Regedit can export and import all or part of the Registry. Early in this chapter, we suggested that you make an extra backup of the entire Registry by exporting it to a .REG file.

Let's take a closer look at .REG files. They're ordinary text files and can be read or edited by Notepad or a word processor (just remember to save them back to disk as plain ASCII text, if you intend to load them back into the Registry). Here's a sample:

```
REGEDIT4

[HKEY_CLASSES_ROOT\CLSID\{645FF040-5081-101B-9F08-
00AA002F954E}\DefaultIcon]
@="C:\\WINDOWS\\SYSTEM\\shell32.dll,21"
"empty"="C:\\WINDOWS\\SYSTEM\\ shell32.dll,31"
"full"="C:\\WINDOWS\\SYSTEM\\ shell32.dll,20"
```

You'll notice several things here. The first line of the exported .REG file is always REGEDIT4. Each key appears on a separate line and is enclosed in square brackets. If the key has subkeys only (as do the fifth and sixth keys) it is followed by other key names in brackets. If the key has a value (as does the first key), its value appears right under the name of the key, in its own line, which starts with the @ symbol.

Editing the Registry is easy in Notepad.

If you wish, you can edit this Registry entry while in Notepad, then save the results to disk. Now you can update the Registry by importing this modified .REG file into the Registry with Regedit. Or, you can simply double-click on the .REG file. If you want, you can keep several .REG files handy, edit them at will and update the Registry in this relatively safe manner. If you are programming, you can create .REG files, place them in the WINDOWS\ START MENU\PROGRAMS\STARTUP folder, and have them upgrade the Registry every time you start Windows. For example, you can change the wallpaper randomly so that each time you start Windows 95 a new background picture is displayed. You can also adjust the default system sound and many other system settings in this fashion, as discussed in the next chapter.

So far, we've only scratched the surface of the Registry. In the following chapter you'll find many tips on customizing your desktop, most of which require hacking the Registry. Since the Registry is a largely undocumented feature of the Windows 95 operating system, new tips will surface as people experiment with it. If you want to make the best of it, you must keep an eye on computer magazines and Internet sites (no, you will not find a single tip on the Registry on MSN). Ventana's Online Companion is a good starting point for any advanced Windows 95 user looking for new tips.

POLEDIT: FOR PARENTS & OTHERS

You can make the changes described in the preceding subsection (displaying no icons on the desktop) even more easily using a program called Poledit (the System Policy Editor). Using the Policy Editor you can also control just how much access your children or others have to your computer. Just as Regedit (the Registry Editor) is intended to be used by professionals or sophisticated users, Poledit is intended for use by network administrators. However, Poledit can be used on a single computer. We'll cover the network-specific elements of Poledit in Chapter 5. In this chapter, we'll see what you can do with Poledit on an un-networked machine.

Poledit provides lists of options in plain English. Most of the adjustments you can make with Poledit are restrictions, for example, preventing the user from leaving Windows to access DOS, or from using the Run option on the Start menu.

If you have a CD containing Windows 95 (Poledit isn't available to users who installed Windows via disk), you'll find Poledit in the \ADMIN\APPTOOLS folder. After you've found Poledit on the CD using the Explorer, run Poledit by double-clicking on it. The System Policy Editor window appears (see Figure 2-11). Click on its File menu. Choose Open Registry.

TIP

It's easy to make changes with Poledit. Unlike Regedit, all the names, values, and data are conveniently hidden from you. All you do is click on Poledit's File menu, then choose Open Registry. Then double-click on the Local User or Local Computer icons to see an easily navigated and easily modified set of options.

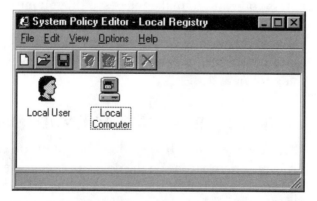

Figure 2-11: On a single-user non-networked computer, you'll see only two icons in Poledit—the Local User and the Local Computer.

To get rid of your permanent desktop icons, double-click on the Local User icon in Poledit, and then look for SHELL\RESTRICTIONS. Click on Hide all items on desktop.

TIP

When you make changes using Poledit, you generally don't have to shut down and restart Windows to see the effects. Just click on the File menu in Poledit, then choose the Save command. The Registry will be immediately updated and, in many cases, your settings will immediately take effect.

FORBIDDEN ZONES

With Poledit you can restrict access, forbidding users to make changes or access areas within the machine. If you've got children and you want to control their admittance to various locations on your machine, or to various programs or services, play around with Poledit and become your own network administrator. You can do all this, even if your computer stands alone and isn't part of any network. The following sections explain some potentially useful settings.

Preventing Mangled Desktops

In Poledit select Control Panel, then Display, and you can immobilize various desktop properties. Figure 2-12 shows how to prevent users from accessing the properties of the machine's desktop.

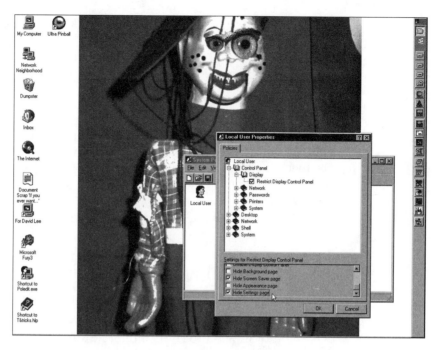

Figure 2-12: A user can remove the background puppet image but not adjust any resolution settings because the Restrict Display Control Panel is selected.

As shown in the Settings for Restrict Display Control Panel list box at the bottom of Figure 2-12, the several pages of the Desktop Properties dialog box for your desktop can be selectively placed off limits. There are four tabs displayed when you right-click on your desktop. They are: Background, Screen Saver, Appearance, and Settings (if you've bought Microsoft Plus!, that will be there too). Any or all of these pages can be restricted by clicking in the check boxes next to their names in the list at the bottom of the Local User Properties dialog box. For instance, if you click on Hide Screen Saver and Hide Settings, anyone right-clicking on the desktop and choosing Properties will see an abbreviated version of the usual Display Properties dialog box (see Figure 2-13).

Put parts of your desktop property sheet off limits to other users.

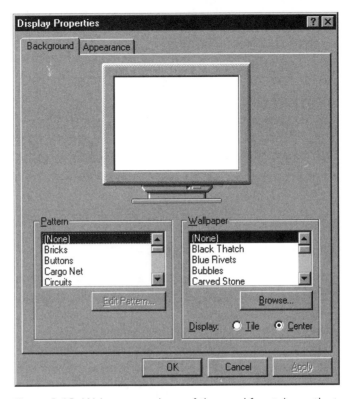

Figure 2-13: We've removed two of the usual four tabs on the top of the Display Properties dialog box.

If you click on the first option in the Settings for Restrict Display Control Panel list at the bottom of Figure 2-12, Disable Display Control Panel, the entire Display Properties dialog box will refuse to show itself, as you can see in Figure 2-14.

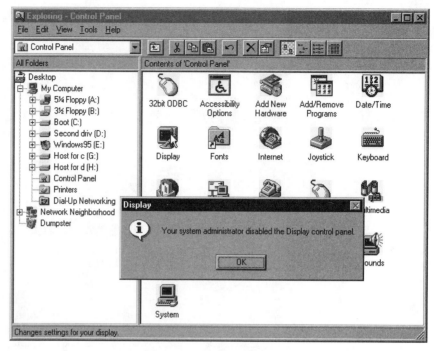

Figure 2-14: Now neither the Display icon in Control Panel nor right-clicking on the desktop reveals the Display Properties dialog box.

Setting Printer Restrictions

Click on Control Panel | Printers and you can restrict the General and Details printer property pages (leaving the Paper, Graphics, Fonts, and Device Options pages available and modifiable). In addition, you can forbid the deletion or addition of printers. Figure 2-15 shows the Restrict Printer Settings option.

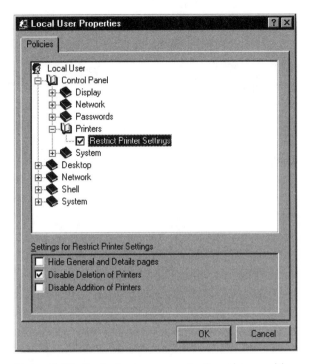

Figure 2-15: Control user access to the printers with the settings for Restrict Printer Settings options.

Guarding System Settings

If you don't want other users messing around with device drivers, IRQ settings and the like, suppress the System properties. The System icon in the Control Panel area of Poledit is a gateway to a property sheet that provides information and permits the adjustment of a variety of sophisticated settings. In Poledit, click on Control Panel | System, then click Restrict System Control Panel. Now you can make either the Device Manager or Hardware Profiles pages disappear. You can also make the File System or Virtual Memory buttons on the Performance page invisible.

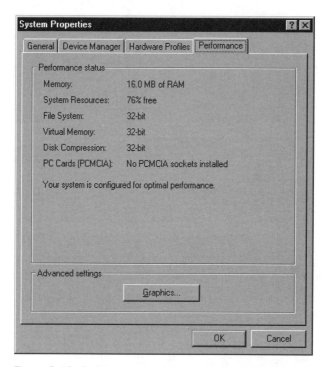

Figure 2-16: Ordinarily two additional buttons, File System and Virtual Memory, are visible along the bottom of this property sheet.

Setting Serious Strictures

When someone clicks on the Start button in Windows 95, there's a selection on the menu that pops up called *Programs.* If he or she moves the mouse pointer up to it, an entire set of submenus can pop out. Most importantly, the user can get to Accessories where there are system tools and other dangerous executables that you might not want them fooling with. Usually, the Programs menu displays everything that's in the Windows | Programs | Start Menu folder.

You can eliminate or restrict access to this Start | Programs menu, diverting it from the usual location (the Windows | Programs | Start Menu folder). Instead, you can point it to another folder where it finds what to show the user. First, you must create a folder to hold any programs you want included on the

Start|Programs list Start the Explorer, and on the File menu, choose New Folder. Open this new folder after you've named it, and put into it any programs or shortcuts you want the user to see when clicking Programs on the Start menu.

Now go down into the Local User\Shell\Custom Folders zone in Poledit. Click on Custom Programs Folder and it will ask you for the "Path to get programs from." Provide the path to your new custom folder. For example, if you named your folder betty and created it on drive C:, you'd type **c:\betty**.

■ ■

TIP

Oddly, following the preceding steps does create a custom Programs menu item on the Start Button menus list, however, the *original default Programs menu also appears as a folder* at the very top of the Start pop-up menu (above any executable programs you've put on Start). To suppress this default Programs menu, you must select the Hide Startup Menu Subfolders option, the third item listed under Local User\Shell\Custom Folders in Poledit.

■ ■

Limiting Access to Desktop Shortcut Icons

Poledit's Local User\Shell\Custom Folders zone also permits you to set up and point to a specialized folder holding the shortcut icons you'll permit on the desktop. Ordinary icons like My Computer and Network Neighborhood aren't affected by this setting, but all *shortcuts* and scraps are affected. To limit access to desktop shortcuts, click on Custom Desktop Icons in Poledit's Local User\Shell\Custom Folders area.

Customizing the Autostart Programs

In the folder Windows\Start Menu\Programs\StartUp section of Poledit you'll find any applications or utilities that you want to automatically run when Windows 95 starts up. This is the equivalent of the RUN= setting in Windows 3.1's WIN.INI file.

If you want to create a custom startup set, follow the steps listed earlier for creating a custom folder, then, in Poledit's Local User\Shell\Custom Folders zone, select the Custom Startup Folder option.

Massive Start Menu Restrictions

You can restrict many of the elements of the Start Menu (see Figure 2-17). These include Run, Printers, Control Panel, or taskbar under "Settings"; the Find command; the disk drive icons within the My Computer icon; the Network Neighborhood icon and other network features; all of the icons on the desktop (discussed earlier in this chapter under "Eliminating My Computer"; and the Shut Down command. If the Shut Down is selected in Poledit, the user can't select Shut Down from the Start menu (or press Alt+F4) to get Windows to shut down. Instead, they'll see the message in Figure 2-18.

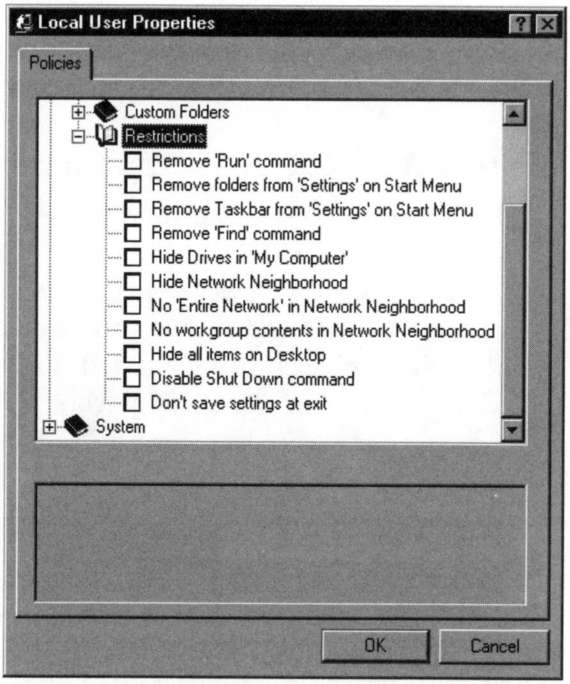

> You can virtually geld the Start Button and its associated features.

Figure 2-17: From this location in Poledit, you can pretty much control what the user can or can't do—including even shutting down Windows itself.

Figure 2-18: A user will see this message if you've forbidden them to shut down the machine.

To invoke any of these restrictions, run Poledit and go down to this location: Local User\Shell\Restrictions.

Adjusting the Don't Save Settings Option

The Don't save settings at exit option can be particularly valuable if the kids like to mess around with your Explorer or folder settings. With this option turned on, they can resize, change to Large Icon view, or do whatever they want. They can play around to their heart's content, but all your Explorer/Folder view settings will be restored to normal the next time the computer is turned on. To implement this, run Poledit and go down to this location: Local User\Shell\Restrictions. Click on Don't save settings at exit.

Restricting Access to Applications

If you feel the need to be in complete control of which applications or utilities you'll permit the user to run, look for the Only Run Allowed Windows Applications option under Local User\System\ Restrictions in Poledit. (Read the warning below before trying this.) When you click on this option, you'll see a small dialog box into which you can add the applications you're making active. Note that you are not to supply the *path* (C:\CSERVE\WINCIM.EXE); instead, merely provide the name of the application (WINCIM.EXE). Remember to include the extension .EXE.

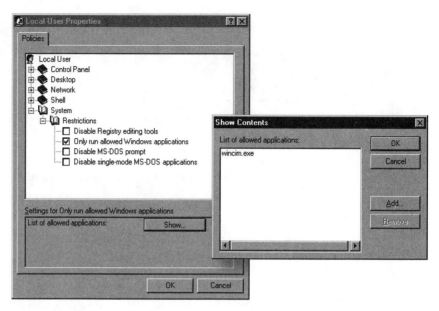

Figure 2-19: Now the user can only run the Windows applications listed here, no others.

WARNING

Turning on this "Only Run Allowed Windows Applications" option can be risky—it can create a chicken-egg paradox and lock you out of your machine. Here's what can happen. Suppose you establish that users can use only, say, CompuServe and no other program. WINCIM.EXE is the only program you list using Poledit as shown in Figure 2-19. This change takes effect as soon as you close the windows on Poledit. Fine, only CompuServe can be activated. *So how do you reverse this condition?* How do you get control of your computer again? Restart it and only CompuServe runs. Windows's Find works, but when you find something you can't run it. Hotkeys don't work, unless you have one for CompuServe. The MS-DOS gateway doesn't work, nor does Run, any Start Up utilities, nor the Explorer. Above all, *Poledit* won't run—so how are you going to reverse this setting? All you'll see when you try to run Regedit or any program other than CompuServe will be the message in Figure 2-18.

Probably the easiest way to restore your previous settings in this situation is if you have a copy of Poledit on your hard drive. Shut down the computer, and press F8 while the computer is starting up (before the Windows logo shows). Choose Safe Mode, then run Poledit, and de-select the "Only Run Allowed Windows Applications" option.

The second easiest fix requires that you have made a backup of USER.DAT and SYSTEM.DAT before you ever turn on the "Only Run Allowed Windows Applications" option. If you backed up these files, shut down the computer and press F8 while the computer is starting up (before the Windows logo shows). Choose Command Prompt only and copy your backup .DAT files to overwrite the USER.DAT and SYSTEM.DAT files on your hard drive.

Alternatively, if you don't have backups of the .DAT files, you can shut down, then press F8 as described above, but choose Safe Mode. This should allow you to use Regedit. (You probably didn't copy *Poledit* from your CD to your hard drive. After all, that might tempt the users you're trying to restrict. They might discover it and use it.) In any case, run Regedit, search for RestrictRun, and delete it. As shown in Figure 2-20, click on it in the right pane in Regedit, and then choose Delete.

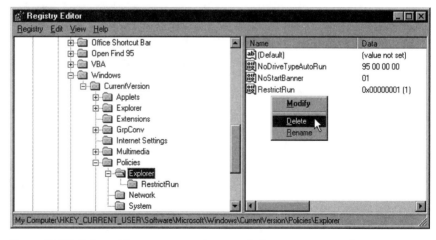

Figure 2-20: Delete this entry to regain control of your computer after you've turned on the Only Run Allowed Windows Applications option.

Disabling Regedit

Another option in Local User\System\Restrictions in Poledit is Disable Registry editing tools. Enabling this option prevents the user from running Regedit, but Poledit still runs, so you can at least reverse this prohibition itself.

Controlling Access to DOS

The final two options in Poledit's Local User\System\Restrictions section affect the user's access to DOS or DOS applications. The Disable MS-DOS prompt prohibits running a DOS session within Windows. The other option, Disable single-mode MS-DOS applications, inhibits those MS-DOS programs that take over the machine and pretend that Windows isn't running. The distinction between these two settings is that if you allow the user access to the MS-DOS prompt, but not to single-mode programs, the user can do things like MOVE, COPY, etc. from the prompt, or run Windows-aware DOS programs (in other words, programs that are less likely to bring down the system). However, locking the user out of DOS mode completely may provide an added level of security, preventing the user from making changes to the system setup. For example, a system administrator might forbid something in Windows, but a savvy user could well circumvent that restriction by dropping to the DOS prompt to change something.

MOVING ON

In Chapter 2 you've learned the basics of the Registry. You've seen how the information is organized in the Registry, how to find and modify values, and have reviewed a few examples. In the following chapter you will find out how to use the Registry to customize your computer in ways that are not possible outside the Registry. You will find many practical examples, as well as discussions of the most important new features of the Windows 95 user interface, including shortcuts, shortcut menus, and file associations.

Chapter 3

Extreme Customization

In this chapter we are going to build on what you learned about the Registry in Chapter 2, looking at the elements of the Windows desktop and showing you how to customize it. This chapter is not about trivial customization techniques on the desktop. It's a collection of techniques we believe every power user wants to know. We will show you ways to alter the behavior of many of the desktop's functions to accommodate your needs. We'll show how to take control of your file types, how to modify the shortcut menus, and in general how to make Windows 95 work *your* way.

The default desktop that appears the first time you run Windows 95 is simply a starting point, the simplest and least objectionable desktop that Microsoft could provide to millions of users. It's up to you to create a desktop that suits your needs and the way you work, a desktop that makes you more productive, more efficient and, why not, happier than your previous Windows environment did.

You can customize numerous items on the default Windows 95 desktop and we'll show you many of them in this chapter. The changes you'll learn about here can be classified in two major categories: cosmetic changes and functional changes. Cosmetic changes have to do with the appearance of the desktop. We're sure most of you are already using your own wallpaper and have fooled around with the various sound schemes—especially if you have purchased the Microsoft Plus! too. Functional changes have to do with the arrangement and function of the objects on the desktop. By making functional changes you create an ideal environment for your working habits. Of course, there's no hard line between the two categories. Most people appreciate beauty and a beautiful environment is their first concern when they move to a new office. Having an aesthetically pleasing desktop will also help you work more efficiently. Others don't care about the environment. All they care about is function. In Figure 3-1 you see a desktop with a true color wallpaper, large, true color icons, and a customized desktop shortcut menu. These are some of the techniques we are going to present in this chapter. We'll start with the simpler customization techniques and move on to more advanced ones.

Practically every item on the Windows 95 desktop can be customized.

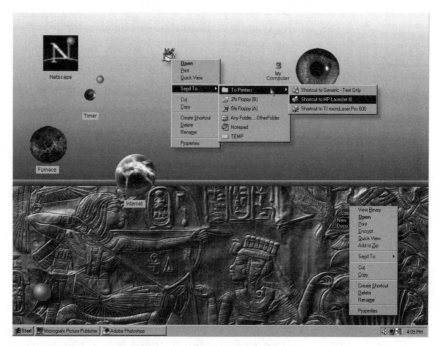

Figure 3-1: A fully customized Windows 95 desktop.

For the advanced user this chapter offers a collection of useful techniques that involve the Registry. These techniques can also help you develop a better understanding of the Registry, so that you can do your own tricks with it. It's true that the most impressive customization techniques involve the Registry, but editing the Registry is not the only way to customize your system. In addition, some very simple techniques can prove extremely useful for you, and we'll look at these as well. Don't overlook the usefulness of some techniques that don't involve the Registry. If they do the trick and help you out, then that's what you need. Sooner or later you'll have to hack the Registry to get the job done (you are a power user, after all), but don't jump there just yet.

For many of the techniques that can be accomplished outside the Registry, we will also show you the Registry entries that are modified. It is important to know how your system's settings are stored in the Registry. For instance, you can automate many tasks through the Registry. Here's an example. One of the simplest customization techniques is to change the desktop's wallpaper through the Display Properties dialog box. If you know which entry in the Registry controls the wallpaper (see Chapter 2), you can write a brief program that randomly selects a .BMP file in a specific folder on your hard disk and turns it into a wallpaper automatically. Every time you start the computer, this program displays a new wallpaper.

IT'S YOUR DESKTOP, AFTER ALL

In the first section of this chapter we are going to look at ways to customize the appearance of the desktop, how to change the icons of some permanent fixtures on the desktop (like the Recycle Bin, for example), how to customize sounds, and finally how to take control of the startup and shutdown procedures. We discuss palettes in detail and thoroughly explain the way Windows 95 aligns the icons on the desktop and how you can change the spacing of the icons on the desktop.

The default desktop is Microsoft's suggestion for a minimal, functional desktop. Microsoft couldn't provide a fancy desktop that would please everybody. Instead, they gave us the bare minimum and a number of tools to customize its various aspects and make it work for you.

Note: Actually, Microsoft provides some additional tools to customize the desktop, by means of the Microsoft Plus!. We found that the Microsoft Plus! is a memory hog and should be used on high end systems only. After the release of Windows 95, Microsoft made another set of tools, the PowerToys, available. PowerToys is a collection of useful tools for handling several aspects of the operating system. We believe these tools will eventually become part of the operating system. Unlike Microsoft Plus!, PowerToys are available at no charge, but they can't be distributed. You must get on Microsoft's network to obtain them.

The Right Background for Your Work

One of the first things you do (or, would like to do, but are usually not allowed to) when you move into a new office is to change its appearance. You paint the walls with a different color, change the posters and the curtains, get a new desk, and so on. You want to make changes that can help you feel that it's your own office and not someone else's. First you want to feel at ease, and then you get down to work.

It's the same with your new operating system. Personalize its appearance to increase your comfort and efficiency. No one is going to tell you what you should and shouldn't do. You can customize it as much as you wish, as long as your hardware permits it. Windows 95 lets you change the appearance of the desktop through the Display Properties dialog box shown in Figure 3-2. To get to the Display Properties dialog box, right-click on the desktop and select Properties. By default, this dialog box has four tabs: Background, Screen Saver, Appearance, and Settings. If you've installed Microsoft Plus!, you'll also see the Plus! tab for its options.

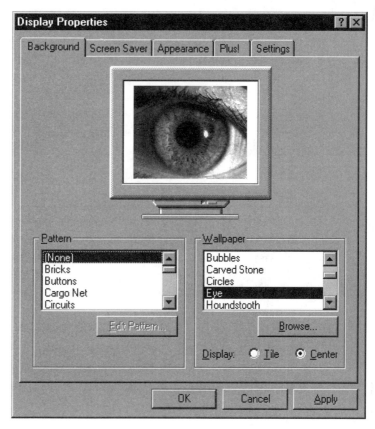

Figure 3-2: The Display Properties dialog box is your starting point for customizing the desktop.

Your desktop's background should be a simple design that isn't distracting.

On the Background tab you can set your desktop's background color, or add a pattern or a wallpaper. We generally recommend that you avoid using patterns, because on most monitors they induce eye strain. Your wallpaper should not be very busy either.

The next tab, Screen Saver, lets you set a screen saver and a password for it. The screen saver is an interesting animation that starts running after a certain interval of inactivity on the keyboard and the mouse. Screen savers can be considered a security feature, especially in an office environment. If you don't want other people to see what's on your screen, but at the same time you don't want to close every open document and shutdown your computer every time you leave your desk, set a password on the Screen Saver tab. Unless someone knows the password, he or she won't be able to get past the screen saver. (As we mentioned, the screen saver starts running after a predetermined interval of keyboard and mouse inactivity. To be considered a security feature, there should be a way to activate it immediately. To do so, you need Microsoft Plus!)

Appearances Matter

The Appearance tab in the Display Properties dialog box, shown in Figure 3-3, lets you modify the appearance of some of the basic elements of the desktop. The Windows default values may not be the optimal ones for you. Take a look at the captions of the various windows on your desktop. Would you prefer a better color combination? One that would make the text stand out? How about the Minimize, Maximize, and Close buttons on the top right corner of the windows? Are they perhaps too small for you? Most of us wouldn't consider the mouse as an extension of our hand. If you're over thirty, chances are you don't have the dexterity of a kid in handling the mouse. So, you may need some help to get to those buttons, which get really tiny as you increase your monitor's resolution. The same is true for the scroll bars' buttons. If you intend to click on the up and down buttons to move the contents of a window, but half the time you hit the scroll bar itself, then you might prefer larger buttons. And how about the menus? Can you read them easily? Or would you rather give up some of your document area to have larger menus?

Adjust the appearance of each element on the interface according to your hardware and your preferences.

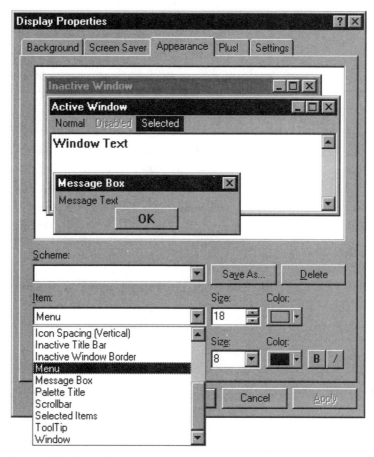

Figure 3-3: Depending on your monitor's resolution and size, you can adjust the size of the elements of the interface, so that they're easy on your eyes.

To change the appearance of your desktop, first select the item you want to modify by expanding the Item drop-down list box (as in Figure 3-3). Then adjust the proper parameters (its size, color, and font). To make the application names on the title bars stand out, choose blue as the item's color and yellow as the text color. Yellow on blue or black, for example, is unusual, almost extreme, but more noticeable than white on black.

Are the menu captions too small for you? Select Menu from the Item list box and change the font size. The height of the menu bar will be increased accordingly, to accommodate the new font size.

To make the three buttons on the top right side of a window easier to reach, select Caption Buttons from the list box and change their size. Again, the window's title bar height will be adjusted automatically to accommodate the new button sizes.

Every time you discover an element of the interface that is not working conveniently for you, you can try to change it on the Appearance tab of the Display Properties dialog box. You can fix only the elements of the Windows interface here. If you don't like the icons on the toolbar of your favorite application, don't blame Windows for that. See what you can do from within your application. When you change the default icon size in Windows, only the icons on the desktop are affected. The icons in your application won't be resized.

Your Screen Settings in the Registry

Let's see now how the Display settings are stored in the Registry. Start Regedit and follow the path to HKEY_CURRENT_USER\ Control Panel\desktop, as shown in Figure 3-4. (If you need to brush up on accessing the Registry, refer to Chapter 2.)

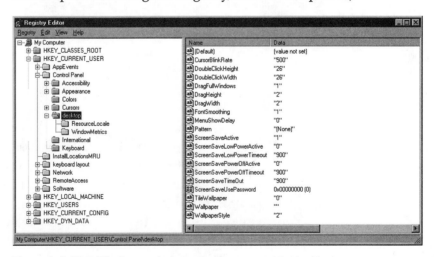

Figure 3-4: Your Display settings as they are stored in the Registry.

The data for the Wallpaper value is the name of the .BMP file to be used as wallpaper, while ScreenSaveTimeOut (expressed in seconds) is the interval of inactivity after which the screen saver is displayed. By using any programming language under Windows (or even DOS) you can easily create a .REG file that selects an image from a collection of .BMP files and turns it into wallpaper by assigning its pathname to the Wallpaper value in the Registry. To display a different wallpaper every time you start your computer, place this REG file into the Startup folder.

Use the Registry to adjust the appearance of the elements you can't change from the Display Properties window.

You'll also find other useful values within this subkey, like DragfullWindows. Its default value is 0, so that when you drag a window, only its outline is displayed. If you have a fast machine, set this value to 1 to see the entire window as you drag it.

Name Value:
HKEY_CURRENT_USER\Control Panel\desktop\DragfullWindows
Data Value:
```
0        Outline dragging
1        Window dragging
```

The left pane of Figure 3-4 contains other interesting subkeys, like Colors. Open this subkey by double-clicking on it and you'll find the color values for every Windows element, including the color of an active or inactive title bar and the color of the menu text. Their actual values are three numbers, which designate the Red, Green, and Blue component of each color (its RGB value). Each number represents the intensity of the corresponding primary color and its value can go from 0 (absence of the specific color) to 255 (maximum intensity). The value "0 0 0" for example, corresponds to black (all colors components have zero intensity) while "255 255 255" corresponds to white. A pure red tone is represented as "255 0 0" and a mid-yellow tone is represented as "0 128 128" (no red, and equal percentages of green and blue). You can easily find the RGB value of any color by opening the Color dialog box, which is available from the Display Properties window. Just open any color box in the Appearance tab and you'll see the Color dialog box.

Expand the first subkey under HKEY_CURRENT_USER (the AppEvents subkey) and you will find the names of the events that can trigger various sounds. We will discuss the various events and their sounds in the section "Customizing Sounds."

Resolution & Color Depth

The Settings tab of the Display Properties dialog box is related to your hardware and it lets you set up the resolution and color depth of your monitor. You can set two parameters here: Color palette (number of colors) and Desktop area (resolution). The Change Display Type button lets you change the display adapter and monitor type. Let Windows figure out the monitor type, for you can actually harm the monitor if you don't know what you are doing here.

The larger the resolution, the more windows you can open on your desktop, or equivalently, the more information each can display. The more colors you can display, the more life-like the displayed images will be. The choice may seem obvious: as many colors as possible and as large a desktop area as possible—but it's not so simple.

To begin with, the number of colors and resolution are not independent—not for most users, at least. If your computer has less than 2MB of Video RAM (and most systems sold today have 1MB of VRAM), you can't increase both the resolution and number of colors at will. The amount of VRAM determines the largest resolution and the maximum number of colors that can be displayed for each resolution.

The best resolution for a typical Windows user is 800 x 600 pixels. The previous standard, 640 x 480 is no longer adequate. There are already a few notebook systems that can display 800 x 600 pixels and before too long we'll see the first notebook monitors with a resolution of 1024 x 768. If your monitor size allows it, choose a resolution of 1024 x 768. Resolution is the number of pixels you can display on your monitor. Since the monitor size doesn't change, as the resolution increases, the pixel size gets smaller and smaller. A small monitor just doesn't have the room to fit all

On most systems you can't increase both the resolution and color depth simultaneously.

those pixels comfortably, and the images may become "wavy," and the colors may start leaking. These unpleasant side effects may offset any benefit that results from increasing the resolution.

TIP

You've upgraded your computer's RAM to run Windows 95 and you probably bought a new hard disk too. But are you happy with your new monitor? If you would like to increase the resolution, make sure both your video adapter card and monitor can handle it. Your eyes are worth more than any computer system, so go for a 17-inch monitor. Don't skimp on the essentials.

When you increase the resolution, the same image can fit in a smaller area of your monitor. Therefore, you can see more of your desktop (the area that otherwise would be outside your monitor). It's similar to looking at a large object from various distances. If you are too close to the object, you can't see much. As you move farther away, you can see more of it.

Today's graphics cards can reach resolutions of 1280 x 1024, sometimes even more. The average user doesn't need that kind of resolution. If you are using CAD or DTP applications, you may actually need an extremely high resolution, along with a very large (probably 21-inch) monitor.

The other related setting is the Color Palette (or color depth), which indicates how many colors you can display simultaneously. As you may have figured out by experimenting with various resolutions, there's a tradeoff between resolution and number of colors. Here's what happens. What you see on your monitor lives in a special memory, called Video RAM, or VRAM. The computer doesn't draw directly on the screen. Instead, it draws in the VRAM, a special memory on the video adapter card. The video adapter circuitry then reads the contents of the VRAM and displays the actual image on the monitor. VRAM holds the description for every pixel on the monitor. The more pixels you want to display, the more VRAM you need, and the more colors you want to be able to see on your monitor, the more VRAM you need.

There's a tradeoff between resolution and number of colors you can display, depending on your video adapter card's memory.

Here's why. If you set your system so that it displays 16 colors, you need only Four bits per pixel. Four bits are enough to represent one of 16 values, so each byte in the VRAM holds the description (color) of 2 pixels. If you set your system to display 256 colors, you need 8 bits (a byte) per pixel. For the highest quality color, the so-called True Color, you need 3 bytes per pixel (the RGB value we talked about in the previous section). For the same resolution, you need twice as much VRAM memory to display 256 colors as you would to display 16 colors. And for True Color you need six times as much VRAM. Most systems today come with 1MB of VRAM. For the smallest possible screen size (640 x 480), Windows must store 640 * 480, or 307,200 pixels. For 256 colors, each pixel requires a whole byte, which means 300KB. You can also display True Color with 1 MB of VRAM at the same resolution, since the required amount of VRAM is 3 * 300, or 900 KB.

Let's see what happens when you raise the resolution to 800 x 600 on a system with 1MB of VRAM. You need 800 * 600 bytes, or approximately 480KB, to display 256 colors. How about True Color images? Given that you need 3 bytes per pixel, the required amount of VRAM (480 * 3, or 1.4MB) exceeds the available VRAM and there's nothing you can do about it. Windows 95 doesn't even make this option available to you if you set the resolution to 800 x 600. If you raise the resolution to 1024 x 768 you will still be able to display 256 colors, but no more. Go for an even higher resolution (1280 x 1024) and you can't even display 256 colors. You are limited to merely 16 colors.

The amount of VRAM on your system determines the maximum resolution and maximum number of colors for a given resolution. Or, if you prefer, it determines the maximum resolution for a given color depth. The only way to avoid this tradeoff is to add more VRAM to your system—if your system can take it. Depending on the manufacturer, some systems can be upgraded with extra VRAM, some not. The cost of a new SVGA graphics card, however, is not prohibitive. For less than $200 you can add a new graphics card that not only has more memory, it accelerates graphics operations too (more on accelerating Windows graphics in the next chapter). Notice also that the display's settings under Windows 95 change on the fly. You no longer need to restart your computer, as was the case with Windows 3.1*x*, for the new settings to take effect. If your system can't change the display settings on the fly, you are probably using an older version of the video drivers. You should re-install the video adapter card from within Windows 95, or contact the manufacturer for an updated version of the drivers.

Palettes & True Color

At this point we must digress a little and explain how the various color depths affect the way you work. Sixteen color displays are fairly limited. They can be used to display icons and simple, geometric images, but not high-quality graphics (and modern operating systems rely heavily on high-quality graphics). They also use the same basic 16 colors that span the entire spectrum. One of the reasons the icons used in Windows 95 are so plain is because Microsoft uses the 16 basic colors, so that they can be displayed on every system.

The colors of a palette are not fixed. They are limited to 256, but can be any of 256 color values.

The situation is much better at 256 colors. With 256 colors you can display fairly good quality images, but there's another problem. There are no 256 basic colors. The system can display practically any color, but no more than 256 of them at once. The 256 colors in use at any time, form a so-called *palette* and such a system is also called *palette capable*.

If you want to display an image of the ocean, the system will select many tones of white and blue to form the best possible palette for the given image. Should the actual image contain more than 256 colors, Windows will approximate some of them, because it can't display them all. The total number of colors in the image can't be more than 256, but the system has the freedom to select the most appropriate 256 colors for the job. And Windows 95 does an excellent job in selecting the most appropriate colors for the image you want to display.

117

Problems arise when you want to open a second image, with drastically different colors. What if you keep the ocean image on the screen, and you open an image of your last Christmas party next to it? The new image needs different colors, and the total number of colors required by both images probably exceeds the limit of 256. The effect is all too familiar to users of 256-color systems: an image with some or most of its pixels having the proper colors and the rest of them having irrelevant colors. Every time you open a new image, or move the focus to an existing one, Windows creates the best possible palette to describe the new image. The other one is displayed with the wrong palette and looks unreal. The image's colors are still available and all you have to do is select it to see it displayed correctly. Figure 3-5 demonstrates this effect, although it doesn't look as bad when printed in monochrome.

Figure 3-5: Opening multiple images with drastically different colors on 256 color systems will produce unpleasant side effects.

Avoid wallpapers on 256-color systems, because Windows has to work extra hard to display them correctly at all times.

This palette problem may become annoying if you are using a colorful wallpaper. The moment you open an image, the wallpaper's colors look awful. The solution: Avoid using colorful wallpapers with 256-color systems (or use a simple wallpaper with a few colors only). Not only will your desktop look the same at all times, Windows itself will have more freedom in choosing the proper colors for your images.

In between the palettes and True Color, there's another quality, called *High Color*. High Color images use 16 bits (2 bytes) per pixel and they are closer to True Color images than they are to palette images, yet they are not as good as True Color images. High Color systems can display up to 65,000 colors, as opposed to the 16.8 million colors of a True Color image. It takes an image with dimensions 256 x 256, in which all pixels are colored differently to exhaust all 65,000 colors. For all practical purposes, High Color systems are as good as True Color systems (unless you make a living by processing images, of course).

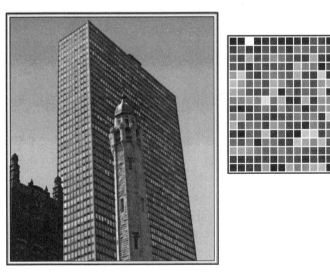

Figure 3-6: A typical image displayed on a 256-color system, along with its palette.

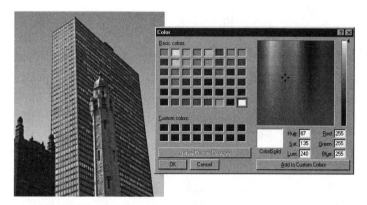

Figure 3-7: The same image on a True Color system. Notice the freedom in choosing colors (being able to specify any color, instead of having to select one from the palette).

If you are using a 256-color system, you will notice that palette manipulation doesn't affect the colors on the various elements of the windows on the screen. To make sure that its interface elements (frames, buttons, status bars, icons, etc.) are always displayed correctly, Windows 95 reserves 20 colors for its own use. Palettes, therefore, contain 236 colors that can actually be manipulated.

Adjusting the Mouse

Use the Registry to adjust the mouse's spatial tolerance to double-clicks.

Another item you may wish to adjust is the mouse. Using the Mouse Properties sheet (double-click on the Mouse icon in the Control Panel) you can adjust most of the mouse properties, including the time interval that differentiates a double-click from two single clicks. There's no provision, however, for a similar spatial interval. How many times did you attempt to double-click while the mouse wasn't still? Wouldn't it be a little easier if there was some "slack," some small allowable movement between the two clicks?

It *is* possible to generate a double-click, even if the mouse doesn't remain still between two clicks. As you might expect, this feature is hidden in the Registry. Open the Registry and look for the Name values DoubleClickHeight, or DoubleClickWidth, which are both under the key HKEY_CURRENT_USER\Control

Panel\desktop. If these values do not exist, select the desktop key and add two new String Values: DoubleClickWidth and Double-ClickHeight. Then set the Data values for both DoubleClickHeight and DoubleClickWidth in pixels (the number of pixels you allow the mouse pointer to slide during a double-click operation). After this edit, your Registry should look like the one in Figure 3-8.

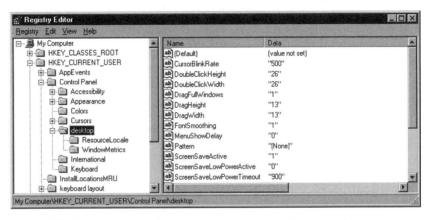

Figure 3-8: Making spatial adjustments to the double-click operation.

We can see no reason to favor one direction over the other, so we suggest you change them both to the same value. Testing this feature isn't going to be easy, but you will notice an improvement in your double-clicks.

Key:
HKEY_CURRENT_USER\Control Panel\Desktop
Name Value:
DoubleClickWidth, DoubleClickHeight
Data Value:
The pixel differential between the two clicks of a double-click

Arranging Icons on the Desktop

Windows uses an invisible grid to line up the icons on the desktop.

Windows 95 neatly places the icons that appear on your desktop on its own. As you create and place additional objects on the desktop (folders, shortcuts, etc.), you'll realize that it's not so easy to keep them properly arranged. Did you ever try to align two icons vertically or horizontally? You probably did and you discovered how difficult it is, until you figured out the Line Up Icons command in the desktop's shortcut menu. Each time you issue this command, all icons move a little so that they align vertically and horizontally. It seems like Windows has a hidden grid on which it aligns icons, which is indeed the case. In Figure 3-9 you see this fake grid superimposed on a typical desktop. Notice that the icons' captions must also fit in their corresponding boxes.

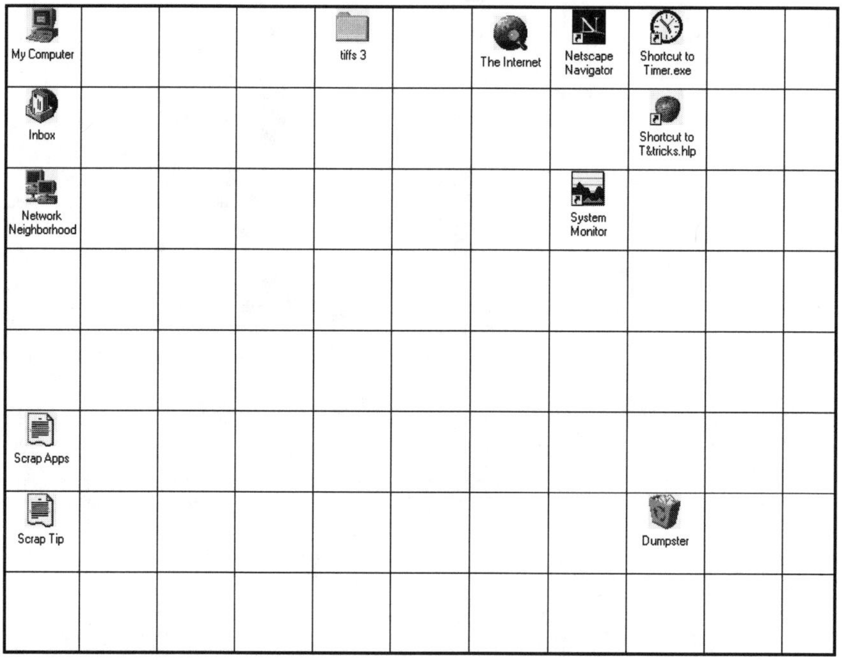

Figure 3-9: The grid Windows uses to align the icons on the desktop.

The size of this grid is changeable. Right-click on the desktop and select Properties to open the Display Properties window. Select the Appearance tab and then drop down the Item list box. There are two items, called Icon Spacing (horizontal) and Icon Spacing (vertical). Their values are the vertical and horizontal sizes of each box in the grid, excluding the icon size. Their default size values are 43 pixels. Given that the icon size is 32 pixels, the dimensions of each box are 75 x 75 pixels. If the icons' captions

You can change both the spacing of the icons and their sizes through the Registry.

can't fit in the space provided and they overlap, as the ones in Figure 3-10, change the values of these items. By doing so, you are actually changing the dimensions of the invisible grid Windows uses to align the icons. The box's dimensions also determine how the icons' captions are displayed. A larger horizontal dimension would allow longer lines of text under each icon. If you can afford to offer more space to the captions, do so. Increase the horizontal icon spacing until you are satisfied with the way Windows displays the captions.

Figure 3-10: Even the Line Up command won't help this desktop. It's time to change the spacing of the icons.

TIP

There's another option in the desktop's shortcut menu, Auto Arrange, under Arrange Icons. If you check this option, Windows places all icons in columns, regardless of their previous arrangement on the desktop. You should place the icons on the desktop yourself and group them according to their functions, rather than let Windows be responsible for their placement (by grouping together all communications applications separately from your image processing applications, or the utilities). From time to time, click on Line Up icons to force them into the closest grid box. (Unfortunately, we don't know of any key in the Registry that will force icons to be lined up automatically).

Using the Registry to Change the Grid Size

You also can set the desktop's grid size from within the Registry. But why do it? We are not suggesting that you use the Registry for changes that you can make easily and more safely otherwise, but we'll show you how it's done anyway. Windows 95 uses an interesting metric to adjust sizes and you should be aware of it, if you plan to make extensive modifications to the Registry.

Run Regedit as described in Chapter 2 and search for the string IconSpacing with the Find command on the Edit menu. When it finds IconSpacing the Registry Editor window looks like the one in Figure 3-11. IconSpacing is the horizontal spacing and IconVerticalSpacing is the vertical spacing of the icons. Their values are negative and they obviously aren't pixels. For most display options, Windows uses a unit called *twip*, which stands for twentieth of a point. A point is a typographical unit of measurement and there are 72 points in an inch. Therefore, there are 20 * 72, or 1,440 twips in an inch. Windows uses twips to arrange objects on the screen. Not only are the icon spacing values expressed in twips in the Registry, they also include the icon size as well. Just ignore the negative sign in front of the icon spacing values. It has to do with the orientation of the twips and you should enter the negative of the desired value.

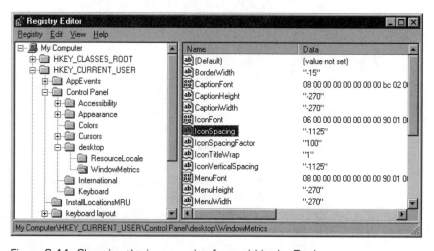

Figure 3-11: Changing the icon spacing from within the Registry.

But there's another complication. How can you express sizes in twips, when all screens don't have the same size. And why does the Windows interface let you use pixels to express the icon size? The default size of the grid is 75 pixels and the Registry says it's "-1125" which really means 1125 twips. (If this number is different on your system, keep reading). If you divide 75 into 1125, you'll get 15, the number of twips per pixel. Once you decide how many pixels you want your grid size to be, multiply this number by 15 (or whatever this number happens to be for your system) and you have expressed the same size in twips.

At this point you may be ready to ask the following question: If there are 15 twips per pixel, what happens when I change resolution? The screen size isn't going to change, while the number of pixels is going to increase (if the resolution is increased). Do I still have 15 twips per pixel? Increasing the resolution will inevitably change another metric, the dpi (dots per inch). Go back to the Regedit program and this time search for DPILogicalX in the Registry. This entry is under the key HKEY_LOCAL_MACHINE\ Config\0001\Display\Settings and its Data value is 96. It is the number of pixels in a "logical inch." Because Windows doesn't know the actual size of every monitor out there, it uses a logical inch. A logical inch is close to a physical inch, but not exactly. In printing, though, a logical inch is exactly equal to a physical inch. To satisfy your curiosity, you can divide 1,440 (twips per inch) by 96 (pixels per inch) to find out how many twips there are in a pixel. There are 15 twips per pixel as before.

The Logical Inch

We have pixels, we have twips, and we have dpis (logical inches). Isn't the Windows display a bit complicated? Yes, but not for the end user, however. It's complicated for developers, but end users don't see much of this. However, as a power user you certainly want to understand how the display works and how to best exploit its capabilities.

The logical inch is a fundamental concept in WYSIWYG systems.

Pixels are the smallest items on the display and they determine the detail you see on the monitor. Dots, on the other hand, are the smallest items on a printer. Ideally, each pixel on the screen should correspond to one dot on the printer. Then everything we see on the monitor would appear exactly the same on paper (this would be the ultimate WYSIWYG—What You See Is What You Get). A rather common (if not low) resolution for a laser printer today is 300 dpi (dots per inch), which means 8.5 x 300, or 2,550 dots across the page. Obviously, there's no monitor that can handle that kind of resolution. So, how can we see on our monitor what will appear on paper? This is where the logical inch comes into play.

A logical inch is an area on your monitor that corresponds to one inch on paper. A logical square inch on the monitor contains the same information (image, characters, etc.) that appears on an actual square inch of paper. Of course, since monitors can't display as many pixels as printers can print dots, Windows approximates this image with fewer dots, or pixels.

Let's see how you can change the logical inch on your system and how it affects your display. Open the Display Properties dialog box and click on the Settings tab. Change the Font Size setting by clicking on the Custom button. "But I can set any font size from within my application, so why would I want to change it here as well?" you ask. Well, what you are actually changing here is the *logical inch*, but Microsoft didn't want to scare users. So, they call it font size.

Click on the Custom button and you'll see a window with a logical inch, similar to that of Figure 3-12. A logical inch is actually larger than a physical inch (measured on your monitor, of course; don't use the dimensions of Figure 3-12 as basis for any comparisons). The logical inch can be scaled. Scale it to 125 percent of its original size and see what happens on the monitor. The items are not as close together as they were before. What used to fit in a 1-x 1-inch area on the monitor before, now fits in an area 1.25 x 1.25 inches. The result is a display that is easier to read. The resolution (or the degree of detail) is still the same, but the objects are less crammed on the monitor.

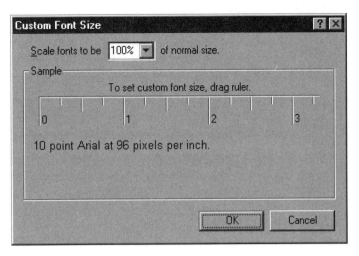

Figure 3-12: Changing the logical inch will result in a more (or less) crowded display.

What has really changed are the DPILogicalX and DPILogicalY units. If you look them up in the Registry, their new value is 120 (which is 25 percent more than 96). If you line up the icons on the desktop now, you'll see that you can't fit as many icons across the monitor as before. There's 25 percent less room than before! The size of the desktop grid is not 75 pixels anymore, but 94 pixels! That's 25 percent more than 75. To verify it, select the Appearance tab. The value of the Icon Spacing is now 62. Add to it the size of the icons (32) and you have 94 pixels. Scale the logical inch to 150 percent and the grid's size will become 112 pixels.

As we've mentioned earlier, the desktop is a metaphor of your actual desktop. As such, it wouldn't make much sense to measure its size in pixels. If you want more space on your desktop, you either remove some of the items on it, or you order a new, larger desktop. Changing the size of the logical inch is how Windows provides you with a larger desktop. Think of it as an illusion.

The real question is: Should I change the logical inch, and when? Feel free to change it if, for a given resolution, your desktop is crammed. If you increase the logical inch, the font sizes will be scaled accordingly. Increase the size of the logical inch and then open a document with your word processing application. The

Changing the logical inch doesn't affect the actual size or formatting of the document, just the way it looks on the monitor.

fonts are larger too. They are still 10 or 12 points, which means they will be printed properly, but they appear larger. Everything has been scaled up by 25 percent. This is what the logical inch buys you: a more convenient display. In Figures 3-13 and 3-14 you see the same document in Word, at two different scales of the logical inch (the resolution is 1024 x 768 in both cases). The document will be printed identically in either case. But which window would you rather work with? Logical inches determine how much information you can fit in a given area on your display. By scaling up the logical inch you get more detail, since the same information can fit in a larger area of the display, therefore it can be represented with more pixels. The downside is that you can't fit as much on the entire screen. By scaling it down, you get the opposite effect.

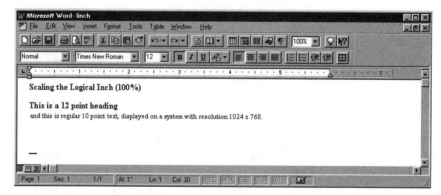

Figure 3-13: A typical formatted document displayed with the default logical inch (100%).

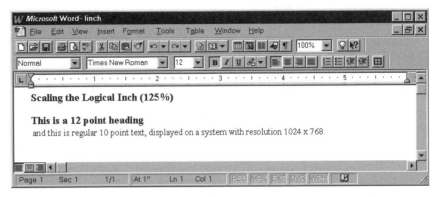

Figure 3-14: The document of Figure 3-13, after the logical inch was scaled up to 125 percent. The actual resolution is the same for both images (800 x 600).

Figures 3-13 and 3-14 also explain why Windows calls the logical inch "font size." The most obvious effect of scaling the logical inch is a change in font sizes. Because most users are quite familiar with font sizes, Microsoft thought there was no reason to introduce another (rather obscure) concept, like "logical inches."

TIP

Some people use a crude font, like Courier at 12 points, to compose their documents, and then format them. Formatted documents are not as easy to read on a display with the default logical inch (10 point Arial is too small to be legible on most monitors), so they use an easy-to-read font while they compose the document and when they are finished they format the text. If you scale up the logical inch, then you'll be able to read the formatted text just fine.

Changing the Icon Size

There are other interesting settings in the HKEY_LOCAL_ MACHINE\Config\0001\Display\Settings branch of the Registry and most of them are expressed in twips. One of them is called Shell Icon Size (this one is expressed in pixels). Change the value of Shell Icon Size to 64 to make the icons on your desktop four

If you want to display large icons, don't enlarge the existing ones; design new ones that look good at the desired size.

times as large (twice as large in every direction). Then close the Registry and restart Windows. The large icons don't look quite right (see Figure 3-15). The reason they are distorted is because they were designed to be displayed at their default size, which is 32 x 32. Those users familiar with image processing software will immediately object to that. Picture Publisher, for example, does a fine job of resizing images. Why can't Windows do better? Because unlike Picture Publisher, or Photoshop, Windows uses a quick and very simple technique to resize icons. Besides, icons contain only 16 colors, and there's not much you can do in terms of image processing with 16 colors.

Figure 3-15: Icons were designed to be displayed at their default resolution. This is what happens if you make them bigger.

Don't use icons with more than 16 colors if your system doesn't support High Color or True Color. Every time you open an image they will look really strange.

The situation is not hopeless, though. You can change not only the size of the icons, you can change the icons themselves. Any .BMP file can be turned into an icon. All you have to do is enter the .BMP filename where normally an icon name would appear in the Registry, or any dialog box where you're supposed to enter an icon name. It is possible, therefore, to enlarge the icons (make them 48 x 48, or 64 x 64) and use your own bitmaps for them. Moreover, you can use more than 16 colors. Use 256 color bitmaps to make your icons stand out. Unfortunately, this isn't going to work on 256 color systems for the reasons we have already explained in the section "Palettes & True Color." The desktop of Figure 3-1 contains large, True Color icons.

Changing the Icons of the Desktop Items

Now that you know how to create large, colorful icons you are probably wondering how to change the various icons already on the desktop. For shortcut icons there's no problem. Right-click on them, select Properties, then Change Icon from the Shortcut tab. Select any icon or .BMP filename and assign it to the shortcut. Changing more persistent icons, like the InBox, or My Computer's icon calls for Registry modifications. To change the icons of the permanent fixtures of the Windows desktop, you must locate and change the following values in the Registry:

Name Value:
```
HKEY_CLASSES_ROOT\CLSID\{00020D75-0000-0000-C000-
000000000046}\DefaultIcon
```
Description:
```
Change Default Value to the icon you want to use for the InBox
folder
```
Name Value:
```
HKEY_CLASSES_ROOT\CLSID\{208D2C60-3AEA-1069-A2D7-
08002B30309D}\DefaultIcon
```
Description:
```
Change Default Value to the icon you want to use for the Network
Neighborhood folder
```
Name Value:
```
HKEY_CLASSES_ROOT\CLSID\{20D04FE0-3AEA-1069-A2D8-
08002B30309D}\DefaultIcon
```
Description:
```
Change Default Value to the icon you want to use for the My
Computer folder
```
Name Value:
```
HKEY_CLASSES_ROOT\CLSID\{645FF040-5081-101B-9F08-
00AA002F954E}\DefaultIcon
```
Description:
```
Change Default Value to the icon you want to use for the Recycle
Bin folder
```

There's another place in the Registry with icon descriptions. They are the icons that are not unique to an application and are repeated on the desktop (such as folder icons, shortcut icons, and

so on). You will find them under the key HKEY_LOCAL_
MACHINE\SOFTWARE\Microsoft\Windows\CurrentVersion\
explorer\Shell Icons. This key contains a number of Values, which
correspond to the various icons Windows uses for special files or
folders. If you have installed Microsoft Plus!, you will find a
number of values there. If not, you will have to add the few values
we suggest.

TIP

If you have installed Microsoft Plus!, you will find some 30 values under
the Shell Icons subkey. They correspond to various icons the system
uses and you are free to change any of them. To view all the icons,
pretend you are changing the icon of a shortcut. Click on the Browse
button and take a peek at the icons in the files WINDOWS\SYSTEM\
COOL.DLL and WINDOWS\SYSTEM\SHELL32.DLL.

Here are the values you will most likely want to change:

Key:
HKEY_LOCAL_MACHINE\SOFTWARE\Microsoft\Windows\CurrentVersion\
explorer\Shell Icons
Name Value:
3 Is the name of the icon that Windows uses to display folders.
8 Is the name of the icon that Windows uses to display disk
   drives.
29 Is the name of the (tiny) icon that Windows overlays on the
   normal icon of a shortcut.

Notice the syntax of these values: C:\WINDOWS\SYSTEM\
COOL.DLL,10 means the 11th icon in the COOL.DLL file (their
numbering starts with zero). If you haven't changed any icons
before, you will find it rather strange that .DLL files contain icons.
You can find icons in both libraries and executable files (with the
extension .EXE). You can find out whether a .DLL or .EXE file
contains icons by using an icon viewer, or the Program Property
tab of the Properties dialog box. Just right-click on a shortcut,

select Properties, and then pretend you are changing the shortcut's icon. You can select any .DLL file and view the icons in it. Not only that, but you can also determine the order of a given icon in the file.

You can find many icons in various Windows 95 DLL files, but you can also create your own icons.

Windows uses mainly two sources for icons, the files COOL.DLL and SHELL32.DLL. Another source for interesting shortcuts is the file PIFMGR.DLL. You will find the icons in this .DLL very useful for MS-DOS applications. You may also find collections of stand-alone icon files. They have the extension .ICO and are really easy to create. We have included an icon editing application on the Companion CD-ROM called MuAngelo. MuAngelo will also help you create your own cursors, as well as animated cursors. Animated cursors have the extension .ANI and can be used in any place you would normally use plain, static icons. There are sequences of static icons, which the system displays in rapid succession. If you think you would enjoy an animated pointer instead of the static hourglass, give them a try.

The previous changes will not take effect immediately, even if you restart your computer. Windows maintains a copy of the icons in use in a hidden file. For the previous changes to take effect, you must first delete the file ShellIconCache in the Windows folder and then restart Windows. Don't be surprised if you have to perform these steps twice. We don't know why, but sometimes we had to remove the ShellIconFile and restart the computer twice, before the new icons could be displayed on the screen.

Changing the little arrow that denotes a shortcut is a little tricky and we will explain the process in the section "Customize the Shortcut's Icon."

After using Windows 95 for a while, you'll notice that all folders are depicted with the same icon. If you have many folders open and you attempt to switch to one of them, you'll see something like Figure 3-16. Now just pick the correct folder. It's easy, if you read their names, but it would be much easier if each folder had a different icon.

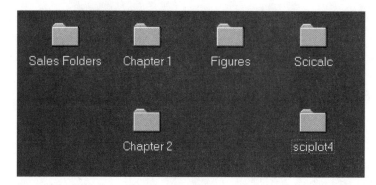

Figure 3-16: No matter what a folder contains, their icons are all the same.

Unfortunately, there's no way to specify different icons for your games and correspondence folders, short of creating shortcuts to the folders and then changing the shortcut's icon.

Another shortcoming of the Windows 95 interface is the fact that open folders have the same icons as closed ones. This isn't a big problem, since clicking the desired folder's icon will either open the folder, or bring it on top if it's been opened already. But in a visually rich environment, such as Windows 95, open folders should be depicted differently from closed ones. As far as we know, there's no way to change this behavior.

Creating .BMP Thumbnails

You can ask Windows to turn .BMP images into their own icons through the Registry.

Here's another trick for those of you who use .BMP files frequently. Thumbnails are small images, which are displayed in the place of an icon, next to an image filename. By using thumbnails, you can easily spot the image you need, instead of opening half of them, before you hit the right one. Any .BMP image can be turned into a thumbnail, which will show as an icon on the desktop. The technique described here applies only to .BMP files.

Open the Registry and follow the path: HKEY_CLASSES_ROOT\Paint.Picture\DefaultIcon. This is the default icon for a .BMP image. To make an icon the same as the image, assign to this key the value "%1" (which is the filename). Close the Registry, press F5, and open a folder with .BMP files. For the reasons we explained in the section "Palettes & True Color," this trick works best with High Color and True Color systems.

Key:
HKEY_CLASSES_ROOT\Paint.Picture\DefaultIcon
Name Value:
(Default)
Data Value:
Set it to %1 to make the image's thumbnail become its icon.

Customizing Sounds

An interesting feature of the Windows operating system is the freedom it offers you to selectively assign sounds to many events. We assume you are familiar with the Sounds Properties dialog box of Figure 3-17. To open this window select Settings from the Start menu, then Control Panel and double-click on the Sounds icon.

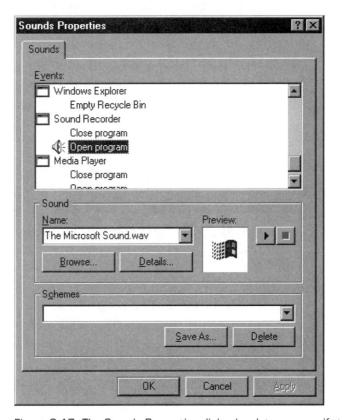

Figure 3-17: The Sounds Properties dialog box lets you specify the sounds triggered by various Windows events.

Avoid assigning sounds to trivial events. Reserve them for selected events of selected applications only.

The Sounds Properties dialog box lets you assign sounds to various Windows events. At the top of the dialog box, you see the events that are generated by Windows and any application that runs under Windows. For example, if you assign a sound to the Open Program event, every time a new program starts, this sound will be played. Or, even worse, the Menu command event: Do you really want to hear a sound every time you open a menu and select a command? You'll get tired of the same sound and the frequency of it. We recommend you assign a sound to events that occur less frequently, such as a program error, or a shutdown event, but having your computer make a sound for every trivial event is overkill.

With some digging into the Registry, you'll discover that it is possible to add sounds to selected events for selected applications only. For example, you can add a sound to your word processor's Open event, which is heard every time you start your word processor, but not when you start any other application. Or add a sound to the Close program event of your communications application, which will remind you to check your telephone's status, to make sure it was hung up.

Let's open the Registry and find out where the names of the events and corresponding sounds are stored. Follow the path HKEY_CURRENT_USER\AppEvents\Schemes\Apps. Your Regedit window should look like the one of Figure 3-18. Under Apps you'll find the Default key, which contains all the system sounds, and the Explorer key, which contains sounds for specific events while you're in the Explorer program, and possibly more application names.

Under each application name you'll find a list of events that trigger sounds. Under Explorer, for example, you'll find the name of the sound file that is played every time you empty the Recycle Bin. If you're like most users, you'll change the default sound to something more obscene.

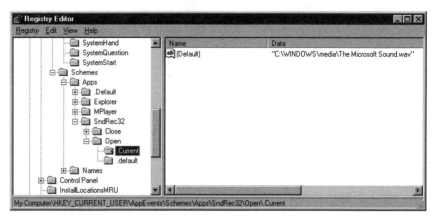

Figure 3-18: This is where the event sounds are stored in the Registry.

These sounds can also be altered from within the Sounds Properties window, shown in Figure 3-17. What you can't do with the Sounds Properties window, though, is add your own applications to the list. But since we found out how the sounds are stored in the Registry, why bother with the Sounds window?

To find out what events Windows generates, look under the key EventLabels. This is a list of event names; you can't assign sounds here. First, add the application name to which you want to assign a sound to the key HKEY_CURRENT_USER\AppEvents\Schemes\Apps. Then, open this key and add one or more subkeys, with the names of the events to which you want to assign sounds (like Open, Close, Maximize, etc.). Open the new subkey again and create yet another subkey under it, named .Current (don't omit the period in front of its name). Now, you can finally assign a sound file to the event(s), by assigning the name of the sound file to the .Current value of the corresponding event. Or, if you prefer, open the Sounds Properties window, which will contain the application names you've added to the Registry, and specify the events you want to trigger sounds.

Let's see how you can add a sound of your own to the Close program event of the Netscape application. Netscape is an online communications application that lets you communicate with the vast world of the Internet (you'll find more about the Internet in

Use the Registry to add sounds to the events of your favorite applications.

Chapter 7). Netscape uses the modem to communicate with other computers, so it wouldn't be a bad idea to have Netscape play a pre-recorded sound that reminds you to hang up the modem when Netscape shuts down. Here are the steps you must follow:

Open the key HKEY_CURRENT_USER\AppEvents\Schemes\ Apps. Under it, you'll see the applications, certain events of which cause sounds to be played. Add a new key and name it "Netscape" (this is the name of the application to whose Close event we want to assign a sound). Now add another subkey under Netscape and name it "Close" (it is the event's name). Finally, add the .Current subkey under Close and change this subkey's default value to the name of the .WAV file you want to hear every time you close the Netscape application.

You can assign sounds to practically any event, as long as the event's name appears under the key EventLabels. Notice that once the new application name has been added as a key under Apps, you can assign sounds to the application's events from within the Sounds Properties window as well.

Key:
HKEY_CURRENT_USER\AppEvents\Schemes\Apps
Description:
Contains a list of applications and the events that cause a sound to be played back

Customize StartUp

This section discusses some of the aspects of the Windows 95 startup process and how you can customize them.

Turn Off the Little Bouncing Arrow

Do you really need the little bouncing arrow telling you where to start every time you turn on your computer? We doubt it. Actually, we found it annoying from day one. Who needs to be told "Click on Start to Begin?" Here's how you can eliminate it for good.

Run the Registry Editor and follow the HKEY_CURRENT_ USER\ Software\Microsoft\ Windows\ CurrentVersion\ Policies\ Explorer path. Add a new Binary Value, called No-StartBanner (if it's not already there) and assign the data 01 00 00 00 to it.

Name Value:
HKEY_CURRENT_USER\Software\Microsoft\Windows\CurrentVersion\
Policies\Explorer\NoStartBanner
Data Value:
00 00 00 00 Default startup
01 00 00 00 Suppresses the "click here to begin" animation

Eliminating Tips at Startup?

Another annoyance that occurs at startup is the display of a trivial tip. There are only a few dozen tips and you will not see more advanced tips as you become more familiar with your computer. Most of you have already turned off this "feature," but here are a couple of suggestions.

How about reading them all and then disabling them? Open the Registry and search for the word "tip." You will find several keys that match your search criteria before you hit the section with the actual tips, as shown in Figure 3-19 (the tips are under the key HKEY_LOCAL_MACHINE\Software\Microsoft\Windows\ CurrentVersion\explorer\tips).

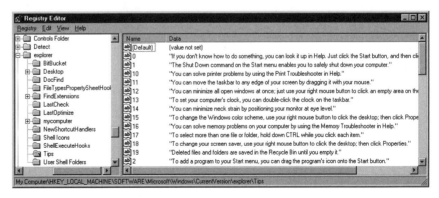

Figure 3-19: This is where the tips are stored in the Registry.

It's easy to change the default Windows 95 tips through the Registry.

It's not easy to read the tips in the Registry, but you can export this branch of the Registry to a text file and view it with your word processor. Click on the "Tips" key in the left pane to select it and then select Export Registry File from the Edit menu. In the Save File dialog box that appears on your screen, enter a filename and click OK. Although the file with the tips has the extension .REG, it is a regular text file. Open it with Notepad or Wordpad, read the tips (in case you missed a good one) and then disable them.

If you want to use the proper entry in the Registry to disable the tips, search for the "Show" key. Repeat the search with the F3 key until you reach the: HKEY_CURRENT_USER\SOFTWARE\Microsoft\Windows\CurrentVersion\Explorer\Tips subkey. The data setting of the Show value is 01 00 00 00. To disable the tips, change this setting to 00 00 00 00. (If you've already turned the tips off from your desktop and you want to turn them back on, set the value back to 01 00 00 00.)

Name Value:
HKEY_CURRENT_USER\SOFTWARE\Microsoft\Windows\CurrentVersion\
Explorer\Tips\Show
Data Value:
00 00 00 00Disables tips at startup
01 00 00 00Enables tips at startup

Under the same subkey, you'll find the Next value. This is the number of the tip to be displayed the next time the computer is turned on. We'll use this value in the section "High Visibility Reminders."

Name Value:
HKEY_CURRENT_USER\SOFTWARE\Microsoft\Windows\CurrentVersion\Explorer\
Tips\Next
Data Value:
The number of the tip to be displayed next time you start
Windows

Displaying Your Own Tips

You can change the list of default tips and have your own tips displayed at startup. Open the .REG file to which you exported the original Windows 95 tips with a word processor and edit it to your heart's content. Then, you can import the file back to the Registry to replace Microsoft's tips. An even easier way to update the Registry is to simply double-click on the .REG file's icon (as long as the file's extension is .REG). If you come up with a collection of interesting tips for advanced users, you can distribute your .REG file to friends, or coworkers. If you manage a network, or part of your working day is spent in assisting other Windows users, you can anticipate their needs by turning the answers to their questions into tips.

High Visibility Reminders

If you don't need any tips at startup, change them into reminders for the next time you turn on your computer.

Here's another idea for a practical use of the Registry's tips. You can turn the first tip into a reminder, such as "Call accountant," or "Review Tom's reports before noon today!". Export the tips into a .REG file (REMINDME.REG, for example) as we did in the previous paragraph and edit the first tip (tip #0), whenever you want to leave a reminder to yourself for the next time you turn on your computer. Then double-click on the .REG file's icon to update the Registry. That's all there is to it. To make sure Windows will display your reminder, and not another tip, set the value Next to 0.

Here are the contents of a .REG file that causes Windows to display a reminder the next time it starts:

```
REGEDIT4
[HKEY_CURRENT_USER\Software\Microsoft\Windows\CurrentVersion\
Explorer\Tips]
"Next"=hex:01,00
"Show"=hex:01,00,00,00
[HKEY_LOCAL_MACHINE\SOFTWARE\Microsoft\Windows\CurrentVersion\
explorer\Tips]
"0"="that Mom is coming to visit next week?"
```

Notice that you need not specify all the tips, just the one you want to modify.

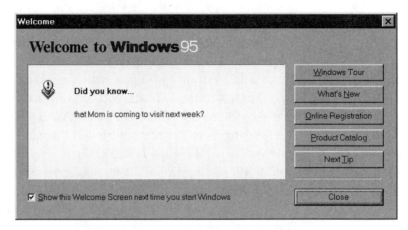

Figure 3-20: Turn the trivial Windows tips into reminders that appear the next time you start Windows 95.

Customizing the Startup & Shutdown Screens

If you've grown tired of the tips and other trivial startup sequences, you would probably like to change the default Windows startup and shutdown images. These images are ordinary .BMP files you can edit with any image processing application or replace with your own .BMP files. The only problem is that they don't have .BMP extensions as they should. They use the .SYS extension, so that they will not be deleted accidentally. The image displayed when Windows starts lives in the root directory and is called LOGO.SYS. The other two images, displayed when Windows shuts down (the one that asks you to wait while Windows shuts down and the final one that informs you that it is safe to turn off your computer) can be found in the Windows folder and are the files LOGOW.SYS and LOGOS.SYS respectively. To edit them, change their extension to .BMP, load them in your favorite image processing application and when you are finished editing them, save them and change their extensions back to .SYS. Or, back up the original .SYS files, create your own .BMP images and rename the new ones with the names of the original with the .SYS extension.

Display your own images during the startup and shutdown process.

TIP

If you decide to change these images, make sure the images that replace them have dimensions 320 x 400 and contain no more than 256 colors. Also, if you are using DriveSpace, the LOGO.SYS file is on the host drive (usually G:) and not on the C: drive (there is a LOGO.SYS file on the C: drive, but it's not the one Windows uses). Also, if Windows 95 can't understand the replacement images for any reason, it will boot in DOS mode!

Creating a Foolproof Startup Procedure

The Startup folder contains all the programs that are executed when the system starts. All you have to do to make a new program run at startup is to drag and drop the program's icon in the Startup folder and create a shortcut. (The Startup folder is in your Windows\Start Menu folder.) If other users fool around with your Startup folder (perhaps someone is removing your antivirus software or other maintenance tools from the Startup folder to shorten the startup process) you can make it harder for them to foul up your machine. To place the programs you want absolutely to be executed at startup in the Registry open the HKEY_LOCAL_MACHINE tree, select SOFTWARE, then Microsoft, then Windows, then CurrentVersion, and finally Run. Any applications here will run at startup regardless of the contents of the Startup folder.

Name Value:
`HKEY_LOCAL_MACHINE\SOFTWARE\Microsoft\Windows\CurrentVersion\Run`
Data Value:
`Any programs listed here will be executed at startup`

Notice that you are not restricted in specifying only the name of a program. If you want to play a sound every time the system starts, just add the corresponding .WAV file in the Startup folder, or in the Run key. Windows knows what to do with it.

Keep Your System Always Up-to-Date

Modify an entry in the Registry to have Windows 95 automatically update the desktop every time a disk is swapped, or a new file is created.

Let's say you've opened the folder of the A: drive, or the CD-ROM drive. If you change a disk in your drive, or place a new CD in the CD-ROM drive, while its folder is open, you will not see the contents of the new disk, or CD immediately. You must first press F5 or select Refresh from the View menu. Wouldn't you rather have the system update the folders the moment their contents change? The Registry maintains an entry which controls whether the contents of the various folders are updated automatically, or not. It's called UpdateMode and its value is 01 (which corresponds to manual refresh). Change its value to 00 and the contents of your folder windows will reflect the actual contents of your disks, at all times.

To locate this entry in the Registry, open HKEY_LOCAL_ MACHINE, then System, then CurrentControlSet, then Control and finally click on Update. Change the Data setting for the UpdateMode value from 1 to 0 to make Windows 95 refresh the desktop automatically, every time a file is created or a new disk is inserted in a drive. Notice that automatic update applies not only to external events, but to changes you make in the Registry as well (although some changes in the Registry will not take effect until the next time you start your computer).

Name Value:
HKEY_LOCAL_MACHINE\System\CurrentControlSet\Update:
Data Value:
0   Automatic refresh
1   Manual refresh

Maintaining a Neat Desktop

After working with several applications and documents for a while, you'll realize that the desktop looks just like your real desktop! It's messy, documents are all over the place, and you can't reach the ones you need without putting away some of the open documents. What do you do when your screen looks like the one in Figure 3-21 and you need access to the desktop? A friend called to let you know that he's sending a fax, and you must start the Exchange program. Or a client calls and you need access to the documents, which you carefully placed in a special folder right on the desktop (so that you could reach them quickly). Your idea of placing the most needed documents on the desktop was a great one and the desktop looked attractive and organized—that is, before you started opening applications and documents.

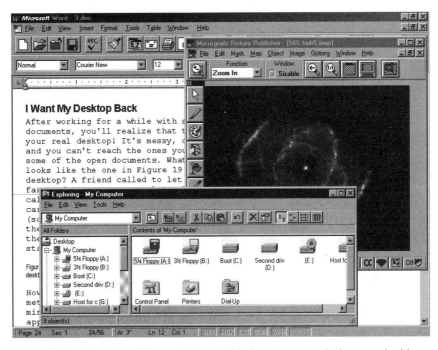

Figure 3-21: It's easy to fill your desktop with documents, and when you do, it's not always easy to get to the desktop.

The Windows 95 desktop is very much like your real desktop: you have to dig through the open documents to find something on the desktop.

How can you get your desktop back? Fortunately, there are a few methods to choose from. To begin with, you can start minimizing the open applications. The problem with this approach is that you have to click on a tiny space, and half the time you'll be maximizing applications instead of minimizing them. It's so easy to miss that tiny spot (the Minimize button) on the right top corner of an application, especially if you are using a resolution larger that 640 x 480 (unless, of course, you've changed the default button size as described in the section, "Appearances Matter," earlier in this chapter).

Your second choice is to right-click on an empty area of the taskbar and select Minimize All Windows. Doing so minimizes all active applications. After you've reached the desktop, you can restore the applications to their original sizes by selecting each application's button from the taskbar, or by selecting Undo Minimize All from the taskbar's right-click menu.

 WinShade is a Windows 95 desktop utility (included on the Companion CD-ROM) that makes it easy to move large windows out of the way. Rather than minimizing an application to view another, WinShade allows you to click on the title bar and reduce the window to its smallest vertical dimension. In most cases the window "rolls up" into its title bar, leaving only a thin horizontal window on the desktop. After working in another application, you can click back on the rolled-up window's title bar and the window will expand to its previous dimensions. WinShade works with almost all windows, including dialog boxes, child windows, and even maximized windows.

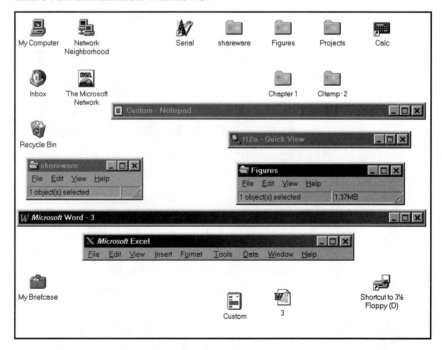

Figure 3-22: On this desktop, applications have been "rolled up" with WinShade to make the desktop accessible.

To install WinShade, create a new folder called WinShade, move the WINSHADE.ZIP file there and unzip it (then you can delete the WinShade95.zip file). To run WinShade, simply double-click the WINSHADE.EXE icon. Or if you want to run WinShade on startup, drag WINSHADE.EXE into your Startup folder to create a shortcut to the application. Restart Windows 95 and you're all set.

The Task Manager

Do you miss the Task Manager from Windows 3.1x? It's still there, only it's a bit different. You can't start it by double-clicking on the desktop, as was the case with Windows 3.1x. However, you can create a shortcut and assign a hotkey to it. Task Manager was replaced by the taskbar, but it provides the same functionality and can be displayed anywhere on the screen (you can even keep it on top of all other windows, if you like).

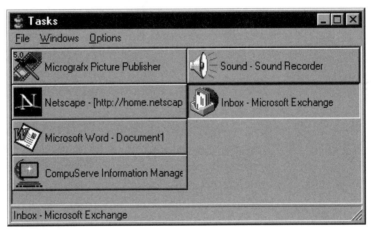

Figure 3-23: The Task Manager is hidden in the Windows folder, but it's just as useful as ever.

To start the new Task Manager, run the program TASKMAN.EXE in the Windows directory, or, even better, drag the file to the desktop to create a shortcut. If you use it frequently, place a shortcut to Windows\TASKMAN.EXE in your Startup folder.

WORKING WITH FILES

So far we've discussed ways to customize and maintain some order on your desktop, which is just the surface of the operating system, as well as some features such as event sounds and mouse clicks. In this section we're presenting a collection of techniques related to file manipulation. We will only present a few interesting topics, like the differences between My Computer and Explorer and how to make Windows 95 generate easier to understand filenames under DOS. We will also explain file associations and show you how to best exploit them.

What you'll be doing most of the time on your desktop is file manipulation: moving files around, searching for the files you need, deleting files you don't need any more, and so on. As you already know, there are two places to start: My Computer and Explorer. They look very much alike, because they're both the same program. They do the same thing and even have the same menu. Their only difference is the Tools option, which is present in the Windows Explorer only and contains commands for connecting to network drives. Since the network drives are not on your computer, this menu has no reason to exist on My Computer.

There's another major difference between the two programs. My Computer offers a single pane in which you can view the files of the current folder only. Windows Explorer, on the other hand, provides a bigger picture, with the directory structure on the left pane and the current folder's contents on the right pane. Moreover, you can easily expand, or collapse, a folder with the plus and minus keys on the numeric keypad respectively.

Explorer and My Computer are the same program with a different front end.

■ ■

TIP

You can expand the entire directory structure of a disk by selecting it and pressing the asterisk key (*) on the numeric keypad.

■ ■

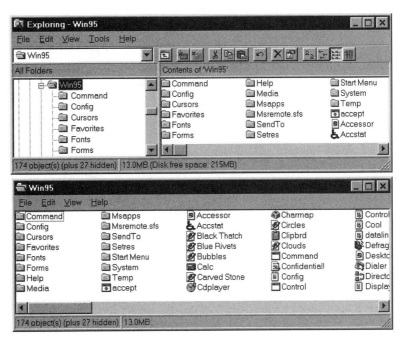

Figure 3-24: Two views of the same object.

TIP

With both the Explorer and My Computer, it is possible to move to a specific folder by typing the first few characters of the name of the folder. This is tricky, though, since you must type the characters rather quickly. If you pause for a second or so, Windows thinks you are typing the name of another folder.

If you are a DOS user and want to know your exact location on the disk, use the Windows Explorer. If most of your folders live on the desktop and you don't want to look up program names or auxiliary files, use My Computer. However, since the subdirectory view of the Explorer doesn't hurt anything (you can simply ignore it) why not make My Computer behave the same as the Windows Explorer? Just hold down the Shift key as you double-click on My Computer.

■ ■

TIP

To switch to the Explorer from within any folder, right-click on the
Control menu and select Explore.

■ ■

The difference between My Computer and the Windows Explorer is the same as the difference between the Windows 3.*x* File Manager and the numerous third-party File Manager replacements. Every management tool was better than File Manager. And the Windows Explorer is better than My Computer. You may wonder why My Computer was included in the operating system. And why you can't even remove it from the desktop? Because, someday in the future, directories and disk structures will be history. We'll be working with documents and the operating system will be handling "details" such as where the files are stored, subdirectories, and the rest. So, My Computer will help you transition more comfortably to the operating systems to come. There won't be any reason for DOS windows either. But, today, we just can't overcome our DOS legacy and pretend DOS isn't there. How many times did you switch to DOS to use File Managers like Norton Commander to move files around or delete them en masse? DOS is still alive, and will continue to be around, as *we* DOS users are alive and active.

Minimize the Open Folders on the Desktop

Browsing through your hard disk to locate a file or an application with My Computer may leave you with a messy desktop. If the file you're looking for is three or four levels down in a subdirectory, on your way there you'll leave three or four open folders on your desktop. Fortunately, Microsoft has built some neat mechanisms into Windows 95 to minimize the clutter. By default, every folder you open remains open until you close it by clicking on the Close icon, or pressing Alt+F4. This is the Multiple Window Browse mode. To change it, you can select Options from the folder's View menu and check the box "Browse folders by using a single window that changes as you open each folder" as shown in

Figure 3-25. This setting is global and can be changed from within any open folder. From now on, every time you open a folder by double-clicking on its icon, the contents of the new folder will replace the contents of the parent folder, in the same window.

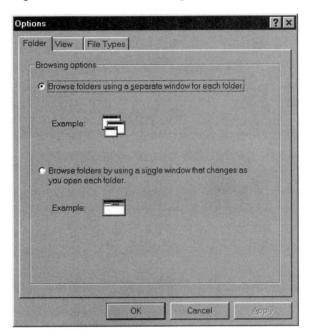

Figure 3-25: Forcing My Computer to use the same window for each folder, instead of opening a new one.

You can force Explorer to use a single pane for each new folder you open.

Neither mode, however, will suit all your needs. That's why you can overwrite either mode by holding down the Ctrl key as you double-click on a folder's icon. For example, if you normally have your machine set for single window browsing, but for some reason need to open a folder in its own window, simply hold down the Control key as you double-click on that folder. The same goes for keeping a normally multi-windowed machine restricted to the open window.

My Computer's default view of your hard disk is a rather spasmodic one, because you don't know where you stand. Old DOS users need to know where they are within their disk's structure. You can make Windows 95 display the full path of the current folder by opening the View/Options dialog box, (see Figure 3-25) selecting the View tab, and checking the "Display the full MS-DOS path in the title bar" box, as shown in Figure 3-25. By seeing the full pathname of each open folder, you know for sure whether the current Tools folder contains your Internet tools, or some programming tools.

How to Make Better DOS Filenames

Windows 95 uses long (up to 260 characters), meaningful filenames. If you use only Windows 95, then stick with long filenames and forget the 8.3 restrictions of the old DOS world. You'll be wondering how you managed for so many years without longer filenames (i.e., without a Macintosh). But many of us can't live without DOS. It's probably a habit we can't kick overnight— all these file management utilities are still alive. In fact, most Windows 95 users will switch to DOS to perform massive file shuffling. DOS, however, hasn't changed and it still doesn't understand long filenames. Windows 95 therefore, must translate and truncate long filenames into short, cryptic names for DOS.

At the DOS prompt, the filename "Great Tips for Windows 95.DOC," for example, will be translated to "GREATT~1.DOC." It's no longer clear whether the file contains great tips for Windows 95, or the Internet. Can we do any better? As long as DOS doesn't support long filenames, you can do very little, but a little is still better than nothing. You can at least get rid of the tilde symbol and the following digit. You can ask Windows 95 to rename the Great Tips for Windows 95.DOC file as "GREATTIP.DOC" so the last two characters aren't wasted. And two out of eight is a significant gain. Of course, if you have another "Great Tips" filename, it will be truncated to "GREATTI1.DOC" and so on. You should also name your files so that the first word makes them different than other files with similar names. For the previous example, a name like "Win95 Great Tips.doc" would result in a better DOS filename.

To change the rules Windows 95 uses to truncate long filenames into their DOS equivalents, open the Registry, follow the HKEY_

Change an entry in the Registry and you'll never see filenames with tildes in a DOS window.

LOCAL_MACHINE\System\CurrentControlSet\Control path and select the File System key. Right-click on the right pane of the Regedit window and in the pop-up menu select New, then Binary Value. Type **NameNumericTail** to add the new Name and press Enter. Double-click on the new value Name and enter 0 (zero) as its Data. You have just created a whole new, undocumented entry in the Registry, which will cause the DOS versions of the long filenames to be as close as possible to that of the long name. Of course, if the short versions of more than one file happens to be the same, Windows will append sequence numbers to the filenames.

While we're at it, we should mention a little known fact: the DOS version that ships with Windows 95 understands long filenames, although it prefers the short ones. Figure 3-26 shows a DOS window. Notice the short DOS filenames on the left and their long versions on the right. You can use long filenames in DOS commands, as long as you enclose them in double quotes, as in the following command lines:

```
dir "My Daily Correspondence"
or
cd "Employee Reports"
```

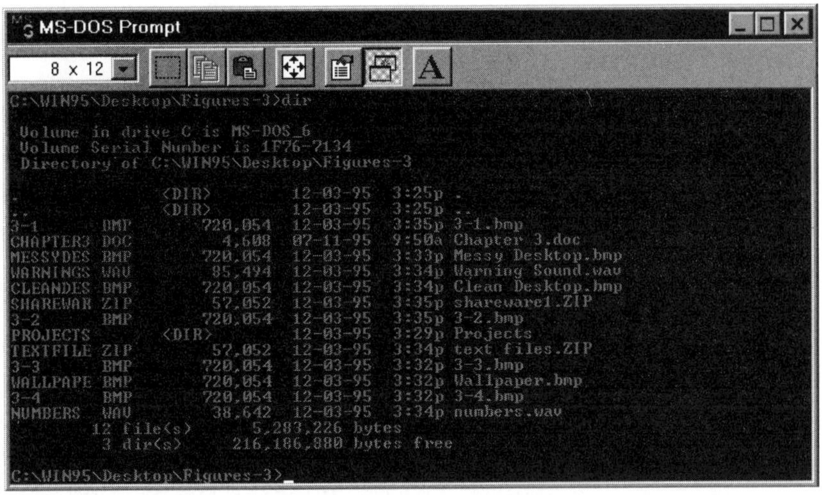

Figure 3-26: Make Windows 95 create better short filenames for DOS.

We frequently use long filenames in DOS sessions because it beats having to figure out how DOS has shortened the long version of a directory or filename.

Key:
HKEY_LOCAL_MACHINE\system\CurrentControlSet\Control\File System\
Name Value:
NameNumericTrail
Data Value:
0   omits the tilde (~) character and sequence number in short
    version of long filenames
1   restores the Windows 95 default method of creating short
    filenames

Finding Files

Another very useful feature of the Windows 95 operating system is its ability to search for any file, based on a number of criteria, such as filenames, file sizes, and dates. Moreover, the search criteria can be saved in special files so you can perform the same searches without having to explicitly enter every one of the criteria. The search files have the extension .FND and they are created every time you issue the File\Save Search command.

Create FND files for the most common searches you perform on your disk(s) and use them again and again.

A very useful item to have on the desktop, or in a special folder, is the search criteria you use most often. Let's say you reclaim disk space every week or so, by removing huge or unused files from your disk. Under Windows 3.1*x* there was no easy way to locate all .TMP files, whose sizes exceed 1MB. Windows 95 makes this operation easy. Images and animation files can quickly eat up your disk space. Create a search to locate these items, similar to the one shown in Figure 3-27, and then save it with the File\Save Search command. A new .FND file will be created on your desktop, with an unusual long name: "Files named @.avi, @.bmp, @.jpg.fnd". Rename it something less cryptic, such as "Large images" and move it into the Frequent Searches folder. Every time you want to perform the same search on your disk, double-click on this file's icon and you'll see the Find window on your screen, with all the search criteria in place.

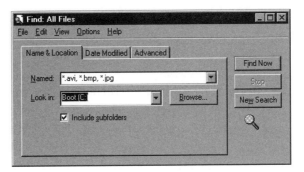

Figure 3-27: Searching for multiple file types on a drive.

One feature missing from the Find program, though, is the exclusion of certain file types. It would also be useful for the .FND files to be editable, so that we could automate our searches.

Multiple Program Associations

A good deal of the friendliness and ease of use of Windows 95 comes from its file-program associations. Files can be associated to applications, so that every time you double-click on the file's icon the application starts and loads the specified file. This technique has been in use since Windows 3.0, as the operating system had no way of knowing which application created a document. That's why all documents must have a proper extension, even though the extension is now typically not shown in file or Explorer windows. (If Microsoft is going to live up to its promise to deliver a docucentric operating system, it will have to get rid of file associations and extensions. The operating system should be able to keep track of the application that created each document without such "obvious" hints, like file extensions.)

At times, you may want to open the same document with different applications, for different purposes. For instance, you may want to use Paint Shop Pro to view bitmap images (files with the .BMP extension) and Picture to edit them (draw frames, place annotations, and so on). By default, Windows associates each file type with a single application. It is possible to associate any given

A document type can be associated with multiple applications and they can all appear in the document type's shortcut menu.

155

file type with multiple applications, and we'll explain how it's done. Of course, one of the associated programs will start with a double-click on the file's icon, but you can see all associated applications and select the one you want by right-clicking on the icon. In Figure 3-28 you see the right-click menu of a .BMP image on a plain Windows 95 system and on a customized system. The Open to Edit command opens the file with Paint (the painting application that comes with Windows 95). The Open to View command opens it with Paint Shop Pro (or any other image processing application you prefer).

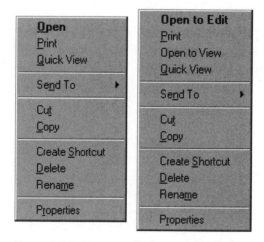

Figure 3-28: Assigning multiple associations to a file type.

You can add your own commands to an icon's shortcut menu in two ways. One of them, you guessed it, involves the Registry. Let's start with the simpler method, from within the Explorer.

In the Explorer, open the View menu and select Options. Then click on the File Types tab and you'll see a list with registered file types. Double-click on the file type you want to work with (Bitmap Image in our example) and the Edit File Type dialog box appears (see Figure 3-29). The Actions list contains the various actions, which appear in the corresponding file's shortcut menu. Most file types have a single action, called Open. The second most common action is Print. .BMP files can be opened and printed. To see which application carries out each action, double-click on the action's name. .BMP files are opened with the Paint application, as you can see in Figure 3-29. (You may also see the Quick View option, if you have installed the Quick View accessory. Quick View is inserted there by the system. If Quick View understands a specific file type, its name will appear in this file's shortcut menu.)

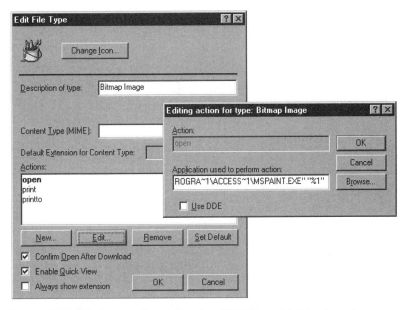

Figure 3-29: Manipulate the actions for .BMP files with this dialog box.

Add a new action by clicking on the New button. You'll be prompted for the name of the action and the corresponding application. In this case you would enter "View Image" as the action name and "c:\graphics\psp.exe" "%1" in the Application box (replace the application name with the appropriate pathname on your system). %1 stands for the name of the selected file and is passed to the application as its first argument, so that it opens the selected file automatically. While you're editing the .BMP file type's actions, you may as well rename the Open command to "Edit Image." Since there's no Rename button, you must first delete the original "Open" action and then add a new action and name it "Open to Edit" or "Edit Image."

You can also use descriptive names for each associated application in a document's shortcut menu.

Of all the actions, one appears in bold. This is the action the system will take when you double-click on a .BMP file's icon. Select the action you want to become the default one and click on the Set Default check box.

TIP

Don't change the default action, unless you have good reason to. The default action for the .WAV file type (sounds) is Play. If you place a .WAV file in the Startup folder, it will be played every time you start your system. Windows knows what to do with the .WAV file, only because its default action is Play. Change it to Open and Windows will open the Sound Player application at startup.

While editing an action, you'll also notice a check box called DDE. If you check it, you'll see a few more options, as shown in Figure 3-30. DDE (Dynamic Data Exchange) is a mechanism for sending commands to a running application. The application that receives the commands must be DDE-capable, in other words be able to understand the set of DDE commands.

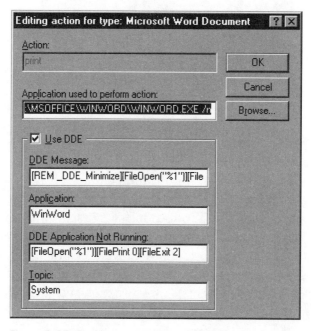

Figure 3-30: Passing commands to a running application.

Use DDE to tell Windows that if the application associated with the specific file type is already running, it shouldn't start another instance of the application. Instead, it should send the appropriate DDE command to it. Take a look at the Print command of .DOC files (in Figure 3-30). The DDE message is [FileOpen("%1")] [FilePrint()][DocClose(2)]. This is the command Windows sends to Word for Windows if it's already running. If Word isn't running, Windows uses the next string, [FileOpen("%1")][FilePrint .Background = 0][FileExit(2)]. Windows will start the application, have it open the file, print it in the background, and finally shut down the application (instead of just closing the file, as in the previous case).

DDE commands are fairly easy to understand and they usually correspond to menu commands of the application. To find out whether an application supports DDE commands, and which ones, you must consult the application's help files, or the documentation.

The second method of associating file types to applications, which involves the Registry, is explained later in the chapter, in the section, "Icon Shortcut Menus."

Multiple File Associations

It is also possible to associate multiple files with a single application. For example, Windows 95 understands two types of bitmap images, .BMP and .PCX files. Moreover, it uses the Paint application to open both file types—look up the associations of Bitmap Images in the File Types dialog box. Adding multiple file associations to the same application can't be done through the File Types tab of the Explorer's Options dialog box, but it can be easily accomplished with the help of the Registry.

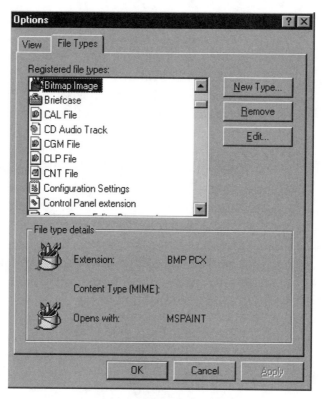

Figure 3-31: Bitmap Images are files with extensions .BMP and .PCX—unless you add more file extensions for this file type.

You probably think the authors of this book haven't looked at the list of registered files. It looks like there are so many, but there are times when you do need to add more file types. If you have used image processing applications under Windows 3.*x*, you probably remember the .DIB (Device Independent Bitmap) extension. You may even have .DIB files on your disk, but Windows 95 can't open them when you double-click on their icons. .DIB files are really .BMP files with a different extension. Paint could read them, if they were only registered. If you look at the list of registered file types in the Registry, there's no .DIB key. (If this key exists in your Registry, it's because one of your image processing applications placed it there.)

Use the Registry to add new file types and the applications that can handle them.

Let's see what's involved in adding a new file type in the Registry and associating it with an application. Since .DIB files are the same as .BMP, let's open the .BMP key and see its value. Find the .BMP key under HKEY_CLASSES_ROOT and click on it to see its default value. It's Paint.Picture, which is the class name. Let's go down the list of file types to see how Windows handles files of the Paint.Picture class. Expand the key to see its subkeys. One of them is Shell. Expand the Shell subkey and its subkeys, as shown in Figure 3-32. What you see here are the operations Windows can carry out with files of the class Paint.Picture. To make sure Windows can handle .DIB files as well, all we have to do is create a new file type (.DIB) and make it part of the Paint.Picture class.

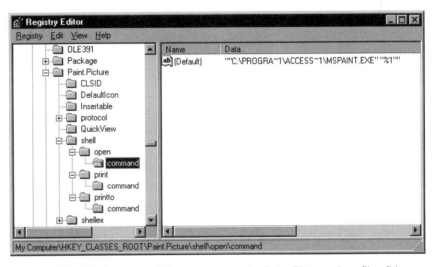

Figure 3-32: Windows uses Paint to process the Paint.Picture class files (bitmap images).

Let's add a new key for the .DIB extension under HKEY_CLASSES_ROOT. To do so, back up to the top of the current branch and right-click on it. From the pop-up menu select New | Key. Name the key ".DIB." After naming the key, change the Data entry for Default to "Paint.Picture" (don't use quotes in either case). Now close the Registry and press F5 to make the changes take effect. If you open the File Type dialog box again and select Bitmap Image, you'll see that the Bitmap Image file type encompasses three extensions: .BMP and .PCX as before, plus the .DIB extension. Any action the system could perform on .BMP and .PCX files, it can now perform on .DIB files as well.

BELOW THE SURFACE

Now it's time to get down to some powerful techniques that can help you make the most of your new operating system. As you recall, in Chapter 1 we described Windows 95 as a docucentric operating system, which means that with Windows 95 your attention is shifted from the applications to the documents, which is why you are using a computer in the first place.

The two elements of the new Windows interface that will have the most impact on the way you work are the folders and the shortcuts. They allow you to organize your documents in any way that suits your needs, as opposed to your machine's needs. The ability to have folders within folders and use shortcuts to get to your files and programs was a desperately needed feature, which finally arrived with Windows 95. (By the way, this feature was part of every other major operating system in the days of Windows 3.1x). The desktop is no longer an application launching instrument. It has become a place where you can get your work done and it happened thanks to the functionality these two elements provide.

Folders & Shortcuts

DOS, as well as Windows 3.1x users are quite familiar with directories and subdirectories. Although Windows 3.1x used folder icons to represent subdirectories, they were fairly limited and users couldn't organize their files to folders. They had to be aware of the locations of their files on the disk. In other words, they had to be familiar with the structure of their hard disks. This situation is changing with Windows 95 and will change completely when the new version of Windows (code named Cairo) is released. Let's start our discussion by comparing folders to subdirectories.

Folders vs. Subdirectories

To old DOS users, a folder is simply the icon of a subdirectory. In the Windows 95 paradigm, however, a folder is a way to organize files. A Windows folder may contain related files, regardless of where they actually reside on the disk.

Folders are quite similar to subdirectories, with the exception that they may contain shortcuts to other files, which live in different folders.

The actual folder is a subdirectory, no matter how you look at it. Every time you create a new folder (and there are many ways to create folders in Windows 95), a new subdirectory is created. You can easily locate the name of each folder in a DOS window and view its contents. Every time you save a file in a given folder, a new file is added to the specific subdirectory. Likewise, every time you move or copy a file to a folder, a new entry is created in that folder. Folders are subdirectories and their contents are the files in them. So far, the two views are consistent. But folders can also contain shortcuts, which are pointers to files. The topic of shortcuts is explained in Chapter 1, but it's worth looking at them again. Shortcuts are Windows 95's way of maintaining multiple views of files, wherever the user needs them.

What's a Shortcut?

A shortcut is a shorter, easier way to get to your destination. With computers, the destination is information. Let's say you keep the most frequently used files in folders right on your desktop. One of them is Customers. When a customer calls, you open this folder and all the information you need is right at your fingertips. If you write a report and you need some information about your customers, just open the Customers folder and find what you need. Another folder might be called Marketing and contains all the information you need when you talk to the people in the marketing department. The files in each folder need not reside in the same subdirectory—in fact they shouldn't. The actual files may reside on your company's server. All you need is a way to view the files you need.

The two folders in our example may contain common files too. For instance, the Price List file is needed in both folders.

163

Obviously, there shouldn't be two versions of the same file on the disk. What you need is two shortcuts, one in the Customers folder and another one in the Marketing folder and you will be able to see the same file from two different places. Any changes made to the Price List file will be available to you from within either folder.

The Customers and Marketing folders do not contain the actual files, but shortcuts to them. By double-clicking on a shortcut, you open the corresponding file with the appropriate application, without knowledge of the file's or application's physical location on the disk. Windows 95 takes care of these details. All you need is a way to organize your files so that you can access them instantly. And that's exactly what shortcuts do. They provide the means to organize the files according to your needs, regardless of their physical organization on the disk.

Your network's administrator may choose to move some files around. He or she may move some of the marketing department's files to another server. The best part of shortcuts is that your view of the company's files doesn't change. Windows 95 updates the shortcuts and your view of the files remains the same.

Do you see the relationship between folders and shortcuts? Folders alone would be just pictures of the actual subdirectories they correspond to. They would allow you to organize your files on the disk, but you would still have to be aware of the directory structure of your disk. What would you do about the Price List folder? Maintain two copies, one in each folder? Or just remember to look for it in another folder? Without shortcuts, Windows 95 folders wouldn't be any more useful than the plain old folder in Windows 3.*x*—with the exception that in Windows 95 you can have folders within folders.

Let's take one more step in this organizational scheme. Say the customers' names are stored in a database. In some cases, you would rather view them in a spreadsheet organization, a table with one customer per row. You can place a shortcut to an Excel spreadsheet, which in turn is "linked" to a database. Every time you want to view your customers' names, you double-click on the shortcut to the Excel file. Excel starts, retrieves your customers from the company's database, and there you have them. We will

Shortcuts enable you to organize your files and folders according to *your* needs, regardless of their locations on the drive(s).

talk more about linking applications to one another in Chapter 8, but the idea is that you no longer need to be aware of the physical organization of your data on the disk, as long as you provide the appropriate links to the information you need. Your shortcut to the customer names is not even a file! It's a program that knows how to retrieve the data you want and present them to you in any form you like.

Finally, shortcuts can be easily moved around, even deleted. When you delete the shortcut to the Price List file in the Marketing folder, you simply can't access that file from within the specific folder. The actual file doesn't cease to exist and you can still access it from within the Customers folder or by specifying its complete pathname. Re-establishing a shortcut is as simple as locating the actual file on a disk with the Explorer. Moving shortcuts around is also easier than moving, or copying, the actual files. Shortcuts are small, 1KB files.

Shortcuts represent a milestone in the evolution of Windows. They introduce a conceptual model for organizing your files and your view of the hard disk will never be the same again. Earlier operating systems, including DOS, required that the user understand the physical organization of the files on the disk. Under DOS, for instance, you can't open a file or start a program, unless you know its exact location on the hard disk. The PATH command introduced some convenience, but it didn't solve the problem. Windows 3.x introduced the concept of file associations so you could start an application by double-clicking on a file's name (there wasn't any need to know where the application was stored), but it didn't allow much freedom in organizing files on the hard disk. One of the major shortcomings of Windows 3.1x was the fact that you couldn't place folders within other folders. It was impossible, therefore, to organize one's files in meaningful ways that suited the user's needs, rather than the computer's needs.

Shortcuts to Everything

When should you be using actual objects and when should you be using shortcuts to them? Whenever it's convenient. If there's a particular program you use often, place a shortcut to it on your desktop. If there's a file you frequently need, do the same. You can set up your environment so that there are no folders or files on your desktop, just shortcuts. Shortcuts let you create your own view of the hard disk and not be aware of the files' physical locations. Ideally, there should be only shortcuts on your desktop. If you keep creating files on the desktop, you'll realize that they all live in the Windows\desktop folder and manipulating them with Explorer will be more difficult than it should.

Another benefit of using shortcuts is the fact that they are more conducive to customization than folders and files. As you recall from our discussion of the desktop's icons, you can't assign different icons to different folders. The default icon is a picture of a plain manila envelope. Even if you change the icon, it will be the same for all folders. To create a shortcut to a folder, right-click on it and open the Properties dialog box, shown in Figure 3-33.

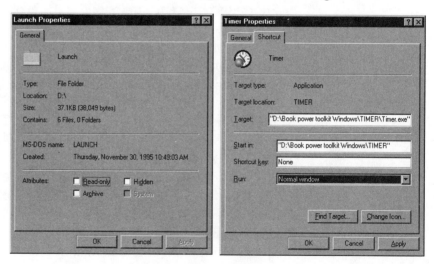

Figure 3-33: The properties of a folder (right) and the properties of a shortcut to a folder (left).

You can change not only the shortcut's icon, you can even assign a shortcut key to it. (So, why can't you do the same with folders? We can think of no technical or practical reason that prohibits extensive customization options for folders. We believe it's simply an incentive from Microsoft to make people use shortcuts on their desktops.)

More Uses for Shortcuts

Shortcuts are not limited to files and applications. You can create shortcuts to various peripherals, such as the disk drives and printers. To look at the contents of your floppy disk you must start My Computer and double-click on the icon of the A: disk drive (or the ZIP drive, or the tape drive). If you work frequently with floppy disks, you can create a shortcut to the drive A: on your desktop and double-click on its icon instead.

Shortcuts are not limited to files and folders. You can create shortcuts to printers, remote drives, even your favorite Internet sites.

To create a shortcut to drive A:, right-click on the desktop and from the pop-up menu select New | Shortcut. In the dialog box of the Shortcut Wizard type **A:** in the Command line box. Then move to the next window and enter the name of the shortcut. Windows itself will propose the name "3 1/2 Floppy (A)" (if your drive is a 3 1/2 inch drive). Enter another name if you wish and click on Finish. You have just created a shortcut to the drive A: and you can view the contents of the floppy disk in A: by double-clicking on its icon. Notice that Windows has used the icon of the drive A: that appears in the My Computer folder to depict the new shortcut. If you don't like it, you can change the icon of the shortcut (the little arrow on the lower left corner doesn't help much). If you choose to keep the A: folder open at all times, you can ask Windows 95 to update its contents automatically every time a new floppy is inserted in the A: drive (see section "Keep Your System Always Up-to-Date" for more information).

You can do the same with your network hard drives, your CD-ROM drive, and your printer. If you create shortcuts to your printers, you can print a document to a specific printer by dragging and dropping its icon on the printer's shortcut. You can create shortcuts to network printers as well.

You can even create shortcuts to other network computers. Just locate them with the Find Computers command and create a shortcut on your desktop (this command isn't even available to you unless you are connected to a network).

Customizing Shortcut Icons

The two characteristics of shortcut icons are a little arrow on the lower left corner and their names—they always begin with the "Shortcut To" string. You can change these defaults if you want, and here's how.

Getting rid of the "Shortcut To" prefix is easy. Create a shortcut to anything and delete the "Shortcut To" prefix from its name. Repeat the same process eight times and by then Windows has learned. It will never again prefix the names of the shortcuts with the "Shortcut To" string.

Removing the little arrow requires some digging in the Registry. Run Regedit and follow the path: HKEY_LOCAL_MACHINE\ SOFTWARE\Microsoft\Windows\CurrentVersion\explorer\Shell Icons. This subkey contains a number of values, which correspond to various icons Windows uses for special files or folders, as explained in the section, "Change the Icons of the Desktop Items." The value you want to change is 3. It is the icon that appears in the lower left corner of a shortcut's icon. By default, it's a bent arrow.

This arrow is really another icon, overlaid over the actual icon. To be effective, it must have the same dimensions as the icon it will be overlaid upon, and a white background. If your icons have the default size of 32 x 32, then the shortcut icon must have the same dimensions, but most of this area must be empty. If you make a smaller icon, say 8 x 8, Windows will enlarge it to make it the same size as the normal icon, and it will actually cover the entire icon.

The transparent part of the icon must be painted white. Windows will use this color to show the actual icon through. In Figure 3-34 you see a few shortcuts marked with two different symbols: a little sphere and two diagonal lines in their lower left and upper right corners. These icons are .BMP files with the same dimensions as the shortcut's actual icons.

One of the benefits of using shortcuts is that you can customize their appearance—something you can't do with files and folders.

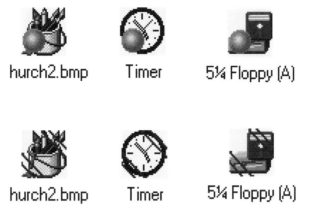

hurch2.bmp   Timer   5¼ Floppy (A)

hurch2.bmp   Timer   5¼ Floppy (A)

Figure 3-34: You can use any symbol you like to identify shortcuts.

THE OBJECT-ORIENTED NATURE OF THE DESKTOP

We kept the best for last. Windows 95 is an object-oriented operating system—at least much more so than Windows 3.1 was. Actually, not even Windows 95 is fully object-oriented, but it is getting there. Every new major release of Windows is closer to a fully object-oriented operating system.

By now, you must have heard the arguments from Windows 95 critics. It's just the old operating system in a better looking package, a better surface but the same old core, and so on. For the most part, this criticism is valid. There are a few areas in the operating system, though, that go way beyond "better looking." And Windows 95's ability to manipulate objects makes this criticism invalid. The last part of this chapter deals with the object-oriented nature of Windows and we will show you how to make the objects work for you.

Right-Clicks Are for Objects

We've already talked about shortcuts, a major new concept in working with Windows 95. Another major change in Windows 95 from Windows 3.x is the use of the right mouse button. Where Windows 3.x almost exclusively uses the left mouse button, Windows 95 makes use of both buttons. The right-click (or other-click, as it is sometimes referred to) changes the way you are used to working with Windows and can, more than any other tool, help you customize your desktop. In short, the right-click (or shortcut menu, as it is frequently called) is the most obvious manifestation of the object-oriented nature of Windows 95.

As you may have realized from using Windows so far, the right-click deals with objects. Just about everything you see on your desktop is an object. So what's an object? From the user's point of view, it is an entity that can perform certain tasks and react to changes in its environment. If you right-click on an icon, for example, you will see a menu, with different options, depending on the nature of the object. In Figure 3-35 you see the right-click menus of two drastically different objects: an image file and a folder.

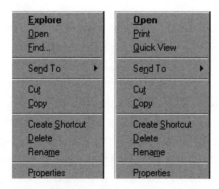

Figure 3-35: Different objects do different things; but they know what they can do.

The most common operations you can perform on an object appear in its right-click menu.

The image can be opened and printed only (you may see more, or fewer, options on the menu when you click on an image). A folder can be opened, but it can also be explored and searched. As you can see an object knows the actions it can perform and every time you right-click on it, it presents a list of these actions to choose from.

In Figure 3-36 you see an even better example of the way objects behave. Word for Windows 95 can spell-check a document as you type it. Misspelled words are marked with a curly underline. Right-click on a misspelled word, and a list of suggestions pops up. Right-click on a correctly spelled word and you'll get the usual list of editing and formatting commands. An entity that can react to external changes has to be an object.

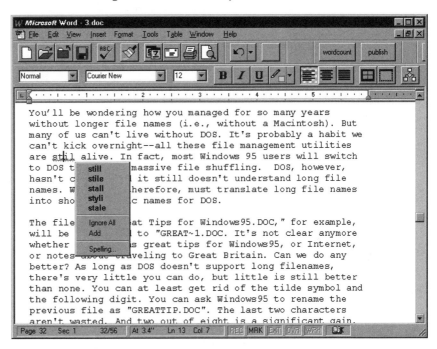

Figure 3-36: Why would you right-click on a misspelled word, if not to ask for suggestions?

It's easy to understand why a folder, or a file, is an object. But a single word? Yes, a single word in a document is an object (or, at least, it behaves like an object). If the previous demonstration didn't convince you, just select a word from a WordPad or Word document and drag it onto the desktop. Windows creates a new document with the same structure as the original document, in which it stores the selected text. Double-click on this new document and the corresponding application starts. The document you created by dragging and dropping a piece of text on the desktop is called *scrap*—another very handy feature of the Windows 95 interface, discussed in the section "Compose With Scraps."

Right-Clicking & Right-Dragging

Left-clicking is a very familiar operation and it hasn't been enhanced in Windows 95. It is used to drag documents, make selections, and so on. Double-clicking is still the way to start applications. But right-clicking opens another world of possibilities. It reveals the object-oriented nature of Windows 95. The choices you see in the right-click menu are the actions an object can perform, and they differ depending on the type of object that was right-clicked. You can right-click even on the desktop, because the desktop is itself an object.

Right-clicking introduces another object-related operation: right-dragging. If you grab an object by clicking on it with the right mouse button and you drag it to its destination, a menu appears, similar to the one in Figure 3-37. This menu contains the available options, depending on the nature of the object being dragged and the object on which it is dropped. The old drag and drop operation has its own, built-in rules. If you drag and drop a file onto a folder, the file is either moved or copied. If both the file and the folder are on the same disk drive, the file is moved. When they are on different drives, the file is copied. Hold down the Shift key, and the file is copied, even when it's on the same drive as the folder. Even if you remember these rules, how can you be sure that a folder on your desktop is on your hard disk, the floppy, or a network disk?

Figure 3-37: Right drag an object to its destination and a pop-up menu will display your options, depending on the nature of the source and destination objects.

Welcome to drag and drop with the right mouse button. Using the right mouse button, pick up the object you want to move, and drop it on its destination. A small shortcut menu will appear, from which you can select the desired action. The menu's contents vary, depending on the nature of the two objects. If you right-drag a file over an application (or a shortcut to an application, for that matter) the menu options are Open With (starts the application which then opens the file) and Cancel. If the destination is a folder, the options are Move Here (the default), Copy Here, Create Shortcut Here, and Cancel. Finally, if the destination doesn't know what to do with the file—if, for example, you drop the file on another file or on My Computer—nothing will happen; you won't even see a shortcut menu.

Right-clicks reveal the intelligence built into the objects and you should freely use the right mouse button. It can't hurt you (no action will take place unless you specify so from the pop-up menu) and you may find that more options are available than you thought. In the following sections we'll discuss the two types of shortcut menus you see when you right-click: the icon shortcut menu, which pops up when you right-click on an icon, and the desktop's shortcut menu, which pops up when you right-click on the desktop. We'll show you how to customize them both to suit your needs.

Icon Shortcut Menus

Every time you right-click on a document's icon (whether on the desktop or within its own folder), you get a menu with useful options, such as printing it, or sending it to a mail recipient, and so on. These actions apply to every file you create. For specific processing, you must open the file with the application that created the file, or an application that understands the file's format. A few operations apply to (nearly) all types of files. Compression is one of them. If you've installed WinZip, the most widely used file compression application today, a new entry is added to the right-click menu, as shown in Figure 3-39. The Add to Zip option was added by WinZip and lets you compress files right on the desktop. No need to start the WinZip application and look for the files to compress. (If you don't already have the WinZip application, you can find it on this book's Companion CD-ROM.)

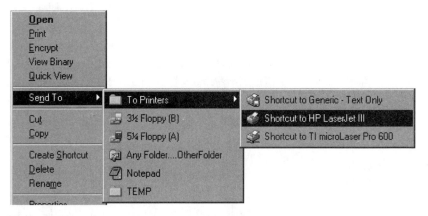

Figure 3-38: You can customize an icon's shortcut menu by adding your own commands to it, or new destinations to its Send To submenu.

You may have useful applications of your own that you would like to add to this menu. If you share your computer, or a file server, with others, you may be encrypting documents routinely. Adding an Encrypt command to the right-click menu of .TXT and .DOC files could save you a number of mouse clicks and keystrokes every day. We've shown how to do this from within the File Types dialog box, in the section "Multiple File Associations." This time we'll show you how to add a new command to the shortcut menu from within the Registry.

First, you must figure out which files can be processed by your program. Let's say you wish to encrypt text documents only (the ones with extension .TXT), or Word documents (the ones with extension .DOC). You can also add menu options for all file types, and we'll see later how this is done, but we find it more helpful and functional to add certain commands to the shortcut menu of the file types they apply to (it doesn't make much sense to encrypt program files, for example).

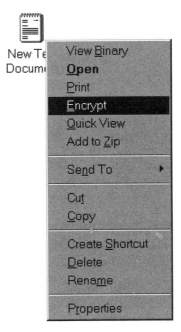

Figure 3-39: If you encrypt text files often, make the Encrypt command an option of the shortcut menu.

Run the Regedit program and click on HKEY_CLASSES_ROOT. You'll see a list of all the file types your system recognizes. One of them is .TXT (notice the period in front of it). Click on this key and you'll see on the right pane its default value Data, which is "txtfile," the class name of text files. There could be other file extensions such as .ASC, or .TEXT with the same class name. Windows 95 not only allows long filenames, but long extensions too. The new menu option we are going to add to the New submenu will apply not only to files with the extension .TXT, but to all files belonging to the class txtfile (even if they aren't registered at the moment; the menu option we are going to add now will apply to all registered files belonging to the class txtfile).

Now move down the list, to the key txtfile and expand its subtree by clicking on the plus icon. You will see the DefaultIcon key (which is the location of the icon Windows uses for text files, and can be easily changed) and another subtree, under "shell." Expand this subtree and you'll see the entries for the Open and

Print options. They contain the commands that carry out the "open" and "print" operations.

To add a new command, click on the shell key and from the Edit menu select New | Key. As soon as the new entry is created, type in the name of the command, **Encrypt**. Then, while the Encrypt key is selected, create another key under it (open the Edit menu and chose New | String Value). This time name the key "**command.**" Finally, double-click on the command key to see its default value. As expected, this key has no value. Here you must enter the name of the program that will carry out the Encrypt command. Double-click on Default (in the right pane) and enter a string with the program's pathname (such as "encrypt.exe %1", or "c:\win95\ tools\encrypt %1". %1 is the file's complete pathname, which is passed to the program as its argument (see Figure 3-40).

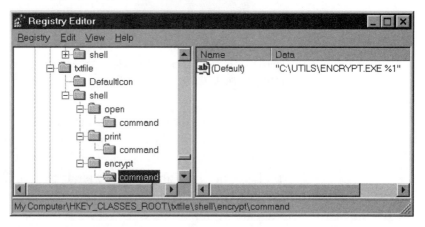

Figure 3-40: Adding a new command to a specific file type's right-click menu.

Now close the Registry Editor window, press F5 to activate the changes you just made and locate a text file's icon on the desktop or in a folder. Right-click on the file and presto: the menu contains the new option, Encrypt. If you have an encryption program and have entered its pathname correctly, when you select the new option, the encryption program starts. Of course, the application must accept command line arguments, such as "encrypt myfile.txt".

If Windows can't locate the application, it will prompt you with a dialog box and let you locate the application (see Figure 3-41). The encryption program should encrypt the original file and create a new, encrypted file with the same name. To open this file with a word processor, you must first decrypt it (restore it back to its original form) and then open it. If another user tries to view the same file with any other application, even Quick View, he or she will see nonsensical text on the screen.

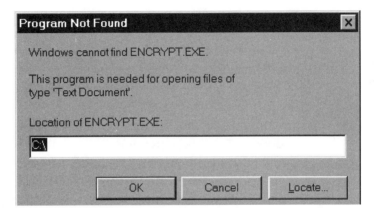

Figure 3-41: If Windows can't find the command to carry out a task in the right-click menu, it asks you to locate it.

Suppose your encryption program processes .TXT files and creates new ones, with the same name and extension .ENC. You can register the new file type and add a Decrypt command to the new file type's shortcut menu. Moreover, you can remove the Open and Print commands for this file type, because you won't need to open or print an encrypted file.

This method is substantially more complicated than the one we described earlier, but it will come in handy when you want to automate the process. If you want to add the same action to several file types, or across a number of workstations on a network, you can create a .REG file with the required pairs of keys/ values and distribute it. The users will have to double-click on the icon of the .REG file to update his or her Registry.

Associating an Application With All File Types

The Registry makes it possible to add new commands to all file types (something you can't do with the File Types dialog box). Let's say you frequently use a binary file viewer to view all types of files. A binary file viewer is an application that displays the contents of any file either as characters, or as hex numbers. If you've ever discovered a file on your disk and none of your applications could understand it, you could benefit from a binary file viewer. Quick View will work with most file types, but what about the file types it can't handle? When Windows runs into a file it can't open with Quick View it offers you the option Open With and you must select the program that can open the specific file from a list of applications. A View Binary option in the right-click menu should come in handy.

Our goal is to add an action to all file types (going through each and every file type separately is obviously out of the question). The Registry provides the * key under the HKEY_CLASSES_ROOT branch. This is the generic extension that encompasses all file types. Every action you assign to this file type will be available in the right-click menu of any file on the desktop. However, no such file type exists in the File Type tab. If you look at other registered files type that appear in the File Type tab, you'll find out that their Registry keys include the EditFlags value. Add a new Binary Value to the * key, and set its Data value to 02 00 00 00. This will make the * file extension appear in the dialog box, in which you can set the appropriate actions. Close the Registry and press F5.

Now you can start Explorer, or My Computer, select Options from the View menu, and click on the File Types tab of the dialog box that pops up. The "anyfile" file type will be listed. Click on Edit to enter the desired actions. The Edit File Type dialog box (shown in Figure 3-42) will be initially empty. Enter a new action, such as View & Binary (the & symbol makes B the shortcut key), and the name of your binary viewer application (for example, "c:\utils\hexview.exe %1"). Because the asterisk isn't quite as intuitive as a file type name, change it to Anyfile (or any other appropriate string).

With a few changes in the Registry you can add more shortcut menu options to all file types.

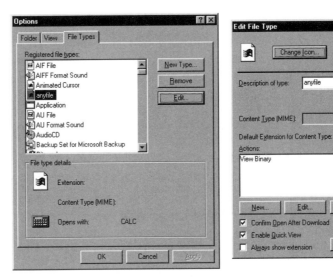

Figure 3-42: Adding a View Binary option to every file's menu.

If you right-click on any file's icon, you'll see the menu shown in Figure 3-43. Select View Binary to see the contents of the file in hex format. Notice also, that the View Binary option doesn't appear in the right-click menu of other objects, such as folders, printers, and so on.

Figure 3-43: The View Binary option is now available from within every file's right-click menu.

Changing the file's (or folder's) right-click menu is not a trivial undertaking, but it will come in handy in some situations. Some Windows applications are not as considerate, and they take over your system upon installation. You may run into an image processing application that changes the associations of all image files. Sooner or later you will have to remove the actions placed in your right-click menus by applications that think they know everything. Now you know how to do it, either via the Files Types dialog box, or the Registry.

K eep your right-click menus lean by removing the options you don't need.

The Send To Submenu

Another customizable item on the shortcut menu for an icon is the Send To submenu. The Send To submenu can help you automate many daily tasks. When you first installed Windows 95, the Send To submenu had just a few options. You could send the file to the floppy disk drive (make a copy), to the printer (if you installed one), to the Briefcase, and to a mail-recipient (only if the Exchange program was installed).

The destinations of the Send To submenu are stored in a folder, appropriately named Send To, under your Windows folder. Everything you place in this folder becomes a destination for the Send To command. If you add a folder to the Send To folder, you will get nested destinations in the Send To folder, as shown in Figure 3-44. Let's say you have access to a number of printers on your network. Instead of cluttering the Send To command with the names of all printers, create another submenu, Print To, which leads to the individual printer names, from which you can make your final selection.

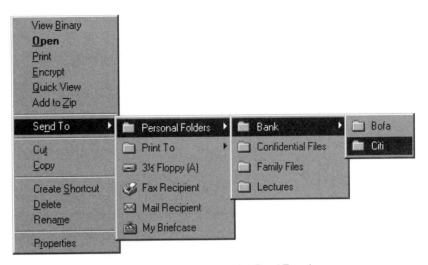

Figure 3-44: You can easily nest options in the Send To submenu.

If you prepare lots of short documents, or notes, which will be later added to a few folders, add these destinations to the Send To menu, as shown on the right-hand side of Figure 3-44. You don't have to place the actual folder within the Send To folder—actually, you shouldn't. The Send To folder should contain shortcuts to the various destination folders instead.

Can You Send To Your Desktop?

Is there something missing from your Send To submenu? Hard to believe, but Microsoft omitted the most common destination: the desktop itself. Go ahead and add this option:

Through My Computer, or the Explorer, open the Send To folder (it's in the Windows folder). Then open the Windows folder and right-drag the desktop folder on the Send To folder. At the destination, select "Create Shortcut(s) here" from the pop-up menu. Windows will assign a long name to the shortcut (as usual), but you can change it to any string that best describes the new destination, as you can see in Figure 3-45.

The Send To menu need not be a long list of options. You can organize it as a series of cascading menus.

Figure 3-45: You can make the desktop folder a destination in the Send To submenu.

Alternatively, you can obtain the PowerToys, which add the option "Send to Any Folder" to your Send To submenu. When you select this option, the Explorer window will appear and you can select the destination. This is a useful, general tool for moving files around, but it shouldn't stop you from placing the most common destinations for your files into the Send To submenu. And one of the most common destinations, is indeed the desktop.

The Desktop Shortcut Menu

Besides the shortcut menu that appears every time you right-click on an icon, there's another similar menu, the desktop shortcut menu, which appears every time you right-click on the desktop and is shown in Figure 3-46. The contents of the desktop's right-click menu are stored in the Registry, and they can be modified too, by adding new entries, or removing existing ones.

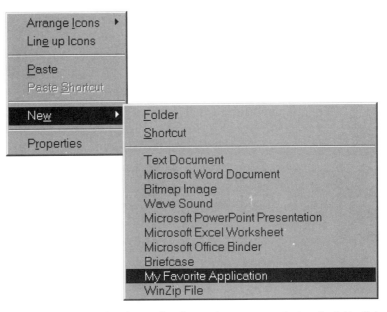

Figure 3-46: Don't let the applications take over your desktop's right-click menu. Add the commands *you* need the most.

TIP

Avoid creating new files on your desktop, unless you want them to be available at any time, or you are sure you'll move them to folders they belong to later on. Create the files in their proper subdirectories and place shortcuts on the desktop. All files you see on your desktop reside in the subdirectory Desktop, under the Windows directory.

Use the Registry to remove the unwanted options from the desktop's New submenu.

This menu contains a New submenu, which lets you create new documents on the desktop, without launching an application. As you can see in Figure 3-46, as you install new applications, they add their own file types to this submenu. Pretty soon you'll end up with a huge New submenu which will complicate, rather than simplify, your work. Most of the options shouldn't even be there. For example, I am using Visual Basic on a daily basis, but I never have to create a new project from the desktop. I start Visual Basic and then create a new project. The mere presence of the option

Visual Basic Project in my New submenu is of no use to me what-soever. (If you haven't installed Visual Basic on your computer you aren't going to see this option, but as you install new applications, they will add new options to the desktop shortcut menu.) The same is true for the Wave Sound option. If I want to create a new sound file, I go directly to a sound recording application.

Removing unwanted options from the New submenu is quite easy. Let's start by removing the option Visual Basic Project. Open the Registry and search for the string "Visual Basic Project". Unless you've hacked your Registry extensively in the past, the key you are looking for is the first one to be found. It is the key HKEY_CLASSES_ROOT\VisualBasic.Project. It's default value is "Visual Basic Project" (which is the option that appears in the New submenu). Because the Default value can't be removed, we need another key in the Registry. We must find out where Windows 95 keeps the list of the applications whose files appear in the New submenu.

There's no such place per se, but look for the string "Visual-Basic.Project" (to locate this string back up to the top entry in the Registry's left pane and select it). The key that contains this value is ".VBP." It's the class name for Visual Basic projects. This key contains a subkey, called ShellNew. That's how Windows knows whether to display an entry for Visual Basic projects. If a key under HKEY_LOCAL_MACHINE\SOFTWARE\Classes contains the ShellNew subkey, the corresponding file type appears in the New submenu. Delete the key ShellNew, close the Registry and then press F5 to activate the changes. Now you can open the New submenu by right-clicking on the desktop and see for yourself that the New submenu doesn't contain the Visual Basic Project entry any more. Similarly, you can remove other unwanted entries from the New submenu. The steps of this example were specific to the Visual Basic Project entry of the desktop shortcut menu. To remove other entries from this menu, find the class name of the corresponding file type and then delete the ShellNew subkey under the specific class name.

Don't Just Create Documents—Launch Them

We've seen how to remove unwanted entries from the desktop's New submenu. To make the New command really useful, there must be a way not only to create a new text document, but to start an application to edit it (or process it if it's an image, render it if it's a three-dimensional scene, and so on). As usual, to fix something in Windows 95, we must descend into the Registry and do some magic.

Wouldn't you rather start Notepad instead of creating a new text document on the desktop?

We will describe this procedure in detail, so that you can modify the Registry for your own file types later on. We are going to modify the behavior of the desktop shortcut menu, so that when you select New | Text Document, it doesn't just create a new text file, but it starts NotePad instead.

Open the Registry and search for the string that you want to hack in the desktop shortcut menu. The name of the command that creates a new text document is Text Document. Open the Edit menu in Regedit, select Find and enter the string "text document" (the search is not case-sensitive). Regedit may find other instances of this string, such as "Rich Text Document." Keep searching (press F3 to locate the next occurrence of the string), until you find an exact match. It will be under the "txtfile" key (the complete path is HKEY_CLASSES_ROOT\txtfile). As we mentioned in the previous section, this is the class name for text files. It's a special string that Windows uses to uniquely identify text files, regardless of their extensions. Under this key, you'll find two subkeys: DefaultIcon and Shell. The DefaultIcon key points to the file that contains the icon of the text files. The other key, Shell, contains two subkeys: open and print (unless you, or an application, have added more commands). You may notice that these are the two commands that appear in the menu that pops up every time you right-click on a text document's icon. Under each subkey, there's another subkey, called command. Its value is the name of the program that performs the corresponding action (opening or printing the file).

Let's sidetrack for a moment. Do you remember where else you saw these actions? In the Explorer's Options command, of course. If you start the Explorer, or My Computer, and select Options from the View menu, you'll see a dialog box with three tabs. One of them is called File Types. Click on that tab and you'll see the list of all registered file types. Find the "Text Documents" entry, double-click on it, and you'll see the Edit File Type window, shown in Figure 3-47. Double-click on Open and you'll see the command that carries out the specific action in the "Application used to perform action" box. NOTEPAD.EXE is the name of the program that opens this specific file type. If you change the application name here, the corresponding value in the Registry changes. Similarly, if you change the value in the Registry, the application name in the Edit File Type window changes.

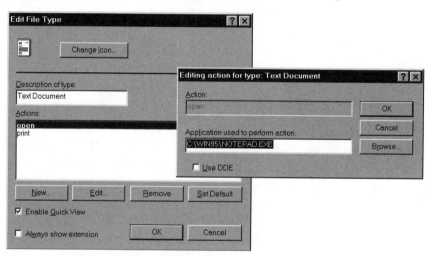

Figure 3-47: What does Windows do when it meets a text file?

We've found the name of the application that opens a document of the specific type (i.e., when the document's icon is double-clicked, or the Open command is selected from the object's short-cut menu). All we have to do now is make sure that this command is executed each time the user creates a new file by selecting New | Text Document from the desktop's shortcut menu. Back up to the top level in the Regedit's left pane and this time search for txtfile. Keep searching until you find the key .txt (ignore the .DIC and possibly other keys along the way). Open the .txt key and you'll see the ShellNew subkey. Here's all the information Windows needs every time a new Text Document is created. This key contains two values: (Default) and Null File. All we have to do is add a new entry, called (what else) "command." Create a new key under ShellNew and assign to it the pathname of the NOTEPAD application (make sure to type in the correct pathname for your computer, as it is displayed in the Edit File Type window). Figure 3-48 shows what your Registry should look like after this change.

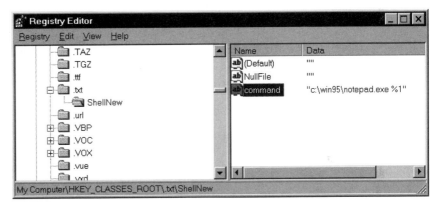

Figure 3-48: Changing Windows 95's default behavior for text files.

Close the Registry, press F5, and then right-click somewhere on the desktop. From the pop-up menu select New | Text Document. This time Windows doesn't simply create a new text file's icon on the desktop, but it actually starts NOTEPAD with a new file. The name of the file is "Untitled.txt."

This concludes our discussion on modifying the desktop's right-click menus. You've learned how to modify the New submenu, how to make it start applications instead of creating new, empty documents, and how to clean up the New submenu. You've also learned how to manipulate an object's shortcut menu through the File Types dialog box and the Registry. Now, you're ready to customize these two powerful menus and place the operations you perform most frequently right at your fingertips.

Compose With Scraps

Don't mind their name, scraps are another extremely useful element of the new interface. A scrap is a special object (part of a document) that can be moved around, from application to application, similar to the contents of the clipboard. Scraps have two distinct advantages over clipboard items. First, there can be multiple scraps, while the clipboard can hold only one item at a time. Every time you copy (or cut) something to the clipboard, its contents are replaced. This means that you must know what's on the clipboard and use it before you place something else there. The second advantage of scraps is that Windows knows which application created them and can start that application when you double-click on a scrap.

To create a scrap, select part of a document, drag it and drop it on the desktop, or any open folder. (Note: In order to create a scrap the source must be in a program that is OLE-enabled.) A new file is automatically created with the same type as the file in which the scrap originated. If you created the scrap from within Word, a new .DOC file is created. Double-click on it to verify that it is indeed a Word file.

Different applications use different operations to create scraps.

If you right-drag the selection to the desktop, you'll be offered additional options in the usual pop-up menu. You can create a copy of the scrap (the default action), move the scrap (it will be cut from the original document and placed in its own file), or create a shortcut to the document itself.

Creating a scrap can be tricky sometimes, depending on the application. With Word, all you have to do is select some text, release the mouse, and move the pointer over the text. Then you can press the left or right mouse button and drag the text on the desktop. With Excel, though, you must be a little more careful. After you make a selection, you must move the pointer on the frame of the selection. When the pointer becomes an arrow, you can drag the selection onto the desktop. If you attempt to drag the selection as you would in Word, you simply make another selection.

Scraps are useful when you try to compile information from various sources. Suppose you've downloaded a bunch of text files and images from the Internet and you want to sort through them, extract the information you need, and place it in a new document. You can go back and forth using the Copy and Paste commands, or you can go through the information and every time you find something you need (be it a paragraph, an image, or part of an image) put it on the desktop as a scrap. When you're done, create a new document and start dropping the scraps into it. Scraps are not linked into documents as objects. Their contents are inserted into the file, as if they were brought from the Clipboard.

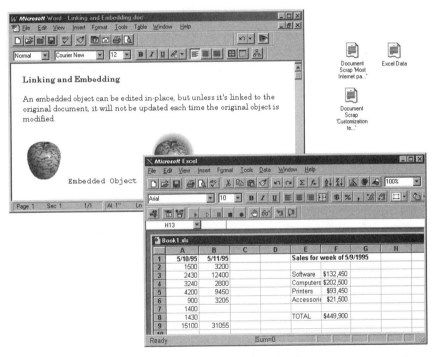

Figure 3-49: Select all the information you need on the desktop as scraps and then place them in a new document.

Feel free to fill your desktop with scraps. Their lifetime is short (you don't need them any longer than you would need the contents of the clipboard, but you have to delete them yourself). Once you are finished, move them to the Recycle Bin and the desktop is instantly cleaned up.

Keep in mind that only Windows 95 applications can handle scraps. If you are using Windows 3.*x* applications, you are pretty much stuck with the clipboard. Notepad, for example, can neither create nor accept scraps. If you drop a scrap on a Notepad window you'll see all the information Windows stores in a scrap file— for all intents and purposes an unusable file. Some Windows 95 applications can't handle scraps either (Paint being one of them).

MOVING ON

Chapter 4, "Tuning Up Windows," investigates all the ways you can fine-tune and optimize key peripherals under Windows 95. This includes time-savers that will increase your efficiency, along with various ways to maximize your system's performance. You'll learn how to install and cleanly uninstall applications; ways to keep your disk drives in good shape and running at top speed; and how to optimize your swap file. You'll also learn about short-cut launching, printer management, disk compression, and more.

Chapter 4

Tuning Up Windows

In this chapter we're going to investigate all the ways you can
fine-tune and optimize key peripherals under Windows 95. This
topic includes time-savers that will increase your efficiency and
help you maximize your system's performance. You'll learn how
to install and cleanly uninstall applications and discover ways to
keep your disk drives in good shape. We'll start with a frequently
overlooked time-saver—shortcut application launching.

SHORTCUT APPLICATION LAUNCHING

Windows 95 includes a highly useful option—launching applica-
tions via Shortcut Keys that you can define. To do this, right-click
in the Explorer on the icon of an application you use frequently.
Then choose Create Shortcut. Now right-click on the new
Shortcut's icon, choose Properties, and click on the Shortcut tab.
You'll see a property sheet dialog box like the one shown in
Figure 4-1.

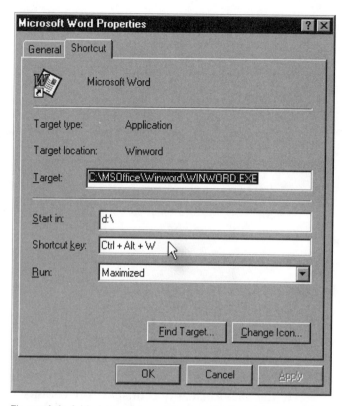

Figure 4-1: Add shortcut launching to your favorite programs.

Click on the input box labeled Shortcut key and press the letter of the alphabet that you want to use to launch this program. Ctrl+Alt will automatically be added to your keypress. It's generally easiest to remember the key combination if you use the first letter of the program—*W* for Word for Windows, for example. Thereafter, whenever you press Ctrl+Alt+W, Word for Windows pops up, even if you're within another application when you summon it.

Ctrl+Alt was selected as the method for launching because it would not interfere with the Alt+*underlined letter* shortcut used throughout Windows as a way of accessing menus. Nor would it conflict with the Ctrl+*any key* widely used by Windows applications to trigger special features, launch macros, and so on.

OVERALL SYSTEM PERFORMANCE

Use the System Monitor to see what's going on in your computer.

You can observe your computer's performance with a Windows 95 utility called System Monitor. To determine if you installed it, click on the Start button, then Programs, then Accessories, and then System Tools. If you don't see System Monitor listed there, that means you didn't elect to install it during Windows setup. To install it now, click on Start, then Settings, and then Control Panel. Click on Add/Remove Programs in Control Panel, then click on the Windows Setup tab. In the list box, double-click on Accessories and locate System Monitor. Click on the check box next to it, then click OK twice.

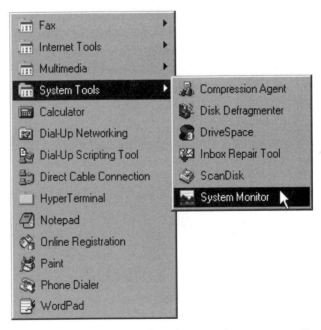

Figure 4-2: Look on these Start button submenus to see if you've installed System Monitor.

System Monitor allows you to conduct before-and-after tests to see the effects of changes you make. Perhaps you'll fiddle with the swap file, add more memory, install a new hard drive, or start using a new application. Maybe you just want to check to see if a utility you run in the background is slowing down your system.

Run System Monitor to get a picture of how resources are being used in your machine at the current time. What you look at and how you see it are up to you. You can monitor several dozen aspects of your machine's behavior. They are organized into three primary categories: File System, Kernel, and Memory Manager. There are also three additional categories, Microsoft Network Client, Network Server, and Network Monitor, you might or might not see depending on whether, and how, the machine is connected to a network: Let's first take a look at the File System report.

Checking File System Statistics

Click on the System Monitor's Edit menu, then choose Add Item. Click on File System, and then select the top item, Bytes read/ second, by clicking on it. Hold down the Shift key while you click on the bottom item, Writes/second. Now that all five measurable File System factors have been selected, click on OK (Figure 4-3). To see the measurements over time, click on the View menu and choose Line Charts. To adjust how often the display is updated, click on the Options menu and choose Chart.

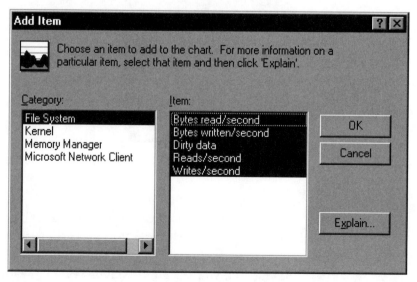

Figure 4-3: Viewing five statistics about your disk access.

Let's try an experiment. We'll copy the same 8MB file from one hard drive to another, and then from a hard drive to an Iomega Zip drive (a removable-medium peripheral that is somewhat slower than an ordinary hard drive). As you would expect, the copying is faster between hard drives—illustrated by the higher and narrower chart activity in Figure 4-4. Compare the chart in Figure 4-4 to that in Figure 4-5.

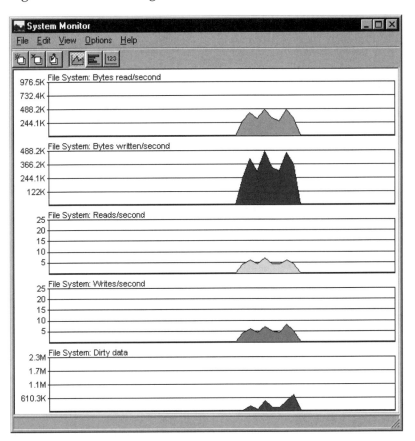

Figure 4-4: Data copied between two internal hard drives is read and written relatively quickly.

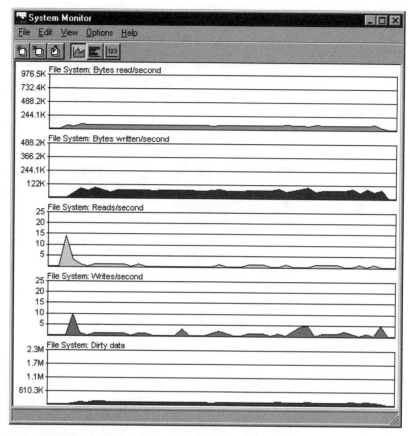

Figure 4-5: The same 8MB file that was monitored in Figure 4-4, but here copied from a hard drive to a Zip drive.

The vertical axis represents the volume of data being transferred; the horizontal axis displays the passage of time. So, higher, spiky activity indicates a greater amount of data being sent in less time. The five charts shown in Figures 4-4 and 4-5 correspond to the options selected in Figure 4-3. Copying the 8MB file between internal hard drives took 17 seconds; copying it from a hard drive to a Zip drive took 110 seconds. The first two charts in Figure 4-5 illustrate that the Zip drive reading and writing of bytes was at a rate of approximately 70K per second, whereas the first two charts in Figure 4-4 show the bytes being transferred at approximately 490K per second.

The bytes read/second result and bytes written/second should, of course, be roughly the same for any given file transfer. Clearly, data can't be written any faster than it is read. The "Dirty Data" chart in Figures 4-4 and 4-5 illustrates data in a RAM cache inside the computer, waiting to be sent to the target drive—in other words it illustrates where and by how much the source drive is being read more quickly than the target drive can absorb it.

Reviewing Kernel Statistics

In the System Monitor window, open the Edit menu and click Add Item. In the Add Items dialog box, click Kernel in the Category list, then choose all three choices in the Items list. You'll then see the display shown in Figure 4-6.

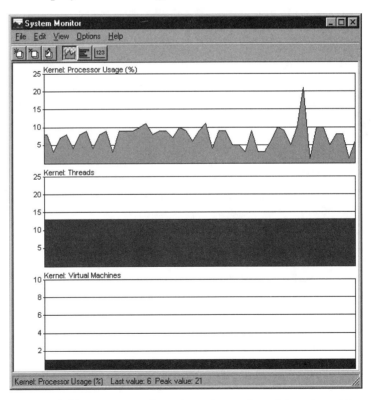

Figure 4-6: Your processor in action—the number of threads and the number of virtual machines.

The Kernel is a major section of the Windows operating system and includes the activities of the microprocessor, DOS sessions (Virtual Machines), and Threads (programs that are running simultaneously and are sharing time on the machine). The spike at the right of Processor Usage was caused by pressing PrintScrn to capture the screen and copy it to the clipboard. If you click on the MS-DOS icon, you'll find that the Threads and Virtual Machine displays each grow. In Figure 4-6, Threads would go up to four and Virtual Machines would go up to two. Interestingly, Processor Usage would go to 100 percent and would stay there until you shut down the DOS session.

A DOS session drives Processor Usage all the way up to 100 percent, where it stays until you shut down the session.

Note: a *virtual machine* is like a separate "computer" that's created within your computer and is running more or less independently. When you run a DOS program or go to the DOS prompt by clicking on the MS-DOS icon, a virtual machine is created. Among other things, this walling off of DOS within its own separate "computer" prevents side effects or interference between DOS virtual machines or between the DOS virtual machine and the other virtual machine within which Windows is running. Figure 4-7 shows the effect of shutting down a DOS session.

TIP

If you suspect that one of your applications is responsible for slowing down the entire system, here's what to do. If Processor Usage stays high even while nothing is going on (you're not typing, moving the mouse, downloading something, or otherwise keeping the system busy), press Alt+Tab, switching to the application you suspect is retarding the computer. Shut that application down. If Processor Usage drops, that application was the culprit. The solution is to upgrade to a newer version or use that application selectively (when you don't need to run other applications), knowing it will hog the machine.

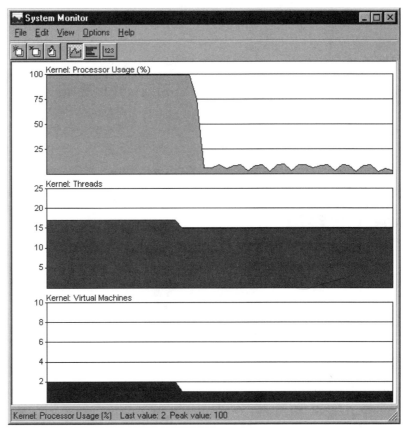

Figure 4-7: When you shut down a DOS session, Processor Usage falls from 100 percent to the normal windows 10–15 percent you'll see while running the System Monitor.

Understanding Memory Manager Information

In Figure 4-8, you can see the effect of opening two applications on your computer's various memory zones. There's a stairstep shape in five of the charts—Allocated memory, Locked memory, Swapfile in Use, Swapfile Size, and Swappable Memory.

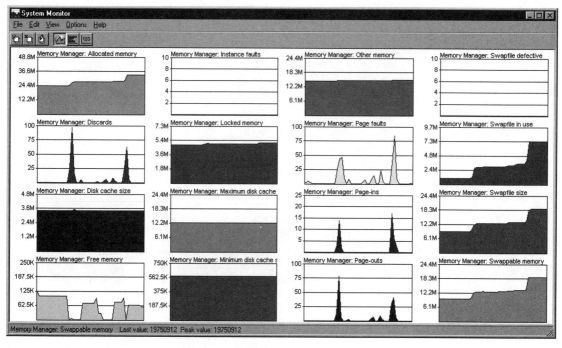

Figure 4-8: All 16 of the memory charts in view at the same time.

Several of the memory charts are of particular interest. Locked Memory is being governed by applications or Windows itself, and can't be "paged" or swapped to and from disk. It's similar to memory under DOS that's been appropriated and is, therefore, no longer free for other uses. The Locked memory statistic includes the disk cache. The cache is dynamic in Windows 95: it adjusts itself as necessary up to the limits imposed by the amount of RAM you have in your computer. To find out the exact amount of truly locked memory, subtract the disk cache Size from the Locked Memory. For instance, in Figure 4-8 the disk cache size is 3.5MB and the locked memory is 5.3MB. Therefore, the amount of memory that's actually locked (ignoring the cache) is 1.8MB.

Compare the Locked memory chart with the Allocated memory chart. Allocated memory is the sum of the Other memory and the Swappable memory. (If you notice that Allocated memory changes during inactivity in your computer, this means that the disk cache is resizing itself.) If the statistics for Locked memory are always close to the statistics for Allocated memory—your computer would likely benefit from additional RAM. In Figure 4-8, Locked memory is 5.3MB and Allocated memory is 33MB, so there's plenty of room.

IMPROVING I/O

I/O, input/output, has a major effect on the perceived performance of your machine. How quickly data flows between the computer and the hard drive or CD-ROM drive can make your computing smooth and efficient, or annoyingly slow. With a slow and out-of-date CD-ROM or hard drive that has a slower I/O speed, system performance will seem sluggish even if you have the latest, fastest video system and a hot Pentium computer.

First, take a look at System Properties.

When you turn on the computer, Windows 95 looks in AUTOEXEC.BAT and CONFIG.SYS. If it finds a driver (software that tells Windows how to communicate with a hardware peripheral such as a CD-ROM drive) or a TSR it doesn't recognize, Windows goes into MS-DOS compatibility mode to make sure that the system will at least run, if sluggishly. Unfortunately, this performance degradation can spread, slowing down even those peripherals that do have proper Windows 95 "protected mode" drivers installed. (Peripherals that have protected mode drivers installed will not need to be listed in AUTOEXEC.BAT or CONFIG.SYS.) Your goal is to get a Windows 95 driver and re-move from AUTOEXEC.BAT or CONFIG.SYS the reference to the older driver that will no longer be needed once you've installed a Windows 95–compatible one.

The first place to check to determine whether system performance is being degraded by a driver or TSR is the System Properties. On the desktop right-click on My Computer, then choose Properties. Now click on the Performance tab. You should see statistics similar to those in Figure 4-9.

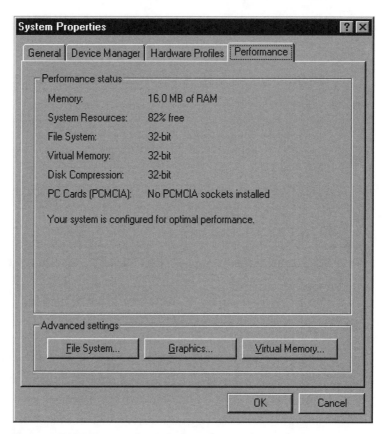

Figure 4-9: Ideally, your Performance sheet should say "Your system is configured for optimal performance" like the one shown here.

If you see "Your system is configured for optimal performance," that means that your CD-ROM unit and hard drives are all using the best and fastest I/O, namely 32-bit data transfer. If you see a report saying "File System Some drives are using MS-DOS compatibility," you should try to obtain Windows 95 drivers for your hard drive or CD-ROM unit or any other peripheral that's using a "real mode" driver. Take a look at your AUTOEXEC.BAT and CONFIG.SYS files. Click the Start button, then choose Run. Type **Sysedit**. Do you see a reference to this, for example:
C:\WINDOWS\COMMAND\MSCDEX.EXE/D:MSCD001 /M:15

If you do, it means that your CD-ROM is using a less-than-optimal driver. Your AUTOEXEC.BAT should be relatively clean, like this:

```
PROMPT $p$g
set tmp=c:\t
set temp=c:\t
set tem=c:\t
path C:\WINDOWS;C:\WINDOWS\COMMAND;C:\WINDOWS\SYSTEM;C:\UTILS;
c:\batch;c:\n
```

Likewise, CONFIG.SYS should also be bare. DOS=high might be its only entry.

TIP

Files that were typical in Windows 3.1's AUTOEXEC.BAT and CONFIG.SYS can safely be removed when you use Windows 95. These include SHARE and anything to do with SMARTDRV.

If you do have some drivers in your AUTOEXEC.BAT or CONFIG.SYS files, take a look at the IOS.INI file in your Windows directory. Windows 95 can replace all the drivers and TSRs listed in this file. Use the Add New Hardware feature in Control Panel to delete or add drivers.

TIP

Most equipment vendors have Windows 95 drivers available for their peripherals by now. Contact the vendor or look in CompuServe, America Online, or the Microsoft Network for new drivers. There'll be a README file telling you how to install the new driver.

A single DOS-style driver can cause *all* drives to switch to real mode, including virtual memory, thus slowing down the entire system. For example, if a real mode driver is in your AUTO-EXEC.BAT file, you might see the report in Figure 4-9 change to the one in Figure 4-10.

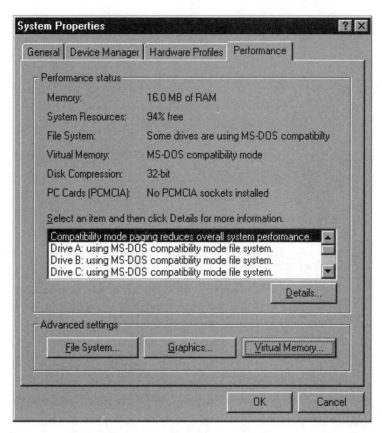

Figure 4-10: All the drives in this computer are now running slowly as real mode drivers.

When you turn on the computer, Windows 95 looks in AUTOEXEC.BAT and CONFIG.SYS. Finding a driver it doesn't recognize (or a TSR, terminate-and-stay-resident program), Windows goes into MS-DOS compatibility mode to make sure that things will at least work, if sluggishly. Unfortunately, this can spread, slowing down even those peripherals that do have proper Windows 95 protected mode drivers installed (you won't see them listed in AUTOEXEC.BAT or CONFIG.SYS). Your goal is to get a Windows 95 driver, and remove the reference in AUTOEXEC.BAT or CONFIG.SYS to the older driver that will no longer be needed once you've installed the Windows 95–compatible one.

SWAPPING

You might notice from time to time that your hard drive is working spontaneously. You didn't load or save a file, open the Explorer, or otherwise do anything that could explain this disk activity. In fact, the hard drive can get active for what seems like a long time (a minute or two) and for no apparent reason. This self-induced disk activity happens for several reasons. It occurs while you're working on something like a text document (in this case, it might be paging between RAM and the hard drive, for example). That's understandable. But disk activity can also occur even if you've just been sitting there doing nothing with the computer for several minutes. You didn't load or save a file, you didn't start some process in an application. You've been quiescent but the drive all of a sudden starts working.

Windows 95 sometimes mysteriously starts using your hard drive, all by itself.

Unexpected disk activity isn't a bad sign; it doesn't mean that the drive is "thrashing" because you have too little RAM or too little free hard drive space and it must swap (thrash) back and forth more than it should. It's typical of Windows 95 to take care of various tasks when it detects inactivity. It might be sending data that it thinks you might need next, but isn't of top priority. It might be swapping portions of itself out to disk and back, as needed. Whenever you change a document, that document then becomes "dirty" meaning that the version on your screen differs from the version stored on disk. Windows 95 is more energetic than earlier versions of Windows about saving dirty data to disk while the system is idle. This background page swapping occurs even if there's plenty of room left in RAM.

However, if you notice lots of intense disk activity when you *are* accessing the drive or working in an application, there's a problem. You're using real mode drivers (most likely the culprit), have too little RAM, or too little free hard drive space for a swap file of reasonable size. In a word: too much unnecessary swapping is going on. This *is* thrashing, properly so called, and it does slow down your work. You have to wait for the disk drive to finish its job before you can proceed writing or drawing or whatever you're doing. In other words, the entire system is held hostage to inefficient swapping.

In order to take care of business, Windows 95 attempts to make the best use of RAM as it possibly can. However, five or six huge graphics files can, for example, easily exceed the amount of memory in your machine. Or if you're running several applications simultaneously, where are they all to fit? Accessing RAM is much faster than accessing the disk drive, but Windows realizes that you want more memory than is provided merely by the amount of RAM in your system. It therefore *pages* or *swaps* portions of RAM onto the hard drive.

The Windows 95 operating system gives each application as much memory as it needs (up to 2GB per process if your computer can provide that much). As you start more applications, or open more and more files, Windows eventually runs out of memory. Windows has to do something so that the applications can keep working, regardless of whether there's enough memory or not. (In a sense, there's never enough.) To handle this situation, Windows uses a section of the disk as memory. The applications, however, are not aware of this. They, themselves, never have to go to the disk to look for the information they need except when a document is first opened.

Windows divides the physical memory into segments of fixed length, called pages. When an application requests a piece of information from memory, Windows checks to see if the page where this piece of information resides is in physical (RAM) memory. If it does, the application goes ahead and reads it. If not, Windows has to get the requested information from the swap file. Knowing that the next piece of information that the application requests will most likely be close to the previous one (programs generally don't just jump erratically all over the memory) Windows brings in not only the requested piece of information but also the entire page that contains it. Unfortunately, though, no RAM is available at this point, so Windows has to make room for the new page. And the only way to make room for the new page is to remove another page from memory.

Using a complicated procedure, Windows calculates which page most likely will not be used in the near future, and this is the one it removes (it is generally the page that has been least recently used). This is called *demand paging* (pages are swapped between the memory and the disk on demand). Another factor Windows uses in determining which page to remove, is whether a page has been written (information saved to) since it was placed in memory. Pages that were not written to, can be simply replaced. Dirty pages, those containing new information, must be read into the swap file on the hard drive before they can be replaced in memory. Paging, or swapping, is a very efficient method for running multiple applications on a computer with limited memory (and that's practically every machine).

In Windows 3.1, the swap file was a fixed portion of the hard disk, walled off from the rest of the disk. In Windows 95, the swap file is dynamic, growing and shrinking in response to the demands made on it by whatever's happening in your computer at the time. The swap file zone on the hard drive is also called *virtual memory* because it's not really RAM, but endeavors to mimic it and, thereby, to extend it.

In Windows 3.1, you were advised how large to make the swap file—Windows recommended a figure approximately four times as much as the amount of RAM you had. If you had 8MB of RAM, Windows suggested that the optimum swap file size for your machine was 32MB. In no case, however, should the swap file exceed 50 percent of the remaining free space on the hard drive.

By contrast, the swap file in Windows 95 is not fixed as it was in Windows 3.1. In Windows 95, the swap file grows and shrinks as demands are made on it while you're working with the computer. Another difference is that in Windows 3.1, the swap file could not be located on a compressed drive; in Windows 95, it can (though the swap file itself isn't compressed because it notifies the compression software that it shouldn't be).

The Windows 95 swap file is dynamic.

Optimizing Your Swap File

Although Windows 95 generally makes its own decisions about
how much space to allocate and where to locate its dynamic swap
file, you can make adjustments that will improve performance.
For example, let's assume that you have two hard drives and one
is faster than the other. You should tell Windows 95 to locate the
swap file on the faster drive. Likewise, if there's very little space
left on one drive, move the swap file to the other drive.

First, find out where the swap file is. Click the Start menu button,
then select Find. Click Files or Folders. The Find All Files dialog box
appears. In the Named text box of the Name & Location tab, enter
the name of the Windows 95 swap file, WIN386.SWP, and click Find
Now to search for it. Most likely, Windows will find it on your
C: drive.

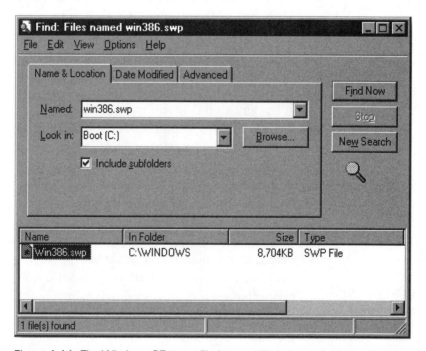

Figure 4-11: The Windows 95 swap file is most likely located on your C: drive. If
you have a faster drive, move the swap file there.

Notice in Figure 4-11 that the swap file is currently about 9MB large. However, if you start another application running, it might double in size.

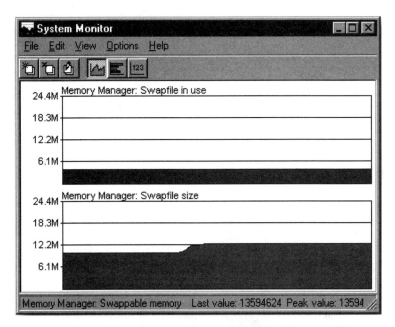

Figure 4-12: Loading in a new application raised the Windows 95 dynamic swap file from 10 to 12MB, though actual usage remains constant.

Say that you found your swap file on the C: drive, but you have a second, faster drive named D:. Here's how to move the swap file to that faster drive. Right-click on My Computer, choose Properties. Click on the Performance tab. Select Virtual Memory.

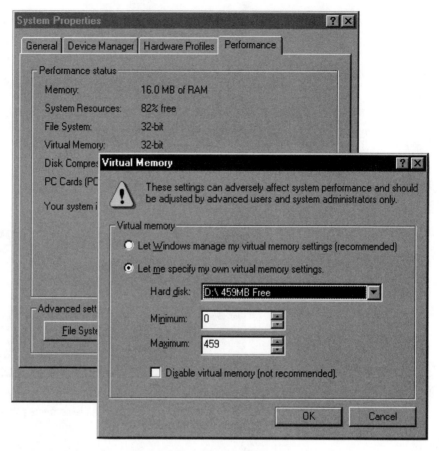

Figure 4-13: You can, and you should, stipulate that your swap file be located on your fastest hard drive.

Click on the "Let me specify my own virtual memory settings" option. Change the Hard disk setting so that it specifies your fastest hard drive. The only reason you should leave the swap file on a slower drive is if the faster drive has little remaining free space (less than, say, 30MB). Interestingly, after you restart the computer, the "Let me specify my own virtual memory settings" option will have returned to inactive status; it will be grayed out, but your hard disk for virtual memory is now D: as you requested.

Don't fool with the Minimum or Maximum settings in the Virtual Memory dialog box—let Windows 95 determine those.

OPTIMIZING DISK FILE ACCESS

You can change three settings in the File System Properties dialog box to customize the way that Windows 95 handles hard drive access. These options are chosen for you during Windows 95 setup, when you indicate the kind of computer you're using. However, you can adjust them. To do so, right-click the My Computer icon on the desktop, and choose Properties. In the System Properties dialog box, click on the Performance tab, and click the File System button to display the dialog box in Figure 4-14.

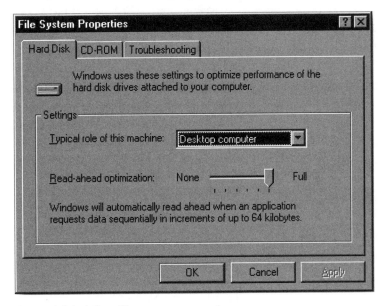

Figure 4-14: Adjust file system access here.

Tuning Up Hard Drive Access

The three possible settings for "Typical role of this machine" are:

❐ **Desktop computer:** Choose this setting for either a lone computer, or a computer attached to a network (as a client, not the central server to which all other machines on the network are attached). The computer is powered by being plugged into a wall socket, not a battery. This setting utilizes a moderate amount of caching. The PathCache is a location in which the most-recently accessed disk paths are stored (so they don't have to be looked up via a slower search of the file allocation table, or FAT). PathCache is set to 32 paths. The NameCache saves the most-recently accessed filenames and works, of course, with the PathCache. The NameCache is set to 8KB.

❐ **Mobile or Docking System:** A portable or dockable computer—reliant on battery power and constrained by a limited amount of RAM. The caches are kept small and, in addition, are more frequently flushed to disk. PathCache is set to 16 paths. The NameCache is set to 4KB.

❐ **Network Server:** Use this if you have a powerhouse machine, sharing work among attached clients on a network. By contrast to a portable or even a desktop, servers are expected to handle larger disk access tasks and therefore contain considerable RAM. PathCache is set to 64 paths. The NameCache is set to 16KB.

Read-ahead optimization should be left as is. This setting is designed to speed access to some types of files. Essentially, by sliding the bar for this setting, you're telling Windows how much data to read into the available buffers at one go—in effect, you're telling Windows to assume that you'll be coming back for more data after it reads what you've requested. This is great for files that require lots of sequential reads, like word processing or spreadsheet files. It's not so good for database files and things of that sort. If you do choose to noodle with the settings, you won't hurt anything. Just reset it the way you found it if you notice your computer's performance degrading.

Technically, if you choose read-ahead optimization, Windows will completely fill the buffers every time it reads from the disk. For example, if you have 32K of buffer space available and you're only interested in seeing 1K of data—Windows will nevertheless read enough off the disk to fill the 32K buffers.

CD-ROM Optimization

Next to the hard disk optimization tab in the File System properties sheet is the CD-ROM page. This enables you to specify the size of the cache that will be used to speed up data access from the CD. The optimum setting here depends on how much RAM you have. Right-click on My Computer and choose Properties. Click on the Performance tab and choose File System, then move to the CD-ROM tab. The supplemental cache can be set within a range of 214 to 1238K. In general, if you have 8MB or less RAM, you should set the supplemental cache to a low value, such as 214K. If you have 8 to 12MB, choose 470 or 726MB; if you have more than 12MB, push it all the way over to 1238K. Also be sure that the setting under "Optimize access pattern" reflects the speed of your CD-ROM unit. Windows 95 CD-ROM caching performs better than Windows 3.1 did. MSCDEX is no longer used. The cache is now both larger and smarter.

MSCDEX is no longer used.

Troubleshooting

The third tab in the File System Properties dialog box is Trouble-shooting (shown in Figure 4-15), and, unless you're having hard drive problems, leave these settings alone (unchecked). Checking them can slow your system.

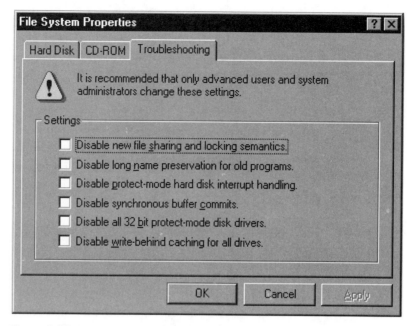

Figure 4-15: Leave these settings unchecked unless you're having hard drive problems.

The bottom one, "Disable write-behind caching for all drives," has the effect of turning off the delayed, intelligent flushing feature. In other words, any dirty document is flushed immediately to disk. This setting insures that no data is lost no matter what happens—even if you lose power from a lightning strike. But the price is high: You lose all the performance benefits of smart caching.

Adjusting Graphics Settings

Fool around with the graphics settings (accessed from the Performance tab in the System Properties dialog box) only if you are having problems with the mouse pointer or other graphics problems during the Windows boot process. Windows 95 assumes that your video card has some built-in capabilities, that it is Windows-compliant, and that it can take on some of the display calculations, thereby relieving Windows and your computer's CPU (the main computer chip, the microprocessor Pentium or 486, or whatever

CPU you have) from these responsibilities. However, maybe your video card can't do some of these things. If so, you might be able to remedy the situation by forcing Windows itself to take on some of the tasks. To access these settings, right-click the My Computer icon on the desktop, and choose Properties. Click on the Performance tab in the System Properties dialog box, and then click on the Graphics button to access the Advanced Graphics Settings dialog box shown in Figure 4-16.

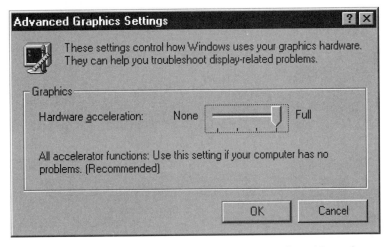

Figure 4-16: If your computer is working well, don't adjust this setting.

There are four settings that you can choose for the Hardware acceleration option. The Full setting at the far right is the normal setting. If the system is working well and you're not experiencing any graphics-related problems, leave this setting at Full. If you are having any of the following problems, try adjusting the slider to the various notches. Each notch adds limitations. The problems that adjusting the graphics settings will solve are:

❑ If your mouse pointer is disappearing, freezing, or otherwise behaving strangely, try moving the pointer shown in Figure 4-16 over one notch to the left (from the Full setting). With this setting, Windows no longer assumes that your video hardware can be responsible for the mouse pointer.

❒ If your applications are reporting errors that seem related to video functions, try the second notch over from the right.

❒ If, when you start Windows, you get the error message "Invalid page fault in module..." or you often find that the computer freezes up and won't respond to mouse moves or keyboard input, move the pointer all the way to the left to the None setting. At this setting, no video hardware acceleration is activated and, thus, the entire burden falls on Windows and your computer's CPU.

TIP

Be aware, however, that Windows runs faster if your video card does, in fact, contain the necessary hardware support for various video behaviors. If you do find that changing these graphics settings solves a problem, you nonetheless might consider purchasing a new video card. Video cards are no longer expensive and sometimes updating your video card can be one of the most cost-effective upgrades to perceptibly improve the efficiency of the entire computer. After all, if the screen can't display information as fast as the CPU can transmit it, it doesn't matter how fast the CPU is; information will only get to you as fast as your screen can relay it.

OPTIMIZING A PRINTER

For most people, the primary issue when adjusting printer settings is: How much hard drive space do I devote to a spool? (*Spool* is another name for cache, a place where data is temporarily pooled in order to free up resources.) A large disk spool returns control of the computer to you more rapidly when you print something. But the drawback is that this option both slows down the print job itself (your document will not come out of the printer as quickly) and it also requires more free disk space. A small spool does the opposite.

Windows uses an Enhanced Metafile (EMF) language to describe how to build a printed page. A metafile contains a description of your text or image, rather than a literal picture like a dot-for-dot copy of the original. An EMF description, might say: draw a 2- x 3-inch rectangle 5 inches down from the top and 3.45 inches over from the left, then fill it with blue dots.

The printer driver is responsible for converting the metafile into the codes used by a particular printer to achieve the effects described in the metafile. With no buffering, this conversion takes up all the computer's time, resulting in a seemingly frozen computer while the printing churns slowly out.

Before Windows 95, background print spooling was essentially an illusion. In Windows 3.1, the Print Manager applet could make printing *appear* to occur in the background, allowing you to continue using your computer while it printed. Instead of feeding the printer codes directly to the printer, they were stored on the hard drive, and the Print Manager spooled a little bit of this data to the printer every so often (during idle time, i.e., those moments when you're not typing or editing or an application isn't doing anything). By cooperating in this way with other running programs, the Print Manager created the illusion of background print spooling. This method, of course, increased the overall time it took for the document to print.

Windows 95 improves on the old Print Manager spooler in several ways. First of all, it's written using 32-bit programming and is fully integrated into the printing system. As a result, it multitasks much better (allows you to perform other tasks, i.e., do other things with the computer at the same time it's working). It also doesn't require running a separate print manager program. Thanks to the new printing system, you don't notice as much halting or jerkiness if, for example, you are scrolling through a document while printing.

Second, instead of waiting for the printer driver to convert the entire metafile to a spool file, Windows 95 can spool the Enhanced Metafile first. That way, the printer driver can also do its work in the background. (Some printers can even accept Enhanced Metafiles directly.) You can also set up a printer to start printing as soon as the first page is spooled, so you don't have to wait as long for printing to begin. It can simultaneously print and add new data to the spool file. All of these changes make printing with Windows 95 smoother and more efficient than it was with Windows 3.1*x*.

The idea is to get the page description out of the way and off the system as quickly as possible so you can resume working with the computer. If you're interested in *printing* as quickly as possible (and getting back the computer isn't a major issue), you can choose that setting.

TIP

You can also set up a printer to avoid Enhanced Metafile (EMF) spooling, in case this process causes problems with a particular program. After all, it's a new technology. With Raw spooling, printing works similarly to Windows 3.1; the entire metafile is first converted to printer codes, which are then spooled to the hard drive for background printing. PostScript printers already use a special type of metafile—a PostScript program file—to describe a page's layout to the printer. That's why Postscript printers don't have a separate EMF spooling method, they always use Raw spooling.

Setting Up a Printer

Printer settings in Windows 95 are controlled through the Properties dialog box for the printer. We'll now look at how to use this Properties dialog box to make adjustments to printer performance.

You might install a new printer months after setting up Windows 95. (Some people even have three printers attached to their computers—one for high-quality business letters and graphics, one for quick rough drafts, and one for color.) Indeed, any time you want to install a new peripheral such as a sound card or printer, you don't have to run the entire Windows Setup program again. Instead, you can double-click the Control Panel icon labeled Add New Hardware.

Unlike earlier versions of Windows, Windows 95 has no generic Windows Setup option in the Control Panel. You could, however, use your original Windows 95 CD or disk to run Setup again. When you want to make fundamental changes to the peripherals attached to your computer under Windows 95, look for the Add/Remove Programs and Add New Hardware icons in the Control Panel (click Start, then Settings, then Control Panel). There are separate setup routines for various parts of Windows, but no umbrella setup program. To install a new printer, there's an even simpler tactic: you just click on Start and then select Settings | Printer. Choose Add New Printer. Sometimes you'll want to follow the process of "installing a new printer," but you're not really adding any hardware. Printer manufacturers sometimes offer an updated device driver, which makes their printer run faster or adds new features. This is just a file that will replace the older device driver. To make this replacement, follow the steps below for installing a new printer, helpfully provided for you by Windows 95 with a Printer Installation Wizard that appears when you choose Add New Printer.

Adjusting Printer Properties

By far the most common adjustment you'll want to make to a printer is adding new fonts (typefaces) to it, to give your documents character and variety (see "Fonts Tab" later in this chapter for more information). However, you might want to change the title that appears beneath the printer's icon or the orientation of the paper, and so on. You can make these changes in two ways: from within an application or from the Windows desktop. But applications usually offer a limited subset of the printer's properties, so usually you'll want to access the printer property sheet.

Click on the Start button, then Settings, then Printers. You'll see the Printers folder. Right-click on your printer's icon and select Properties. Then you'll see the tabbed window shown in Figure 14-17 (yours may look a little different, depending on the features of your printer). Here you can access a full range of your printer's features. Note that the options available on the various tabs of the Properties dialog box will vary depending on the type of printer.

219

General Options Tab

For the moment, we'll assume that you're using some sort of laser printer. The General Options tab of the printer's Properties dialog box shown in Figure 4-17 simply shows the name of your printer (you can type in any name here you wish; it's merely the title that appears below the icon). Especially useful is the Comment field. As you can see, we noted the date when we last changed the printer's toner cartridge (the "ink" of a laser printer). You could also write notes to yourself describing the location (on a network) of this printer.

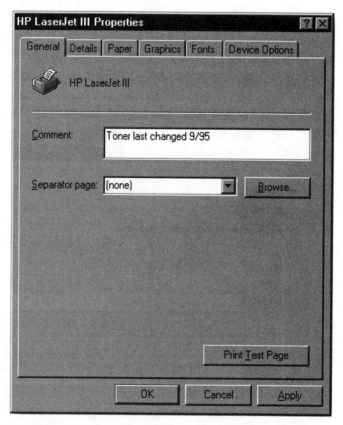

Figure 4-17: Here you can change the icon's title, insert a separator page, or print a test page.

Separator Page

The General tab also enables you to tell the printer to use a separator page. A separator page, if you want one, is inserted between each document printed. This page helps you keep different documents apart when a printer is busy turning out multiple copies or documents from various people on a network. You could also use it as a simple title page. Windows 95 offers two styles. To access them, click on the drop-down arrow on the Separator Page list.

Separator pages simplify sharing a printer on a network.

The Full option prints a nice, bold Windows logo and, using a large bold typeface, the title "Windows 95 Separator Page." Below that it prints the name of the document, who it was printed by, and the date and time of printing. The Simple option prints the same information, but without the logo and in the small regular typeface of the document's text. The Simple option isn't nearly as easy to spot when you're flipping through a stack of pages, so it doesn't achieve the main purpose of a separator page.

If you want something really distinctive, click on the Browse button of the General Options page to locate a Windows Metafile (.WMF) graphic to use on the separator page. You could use a drawing, your company's logo, or whatever. The separator, however, must be a Windows Metafile-style graphic. Unfortunately, perhaps, the Windows Metafile graphics file type hasn't really caught on. Few graphics programs allow you to save pictures in that format; even Microsoft Paint doesn't. (CorelDRAW!, though, does a good job if you want to edit a .WMF file.) Also, many applications (including Microsoft Office) provide .WMF files as part of a clip-art collection. (To see if you've got .WMF files on your hard drive, click on the Start button, then Find. In the Named text box, type in: **.WMF** and then select Find.)

The Details Page

When you click on the Details tab of the printer's Properties sheet, you'll see the options shown in Figure 4-18.

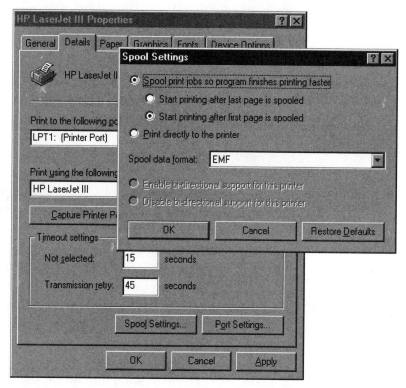

Figure 4-18: You decide the trade-off between multitasking and printer speed.

The Details options govern how your documents are sent to the printer (which printer, how fast, and what delay). In the top drop-down list box, you can select which printer you want to send your documents to—if more than a single printer is available.

You can also select different drivers. This list, however, will display a separate driver for all printers available to your computer. This is a way to divert the document from your printer to a fax machine, for example.

"Capture printer port" means mapping the printer to a network drive.

The Capture Printer Port button allows you to map a printer to a network drive, which is necessary for MS-DOS applications and some older Windows applications. Most Windows applications are designed to print to a specific printer, not a specific printer port (such as LPT2:). DOS, however, can print only to a port.

A network printer is not physically present, so the Capture Printer Port button fools MS-DOS into believing that your LPT2: port (which most computers don't really have anyway) is a local printer. In fact, the printer data sent to LPT2: is re-routed to a network printer. If you don't have a printer attached to your local computer, you can capture LPT1: and redirect it to a network printer. If you do have a local printer, you'll probably want to redirect LPT2: or LPT3: instead.

When you send a document to the printer, the Timeout settings on the Details tab determine Windows 95's behavior. The upper setting, Not Selected, takes effect when the printer is detected to be physically unavailable. It governs how many seconds Windows should wait for a printer to come online. (For example, if the printer's power is turned off, how much time should pass before you're notified of that fact.)

The Transmission Retry setting determines how many seconds Windows waits before reporting that the printer isn't responding or isn't yet ready to print. Printers need some time to digest and understand documents before they actually start ejecting pages. You should increase this setting if you get timeout error messages when printing large or complex documents.

Spool Settings

The only reason for changing any of these default spooling settings is if you're having problems printing, or if your printer's manual instructs you to.

To choose when, if, or how the spooler intervenes in the printing process, click the Spool Settings button at the bottom of the Details tab of the printer's Properties dialog box. This displays the Spool Settings dialog box.

Most people will want to leave spooling on because it returns the computer to your use (unfreezes it) more quickly when a document is sent to the printer. When you first print a document, Windows wants to focus all its attention on formatting it. If spooling is turned on, the resulting formatted document is saved to a temporary file on your hard drive where Windows can work on it in the background, and control of the computer is returned to you—you can type and move the mouse. In the background, without affecting your interaction with the computer, Windows feeds the contents of that file to the printer.

Likewise, the EMF setting is faster than Raw for most printers. EMF results in smaller spool files. Without EMF, the entire burden of translating codes (such as italics) falls on the printer.

TIP

Some applications get confused by the new EMF spooling and in some cases, Windows 95 automatically notices the problem and turns EMF spooling off. One example of this is if you have older versions of Adobe Type Manager installed. In that case, Windows 95 is forced to turn off EMF spooling. (However, Adobe has been working on a new version of ATM, so this problem will be fixed soon.)

You could also choose to print directly to the printer (avoiding spooling entirely), but why would you want to do this? The spooler uses only a few megabytes on your hard drive, and uses them only temporarily; after the printing is finished, the hard drive is cleaned of the spooler's activities. What's more, if you turn off spooling, you can't pause print jobs in progress. Resort to this option only if you are having problems getting your printer to work.

The "Start printing after last page is spooled" option unfreezes the computer faster than ordinary spooling. All formatting is calculated by the computer, and then the printer file is saved to the disk. Nothing is sent to the printer until the entire document has been saved. This option, however, can require a large temporary (spool) file on your hard drive, particularly for large or complex documents.

The Bi-directional options will be gray and not respond to mouse clicks unless your printer is capable of two-way communication with the computer. If your printer can send messages, these options can be useful if problems occur; therefore, you should leave this option turned on.

If your printer is bi-directional, use that option.

Port Settings

Finally, you also can set the correct printer port by clicking the Port Settings button in the lower-right corner of the Details tab of the printer's Properties dialog box. The Port Settings option allows you to specify whether printing from MS-DOS windows should also be spooled. (Turning off this option can sometimes speed up DOS print jobs, but can also cause conflicts when you try to print from Windows while the DOS program is printing.)

The Paper Tab

Ordinarily, you'll use your word processor to make any adjustments to margins, envelopes, feeder, page size, and page shape. Word processors have access to the Windows Setup information. However, you can optionally adjust the choices in the Paper page of the printer's Properties sheet.

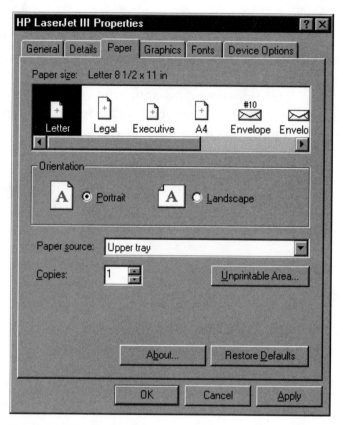

Figure 4-19: In the Paper tab, you can adjust the virtual margins of the document.

You can put various sizes of paper into most printers—from a business card to a one foot by infinite roll of computer paper. What's more, the printer can print on these various sizes without your changing any settings. The purpose of setting a paper size, orientation, and margins is so your word processor formats the text (or graphic) to stay within the physical boundaries of the paper and to provide a blank margin that frames the text (or graphic) the way you like.

If you see an icon labeled Custom in the Paper size panel at the top of the Paper tab, you can click on it and define a unique paper size. PostScript printers, for example, permit various custom paper sizes, including huge formats that are used with *imagesetters* (typesetting machines).

In the Orientation section in the middle of the Paper tab, you can set how your text is printed on the page. You can choose Portrait or Landscape. Click on Portrait if you want to print the long way on the paper—the shape that most artists use to create human portraits. Click on Landscape if you want to print so the page is wider than it is high—the way landscape scenes are painted. Portrait is by far the most common because people have a harder time locating the next line when lines of text are extremely wide. Landscape, however, can be superior for printing graphics or if you are designing a newsletter with two side-by-side pages. Just fold a 14- x 11-inch page in half, and you have a four-page 7- x 11-inch newsletter format.

Some printers have several trays holding different sizes of paper or envelopes. You can specify which tray should be the source of the paper for a particular print job by choosing from the Paper source drop-down list. The options listed here depend on your printer model. You can also request that multiple copies be printed.

Click on the Unprintable Area button to specify margins. The word processor is forced to keep the text or graphics within this frame of blank space. In other words, you can specify how far over from the left side of the paper the document should be printed and how far down from the top, over from the right, and up from the bottom of the paper. Most laser printers have a quarter-inch unprintable area on all four sides of a page because their grippers and rollers need space to move the page and because the image area of the printer's drum is slightly smaller than a page. You'll find that photocopiers also have a narrow unprintable region, and some even automatically reduce a page to fit. Inkjet printers typically have a larger unprintable region of about one-half inch on the top and bottom.

The margins are adjustable for the Hewlett-Packard LaserJet in increments of 1/100 of an inch and default to one-quarter inch on all sides except the top, which is a bit less than one-fifth inch. On many printers, you cannot reduce the margins to the very edge of the paper. One-quarter inch is about the narrowest possible margin permitted; this thin zone is truly unprintable unless you fool the printer by claiming to be using a larger piece of paper than you really are.

The Graphics Tab

Dithering is an effort to simulate missing colors or shades of gray.

In the Graphics tab of the printer's Properties sheet, you can tell Windows what kinds of compromises it should make if an image must be printed at a low resolution. Note that this discussion assumes you are not using a PostScript printer. A PostScript printer bypasses the universal printer driver, and uses a different set of dialog boxes. Also, some printers aren't capable of any dithering. If you don't see dithering options listed on the Graphics page of Printer Properties, that means your printer won't dither.

Dithering

The Dithering option of the Graphics tab of the printer Properties dialog box conveys to the printer what it should do if you send it a graphic that's more complicated than it can directly reproduce. *Complicated* in this context means that some printers can print, for instance, only 64 shades of gray (or that many different shades of color). However, you might want to print an image with 256 shades. Dithering is a compromise—a way to display in-between shades by adding patterns (crosses, scattered dots, and other patterns) to lighten areas that, in the original graphic, are really a shade of gray that the printer cannot reproduce. You also can use dithering to improve the quality of color printing.

TIP

A printer can't really print shades of gray. It can only impress black or white dots (pixels) on the paper. After all, the black ink or toner powder used in a printer is just that: black. There aren't 64 or 256 little nozzles connected to as many wells filled with different shades of gray. By arranging clusters or checkerboard patterns of black and white dots, a printer can fool the eye into seeing shaded regions. The size of the printed dots affects how smoothly and how finely the shaded patterns can be produced, so a typical 300 dpi (dots per inch) laser printer can display only 64 shades or fewer. By quadrupling the resolution, a 600 dpi printer can display 256 shades of gray. Color printers also use these techniques to create a range of pseudo-colors out of just three primary colored inks.

Dithering is also sometimes seen on the computer screen if you're displaying, for instance, a True Color image on a 256-color display card or a 256-color image on a computer that can display only 16-color graphics. However, the Dithering option on the Graphics tab of the Printer Properties will affect only the printer, not the screen.

Your choices for dithering are None, Coarse, Fine, Line art, and Error diffusion. See Figures 4-20 through 14-24 for examples of these options.

Figure 4-20: This is the undithered original. Your image will be close to this quality if you select the Fine setting. Better yet, if the image is of high quality and your printer is capable of very high resolution (above 600 dpi, dots per inch), choose None and don't dither at all.

Figure 4-21: If you choose None on a low-resolution printer, the printer will make its own decisions if it has to compromise on shading. Here's one possible result.

Figure 4-22: This image is printed at the Coarse dithering setting. Coarse can actually yield a perception of more shades of gray than the None setting, but the whole picture looks blotchy. Some gradients, which should be smooth transitions from light to dark, take on a camouflage look—see the letter "K" here.

Figure 4-23: If you set dithering to Line art, you'll see no grayscale shading at all—just black and white.

Figure 4-24: Error diffusion creates cross-hatches, noodle patterns, irregular blobs, something like rough paper. This setting can be a good compromise if your printer must dither. Error diffusion is similar to the *halftoning* effect you see in newspapers. PostScript printers can perform true halftoning.

The results of the various dithering options are usually unfortunate, but better than nothing. Each attempts to soften the blow when reducing the resolution (detail) to accommodate a printer with fewer dots per inch than the original image enjoys. Something's got to give if you try to write a letter with a brick. Of all the options, error diffusion is often the best, but you really should experiment. Send various images to your printer, using these various dithering options, to see what produces the best results with different kinds of graphics.

Resolution

On the Graphics tab, you can adjust how cleanly images will be reproduced by adjusting the Resolution setting. Rough printing is faster and can be used if you want to see just a draft of a drawing. For the final product, though, you'll want to use the maximum *resolution* of which your printer is capable—the highest available dpi setting on the Resolution drop-down list.

High resolution means detail; can you see eyelashes, blades of grass?

Resolution determines how much detail you can see. The lowest resolution, 75 dpi for many printers, produces a cruder, rougher graphic than higher settings. Some printers can achieve a density of 600 or even 1,200 dpi with special interpolation. The fewer dots per inch that are printed, the looser, more blurred, and less detailed the result.

Again, which options you'll see on this Properties sheet depends on the capabilities of your printer. For example, an Apple Personal Laserwriter NTR has no Intensity option in the Properties dialog box. However, there are options for Halftoning, special options (like printing a negative or mirror image), and scaling the printed image.

Intensity

The final setting on the Graphics tab, Intensity, is similar to those found on photocopier machines—you can use this setting to compensate for printing that's too light or too dark. Ordinarily, you can leave this slider alone, but if your printer ink cartridge or toner is getting old, you might want to increase this setting. You'd probably be better off simply replacing the ink in your printer, and restoring the slider to the midpoint between dark and light. Adjusting Intensity can be a great way of lightening images that print too muddy or too dark, as an alternative to retouching the picture in a Paint program. Keep in mind that both Dithering and Intensity apply only to printed images printed in grayscale or color; these settings won't affect line art, text, or solid black objects.

The Fonts Tab

The Fonts tab in the printer's Properties dialog box is printer-specific. The options here differ from printer to printer: this page designates what cartridges, if any, the printer can accept and what printer-specific fonts, if any, are available. You can easily ignore this Fonts page entirely because it represents an older technology, font cartridges. Also, printer-specific fonts are old hat—written in proprietary *font languages,* which are largely dying out and being replaced by Windows's TrueType language and other standards. Instead of managing the kinds of fonts governed by this tab of the printer's Properties sheet, simply click on the fonts icon in the Control Panel to manage TrueType fonts, which are available to all the printers connected to your system. (See the "Windows Fonts" section, later in this chapter.) There are, though, two TrueType settings on this printer Properties sheet tab that you should be aware of.

TrueType fonts are typefaces conforming to a standard established by Microsoft and Apple. All TrueType fonts are stored in the Motorola big endian format and are binary-compatible across many platforms. These fonts are also *scaleable* (you can freely resize them from tiny 8 point to huge 120 point). Also, TrueType fonts look essentially the same when displayed on the screen as they do when printed. The type *can* be a little ragged around the edges if printed or displayed in low resolution. For example, if you select 75 dpi in the Graphics tab of the printer's Properties dialog box, curves and diagonals within the characters stairstep and look rough. Similarly, some screen resolutions can produce ragged characters as shown in Figure 4-25.

Figure 4-25: The character on the left is ragged or "stairstepped" as it's called. The character on the right illustrates font smoothing (anti-aliasing).

TIP

If you install Microsoft Plus! for Windows 95, you can turn on font smoothing, which produces smoother lines and curves, especially with large typefaces, on your computer screen. It doesn't suffer from the usual problems induced by anti-aliasing—blurry characters at body text sizes such as 10 or 12 point.

Soft Fonts or Graphics?

The TrueType options in the Fonts tab of the printer's Properties sheet determine how Windows sends characters from the computer's hard drive to the printer. Normally, you should leave the default setting "Download TrueType fonts as bitmap soft fonts" selected because your documents will print faster.

For example, if you select a TrueType font from within a word processor, and then start printing a document, the font is loaded into your printer. Windows reads the font off the disk drive and sends it as a description of how that font should be geometrically reproduced. Many printers are capable of accepting such a description and then reproducing the look of the characters. This description is similar to telling someone how to print a black square by saying: "Start with a black dot 5 inches over from the left of the paper and 4 inches down from the top. Then draw a line 2 inches to the right, 2 inches down, 2 inches left, and 2 inches up. Now fill with black." Such a description can be transmitted to the printer rapidly.

TrueType should be sent to the printer as a soft font, not as graphics.

The alternative, printing TrueType fonts as graphics, is essentially like taking a snapshot of each page of your document and sending a dot-by-dot message to the printer. (This "snapshot" approach is almost always the way a drawing or other graphic is sent to the printer. Many printers are not equipped to reconstruct a drawing from a description.) To print a graphic, the computer sends a stream of information, dots that are reproduced by the printer. If you've chosen 300 dpi resolution (in the Graphics tab of the printer's Properties sheet), a 2-inch black square is reconstructed by the computer saying, in effect, "Start at this position on the paper. Now: black dot, black dot, black dot . . ." 600 times for the first line across the top. Stop. Start at this new position: black dot, black dot . . . then repeating this 600 more times to go down 2 inches. A total of 360,000 pieces of information sent to the printer are required to print those black dots. This approach is obviously slower because the computer has much more information to pass along to the printer.

In general, it makes sense to leave the "Download TrueType fonts as bitmap soft fonts" option selected. However, if you are printing documents with many graphics but very little text, you might speed the printing if you select the alternative "Print TrueType as Graphics" option. The increase in speed, however, isn't much in most cases. Also, you can achieve some special effects (graphics partially covering characters) using this option, but you have more control over such effects using a drawing/ retouching program such as CorelDRAW! or Photoshop. Overlays are far easier to construct within a graphics application than via overprinting.

A more practical and efficient approach to adding fonts is to install fonts into Windows 95 itself, and let the Print Manager in Windows convert the fonts to codes that your particular printer understands. To install Windows fonts, click on the Start button, and select Settings | Control Panel. When the Control Panel appears, click on the Fonts icon. A window then opens showing all the fonts you currently have installed. Select File | Install New Font. After you select the fonts from the Add Fonts window, click OK. The fonts then are sent to your Fonts folder.

TIP

Windows's native TrueType font files end in .TTF. Printer-specific fonts end in .FON or .FNT or a bevy of other filename extensions.

The Device Options Tab

The Device Options tab of the printer's Properties dialog box, shown in Figure 4-26, enables you to select additional options for your particular printer. What appears on this tab depends on the memory—how much RAM—your printer contains. The printer's RAM is just like the RAM in your computer. (Remember that most printers have microprocessors and RAM; they are "computers," too. They are dedicated to the process of producing documents rather than being general-purpose machines like your main computer.)

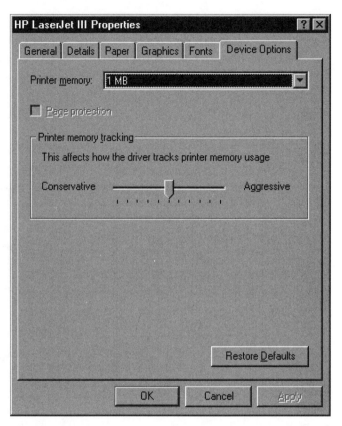

Figure 4-26: The options you see on the Device Options tab of the printer's Properties dialog box depend on your particular printer.

You may need more printer memory if you frequently print complex graphics.

All printers have some memory, but you can add additional memory to some printers, just as you can to computers. But why would you want to? Printing ordinary text is generally no problem at all, but graphics can create huge files, requiring several megabytes to hold a single page. Some printers' memory can be expanded to contain as much as 4 or 5MBs to hold such complex graphics, but even they can struggle to print the most difficult graphics. If the work you do frequently results in an "Out of memory" or "Page too complex" error message from your printer, consider investing in additional RAM for the printer. In some cases, you can add RAM via a cartridge; in other cases you must open up the printer and push in a memory board.

The list box at the top of the of the Device Options tab displays the amount of memory that was included with your particular printer when you bought it (the default amount). In the case of the LaserJet III, it's 1MB. If you add more memory, you must let Windows know by clicking on this list box and selecting the correct total of RAM from the drop-down list. Note that some printers communicate with Windows 95. If you have this kind of printer, this memory-adjusting option will be unchangeable (by clicking), and Windows will already display the correct RAM.

If printing complex documents requires so much memory, why not divide the graphic in pieces and feed the printer the pieces one at a time, like a bucket brigade? The next option on this window, Page protection, permits you to zone off some of the printer's memory (into a "page"). (Again, what options appear here will depend on your particular printer.) If you get an "Out of memory" message from your printer when you try to print a complicated graphic, try clicking on Page protection. In some cases, selecting this option makes it possible to print the large document. Ordinarily, leave this option unchecked. (If your printer doesn't have enough RAM, checking the Page protection feature isn't possible, and this check box remains gray (disabled), so you can't click it.)

The final option on the Device Options tab is a fudge factor. The Printer memory tracking slider allows you to tell your printer's driver how conservative to be when estimating the amount of printer memory required to print each page sent to the printer. If you get an "Out of memory" message when trying to print a complex page, this memory-tracking option is your last resort, short of adding RAM to the printer. Try moving the slider to the right toward Aggressive. Among its other duties, a printer driver predicts how much printer RAM a page requires, before it releases that page to the printer to be printed. If the driver calculates that a page will exceed the RAM available in your printer, it won't waste your time by sending the page on and having the printer grind away and then fail to print. Instead, the driver immediately notifies you that there's insufficient printer memory to print this page. However, the driver can't always predict accurately. It might be too conservative, and some borderline-sized pages might actually print, even though the driver doesn't think they could.

If you set this slider too far toward Conservative, you won't have to wait until the slower printer fails to print a complex page. The drawback is that some pages that could have printed will be reported as too complex by the driver before the printer ever gets a chance to even try. Set the slider too far toward Aggressive, and you'll cause the driver to send pages off to the printer that the driver estimates are going to overflow the printer's memory. The drawback here is that the printer will waste your time while it tries, and sometimes fails, to absorb these dubious pages.

USING THE FILE SYSTEM TOOLS

Optimizing the performance of your machine can be assisted by several tools provided with Windows 95. These utilities— ScanDisk, Defragmenter, and DriveSpace—offer improved efficiency and increased protection for your hard disks and other kinds of floppy and removable disks you use with your computer.

A hard disk drive is a remarkably sturdy device, considering that it is heavily used, spins rapidly and must hold delicate data in a high-density environment. Although the disk is sealed, things can go wrong. A major software component of a disk drive is the FAT (File Allocation Table), which is where the operating system maintains the details about the location of files on a drive—where the clusters are and where the data is and where there's free space. But there can be problems: the FAT can be damaged by electrical surges, applications that accidentally overwrite it, or other mishaps. If that happens, Windows no longer has a completely accurate blueprint of the hard drive. The next time a file is saved to a disk with a damaged FAT, the operating system might overwrite an existing file—mistakenly thinking that this area was free space. When that happens, two files are at least partially sharing one or more clusters, but only one of them can actually claim to have authentic data in that cluster. The other, older file has been, at least in part, overwritten. This condition is called *cross-linking*. To complicate matters, should you delete the older, injured file, the operating system gets even more confused and lists the entire space as now available for new disk saves. At this point, there's a vulnerable space within the second file.

The solution to this problem used to be CHKDSK, a DOS program that looked at the real estate claims made by each file, then reported any two or more that were occupying the same space. It could not detect which of the two files was, in fact, whole. CHKDSK reported the crosslinks to you, so you could look at the bad files yourself, but it could not repair them.

CHKDSK has been superseded by ScanDisk.

In addition to crosslinks, CHKDSK could also compare the FAT's list of space in use with areas that CHKDSK found weren't actually in use. In these cases, it offered to free up unused space on the disk. Data from this unused space was then saved in the root directory for you to examine. Sometimes you could still retrieve information from these fragments of data. For example, if it were a .BMP file, you could rename it from CHKDSK's default name (FILE0000.CHK) to BAD.BMP and then load it into a graphics program. Part of the file was damaged, perhaps all of it, but other parts could be okay. With text files, just load them into Notepad and look around. If you've got a good copy of this text you see inside, delete this file. If, however, this is chapter three of your term paper—well, at least you won't have to redo the entire thing. Fragments, maybe large chunks, of it are right here ready to be cut and pasted into your word processor.

You couldn't use CHKDSK under Windows; you had to be in DOS. CHKDSK is still around if you drop out of Windows 95 into DOS mode, but why bother when you have ScanDisk? Among other things, ScanDisk can deal with Windows 95's new long filenames. But probably its greatest value is that it *can* fix crosslinked files to an extent. It copies both files to new filenames, and then fixes the link. Of course the new files might both be damaged.

ScanDisk works on anything that the operating system treats like a disk file: Zip drives, hard drives, floppies, RAM drives, and memory cards. It goes beyond CHKDSK in capability, fixing errors in long filenames, the FAT, lost clusters, the directory structures, crosslinks, areas on the drive that are permanently damaged physically (marking them so the FAT won't try to store future files there), and the components of compressed drives (DriveSpace or DoubleSpace).

To run ScanDisk, you can right-click on a drive's icon in the My Computer window, then choose Properties and the Tools tab. Click on Check now. (Alternatively, you can get to ScanDisk via the Start menu: Click on Programs, select Accessories. Select the System Tool, then click ScanDisk.) No matter which method you use, the ScanDisk window appears, as shown in Figure 4-27.

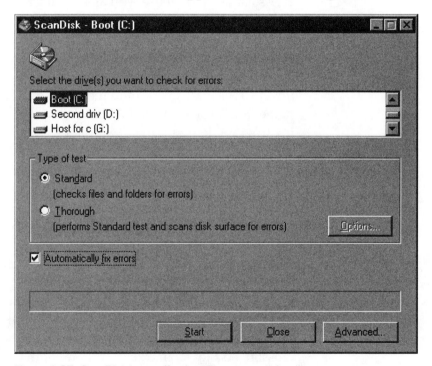

Figure 4-27: ScanDisk is an effective all-purpose disk utility.

Within the ScanDisk window, just click on the drive (or hold down the Shift key and click on several drives), then click on the ScanDisk Start button. Also click on the Automatically fix errors box—it's hard to imagine a situation when you wouldn't want an error fixed.

Hard drives have an expected life of four to six years. As they get older, the usual problem is that more and more of the surface becomes corrupted and physically unusable. You should generally run ScanDisk with the Standard option active. However, if you're frequently getting errors on a drive, you might want to try the Thorough option. When you select that, a second window of options pops up. To speed up the Thorough ScanDisk test, you can check the system area only (just the FAT and directory zones). Or you can have ScanDisk check only areas containing files. Another way to speed up this "thorough" version of the ScanDisk testing is to have it avoid write-testing. It then merely sees if it can read the entire surface of the disk, without attempting to verify that data can be written and then correctly read back. Why not go all out and get a thorough physical while you're at it?

During this physical scan, any spots on the drive that are found to be unusable are cordoned off. The thorough version of the scan takes about 30–40 minutes on an average 400MB drive. So it's about as time-consuming as running the defragmenting utility described later in this chapter.

Note that an area discovered to be bad is copied to another location, a good location, on the drive. Some few legacy (old, very old) applications and Windows 3.1's Swapfile should not be rearranged; but unless you're faced with those situations, don't worry about the Automatically fix errors option—leave it on.

Advanced ScanDisk Repairs

ScanDisk has a button labeled Advanced. When you click on it, you can further customize how ScanDisk behaves.

Figure 4-28: If you wish, adjust ScanDisk's behavior in this screen.

You might as well turn off the Display Summaries option if you've chosen to have ScanDisk automatically fix errors. However, if you're curious to see if there *were* any errors, leave this option on, but select Only if errors found. Other than that, the report at the end is merely a description of the size of your drive, the number of files, the amount of free space, and so on. And this report is *modal*—it pops up onscreen and won't go away until you click on it. Obviously, modal reminder screens are annoying if you want to continue merely working in some application and don't care to be interrupted to answer the message. Likewise, if you have Microsoft Plus (and have set the System Agent to automatically run ScanDisk in the background), or if you put ScanDisk in your Windows\Startup directory so it runs every time you run Windows—you won't want that modal window popping up.

ScanDisk by default creates a text file log of what it finds. If you're tracking the entropic collapse of an aging disk (so that you can make a decision about when to retire it and replace it with a new one), you might want to choose the Append to log option so you'll have a history of the corruptions that ScanDisk discovers. Otherwise, Replace Log is a good compromise. You don't grow a huge file, but you do have a record of the last scan. You can find SCANDISK.LOG on your boot drive in the root directory, probably C:. Here's a typical log after running a thorough scan:

```
Microsoft ScanDisk for Windows

NOTE: If you use an MS-DOS program to view this file, some
of the characters may appear incorrectly. Use a Windows
program such as Notepad instead.

Log file generated at 14:08 on 11/21/1995.

ScanDisk used the following options:

 Thorough test

 Automatically fix errors

Drive G: (host for drive Boot (C:)) contained the follow-
ing errors:

ScanDisk did not find any errors on this drive.
```

```
Drive Boot (C:) contained the following errors:

ScanDisk did not find any errors on this drive.
```

If ScanDisk finds crosslinked files, you'll probably want it to save copies of the data in those corrupted files prior to fixing the linking problem. This way, you can sometimes recover data from these FILE0000.CHK files that ScanDisk creates to store recovered data. So leave the default option, Make copies, selected.

Likewise, you'll probably want to take a look at any lost file fragments, zones that were listed in the FAT as being in use, but are not, in fact, part of any currently valid file cluster chain. Again, you can take a look at the data to make sure you have better copies of whatever's there. Once sure you will never need this data, delete the .CHK file(s) that ScanDisk has created.

Allow ScanDisk to check for and resolve any discrepancies between older DOS-style 8.3-character filenames and Windows 95's new 260-character long filenames.

TIP

The new longer filenames are limited to fewer than 260 characters because the *path* to the file is also included in the character count. Thus, C:\MYFILE actually uses up 9 characters.

You could also have ScanDisk locate any invalid (wildly inaccurate) times and dates, such as February 40, 1856. The host drive (the partition that governs a compressed drive) should be checked prior to checking the compressed drive. Leave this option, Invalid dates and times, selected.

THE DISK DEFRAGMENTER

When Windows saves one of your files for the first time, the FAT tells it where there's empty space on the disk for the file to be placed. You might prefer that the file be copied onto contiguous clusters. A contiguous chain of clusters can be read back into the computer more quickly than noncontiguous clusters. Copying a file to contiguous clusters isn't always possible. Every time a file is deleted from the disk, its space is marked as freed up. However, given that files are of different sizes, you can see that these spots of free space become, over time, increasingly varied in size and position. Imagine, for example, that you wrote a few pages in a new document, then saved it to disk. It fits nicely into a cluster or two that are vacant. But if you continue writing, the text could grow larger than the empty space originally selected to store that file.

Defragment once a month or more.

When, as often happens, a file must be located in two or more areas on the disk, that file is said to be *fragmented*. If there's a fair amount of fragmentation, you'll improve your disk's response time by defragmenting the drive.

You can access the Defragmenter in two ways. You can right-click on a drive's icon in the My Computer window, then choose Properties and the Tools tab. Click on Defragment now. Alternatively, you can access the Disk Defragmenter from the Start menu. On that menu select Programs, then select Accessories. Select the System Tools choice, and then choose Disk Defragmenter. The Disk Defragmenter window appears.

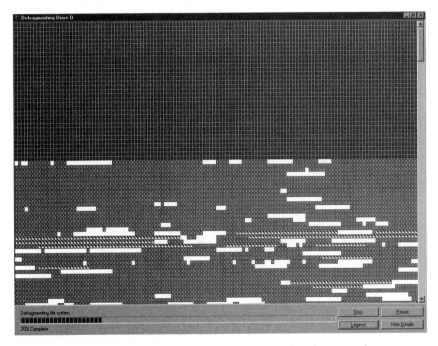

Figure 4-29: Defragmentation in action. The dark section shows contiguous (defragmented) file clusters. The white sections are free space. The gray is data in its obviously fragmented state. Boxes with small dark squares in their upper right are immovable—they're supposed to stay where they are.

If your disk is relatively free of fragmentation, Windows 95 tells you that you need not defragment it at this time. No harm done. If you use your computer fairly regularly, it's a good idea to use the

Defragment Disk utility once a month or so, just to see if defragmentation is advisable. You don't want to defragment unless necessary—it takes quite a while, about as long as ScanDisk takes to run with its Thorough and Write-testing options turned on. For a typical 400MB disk, this ranges from 30–40 minutes.

You can defragment more quickly by clicking on the Advanced button on the Disk Defragmenter window. The default is a full defragmentation. This not only makes all the clusters in all files' chains contiguous, it also moves all data to one zone and leaves the rest of the drive with contiguous empty space. Alternatively, you can partially defragment by doing it only to the files (not moving the free space to a separate zone), or by choosing only to consolidate the free space.

DISK COMPRESSION

If you've had, or read about, unpleasant experiences with disk compression—a slowdown of the drive's response time, data instability, increased risk of losing data or whatever—consider using DriveSpace, Windows 95's well-tested and speedy compression utility. You're unlikely to experience any problems with DriveSpace, and you'll probably double the usable size of your hard drive.

As we move toward high-definition TV (HDTV), graphic Internet communications, real-time 3D rendering, digital movies on CD, and other data-intensive transmission and storage systems, finding ways to fit information into ever smaller spaces has become essential. For example, although relatively few people still watch over-the-air TV, owners of local television stations have not wanted to give up their franchises. The interaction between this powerful lobby and congress is too complex, lengthy, tedious, and alas, predictable to recount here. Nonetheless, an ultimate result of their confluence is that HDTV is required to fit itself within the 6MHz bandwidth currently used by local low-fi TV. Never mind that HDTV requires 12MHz. So, engineers had to figure out a way to *compress* the high-resolution signal.

There are various ways to compress data. For example, if people are talking, only their mouths are moving most of the time and, therefore, you can compress by making a notation that for five frames, perhaps, the sky and the car don't shift position or color or shape. Only the mouths must be redrawn. In other words, a few mathematical descriptions of the unchanging regions, descriptions requiring only a few bytes, can replace megabytes of scenery.

There are additional techniques. For one thing, words are repetitive. The amount of compression possible by comparing congregate repetition depends on the writer's style. Obviously, though, you could save space by replacing the word *compression* in this section of the book with a 2- or 4-byte numeric substitute. And, too, the two-letter combination *th* occurs 3 percent of the time on average within any English text; among words, *the* occurs 6.5 percent of the time with *of* (4 percent) and *and* (3.1 percent).

The compression tradeoff: more disk space or faster disk access.

Of course, there are tradeoffs. It takes time to compress or decompress data. On the other hand, when packed tight, that data can be transmitted faster between the hard drive and the computer or, for that matter, over modems, TV cable, or any other delivery system.

Compressing a hard drive is even more efficient than other compression techniques because of a strange fact about file storage on disk: there's considerable room for improvement. The FAT is limited—it can keep track of a total of only 65,535 allocation units (clusters) on the hard drive. Therefore, the size of the hard drive determines the cluster size. The clusters are 2,048 bytes large on a hard drive smaller than 128MB, but a 1GB hard drive's clusters are 32,768 bytes large. Here's the inefficiency: If a file is 2,049 bytes large, it takes up two clusters on a 127MB disk drive. This means that 4,096 bytes on the hard drive are marked in the FAT as used, but nearly half of them are wasted space.

Compression solves this problem of waste by storing the contents of your hard drive as one giant file. At what cost? The user is uninvolved in the compression/decompression activities, but on slower computers (anything less than a 100MHz 486, for example), there is a perceptible decrease in access speed. Recall, too, that any slowdown is ameliorated because there's less data to send back and forth between the computer and the hard drive. A file half as large after compression transfers twice as fast.

Given that compression has now reached a state of high efficiency and safety, you might as well use it. In Windows 3.1, many people relied on DoubleSpace or Stacker and achieved a compression ratio of 2:1.

Windows 95 can work with hard drives compressed with DoubleSpace or Stacker. However, there are two new, better compression utilities available to Windows 95 users: DriveSpace versions 2.0 and 3.0. DriveSpace 2.0 comes with Windows 95 and compresses drives as large as 512MB. However, version 3.0, available in the add-on product Microsoft Plus! compresses drives up to 2GB. DriveSpace 3.0 is also more efficient than version 2.0. In the following discussion, we'll focus on version 3.0—it includes all that version 2.0 can do, and more.

Taking the Leap

Once you've decided to compress, it's easy to do. First, of course, you should back up all your *data* files. You can reinstall your programs from their original CDs or disks, but you can't recover letters you've written or pictures you've drawn. Just in case something goes wrong, you should make a safety backup. That done, you can access DriveSpace in two ways. Click Start | Programs | Accessories | System Tools | Drivespace. Or run Explorer, right-click on the hard drive's icon, and choose Properties (Figure 4-30). Then click on the tab labeled Compression.

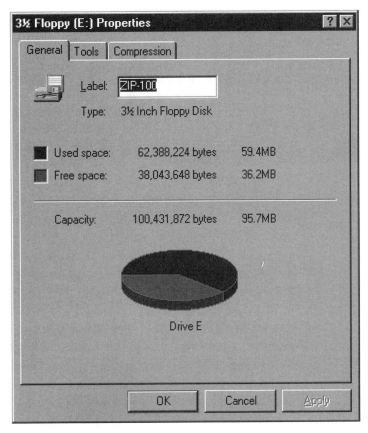

Figure 4-30: If you look at its general properties page, you'll see that this Zip drive is, when uncompressed, 100MB large.

When you first look at the Compression tab of a drive's Property sheet, you'll see a description of the potential additional space, as shown in Figure 4-31.

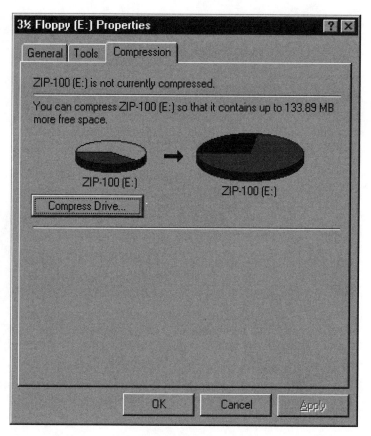

Figure 4-31: This 100 MB drive can gain an additional 133MB via compression.

When you click on the Compress Drive button, you're shown a comparison of the status of the drive before and after compression.

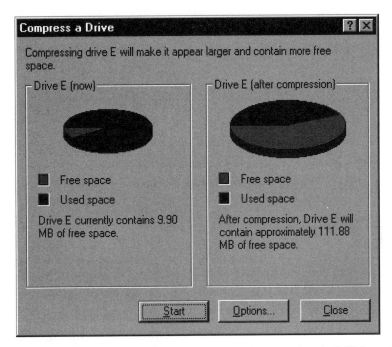

Figure 4-32: On this 100MB Zip drive, there is currently only 9MB free. After compression, it will have 111MB free for additional file storage.

If you click on the Options button, you can change the drive letter for the "host drive." If you are planning to add a second hard drive, you might want to use a higher letter of the alphabet for the host drive (two virtual drives are used for each compressed physical hard drive). Also, if you want uncompressed storage space on the host drive, you can type in an amount beyond what Windows 95 suggests. Such free space can be used as always, though it's rather inconvenient to keep switching drives to locate files. If you want this drive compressed in the older, less efficient format, choose Use DoubleSpace-compatible format.

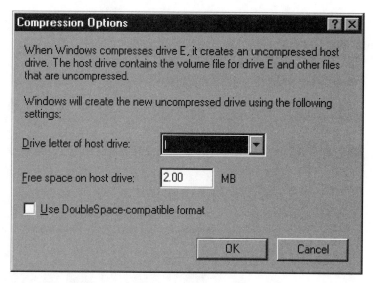

Figure 4-33: The Compression Options window.

Finally, to see a detailed report of a drive's status after a drive has been compressed, right-click on that drive's icon, then choose Properties and the Compression tab.

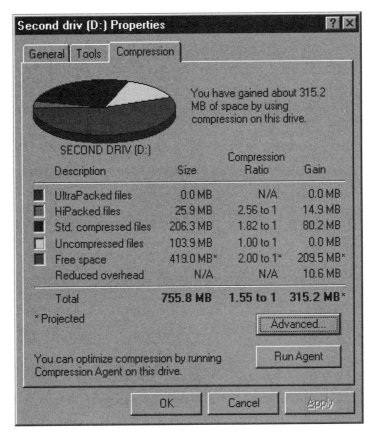

Figure 4-34: When a disk has been compressed, this page offers a summary of the elements of the compression, and can even suggest further compression.

As you can see in Figure 4-34, DriveSpace 3.0 offers three levels of compression: Standard, HiPacked, and UltraPacked (discussed below, in the section, "The Compression Agent"). Click on the Advanced button to see the various options in Figure 4-35.

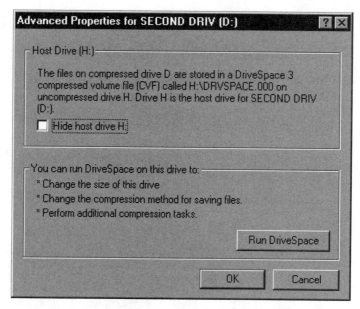

Figure 4-35: Additional tweaking of an already-compressed drive is possible.

The first option shown in Figure 4-35 is Hide host drive. This avoids the clutter of seeing the host drive listed in Explorer or My Computer—you don't have to keep ignoring these essentially pointless drive listings. (They will still be visible from DOS, or within the Properties of the drive that's hosted.) The one drawback of choosing this option is that you can't then use any of the *uncompressed* extra space that you might have left on this drive after compression. Usually, though, this is a non-issue. There's not that much useful space.

Managing Compressed Drives in the DriveSpace Window

Click on the Run DriveSpace button and you'll see the DriveSpace window. (You can also get to this window by clicking on Start | Programs | Accessories | System Tools | DriveSpace.)

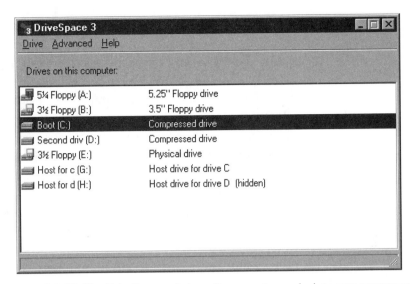

Figure 4-36: The DriveSpace window allows you to manipulate your compressed drives.

In the DriveSpace window's File menu, you can choose to compress or decompress the selected drive. You can also adjust the amount of free space, meaning that you can give some of the host's uncompressed free space back to the compressed drive, or vice versa. If, for instance, you originally compressed the drive and at that time chose to give 30MB of free space to the host, you might have since discovered that you never use this free space. You can correct this by returning some of the host's free space, making it available on the compressed drive. Remember that 30MB of free space on a host usually results in about 60MB of free space on a compressed drive.

You can also take a look at the general Properties of a drive (in the File menu), or upgrade a drive that has been compressed by DoubleSpace or DriveSpace version 2.0 to DriveSpace 3.0 compression (well worth doing). Finally, you can choose to format the drive—thereby removing all its contents.

In the Advanced menu shown in the menu bar in Figure 4-36, you can mount or unmount the drive. Ordinarily, Windows automatically takes care of this mounting (a mounted drive is made available for use) of any compressed drives. However, you could choose to mount and unmount compressed drives manually. Mounting and unmounting applies to drives, such as floppies or dockable units that were not present when you turned on your computer. Typically, you let Windows do this for you, but it might provide some measure of security if you selected the manual mounting alternative.

The Create Empty option on the Advanced menu creates a new, empty compressed drive, and the Delete option does just that: Deletes the selected drive. The Change Ratio option is somewhat misleading—you can't really change the actual compression ratio here. All you can do is change the estimate that DriveSpace uses to calculate the amount of free space. This value will always be merely an estimate on a compressed drive because Windows can only base the free space figure on what sort of compression has so far been achieved by the files currently stored on this drive. Generally, text files compress considerably (a 6:1 ratio), but you might start saving a lot of .ZIP files that don't compress at all since they're already compressed. In this case, and only this case, you might want to adjust this Change Ratio option—to reflect the fact that you intend to use the rest of the drive for a file type that differs radically in compression potential from the files already saved. In this way, you'll then get a more accurate free space figure. However, most people use hard drives in a highly varied and dynamic way—storing all kinds of files and adding, deleting all the time. For most people, there's no real point to adjusting the Change Ratio.

The Change letter option permits you to give the host drive a new drive letter designation. You could rename it from E: to G: for example. However, if Windows files are stored on the compressed drive, you won't be permitted to make this change. Usually you can change the host drive designations, but not compressed drive letters.

Choose Change ratio to adjust how Windows estimates free disk space.

Click on the Settings option in the Advanced menu and you'll see the dialog window shown in Figure 4-37.

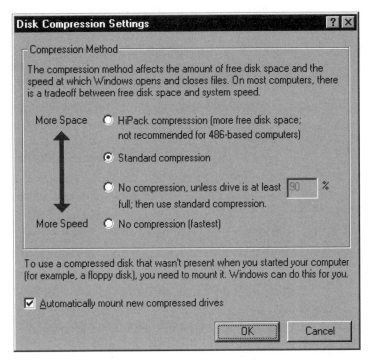

Figure 4-37: In the Disk Compression Settings dialog box, you can tell DriveSpace just how much compression you prefer.

When you choose Standard compression, DriveSpace 3.0 uses the same techniques as DriveSpace 2.0, but if you choose HiPack you'll get, on average, about 15–20 percent more compression. HiPack generally shrinks files to slightly more than half their original size. UltraPack shrinks files typically to one-third their original size. Is it worth it? There is a slight additional reading time penalty, and an even greater writing time penalty. And, when you first HiPack a file it takes much longer than when you first compress a file in Standard mode. Microsoft notes that HiPack is not recommended for 486 computers. Another interesting option is to request that files remain uncompressed until the disk is a certain percentage full. This way, you get maximum speed, but you also build in a way to reduce disk consumption should the disk get crowded.

Why is there a No compression option? Recall that we pointed out earlier an inefficiency of the FAT system of disk management: If a file is 2,049 bytes, it takes up *two* clusters on a 127MB disk drive. This means that 4,096 bytes on the hard drive are marked in the FAT as used, but nearly half of them are just empty, squandered space. The No compression option means only that the *data* is left uncompressed. You'll still gain all that squandered empty space created by the FAT because DriveSpace causes the data to be saved in units of 512 bytes. The result: the maximum wasted space in any given case is 511 bytes, not thousands. (Recall on a 1GB drive, each cluster is 32,768 bytes—potentially wasting as much as 32,767 bytes in various locations around the drive.) It's well worth using DriveSpace, even if you choose No compression which, properly speaking, means *no file compression*.

THE COMPRESSION AGENT

Microsoft Plus! includes an agent. The idea behind agents is that you tell them what to do, and, thereafter, they automatically carry out your instructions. The Compression Agent can act as an intelligent assistant, refining and expanding your compression options. The primary task for which the agent is designed is background *re*compression.

You have options to move up to higher levels of compression or to clarify just how and when you want files compressed. You mustn't think of a compressed drive as a monolith. As we will see, you can redefine the level and extent of compression any time you want. Start the Compression Agent by clicking on Start | Programs | Accessories | System Tools. Click on Compression Agent. If you've not yet run the Compression Agent, you'll see the empty report shown in Figure 4-38.

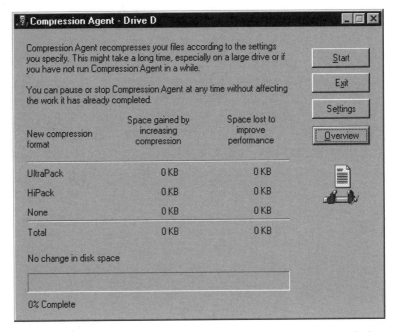

Figure 4-38: Until you run Compression Agent, there will be no statistics on this page.

If you have a Pentium or a 100MHz 486, you're unlikely to notice any slowdown in file saving or loading.

Note that by dividing its report into two columns labeled "Space gained by increasing compression" and "Space lost to improve performance," the Compression Agent neatly reveals the essential tradeoff here. But remember, if you have a Pentium or a 100MHz 486, you're unlikely to notice any slowdown in file saving or loading.

TIP

Unlike previous defragmenters and compression utilities, Windows 95's Defragmenter, the Compression Agent and DriveSpace are quite sturdy. You can pause them or shut them down at any time with no harm done to your disks or data. They'll neatly clean up any loose ends and halt or exit without any damage to your hard drive. Of course a power failure is another story. Though running the Compression Agent can take a long time, especially the first time, you can run it in several sessions if you want. And the Agent itself is designed to run at night after you've left the computer alone.

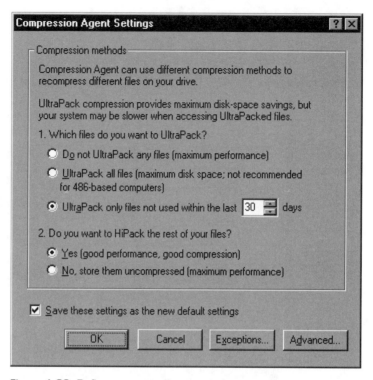

Figure 4-39: Define your overall compression strategy.

Let's try compressing a disk. Click on the Settings button. Now take the quiz, remembering that you can always go back and redefine the various options in the future should you wish. You can UltraPack all files, none, or only those that have remained unused since a certain date. This last option makes good sense. Because many of your applications and old text or graphics files aren't actively being used, why not really freeze dry them so you get more disk space. Then, should you ever actually use these files, they'll load in a little slower but, at that point, they'll be recompressed as Standard compressed files. This way, should you start using some data actively again—after a long period of ignoring it—it will be compressed by the lower density, but more quickly transferred, method.

The next question is, Do you want to HiPack the remaining files? This, too, is a good idea if your machine is relatively fast.

Now to really get specific. You can define exactly what you want compressed, and how. Click on the Exceptions button and you'll see the window shown in Figure 4-40. Exceptions are ways of excluding various kinds of files from compression.

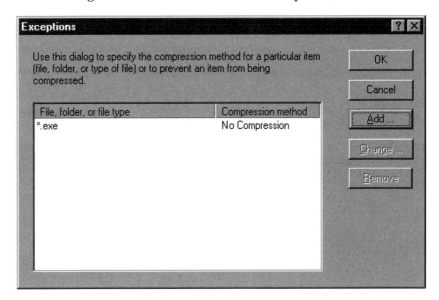

Figure 4-40: You can exclude files, folders, or types of files from any compression option.

To specify an exception, click on the Add button shown in Figure 4-40 and you'll see Figure 4-41.

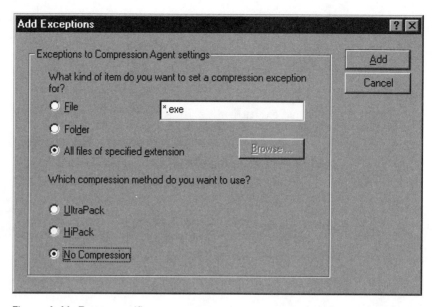

Figure 4-41: Be as specific as you want; you can even exclude just a single particular file.

Because programs, applications, and utilities (all .EXE files) rarely compress much anyway, we've decided to exempt them (all .EXE files) from compression. Once they're exempted, they'll load in at the highest speed. Obviously you could use this exemption feature to get very precise and complex notes about your instructions to the Compression Agent. You could tell it to UltraPack all .BMP files because you don't use them very often and because graphics files compress so well. You could tell it to avoid compressing files that you notice seem slow to load or save. The best tactic is probably to make decisions in the field: start out with aggressive compression, then exclude files, folders, or categories of files (extensions such as .DOC) that you feel are retarding your work.

The Advanced button (see Figure 4-39) offers two additional options.

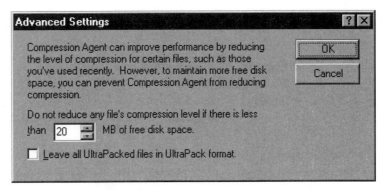

Figure 4-42: You can freeze the compression strategy if disk space gets tight.

Compression methods are dynamic, and intelligently chosen to suit the situation.

Using the options shown in Figure 4-42, you can cause all files to remain compressed at their current levels, should the disk get close to full. In effect, this prevents the Compression Agent from trying to manipulate the situation when that would most likely result in it making inefficient decisions. This setting overrides any other settings, such as the exceptions described previously.

Normally, if you access a file that was UltraPacked, it will be saved back to disk in HiPack or Normal compression, simply because you've told the Compression Agent to HiPack only those files that have not been recently accessed (see Figure 4-39). However, if you click on the check box in Figure 4-42 labeled "Leave all UltraPacked files in UltraPack format," such files will not revert to less intense forms of compression. Note that this option doesn't override other options; it's overruled by any conflicting settings you've created in the Exceptions window.

After you've made all your decisions, exceptions, and settings, click on the Compression Agent's OK button to start the compression process. It takes some time. Suppose that you wait about 20 minutes, becoming increasingly less fascinated watching the percentages as they shift the balance between "Space gained by increasing compression" and "Space lost to improve performance." So you decide to stop the Agent. No harm done. You can click on the Stop button and Agent will remember where you stopped, prepared to pick up where it left off later should you restart the Agent at a more convenient time.

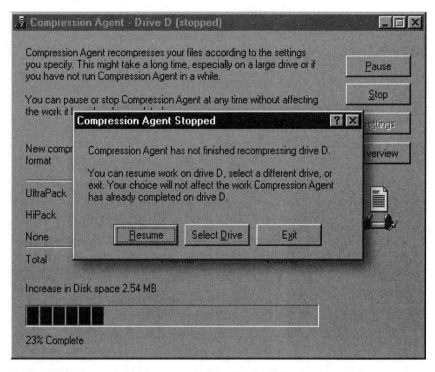

Figure 4-43: If you decide to pause or stop the Agent during it's activities, no harm will be done. You can always restart it later and it will resume where it left off.

THE SYSTEM AGENT

If you get bored watching compression, why not tell the Compression Agent to do its business after hours? You can have your disk cleaned up nightly, after the office is closed down, and, like an effective cleaning crew, Agent will move in and fix everything up nice and tidy. To reschedule the Compression Agent, use the System Agent.

If clicking on Start I Programs I Accessories I System Tools doesn't reveal System Agent, you'll have to get out your Microsoft Plus! CD and run its setup program. Once that's running, install the System Agent and then run it.

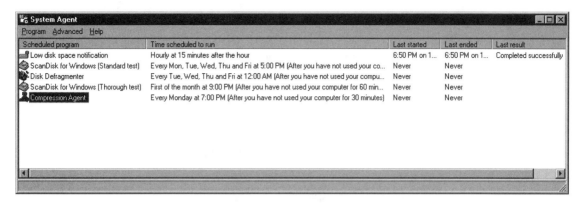

Figure 4-44: The System Agent acts as a central scheduler for several utilities.

As you can see in Figure 4-44, you can schedule ScanDisk, the Defragmenter, and DriveSpace. The System Agent doesn't insert itself into the Windows\Start Menu\Programs\Startup folder. It *does* autorun when you start Windows, and you'll find its little icon on the taskbar over on the right side. Double-click on that icon to adjust the behavior of the System Agent. Click on the System Agent's Program menu and you can tell it to run *any* program of your choice at any time. The Program menu on the main System Agent screen (Figure 4-44) also includes options to Run Now (run the selected program immediately, without affecting its other settings); Disable (disable the currently selected program); and Remove (delete the selected program).

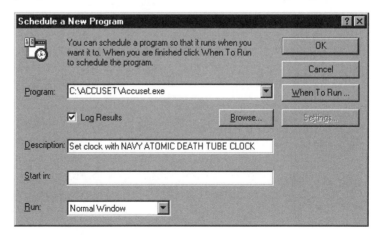

Figure 4-45: You can run any program you want to run, whenever you want to run it.

When you decide to schedule a new program, first tell the System Agent which program you want to run. The Start in option shown in Figure 4-45, allows you to define a different folder from the one in which the program itself resides. This is of importance if the application you're scheduling cannot find files it needs that are located in some folder other than the one in which it resides.

Now, to schedule this program, click on the When To Run button and you'll see the window in Figure 4-46.

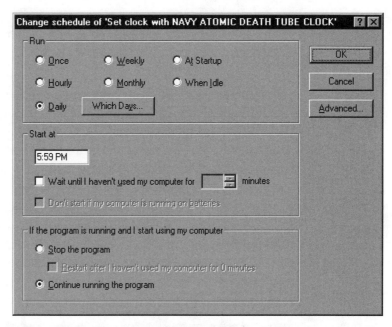

Figure 4-46: You've got more or less limitless options when scheduling a program.

You describe the interval—how often a program will be run—by the Agent. It can be anything between once, to whenever the computer is idle, to every week or month, or on particular, odd days. Then you tell it when to run. You also specify whether it should wait until the computer is idle for a specified time, or refuse to run if the computer is battery-powered. Then you can specify that it not run if you're typing or moving the mouse, and how long to wait, after you've stopped communicating with the computer, to try again. Now click on the Advanced button.

Advanced Options

─ Deadline ───────────────────────────────────

If the program cannot run at the start time, System Agent will keep trying to start the program until the time you specify.

6:59 PM

☐ If the program is still running, stop it at this time

☐ Notify me if the program never started

─ Run repeatedly between the start time and the deadline ─

☐ Run the program every 10 minutes

☐ Stop the program if it is still running after 10 minutes

[OK]
[Cancel]

Figure 4-47: You can be really specific about a scheduled program's behavior.

Your control over the agent can be highly specific.

In the Advanced Options dialog box shown in Figure 4-47, you can further refine your scheduled program's behavior in highly precise ways. If you want it to quit trying (and failing to run) after a certain amount of time, specify that. Do you want it to just stop? Or would you like to see a message onscreen? It's up to you. If you do want a message, you'll see a dialog box like the one shown in Figure 4-48.

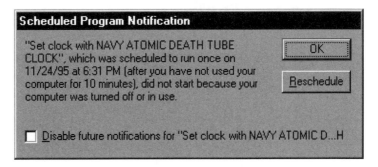

Scheduled Program Notification

"Set clock with NAVY ATOMIC DEATH TUBE CLOCK", which was scheduled to run once on 11/24/95 at 6:31 PM (after you have not used your computer for 10 minutes), did not start because your computer was turned off or in use.

☐ Disable future notifications for "Set clock with NAVY ATOMIC D...H

[OK]
[Reschedule]

Figure 4-48: If you so request, System Agent will tell you why and when a scheduled activity couldn't be accomplished.

If you click on the Reschedule button shown in Figure 4-48, you'll see the help screen shown in Figure 4-49.

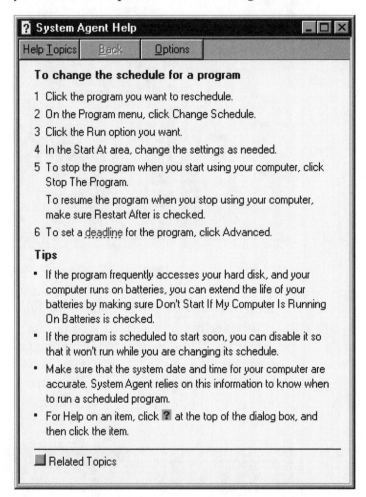

Figure 4-49: Here are your alternatives if you're trying to reschedule a program that failed to run.

The Advanced Menu

The Advanced menu on the main System Agent screen (see Figure 4-44) has provisions to suspend the System Agent (preventing it from carrying out any scheduled tasks) and stop using the Agent (to remove it from memory, from the taskbar, and prevent it from running at startup). If you choose to stop using the System Agent, the only way to start it again is to click on Start | Programs | Accessories | System Tools | System Agent. The final option on the Advanced menu is to view the System Agent's log. Here's a typical sample:

```
Set clock with NAVY ATOMI...H TUBE CLOCK
Started 11/24/95 at 6:29 PM

Set clock with NAVY ATOMI...H TUBE CLOCK
Finished 11/24/95 at 6:29 PM

Result: (0)

Compression Agent        0  Started 11/24/95 at 8:51 PM

Compression Agent           terminating automatically...

Compression Agent        0  Finished 11/24/95 at 9:01 PM

Result: The process was interrupted before completing(3)

********** Most recent entry is above this line **********
```

ADDING & REMOVING PROGRAMS

Windows 95 expects applications to keep track of which files they install during setup, what new keys and data they add to the Registry, and whatever other effects they have on the operating system or hard drive. Should you later want to remove that program, all traces of it can thus be cleaned off your disk drive.

Why not just delete the folder in which the program and any of its ancillary files reside? The reason for an uninstall utility is that applications don't necessarily install all associated files in their own folder. Sometimes they create additional folders or put files in the Windows\System directory. They also often create Programs submenu entries on the Start menu, do things to the Registry, perhaps put their icon on the taskbar, and create other side effects. If you want to remove an application from your computer, you want all these elements of the application removed as well. Simply deleting the application's folder won't clean up all these other items.

Another reason for tidy, graceful, mannerly uninstallation is that applications are increasingly sharing resources. There's no point to having separate e-mail facilities built into your word processor, another e-mail utility within your database program, yet another for your Internet browser, and so on. One e-mail utility should be accessible to all your applications. You'll therefore want to uninstall redundant utilities such as unused e-mail programs.

Each individual application need not stuff RAM memory with all of its various features if these features are rarely used. In other words, the whole program need not come in from the hard drive and take up space in RAM. For example, when you load in a graphics program like Fractal Design Painter, it doesn't need to load up your RAM with programming code for every last trick in its huge repertoire of tricks. Painter can filter and distort an image in many, many ways. But you're unlikely to use most of these filters very often. So why should this program bring from your hard drive the programming for every last thing it can do? How many times a month will you apply a fisheye lens or superimpose mosaic cracks onto a graphic image?

In Figure 4-50 you see the before; in Figure 4-51, the after. We've applied a spotlight filter to this image. But does anyone apply this special effect often? There is no reason to move the spotlight filter (along with dozens of other filters) into RAM along with Painter— just put the core of Painter into RAM, then load any filters that the

Often it's enough to merely load part of a program into RAM.

user requests, when they're requested. When you start reading a book you don't also take down from your library shelves a dictionary, atlas, encyclopedia, and all your other reference works, just in case you might want to use them. Instead, you go get a specialized book only when you need one.

Figure 4-50: Fractal Design Painter can take this "little church in big woods" and do some rather dramatic things to it.

Figure 4-51: Throwing a spotlight onto the church is theatrical—it creates an impressive, tense scene—but how often will you be spotlighting an image?

During their setup, applications often load in a number of additional files beyond their primary .EXE file. In theory, Windows 95 programs are supposed to tell the Registry which files they load and any other changes they introduce to the computing environment. This way, if you decide to remove the application later, you can get rid of *everything*. Often, ancillary files take up more space than the .EXE file itself.

Alas, most of your programs won't be properly registered. All Windows 3.1 versions of programs haven't heard of registering their various files. Likewise, some Windows 95 applications don't follow the rules and properly register their components. Perhaps the authors of these applications feel that no one would ever consider uninstalling their brilliant work.

You can count on Microsoft applications, though, to properly declare themselves to the Registry during setup. To see which of your applications have followed the rules, click on Start | Settings | Control Panel. Then click on the Add/Remove Programs icon. However, this declaration is merely a single reference in the Registry. It usually describes the location of the application's setup program, and, in some cases, contains an additional reference at the end to a file that contains a description of what was done during the setup process.

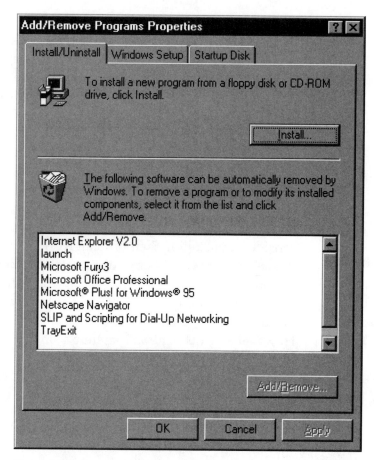

Figure 4-52: The programs that have been properly registered will appear in this list, ready to be uninstalled.

There's no standardized list within the Registry of the components of an application that should be removed from the hard drive. A clean removal is left up to the designer of each individual application. However, there *is* a list in the Registry of applications that have formally declared themselves uninstallable. This list is found in HKEY_LOCAL_MACHINE\SOFTWARE\Microsoft\ Windows\CurrentVersion\Uninstall. Search for the list by starting the Regedit program and pressing Ctrl+F then typing **Uninstall**. (See Chapter 2, "The Registry," to learn more about editing the Registry.) Your first hit during the search might be the Uninstall directory under Setup, but just press F3 to continue until you locate the Uninstall folder in the Registry. You'll see the same list of applications that you see when you click on Add/Remove Programs in Control Panel. These are the well-behaved applications, the ones that allow for a graceful exit should you decide you don't need them any more.

The uninstallation process is largely left up to the discretion of each software manufacturer.

How does an application know what to remove from the hard drive during an uninstallation? Again, there's no standardized approach. This job of cleaning up after itself is left to the devices and discretion of each application's creator. Some developers keep a list, in an ordinary text file, of the files they installed and that, consequently, should be removed. An application created in Visual Basic, for example, creates a .LOG file with a rather plaintive request at the top that the user not delete the file:

%% PLEASE DO NOT MODIFY OR DELETE THIS FILE! %%
%% This file contains information about the installation of an application. %%
%% It will be used to automatically remove all application components from your computer if you choose to do so. %%

```
NOTE: Beginning of the bootstrapper section

CONFIG: Title: "launch"

ACTION: TempFile: "C:\WINDOWS\setup132.exe"
(File was not found or was an older version - new file
copied)

ACTION: RegKey:
"HKEY_LOCAL_MACHINE\SOFTWARE\Microsoft\Windows\CurrentVersion",
"SharedDLLs"

ACTION: SharedFile: "C:\WINDOWS\SYSTEM\stkit432.dll"
(File currently on disk was already up to date)
```

ACTION: SharedFile: "C:\WINDOWS\SYSTEM\VB40032.DLL"
(File currently on disk was already up to date)

ACTION: SystemFile: "C:\WINDOWS\SYSTEM\ven2232.olb"
(File currently on disk was already up to date)

ACTION: SharedFile: "C:\WINDOWS\SYSTEM\olepro32.dll"
(File currently on disk was already up to date)

ACTION: SystemFile: "C:\WINDOWS\SYSTEM\msvcrt20.dll"
(File currently on disk was already up to date)

ACTION: SharedFile: "C:\WINDOWS\SYSTEM\msvcrt40.dll"
(File currently on disk was already up to date)

ACTION: ExeSelfRegister: "C:\WINDOWS\setup132.exe"

ACTION: DllSelfRegister: "C:\WINDOWS\SYSTEM\olepro32.dll"

NOTE: End of the bootstrapper section

NOTE: Now spawning the main Setup program
'C:\WINDOWS\setup132.exe'....

ACTION: CreateDir: "C:\Program Files\launch"

ACTION: SharedFile: "C:\WINDOWS\SYSTEM\COMDLG32.OCX"
(File currently on disk was already up to date)

ACTION: SharedFile: "C:\WINDOWS\SYSTEM\MFC40.DLL"
(File currently on disk was already up to date)

ACTION: SharedFile: "C:\WINDOWS\SYSTEM\TABCTL32.OCX"
(File currently on disk was already up to date)

ACTION: SharedFile: "C:\WINDOWS\SYSTEM\RICHTX32.OCX"
(File currently on disk was already up to date)

ACTION: SharedFile: "C:\WINDOWS\SYSTEM\COMCTL32.OCX"
(File currently on disk was already up to date)

ACTION: SharedFile: "C:\WINDOWS\SYSTEM\THREED32.OCX"
(File currently on disk was already up to date)

ACTION: PrivateFile: "C:\Program Files\launch\launch.exe"
(File was not found or was an older version - new file
copied)

ACTION: DllSelfRegister: "C:\WINDOWS\SYSTEM\COMDLG32.OCX"

ACTION: DllSelfRegister: "C:\WINDOWS\SYSTEM\MFC40.DLL"

ACTION: DllSelfRegister: "C:\WINDOWS\SYSTEM\TABCTL32.OCX"

ACTION: DllSelfRegister: "C:\WINDOWS\SYSTEM\RICHTX32.OCX"

ACTION: DllSelfRegister: "C:\WINDOWS\SYSTEM\COMCTL32.OCX"

ACTION: DllSelfRegister: "C:\WINDOWS\SYSTEM\THREED32.OCX"

ACTION: ExeSelfRegister: "C:\Program
Files\launch\launch.exe"

ACTION: ShellLink: "", "launch"

ACTION: RegKey:
"HKEY_LOCAL_MACHINE\SOFTWARE\Microsoft\Windows\CurrentVersion",
"App Paths\launch.exe"

ACTION: RegValue:
"HKEY_LOCAL_MACHINE\SOFTWARE\Microsoft\Windows\CurrentVersion\
App Paths\launch.exe", ""

Notice how the various files used in this application are treated differently. Some of these files, like VB40032.DLL, are not copied onto the hard drive. Files like this *are* needed by this application, but they are already there on the disk. This means that some other application has already installed this .DLL and, equally important, that this version is the latest version. Recall that many programs these days are written using a technique that's all the rage: object-oriented programming (OOP). One implication of OOP and of OLE (Object Linking and Embedding—see Chapter 8, "Compound Documents & OLE, for much more on this topic) is that common tasks should be broken down into self-contained, reusable *objects.* Put simply, this means that a single object (a library of programming, a typeface, a utility, etc.) should be usable by various applications, even if they aren't written by the same people and come from entirely different software companies. The idea is that there should be one spell-checker resident on your hard drive and any of your applications that could benefit from spell-checking should have access to it. This has several obvious advantages: you don't have to remember different syntaxes or approaches when spell-checking; you don't have to fill your hard drive or RAM with redundant programming; and, not least, nobody has to waste time writing yet another spell-checker.

So, during setup, an application might intend to copy to disk some support utility library (an object) like VB40032.DLL. But finding it already on the disk, and dated the same or later than the one it wants to copy, the application doesn't copy this file. During uninstall, this means that this same object will not be uninstalled because it is used by another application or applications. Only the application that copied an object to the hard drive during setup is permitted to delete that object.

The registration information in the .LOG file describes several activities. The DLLSelfRegister key is for custom controls, .DLL's, .OCX's, or any other object that is capable of *registering itself* (contains programming that informs the Registry of itself). The EXESelfRegister key is quite similar, but in this case the file is an

Only the application that copied an object to the hard drive during setup is permitted to delete that object.

.EXE object, a file that is self-registering and that has an .EXE extension (the file is not an executable program, though, in the traditional sense). The Remote key is for remote OLE Automation (see Chapter 8) support files. These files end in a .VBR extension.

Where's the Info?

Where do applications keep their uninstall information? As we've seen, Visual Basic applications use a .LOG file. Others use .STF files, short for Setup Text File or *stuff*. Still other applications use a private section within the Registry (Windows 95 applications are encouraged to store information in the Registry, including this kind of information, but most don't at this point). The amount of information stored by some Microsoft applications is truly colossal. Here's a sample from the .STF file of a relatively straightforward type of program, the game Fury3:

```
App Name       Fury3.EXE
App Version    1.95.07.30 (1033)
Frame Bitmap   "Fury3_32.dll, 121"
Frame Caption Microsoft Fury3 Setup
Dialog Caption Base Microsoft Fury3
Usage String  Type SETUP to install on your local computer.
About Box String   Microsoft Fury3 for Windows 95
\n\nCopyright (C) 1995 Microsoft Corp.
Check Modules
Source Directory     E:\
MSAPPS Mode   local
MSAPPS Connect       server
Inf File Name Fury3su.INF
Help File Name       ACMSETUP.HLP


Setup Status "N_!@Ã„Ù?_zep__S;aJ_TóI  | èqA•L£ ˆîPÚ/
¢_ÂŸÑÙ™W ˏ†ÏÒXcëÊ÷˜ÌàONpê+§yp_òÊ1÷ò|8_¿_Y+ O_SÍG_Ü÷'+
N4w¢Z¥è¢'B?QO^ã_V/A9^J^,ˏI•1>¿¿m6,â""¥_P®Ï ˏk=jxè
ëâ"&ÂÄw∂#^Ja_ "âL¿ä@_txPòJ}"
```

```
Maximum Object ID    200
Admin Mode Root Object ID
Floppy Mode Root Object ID 6 : 3
Network Mode Root Object ID
Maintenance Mode Root Object ID  7 : 3
Network Maintenance Mode Root Object ID
Batch Mode Root Object ID 6 : 3
Install Date  1995.10.20.17.08.28
Setup Version 1.20.0.1907
Check Modules 2
```

```
ObjID  Checkbox State    Title Description  Object Type
Object Data   Bitmap Id    Vital Attribute     Shared
Attribute     Configurable Directory    Destination
Directory     Check Directory      Installed By Install Data
Install Directory
3                       AppSearch    "C:\Fury3<%p\Microsoft
Games\Microsoft Fury3>,Fury3.EXE,1.0.0.0,100,yes,yes,"
                        C:\Program Files\Microsoft
Games\Microsoft Fury3\         us         C:\Program
Files\Microsoft Games\Microsoft Fury3\
4                       SearchDrives fixed
```

```
6 yes  Floppy Installation Floppy AppMainDlg   9 10 11 : 12
13 30 51 44                    yes     C:\Program
Files\Microsoft Games\Microsoft Fury3\        us
C:\Program Files\Microsoft Games\Microsoft Fury3\
7 yes  Maintenance Installation  Provides the ability to
Add or Remove application components   CustomDlg    14 18
20 22 24 : 30 51                       yes    C:\Program
Files\Microsoft Games\Microsoft Fury3\
```

```
9 yes  &Typical (recommended)    Installs all game files
to your hard disk (video clips remain on the CD). Requires
55 MB of available hard disk space.    Group 14 18 20 22
"furybb32.dll, 111"              yes              us
```

C:\Program Files\Microsoft Games\Microsoft Fury3\
10   &Compact   Installs the minimum required files to
your hard disk. The CD must be inserted to play the game.
Requires 10 MB of available hard disk space. Group 14 20
22"furybb32.dll, 113"   yes
nyi
11   C&ustom   Installs only selected files to your
hard disk.   CustomDlg   14 18 20 22 24
"furybb32.dll, 112"   yes   us
  C:\Program Files\Microsoft Games\Microsoft Fury3\
12   CustomAction
"""fury3_32.dll""",""Detect256Color""","
            us   C:\Program Files\Microsoft
Games\Microsoft Fury3\
13   CustomAction
"""fury3_32.dll""",""Detect486""",""Fury3 requires at least
a 486 processor."""
us   C:\Program Files\Microsoft Games\Microsoft Fury3\
14yes Fury3 Program Files Installs program files required
to run Fury3. Group 15 16 17 29 120   vital
            us   C:\Program Files\Microsoft
Games\Microsoft Fury3\
15yes   CopyFile   """fury3""",""Fury3Exe"""
            %D   us   C:\Program
Files\Microsoft Games\Microsoft Fury3\
16yes   CopySection """setup32"""
            %D\Setup   us   C:\Program
Files\Microsoft Games\Microsoft Fury3\Setup\
17yes   CopySection """fury3System"""
            %D\System   us   C:\Program
Files\Microsoft Games\Microsoft Fury3\System\
18yes Fury3 Data Files   Installs all data files (installation is NOT required. Data files will be used on the
CD if they are not copied to your hard disk.) CopySection
"""HighResSystem"""   %D\System

us   C:\Program Files\Microsoft Games\Microsoft
Fury3\System\
20yes   Readme Installs last minute product and troubleshooting news.   CopySection   """readme"""
       %D   us   C:\Program
Files\Microsoft Games\Microsoft Fury3\
22yes Help Files   Installs Online Help files.
CopySection   """help"""   %D
    us   C:\Program Files\Microsoft Games\Microsoft
Fury3\
24no   Video Clips Installs all video sequences. Installation is NOT required for video clips to run. They will
be played from the CD if they are not copied to your hard
disk.   CopySection   """AVIs"""
%17\Story   nyi
29yes   Group 31 32 110 91
          us   C:\Program Files\Microsoft
Games\Microsoft Fury3\
30yes   WriteTableFile   setup.stf
     no   %D\Setup   us   C:\Program
Files\Microsoft Games\Microsoft Fury3\Setup\
31yes   CopyFile   """fury3System"",
""pid"""   %D\System
us   C:\Program Files\Microsoft Games\Microsoft
Fury3\System\
32yes   StampCDInfo   "31,106,196"
                   us   C:\Program
Files\Microsoft Games\Microsoft Fury3\
44yes   === Billboards ===   Group 45
                   us   C:\Program
Files\Microsoft Games\Microsoft Fury3\
45yes   AddBillboard
"""furybb32.dll"",""1011"",""FBillbrdDlgProc"""
                        us   C:\Program
Files\Microsoft Games\Microsoft Fury3\
51yes   Group 79 81 83
          us   C:\Program Files\Microsoft

```
Games\Microsoft Fury3\
79yes  AVIs          CustomAction """fury3_32.dll"",
""WriteIniFilePointer"", ""17,Fury3.ini,CD-
ROM,CDROMPath,story,fury3\system\"""
              us              C:\Program Files\Microsoft
Games\Microsoft Fury3\
81yes  Path to Startup.pod      CustomAction
"""fury3_32.dll"", ""WriteIniFilePointer"",
""17,Fury3.ini,CD-
ROM,startupPodName,startup.pod,fury3\system\"""
                            us              C:\Program
Files\Microsoft Games\Microsoft Fury3\
83yes  HD High              CustomAction """fury3_32.dll"",
""WriteIniFilePointer"", ""17,Fury3.ini,CD-
ROM,gamePodName,fury3.pod,fury3\system\"""
                    us              C:\Program
Files\Microsoft Games\Microsoft Fury3\
91yes  Registry Information      Install registry informa-
tion    Group 92 93 94 95 96 97 98 99
              us              C:\Program Files\Microsoft
Games\Microsoft Fury3\
92yes              AddRegData   """HKEY_LOCAL_MACHINE"",
""Software\Microsoft\Windows\CurrentVersion\Uninstall\
Fury3"",""DisplayName"",""Microsoft Fury3"",""""
                    us              C:\Program
Files\Microsoft Games\Microsoft Fury3\
93yes              AddRegData   """HKEY_LOCAL_MACHINE"",
""Software\Microsoft\Windows\CurrentVersion\Uninstall\
Fury3"",""UninstallString"",""%s\setup.exe /m"",""""
                    %D\setup              us
C:\Program Files\Microsoft Games\Microsoft Fury3\setup\
94yes              AddRegData   """HKEY_LOCAL_MACHINE"",
""Software\Microsoft\Fury3\Installroot"",""Path"",""%s\
fury3.exe"",""""                            %15
us     C:\Program Files\Microsoft Games\Microsoft Fury3\
95yes              AddRegData   """HKEY_LOCAL_MACHINE"",
""Software\Microsoft\Fury3\Version"","""",""1.0"",""""
                    %D\setup              us
```

```
C:\Program Files\Microsoft Games\Microsoft Fury3\setup\
96yes            AddRegData   """HKEY_CLASSES_ROOT"",
"".fff"","""""",""Microsoft.Fury3.Game"",""""""
                us          C:\Program
Files\Microsoft Games\Microsoft Fury3\
97yes            AddRegData   """HKEY_CLASSES_ROOT"",
""Microsoft.Fury3.Game\shell\open\command"",""""",""%s\fury3.exe
%%1"",""""""                        %15          us
   C:\Program Files\Microsoft Games\Microsoft Fury3\
98yes            AddRegData   """HKEY_CLASSES_ROOT"",
""Microsoft.Fury3.Game\DefaultIcon"",""""",""%s\fury3.exe,8"","""""
                %15          us          C:\Program
Files\Microsoft Games\Microsoft Fury3\
99yes            AddRegData   """HKEY_CLASSES_ROOT"",
""Microsoft.Fury3.Game"",""""",""Microsoft Fury3 Saved
Game"","""""                                    us
   C:\Program Files\Microsoft Games\Microsoft Fury3\
110    yes              Group 111 112 113 116
                        us          C:\Program
Files\Microsoft Games\Microsoft Fury3\
111    yes              CustomAction """fury3_32.dll"",
""GetPathFromReg"",
""HKEY_CURRENT_USER,Software\Microsoft\Windows\CurrentVersion\
Explorer\Shell Folders,Programs"""
                us              C:\WINDOWS\Start Menu\Programs\
112    yes              InstallShortcut
"""%15\fury3.exe"", ""Microsoft Fury3"""
       %111\Microsoft Games            us
C:\WINDOWS\Start Menu\Programs\Microsoft Games\
113    yes              Group 114
   %S      us      E:\
114    yes              InstallShortcut
"""%113\mmcat\mmcat.exe"", ""Microsoft Multimedia Cata-
log"""                        %111\Microsoft Games
   us          C:\WINDOWS\Start Menu\Programs\Microsoft
Games\
115    yes    Fury3 Desktop Shortcut          YesNoDlg
```

Would you like a shortcut to Fury3 placed on your desktop?
                                    us   C:\Program
Files\Microsoft Games\Microsoft Fury3\
116   yes   Depend 115 ? 117 118
                                    us   Yes   C:\Program
Files\Microsoft Games\Microsoft Fury3\
117   yes   CustomAction """fury3_32.dll"",
""GetPathFromReg"",
""HKEY_CURRENT_USER,Software\Microsoft\Windows\CurrentVersion\
Explorer\Shell Folders,Desktop"""
              us   C:\WINDOWS\Desktop\
118   yes   InstallShortcut
"""%15\fury3.exe"", ""Microsoft Fury3"""
        %117   us   C:\WINDOWS\Desktop\
120   yes   Group 121 122 123 124 125 126
                                    us   C:\Program
Files\Microsoft Games\Microsoft Fury3\
121   yes   CustomAction """fury3_32.dll"",
""KillFileType"", ""15,data*.FFF"""
              us   C:\Program Files\Microsoft
Games\Microsoft Fury3\
122   yes   CustomAction """fury3_32.dll"",
""KillFileType"", ""15,data\score.dat"""
                          us   C:\Program
Files\Microsoft Games\Microsoft Fury3\
123   yes   CustomAction """fury3_32.dll"",
""KillFileType"", ""15,*.FFF"""
        us   C:\Program Files\Microsoft
Games\Microsoft Fury3\
124   yes   CustomAction """fury3_32.dll"",
""KillFileType"", ""15,data"""
        us   C:\Program Files\Microsoft
Games\Microsoft Fury3\
125   yes   CustomAction """fury3_32.dll"",
""KillFileType"", ""15,*.gid"""
        us   C:\Program Files\Microsoft

```
Games\Microsoft Fury3\
126     yes                     CustomAction """"fury3_32.dll"",
""KillFileType"", ""15,*.fts"""
```

These .STF files vary greatly in size, though none is as small as you might think. The Fury3 .STF file is 9KB large, however the Microsoft Office .STF files can be half a megabyte large. But wait, there's more. Other applications store their uninstall information in .INF files located in the WINDOWS\INF folder. You'll find one there for the Microsoft Internet Explorer named IERMV2.INF. The reason for the huge size of these files is that they contain a list of much more than merely the objects and files that were copied to the hard drive during installation. Beyond that, they also describe OLE relationships and other details: items, for instance, that were changed or added to the Registry. If you're browsing through one of these .STF or other setup/uninstall logs, look for AddRegData to see the adjustments that the setup activities made to the Registry. This is a good way to locate settings that you can adjust by editing the Registry (but always first make a safe copy of the Registry first—see Chapter 2). Obviously, a well-behaved program will remove all traces of itself from the Registry as well as from the hard drive.

MOVING ON

The following two chapters deal with computer communications and local area networks. Because Windows 95 was designed to communicate from the ground up, Chapter 7, "Customizing Applications," covers Windows 95's built-in communications capabilities. We'll cover the communications tools that come with Windows 95 and will show you how to use your computer to dial other computers and online services with our modem. You will learn about Windows's scripting language, how to use the Phone Dialer to automate your phone calls, and how to use dial-up networking to connect your PC to other computers, or networks. In the last section of the chapter you'll learn how to connect to the Internet and how to build networks over the Internet, all for the cost of a local phone call.

Chapter 5

Communicating With the World

One of the most interesting aspects of Windows 95 is its built-in capability to communicate with other computers, networks, and the Internet. While in previous versions of Windows communications capabilities were merely add-ons, with Windows 95 they have become part of the operating system. As a result, it's much easier to set up Windows 95 to communicate with online services, send and receive faxes, even build networks over telephone lines with the help of the modem. You can also connect two Windows 95 systems directly with a serial or parallel cable (direct cable connection, as it is called, is presented in the next chapter).

Behind the greatly enhanced communications capabilities of Windows 95 is TAPI, the Telephony Applications Programming Interface, which is a standard for developing applications that use modems and telephone lines. From a user's point of view, TAPI is Microsoft's strategy for integrating computers and telephony—not just modems but telephone lines, too. At some point, your computer will be fully integrated with traditional telephone services, and it is TAPI that will make it possible. For instance, a computer could replace a traditional PBX (private branch exchange) system that manages multiple phone lines at a business location and accept phone calls, provide automated answering services (much more complicated than the prerecorded messages you hear today), route the calls, and more. Couple this with voice recognition technology, and you'll get a good idea of the degree to which TAPI will integrate computers and telephony. The day your computer will be speaking and able to read out your messages over the phone is surprisingly close. TAPI is an advanced topic to be discussed in detail in this book, but after we look at the various communication components of Windows 95, we'll discuss the role of TAPI in the operating system with a few examples, which will help you understand how TAPI improves Windows 95 communications capabilities.

This chapter is more than an introduction to Windows 95 communication capabilities. Because the chapter will cover some more advanced topics, we assume that you already have a modem installed in your computer and that you know how to use a communications program to connect to an online service, such as CompuServe or America Online. Many of you may have already subscribed to the Microsoft Network. We also assume some familiarity with the Internet. You will find information in this chapter about connecting to the Internet, but it's not intended for beginners. Instead, this chapter will focus on a rather advanced technique known as *internetworking*, building networks over the Internet.

Internetworking is an exciting technique for building networks over the Internet

In this chapter, you'll find information about the communications components of the Windows 95 operating system. Once you understand how Windows 95 is built for communications, you'll be able to exploit it fully. You'll find out how to customize your modem connections through the Registry, how to use the built-in dial rules to simplify long distance dialing with calling cards, and how to automate the process of logging in to other computers. Then we'll talk about a new Windows 95 component, Dial-Up Networking. Dial-Up Networking lets you connect to other computers over the telephone and create small networks. Finally, we will show you how to use internetworking: how to build networks over the Internet. It's an exciting new development in Internet services, and we believe you'll find it very useful if you are working with people over a wide geographical area.

THE MODEM

Let's start with the simplest component, the modem. As we mentioned in the introduction, one of the major improvements in Windows 95 over Windows 3.1*x* is the built-in support for communications. Whereas modem support was an add-on to the previous versions of the operating system, it is built in to the Windows 95 system, as a communications subsystem, similar to the printing subsystem that enables you to set up a printer and ensures that all applications can print to it. You no longer have to set up a modem through the various communications applications you're using. Instead, you set up a modem once through the Control Panel, and it is available to all applications. If you need to change the modem's dialing properties, do it once in Windows 95, and all communications applications will use the new properties. You need not maintain multiple dialing profiles, as you probably did with every Windows 3.1*x* communications application. Do it through the Dialing Properties choice in the Modem Properties dialog box, and the profiles will be available to all communications applications. If you are using a calling card to charge your calls, you can define the "rules" for dialing with your calling card, and every Windows 95 application that uses the modem will dial using these rules.

Setting up a modem under Windows 95 is a straightforward procedure. Open the Control Panel folder (click on Start, then Settings), and double-click on the Modem icon. Through the Modem Properties dialog box, shown in Figure 5-1, you can change the properties of your modem or install a new modem (by clicking the Add button). Windows 95 supports most modems you can buy, so let it figure out the best settings. If you have problems installing it, take a look at the next section, "Troubleshooting Modems."

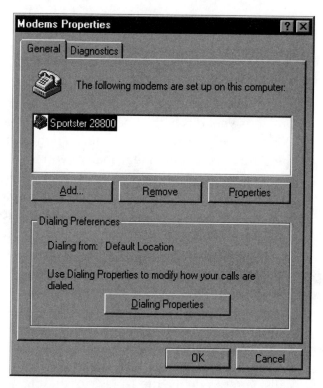

Figure 5-1: Set up a new modem or change its properties from this window.

Setting up a modem isn't any different than setting it up with applications running under the previous Windows versions, with the exception that now you set it up for Windows 95 and not for individual applications. Moreover, Windows 95 will automatically pick parameters and capabilities that you had to enter manually before. What's new is the ability to set up calling locations and to use the dial-up scripting tool to create scripts for BBS connections and the like. Before we move on and discuss those new capabilities, however, we would like to present a few troubleshooting ideas, including working with the modem entries in the Registry.

Troubleshooting Modems

The most common problem you'll encounter in setting up a modem is that Windows doesn't recognize a particular model and thinks it's a standard modem. Your communications applications will still work with the standard modem settings, but you may not achieve maximum throughput, and you won't be able to take advantage of advanced features, such as error control and compression. The best you can do to remedy this problem is to find out whether your modem is compatible with a major brand modem, such as Hayes or U.S. Robotics. If it is, don't let Windows select it automatically after you click the Add button in the Modem Properties dialog box. Instead, check the "Don't Detect my modem. I will select it from a list" option in the Modem Installation wizard, and select the modem model you want to use from the list that Windows displays on your screen. If you don't see your modem in the list, select a similar one from the same manufacturer. Or, if your modem is compatible with a major brand, such as Hayes or U.S. Robotics, select one of these. There's a good chance it may work.

If you still can't use the advanced features of your modem, contact the manufacturer. If it's a really old modem, you'll probably be better off buying a new one, whose exact model appears in the Windows 95 list; or check whether the manufacturer provides Windows 95 drivers, and get the drivers if they're available.

Use the Registry to change the initialization steps for your modem.

Eventually, you may have to get to the Registry (see Chapter 2 to learn more about working with the Registry) to solve persistent problems, and just modify your modem's behavior. Each modem you have installed on your computer has its own entry, under the following key in the Registry: HKEY_LOCAL_MACHINE\ System\CurrentControlSet\Services\ Class\Modem. For each installed modem, Windows 95 creates a new subkey, \0000 for the first one, \0001 for the second, and so on. These keys contain the AT commands that Windows 95 uses to initialize the modem, dial, and answer incoming calls. The Registry entries for the modem on one of our computers is shown in Figure 5-2.

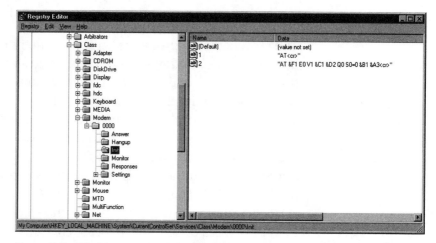

Figure 5-2: This is where the Registry stores information about your modem.

The Init subkey contains the commands to initialize the modem. The commands for the 0000 modem (shown in Figure 5-2) initialize the modem as follows. First, Windows sends the AT command. The modem should respond OK. Then, the computer sends the AT&FE0V1&A3&B1&D2&S0 string, followed by a carriage return character (<cr>). This string contains multiple commands, the first unique one being &F (all commands start with the AT string). The &F command tells the modem to restore its default settings. The next command is E0, which tells the modem to disable echo. The V1 command tells the modem to report the results in verbose mode, as opposed to numeric codes, and so on.

The vast majority of modems support the AT command set. Each AT command starts with the string "AT" (for ATtention) and is followed by a few characters. The command to dial, for example, is ATD (ATtention Dial). Multiple commands can be appended to each other without repeating the AT prefix, as you see in the initialization commands for the modem in Figure 5-2. The description of all AT commands your modem understands can be found in the modem's documentation.

For example, one command you might want to add for the 0000 modem's Init subkey in the Registry is ATX3. This command tells the modem to ignore the dial tone and is required to make your modem work overseas. This is because dialing tones are not the same from country to country, and your modem may not recognize a particular tone from another country. Add ATX3 as a new value, as shown in Figure 5-3, to resolve this problem.

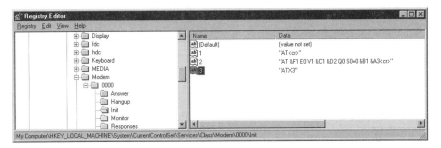

Figure 5-3: Add a new value for the modem section of the Registry to make your modem work in countries that have different dial tones.

The Answer subkey contains the ATA command, to answer an incoming call, and the Hangup subkey contains the ATH command to hang up the phone. If your modem requires additional commands for any of these operations or it has additional features that Windows 95 didn't discover during installation, this is the place to put them.

CONNECTIONS & DIALING PROPERTIES

Before you can communicate with other computers via your modem under Windows 95, you must set a number of properties, collectively known as *dialing properties*, which are specified in the Dialing Properties window, shown in Figure 5-4. The dialing properties are the Dialing Location (where you dial from) and how you dial the desired number from a given location (whether a prefix is required, if your phone uses pulse or tone dialing, and so on). You can get to this window either from within the Modems program (in the Control Panel), or through a dial-up connection. Changes you make to the dialing properties through the Modems program in the Control Panel affect all connections. Changes you make through a connection apply to the specific connection only. In the following paragraphs, we describe how to set up calling locations, the rules for calling card dialing, and how to automate your modem connections. We will also discuss two applets included in Windows 95, the Phone Dialer and HyperTerminal.

Your Calling Location

When you use a modem to dial out, you must enter information specific to the location you are calling from. For instance, Windows needs to know whether you are using tone or pulse dialing, whether a prefix is needed to get an outside line through the phone center (or a hotel room), whether the call will be charged to a calling card, and so on. These properties are specific to the place from which you make the call. If you dial from home, you don't need to dial a special number to get an outside line. If you call home from overseas, you may have to use pulse dialing. If you have a desktop computer at home or the office, a single dialing location is all you need. If you are using a notebook computer, however, these properties must be changed, depending on where you dial from. Most Windows 3.1x communications applications would allow you to create various user profiles and recall the one you need. The profiles, however, had to be entered separately in each communications application.

Windows 95 needs to know not only where you want to dial, but also where you dial from.

Windows 95 lets you enter the information that applies to the location you dial from in the properly named My Locations tab in the Dialing Properties dialog box (shown in Figure 5-4). Every Windows 95 application that wants to use the modem will ask Windows to do the dialing, and Windows will use the properties of the current dialing location.

The Dialing Properties dialog box lets you define the various properties of a location, to simplify dialing from the specific location (be it your office, a hotel room, or home). If you travel frequently and have to use your computer on the go, you know how confusing it is having to modify the dialing rules when you connect your notebook to a hotel room telephone outlet or to the telephone system of another company.

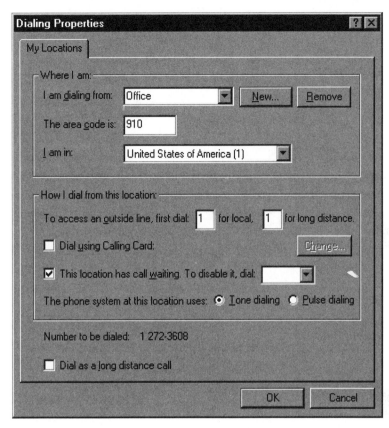

Figure 5-4: Specify your Dialing Properties to help Windows dial correctly for you.

To bring up the Dialing Properties dialog box, double-click on the Modems icon in the Control Panel, and from the Modem Properties window, click on Dialing Properties. You can also open the Dialing Properties dialog box by double-clicking any connection icon in the Dial-Up Networking folder and then clicking on the Dialing Properties button. You can define various locations (using the New button next to the I am dialing from drop-down list), each one with different characteristics and save them with different names. For example, when you want to connect from a hotel room, create and then select a hotel dialing location, which will first dial 9 (or another number or, possibly, a sequence of numbers) to get a line. Then, the hotel location should dial the number you want to call, area code first. When you return to the office, change the dialing location to office. This location could, for example, dial 1 to get an outside line.

A very important element in the Dialing Properties dialog box is the option to specify the calling card you use to charge the calls as part of a dialing location. If you check the Dial using Calling Card box, you must select a carrier and a calling card number. When calling from different locations, you may also use different calling cards (one for home, another for the office, and so on). To specify your calling card, check the "Dial using calling card" check box, then click on the Change button of the Dialing Properties dialog box to display the dialog box shown in Figure 5-5. Once you've specified the correct calling card and card number for a dialing location, Windows 95 will automatically dial the correct long distance carrier and provide the right card number every time it dials from the specific location, as long as the application you use to dial was written for Windows 95 and uses TAPI.

Use as many dialing locations as needed to make sure you dial correctly, wherever you are.

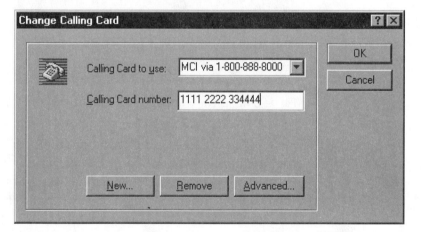

Figure 5-5: Specify your calling carrier and card number to have Windows 95 automatically charge the calls.

Calling Card Dialing

Besides the information you supply about the dialing location, Windows 95 lets you enter information about charging the call. If you are using a calling carrier for long distance calls, you will appreciate Windows 95's automation for dialing out with a calling card. You know how it is when you dial with a calling card. First you have to dial the 800 number, then the number you want to reach, then the card number. Unlike some telephones, your computer can't read the card number, but fortunately it can be told how to dial using a particular calling card.

Windows 95 comes preconfigured for many calling card carriers and methods. If you open the Change Calling Card dialog box and display the Calling Card to use list, you'll see a list of calling cards (AT&T, MCI, Sprint, and more). If your calling card is listed, select it, enter your Calling Card number, click OK, and you're finished. If you have problems using the preconfigured calling card methods or want to specify different calling procedures, you must use single-character dialing commands, which are shown in Table 5-1.

comma (,)	Pauses for two seconds. Use multiple commas to pause for any (even) number of seconds.
@	Wait for the phone to ring.
$	Wait for the calling card tone (the first tone you hear after dialing an 800 number, which tells you that you can dial the number you want to reach).
E	The country code.
Figure	The area code.
G	The local phone number.
T	Dial using touch tone.
P	Dial using pulses (you may need this setting if you are trying to dial from overseas).
Windows	Wait for a dial tone.
H	The calling card number.

Table 5-1: Calling card dialing commands.

For example, if you use MCI for your long distance calls, here are the steps your computer needs to use to make a call:

The dialing rules are actually commands to the modem.

1. Call MCI's 800 number.
2. Wait for the so-called bong tone.
3. Dial the number you want to reach.
4. Then wait for another bong tone.
5. Dial your calling card number.

My MCI calling number, 1-800-444-9595, is not listed in the list of calling cards. To use this calling card method, you'd have to click on the New button in the Change Calling Card dialog box and enter the new calling card name, as shown on the left window of Figure 5-6.

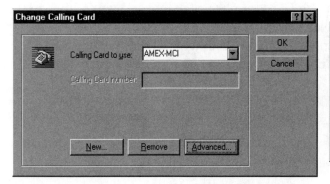 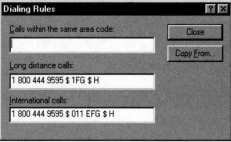

Figure 5-6: To add a new dialing rule, create a new calling card, and specify your own rule.

Click OK, then enter your calling card number in the Change Calling Card dialog box. Click on the Advanced button to display the dialog box shown on the right side of Figure 5-6, where you enter the dialing rules for local, long distance, and international calls.

When you use the calling card rules specified in the right side of Figure 5-6, the computer will use the new sequence whenever it dials. First, the computer dials the 800 number, then waits for the bong tone, then dials 1, the specified area code (F) and phone number (G), and waits again for another bong tone. Finally, it dials the calling card number (H). For international calls, instead of 1, it dials 011 and then the country code (E). The rest is the same. And of course, I didn't bother to enter any rules for local calls. Notice that you don't have to enter the phone number you are dialing, just the code G. The application provides the actual number. The steps for charging the call to the calling card are performed by Windows itself, no matter which application is used to dial. However, you can only use Dialing Locations with applications written for Windows 95. Older communications applications can't avail themselves of this feature.

■ ■

TIP

Your modem may not understand the bong tone. In that case, replace the $ character with several commas to make the computer wait. The long distance rule would be 1 800 444 9595,,,,,1FG,,,,,H.

■ ■

Making Connections

Even more important than the dialing properties are the various connections. You probably want to dial many locations. Windows 95 lets you specify different connections (sometimes also called *connectoids*), one for each destination. If you use multiple Internet Service Providers or connect to a number of BBSes, you can define a different connection for each one. Different connections have different properties to match the requirements of the modem on the other end. By setting up a connection icon for each type of service you want to connect to, you can connect to any given service by double-clicking on the appropriate icon.

To create a new connection, open the Dial-Up Networking folder (Start | Programs | Accessories | Dial-Up Networking). When the Dial-Up Networking folder opens, double-click on the Make New Connection icon. Alternatively, you can select the Make New Connection command from the Connections menu. A wizard will prompt you to enter the name of the connection and the number to be dialed, including area code and country code (if needed). Each new connection has a name and the number to be dialed and is represented in the Dial-Up Networking folder with a different icon. In Figure 5-7 you see the connections on one of our computers. Each time we want to connect to one of the sources described by the Connection names, we double-click on the corresponding icon.

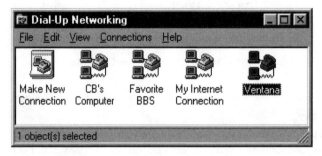

Figure 5-7: Create a new connection for every computer, BBS, or online service you want to connect to.

Each connection has its own properties, which are determined by the requirements of the modem at the other end of the connection. To set the properties for a connection, you must right-click on its icon and select Properties. The dialog box shown in Figure 5-8 will be displayed. The Configure button lets you set the modem's properties (which modem to be used for the connection if you have more than one modem connected, data bits, parity, and so on). Click the Server Type button to specify the protocol to be used in a connection to a server. We'll provide examples of server connections later in the chapter.

Each connection can use its own settings, even a different modem.

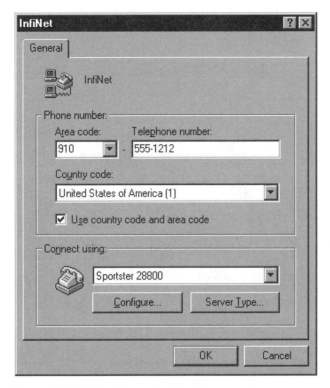

Figure 5-8: Setting the properties of a connection.

Connections are related to dialing locations, too, but not tied to them. You can assign a different dialing location to any connection. When you double-click on a Connection icon to connect to another computer, you see a dialog box similar to the one in Figure 5-9. To change the dialing location, click on the Dial Properties button.

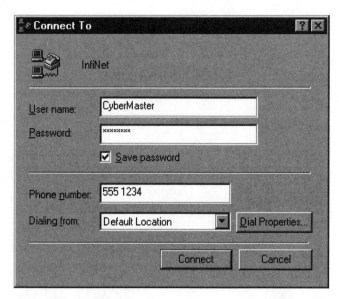

Figure 5-9: You can dial each destination from various locations by selecting the appropriate dialing location.

Moreover, each time you change the dialing location for one connection by choosing an existing location from the Dial from list, the new dialing location becomes the default for all other connections, too.

Automate Connections With Scripts

The so-called connectoids in Figure 5-7 simplify the process of dialing other computers, but there's more. Windows 95 includes the Dial-Up Scripting tool, a utility that lets you automate your login process. It's a scripting language for sending commands through the modem and receiving input from the modem. A Dial-Up Network script is a sequence of commands you send *through* the modem, not *to* the modem. So scripting commands are not cryptic AT commands the modem understands. They are almost as understandable as statements in the English language. Your computer translates scripting commands to AT commands and feeds them to the modem.

Every time you dial an online service or BBS through the modem, you must repeat the same steps to get connected. Wait for the prompt, enter your username, wait for another prompt, and then enter your password. After you have logged in, you must select a menu option or type a command to start a program. Some online services (such as CompuServe and America Online) provide their own front ends, which take care of these steps. Some Internet Access Providers require that you log in manually and then enter the name of a program to run. In such a case, you can write a Dial-Up script that provides the username and password and even performs other actions after login.

Let's start by exploring the DU scripting commands, and then we'll see a few examples of complete scripts. Each DU script is a sequence of commands, forming a short program. This program is enclosed between the keywords *proc main* and *endproc*. The two most important commands in DU scripting are *transmit* and *waitfor*. The transmit command sends a string (a piece of text) to the other end, and waitfor instructs the modem to wait for a specific string to arrive from the other end. The command:

```
transmit "^M"
```

sends a carriage return character, which many online services require before they establish communications. The command:

```
waitfor "User Name"
```

waits until the modem receives the string "User Name". Most online services will print several lines of text before they prompt for the username. The waitfor command ignores all text lines until the string "User Name" arrives at the modem. Notice also that the strings in both commands are case-sensitive. The previous command will not recognize the string "User name" and will keep waiting.

These two commands may be all you need to automate the login procedure for many services. Create a text file with any name and the extension .SCR, and type the following in it:

Each Dial-Up Networking script must be enclosed in a pair of proc/end proc commands.

```
proc main
waitfor "Login:"
transmit $USERID
transmit "^M"

waitfor "Password:"
transmit $PASSWORD
transmit "^M"

endproc
```

You must modify the prompts to match the ones you see in your logon window. Notice that you don't have to type your actual username and password (anyone can read a text file). They will be picked up from the corresponding boxes of the Connect To dialog box (see Figure 5-9). Of course, you can use $USERID and $PASSWORD in your scripts only if you have entered the User Name and Password values in the Connect To dialog box.

There are more commands, even control flow statements, to the dial-up scripting language. For a complete list of the scripting commands, see the help file of the Dial-Up Scripting tool. Here are the ones you'll be likely to use most often.

❒ **delay <n seconds>:** Pauses for n seconds before executing the next command. For example, delay 2 will pause for two seconds.

❒ **getip [index]:** Reads an IP address and uses it as the workstation address. The [index] argument is optional and specifies which IP address to use as the workstation address if more than one is received. For example, getip 2 retrieves the second IP address sent by the remote computer. To use this IP address for the session, combine the getip with the set ippaddr command: set ippaddr getip 2.

❒ **halt:** Causes the script to stop running. A terminal window will appear on your screen, and you can enter information manually. To resume, click on the Continue button.

❒ **;:** Indicates a comment. All text preceded by a semicolon is ignored.

You can send any printable character to the other computer, plus a few special characters. Special characters are specified with the caret symbol (^), followed by an ordinary character. If the value of the ordinary character is between the ampersand (@) and the underscore (_), the ^character sequence is translated to a single-byte value between 0 and 31. For example, ^M is converted to a carriage return (ASCII 13). If the character is between a and z, the ^character sequence is translated to a single-byte value between 1 and 26. There are a few more special symbols: <cr> (for carriage return), <lf> (for line feed), \" (inserts a double quote in the string), \^ (inserts a caret in the string), \< (inserts a < in the string) and \\ (inserts a back-slash in the string).

You can also combine the previous, as well as regular characters, in the same string. The command:

```
transmit "CHARLES^M"
```

sends the string CHARLES followed by a carriage return. The command:

```
waitfor "<lf>Password<cr><lf>"
```

waits to receive the prompt Password in a single line. (It won't react to the string "Password" if it's embedded in the text.)

Here's another simple DUN script to connect you to an Internet account and start a PPP connection:

```
proc main
waitfor "Login:"
transmit $USERID
transmit "^M"

waitfor "Password:"
transmit $PASSWORD
transmit "^M"

transmit "ppp^M"

endproc
```

In this script, ppp is the name of the command required to start the Internet connection. Replace it with any command you type in your account after you log in.

Let's see how you can create a script and assign it to a dial-up connection. From the Start menu, select Programs, then Accessories, and then Dial-Up Scripting Tool. The Dial-Up Scripting Tool dialog box is shown in Figure 5-10.

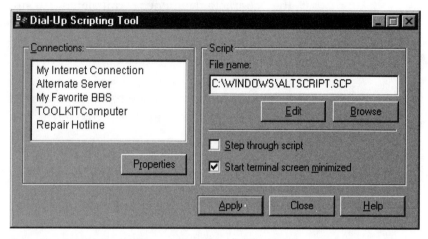

Figure 5-10: The Dial-Up Scripting Tool dialog box is where you assign scripts to the various dial-up connections.

If the Dial-Up Scripting Tool isn't installed on your computer, install it from the Windows 95 CD-ROM. Run the Add I Remove program from Control Panel, click on the Have Desk button and locate the file\ADMIN\APPTOOLS\DSSCRIPT\RNAPLUS.INF on the CD. From the list of available components select Scripting for Dial-Up Networking and click on Install.

On the left of the dialog box, you see the list of existing connections. Select the connection you wish to automate with a script, and enter the name of a script file in the text box on the right. If the script file exists already, you can click on the Browse button to locate it on the disk. If you type the name of a new file, the Dial-

Up Scripting tool will prompt you with a message saying that the file does not exist and ask you whether you want to create a new one. Click on the Yes button, and a Notepad window opens, in which you can enter the dial-up script. When you're finished, save the script to a file with the extension .SCP. Make sure Notepad doesn't use its default extension (.TXT) or the Dial-Up Scripting Tool won't be able to locate the file. If you want to edit an existing script, type its name in the text box, and click on the Edit button.

Because there's a good chance your first attempt to automate the login process will fail, step through each command in the script and see how it works. To do so, check the Step Through Script check box in the Dial-Up Scripting Tool dialog box.

You can single-step dial-up scripts to debug them.

To step through the script, go back to the Dial-Up Networking folder, and double-click on your connection's icon. Make sure the username and password are listed, and click on Connect. A terminal window will appear as soon as the two modems make contact, and you can step through the script by pressing F7. Watch the results, and keep track of the errors. If there are errors that make the login process impossible, press F3 to cancel the script. To fix problems in your script, you can either edit the .SCP file with Notepad or enter the script's filename in the Dial-Up Scripting Tool dialog box, and click on the Edit button.

Once your script works reliably, turn off the Step Through Script option in the Dial-Up Scripting Tool dialog box. Every time you double-click on your connection's icon from then on, the script runs automatically. However, some Internet Service Providers change their logon screens from time to time. If you find out that a good script doesn't work anymore, login manually, and see what has changed in the logon screen. You may find a message for you, and you must press Enter or Esc to move on.

The Phone Dialer

Once you have entered your dialing card and location information in your computer, why not use the computer for making voice calls as well? That's exactly what the Phone Dialer does. Of course, in order to use the Phone Dialer to dial for you, the phone must be connected to the modem.

The Phone Dialer is an accessory. To use it, click on Start, then Programs, Accessories, and finally click on the Phone Dialer Accessory. You can enter any number you want your computer to dial in the Number to Dial box and then click the Dial button (see Figure 5-11). To simplify the dialing process, you can use the Speed dial buttons. To assign a number to a Speed dial button, click on a free button, and you'll be prompted to enter a name for the button and the number to be dialed. Then every time you want to call this number, just click on the corresponding Speed dial button. To change the button's name or its number, choose Speed Dial from the Edit menu.

The Phone Dialer application is rather limited because it allows you to store only 10 speed dial numbers. Most telephones can store more than 10 speed dial numbers, and you have to pick up the phone anyway to talk to another person. Why bother with the telephone dialer? Despite its limitations, the Phone Dialer can be put to good use by reserving it for the 10 most cumbersome numbers you dial on a frequent basis. Moreover, the Phone Dialer is TAPI-compliant, and it will use the calling rules, such as using a specific calling card you've specified for the various dialing locations through the Dialing Properties dialog box. So using the Phone Dialer in such a case can save you the trouble of going through the whole calling card routine. To set the proper dialing location in the Phone Dialer, click on the Dialing Properties command of the Tools menu.

Figure 5-11: The Phone Dialer applet makes use of the dialing properties of each location to simplify your calls.

Did you ever go through an automated telephone system and dial 2 to access the service department, then 1 for computer hardware, 2 for software, 0 for an operator, and so on? You can put the Phone Dialer to good use by letting it dial the lengthiest numbers like these for you. Once a real person is on the other end (some automated phone systems don't even provide the option to talk to a human), you can pick up the phone and start talking.

Let's say you need assistance from a computer company. You dial their 800 number, you first hear a message, and then you are given a number of options. The option you need is 3 (hardware support). You dial 3, and then you are asked to press a person's extension (if you know it) or stay on the line. Once you have determined the extension you need (let's say it is 1223), you can automate this call by dialing 1-800-555-4444-3-1223 and get right to the person you want to talk to. You can't do that with a regular telephone, because you must pause between numbers or wait for a tone. The three modem commands you need to automate this process are: comma (,) which pauses for two seconds; the @ sign, which pauses dialing until there's silence on the line; and the character W, which waits until the modem hears a bong tone.

To automate this call with the Phone Dialer, set up a new speed dial number (call it "Support"), and enter a number to be dialed: 1,800,5554444@3W1223 (just as an example, of course). To automate certain calls, you must first dial the 800 number yourself, find out when you have to wait for a message to end before dialing, and then enter the appropriate string for the Phone Dialer. After you get it right, assign it to a speed dial number, and you'll never have to do it manually again. Let your computer go through the maze, and you can pick up the phone when you've reached the person you want to talk to. Keep in mind that the longest string you can fit in the Phone Dialer is 40 characters.

U se the Phone Dialer to sort through the maze of automated telephone systems.

HyperTerminal

The basic communications application that comes with Windows 95 is a terminal emulator, called HyperTerminal. With Hyper-Terminal you can connect to a bulletin board or an online communications service and download files. However, you can't connect to another computer running HyperTerminal. The version of HyperTerminal bundled with Windows 95 can't handle incoming calls, so don't throw out your old communications application yet. It will come in handy when making a direct connection to a friend's computer and exchanging files. (An improved version of HyperTerminal, the Personal Edition, is included on the Companion CD-ROM to this book.)

The neatest feature of HyperTerminal is that it creates a small icon for each connection you define (much as you can create an icon for each Dial-Up Networking connection you create). Hyper-Terminal comes with three predefined connections: CompuServe, MCI Mail, and AT&T Mail, as shown in Figure 5-12. To connect to one of these online services (in plain text mode, of course), double-click on the corresponding icon. To define a new connection, double-click on the HyperTerminal icon, and the dialog box on the left in Figure 5-13 will appear. Select a name and an icon for the connection, and click on OK. Then in the dialog box shown on the right in Figure 5-13, you must specify the number you want the computer to dial, and you're set.

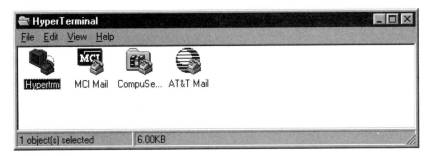

Figure 5-12: HyperTerminal comes with several predefined terminal connections.

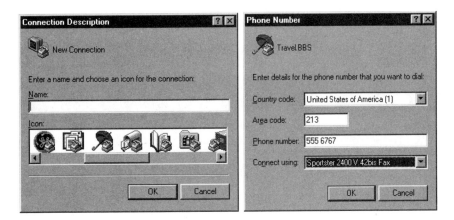

Figure 5-13: The two HyperTerminal dialog boxes for specifying a new terminal connection.

Despite its limitations, HyperTerminal offers a variety of file transfer protocols, since this is the primary reason for using it. It supports the Zmodem protocol (the fastest and most popular data transfer protocol), Xmodem (the most common error-correcting protocol), Ymodem, and Ymodem-G (a variation of the Ymodem for modems with hardware error control).

We mentioned in the introduction that HyperTerminal can't handle incoming calls—it can't answer the phone when another computer calls. However, it is possible to connect two computers with HyperTerminal using a technique, which we describe next.

Open the HyperTerminal folder (Start | Programs | Accessories | HyperTerminal), and create a new connection by starting the HyperTerminal application and selecting New Connection from the File menu. Name it Direct or Answer, and do not provide a phone number for this connection. Instead, click on the Connect Using drop-down list, and select Direct to Com1 (or Com2, depending on where your modem is connected). Once you've chosen a direct connection to the computer's serial port, you'll be asked to enter the port's characteristics, such as speed, data bits, and so on. Set these parameters according to your modem's characteristics. The Direct Connection established a communications link between HyperTerminal and the modem. (It is also used to create direct cable connections, which are described in the next chapter.) Assuming that the direct connection is made to the port on which the modem is attached, you can send AT commands directly to the modem. Issue the command AT to check the connection. The modem should return the string "OK", which will be displayed on HyperTerminal's window.

To instruct the modem to answer an incoming call, issue the ATS0=1 command. This command puts the modem in the auto-answer mode. The next incoming call will be answered by your computer. If a friend calls using HyperTerminal, your computer will reply, and you can exchange files with the Transfer command. One of you should be sending the files and the other one receiving. You should also make sure that you are both using the same file transfer protocol. This isn't the most convenient connection, but it will come in handy if you want to exchange files with users who don't have e-mail capability. You can also use scripts to automate the exchange of data on a regular basis.

DIAL-UP NETWORKING

We've seen how to set up a modem and how to define the Dialing Properties. You can use the modem to connect to your favorite online services or the Internet (we will discuss the Internet connection shortly). Communications are an integral part of the Windows 95 operating system and there's more to it than just setting up a modem. An exciting capability of Windows 95 is Dial-Up Networking. Dial-Up Networking allows you to use a network, or another computer, as if you were actually connected to the network, even though you are in another city or on another continent.

Dial-Up networking is another subsystem, intended to solve the problems of so-called mobile computing. A constantly increasing number of users have to travel, yet stay connected—to their offices, their online services, and the Internet. They are the mobile users who face new challenges every day. You've seen them work with their notebooks on the airplane, and you've seen them rush to the VIP lounge at the airport to connect their computers to phone lines and send data.

The number of mobile users increases steadily (eventually, we'll all become mobile users), and the folks at Microsoft didn't ignore the needs of the mobile users. Windows 95 includes Dial-Up Networking and a few applets to simplify the lives of mobile users. Dial-Up Networking is Windows's built-in capability to network with other computers via a modem and a telephone line. This means that you can not only stay in touch with your work team, but you can actually be with them constantly, even when you travel. All you need is a modem connection to one of the computers on the network.

Dial-Up Networking is a Windows 95 subsystem, just like the printing and messaging subsystems.

Logging into Another Computer Over the Phone

In this section we will show you how to use the modem to connect two computers to each other and share their resources (disks and printers). Connecting two computers with a communications program is still an option (as we explained in the section,

"HyperTerminal"), but with the communications capabilities built into Windows 95 you can do more than simply upload and download files. You can network the two computers. (Networking is covered in more detail in the next chapter.) In this chapter, we'll discuss a few simple, yet practical ways, to network computers over a telephone line. Later in the chapter, we'll also show you how to build small networks over the Internet, for the cost of a local phone call.

The simplest Dial-Up Network (DUN) you can build is to connect two computers: your notebook on the road with a desktop at work, or your computer to a friend's computer. Let's see what's involved. The two computers to be connected must be configured differently. One of them, the computer that will answer the incoming call, is the DUN server computer. The other one is the DUN client computer, which will call and request the services of the DUN server computer. Client support comes with Windows 95. The DUN server computer, though, requires the Microsoft Plus! package, as explained in the following section. Once the client and server are both set up, you can dial the DUN server from the DUN client. You can create as many Dial Up Networks as you wish. Just create a new DUN client connection in the Dial Up Networks folder for each computer you want to connect to. If you are setting up your computer as a DUN server, though, you don't need multiple connections. Finally, you can have several DUN client connections and a DUN server connection—but you can't use them at the same time.

Setting Up a DUN Server

The server you set up will usually be your desktop computer at the office. It may be connected to a network server itself. In such a case, you may wonder why you shouldn't just dial in and connect directly with the company network server computer instead of the desktop in your office. Because most companies use small networks, connecting a portable computer to a network server computer isn't of much help. Chances are many users will be trying to access the same network server computer over the phone. The individual desktop machine you connect to instead (your dial-up server), which later connects you to the rest of the network, won't be as busy as the network server, so you can use the desktop's resources without worrying about network traffic. A network server computer usually runs an operating system that supports multiple connections to the network. This is Windows NT (with the Remote Access Server), Windows for Workgroups RAS, LAN Manager, and NetWare Connect (and, of course, UNIX systems). You'll find more about remote connections to networks in the following chapter, but if what you want is to connect to your office or home computer while you're on the road, the information in this chapter may be all you need. We will discuss only how to connect Windows 95 machines.

A dial-up network requires a server and a client machine.

To set up a DUN server computer, you must install the Dial-Up Networking Server from the Microsoft Plus! CD. Start the Microsoft Plus! setup program, and check the Dial-Up Networking Server option. Don't change the other options. If some of them were already installed, unchecking their boxes will cause them to be removed. Then click the OK button to finish. The DUN Server package consists of a single .DLL file—yet you need the Microsoft Plus! CD to install it.

Now open the Start menu, select Programs, then Accessories, and then Dial-Up Networking. The Dial-Up Networking program will start. If you click to display the Connections menu, you'll see the last command is Dial-Up Server, as in Figure 5-14. This command is available only if the DUN server is installed. Moreover, this is the only place on the desktop from which you can access the DUN server.

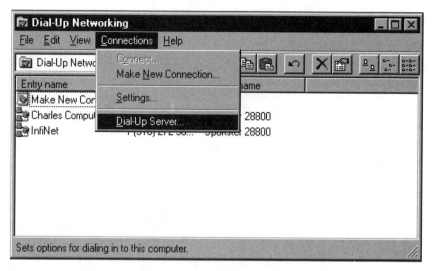

Figure 5-14: The last command on the Connections menu appears only if the DUN server is installed.

Select the Dial-Up Server command from the Connections menu, and you'll see the Dial-Up Server dialog box, which is shown in Figure 5-15. To set up your computer so that it will answer incoming calls as a DUN server, select the Allow Caller Access option button. You can also set a password for the client computer by clicking the Change Password button.

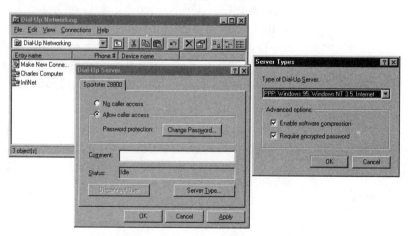

Figure 5-15: Configuring your machine as a DUN server. The Server Type button leads to the Server Types dialog box on the right.

Click on the Server Type button to set additional parameters through the Server Types dialog box (also shown in Figure 5-15). The protocol should be "PPP: Windows 95, Windows NT, Internet". Leave the other two boxes (Enable software compression and Require encrypted password) checked.

Your computer is ready to accept incoming calls from DUN clients, and you'll need to leave the computer on to enable it to accept incoming calls. Unfortunately, you will not be warned as to when a DUN client connects to your computer. To find out if a client computer is connected to your machine, open the Dial-Up Server dialog box (by selecting the proper connection from the Dial-Up Networking folder and then the Dial-Up Server command from the Connections menu), and look at the Status box. Figure 5-16 shows what this dialog box should look like after Caller Access has been enabled and another user is accessing the computer. You will also notice when a client is connected to the DUN server because the connection may slow the server's performance.

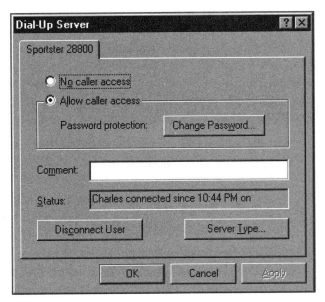

Figure 5-16: Someone's using your computer as a DUN server.

Sharing Resources

The last step in setting up a DUN server is to prepare the resources you want to share with the client computer. By default, your server computer's resources can't be shared. To make them available to other users on a network, you must share them. Resource sharing is a major topic in networking and is discussed in more detail in the next chapter. We'll show you how to share devices here so that you'll be able to follow the examples in this section. For more information about sharing resources between connected (or networked) systems, see Chapter 6.

The two types of devices shared over a network are disks and printers. To share an entire disk, right-click on its icon in the Explorer window (or the My Computer window), and select the Sharing command (which is not available on stand-alone systems). Check the Shared As radio button, and enter the name of the resource you want to share. This is the name of the shared disk the client computer will see. Notice that you don't have to share an entire disk. You can share a single file, a number of files, a folder, and any number of folders. If you are using a DUN so that you can work with a friend on a common project, place all related files in a folder and share this single folder. The user of the client computer will have access to the files he or she needs but not to any other files. Do the same for the printers you want to share in the Printers window. (To display it, click on the Start button, then choose Settings, and click on Printers.) If you want to share a file or other device (such as a backup unit), right-click on its icon in the Explorer window, and look for the Sharing command. If it's there, the device can be shared.

You should try to share your resources as read-only. If you can't, assign a password to them.

Setting Up a DUN Client

Let's look now at the client side of the DUN. The first step is to set up a new dial-up connection to the computer you want to dial. Open the Dial-Up Networking folder (Start | Programs | Accessories menu), and double-click on the Make New Connection icon. The Make New Connection wizard will take you through the steps for creating the connection, assuming you have already set up a modem. All you have to do here is plug in the number you want to dial and give your connection a name, such as Bob's Computer.

Now you must make sure that the right protocols are being used. That's simpler than it sounds, if you understand that Windows 95 is using the modem as a network interface card. Once you decide which protocol you want to use, you must bind it to the Dial-Up Adapter. Double-click on the Network icon in the Control Panel, and you'll see the Network dialog box shown in Figure 5-17. The NetBEUI and IPX/SPX protocols should be listed. If they aren't, install them by clicking on the Add button (you'll need your Windows 95 CD, as well).

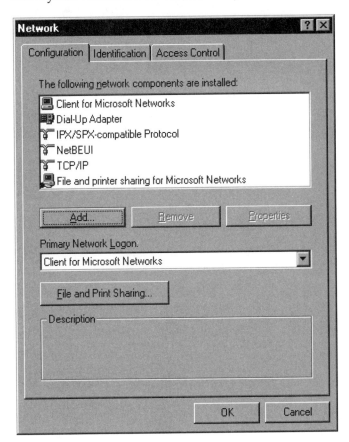

Figure 5-17: To use DUN, make sure that both NetBEUI and IPX/SPX are installed.

From the Select Network Component Type dialog box, select Protocols, and you'll see the dialog box shown in Figure 5-18. Click on Microsoft in the Manufacturers list and on the IPX/SPX-Compatible Protocol in the Network Protocols list. Then click OK to add this protocol. Repeat the same process, only this time select the NetBEUI protocol, and add it to the network components.

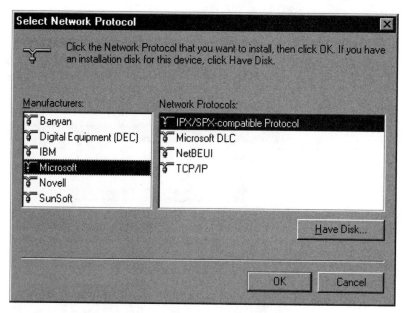

Figure 5-18: The protocols you need to add for DUN support are Microsoft's NetBEUI and IPX/SPX.

Go back to the Network dialog box shown in Figure 5-17, select the NetBEUI protocol, and click on the Properties button. You'll see the NetBEUI Properties window, which has two tabs. Select the Bindings tab, make sure the Client for Microsoft Networks box is checked, and then click OK. Do the same for the IPX/SPX protocol, too. Figure 5-19 shows what the Bindings dialog box for the NetBEUI Properties should look like. The Bindings tab of the IPX/SPX Properties dialog box should look similar.

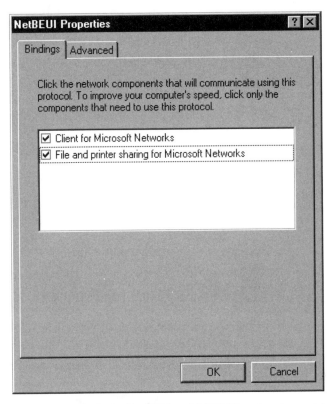

Figure 5-19: Both the NetBEUI and IPX/SPX protocols must be bound to the Client for Microsoft Networks service for DUN.

If the Client for Microsoft Networks box doesn't appear in the Properties dialog box for one of the protocols, you must install that, too. To do so, select Add in the Network dialog box as before, and this time select Client from the Select Network Component Type dialog box. A list of clients will appear, similar to the list of protocols shown in Figure 5-18. Select the Microsoft in the Manufacturers list and Client for Microsoft Networks from the list on the right, and click on OK. Then go back and bind the new component to the NetBEUI and IPX/SPX protocols.

As with the server computer, you must also decide which resources on the client computer you are going to share. A DUN provides two-way communications between the two computers, so that both the server and the client can see each other's shared resources. Follow the approach described in the section above "Sharing Resources" to share some of the client computer's resources.

Connect & Use the Shared Resources

Before you call the server computer using the client computer, make sure you have the following information:

- ❏ The server computer's name.
- ❏ The names of the shared resources on the server computer.
- ❏ The passwords for each shared resource.

If you forgot your computer's name, you can find it in the Identification tab of the Network dialog box.

To find out the name of your computer, double-click on the Network icon in the Control Panel. In the Network dialog box, select the Identification tab, and you'll see your computer's name and the workgroup name, as shown in Figure 5-20. This is the place to change them as well. The name of the server computer must be made known to you by the person on the server computer (and you must tell the other person the name of the client computer).

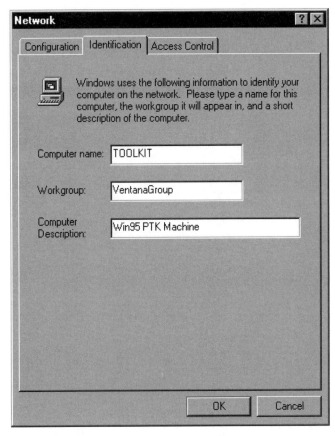

Figure 5-20: A computer's name and its workgroup name appear in the Identification tab of the Network dialog box.

To find out which of the resources on the client computer are shared (i.e., you can access), open the Explorer window, and look at their icons. The shared resources have an icon of a little hand at the lower left corner. The same shared resources at the server's end have the icon of a wire network connection. In the screen shown in Figure 5-21, the drive C:, the folder New Project (on the desktop), and the TI printer are shared. The TI printer is physically connected to the server computer and shared by the client computer, whose desktop appears in the figure. As we will explain in the section "Setting Up an Internetwork," Windows 95 will actually install the appropriate drivers on your computer the first time you attempt to print a document to the remote printer. The C: drive and the New Project folder are resources on the client computer that are accessible from the server computer.

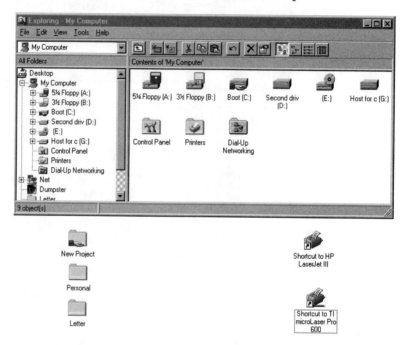

Figure 5-21: Shared resources are depicted with special icons on the desktop.

To connect to the server computer, create a new dial-up connection to that number. To do so, open the Dial-Up Networking folder, and double-click on Make New Connection. Enter a name for the connection and the phone number of the remote computer in the appropriate boxes, and then double-click on the new Dial-Up icon to connect.

If all goes well, you should be able to use the other computer's resources. To test your connection, open the Start menu, and select Find I Computers. In the Find dialog box, enter the name of the

DUN server computer you are connected to, with two slashes in front of its name. If the server computer's name is TOOLKIT, search for \\TOOLKIT. If it's found, you're connected, and you can use the server computer's resources.

If the connection doesn't work, repeat all the steps we described for setting up both the server and client computers, and restart the computer. If this doesn't solve the problem, the problem most likely lies in the connection. Make sure the two modems see each other and they are locked. If you need more help, start the Dial-Up Network Troubleshooter, which is an interactive troubleshooting guide, and it will take you through the steps of troubleshooting the most common networking problems. You can press F1 (the help key) at any time and look up the topic Network Trouble-shooter.

If you can find the other computer, start a chat session with the other end. This is a way to make sure that Dial-Up Network is working. Even if the two computers can see each other, a few minor problems may still have to be resolved. Being able to chat with the user on the other end will help you lick any problems. (Unless, of course, you both have second telephone lines, in which case you can talk to each other.) Once both the server and client computers have been configured properly and they can see each other, there's no need for a user to be present at the server computer. If the server computer is on and set to accept calls, the client computer will be able to connect.

Chat is a simple application that enables two users to communicate in real-time via two window panes, as shown in Figure 5-22. Each user types his or her messages to the other user in the top pane and sees the responses from the other end in the bottom pane.

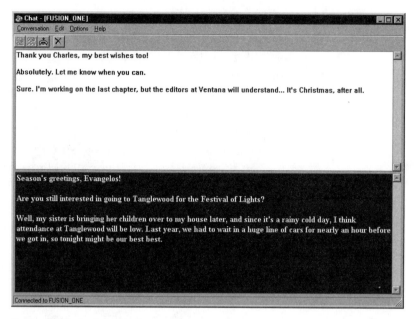

Figure 5-22: A chat session.

The WinChat application can be found in the Admin\Other subdirectory of the Windows 95 CD. To install it, start the Add | Remove Programs tool in the Control Panel, and select the Windows Setup tab. Click on the Have Disk button and the Browse button to locate the file WINCHAT.INF in the Admin\Others subdirectory of the CD. Click on OK, and the WinChat application will be installed as an Accessory. To start it, select Programs from the Start menu, then Programs, Accessories and finally click on the program's name.

To request a conversation with the other user, start WinChat, and select the Dial command from the Conversation menu. In the dialog box that appears, enter the other user's name. If the other end attempts to call you, you will hear a ring through your computer's speaker, and the WinChat program's icon will start flashing to get your attention. Open the application, and select Answer from the Conversation menu.

Another application that comes with Windows 95 for exchanging messages with other users is WinPopup. WinPopup is even simpler, and it lets you send messages to other co-workers in the same workgroup. WinPopup displays a small window in which you type a message, specify the name of the recipient, and the message is sent. It's a way to catch someone's attention, especially if he or she doesn't regularly check the mail. Notice that WinPopup lets you enter either a computer name or a username.

Map the Remote Network Drives

The first thing you want to do once you've established a connection to the server computer is to map the other computer's shared drives, which usually have long names (such as "E: on Ventana's Server"). Once the two computers are connected, however, it's easier to work from the client computer if you designate single-letter drive names to the shared resources. By doing so, you make the remote drive appear as if it is permanently attached to your client computer. You don't have to map the shared drives, but, at the very least, it's much easier to type a single character than an entire string in a FileOpen dialog box. Open the Map Network Drive on the Explorer's menu bar, and select the Map Network Drive command from the Tools menu or click on the Map Network Drive icon. A dialog box will be displayed as shown in Figure 5-23, with the first available drive letter and an empty box, in which you can enter the name of the remote drive you want to assign to this letter.

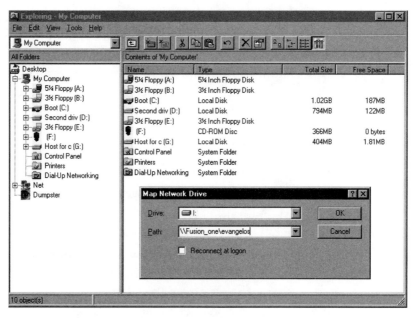

Figure 5-23: Mapping network drives to single-letter drive names.

You can also instruct Windows to reconnect to certain remote drives every time you log on to your machine. If you check the Reconnect At Logon check box in the Map Network Drive dialog box, Windows will establish a connection to the remote drive, which requires that the server computer be on and can answer the call. Also, it lengthens significantly the logon process. This option should be used over local area networks, not dial-up networks. For more information on sharing disks and mapping network drives see Chapter 6.

After mapping the network drives, you can start working as if every drive was physically attached to your computer. You can open files on the remote computer, place files and scraps on the remote computer's desktop, even print your files from the remote computer. If one of the remote drives is mapped to the local drive name d:, you can access any file on that drive with its full pathname (F: being the drive name). You can also refer to remote files with the so-called UNC filename (UNC stands for Universal Naming Convention). Suppose the name of the server computer is

If you map the remote drives, you can access them with their UNC names.

TOOLKIT, and it contains a shared folder named PROJECTS. To open the file COMMPROJECT in the PROJECTS folder on the remote computer, enter the name \\TOOLKIT\PROJECTS\ COMMPROJECT in any program's File Open dialog box. The UNC name starts always with two slashes followed by the name of the computer, and then comes the pathname, as with any local file. If the PROJECTS folder of the TOOLKIT computer has been mapped to drive F:, you can also refer to it as F:\COMMPROJECT.

Of course, there will be a very noticeable delay since data is transferred over the modem, which is extremely slow compared to the hard drive—but you can't have it all. If you are running client-server applications, and not much information has to be moved back and forth, even a DUN network will work. If you want to form a workgroup with a person and you can't set up an actual network, this is as close as you can get. As you will see in the section "Setting Up an Internetwork," you can build a workgroup spanning the globe over the Internet for the cost of a local call.

For a more detailed discussion of the concepts and techniques of workgroup computing, as well as the Windows 95 tools for the mobile user, see Chapter 6.

THE INTERNET

One of the most important aspects of personal computing today is the Internet, the network of networks. The Internet is not a network in the sense of a local area network (or even wide area network) you may be using at your office. It is a way to connect to other computers, no matter where they are located. The Internet has no dedicated servers, no central administration, and no one even knows how many computers are connected to the Internet. You can think of the Internet as the means to connect to other computers. Most people use the Internet to browse Web pages, find information on any topic you can imagine, and even create their own Web pages. Access to other computers on the Internet is rather limited, though. You can connect to a Web page, but you don't see the other computer's resources, just the Web pages the other computer provides. You can exchange mail over the Internet, but it has to go through an Internet Service Provider. Even if the person you want to reach is connected to the Internet at the same time, you can't reach him or her directly. In this section, you'll learn how to reach other computers on the Internet and directly communicate with other users. You've seen how to use Dial-Up Networking to connect to other computers and networks through your modem. Now you'll learn how to do the same through the Internet. The benefit of building Dial-Up Networks over the Internet is that you can share the resources of other computers for the cost of a local call, no matter where the other computer is located.

This section is not an introduction to the Internet. We assume some familiarity with the Internet, and we'll focus our attention on some advanced Internet topics, such as the support for Internet built into Windows 95 and how to build networks over the Internet. We'll also discuss the basic concepts of Internet connections, such as IP addresses and DNS servers and protocols, so that you'll understand what goes on behind the scenes when you are connected to the Internet.

CONNECTING TO THE INTERNET

The simplest and most common method for millions of users who don't have access through a company, college, or university is through an Internet Service Provider (ISP). For many years, the only way to access the Internet was through Unix workstations and mostly from universities. After 1994, though, an amazing explosion of Internet usage made the Information Superhighway a reality.

An ISP is a company that provides you with an account, through which you can log on to the Internet. The ISP is connected to the Internet and acts as a gateway for a number of users who connect through modems to the ISP's computer. All you do is dial your service provider, log in to its computer and establish a connection to the Internet. The ISP's computer is transparent to this connection, which means that you don't have to worry about the ISP computer because you don't even know it's there. Its sole purpose is to give you a connection to the Internet.

Two major types of accounts, PPP and SLIP, are available from ISPs. PPP stands for Point-to-Point Protocol, and SLIP stands for Serial Line Internet Protocol. They both do the same thing, but PPP is preferred, if you have a choice, because Windows 95 works more smoothly with the PPP protocol. We'll show how to connect to both types of accounts.

There are two ways to configure an Internet connection: either with the Internet wizard, which comes with Microsoft Plus!, or manually. The Internet wizard simplifies the process, but we'll show you how to manually configure the Internet connection. As we go through the steps, we also offer an explanation of the terms you'll meet along the way and explain what each component does. You will need this information to work through the last section of this chapter. If you are familiar with Internet terminology, and you understand what each network component does, you may skip this section.

To connect to the Internet through a service provider, you need to make sure two protocols are available in Windows 95: PPP (or SLIP) or TCP/IP.

About Protocols

TCP/IP is a communications protocol that works over many different physical connections.

TCP/IP stands for Transmission Control Protocol/Internet Protocol. The "Internet/Protocol" part says it all: TCP/IP is the fundamental entity underlying the Internet. It is the glue that holds it all together. TCP/IP is a network protocol. It is a standard computers use to send information to each other. The TCP/IP program has been implemented for all operating systems, so any computer can talk to any other computer through TCP/IP. Windows 95 includes the TCP/IP protocol; all you have to do is install it.

But two computers must be connected to each other before they can exchange data. What kind of connections does the TCP/IP protocol support? None. TCP/IP doesn't care about the physical connection. It specifies how applications will exchange information but is totally independent of the actual connection—that is, the medium over which the two computers communicate.

There are other protocols for the actual transmission of information between computers. For serial lines, these are the PPP and SLIP protocols. Both of these protocols allow TCP/IP to run through a serial communications line, such as a telephone line between two modems.

Since Microsoft seems to favor PPP by making it the default during Dial-Up Networking installation, you might as well ask for a PPP account if you have a choice. If you already have a SLIP account, you must install the corresponding support files from the Windows 95 CD yourself (SLIP support is not added automatically when you install Windows 95).

There are two additional protocols related to the PPP protocol, and they are called PAP and CHAP. PAP stands for Password Authentication Protocol, and CHAP for Challenge Handshake Authentication Protocol. If your ISP provides PPP accounts, find out if they support either the PAP or CHAP protocol. These protocols authenticate usernames and passwords automatically so Windows 95 can send the information you have entered in the User Name and Password boxes of the Connect To dialog box (see Figure 5-9). (The difference between them is that PAP transmits plain text, while CHAP uses encryption and is more secure.) If you have a PPP account that doesn't support either the PAP or CHAP protocol, or a SLIP account, you can always automate the login process with a dial-up script, which we explained in the section "Automate Connections With Scripts," earlier in this chapter.

Creating the Connection

Setting up an Internet connection involves three steps:

1. Obtain an Internet account from an Internet Service Provider.

2. Install TCP/IP, and set its properties.

3. Create a new connection, and set its properties.

Since TCP/IP is a network protocol, as we mentioned already, it's part of the network. We must tell our network device that TCP/IP is there, and it must use it to communicate with other computers. In proper network terminology, the TCP/IP protocol must be *bound* to the network adapter. But do you need a network adapter to connect to the Internet? That's where DUN comes in. It makes applications think that the modem is a network adapter. The modem is the dial-up adapter. As far as the applications are concerned, there's a dial-up adapter on the system, and they talk to it with the help of TCP/IP. Once you bind the TCP/IP protocol to the dial-up adapter, you'll be able to communicate with other computers using the TCP/IP protocol. The next step is to create a new connection and configure it to use the PPP or SLIP protocol, which will enable you to communicate through the serial port.

During the installation process, you must have the following information at hand:

- ❏ Your ISP's telephone number.
- ❏ The type of the account (PPP or SLIP).
- ❏ Your username and password.
- ❏ Your hostname.
- ❏ Your ISP's domain name.
- ❏ The IP address of your ISP's DNS server.

Your ISP will surely provide all the information you need regarding the preceding list, but it would help if you understood what each number or name is and what it is used for in the Internet domain.

We've already discussed the two types of accounts. Your username is the name by which you log in to the ISP's computer. Your hostname, on the other hand, is the name by which you are known to the rest of the Internet world. It usually is the same as the username and could be your entire name if it's relatively short (such as JoeDoe), some combination of characters from your first and last names (such as JSeinfeld), or even a made-up name (such as CyberMaster or DragonFly). You can choose any name, as long as it's unique among the subscribers of your ISP. There's bound to be another JoeDoe on the Internet, but his complete address is different. The password is any string you can memorize and keep to yourself.

Your address on the Internet is your username followed by your ISP's domain name. If the domain name is AceNet.com (domain names are case-insensitive), your address on the Internet is something like JoeDoe.AceNet.com, or CyberMaster.AceNet.com. Your e-mail address, which is what other people use to address messages to you is JoeDoe@AceNet.com or CyberMaster@AceNet.com. A message addressed to JoeDoe@AceNet.com must be first delivered to your ISP (AceNet.com) and then to you.

Finally, there's the ISP's DNS server. A DNS (Domain Name System) server is a computer that translates domain names (such as AceNet.com) to IP addresses (such as 132.23.45.90). The Internet Protocol (IP) address is a number that identifies each computer on the Internet. There are probably over 30 million computers on the Internet, and they each have a unique IP address. Since it would be impossible for us humans to memorize IP addresses, we use actual names (the domain names) to describe our computers. These names must be converted to IP address. Some computers on the Internet act as DNS servers: they get requests to convert the actual domain names to IP addresses (or else messages wouldn't be delivered). DNS servers maintain large look-up tables of English-like addresses and IP addresses. Unless a message doesn't have its destination in IP format, it can't get to the Internet. The DNS server has to know every other computer on the network in order to supply the IP address of any domain name. (It's dirty work, but someone has to do it.)

DNS servers are the backbone of the Internet.

Of course, no DNS servers out there have all the information. The trick is that they talk to each other, and if one doesn't know the IP address of the AceNet.com domain name, it knows another DNS server that does.

As we've mentioned already, Internet support was built in to Windows 95. Let's follow the steps of connecting a Windows 95 computer to the Internet through an ISP.

1. Install TCP/IP. If it has been installed already, go to the next step.

   To install TCP/IP, open the Control Panel folder, and double-click on the Network icon. In the list that will appear, double-click on Protocol, and a dialog box listing Manufacturers on the left and Protocols on the right will be displayed. Select Microsoft from the Manufacturers list on the left and TCP/IP from the Protocols list. Click on OK to complete the installation.

2. Configure TCP/IP. Now we must provide some information to the TCP/IP protocol in order to communicate with the other computer.

   Double-click on the Network icon, select TCP/IP, and click on the Properties button. A dialog box like the one shown in Figure 5-24 will appear.

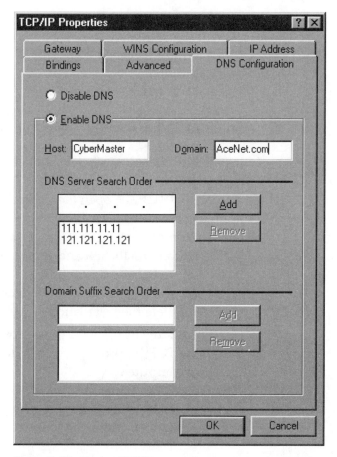

Figure 5-24: Setting TCP/IP properties.

There are six tabs on this dialog box (they're all shown in Figures 5-30 and 5-31). Let's start with the IP Address. If you were given a fixed IP address, enter it here. Most ISPs supply a new IP address dynamically, every time you log in. If that's the case, just check the "Obtain An IP Address Automatically" option box.

Now switch to the DNS configuration tab. Check the Enable DNS option, and enter your hostname (which most likely is the same as your username), the ISP's domain name (which is everything that follows the @ sign in your e-mail address), and the IP addresses of the DNS servers used by your ISP. They must be provided by the ISP. This box contains all the information the specified DNS server needs to properly deliver your messages to you.

In the Advanced tab, check the box Set this protocol to be the default protocol. Then in the WINS Configuration tab, check the Disable WINS resolution check box. (We'll use the WINS option later, when we describe how to set up networks over the Internet.)

Leave the Gateway tab as is, and in the Bindings tab, check the Client for Microsoft Networks service. Click on the OK button, and you are finished with the TCP/IP protocol.

Next you must create a new connection to your ISP. If you have a PPP account, proceed to step 4. If you have a SLIP account, you must first install the SLIP component.

3. Install SLIP.

SLIP support isn't installed automatically during Windows 95 installation.

To install SLIP support, you need the Windows 95 CD. Open the Control Panel folder, and double-click on the Add/Remove Programs icon. In the dialog box that will appear, select the Windows Setup tab. A list of installed components will appear. Click the Have Disk button and locate the following file on the Windows 95 CD: \ADMIN\APPTOOLS\DSSCRIPT\RNAPLUS.INF. and click on OK. The component SLIP and Scripting for Dial-Up Networking will appear in the list of components. Check SLIP item, and then click on Install.

4. Make a new dial-up connection.

The last step is to create a new dial-up connection. Open the Dial-Up Networking folder from the Start | Accessories menu, and double-click on the Make New Connection icon. You will be prompted to enter a name for the connection (such as Internet Connection) and choose a modem. Click on the Next button, and you will be asked to enter your ISP's phone number. Click on the Finish button, and a new Connection icon will appear in the Dial-Up Networking folder.

We're not quite finished yet. You must now set some of the new connection's properties. To do so, right-click on its icon, and select Properties. You will see a dialog box similar to the one in Figure 5-25.

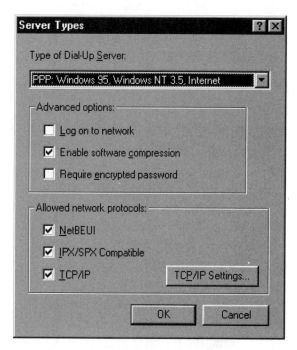

Figure 5-25: Use the Server Types dialog box to set the type of connection you are using in your Internet account.

From the drop-down list, select the type of connection your ISP supports. If you have a PPP connection that supports PAP or CHAP protocol, as explained earlier in the chapter, you should also check the Log on to network box. The new connection will automatically transmit your username and password. If you have a PPP connection that doesn't support either protocol or a SLIP connection, you can always create a script to automate your login process. In the mean time, you must enter your username and password manually. Close the Server Types dialog box by clicking the OK button, and click on Configure in the Internet Connection window. You will see a window with three tabs. Select the Options tab, and check the Bring up terminal window after dialing option. If you can't log on automatically, you must bring up a terminal window in which to type your username, password, and any other command required to start a PPP or SLIP connection on the ISP's machine.

From now on, you can get on the Internet by double-clicking on the Internet icon. If you don't have a PAP or CHAP account, you should also write a short script to automate the login process. One of the examples in the earlier section "Automating Connections With Scripts" is an actual working script. Modify it to match the prompts of your ISP, and you shouldn't have any problems.

We assume you know what to do once you're connected (start your Web browser to view Web pages, exchange mail, and so on). In the rest of this chapter, we're going to present an advanced technique for networking through the Internet.

SETTING UP AN INTERNETWORK

In the last section of this chapter we're going to show you how to build a network over the Internet. This is not exactly a wide area network, but you'll find it extremely useful in several situations. Internetworking is an example of the possibilities you can expect from the Internet. Let's see what internetworking can do for you with an example.

Suppose you are visiting a company overseas, and you wish to stay up to date with all the projects going on at your company in the United States. Exchanging mail with your coworkers is one way to do it, but you'll have to ask for the files you need, let people know that you are working on a specific file, send files back to be printed and distributed in your department, and so on. You can be in touch, but you are not quite a member of the workgroup until you get back home.

Internetworking lets you form workgroups that span the globe for free.

Internetworking is a capability offered by the Internet and Windows 95 to build workgroups over the Internet. It's not a substitute for a real network, it is slow (you are communicating via modems), but it's inexpensive. You can build a workgroup with users on different continents for the cost of a local call. And as Internet connections become faster, internetworking will grow in popularity.

How does it work? It's very simple in principle. When you are connected to the Internet, you have an IP address, which uniquely identifies you. When two computers are on the Internet at the same time, they can exchange information directly. Sure, the information goes through other computers as well, but it's possible to make any two computers appear as if they are connected directly to each other. The Internet Service Providers, or any other computers between them, are quite transparent to the connected users. The kind of network we are going to build here is similar to the one we described in the section "Dial-Up Networking," but this time you can have multiple users in the same workgroup.

Setting up an internetwork is a rather complicated procedure. Explaining each of the many parameters and how they work would make this book extremely technical. We preferred to follow a hands-on approach and show you the steps you must follow to complete an internetwork. In addition, we tested the following procedure with several Internet Service Providers to make sure it works, but we cannot guarantee that it will work for everyone.

The first step in building a workgroup over the Internet is for the users who plan to connect to each other to decide which resources they are going to share with other users. Set up the disks and printers (or any other devices) you want to share, as explained in the section "Sharing Resources" (for a more complete discussion on sharing resources on a network, see Chapter 6). Be sure to assign passwords to the shared resources, because this type of connection is not as secure as browsing Web servers or exchanging mail over the Internet. You'll make these resources available to other users, and the only way to keep strangers out of your workgroup is to use passwords.

Open the Control Panel, and double-click on the Network icon. The Network dialog box (shown in Figure 5-26) will appear. The Client for Microsoft Networks component should be installed, and it should also be selected as the Primary Network Logon.

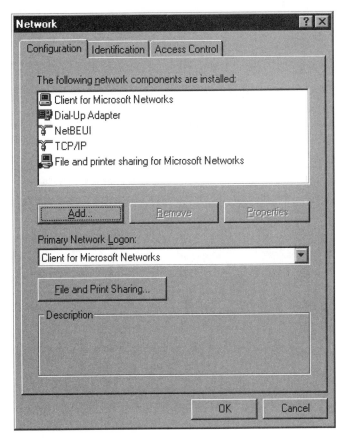

Figure 5-26: This is what the Network dialog box on your computer should look like for Internetworking.

If it's not there, click on the Add button, and you'll see the Select Network Component Type dialog box (Figure 5-27). Select Client, and click on the Add button. This will take you to the Select Network Client dialog box, which has two list boxes. Select Microsoft from the left box, and you'll see a list of network clients in the right box. Select the Client for Microsoft Networks component, and click on OK.

341

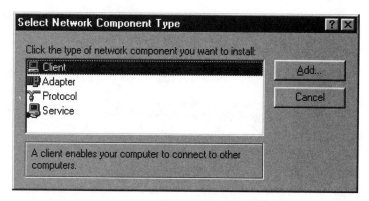

Figure 5-27: The Select Network Component Type dialog box lets you install all the necessary components for internetworking.

Be very careful when networking over the Internet, and assign passwords to shared resources.

Next make sure that the File and printer Sharing for Microsoft Networks service is also installed as a network component in the Network dialog box. If it's not, click on the Add button. You'll see the Select Network Component Type dialog box again. This time select Services, and click on Add. This will take you to the Select Network Service dialog box, which has two list boxes. Select Microsoft from the left box, and you'll see a list of network services in the right box. Select the File and Printer Sharing for Microsoft Networks component, and click on OK. The Configuration tab of the Network dialog box should now look like the one in Figure 5-26. So far, you have asked that your workstation log into other Microsoft networks and be able to share its resources.

Next you must set up a computer name, which other users will use to reach your computer. Click on the Identification tab of the Network dialog box, which is shown in Figure 5-28. Fill in a computer name (the name you see is the one you specified when you installed Windows 95). Fill in the Workgroup entry if you belong to a workgroup or use any name you like if you are not part of a workgroup.

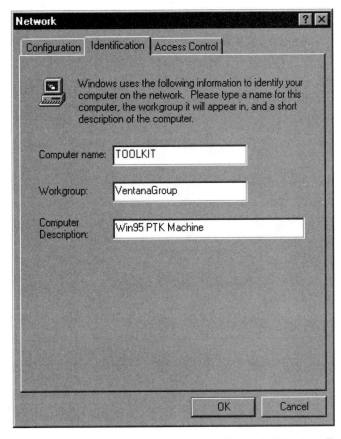

Figure 5-28: The Identification tab of the Network dialog box. Type the name by which you want other internetworked users to reach your computer.

Finally, switch to the Access Control tab (see Figure 5-29), and select the Share-level access control option button. This will allow you to specify passwords for each of the resources you'll be sharing. Unlike local area networks, which are administered and the names of users are known, you don't know in advance the names of the users that you'll be connecting to, so you can't specify user-level access control.

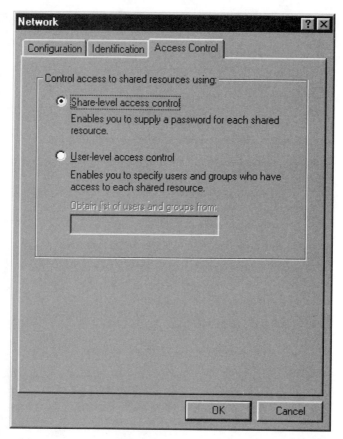

Figure 5-29: For internetworking you must enable Share-level access control.

Now go back to the Configuration tab of the Network window, select the TCP/IP component, and click on Properties. You'll see another dialog box with six tabs this time: Gateway, Bindings, WINS Configuration, Advanced, IP Address, and DNS Configuration. The default entries for most tabs are what you need, but make sure they have the proper values. Figures 5-30 and 5-31 show all six tabs of this dialog box, so that you can compare their contents to yours and adjust the entries on your system accordingly.

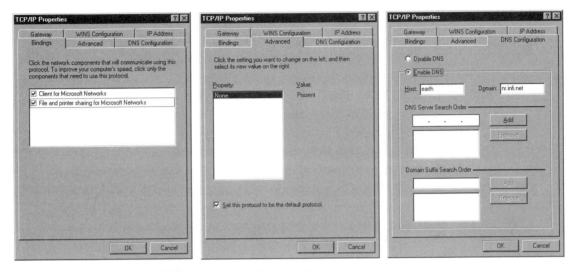

Figure 5-30: The first three TCP/IP Properties dialog box tabs.

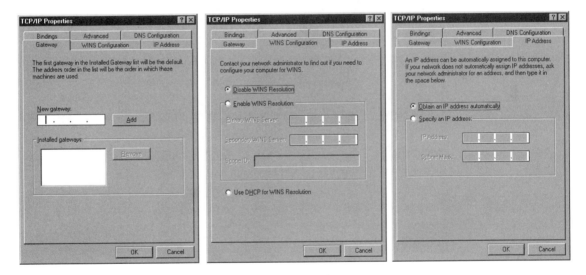

Figure 5-31: The rest of the TCP/IP Properties dialog box tabs.

The IP Address tab specifies whether your Internet Service Provider always assigns the same IP address, or whether a new IP address is automatically assigned to you every time you connect. Check the corresponding box, and if it's always the same enter its value in the IP address box. The subnet mask applies only to fixed

IP addresses, and you should get it from your Internet Service Provider (it is usually 255.255.255.0). If you are assigned a new IP address dynamically every time you log on, just check the first option button.

That's all you have to do here. Depending on which components were already installed, Windows may ask you to restart the computer. Don't do it yet, because you have to change more settings, which also require that the computer be restarted. Right-click on your connection to the Internet Service Provider, and select Properties. In the Connection Properties dialog box, you'll see a button called Server Type. Click on this button, and the Server Types dialog box will appear. Make sure it matches the contents of the Server Types dialog box shown in Figure 5-32.

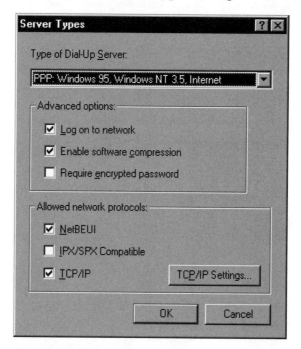

Figure 5-32: This is what your Server Types dialog box should look like for an internetwork connection.

It seems we've fiddled with just about any network and communication setting we could get our hands on. Aren't we finished yet? Now comes the tricky part. We must tell Windows which computer it should contact. If you only want to make your resources available to other users, you can stop here. But if you want to use other people's resources, go on. At this point you can restart your computer for the changes to take effect.

This time we are going to edit two files, which reside in the Windows directory. They are called HOSTS and LMHOSTS (without extensions). If they don't exist, you must create them. In them, you must store the IP addresses of the persons you wish to connect to. Chances are you don't even know your own IP address, let alone someone else's IP address. (We told you this was the tricky part.)

There are two options here. If the person(s) you want to talk to have a fixed IP address, you need to determine what it is and plug it into HOSTS and LMHOSTS. If the IP address is not fixed, though, and is a different one every time this person logs on the Internet, you must learn it and update these files for every connection. That takes the edge off internetworking, doesn't it? It may not be as bad as it sounds. Your provider may give you a fixed IP address, even if it assigns one dynamically to you right now. If not, this is a limitation you have to live with. If you want to set up a workgroup that spans the country, or the globe, for the cost of a local call, you'll probably learn to live with it!

U se the NBTSTAT command to find out your dynamically assigned IP address.

To find out your IP address, connect to the Internet as usual, open a DOS window, and issue the command:

```
NBTSTAT -N
```

This command displays your current IP address and your computer's name. You must pass it to the person you wish to connect to and ask him or her to do the same and pass his or her IP address to you.

Obviously, if you have only one phone line you can't call the other person to let them know your IP address because you will break the Internet connection. If you log in again, you'll be given a different IP address. The way to get around this problem is to send your IP address to the other end by mail. Because both computers are on the Internet, they can communicate via electronic mail. Exchange two mail messages with the IP addresses and then plug the other person's address in the HOSTS and LMHOSTS files.

These two files contain a line for each computer you want to connect to. Once you've obtained the other end's IP address and computer name, append a new line in the LHMOSTS file, like this one:

```
199.134.23.55 FUSION_ONE
```

where 199.134.23.55 is the IP address and must be replaced by whatever IP address the NBTSTAT-N command reported on the remote computer, and Fusion_One is the remote computer's name. Between the IP address and the computer name must be one or more spaces.

Now append a new line in the HOSTS file, like this one:

```
199.134.23.55 CHARLES.ACENET.COM
```

The IP address must match the address of the corresponding entry in the LMHOSTS file and be followed by the hostname. The hostname is the name of the Internet account of the other machine. This is not the user's name. It is the name the other person uses to log on to his or her Internet provider's computer, followed by the provider's computer name. If the address of the other user is Charles@AceNet.com, the hostname will be Charles.AceNet.com.

TIP

The HOSTS and LMHOSTS files are loaded into the memory at startup. Any changes you make to them won't take effect until the next time you start the computer. To reload them in memory, open a DOS window, and run the command: NBTSTAT -R (the R must be upper-case—the parameter -r will do something completely different). Do not restart your computer to load the new contents of the HOSTS and LMHOSTS files because this will invalidate the new entries (unless both computers have fixed IP addresses).

That is rather lengthy, but you don't have to repeat the steps again, except for changing the IP addresses in the HOSTS and LMHOSTS files. Both computers are already connected to the Internet, so you should be able to connect.

Now you're in business. Connect to your ISP by double-clicking on the appropriate Dial-Up Connection icon, and once you've logged in you're also connected to the remote computer (the other user is already connected to his or her ISP or else you wouldn't have the IP address of the other computer). Let's say the other computer's name is Fusion_One (this is one of the computers we used in our experiments). Open the Start menu, select Run, and type the name of the remote computer in the Open text box with two slashes in front of it, as in \\Fusion_One. A few seconds later you should see a window, like the one of Figure 5-33, with the shared resources on the other computer. The remote computer's disks and printers are yours, too!

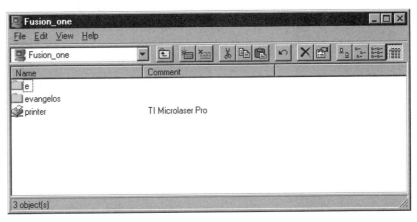

Figure 5-33: Viewing another computer's resources over the Internet.

In Figure 5-33, you can see the shared resources of our good friend Charles who helped us build an internetwork with his computer: his drive (E:), a folder (evangelos), and one of his printers (printer). When sharing a resource, you can assign a name to it. He decided to offer us his hard drive E:, but we also happened to have an E: drive on our computer. Not enough to confuse Windows. As you can see in Figure 5-34, the new drive E: is called E on Fusion_One. Of course, you can always use the Map Network Drive command in Explorer to assign a new name to the shared resources, as explained in the section "Map the Remote Network Drives." Charles's E: drive is mapped to the local drive F, as you can see in Figure 5-34.

We can also print on Charles's printer. It's as simple as printing on our local laser printer, but Charles's printer is a color one and will do a great job with those fractal images! All we have to do in order to print is drop a file from the local desktop on the remote printer's icon. The first time you attempt to print on a remote printer, you'll see a message telling you that Windows must first install the computer before you can use it. Click on Yes, and the Add Printer wizard will take you through the steps, as shown in the lower right window of Figure 5-34. The steps are the same as in installing a new local printer, but you don't have to provide the CD or diskettes with the drivers. Windows 95 will download the files it needs from the other computer.

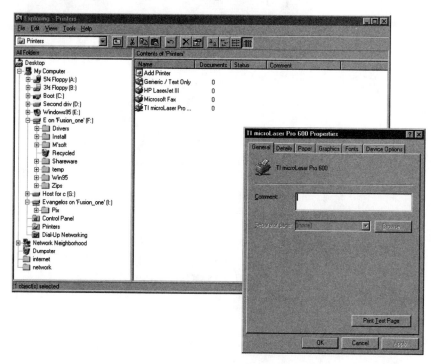

Figure 5-34: Configuring a remote printer on the local desktop.

Wasn't that nice? Windows created a new, fully configured printer on your desktop. You can even access that printer later on, after you disconnect from the remote computer and use it offline. Offline printing means that your printing jobs will be queued and sent to the printer the next time you go online with the same computer.

What can you do with the shared resources? Practically everything you can do with your local resources: open files, run applications, print, and so on. To begin with, you can download any file you want. As you can see in the left pane of the Explorer window in Figure 5-34, Charles has a complete collection of Windows 95 shareware and copies of the latest drivers. It's easy to open two Explorer windows, one with our shareware and another one with Charles's shareware, and download the files we don't have or the ones that are more recent than ours. This beats sending files over the mail, mailing disks, or any other way of exchanging data between computers. We actually have a network.

Another interesting thing you can do over a dial-up connection (whether it is a direct connection or through the Internet) is to install software remotely. This feature is very handy for mobile users, who may need an application that isn't installed on their computer or want to upgrade existing applications. You obviously can't carry around all the disks and CDs you may need in your travels, but what do you do when you need an application that's not on your portable computer?

We could get the files from Charles's machine by mail or by connecting our computers with modems. This, however, requires that we both use a dedicated application. Now Charles can do whatever he wishes on his computer. Well, he can't use the modem, since it's required for our connection, right? Think again! Charles is already connected to his Internet Service Provider, and so is the TOOLKIT computer. Both computers can run any Internet application, such as a Web browser application or electronic mail.

Windows 95 can automatically set up a remote printer.

With internetworking your modem isn't tied to a single machine. It has full access to the Internet.

I Can't Connect!

As we mentioned already, we tested this technique with several Internet Service Providers to make sure it works. But we can't promise you it will work on any configuration. Here's an alternative approach, based on a public WINS server. WINS stands for Windows Internet Naming Server and is a service that maps computer names to IP addresses. WINS runs on Windows NT machines only, and if you are not on a network with a Windows NT workstation, you can't use it.

Fortunately, there's at least one public WINS server (that we know of at the time of this writing). To use this server, go back to the WINS Configuration tab (see Figure 5-35). Double-click on the Network icon in the Control Panel, select TCP/IP from the list of components in the Network dialog box, and click on Properties. In the TCP/IP Properties dialog box, select the WINS Configuration tab. Check the Enable WINS Resolution option, and enter the numbers 204.118.34.6 and 204.118.34.11 as the primary and secondary WINS servers, respectively. These numbers are the addresses of two WINS servers run by Winserve. For more information on these WINS servers and other services provided by Winserve, connect to the www.winserve.com Web page. If you use a WINS server, you don't need the HOSTS file either. However, you must update your LMHOSTS file for each computer you want to connect to. As we explained earlier, you shouldn't restart your computer for the LMHOSTS file to be loaded in memory. Open a DOS window, and issue the NBSTAT -R command.

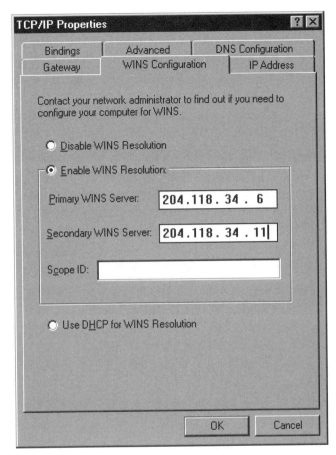

Figure 5-35: Configuring your TCP/IP for using a public WINS server.

Why Internetworking?

So what's the big deal about internetworking? You can do many of the same things with Dial-Up networking and probably faster because you don't have to go through the Internet. The cost of the dial-up connection will be significant if the two computers are not within the same area code, but you'll avoid the inconvenience of having to find out an IP address and plugging it into the HOSTS and LMHOSTS files. Internetworking isn't the most convenient way to network computers, but it has a few advantages.

To begin with, it allows you to connect to any number of computers, not just one at a time. You can add a third and fourth computer to the workgroup quite easily. It also costs less. You can set up a workgroup across the country for pennies. If only there was a better way to handle dynamic IP addresses, internetworking would be easier. Internetworking is a very recent development, and we wouldn't be devoting so many pages to this topic if we didn't think it was promising technology. It will eventually catch up, and the problem of dynamic IP addresses will be somehow resolved. We expect to see companies offering new services in the area of internetworking. Winserve offers internetworking services already, and if you're interested in internetworking, check them out at their www.winserve.com Web page. By the time this book hits the market, even more services may be available.

A FEW NOTES ON TAPI

We mentioned in the introduction to this chapter that the component responsible for Windows 95's communications capabilities is TAPI (Telephony Application Programming Interface). Let's examine the role of TAPI using some examples. Suppose you are using a DUN server to serve connection requests over the phone. When you're finished, you must remember to disable it. If you don't and then attempt to run an old Windows 3.1*x* communication application, you'll find out that the application won't be able to access the phone, even if no calls are incoming. Even CompuServe's front end will report that another application is using the port, even though the modem isn't connected.

To understand what's happening, we must explain how Windows 95 uses TAPI to control serial lines and modems. TAPI is a new layer of functionality in Windows 95, which enables the operating system to control any operation that involves the telephone. We have not yet seen the best of TAPI, which is constantly improving and will integrate computers and telephone lines in a way that was simply impossible with earlier versions of Windows. Support for communications over modems and telephone lines is built into Windows 95, and applications can share the telephone line.

TAPI ensures that a Windows 95 application that simply monitors the phone line doesn't take over the modem.

Of course, you can't be connected to two different sources at the same time, but Windows 95 applications can negotiate which one has control of the modem. You've already seen how to use your computer as a dial-up server to answer incoming calls. The DUN server monitors the modem and replies if another computer requests access to your computer's shared resources. While it's waiting, though, it doesn't stop other applications from using the modem. For example, you can send a fax or connect to the Internet. The DUN server will simply wait as long as you use the Windows 95 built-in faxing mechanism, because there can't be any incoming calls while another application uses the modem.

After the fax is transmitted, the DUN server continues monitoring the line. If you try to start a Windows 3.x application, like Procom or WinCIM, the application will report that it cannot access the serial port to which the modem is connected because another application is using it!—even though the modem is free. Don't try to troubleshoot the application that can't see the modem. These applications were designed for Windows 3.x, and they must take control of the serial port and the modem. And unless they free the serial port, no other application can access it. Windows 95 applications, on the other hand, can negotiate the use of the modem and access it, one at a time. Under Windows 3.x you couldn't have a communications application monitor the line for incoming faxes, while other applications would take control of the modem temporarily and then release the modem. This doesn't happen with TAPI, because Windows 95 controls the modem. An application that needs the modem requests it from the operating system. If no other application is using it, the application that requested the modem can have it.

MOVING ON

In the next chapter we will deal with networking—interconnecting computers to share files and printers, bringing together colleagues for enhanced communication and collaboration. In Chapter 6, "It's a Wired World," you'll find all the information you need to attach your computer to a local area network. You'll find a thorough discussion of workgroup computing, the ideal way for teams and departments to work together more productively. You'll also learn how to set up one or more workgroups within your company and how to manage those workgroups.

It's a Wired World

The 1980s was the decade of the personal computer, a revolution that put computing power into the hands of individuals. The '90s, saw the rapid acceptance of connectivity: tying the individual PCs together to share resources, achieving a kind of power that exceeds the mere sum of its parts. As we cruise into the 21st century, these networks are merging into the fabled Information Superhighway, which ties each personal computer into a fabulous online library, without forcing us to give up the "personal" in personal computer.

WHAT GOOD IS A NETWORK?

Before the age of personal computers, there were only mainframes and terminals. The mainframe performed all the computing. Individual users interacted with the mainframe using a dumb terminal. The terminal's only jobs were to display text sent from the mainframe and relay keystrokes to the mainframe. The network was simply the wiring needed to communicate between the mainframe and the terminals.

The advent of personal computers changed all that. Each desktop has its own complete computer system with its own operating system and software. Every user creates files on his or her own hard drive and prints on his or her own printer. Each user is responsible for installing his or her own software. In effect, each worker is an island, a computing world of his/her own. This was manageable when only a few employees brought a PC into the office to get their job done more efficiently. Now, however, it's commonplace for *every* employee to use a PC.

Networks make employees more productive and help them get the most out of their computers.

Most companies with more than a dozen employees employ a full-time system administrator. This is the "PC guru," "MIS director," "sysop," or perhaps just an employee who knows something about computers. In the days of the mainframe, the system administrator had full control over the computing environment, since the entire computing environment was centralized and contained within a single mainframe. The disadvantage of a mainframe is that it is shared with dozens, if not hundreds or even thousands, of other users. Even the most powerful mainframe, when cut into little pieces, can't match the speed and flexibility of a PC on each person's desk, a real personal computer, not a terminal, with its own CPU, memory, and mass storage.

Put yourself into the shoes of the system administrator facing a transition from a minicomputer or mainframe to a mixed environment of heterogeneous PCs. Each PC has its own operating system software and programs. Some users like to use Excel for spreadsheets and WordPerfect for word processing, others use Lotus 1-2-3 and Microsoft Word. What if you wanted to upgrade all PCs to the same operating system (Windows 3.1 or Windows 95) to run the same software? You'd have to show up at each desk, one at a time, and manually load the software from disks or CD-ROM.

If the PCs are networked together, the administrator might still have to install the software manually at each workstation, but at least the installation software could be stored centrally on the network. And many programs allow automated "push" installations. Driven by a special mini-program called an *installation script*, the install program is sent to each PC on the network, automatically executed, and the software is automatically installed, even customized for particular computers or employees.

Windows 95 makes it much easier for an administrator to manage PCs. Let's say you wanted to inspect and modify some settings in the SYSTEM.INI file of each PC. One way to do this is to edit each file locally, which could get out of hand quickly, especially if there are hundreds of employees, each with a PC. With a network, the administrator can stay at his own desk and access the SYSTEM.INI on the drives shared by each machine. (More on file sharing later.) Even better, Windows 95 allows many network settings to be specified just once in a single file on the network, and the changes are then automatically applied to all the other machines on the network the next time the users log in.

Networks also make the employees more productive and help them get the most out of their computers. To illustrate the advantage of networking, consider the alternative—the dreaded "floppy shuffle."

Internet Terminals: Undoing the PC Revolution?

Ironically, some industry pundits are calling for a return to the old days, in many ways undoing the PC revolution. Instead of owning a powerful personal computer, most consumers would buy an inexpensive "Internet terminal." This box would be little more than a stripped-down PC with very little memory, little or no hard disk space, basic graphics, and "deluxe" optional features, such as a printer or a floppy drive. The idea is that you only need enough hardware to run a World Wide Web browser. Every other application could be run within the Web browser, and the programs themselves would be downloaded on the fly from the Internet and executed locally.

Granted, this scenario has some appealing aspects. The hardware would be considerably less expensive than today's PCs, perhaps even under $500, which would help open up the Internet to everyone. And consumers would never have to struggle with a sophisticated operating system or go through the trials and tribulations of installing and uninstalling software, running out of hard drive space, configuring a DOS game for MS-DOS mode—what have you. ➡

You'd let the experts worry about how the software is configured and delivered to your machine. This client-server model is appealing to some, because it gives central control of most aspects of computing to the system administrators, just as in the old mainframe days. You wouldn't need a big hard drive because the server would store all your files. There wouldn't really be any software installed on your computer because you wouldn't really have a computer—just a Web browser machine.

From the point of view of supporting users, this method makes a lot of sense. It would finally turn computers into appliances, and with new programming languages such as Java or Visual Basic script, Web browsers now have the power to run programs embedded within Web pages.

Doing the Floppy Shuffle

Even the most powerful PCs can be limiting. Without a network, there's no way to share files. Employees rarely work alone; instead, they collaborate. One employee generates a document or spreadsheet, which is reviewed by another. Yet another person may incorporate the document in a report. It may need to go back to the original author or other coworkers for revisions.

For years, many companies relied on floppy disks to do the trick, and far too many small businesses continue to depend on a "SneakerNet." Let's say Mike needs some financial data for a report. He calls up Robin, who copies a spreadsheet to a floppy disk, and walks over to Mike's desk with it. Mike takes the floppy, copies it to his hard drive, and tosses the floppy in a ever-growing stack of "scratch" floppies to be eventually reused. If he discovers a mistake in the spreadsheet, he can correct it, but then he needs to copy the file to a floppy and give it back to Robin. Since Robin has already updated the spreadsheet, she has to carefully compare her version with Mike's.

This scenario gets even more complicated if Robin and Mike work on different floors of the same building, or worse, if Mike works in Cincinnati and Robin operates out of Cleveland. Then the files have be transmitted via modem, the mail, or an overnight delivery service.

Working Together by Sharing Files

With a network, only one copy of the spreadsheet resides in a central location. (For this discussion, it doesn't matter where.) If Mike needs a copy of the spreadsheet, he just looks for it on the network hard drive. He can modify the spreadsheet if he has the necessary permissions (set up by the network manager), and when Robin loads the spreadsheet, she'll see Mike's changes have been incorporated. The network also can prevent more than one person from making conflicting changes to a document at the same time. It also helps prevent "versionitis," which happens if everyone works on his or her own copy of the file without being able to reconcile the differences between versions of the file.

Companies can leverage their investment by sharing equipment.

While today's personal computers typically have large hard drives, many companies prefer to use a huge, shared hard drive, called a *file server*. That way individual PCs don't need big hard drives, and centralized storage makes it much easier to manage files and folders companywide. For example, all the information on the file server can be backed up to tape from a single location. Without a network, every employee is responsible for keeping backup copies of important files, and that's something you simply can't rely on.

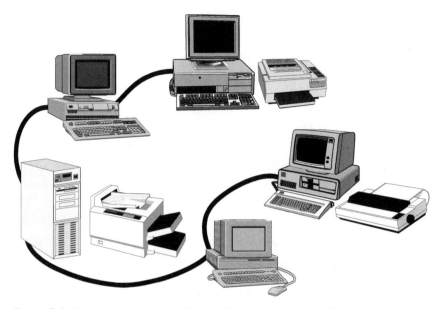

Figure 6-1: A network is a constellation of computers sharing files, printers, and other devices.

Leveraging Your Equipment With Printer Sharing

Instead of each employee using his or her own printer, companies can leverage their investment by sharing equipment. So rather than buy a cheap desktop printer for each employee, the company can purchase a few high-volume sophisticated laser printers and use the network to connect the printers to every computer in the building. Mike doesn't have to change the way he works; he prints his documents as usual, then walks over to the laser printer to pick up his printouts. Employees can also continue to use their personal printers, yet can use the network to share them with co-workers who lack printers of their own. (The printers attached to the two computers in Figure 6-1 can be accessed by any of the other computers on the network.)

Companies can also share other peripherals, such as modems, scanners, and CD-ROM drives. While you can buy devices, such as switch boxes and extended-length printer cabling for sharing printers and modems, inexpensive networks are a much better alternative.

Secure Networking

Networks also provide another important advantage: security. With a centralized hard drive, the network manager can decide who gets access to which files. Individual files or directories (folders) are marked so that only authorized users or groups of users can access the files. Files can be set as read-only to prevent changes except by authorized users, and files, folders, even entire file servers, can be hidden. For example, the accounting system must be shielded from an employee who's curious to find out the salary of a rival.

The initial release of Windows 95 suffered from some security loopholes, which have been fixed by updates from Microsoft. Also, peer-to-peer networking is inherently less secure than using a dedicated file server. We'll tell you what to look out for, and how to seal up any cracks in your security, later in this chapter.

Workgroup Computing

As we mentioned earlier, networks foster group and team computing. Special subnetworks can be set up to allow teams to focus on the documents they work with. It's possible to link together individual PCs into a network, even without a central file server. The files on each employee's hard drive can be read by an employee using a different computer. And the sharing is not indiscriminate. Employees or workgroup managers can decide which files or folders are shared on which computers.

Collaborative computing also relies on software designed to take advantage of networks. For example, if everyone uses the same (or compatible) scheduling software, you can look at another employee's schedule to see if he's available for a meeting or when she'll return from vacation. Workgroup word processing allows you to route a document to a distribution list. Each employee makes changes or notes, which are shown using electronic "post-it" notes or revision marks (underlines for insertions, strike-throughs for deletions). The document is automatically sent to the next person in the team.

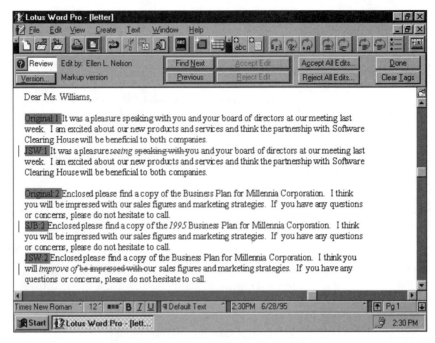

Figure 6-2: Lotus Word Pro is ideal for collaborative editing between members of a team.

Electronic mail (e-mail) is a boon for company communication, making it much easier to send memos and correspondence, and it provides a straightforward mechanism for routing documents. E-mail also provides a link to outside network services and desktop faxing.

Even more exciting, users on a network can use desktop conferencing to communicate face to face using video cameras. Whether you go to the trouble and expense of using video, desktop conferencing gives employees the opportunity to work on the same document at the same time, dynamically. You actually see the other person moving the cursor, highlighting or deleting text, right on your screen, and when it's your turn, the other person can watch as you work. It's as if you both were working on the same computer using dual keyboards and mice.

Other Benefits of a Network

Redirection makes the networked drives seem no different than the real hard drives inside your computer.

While most networks are confined to a single building, larger companies can link their branch offices together, so collaboration is possible even across long distances.

Networks also avoid redundancy. Software can be installed to the file server just once, and with appropriate licensing, employees can run the software from the central location. If software needs to be updated, only the primary copy has to be changed, instead of having to reinstall the software on every computer individually.

HOW NETWORKS WORK

Ideally, a network should be as unobtrusive as possible. At its simplest, a network is a big hard drive out there somewhere (in the file server closet or on another employee's desktop computer). The goal of a network is to make it seem that these hard drives are no different than the real hard drive inside your computer.

Drive Redirection

You're familiar with C:, the drive letter of your computer's hard drive. If you have more than one hard drive or a CD-ROM, you may also have a D: drive or an E: drive. If you're connected to a network, you can also have a drive letter corresponding to a file server or a folder on another computer. Your F: drive would look and act like an ordinary hard drive, but it wouldn't actually be part of your computer. The only requirement to use this drive is that you would have to attach it to the network.

This trick of relocating the server hard drive to your computer is known as *redirection*. You simply "map" a network drive to whichever drive letter you like. (This may have already been done for you by your network supervisor.)

The main server drive (or *volume*) is mapped to a drive letter such as F: on your computer. A server can also map folders (directories) to a drive letter, so that when you open G:\LETTER.DOC, you're actually opening something like F:\WORDPROC\DOCUMENTS\LETTER.DOC. You only see the files, because G: is the "root" of the shared folder F:\WORDPROC\DOCUMENTS.

Windows 95 also makes it easy to browse network drives without using drive letters, which is especially important when you realize that you only have 26 drive letters total. Since you need some drive letters for your own computer, that leaves fewer than two dozen possible network drives or folders.

So instead of using the G: drive to get your documents, you double-click on Network Neighborhood on your Windows 95 desktop, then on the file server's icon, then on the WordProc folder, then the Documents folder. Or you can open a file directly using the Universal Naming Convention (UNC), something like Publications\Word Processing\Documents. But it's up to you (and your network supervisor) which method you use. If you prefer drive letters, you can keep right on using them. We'll get into the details a little later in this chapter.

TWO TYPES OF NETWORKING

A network can consist of multiple workstations all linked to a central file server, or it can simply link the workstations to one another. Both methods have advantages.

Dedicated Networks

Typically, a computer network ties individual PCs into a central hard drive, stored on a special computer called a *server*, or a *file server*, so named because it "serves up" files, just as a waiter serves a meal at a restaurant. But a server isn't limited to this role. It can also run programs for the users of the network. Instead of processing a database file on your local PC, you can just tell the server which records you're looking for, and it can automatically perform the necessary queries and sorting. This is much more efficient because the server has direct access to the data on its own hard drive. This technique is known as *client-server* computing (illustrated in Figure 6-3). Often, such a server is actually called an *application server*.

Figure 6-3: Two models of client-server computing: *server push* means that the network software automatically sends commands and information to your client machine, whereas *client pull* means your machine specifically requests updated data and runs programs on its own initiative.

The server in a large network is dedicated solely to the task of serving up files for users. It's like a master computer, but it's really only another computer on the network with a special job to do. Later, we'll see it's possible to use any computer on the network for sharing files, but on a large network you typically don't have an employee using the file server as a desktop computer. So it's called a *dedicated file server*. An example of a dedicated file server is a computer running Novell NetWare.

Novell NetWare & Microsoft Windows NT

The two most popular network operating systems for IBM-compatible computers are Novell NetWare and Microsoft Windows NT. (Versions of Unix and other network operating systems are also available for PCs, but we can safely ignore them for this discussion.)

Windows 95 provides excellent client support for both NetWare and NT. (A *client* is an individual PC that's connected to a network. If you've implemented a peer-to-peer network, your computer can be both a client and a server, but usually the client is the *user* of a network.)

Novell NetWare does not use MS-DOS, employing instead a unique disk operating system that makes it easy to secure the files

The two most popular network operating systems for IBM-compatible computers are Novell NetWare and Microsoft Windows NT.

on the file server. Even if you boot the file server from a DOS disk, you can't access the files on it. You must attach to the operating system from a client machine to actually use the network, although some management tools run from the file server console (the monitor and keyboard attached to the file server computer).

Windows NT is the "big brother" of Windows 3.1 and Windows 95. Before Windows 95, it was the only Microsoft operating system that could run 32-bit Windows applications. Windows NT is fast gaining ground, displacing NetWare and other network operating systems. Because Windows NT has a friendly Windows-style user interface (and can now run the Windows 95 user interface), it is much easier to set up and maintain. Windows NT is also more powerful, with full multithreaded multitasking and the ability to exploit multiple CPUs (*symmetric multitasking*).

Nondedicated Networking

The disadvantage of peer-to-peer computing is that it lacks centralization.

A popular alternative to server-based computing, *peer-to-peer* networking simply makes the files on each individual computer available to the users of every other computer. So if I had a file on my hard drive to share with you, you'd look on your H: drive, which is actually the C: drive on my computer. But it appears that my hard drive has been mysteriously transplanted into your computer and assigned a drive letter of H: (see Figure 6-4).

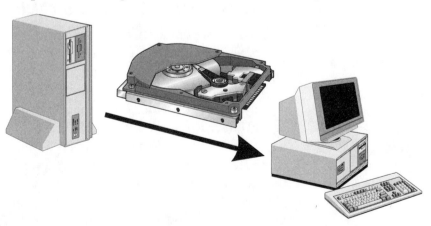

Figure 6-4: Drive redirection is at the core of networking, making my hard drive appear to be attached to your computer.

Peer-to-peer networking also makes it easy to share printers. Even if you don't have a printer, you can print your documents, and they'll emerge from my printer (or vice-versa, if you're the lucky one to have the printer).

The disadvantage of peer-to-peer computing is that it lacks centralization. It can also be inconvenient, because I can't access the files on your computer if you have it turned off.

For this reason, many peer-to-peer networks rely on at least one computer that is turned on all the time and acts, in effect, as a file server. But it's not a *dedicated* file server. You're free to use it as a desktop computer, too. (For best results, elect the fastest computer with the most storage as the main server. That way the local user won't suffer the demands of file sharing too much. Ideally, a nondedicated file server will have another, smaller, hard drive set aside just for the local user.)

WINDOWS 95 NETWORKING

Windows 95 is an excellent tool for taking advantage of a computer network. It includes the desktop networking features of Windows for Workgroups, it interacts with Windows NT, and it fully supports third-party networks such as Novell NetWare.

Windows for Workgroups was a pretty good solution for using Windows on a network, but Windows 95 does so much more.

Windows 95 is easier to use on a network. No complicated steps are required to log in, attach to, or browse a file server—just open up the Network Neighborhood icon on the Windows 95 desktop, and you'll see a list of all the computers you can explore.

Networking is fully integrated into the desktop so you can view files on file servers just by opening a window. You can even use long filenames with most networks, once they're set up properly.

Performance is also enhanced with full 32-bit protected-mode drivers (as opposed to real-mode MS-DOS drivers that gobble up conventional memory) and file system features such as *client-side caching* that speeds network file access by keeping the most frequently accessed network files in memory.

Robustness is improved: no longer will your computer lock up if the file server connection is dropped or if someone accidentally disconnects a cable.

Windows 95 also enhances networking with techniques, such as shortcuts, which let you refer to files on other computers or servers as if they were stored locally on your computer. You can even e-mail shortcuts, so you don't have to tell others where to find a file on a network. Just send them a shortcut to the file; and when they double-click the shortcut, they are automatically connected to the network resource, and the file is opened on their computers.

ABCs OF NETWORKING

It's useful to define some important networking terms for the sake of our later discussion. You'll see how these elements fit together into a functioning network.

Workgroups

What if you don't have (or can't afford) the hardware and software resources required for Windows NT or NetWare? Set up a peer-to-peer network using Windows 95. (You can also use Windows for Workgroups 3.11, but it's an older technology that is completely supplanted by Windows 95.)

With Windows 95 peer-to-peer networking, you have almost all the advantages of a dedicated network. You can even dedicate a computer to act like a file server and use it as a desktop computer when needed.

Windows 95 networking (also called Microsoft Networking—not to be confused with the Microsoft Network online service) revolves around the concept of a *workgroup*, which is often a subset of a larger network. You can mix Windows 95 networking on the same network with Windows NT and NetWare, or you can use it to connect just a few computers.

Usually, only computers within the same workgroup can communicate using Microsoft Networking (see Figure 6-5). The idea is that the accounting department has its own workgroup network, marketing has another, and product development yet another workgroup. A workgroup can be a network unto itself, with each machine in the workgroup only attached to the other machines in that same workgroup. Workgroups can be hooked together to create a larger network, or a larger network can be parceled into workgroups. A workgroup is more of a logical distinction, then, than a physical one. Members of a workgroup see only the files and printers (resources) shared by the members of that workgroup.

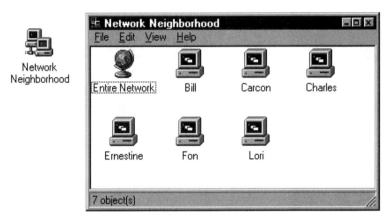

Figure 6-5: When you browse Network Neighborhood, you can see a list of all the other computers in your workgroup.

Workgroup networking is easier to manage and maintain by its users, who aren't full-time network supervisors.

This may seem to be a serious limitation, but it's by design. Workgroup networking is easier to manage and maintain by employees who, after all, aren't full-time network supervisors. If you prefer all the computers in your company work together, all you have to do is use a single workgroup for all of them, instead of individual workgroups for each team or department.

Even if your company uses more than one workgroup, you aren't necessarily prevented from using shared resources on a different workgroup. Using the Entire Network icon in Network Neighborhood, you can view a list of all workgroups.

Clients

A *client* is a user of a network. More specifically, a client is the network software, or driver, that Windows 95 uses to communicate with a network operating system. The two primary clients that come as part of Windows 95 are Client for NetWare Networks and Client for Microsoft Networks.

(We don't want to ignore the contributions made by other network operating systems, such as Lantastic or Banyan Vines, but the fact remains that NetWare and Windows NT are the dominant file server operating systems on this planet. While Lantastic is an excellent peer-to-peer network system, why pay extra for functionality that's already built into Windows 95?)

Only one client can be your *primary* client, but you can be logged into both types of networks at the same time. If you use Microsoft Networking as your primary client, it can automatically log you into a NetWare network at the same time.

Protocols

A *protocol* is the language used to communicate over the network cabling. Traditionally, Microsoft Networking has used the NetBEUI protocol, while NetWare uses IPX/SPX. With Windows 95, Microsoft recognized the popularity and flexibility of IPX/SPX by making it the primary network protocol (although NetBEUI is also installed by default). The protocol used by the client has to match one of the protocols supported by the file server and by other clients on a peer-to-peer network.

Why are protocols important? It's a matter of language, so to speak.

A busy network has to send and receive thousands of files all at the same time. Data is flowing between the server and every computer on the network and also between computers on the network. The network "pipe" can carry only one signal at any given instant, however. If you're opening a large document, does everyone else have to wait until you're finished before they can take their turn?

A busy network has to send and receive thousands of files all at the same time.

No, because all the files are atomized into *packets*. So your 100K spreadsheet file would be split into dozens of smaller subfiles. These packets can be more efficiently routed. If your computer is too busy to retrieve a packet, the file server can resend it. If the packet contains errors, the network can send just that packet again, instead of the entire file. And everyone can access the network at the same time, because your packets are *interleaved* (mixed in sequence) with everyone else's packets.

The network interface card in your computer samples all the packets that travel through the network, but it picks only the packets that are stamped with your address. Your address is a number that identifies your computer (or *node*) on the network.

So we get back to protocols. A network protocol is a standard for formatting and addressing these packets. Because the packets are formatted, the same language has to be used on both ends of the connection. It's similar to word processors—Microsoft Word is not designed to use the same formatting codes as WordPerfect, and attempting to convert documents between the two systems always loses something in the translation.

TCP/IP is fast becoming the world's most popular protocol. It stands for Transmission Control Protocol/Internet Protocol, and its use as the universal protocol of the Internet helps explain its ascendance.

Which protocol is best for networking? For small networks, NetBEUI provides the best mix of performance and flexibility, but IPX/SPX is also a good choice. IPX/SPX can be routed between different file servers, unlike NetBEUI. You'll need IPX/SPX if you intend to link your workgroup network with a Novell network, even if you only use dial-up networking (described in Chapter 5 "Communicating With the World") to make the connection.

TIP

If you're networked to other machines with only the NetBEUI protocol installed, you won't be able to use dial-up networking (DUN) or direct cable connection (DCC) at the same time. NetBEUI gets confused about which network is which. The solution is to add IPX/SPX protocol for use with DUN/DCC. You can also use IPX/SPX for the entire network, as long as each computer has that protocol installed.

TCP/IP's small packet size makes it ideal for slower network connections, so it's preferred for transport between networks on a wide area network (WAN). However, TCP/IP can be difficult to configure and requires a full-time file server to administer the TCP/IP accounts, so it's not suitable for a pure peer-to-peer network.

While you can use more than one protocol on the same network, and even on the same computer, multiple protocols can result in somewhat slower network operation. For our discussion, we recommend IPX/SPX as the best all-around small network protocol.

Adapters

An *adapter* is a device that physically connects you to a network. Usually this means a network interface card (NIC), a plug-in circuit board (similar to a video card, modem card, etc., that you insert inside your computer). Like most plug-in cards, the NIC requires an unused I/O address and usually a unique IRQ setting. The IRQ (Interrupt *ReQuest*) is a special signal sent to the computer by a peripheral to get its attention. Each device has a different IRQ and the computer checks periodically for interrupt request. When it sees one, it interrupts the current operation to service the device that issued the interrupt request.

Your NIC has to be compatible with the cabling used by the network, although it is possible to mix both cabling and different network cards. For our purposes, the type of NIC you buy will use either twisted pair (telephone-style wiring with modular jacks) or BNC (coaxial cable). (See Figure 6-6.) Many NICs support both types of connections.

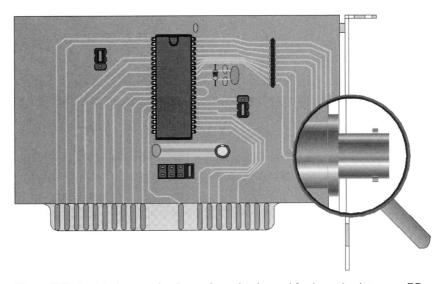

Figure 6-6: A typical network adapter is a plug-in card for insertion into your PC and cabled to other network cards.

The Windows 95 dial-up networking software is itself a kind of network adapter.

You can also buy PCMCIA credit card–type network cards for notebook and laptop computers and network interface modules that plug into the parallel port of a PC or laptop. These are easier to configure, but are more costly and sometimes not as fast as a true network card.

The Windows 95 DUN software is itself a kind of network adapter. It's a software adapter that converts your modem into a network interface device. The DUN adapter takes care of all the details required for placing a call and connecting with the remote computer. Otherwise, it works identically to a network card, except that it's much slower. (The remote computer at the other end of the connection also has to use the DUN adapter or run a program that can communicate with it, such as the Remote Access Server, or RAS, in Windows for Workgroups and Windows NT.)

Services

A *service* is special software that provides utility to a network client. One kind of service is an *agent* that's used by the network to control some aspect of your computer. For example, the Arcada

Backup Agent is a service that can be used by the Arcada Backup software for NetWare or Windows NT to access the files on your computer to back them up to tape.

More typically, the term *service* refers to either File and Printer Sharing for Microsoft Networks or File and Printer Sharing for Novell Networks. You must install one of these file sharing services to allow peer-to-peer networking. If you aren't on a Novell network, use the Microsoft networks file sharing service. It allows each user to set permissions for access to his or her files and folders using passwords. Any user who knows the right password can access your files. This is called *share-level access control*.

If your network is part of a Windows NT network, you can also assign permissions to authorized Windows NT users or groups of users. Windows 95 verifies the user's request using the Windows NT server. This is called *user-level access control*.

With File and Printer Sharing for NetWare Networks, you can choose to set permissions based on NetWare *groups* and *users*. This too is user-level access control.

CONFIGURING NETWORK NEIGHBORHOOD

Perhaps your computer is already configured for Windows 95 networking. If so, you'll be less interested in setting things up than in getting things done, so skip ahead to the section "Logging In." If you're still with me, you're probably interested in getting Windows 95 to work with your network, so let's take a look "inside" the Network Neighborhood icon.

Configuration

To get started, you'll need to access the property sheets for Network Neighborhood by right-clicking on the icon and choosing Properties from the pop-up menu. Don't worry if you can't see this icon on your desktop. You can also access your network settings by using the Network icon in the Control Panel.

Each property sheet is also linked to numerous dialog boxes and controls such as drop-down lists.

After you double-click on Networks in the Control Panel, or right-click to get the properties for the Network Neighborhood desktop icon, you'll get a collection of property sheets collectively called Network Properties. It consists of three property sheets, each with a tabbed heading: Configuration, Identification, and Access Control. Each property sheet is also linked to numerous dialog boxes and controls such as drop-down lists. In this section, we'll focus on the options related to the Configuration property sheet, which is shown in Figure 6-7.

TIP

Even though the property sheets appear distinct, they all share the same OK and Cancel button. So don't press OK unless you've completed working with all three Network property sheets. And don't press Cancel to undo the changes you made in one property sheet, or you'll lose the changes you've made to all property sheets. Of course, this may be just what you have in mind, especially if you were just looking at a sheet and made a mistake.

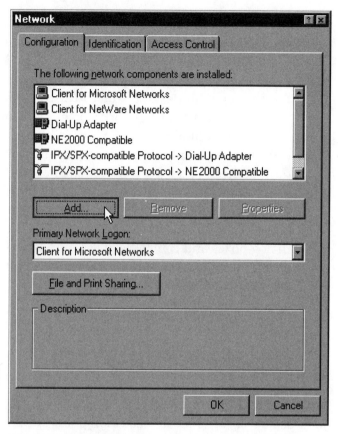

Figure 6-7: You can add, remove, and set the properties for any network component from the Configuration tab of the Network Neighborhood property sheets.

The main feature of this Configuration sheet is a window with a white background that shows all the network components that are currently installed (yours won't necessarily match up with what's shown in the figure). A network component can be a client, adapter, protocol, or a service. You must have at least one client, one adapter, and one protocol to use Windows 95 networking. Before we get into specifics, let's finish describing some other items on the Configuration property sheet.

Use the box labeled Primary Network Logon to choose between the clients you've installed. This is the client that actually logs you in to the network. If you use both the Microsoft networking and NetWare networking clients, choose Client for Microsoft Networks, which will automatically log you in to the NetWare network.

TIP

If you travel with a portable computer, you may want to choose Windows Logon as the Primary Network Logon so that you're not asked for a name and password when you're not connected to the network.

Configuration: Enabling File and Printer Sharing

The Configuration property sheet is also where you enable File and Printer Sharing. You'll want to enable it to set up peer-to-peer networking and share your hard drive and/or printer with other users. File and Printer Sharing uses the Primary Network Logon setting (also on the Configuration property sheet, shown in Figure 6-7) to install either File and Printer Sharing for Microsoft networks, or File and Printer Sharing for NetWare networks. In other words, if your Primary Network Logon is Client for Microsoft Networks and you enable File and Printer sharing, you have added File and Printer Sharing for Microsoft networks.

TIP

Use File and Printer Sharing for Microsoft networks if any of the other computers on the network are running Windows for Workgroups. If all computers in the workgroup are running Windows 95 and are using the Microsoft client for NetWare, you can use the NetWare version of File and Printer Sharing. You can install either type by using the Add button and choosing Service—regardless of the Primary Network Logon setting. We'll explain more about File and Printer Sharing later in this chapter.

Configuration: Adding Components

As we mentioned, the Configuration property sheet is where you set up the software components of your network, the clients, adapters, protocols, and services. Before you can configure a network component, you may need to add it to the list. Just click the Add button to install components, as shown in Figure 6-8.

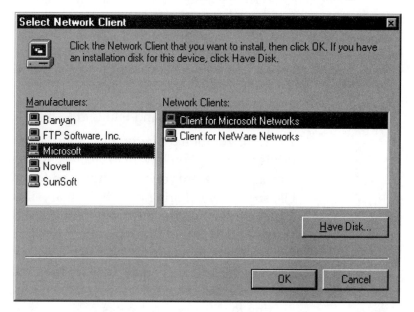

Figure 6-8: Choose the manufacturer on the left and the name of the component on the right. (Use Microsoft as the manufacturer for most components.)

Configuration: Client for Microsoft Networks

Figure 6-9 shows the Client for Microsoft Networks Properties sheet. If your computer is part of a Windows NT network, turn on the check box for *Log on to Windows NT domain,* and fill in the name of your Windows NT server (the domain). You can also choose between Quick logon or Logon and restore network connections. You may prefer the latter if you want to make sure your network connections (mapped drives) are available before you start working.

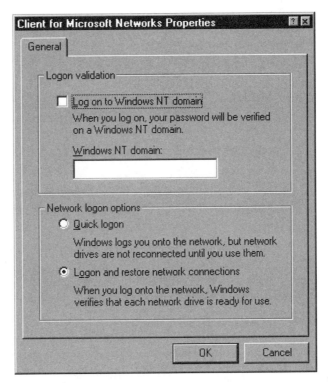

Figure 6-9: You don't have to fill in a domain if you're only using Windows 95 for peer-to-peer networking.

Configuration: Client for NetWare Networks

Windows 95 may install the Client for NetWare Networks, even if you don't attach to a NetWare file server. In this case, you can click on the icon for NetWare and then press the Remove button. This frees up memory.

If you are on a NetWare network, double-click the icon for Client for NetWare Networks to see something like Figure 6-10. Use the General page to type in the name of your NetWare file server. If your location uses multiple servers, you can choose one from a list by clicking the arrow next to the text box. Use the other drop-down box to choose which drive letter to assign to the first NetWare volume (normally F:).

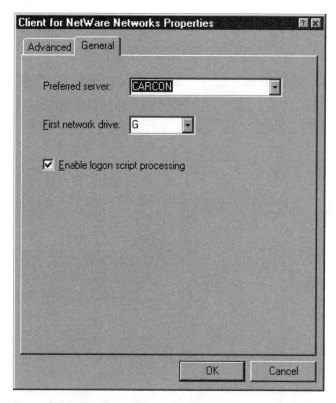

Figure 6-10: The General page for NetWare lets you specify your favorite file server and which drive to use as the first network drive.

TSR programs are forbidden in NetWare login scripts for Windows 95.

Part of logging in to a NetWare file server is executing the *login script*, a special batch file that NetWare administrators use to set up default printer assignments and so forth. You can prevent this script from running by turning off the Enable logon script processing check box. You might need to do this if the login script attempts to start any TSR (Terminate and Stay Resident) programs, which are *verboten* with Windows 95.

TIP

Instead of using the Client for NetWare Networks, you may for some reason need to use the standard DOS drivers (monolithic IPX or ODI). Delete the Microsoft client, and use the Add button to install either the NetWare shell 3.x or 4.x client. (This assumes you've already installed the ODI/NETX network client for DOS in the computer's AUTOEXEC.BAT file.) You'll also need to turn on the option Real Mode (16-bit) ODI Driver on the Driver Type tab heading for the network adapter.

If you do use the NETX driver, remember to add a LASTDRIVE setting to CONFIG.SYS. The NETX client uses the drive following LASTDRIVE for the LOGIN directory. Contrary to common belief, you don't need to always log in using drive F: (with LASTDRIVE set to E:). If you do this, there won't be any drive letters available for Windows peer-to-peer networking. If you set LASTDRIVE=O, the NetWare login directory is mapped to P:, which is perfectly legitimate, and you'll have drive letters between F: and O: available for mapping to non-NetWare resources.

Configuration: Adapter

Next you'll want to verify the settings for your network adapter (shown in Figure 6-7 as NE2000 Compatible). Click on the adapter's name in the list of components, and choose Properties. (You can double-click on any component to access its properties.)

The property sheets for the NE2000 card are shown in Figure 6-11. (The properties for the Dial-Up Adapter are similar.)

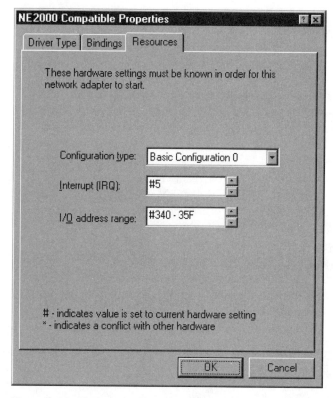

Figure 6-11: Choose the Resources tab to configure your network card.

The Driver Type property sheet lets you decide what type of driver to use. We recommend sticking with the 32-bit drivers unless you're forced to use older Windows 3.1 drivers or DOS drivers.

The Bindings property sheet tells Windows which protocol the adapter uses. Normally, this will be set automatically. A network adapter must be *bound* to (associated with) at least one network protocol.

On the Resources property sheet, use the Up and Down arrow keys, or type the correct values, to configure your card to match its hardware settings (unless it's a plug and play card, which is automatically configured).

The Dial-Up Adapter uses a property sheet named Advanced instead of Resources. Since you won't need to change any of its settings, we'll move on to the properties for your protocol.

Configuration: Protocol

Use the Microsoft TCP/IP protocol to get Internet connectivity.

We discussed why you need a network protocol earlier. The protocol you use must match the protocols used by the computers you want to link with. If the protocol you need isn't shown on the list found within Figure 6-7, click the Add button to create it. When you click Add, a dialog box pops up with a list of protocols to choose from, grouped by vendor. The most common protocols for Windows 95 were developed by Microsoft, so first click on Microsoft, then click on one of the protocols (TCP/IP, NetBEUI, or IPX). For example, add the Microsoft TCP/IP protocol to get Internet connectivity. Use IPX/SPX to connect to NetWare and later versions of Windows NT. Use NetBEUI to connect to earlier Windows NT servers and Windows for Workgroups.

When you've finished adding protocols, you'll be returned to the Configuration property sheet. In the list of components, you'll see one protocol entry for each adapter that the protocol is *bound* to, or associated with. Double-click on a protocol in this list to get its properties, as shown in Figure 6-12.

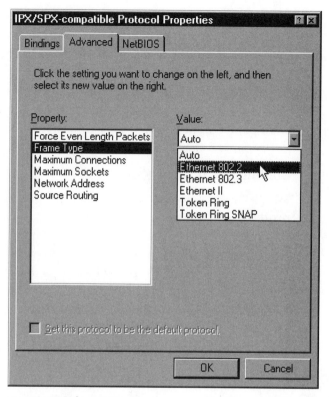

Figure 6-12: IPX/SPX properties let you bind the protocol, enable NetBIOS, and fiddle with advanced settings.

On the protocol's property sheets, click the Bindings tab to link the protocol to an adapter. (You can also bind from the adapter's property sheet, as we mentioned earlier.) Use the NetBIOS tab if you want to turn on NetBIOS support, which isn't used very much these days but is required for some network applications, including WinChat. Exchange also uses NetBIOS, if enabled, to flag urgent messages.

TIP

If Windows 95 doesn't detect the IPX frame type correctly for your network, you may have to choose it manually. Use the Advanced tab of the IPX/SPX Properties sheet to choose a particular frame type, such as Ethernet 802.3.

Configuration: File and Printer Sharing for Microsoft Networks

On a pure peer-to-peer network, there's no one in charge.

If you've chosen to use File and Printer Sharing (discussed earlier), you can double-click on it in the list of components to get its properties, as shown in Figure 6-13. There's only one item shown that you may want to fool with: Browse Master.

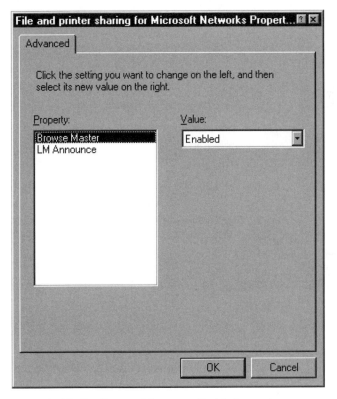

Figure 6-13: Set Browse Master to Enabled on at least one computer for best results with peer-to-peer sharing.

On a pure peer-to-peer network, there's no one in charge. Since there's no server, where is the "master list" of all computers kept up to date? Normally, this is handled cooperatively. One of the computers in the network is elected a *browse master*. The process of choosing a browse master is complicated, but it's usually the machine that's turned on first or has been left turned on the longest. One or more computers are elected as a backup browse master, which update the list periodically from the browse master. If a browse master computer is turned off or logged off from the network, one of the backup browse masters takes over the job of primary browse master.

All this can take up to 15 minutes to be updated, which explains why you sometimes can't see every computer on the network, even if everything is set up properly. Wait 15 minutes before deciding that you need to troubleshoot.

To save time and trouble, you can tell Windows 95 to always use a specific machine as the browse master. For best results, choose the fastest computer, one that is rarely turned off or logged off. From the File and Printer Sharing property sheet, click on the entry for Browse Master, and use the box on the right to set its Value to Enabled.

On the other hand, a slow computer might suffer from serving as a browse master, so you can set the Browse Master property to Disabled. Otherwise, the Value is set to Automatic. With Automatic, Windows is free to elect a browse master. It's like being chosen for jury duty.

Configuration: File and Printer Sharing for NetWare Networks

Your computer can act as a secondary NetWare file server, but it can't replace a real one.

Normally, with File and Printer Sharing for NetWare Networks, shared resources are organized by workgroup. Shared drives are listed along with the other computers in the workgroup. This option is called *Workgroup Advertising*. Alternatively, you can use *SAP Advertising*. With SAP Advertising, your computer appears to be a NetWare file server. It's an exciting feature, because when SAP Advertising is enabled, other computers using the Novell client software NETX can attach to your computer, *even if they're not running Windows 95.* It's a great way to make a device like a CD-ROM available to all users on a mixed network. (If all computers are running Windows 95, you're better off using Workgroup Advertising, which is more convenient for the users.)

You might think this is a way to get a NetWare-type network without paying for a NetWare license and going through all the work of setting up a NetWare network. Unfortunately, it's not that easy. While your computer can act like a NetWare file server, the lists of users and groups have to be obtained from an actual NetWare file server. So your computer can act like a secondary NetWare file server, but it can't replace the real one. This feature is still very handy. Shared printers appear as NetWare print queues, and you can use the standard Novell network management commands (SLIST, PSERVER, FCONSOLE, etc.) to manage the "NetWare" settings for a Windows 95 computer.

Figure 6-14 shows the options for File and Printer Sharing for NetWare Networks. If you're using Workgroup Advertising, set its Value to Enabled: Can be Master. This is equivalent to the Automatic choice we mentioned above—your computer can be elected as the browse master. Use Enabled: Preferred Master if you want to set your computer to be the browse master or Enabled: Will Not Be Master if your computer is too slow to serve as a browse master.

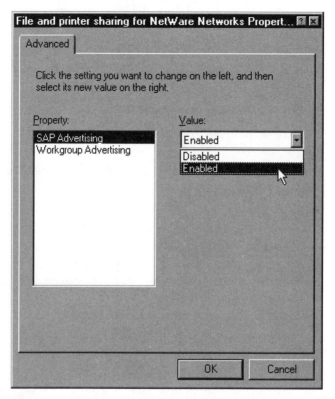

Figure 6-14: Enable SAP Advertising if you want to masquerade as a NetWare file server—but don't use the name of an existing NetWare file server.

For SAP Advertising, all you have to do is choose Enabled or Disabled.

Warning

If you choose the name of an existing NetWare file server for your machine, clients may attempt to log into your computer instead of the main file server. This is one of the security loopholes we mentioned earlier, and it can also create headaches for the network manager, to say the least. So we recommend you avoid it.

Contact Microsoft for an updated driver for File and Printer Sharing for Novell Networks that addresses this security loophole. It's available via http://www.microsoft.com. You can also call the Microsoft FastTips line (1-800-936-4200) and request the update via mail.

Identification

We've now completed a discussion of the Configuration property sheet. The next Network property sheet is called Identification. Assuming you're currently viewing Configuration, click on the tab marked Identification to move to it (Figure 6-15). If the Network property sheets are not visible, you've already clicked OK or Cancel while viewing the Configuration sheet, so bring back the property sheets by double-clicking Networks in the Control Panel or right-clicking the Network Neighborhood icon on the desktop and choosing Properties from the pop-up menu.

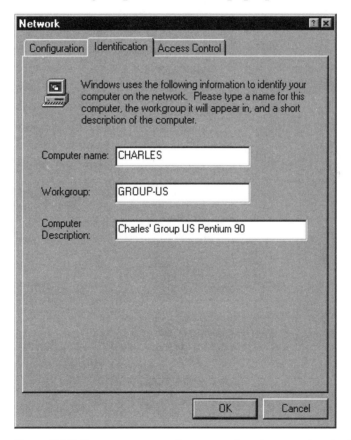

Figure 6-15: Set your computer's name and workgroup using the Identification panel of Network Neighborhood.

You use Identification to "name" your computer and specify which workgroup it belongs to. Remember that by default, you can only "see" computers that use the exact same workgroup name, which helps you limit the scope of a network. However, the Entire Network icon in Network Neighborhood can let you view other workgroups, too, unless this feature has been disabled by the network administrator.

TIP

When setting up a small office network, use any name you like, such as the name of your company. Keep it simple so there's no ambiguity in spelling. Otherwise, you might not realize that two computers are actually using different workgroup names.

Every computer within the same workgroup must have a unique machine name. If every user tends to use his or her own machine exclusively, you'll probably want to name the machine the same as the user's name. If many employees share the same machine, make up a name that meaningfully identifies that computer, such as Compaq 4/33S or even use a fanciful name like TurboMax. You can use up to 15 characters for the machine name; use the Computer Description box to fill in a more complete name, which is also shown when users are browsing the network.

Access Control

When you're finished with Identification, click the tab for Access Control (Figure 6-16). Here you're choosing which security method to use for validating peer-to-peer sharing. If your computer is not part of a NetWare or Windows NT network, you'll have to choose User-level access control. With Share-level access control, you can set up a password for each drive or printer that you're sharing. Any user with the same workgroup can access a drive you're sharing, if they know the password.

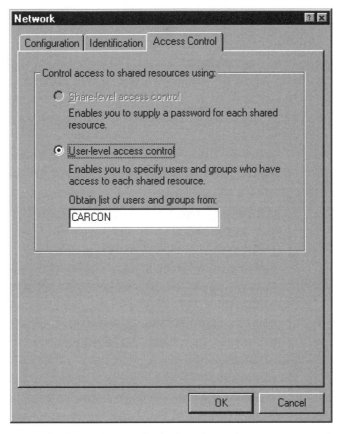

Figure 6-16: Use Access Control to choose between password protection (Share-level) or server-based authentication (User-level).

For enhanced security, consider using User-level access control. This gets a list of authorized users from a NetWare or Windows NT file server. When you share your local drives and printers, you can choose by *name* (username) which users (or groups of users) are allowed access to a particular resource on your computer.

LOGGING IN

Before you can use a network, you have to log in. Your *login* is your username plus a password. You can simply use your first or last name as your username. If you choose the same username and password for your Windows login as your network login, you only have to login once—the Windows login allows access to your password list file, which stores (caches) all the other passwords.

When you first log in to Windows, you are creating your password list file. From that point on, your username and password uniquely identifies you.

A password is a kind of "key" you use to lock up your computer and protect it from unauthorized access. You can have separate passwords for various purposes, such as a password to access your Exchange Inbox, a password to log in to the file server or to log in to your Windows network, or a password to access a shared printer. For convenience, all these passwords can be accessed via a single master password. Imagine the master password as a key to a lock on a box that holds the keys to all the other locks in your house.

Using a single master password, your Windows password, is convenient because Windows remembers your other passwords for you and automatically fills them in when needed (though for the sake of security, the password is shown as a series of asterisks). You may have originally chosen a password the first time you ran Windows 95.

You might wish to silently log in to your computer, so that you don't have to answer the username and password prompts every time you start up your computer. The only way to do this is to enter a blank password when you first login, by not entering any value for the password.

This lets you skip the initial login procedure, but unless you also have a blank password on your Windows NT or NetWare server, you'll still be prompted to enter that password. The only way to have a truly silent login is if you are allowed to access the server without a password, which is not recommended unless you have a reasonably secure business environment with relatively few users. This might be the case for a small peer-to-peer network, for example.

You can configure the password settings for your computer by double-clicking the Passwords icon in the Control Panel.

As shown in Figure 6-17, the Passwords Properties property sheets let you can change your Windows (master) password. The only risk with this scheme is that if someone discovers your master password, your entire security system is vulnerable. You can also change the other passwords that are linked to your Windows password.

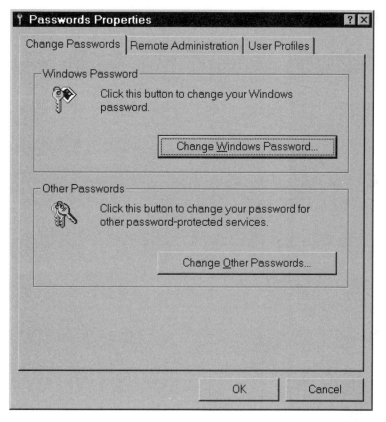

Figure 6-17: The Windows password can control all your other passwords.

Your computer can be configured or even remotely controlled by the system administrator on the network. But to preserve your privacy, you want to make sure that not just anyone can use your computer. The Remote Administration password should be known only to you and the system administrator (see Figure 6-18). Depending on your company policy, it may or may not be possible to change this password. (Some companies enable Remote Administration automatically when they set up Windows 95 on their computers.)

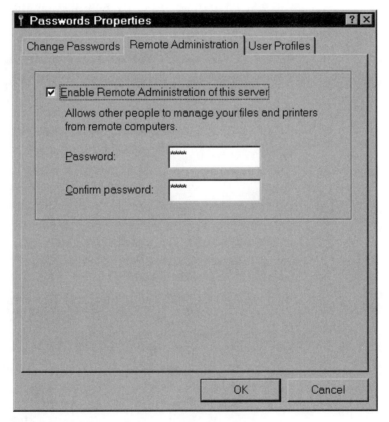

Figure 6-18: Remote Administration settings.

The User Profiles settings, the third property sheet in Passwords Properties (shown in Figure 6-19), are especially significant. By default, the Control Panel settings (and settings like the desktop colors) are always used for your computer, no matter who logs in to use it. But if you select the "User can customize their preferences option," a separate copy of the Control Panel settings is employed for each user. You can create multiple accounts on the same computer, and when users log in, they can have their own custom colors, cursors, network settings, passwords, default printers, what have you. (Actually, you can choose some settings to be shared between users if you like, but the choice is up to you.)

To create additional accounts on the same computer, click Start, then Shut Down, and choose the option "Close all programs" and log on as a different user before clicking Yes. This has the same effect as restarting Windows, but the computer will first ask for a username and password, even if none was previously used. Note that enabling User Profiles forces the login box to always appear (even if you have a blank password), because otherwise Windows can't determine who is using the computer and which custom profile should be used.

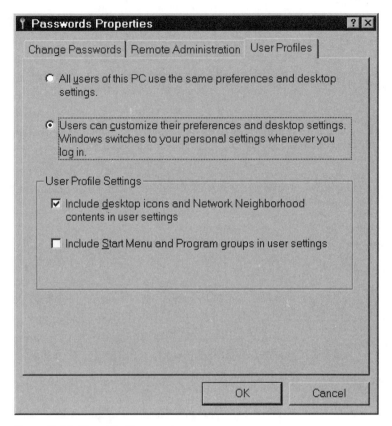

Figure 6-19: User Profiles settings.

TIP

If your network is configured for Windows 95 by the administrator, using Policy Editor (see Chapter 2, "The Registry," for more on the Policy Editor), your user preferences will "follow" you as you move from machine to machine in an organization. Wherever you log in, your personal preferences such as screen colors, desktop icons, accessibility settings, and so on, will be applied to whatever computer you're using.

If you ever need to delete a user's account (password list) from your computer, browse the Windows directory for .PWL files. Deleting a .PWL file removes that user's password list and any custom settings for that individual, at least on your computer.

USING NETWORK NEIGHBORHOOD

The Entire Network icon also shows the names of other workgroups, including your current workgroup.

After you've configured your network and restarted your computer, you're ready to get started with networking. Once again, Network Neighborhood is the key.

Browsing for Computers

Double-click the Network Neighborhood icon on the desktop to open a folder-style view of all the computers on the network, as shown in Figure 6-20. Or you can right-click on the Network Neighborhood icon and choose the Explorer to get an Explorer view. (From within the Explorer, you can just click on the Network Neighborhood icon.)

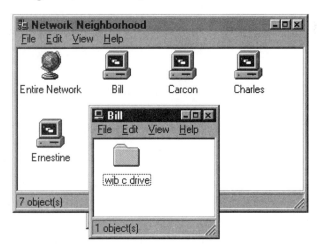

Figure 6-20: The Network Neighborhood folder shows all the computers in your current workgroup. Double-click on an icon to view the shared drives and folders on that computer.

The Network Neighborhood folder normally shows your preferred server (if you're on a NetWare or Windows NT network) and any computers within your workgroup. Your own computer's name is also on the list, although you'll usually use My Computer or the Explorer to access your own computer.

Also shown is an icon for Entire Network. This expands your view to show all the file servers that are part of your company's local area network (LAN), including off-site servers that are part of a wide area network (WAN). When you double-click on a server icon, you may be asked again for a login name and password, unless it's the same as that used by your usual server. The Entire Network icon also shows the names of other workgroups, including your current workgroup. Double-click on any workgroup to see the computers contained within it.

Drilling for Data

Double-click on a machine name to *drill down* the hierarchy and view the drives and folders shared on that machine. These are also called *shared resources*, or simply, *shares*. (The user of that computer must also be using File and Printer Sharing and have previously set up sharing for the drives and printers on his or her computer.)

Or double-click on a file server's icon to view the volumes available on that file server. (Your network administrator can control which volumes you have access to.)

When you see the drive (or folder) that you want to examine, double-click on it. If User-level access control is set for that share, you need to type a password (asterisks are shown as you type) to open it. (You don't need a password if the user didn't choose one or if the share is set for User-level access. However, if you're not one of the users authorized for that share, you won't be able to open it.) The next time you start your computer, you'll have to enter the password again. However, when password caching is enabled (and it is enabled unless your system administrator forbids it using Policy Editor), your computer remembers the password (shown as ****), and all you have to do is click OK.

Mapping Drives

You may find it convenient to *map* a drive letter to a shared drive or folder. You can also map a drive to a volume or folder on a file server. Right-click on the Network Neighborhood desktop icon, and choose Map Network Drive. You can also map a drive from the Explorer or a folder view, if you have the toolbar enabled (View | Toolbar). Just click on the ▣ icon from the Explorer or folder toolbar. You'll get the dialog box shown in Figure 6-21.

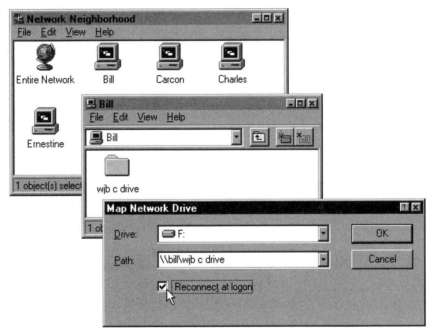

Figure 6-21: Choose a drive and a network share name, and you'll be able to access that drive or folder more conveniently.

Click the box next to Drive to choose a drive letter to assign to the shared drive or folder. In the Path text box, you can type the name of the network resource you want to use or choose it from a list of shares you've used recently by clicking the down-arrow next to the box. This box is blank the first time you use it so you'll have to type a path to the resource.

Universal Naming Convention

You can always open a folder by referring to its UNC name.

Note that there is no Browse button—you have to know how to specify the name of a shared folder. To do this, use the Universal Naming Convention (UNC). For example, if your network file server's name is PRIME, and you want to assign a drive letter to the APPS folder on the WIN volume, you'd use the UNC of \\PRIME\WIN\APPS. For a Windows NT server, the first part of the UNC (\\PRIME) would be the name of a domain on that server. You can also refer to a shared drive on another computer (using peer-to-peer networking) by using something like \\CHUCK\C-DRIVE or \\CHUCK\CD-ROM\WIN95. The second part (after \\CHUCK) is the name of the shared drive, or it can be the name of a shared folder.

Actually, there is an easier way to map drives. Just open the Network Neighborhood folder, navigate to the folder you want to use, and choose Map Network Drive from the File menu (you can also click the toolbar icon). This automatically fills in the path to that resource.

You might need to map a drive when running DOS or Windows 3.1 applications because they probably won't understand UNC names. Drive mappings will eventually be obsolete because Network Neighborhood makes it so easy to browse for folders.

UNC names have another advantage. Sometimes you aren't able to browse the network, for instance if your computer is running low on memory or if the browse master is temporarily unavailable. But you can always open a folder by referring to its UNC name.

TIP

Use Start|Run, and enter a UNC name to jump directly to that folder, opened on your desktop.

If you map drives to network locations, consider adopting standard drive letters consistently in the organization. For example, you could always map drive M: to the mail directory, drive N: to the newsletter folder, etc., or at least use a common mapping for the same machines, such as L: for Lori's machine.

Mapping drive letters this way is often necessary, although difficult to enforce in practice. For example, let's say you have a document containing a picture, linked to N:\MASTHEAD.TIF. But if that document is opened on someone else's computer, the N: drive letter may be used for a different network location. That's why it's important to keep the drive letters consistent across the organization. But what if drive N: refers to a shared directory on Nancy's machine, and Nancy herself tries to work with the document with the embedded N:\MASTHEAD.TIF? Clearly, Nancy wouldn't have a drive N: mapped to her own machine.

The solution is to use UNC names instead. So instead of mapping drive N: to Nancy's newsletter folder, just directly reference the location using UNC: \\NANCY\NEWS\MASTHEAD.TIF.

Finding a Computer

On large networks, use Start|Find|Computer to more quickly locate a shared drive or server. This can be a lifesaver if you're trying to access a computer that's linked via a slow connection, such as dial-up networking, since browsing can be very slow over a phone line. For the same reason, you'll want to rely on UNC names rather than the Browse button when you're opening or saving files from an application.

If you use DOS and Windows 3.1x applications frequently, you'll want to map a drive to the shared drives you use most often.

Accessing the Network From Within an Application

If you're running a word processor or other application, you'll sometimes need to open or save files to a network drive. If you've mapped a drive letter to a network volume or folder, it's ridiculously easy—just save the file to that drive. For example: X:\DOCS might actually map to \\SERVER\SYS\AMIPRO, so that the file is saved to \\SERVER\SYS\AMIPRO\DOCS.

Windows 95 applications use a new version of the common dialog box. To open a file or save a file using a network, just click on the Look in box to open a list of drives on your computer (see

Figure 6-22). Choose Network Neighborhood, and you'll be able to browse the computers on the network, just as if you were using the Explorer.

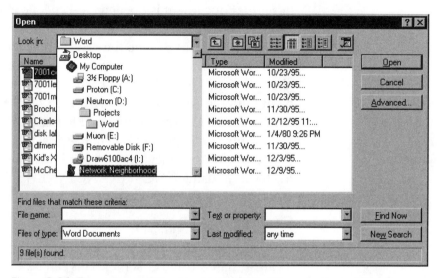

Figure 6-22: The common dialog box for Windows 95 applications makes it easy to browse the network from within the application.

You can also just use the UNC name for the network resources. Choosing File I Open and entering \\DOGIE\ART\BMP\ WISTFUL.BMP opens a file directly, without any browsing non-sense. (If you find you can't save a file you've opened, you may have been granted read-only access to that drive or folder.)

Windows 3.1*x* applications use a cruder method. Some support direct entry of UNC names. If the dialog box includes a Network button, it lets you map a drive to a resource on the fly. You often have to enter the exact UNC name at this point. So if you use DOS and Windows 3.1*x* applications frequently, you'll want to create a permanent drive mapping for the shared drives you use most often.

NETWORK TECHNIQUES

We'll now spend a little time discussing how to take advantage of networking. You'll learn how to share your drives and folders and let others use your printer. And you'll be able to "see" files on other people's computers, and print to their printers, too. We'll then review how to use dial-up networking to log in to the network from off-site (or from home) and see how to attach your notebook computer to a network without investing in a notebook network adapter.

Sharing Drives & Folders

Sharing is a two-way street. It's one thing to be able to access files and folders on somebody else's computer, but others may need to use your computer's files, too. First, don't be worried that you're opening a Pandora's box: you have full control over which folders are shared, and you can use a secret password so that only authorized users can "get in." (Or you can limit access to only certain users.)

Sharing is a two-way street.

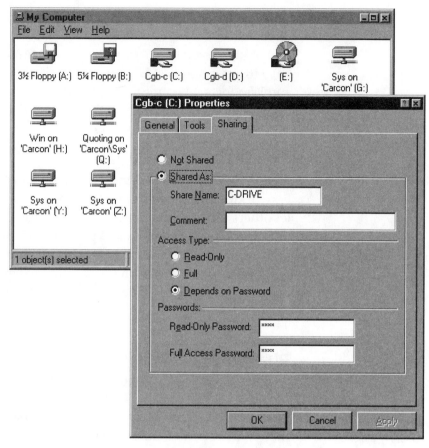

Figure 6-23: Use passwords to protect a shared drive.

The easiest way to share a drive is to first open My Computer. Next, right-click on a drive you want to share, and choose Sharing from the pop-up menu.

You then get the Sharing property sheet shown in Figure 6-24. (You can also open this panel by choosing Properties for a drive and clicking on the Sharing tab.) Or you click the 🖳 toolbar button from the folder's toolbar or from the Explorer toolbar. (Use View|Toolbar, if necessary, to enable this toolbar.)

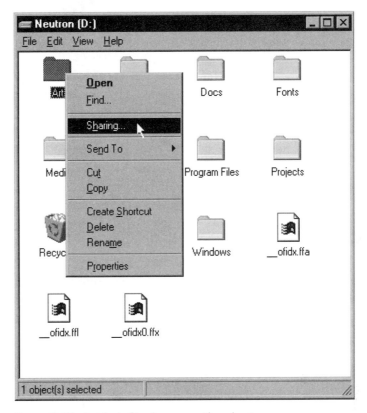

Figure 6-24: A drive's Sharing properties sheet.

TIP

It's possible that your network administrator has disabled peer-to-peer networking for your network, probably for security reasons. If this is the case, you may be out of luck, but bring up the issue with the administrator to be sure.

Sharing a folder works identically. Just right-click on the folder you want to share, and choose Sharing; or click the Share Drive button on the toolbar. The difference is that when you share a folder, the other users see that folder as if it were a hard drive. Only the files in that folder (and any subfolders it contains) are visible.

After you click the Share button or choose Sharing from the File menu (or right-click the shortcut menu), you'll see the Sharing property sheet for that file or folder.

To create a name for the shared file or folder (hereafter simply called a *share*), first click the Shared As option button. By default, the share name is simply the drive letter of the hard drive. You can use any name you like, but it makes sense to be consistent with these names networkwide. For example, if everyone shared his or her drive as C-DRIVE, you wouldn't have to guess when composing a UNC to someone's computer. You'd know to use \\BILL\C-DRIVE when referring to drive C: on Bill's machine.

It's possible to share a drive or folder, yet make the drive invisible to casual users browsing Network Neighborhood. Just add a dollar sign ($) after the share name. If you shared your C: drive as C-DRIVE$, it would not be shown when users browse the network. A user would have to know the hidden name, and use a UNC name like \\LORI\C-DRIVE$\DOCS to access a folder. This adds an additional layer of security, but you'll probably want to use User-level or Share-level access control, too.

Use the Comment box to provide a more meaningful description of the drive if you like. This is shown when someone uses Network Neighborhood to browse your computer.

Share-Level Access

Next, choose the type of access you want to allow. For a CD-ROM, you'd naturally use read-only. Use full access to allow someone unlimited read and write access to your drive. Or click Depends on Password if you want to allow some users to have read-only access, and others to have full read/write access, depending on which password you give them. You might do this to give most users read-only access, say, to a clip-art directory but to allow selected users, such as the artists, to make changes to the files. Normally, you wouldn't bother with two passwords, however.

You don't have to use passwords. Indeed, if your company is "one big happy family," sharing is a lot more convenient without passwords.

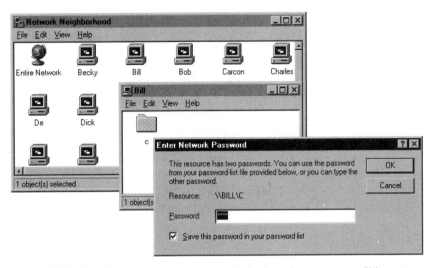

Figure 6-25: If you're accessing someone else's shared resource, you'll have to enter a password first.

If the share is read-only without a password, the user isn't even prompted for a password when the share is accessed. Otherwise, even with a blank password, the user will have to enter that blank password by pressing just the Enter key when prompted for a password. (This alone can foil some unauthorized users, who try every password under the sun, without realizing *there is no password!*)

Password Caching

Your master password unlocks all your other passwords.

Once you've typed a password to access a shared resource, you won't have to type it again, as long as password caching is enabled on your network (and this is the default). With password caching, your master password (the one you use to log in to Windows) unlocks all your other passwords.

The next time you try to open the shared resource, you'll still be prompted to enter a password, but you'll notice that the password entry box is already filled in with asterisks, to hide the cached password. All you have to do is click OK to proceed. If the network administrator has disabled password caching, however, you'll have to enter the password each time.

Because a share can have two passwords, one for read-only access and one for full (read/write) access, keep in mind that the last password you use is the one that's cached. So if on Tuesday you accessed a share using the read-only password, then on Thursday you click OK to accept the cached password, you'll again have read-only access. You'll have to manually retype the full access password if you want to change your access level, bypassing the password cache.

Of course, this shouldn't be an issue, because the point of having separate read-only and full access passwords is that you want to limit access to certain users by only giving them read-only access to your machine. The most trusted users will, most likely, use the full access password.

A better way to set limits according to the user, however, is to work with User-level access control, which lets you choose which users (or groups of users) have what level of access to a particular share.

TIP

The password cache is an encrypted (encoded) file stored with the extension .PWL in the Windows directory of the computer sharing the files. Microsoft discovered that hackers could theoretically break the simple encryption used for password caching and thereby gain access to all the shared resources on your computer. This can only happen if the hacker has access to your computer in the first place, so many don't consider it to be an issue. However, you can acquire an update to the password caching method from the Microsoft Web server (http://www.microsoft.com) that solves this problem by increasing the size of the encryption key from 32 bits to 128 bits. It can also be obtained by mail via Microsoft FastTips, 1-800-936-4200.

User-Level Access

If you configured your computer for User-level access (see the
section "Configuring Network Neighborhood" earlier in this
chapter), the Share dialog box looks like Figure 6-26. Here, you can
pick the names of the users you'd like to give access to your files.

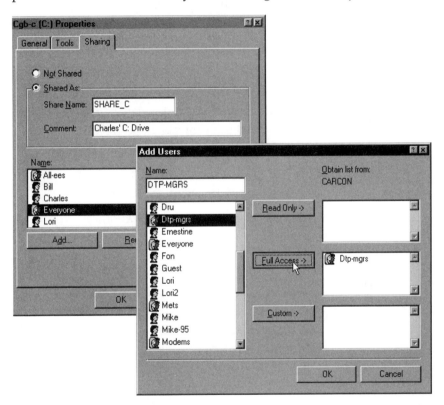

Figure 6-26: You can choose which users can have read access to your files and
which can have read/write access.

If you're accessing someone else's computer, and they share
resources with User-level sharing, you don't need to worry about
passwords. The share is instantly available, as long as the other
computer is turned on and assuming you've been chosen as an
authorized user for the resource. The NetWare or Windows NT file
server on your network takes care of authenticating you (proving

you are who you say you are), but it's still up to the user who is sharing the resources to choose which users will have access. Sharing this kind of authority is too much for some system operators to bear, so you may find that even User-level access has been disabled on your network. Before you jump to that assumption, however, check with the poor beleaguered sysop.

Network Printing

When you share your printer, you're publishing its name on the network.

There are two issues involved in printing over a network. Obviously, you need to know how to access and print to other shared printers, but before this can happen, someone has to share a printer in the first place. So let's first start with that discussion, making your printer available for others.

Sharing *Your* Printer

Sharing your printer allows others on the network to send their files to your computer to be printed. When you share your printer, you're publishing its name on the network. Later, when other users want to print to your printer, they'll add it to their own Printers folder, which will automatically copy the necessary printer drivers. (In fact, it's helpful to completely disregard the concept of printer drivers—the drivers go along with the printers, so just think in terms of printers, not drivers.)

Use Start|Settings|Printers to open your Printers folder. Right-click on the printer you want to share, and choose Sharing to get the sharing property sheet, as shown in Figure 6-27. (Note that there is no toolbar button to share a printer, nor is it available from the File menu. But you can also get to the Sharing page of the printer by clicking on a printer in your Printers folder and choosing the properties button 🖳 from the Printers toolbar or choosing Properties from the File menu. You can also right-click on a printer and choose Properties from the pop-up menu.)

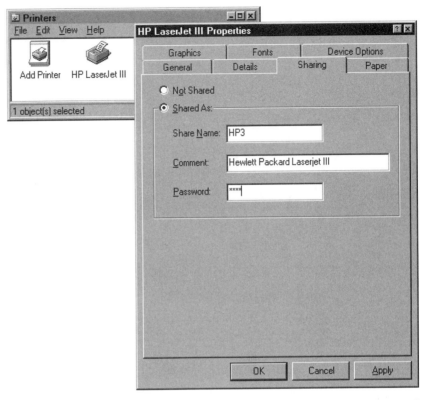

Figure 6-27: The share name of the printer is visible when a user chooses Install Network Printer.

It's also possible to share your printer NetWare-style: other users will see the shared printer as if it were attached to a NetWare file server. Even non-Windows (DOS) users can CAPTURE and NPRINT to your printer. While this can also be done using the Novell RPRINTER utility, the Windows 95 method works much better. All that's required is to use File and Printer Sharing for NetWare Networks and enable SAP Advertising (see above). The share name of the printer becomes a NetWare print queue. For example, if you shared your laser printer as HP3, then a DOS user could redirect his or her printer output to your printer with the command:

```
CAPTURE LPT1: /QUEUE=HP3 /NT /NB /NFF /TI=30
```

Installing a Network Printer

To print to someone else's shared printer, use Start | Settings | Printers to open your Printers folder. Double-click the Add Printer icon, and from the Add Printer wizard, choose Network Printer, then click Next. When you do this, you'll be asked to enter a network path or the name of a file server printer queue (as shown in Figure 6-28).

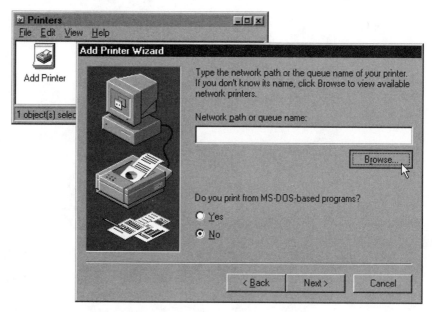

Figure 6-28: Click Browse to quickly find a network printer.

For example, the primary printer on a NetWare file server might be \\PRIME\PRINTQ_0. A printer shared as HP3 would be accessed via \\CHARLES\HP3. More conveniently, click the Browse button. As shown in Figure 6-29, you can navigate easily to the desired computer. Click the ⊞ symbol to the left of the computer name, if necessary, to show the printers shared by that computer.

Figure 6-29: Find the computer that hosts the printer you want to use.

Ideally, Windows 95's Point and Print feature will automatically install the drivers for the printer. After all, the computer that's sharing the printer already has the drivers it needs, so they're passed along to your computer. On a Windows NT or NetWare file server, however, the network administrator has to set up Point and Print. Otherwise, you'll have to choose a printer vendor and printer model from the list of printers (see Figure 6-30). As long as you know the make and model of the network printer, this shouldn't be too much of a hardship.

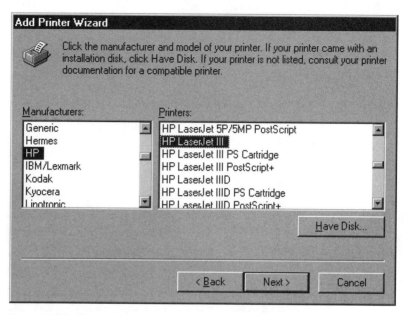

Figure 6-30: Choose the printer's manufacturer on the left and the specific model on the right.

Browsing for Network Printers

Another way to install a printer is to browse Network Neighborhood. When you double-click on the Network Neighborhood icon, you'll normally get a list of computers in your current workgroup, and if you're attached to a Windows NT or NetWare server, you'll see that server's name too.

Drag and drop a file onto a printer to quickly print the file.

To print to a shared workgroup printer, double-click the name of the computer you want to use in Network Neighborhood (or just click on the ⊞ symbol at the left of the computer name). This reveals a list of the resources on that computer, including shared drives, folders, and printers. If you want to be able to use the shared printer, just double-click on it. You can also drag and drop the printer into your Printers folder, accessible from My Computer or via Start | Settings | Printers.

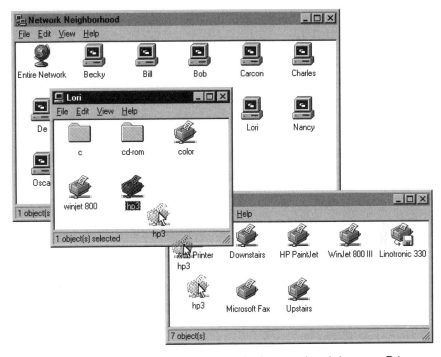

Figure 6-31: You can double-click on a shared printer or drag it into your Printers folder to add it to your computer's list of printers.

When you add a shared printer to your computer, the necessary system software (the printer driver) is copied from the other computer to your computer. In the future, you can print to it from any application—as long as the other computer is turned on and as long as the shared printer remains shared by its owner.

If the printer was shared via Share-level access, you'll need to enter a password to use it, unless the printer was shared without a password. With User-level access, you don't need to worry about a password—you only have access to the printer if you are on the owner's list of authorized users.

There are many variations on this technique. You could have dragged the printer from the workgroup list onto your desktop to create a shortcut to it. And if you want to print a file to that printer, you can drag that file and drop it on the printer shortcut, just as you can do with shortcuts to the printers on your computer.

Dial-up Networking

In principle, dial-up networking (DUN) works exactly like a real network connection, but it's significantly slower. DUN also relies on a host machine at the main network location, which serves as a bridge between you and the main network.

Dial-up networking can be slow.

You can use DUN to connect a computer at your home or branch office to a computer attached to a local area network. It's also possible to use devices such as the Shiva Netmodem to connect to a network without requiring a computer to answer the phone. When connected via DUN, you have all the resources of "being there," including the ability to share files and print to remote printers. But DUN is slow. Plan on running all your applications from your local hard drive, and use DUN only to access documents and data files over the link. Printing to a network printer is also possible but may not be practical if you're printing large files or documents with graphics. We recommend nothing less than a 28,800 bps v.34 modem for DUN.

Because DUN is crucial to Internet access, we've already discussed it thoroughly in Chapter 5, "Communicating With the World." It's also a great way for two PCs to temporarily become networked over the phone lines. However, some applications of DUN are especially appealing if you have a real network.

As long as you have the dial-up server running on one of your PCs, with a telephone line that rings in to the modem, you can call your office PC from home (or on the road while traveling), and access your files. While you don't want to run any applications over the dial-up connection, it's a good way to open files, such as word processing documents. You can edit the files on your local PC, then save it back to the network, avoiding the need to keep a separate copy on your local drive. So far, this isn't any different than ordinary dial-up networking.

But dial-up networking also serves as a kind of gateway. When you're logged into the office network from home, you can access not only the files and resources (such as printers) on the desktop you're calling, you can also use any network resources available to that machine, including access to a NetWare or

Windows NT network, and drives and printers shared by other employees. And your home computer (or laptop if you're traveling) can share its files with the coworkers at your office, although this is much less practical.

To get this benefit from dial-up networking, the name and password you use on your home computer or laptop should be the same as an account on the NetWare or Windows NT server. For a peer-to-peer network, you'll have to make sure you have a unique machine name and belong to the same workgroup. You can confirm this by double-clicking Networks from the Control Panel, and clicking the Identification tab heading.

You'll also want to make sure you have the necessary client software. While you probably won't have a NetWare server in your home or hotel room, you'll need the Client for NetWare Networks installed on your notebook or home computer if you want to access your file server via dial-up networking. (Refer to an earlier section "Configuring Network Neighborhood" to learn how to install this client.) Also make sure that the protocol you're using matches the network protocol at the office. IPX/SPX is usually the best choice for dial-up networking, since it can be routed between file servers, and is NetWare's native protocol and is the now-preferred protocol for Windows NT. Formerly, NetBEUI was the favorite protocol for Microsoft networking, and it's still a good choice, since it supports NetBIOS without any special configuration. If you use NetBEUI, make sure every other computer you want to access also has NetBEUI installed. (Refer to the earlier section "Configuring Network Neighborhood" to learn how to install a protocol.)

Direct Cable Connection

Make sure that the protocol you're using matches the network protocol at the office.

Direct cable connection (DCC) is very similar to dial-up networking, but instead of using modems and the telephone system to make the connection, you have a direct connection between two computers via a cable attached between the two serial ports. You can also use a parallel cable for higher speeds. Indeed, new computers feature enhanced parallel ports (or enhanced capability

419

ports) that permit much faster data transfer, approaching the speeds of a true network. It's a nearly ideal way to connect two computers. DCC is ideal for a home-based network (or one for a very small business), since you don't need to buy network cards or run any wiring. But you can only use it between two computers—so far there's no way to "daisy-chain" a cable to a third computer. For that you'll need a regular network card and cabling.

Let's walk through the steps for setting up DCC. We'll set up a direct cable connection between a desktop computer and a portable notebook computer. It can also be used to link two computers together into a mini-network. To get started, choose Start | Programs | Accessories | Direct Cable Connection. In Figure 6-32, choose which computer will be the host, the one that shares its files, and which computer will be the guest, the one allowed to access those files. Usually the desktop computer is the host and the portable computer is the guest, but this can be reversed at any time.

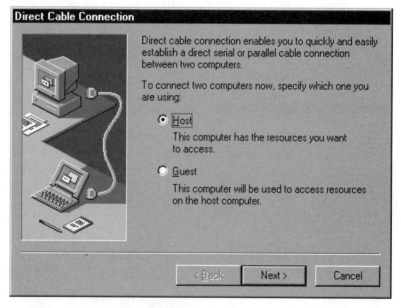

Figure 6-32: Choose host on the computer that has the files you want to access, and configure the other machine as guest.

■ ■

TIP

Both computers need fast 16550 serial ports, or you'll be limited to 19,200 bps when sending files over a serial cable. With a 16550, you can use speeds as high as 115,200 bps.

■ ■

To set up the host, you next need to choose how you're connecting the two computers, via either a parallel "LapLink" style cable or a serial *null-modem* cable. The parallel cable (which plugs into the printer ports on both machines) is fastest, but it has a length limitation of about 10 feet. You can string serial cables much farther without data loss. In Figure 6-33, we've chosen the parallel cable option. At this point, you should go ahead and plug in the cable between the two computers if you haven't already.

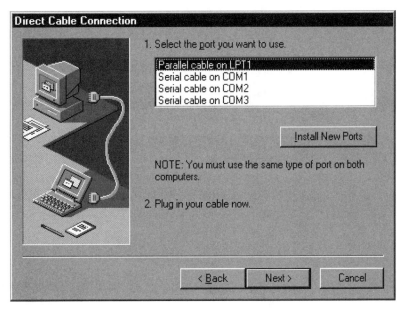

Figure 6-33: Choose a cabling method next.

In Figure 6-34, you'll see that we've set a password by clicking the Set Password button. Realistically, it's doubtful that you need a password, since the connection only exists as long as you have the two computers cabled up. Once you've completed this step, the desktop computer perks up and starts listening for the guest computer.

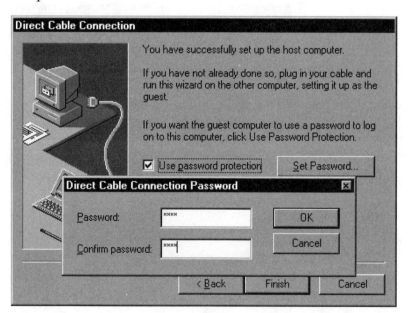

Figure 6-34: Click the Set Password button if you want to have a more secure connection.

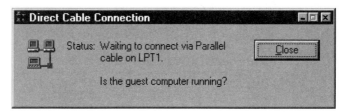

Figure 6-35: The host computer might get impatient if you wait too long to start the guest connection.

You can't actually print to a shared printer via direct cable connection if you're using the parallel printer port for the connection.

When you connect with the guest computer, you might see the warning message shown in Figure 6-36. If you want to view the shared folders on the host computer, you'll need to type the name of that computer (which you configured using Network Neighborhood).

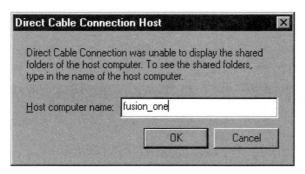

Figure 6-36: If direct cable connection can't figure out the name of the host computer, you'll have to type it.

Finally, you'll see a view of the shared folders on the remote computer. At this point, treat the direct cable connection exactly like any other form of Windows 95 networking. Just as with a direct networking connection or dial-up networking, you won't be able to see anything on the host computer unless that user has installed File and Printer Sharing and has shared some drives or folders.

You can't actually print to a shared printer via direct cable connection if you're using the parallel printer port for the connection. You can either use the serial cable method to connect or add a second parallel port to the host machine.

Synchronizing With Briefcase

The Briefcase in Windows 95 is an anomaly: most people don't even know they need it. If you have a portable computer, you're already familiar with the process of transferring files between your desktop computer and your portable machine. When you're finished with files on the portable computer, you have to remember to transfer the file back to the desktop machine. You also have to manually compare the file dates to see which machine has the most up-to-date version of a file. This process can get tedious if you transfer large numbers of documents between machines or work with the same documents frequently on different machines.

The Windows 95 Briefcase automates the process of transferring files and using the most current versions. If the Windows desktop of your portable computer doesn't include Briefcase, use File| New|Briefcase to create one. Connect your portable computer to your desktop computer via a network adapter, dial-up networking, or direct cable connection. Then drag and drop the "master" files from the desktop computer into the Briefcase folder on the portable computer. You can then edit the documents while you're on the road and later use Briefcase to update the original documents on the desktop computer.

Choosing a Briefcase Host

To make this easier, you can create the Briefcase first on the desktop computer, copy all the files to it, then move the entire Briefcase to the notebook computer. Don't copy the Briefcase file; *move it*—there should only be one Briefcase in use at any given time. Why? Consider if we were talking about a real-world briefcase. You only need one of those, too, in order to move documents from one location to another. Having two briefcases can sometimes be advantageous but can also be confusing. "Which briefcase contains the memo from Thursday's meeting that I've marked up?" you might ponder. Determining which briefcase contains the memo can be especially tricky if you photocopied the memo and kept a copy of it in each briefcase. You'd have to compare the two documents to find out which is the one you've revised.

The Windows 95 Briefcase automates the process of transferring the most current versions of files.

There's nothing to prevent you from using more than one Briefcase.

TIP

If you use a floppy disk to transport your Briefcase, all the files in the Briefcase folder must be able to fit on the single disk. This can some-times rule out a disk as a Briefcase container. (That's why it's more useful to use a portable computer to host a Briefcase.) But if you run Start | Programs | Accessories | System Tools | DriveSpace, you can dou-ble the free space on a floppy disk. Even if you don't DoubleSpace or DriveSpace your main hard drive, doubled floppies can be very conve-nient. The only catch is that you can only read a doubled floppy on another computer than is running DoubleSpace or DriveSpace. This includes PCs running DOS 6.0 or later and, of course, any other Windows 95 machine. (But Windows NT can't yet read DoubleSpace or DriveSpace.)

Thanks to this real-world metaphor, you probably understand why using only one Briefcase is a good idea. However, there's nothing to prevent you from using more than one Briefcase. You could use a separate Briefcase file for each separate project you work on. There's no confusion, and that way each Briefcase might even be small enough to hold all its files on one floppy disk.

TIP

A better alternative for hosting a Briefcase than a floppy disk is to use a removable hard drive, such as the Iomega Zip drive or a Syquest EZ135. These drives use 100MB or 135MB cartridges (respec-tively), making them a nearly ideal place to keep a large briefcase. Get one drive for home and another for the office, and just transport a cartridge between them as needed. Briefcase will help you easily keep the files on both computers synchronized. The drives cost around $200, and the rugged hard-drive cartridges sell for about $15 to $20 each, a pretty good bargain.

How Briefcase Works

We're going to assume you're using a notebook for your Briefcase in the following steps, but a similar technique applies if you host it on a floppy or removable hard-drive cartridge.

1. On the road, you'll edit the files within the Briefcase on the portable computer (don't move the files out of the Briefcase).

2. When you're ready to update the documents on the desktop computer, connect the portable computer to the desktop machine. You can make the connection using direct cable connection or via a notebook network adapter. If the Briefcase is stored on a remote system (if you're synchronizing your files with those of another traveler), use dial-up networking.

3. Use the desktop computer to double-click the Briefcase on the notebook computer to open it.

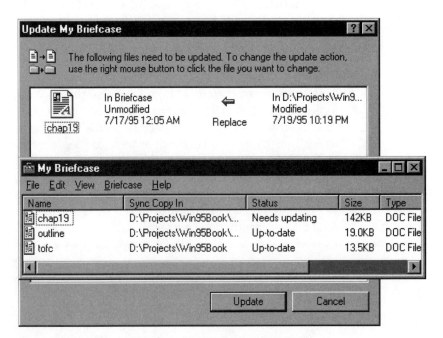

Figure 6-37: Open the Briefcase to update the original files.

Now you're ready to transfer files. You've opened the Briefcase folder, and now you may want to see which items will be updated.

4. Use Details view (View|Details) to see which items need to be updated.

You can update all the files that have been changed, or only the files you've highlighted by clicking on them. You'll choose an option from the Briefcase menu.

5. Use Briefcase|Update All to copy the modified documents from the Briefcase to their original locations on the desktop computer. Or you can select only certain files and use Briefcase|Update Selected.

Sometimes you'll want to take a file "out" of the Briefcase and no longer keep track of its changes.

6. Use Briefcase|Split From Original to break the link between a file in a Briefcase and the original. You can then move that file out of the Briefcase and keep it anywhere you like on the portable computer. Even if you make changes to the file, it will no longer be updated on the original (desktop) computer.

True File Synchronization

The Briefcase forces both computers to use whichever file has been modified most recently.

The Briefcase has another powerful potential: files can be transferred not only between computers, but they can be synchronized, too. What happens if you changed the document on the original (desktop) computer and on the notebook computer in the Briefcase? If you reconnect, you have a problem: you can't just replace the original file, or it would lose its changes, being replaced by the Briefcase version. Generally, the Briefcase is designed to force both computers to use whichever file has been modified most recently, although you can still make this decision for yourself.

Although there is no easy fix for this situation, Windows 95 allows programs to set up special synchronization for files that they create. For example, Microsoft Access for Windows 95 can compare the table files between the two machines. Any records added on the desktop computer are merged with the database in the Briefcase on the portable computer, and vice versa. Both copies are complete and up-to-date. We look forward to more applications that support this feature, especially when applied to contact managers and scheduling software.

We've used an example of using the Briefcase to synchronize files between a desktop computer and a notebook computer. The preceding description only covers the most typical use of the Briefcase. You can also use it to synchronize files between a notebook and a hard drive in the notebook's docking station, or use the Briefcase along with dial-up networking to transfer files more conveniently. With some experience and a little trial and error, you'll probably figure out some innovative ways to put the Briefcase to good use.

NETWORK PRODUCTIVITY

A network is more than a bunch of wires and a server full of shared files. It's about connectivity—linking people together. With a network, you can communicate via electronic mail and pop-up sticky notes. Tasks can be distributed among many workers. You can collaborate with colleagues by forwarding a document from one person to another, even working on the same document simultaneously. Networks make contact and time managers come alive, letting employees pool their resources, find the best times for meetings, and reserve equipment or conference rooms.

The power of networks, when applied to application software, can be tremendous, spawning a whole new industry of "groupware" or "group-enabled" software. For example, Lotus Word Pro was redesigned from the ground up from the original Ami Pro as an ideal word processor for document collaboration. It has features to mark each person's changes in a different color, keep track of which version of a document is most recent, even automatically forward the document from one team member to the next. Co-workers can even embed notes to each other within the document. These notes don't print, but they help employees communicate and work together. (See Figure 6-2 at the beginning of this chapter.)

The Killer App: Electronic Mail

A *killer app* is an application that by itself justifies the use of a computer. Spreadsheets and word processors were the killer apps of the 1980s. World Wide Web browsers are the killer apps of the Internet. And electronic mail, by far, is the killer app of networking. For some, it can also be a major time killer; many become inundated in a sea of excess mail or become overly fascinated with e-mail as a confidant or soapbox. While computing can boost a company's productivity and, in some cases make the business possible in the first place, e-mail overload can actually impair productivity if not properly managed.

Windows 95 includes an excellent e-mail client, called Exchange, based on Microsoft Mail. Microsoft Exchange provides rich electronic mail editing, with full support for fonts, colors, graphics, and embedded objects. It's touted as a universal inbox for all types of e-mail systems, from an in-house Lotus Notes server to a portal to the wide world of Internet and online services.

Exchange goes still further by incorporating electronic faxing via Microsoft At Work Fax. You can send a document to someone's fax machine as if it were a printer—it's literally that simple. And if both parties to the fax are running Exchange, entire editable files can be transmitted via fax, a simple and straightforward way to exchange files without the hassle of running a terminal program. (Third-party programs such as WinFax Pro can also integrate with Exchange, or operate on their own.)

We're going to assume that your company has already installed Exchange at your location or that you've done so on your personal computer. For one reason, the process is virtually automatic—just double-click on your Inbox, and follow the onscreen prompts.

Windows 95 includes an excellent e-mail client, called Exchange, based on Microsoft Mail.

429

Instead, we'll focus on some interesting Exchange techniques and workarounds.

Bug Swatting

First of all, if you've had any experience with Exchange, you've probably noticed that it has a few bugs. The most common problem is an outgoing fax or outgoing Internet mail that stubbornly sits in the Outbox and never goes anywhere. Others find that they can send mail but never seem to receive any. Or you'll find that the fax program won't let you choose a cover page.

Obviously, the best solution to these problems is an updated release of Exchange, and Microsoft is working on this update for release sometime in 1996, along with their full Exchange client, a more feature-rich version for use with the upcoming Exchange Server.

In the meantime, you can attempt to fix the problem by removing Exchange and then reinstalling it. To do this, open the Control Panel (Start | Settings | Control Panel), and double-click the Add/ Remove Programs icon.

Click the tab for Windows Setup, and turn off the check boxes for Exchange and Fax (see Figure 6-38). Then click OK. Windows will whir and grind a bit, as it removes the files for Exchange and Fax, and also as it removes the corresponding entries in the Start Menu. You'll then be asked to restart your computer.

When Windows 95 starts up again, you can reinstall Exchange by reversing your actions. Double-click on Add/Remove Programs again in the Control Panel, and check the boxes for Exchange and Fax. You will be prompted to insert the Windows 95 CD-ROM or disks (unless you installed from a network). Then you'll restart your computer again.

The next time you open your Inbox, you may or may not be asked to go through Exchange setup again, but when Exchange is finally up and running, you may find that it's working much better this time—for now, anyway. A month or so later, some of the bugs may have come back, and you'll have to repeat this

*S*ome people find that they can send mail but never seem to receive any.

method of removing and reinstalling Exchange. (Remember that you'll need to have the Windows 95 CD-ROM or disks on hand during reinstallation.)

A less drastic technique is to remove your profile and rebuild it or remove a component of your profile and then add it back. To do this, double-click the Mail and Fax icon in the Control Panel. By default, it shows you the services installed in your current profile.

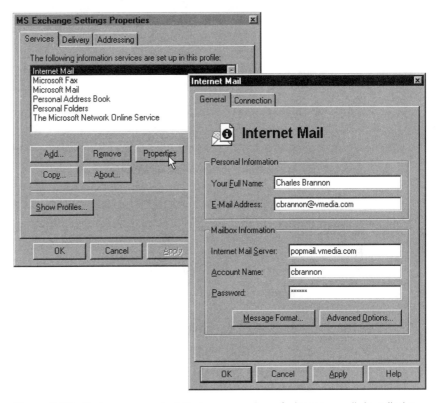

Figure 6-38. Each component of Exchange, such as faxing or e-mail, is called a *service*. Services are grouped together into profiles.

You may have only one profile, but it's possible to create additional profiles. If you share your computer with others, each user can have a separate profile with a separate personal store and personal address book (just choose different filenames for the .PST and .PAB files when setting it up).

If you want to remove or create a profile, click the Show Profiles button (see Figure 6-38). You can then choose which profile to work with, you can remove a profile, or create a new profile.

■■

TIP

To install Internet mail, you'll need an account with an Internet service provider and a copy of Microsoft Plus! for Windows 95, which includes the Internet mail client. You can also obtain the Internet mail and Web browser by downloading MSIE20.EXE from http://www.microsoft.com. It's also available from the WINNEWS forums on CompuServe and America Online.

■■

Another technique that has been reported to improve Exchange's reliability is to use a separate profile for each type of service. Certainly this reduces the value of Exchange as an all-in-one inbox, but whatever works, right? In particular, Internet Mail and Microsoft Fax don't seem to get along together in the same profile.

You should also keep in mind some features of Microsoft Exchange that may sometimes resemble bugs.

When a FAX Won't Send

A less drastic technique is to remove your profile and rebuild it.

When you send a fax, Exchange is designed to immediately compose, render, dial-up, and send a fax. It's possible to schedule a fax for later delivery, however, so if a fax doesn't seem to be going anywhere, click on it, and choose File | Send Options. This lets you verify or change when you want to send the fax. While you have the Send Options dialog box open (see Figure 6-40), you can also change the cover page and the method used for delivery.

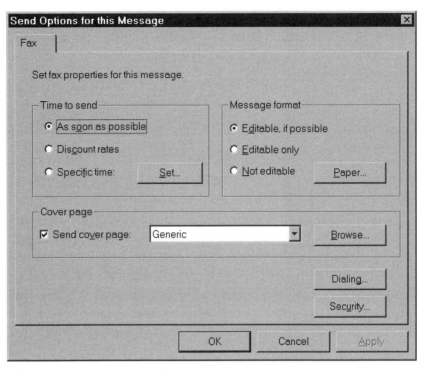

Figure 6-40: Choose Send Options for a file to see how it will be faxed. Use File|Properties instead to change or view the settings for other types of mail.

If an outgoing item of mail still won't send, open your Outbox. (To easily access your Outbox, use View | Folders to open a folder pane to the left of the current mailbox.) Check to see that the item's description is in italics. If you try to read outgoing mail before it's sent and then close the mail editor, the italics are removed, and the item can no longer be routed as mail. To fix this, double-click on the mail item in your Outbox to open it, and use File|Send to resend it.

If all else fails, remember that Exchange is not your only choice. You can get superior faxing abilities with a program such as Delrina WinFax Pro 7.0, or you can use a package such as Eudora for Internet mail instead of struggling with Exchange. This can also be a good alternative if you have 8MB memory or less. Exchange is a bit of a memory hog, and a stripped-down or alternative mailbox package may leave more of that precious RAM available for your other Windows applications and keep your computer running faster, too.

Organizing Your Mail

When you open a mail document, Exchange must start up in order to let you view it.

Another important technique with Exchange involves organizing your mail so that you don't end up with an overflowing Inbox. Use File|New to create a new folder in Exchange. You can also create subfolders inside of other folders by first clicking on the top-level folder you want to have host the other folders.

By default, Exchange manages all mail from all sources, be they fax, Internet mail, company mail, what have you, all in the same Inbox. Pending mail is all held in the same Outbox. These are part of your personal message store (PST). When you create a profile, you'll be asked for the name of this PST, which by default is mailbox.pst. If you prefer to keep your different mail types completely separate, create a separate profile for each mail type, and use a different PST for each one.

So you could have a folder called Pending to hold mail for further action, one called Archived to save old mail that you can't yet bear to delete, a folder called Projects, with subfolders for your various tasks, to hold the mail that's related to each project.

This relies on Exchange's folder mechanism, which resembles the Explorer but actually just mimics it. Instead of using Exchange folders, you can also use your existing hard drive folders to store mail messages. Just drag and drop a mail message to your desktop or to an open folder. It's always copied, so if you don't want to keep two copies of it, delete the one that's still in Exchange. This can be useful if you want to group your project e-mail with the actual documents and shortcuts you use for that project. (However, when you open a mail document, Exchange must start up in order to let you view it.)

Rich Mail

Why limit yourself to plain black text on white "paper"? Exchange offers many formatting features that let you choose various fonts and colors for use in your mail messages and faxes. You can embed a graphic by opening it in Paint or another graphics application, copying it to the clipboard, and pasting it into the message. Or you can use the Insert menu to embed a file (which is shown as an icon) or a registered object.

When you embed an object, the application used to create that object opens up "inside" of Exchange. For example, let's say you want to sign your name at the end of a fax. Compose the fax as usual, then move the cursor to the end of the document, and choose Insert|Object. (You'll access the dialog box shown in Figure 6-41.)

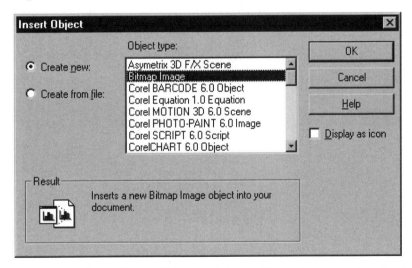

Figure 6-41: Choose Insert|Object, and choose Bitmap image to add a drawing to your mail.

Microsoft Paint opens up inside the New Message editor, as shown in Figure 6-42. You have full access to the toolbox and menus of Paint, and the menus and toolbar for Exchange are also available.

435

Figure 6-42: The beauty of Object Linking and Embedding is *in-place activation*: you embed a type of data, and the program for working with it opens within the original application.

As long as you work within the bounded area of the Paint canvas, Paint remains running. You can use the paintbrush tool to scrawl out your John Hancock. When you're ready to return to the mail document, just click anywhere outside of the Paint canvas. This removes the Paint toolbar and menus and restores you to the message editor. If you want to resize the picture, click on it, and then adjust its size by dragging the sizing handles at each corner of the picture. If you want to change the drawing, just double-click on it to bring Paint back into play. Then click outside of the Paint image to close Paint again, click the Send button ⊠ from the Exchange toolbar, and you're done.

Word Mail

If even these features aren't enough to bring your creativity to life, consider using WordMail, an optional feature of Microsoft Word 95 for Windows 95. It isn't installed if you chose the typical installation—you must use Custom install. So if you don't have a WordMail Options entry on your Compose menu, you'll have to rerun the Setup program for Microsoft Word or Office 95. Choose the option for adding/removing components. Locate Word on the list, if necessary, and double-click on it to see the options available. Turn on the check box for WordMail.

WordMail replaces Exchange's message editor and viewer with a customized Word template, replete with custom toolbars that resemble the mail toolbar. You can do everything with WordMail that you can do with the message editor, but you're using your word processor, which is presumably more familiar to you and certainly more powerful. The only real downside is that Word takes longer to open than the Exchange message editor. You might also miss the convenient one-click color selector on Exchange's formatting toolbar—you must use Format|Font to change the text color in Word.

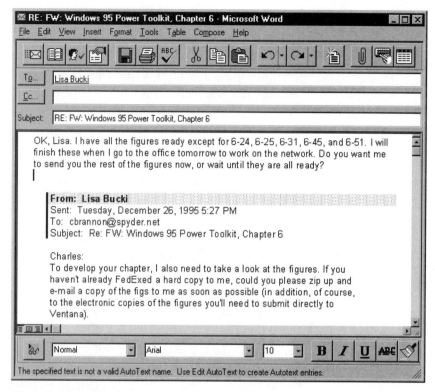

Figure 6-43: WordMail is a powerful alternative for editing and viewing mail documents.

For example, you can easily add a signature to the bottom of every mail message. Just use File | Autotext to create an Autotext entry of AutoSig. Add your name and perhaps your e-mail address or other taglines, and whenever you send a mail message using WordMail, this autotext entry is automatically added at the bottom of the message. If you want to add it manually, name it something other than AutoSig. Move the cursor to where you want to insert the signature, type the Autotext name, and press F3 to expand the Autotext name into the full signature. (Some people prefer to create an AutoCorrect entry instead, since it is automatically expanded whenever you type the word and press the spacebar.)

Schedule+ for Windows 95

Schedule+ can automate tasks such as setting up meetings.

Another handy groupware product is Schedule+ 2.0, which is now part of Microsoft Office for Windows 95. The original Schedule+ 1.0 was included for free with Windows for Workgroups, and registered licensees of Windows for Workgroups qualify for a $20 rebate on the $99 purchase price of stand-alone Schedule+ 2.0.

Schedule+ is a handy time and contact manager (Figure 6-44). While less sophisticated than some stand-alone packages, it is also easier to use than the others. When you first run Schedule+, you'll see a familiar "notebook" style page with times of day running along the left side. You can double-click on any time to enter an appointment, and you can turn on or off a reminder. You can double-click on any day of the calendar to switch to that day. Just these two features are sufficient for some people.

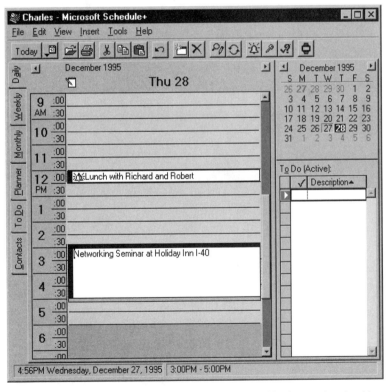

Figure 6-44: Schedule+ is easy to use. It's like a tabbed organizer booklet.

Schedule+ works for your organization only if you can convince, cajole, bribe, or otherwise motivate everyone on your staff to use it for keeping track of appointments, events, and meetings. While any individual user can benefit from keeping his or her schedule (as well as tasks and business contacts) on the computer, the groupware aspect comes into play when you view other people's schedules. By consulting other people's schedules you can find out why Betty can't be tracked down today (she's making a presentation for a client), or why Sr. Lorenzo can't fit in a meeting this week (he's booked up already).

What's more, Schedule+ can automate tasks such as setting up meetings. You run the Meeting Wizard (see Figure 6-45), and give it some guidelines about when and where you'd like to have the meeting and who you would like to invite. Cleverly, Schedule+ accesses the shared schedules of the attendees and finds a time in everyone's schedule when they would be free to meet. (You can see why this only works if everyone uses it religiously.) The Meeting Wizard then sends a meeting invitation to each person. If an invitee elects to attend, you're notified, and the meeting is automatically added to that person's schedule.

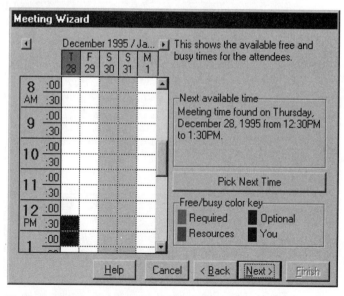

Figure 6-45: The Meeting Wizard is a marvelous application of groupware to practical business needs.

Keep In Touch

It's all too common to be unable to reach co-workers by intercom or in-house telephone call. They're usually on the phone already. What you need is a way to pop up a quick message on their screen, which they can respond to with just a click of the mouse.

Enter WinPopup

You must keep WinPopup running at all times to be able to receive messages.

WinPopup is usually installed automatically when you set up your computer for networking. If it's missing (which you can determine by using Start|Run and entering **WINPOPUP**), you can add it by running Add/Remove Programs from the Control Panel and choosing the Windows Setup tab. Double-click on Accessories to view the accessories installed, and turn on the check box for WinPopup. If WinPopup is already installed, yet doesn't appear, you can add its shortcut to your Startup folder to force it to load every time Windows starts.

When you receive a message, it's taskbar button flashes, or can even pop up automatically to display the message. It's like a multi-page yellow sticky note, since you can receive multiple "WinPops," and move between them with the << and >> toolbar buttons.

TIP

Note that WinPopup runs on its own. You don't need to have Exchange or mail services running. However, both computers must have WinPopup running, even if only minimized on the taskbar, to be able to send and receive pop-up messages. WinPopup can also receive NetWare SEND messages.

Figure 6-46: Click the envelope icon to type a WinPopup message and send it to another user.

To send a message, just click the envelope icon, and type the name of the recipient. You can communicate with others on a Windows for Workgroups, Windows 95, or Windows NT Microsoft network, or with users of a NetWare network even if they aren't running Windows. In the latter case, use the login name of the user to send the message, and note that you're limited to about 70 characters—about a paragraph or so.

You can send a message to a group of users, by using a Net-Ware group name, a workgroup name, or an NT domain name, which is similar to broadcasting, or paging. It can be useful for displaying notices and warnings, such as, "The network is going down at 6:00 PM today for maintenance."

Windows 95 can also use WinPopup to notify you if a networked printer needs your attention. If, for example, it has run out of paper.

If you would like WinPopup to appear on top of whatever else you're doing when you receive a message, choose Options from the Messages menu, and turn on the Pop up dialog on message receipt option. Also consider enabling Play sound when a new message arrives, since new messages are "buried" behind the current message. You have to press the >> button to find the next one, and the audio cue helps you realize when you've received a new one. Turn on Always on top if the WinPopup window tends to get lost in your Windows desktop clutter: it forces the WinPopup window to remain visible (on top) at all times, except when minimized to the taskbar.

Just one reminder: you must keep WinPopup running at all times to be able to receive messages. Resist the temptation to click the Close (X) button when you're finished reading a message. Instead, click the wastebasket icon, which discards the message and automatically minimizes WinPopup to the taskbar.

Have a Chat

Another popular network communication tool is WinChat, which lets you open a window to type in *real-time* to another user. Your typing appears at the top of the screen, and you see the other user's typing in the window below. This can be more fruitful than sending WinPops back and forth, although it can also be a way to goof off and gossip.

Perhaps because of its non-serious side, WinChat is not a standard part of Windows 95. To install it, you'll need the Windows 95 CD-ROM (or the free CD-ROM extras downloaded from http://www.microsoft.com).

Open the Control Panel, and choose Add/Remove Programs. Click on the Windows Setup tab, and then click the Have Disk button. You'll be asked to enter the path of the setup files, so type the location on the CD-ROM (such as D:\OTHER\WINCHAT). You can then turn on the check box for Chat, which copies the chat files and the "telephone ringing" sound effect to your Windows installation.

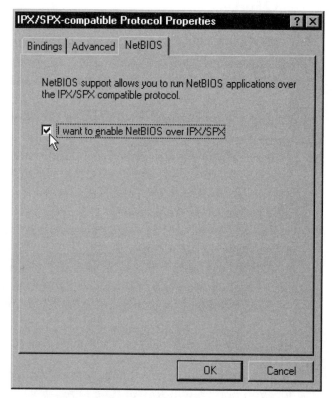

Figure 6-47: Enable NetBIOS support for WinChat.

Naturally, the other users must also follow this technique, but you're not done yet. Chat uses the NetBIOS protocol to send its messages back and forth. If you are using the NetBEUI protocol, you're almost ready to chat, but if you're using IPX/SPX, you'll have to open the Network settings in the Control Panel and choose the Properties for IPX/SPX. Click the NetBIOS tab, and turn on the check box for I want to enable NetBIOS over IPX/SPX. (See the section "Configuring Network Neighborhood" for more information on customizing your network setup.)

If you'd like Chat to pop open automatically when you're called, you need to run the NETDDE utility. The easiest way to do this is to create a shortcut in your \Windows\Start Menu\ Programs\Startup folder to the NETDDE.EXE program.

We discussed WinChat and WinPopup in Chapter 5, but consider how they can be used to enhance network productivity. Employees can have background Chat discussions while they are each occupied on the telephone. A receptionist can use WinPopup to announce that a visitor has arrived, or a secretary might use WinPopup to remind the boss of an appointment. The help desk supervisor can use Chat to walk an employee through the steps to solve a problem. WinPopup can also be good for quick company announcements. For example, if an important mail memo just went out, you can use WinPopup to notify everyone to open their Inboxes and read the memo.

ADVANCED NETWORK TECHNIQUES

We've saved some networking techniques for the end of the chapter because they may be of more interest to network professionals or system administrators. However, even if it's not your job to set up or maintain your network, you'll want to at least be aware of these techniques.

Shared versus Local Windows Installation

Even if you don't implement a common Windows folder on the network, it's still useful and necessary to create a Windows 95 installation directory.

For the best performance, you'll want to install Windows 95 on your local hard drive. Some network administrators prefer to keep a centralized Windows 95 directory on a network drive. They believe that this makes Windows 95 easier to maintain. We don't recommend this option; Windows needs all the speed it can get, and even a sluggish hard drive is much faster than a network connection. Running Windows from a file server also significantly increases network traffic. If your computers are diskless worksta-

tions, you may have no choice but to run Windows 95 from a file
server directory, but the network traffic will get horrendous because
the Windows swap file will also have to be located on the server.

Even if you don't implement a common Windows folder on the
network, it's still useful and necessary to create a Windows 95
installation directory. This allows users to upgrade or re-install
Windows 95 without needing the original disks or CD-ROM. (Of
course, your company must still arrange with Microsoft to obtain
the necessary number of software licenses for Windows 95.)

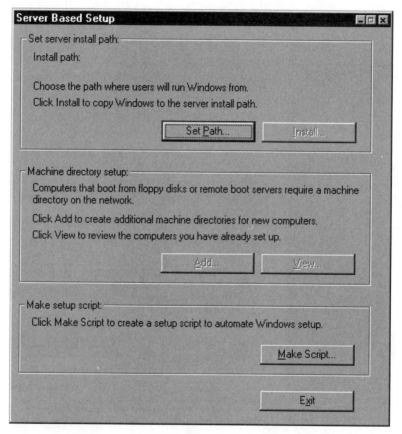

Figure 6-48: NetSetup is ideal for automating network installation.

The easiest way to create a network install directory is to copy the \WIN95 folder from the Windows 95 CD-ROM to the network. Users can run the SETUP program from the network from either DOS or Windows 3.1. Or you could set up a share to a CD-ROM drive that hosts Windows 95.

Expert network administrators will prefer a more optimal method, however. You'll need the Windows 95 CD-ROM. Look in the \ADMIN\NETTOOLS folder, and run the program called NETSETUP. This allows you to create a custom Windows 95 folder on your network drive and an automated batch script for installing Windows 95. It's possible to create a setup script that completely automates Windows 95 setup, which is a lifesaver for administrators of large companies. The Windows 95 files are also decompressed for faster searching and lookup on the LAN.

We can't get into all the complex details of using NetSetup in just one chapter of this book. For more information, open the Windows Resource Kit help file located in the \ADMIN\RESKIT\HELPFILE folder of the Windows 95 CD-ROM, and search for NetSetup. You'll also find sample setup scripts and polices in the \ADMIN\RESKIT\SAMPLES folder.

Setting Network Policies

Policy Editor can hide all desktop icons.

Thanks to Policy Editor, configuring Windows 95 on local workstations is easier than ever. You can even access a computer's registry from your own machine. With Policy Editor, you can set certain default registry settings that are enforced on each user's computer. Policy Editor also lets you improve security. For example, you can prevent a computer from running MS-DOS programs or, in fact, prevent access to any programs except those on the Start menu, and you can lock the Start menu to prevent modification.

Policy Editor can also hide all desktop icons, although this also prevents the use of desktop shortcuts and scraps. You can also prevent access to certain Control Panel items or property sheets.

Run POLEDIT from the \ADMIN\APPTOOLS\POLEDIT folder of the Windows 95 CD-ROM. Use File | Open Registry to modify the policies of your local computer. Then click the ⊞ symbol to the left of each option to expand the list of settings. Click in the check boxes of the policies you want to implement. Figure 6-49 shows some of the shell restrictions you can set up.

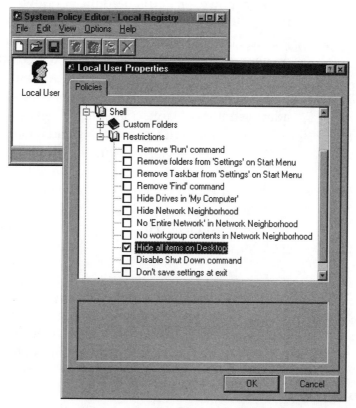

Figure 6-49: Use Policy Editor to control access to Windows 95 features.

You can then save the policy template to a folder that's accessible to all computers, such as the SYS\PUBLIC directory of a NetWare file server or on the domain controller or backup domain controller of a Windows NT server. The template can also be distributed to backup domain controllers so that automatic load balancing can be performed. If you're running only peer-to-peer, you'll have to copy the POLICY.DAT file to the local hard drive of each computer.

Policy Editor can even be used without a network. If you've set your computer to allow a separate login for each user or family member (covered earlier in this chapter), then each user can have a different policy. This lets you, as the administrator (parent) control access to the computer when it's used by the users (children). This is an ideal way to protect your computer from unauthorized (or accidental) operations, such as shelling to DOS.

Since you're probably not the network administrator, we've provided just an overview of Policy Editor (here and in Chapter 2, "The Registry"). For more complete documentation, search for POLEDIT in the Windows 95 Resource Kit help file as we discussed above for NetSetup.

NetWare Techniques

As we said, this chapter has focused on the end-user of a network. If your job is to administer a network, there's no better reference than the *Windows 95 Resource Kit*, published by Microsoft Press. However, there are some useful NetWare techniques that you might want to be familiar with.

Enabling Long Filename Support

Keep in mind that DOS and Windows 3.1 users will only be able to see the short version of a long filename.

A typical NetWare server is designed to support DOS machines, including DOS machines running Windows for Workgroups. NetWare only reserves space in its directory tables for the standard 11-character (8.3) DOS filenames. But once you've become accustomed to Windows 95 long filenames, it seems unfair to have to revert to the old ways when storing files on a network.

Windows NT supports long filenames as a matter of course, but for NetWare servers, you have to first add a *namespace*. This is a chunk of reserved space on the file server hard drive for storing the extra characters in a long filename. For example, Apple Macintosh filenames can be up to 32 characters long, so the Macintosh namespace is used to support Macs that are attached along with PCs to a NetWare network.

A similar issue popped up when Microsoft and IBM first developed OS/2. OS/2, like its successor, Windows NT, was designed to support long filenames, and without support for long filenames from NetWare, this could limit the acceptance of a mixed OS/2 and NetWare network.

The solution was NetWare's OS/2 namespace. We can take advantage of it with Windows 95, too. When the OS/2 namespace is added to a NetWare server, Windows 95 clients can store files using up to 256 characters. Without it, your long filenames are *truncated*, although the method of truncation is not quite the same as with Windows 95.

When you store a file with a long filename on a Windows 95 computer or Windows NT server, the DOS filename is created from the first six characters of the long filename, and then a tilde character (~) and a number (usually 1) is added. So the file December Sales Results would become DECEMB~1. A second file named December Forecast would become DECEMB~2. The same two files on a NetWare server would become DECEMBER and DECEMBE0, respectively, and if you created a third file December Donuts, it would become DECEMB~3 on Windows 95 and Windows NT and DECEMBE1 on the NetWare server.

Keep in mind that DOS and Windows 3.1 users will only be able to see the short version of the filename, and if they save the file back out to the server, the long filename will be replaced by the truncated filename. Because of issues like this, you may not want to use long filenames on your network unless all users are using Windows 95 or Window NT Workstation as their client operating system.

To get started, go to the NetWare file server console, or run the RCONSOLE utility from the client workstation.

Type the following commands at the file server console:

```
load os2
add name space os2 to volume sys
```

This creates the namespace, which can sometimes add up to several megabytes of space so make sure plenty of free space is available on the NetWare SYS volume. If you have other volumes that you'd like to use for long filenames, use the second command again, changing only the name of the volume. This is a one-time setup, but you do have to make sure that the OS2 module is loaded every time the server starts up.

To do this, run INSTALL from the NetWare server, or directly edit the STARTUP.CNF file, and add the command:

```
load os2
```

Because STARTUP runs before the volumes are mounted, you'll need to copy the OS2.NLM file to the DOS partition (C:\) of the NetWare server, or to the boot diskette if that's used instead.

Once you've installed the patch on the NetWare server, you'll have to edit the Registry on each client machine to re-enable long filenames.

As long as you're running NetWare version 3.12 or later, that's all it takes. From this point forward, you can store files using long filenames (up to 254 characters) in directories (folders) on the NetWare server.

A bug in NetWare 3.11 that affects the OS/2 namespace and programs that open a large number of files can make the use of long filenames unreliable. For this reason, Windows 95 running on NetWare 3.11 won't use long filenames even if the OS/2 namespace is running on the server. However, you can obtain a fix for the OS/2 namespace from CompuServe in the NETWIRE forum to fix this.

Look for a file named 311ptd.exe. (It can also be retrieved via the Internet at ftp://ftp.novell.com in the /pub/netware/nwos/ nw311/osnlm directory.) When you run the 311ptd.exe file, it will extract a file called os2opnfx.nlm. Copy this to the SYSTEM folder of the NetWare SYS volume, and use LOAD OS2OPNFX from the NetWare file server to install the patch.

Once you've installed the patch on the NetWare server, you'll have to edit the Registry on each client machine to re-enable long filenames.

1. Start the Registry Editor (using Start|Run, REGEDIT if you don't have a shortcut to it already), and click on the ⊞ symbols next to each entry (as shown in Figure 6-50) to drill down to the following Registry location:

```
Hkey_Local_Machine\System\CurrentControlSet\Services\VxD\Nwredir
```

2. Create a new binary value called SupportLFN.

3. Double-click on the value you created, and set its value to 2. (For more information on Registry editing, refer to Chapter 3, "Extreme Customization.")

TIP

The default value of SupportLFN—even though it's not listed—is 1, which allows Windows 95 to support long filenames only on NetWare versions 3.12 and greater. You can use 0 to prevent long filenames unconditionally.

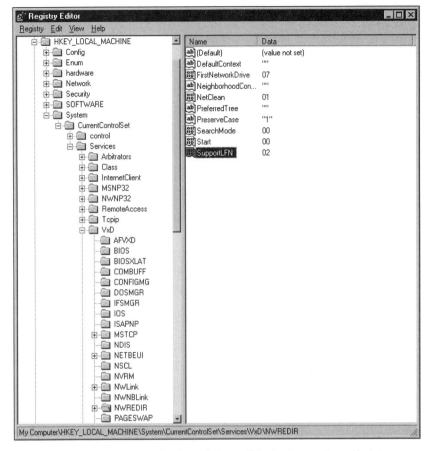

Figure 6-50: Here's how the Registry Editor will look after you've added the new SupportLFN value.

Obtaining NetWare Support Files

Many applications specific to NetWare require the presence of certain NetWare system files. You might also need to use the ODI or VLM drivers in some circumstances. Novell has not licensed these files to Microsoft, so you'll need to obtain the latest versions of these support files and drivers directly from Novell or via the

NETWIRE or NOVLIB forums on CompuServe. You can also find them on the Internet at *ftp.novell.com*. You're looking for DOSUP9, WINDR2, WINUP9, and VLMUP9. (Use later versions if available, such as WINUP10 or WINDR3.) These are self-extracting files. When you copy them to a folder and double-click on them (or type their names at the DOS prompt), the files contained within the master file are extracted to that folder. Look for the README files to learn more about the use of these drivers and system files.

Login Script Issues

When you attach and login to a NetWare server, the server feeds the workstation a series of commands, known as a *login script*. These commands are used to map default network drives and set search paths (similar to the DOS PATH utility), run command-line tools (such as CAPTURE for redirecting a printer port), set environment variables, even display a greeting. If you're logging in using the standard IPX or ODI drivers, there aren't any issues involved, but if you're using Microsoft's Client for NetWare Networks, you should be aware of a key limitation: the login script must not contain any TSRs (terminate and stay resident utilities). This can sometimes cause a Windows 95 machine to lock up. Using TSRs won't work in any case, since the only way to set global TSRs for all DOS sessions is to run them in AUTOEXEC.BAT or in WINSTART.BAT.

One way around this problem is to use the IF command in the login script to test for the DOS version, and skip the TSRs if the login script determines it's running on a Windows 95 machine

Another means to get around the TSR issue is to disable the login script.

(which uses DOS 7.0). This probably won't work, because the SETVER command (loaded by default in CONFIG.SYS) is designed to lie about the version number of DOS in order to force NETX to allow a login. It seems that Novell has always rigged NETX not to run on Microsoft's latest version of DOS (presumably for compatibility reasons), and the SETVER command allows DOS to lie about its version number. Thanks to SETVER, when NETX is run, DOS reports its version number as 5.0.

If you have obtained the latest version of NETX for DOS 7.0/ Windows 95, you can use the SETVER command to remove this prevarication. Just go to any DOS prompt and type:

```
SETVER NETX.COM /D
SETVER NETX.EXE /D
```

This removes the NETX exception from the SETVER table, and you'll be able to use IF NOT DOS_VERSION = "7.0" in the login script to bypass any TSRs.

Another means to get around the TSR issue is to disable the login script. Right-click on the Network Neighborhood icon, and choose Properties (or choose Network from the Control Panel), and bring up the properties for the NetWare client. Click the General tab, and turn off the check box for Enable login script processing. If you do this, you won't be able to access command-line tools such as NPRINT, because there is no drive mapped to them. You can get around this by creating a batch file with the login script commands you need, and putting a shortcut to this batch file (or the batch file itself) in the Startup folder, in \Windows\ Start Menu\Programs\ Startup.

NetWare Goodies

Windows 95 includes special features for NetWare networking. You can access these by right-clicking on a server name in the Network Neighborhood window. Some of these commands are also available for the current server when you right-click on the Network Neighborhood icon:

❑ Use Open to connect and log in to the server.

❑ Use Explore to see what volumes are available on the server, without connecting to the server.

❑ Use Who Am I to see your current user name on the server.

❑ Log Out disconnects you from the server.

❑ Attach As lets you attach to another server in addition to the server you're already using and, in addition, lets you choose a different username and password, if necessary.

❑ Use Map Network Drive to create a drive letter on your local computer that maps to (is redirected to) a drive and folder on the NetWare server. You can map a drive letter to either a NetWare volume, or you can use Connect as the root of the drive to map a drive letter to a directory, yet have the files and subdirectories of that directory appear to be the only ones on the drive.

❑ You can choose Create Shortcut to make a desktop shortcut to the server or choose Properties to view information about the server. (Viewing a server's properties requires attaching to the server temporarily, which uses up one of the available connections until you close the property sheet.)

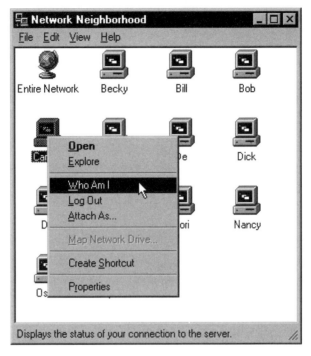

Figure 6-51: Right-click on a server to access special pop-up menu commands.

MOVING ON

Chapter 7, "Customizing Applications," focuses on programming—telling the computer what you want it to do. Probably the most effective introduction to computer programming is by creating *macros*, small programs you can write to customize applications (with considerable assistance from those applications). In the next chapter, we'll look at the basics and, in the process, create some macros that are useful in the real world. Then we'll go on to more advanced topics, including Visual Basic for Applications.

Chapter 7

Customizing Applications

In this chapter we'll explore macro programming, techniques you can use to customize Windows 95 applications. First, we'll introduce the concept—showing you how to tailor your applications to suit your particular ways of working. The rest of the chapter covers important elements of Basic programming—variables, constants, arrays—along with examples of advanced macro programming.

To make this chapter do double duty, many of the examples are useful in their own right. They'll illustrate the techniques being discussed but also can be employed to good effect in real-world applications. We'll begin by exploring a series of macros created in Word for Windows, the most popular word processor, using WordBasic, Word's macro language. (For thorough coverage of all aspects of WordBasic, see the *Microsoft Word Developer's Kit*. You can find it in bookstores or purchase it directly from Microsoft Press at 1-800-MS-PRESS.

Later in the chapter, we'll explore VBA (Visual Basic for applications), a macro language that's quite similar to WordBasic. Microsoft is endeavoring to simplify macro programming by inserting VBA into all its applications, so that you need to learn only one macro language rather than three or four, to work with the Office suite. Previously, if you used AccessBasic or the Excel macro language, you had to switch gears. WordBasic was yet a *third* flavor—different commands, syntax, and punctuation. Now, all Microsoft applications are using VBA, except Word. Doubtless the next version of Word will incorporate VBA as well.

VBA doesn't eliminate the older, individual macro languages in Microsoft's applications. WordBasic will still be there, just as Access still responds to AccessBasic commands and Excel Basic is still included in Excel. But you'll probably want to create all your future macros using VBA—it's better. Visual Basic in general is more robust than other languages when dealing with OLE and other advanced Windows programming.

WHY USE MACROS?

A macro is a computer program. It's not as large or complex as a word processor or spreadsheet program, but it's a program nonetheless. You tell it how to do something for you. Then, forever after, it will carry out your instructions flawlessly.

There are many ways of writing a computer program. Languages like C and Basic are popular for creating stand-alone utilities and applications. However, most commercial applications contain their own, embedded programming languages, called *macro languages*. These languages enable you to create little programs—macros—that work whenever their host application is running. In other words, if you create a macro in Word for Windows, you can run that macro whenever Word is running.

Macros are a sophisticated and powerful way to customize your applications. Macros can make your work with spreadsheets, database applications, word processors, graphics programs, and other applications much more efficient. If you find yourself doing something repeatedly, consider creating a macro.

A Simple Example

For example, let's say that you must frequently type these same two sentences:

We're hoping that you'll enjoy our product line. We look forward to hearing from you.

There's no point in typing those sentences day after day. Let's create a macro to automate this process in Word for Windows. We'll start with this simple example, but as you'll see throughout this chapter, macros can be extremely complex. For now, if you click on the Tools | Macros menu in Word, you'll see a dialog box similar to Figure 7-1.

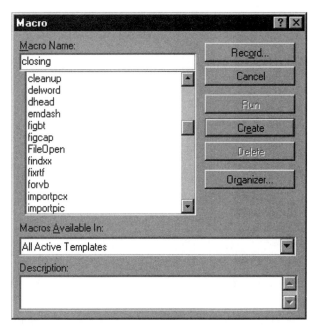

Figure 7-1: Word's macro-creating dialog box.

Type the name you want to give this macro into the Macro Name text box; we used the name "closing" as you can see in Figure 7-1. Now click on the Record button. Then click on OK in the next dialog box that appears. You'll see the small floating toolbar shown in Figure 7-2. It contains two buttons: the button with the square stops the recording; the other button pauses it (in case you want to do something that you don't want to become part of the macro). Also notice that a cassette tape icon attaches itself to the mouse pointer. (Mouse movements, except for clicking on menu items, making selections, and so on, aren't recorded.)

Now type the two sentences that you want to have entered automatically when you run the macro. Then click on the Stop button with the square.

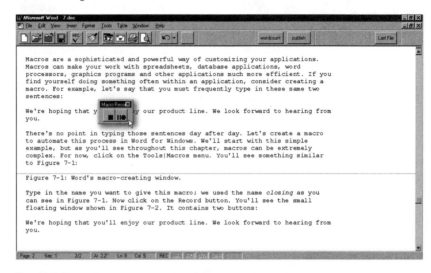

Figure 7-2: While you're recording a macro, this small toolbar with two buttons appears.

Any time you need these sentences in the future, you don't have to retype them. Just run this macro. One way to run it is to click on the Tools | Macro menu, then double-click on closing in the Macro Name list. But there's another, better way, to run macros; you can trigger them with a keyboard shortcut.

Keyboard Shortcuts

The most efficient way to run a macro is to create a keyboard shortcut that triggers it when you press a particular key combination. For example, let's assign Ctrl+E (for "ending") to our closing macro. It's a good idea to use memorable keys, so generally you should try to employ the first letter of the idea or concept you're dealing with. Now click on Tools | Customize, then click on the Keyboard tab. In the Categories list on the left, locate Macros and click on it to select it. In the Macros list on the right, click on closing (see Figure 7-3).

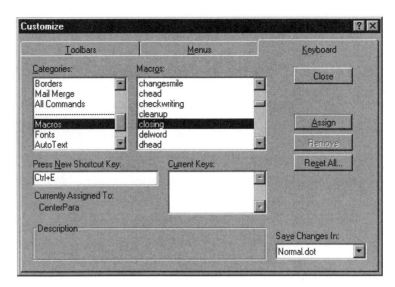

Figure 7-3: Assign frequently used macros to keyboard shortcuts in the Customize dialog box.

Click on the Press New Shortcut Key text box, and press Ctrl+E. Word assigns lots of its features to shortcut keys, before you even start fooling around with them. So you might see Currently Assigned to describe what would happen if you press Ctrl+E or any other key combination that you want to use. If so, decide whether the built-in assignment matters, if you'll ever use it. If not, go ahead, and click on the Assign button. That key combination will be reassigned to your macro. (Note: to remove an entry from the Press New Shortcut Key text box, use the Backspace key.)

Click on OK to close the Customize dialog box, then press Ctrl+E to try out your macro.

Editing a Macro

The closing macro is now part of Word—it's in there whenever you want to run it. But what if you want to change it? Easy. Most applications' macros are written in what many consider the best programming language ever invented, Basic. The great advantage of this language is that most of the commands are in plain English. You'll find words like *stop* and *if* that mean just what they say.

There's no attempt in Basic to create fancy, unnecessary, crypto-mathematical constructs. In Basic, the commands are as close to natural English as possible, and the punctuation and syntax make sense, intuitively for the most part.

Figure 7-4: A macro can be edited just like any ordinary Word document.

Let's change the closing sentences. Click on Tools | Macros, and click on closing in the Macro Name list to select it. Click on the Edit button. You'll see something like this (the line break depends on your current margin settings and the typeface of your current document):

```
Sub MAIN
Insert "We're hoping that you'll enjoy our product line. We look
for"
Insert "ward to hearing from you."
End Sub
```

■■■

Important

All through this chapter we show macro program listings. The computer requires that instructions appear on a single line (don't press the Enter key). However, in this book, the margins sometimes force a line to break into two lines. If you get mysterious error messages when you try to run or test these macros, check to see if you've typed as two lines what should be a single line. The best solution is to cut and paste the macros from this book's Companion CD-ROM. All the programming on the CD has been tested and works as it should.

■■■

Note that if you want to save a macro you've edited for future use, click on the File menu, and select Close.

It doesn't take a computer scientist to translate this Basic command: Insert. It's easy to see what this macro does. It inserts these two sentences at the current cursor location. Sub MAIN and End

Sub surround all macros and mean—"start here" and "end here," respectively. What's between those two lines is what happens when the macro is run. Notice also that you're now in just another Word editing screen—like any ordinary screen. It's merely a new document. You can type whatever you want to change the message. Type **We hope** on top of "We're hoping" (press the Ins key so you can type over the existing text). Then click on File | Close. Select Yes to save your changes. Next time you run the macro, it will reflect your changes.

TIP

There's another way to insert boilerplate text. If you've got some phrases or other text that you often type, try using Word 95's AutoCorrect feature. All you do is select Tools|AutoCorrect, then in the text box labeled Replace, type a few letters that will trigger the replacement. We'll use *cl* to trigger our sentences, short for *closing*. In the With text box, type your two sentences or any text you want (see Figure 7-5). Click on the Add button. When you type **cl** followed by a space, Word inserts your text.

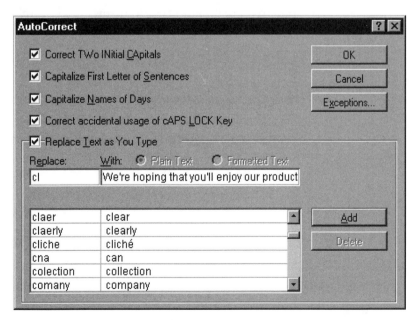

Figure 7-5: The AutoCorrect feature is an alternative way to add instant text.

WRITING A MACRO

Although there's much you can do via macro recording, some truly useful macros must be written from scratch, at least in part. We've seen that editing a macro is merely a matter of changing the words in an ordinary Word document. By extension, you can write a macro from scratch. You need not have recorded the macro example above. All you have to do to start writing a WordBasic macro from scratch is to select Tools | Macro, type a name for your macro, then click on the Create button. You'll see a new Document with necessary Sub MAIN and End Sub, between which you can type:

```
Insert "We're hoping that you'll enjoy our product line. We look for"
Insert "ward to hearing from you."
```

Add as many additional Insert statements as you wish. Note that the number of Insert commands in the previous example depends on your current margin settings—how much information Word can get on a line. The Insert command does not create a new line or new paragraph. New paragraphs (line breaks or carriage returns) are created by the InsertPara command.

Dialog Boxes & Lists

Let's expand on the idea of a pre-packaged instant letter closing. You can create an entire set of optional closings to suit various situations. The Macro dialog box will display the alternative sentences, and the user can click on the desired one. For this, we'll create a dialog box. And, we'll have to write some of this macro (rather than record it).

However, Word will help us out. Word 95 comes with a dialog box editor to make it easier to create just what you want. Select Tools | Macro, then type **closebox** in the Macro Name text box as the name for the new macro, and click on the Create button. Notice that Word puts a Macro toolbar up at the top with various buttons you can use to work with macros. On the far right is a button that launches the Dialog Editor utility. Click on that button.

If the Dialog Editor doesn't come up (you get a message that a file is missing), this means that you didn't choose to install it during Word setup. Get out your Word, or Microsoft Office, CD or diskettes, and run Setup. Choose Add/Remove, then click on Microsoft Word, and click on the Change Option button. You'll see a window like the one in Figure 7-6. Click to select the Dialog Editor.

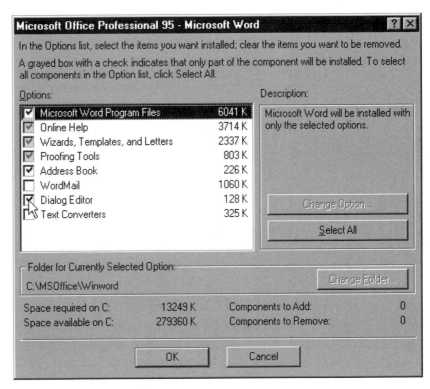

Figure 7-6: Add the Dialog Editor utility by running Word setup.

You'll be able to add various elements to the basic dialog window by clicking on the Item menu. But first, stretch the new dialog box so it's about the shape of the one in Figure 7-7. A blank dialog box automatically appears when you start Dialog Editor.

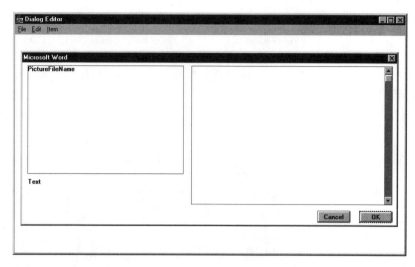

Figure 7-7: Our new custom dialog box, in its design phase.

Using the Item menu, add a Picture Box, Text, List Box, and OK
and Cancel buttons. Reposition and resize them as shown in
Figure 7-7 by mouse-dragging. (Alas, the Text item will resist any
resizing until later. We'll take care of that shortly.)

You need to transform this visual template into macro programming that Word can understand and display. Click on the Dialog
Editor's Edit menu, and choose Select Dialog. This captures the
whole thing. Then click on the Edit menu, and choose Copy. Now
it's in the clipboard.

Go back to the window holding your Word Macro that we
named closebox, and position the cursor on the blank line between Sub MAIN and End Sub. Click on Word's Edit menu, and
choose Paste. You'll see the programming for your dialog box
appear, as shown in Figure 7-8.

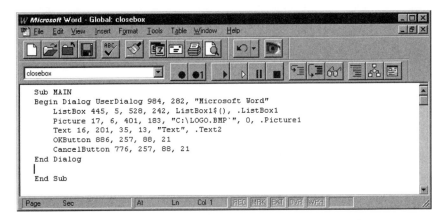

```
Sub MAIN
Begin Dialog UserDialog 984, 282, "Microsoft Word"
    ListBox 445, 5, 528, 242, ListBox1$(), .ListBox1
    Picture 17, 6, 401, 183, "C:\LOGO.BMP`", 0, .Picture1
    Text 16, 201, 35, 13, "Text", .Text2
    OKButton 886, 257, 88, 21
    CancelButton 776, 257, 88, 21
End Dialog

End Sub
```

Figure 7-8: Our visual dialog box has been translated into the Word macro language.

At this point, let's edit this programming somewhat, to get the results we're really after. To provide a different title for the dialog window, change:

```
Begin Dialog UserDialog 984, 282, "Microsoft Word"
```

to:

```
Begin Dialog UserDialog 984, 282, "Closings to official let-
ters…"
```

To tell Word what picture to display in your dialog box, type the name of a .BMP file on your hard drive to replace Picture-FileName.
Change:

```
Picture 17, 6, 401, 183, "C:\LOGO.BMP`", 0, .Picture1
```

to:

```
Picture 17, 6, 401, 183, "D:\CLOSING.BMP", 0, .Picture1
```

(Substitute whatever .BMP file you want to use. Word automatically resizes your image to fit the space.)

Now enter the text that you want to display as instructions to the user. Change:

```
Text 16, 201, 35, 13, "Text", .Text1
```

to:

```
Text 16, 201, 320, 13, "Choose a closing by double-clicking on
it in the list", .Text1
```

Notice that we also adjusted the width by changing 35 to 320. Those first four values for each item describe horizontal position, vertical position, width, and height. A 0, 0 for horizontal and vertical position would put the item in the upper left corner of the dialog box.

TIP

You can position an item in the Dialog Editor by clicking on it to select it, and then using the arrow keys to move it in small increments.

So, by this time, you've got something like this in your macro:

```
Sub Main
Begin Dialog UserDialog 984, 282, "Closings to official let-
ters...."
        ListBox 439, 9, 528, 242, Closer$( ), .ListBox1
        Picture 20, 10, 393, 176, "D:\CLOSING.BMP", 0, .Picture1
        Text 21, 195, 320, 79, "Choose a closing by double-
clicking on it in the list", .Text1
        OKButton 878, 257, 88, 21
        CancelButton 776, 257, 88, 21
End Dialog
End Sub
```

To display the dialog box when the macro runs, we'll need to type in these lines, just above End Sub:

```
Dim dlg As UserDialog
chosen = Dialog(dlg)
```

The first line creates an object named "dlg" that represents our entire UserDialog box as defined above. Then, we pick a word to hold the results when the user clicks on the OK or Cancel button. *Chosen* is a "variable," meaning that it can hold various values. If the user clicks on OK, chosen holds a –1, and if the user clicks on Cancel (or clicks on the x icon to close the dialog box), chosen holds a 0. This variable will come in handy when we decide how to respond after the user closes the dialog box.

In any event, by saying *chosen = Dialog(dlg)*, you tell WordBasic to display the dialog box named dlg. Remember that we've just assigned the name "dlg" to our box. If all this seems a bit much to you, don't worry. You can simply copy this programming—just type it in. It works and can be used to create any number of different, useful dialog boxes, as we will see.

Figure 7-9: Your dialog box, ready to add options in the list box.

Now all that remains is to fill the list box with options that the user can double-click on. To fill in the list, just create an "array variable. (Variables and arrays are discussed in more detail later in this chapter. This special kind of variable can hold a number of values, each labeled by an index number. We'll create a text (string) array by using the Dim command. (See "The Complete Macro" on the following page for the location where you should type this into the macro.)

```
Dim closer$(4)
```

This means that we've created an array called *closer$* (the $ means it will hold text). Further, we've said that it can hold five values (0 to 4). You don't have to use all of them if you don't want to. In the macro editing window, type the actual values, the text that you want in each of the closer$( ) elements. Note that you can single or double space; blank lines are ignored when the macro runs:

```
closer$(0) = "We appreciate your comments and will pass them
along."

closer$(1) = "We hope this matter is now resolved."

closer$(2) = "Our president, Jim Nobles, has resigned as a
result of your letter. We assume this closes the issue."

closer$(3) = "Your question has been submitted to Mrs. Murphy of
our customer service department. She will be in contact with you
when she returns to work."

closer$(4) = "Please consider that our final offer."
```

Now we can refer to these various sentences by their array name *closer$* along with the particular index number of each closer$(0), closer$(1), and so on. However, all we have to do to put this array into the list box is name it within the specifications of the list box created when you pasted the dialog box specifications:

```
ListBox 439, 9, 528, 242, Closer$( ), .ListBox1
```

Finally, the macro has to react to what the user clicks on when the dialog box is displayed. First, we say that *if chosen* equals –1 (meaning that the user clicked on the OK button), then Insert (type) the array item (*closer$*) indexed by whatever is currently selected (highlighted) in the list box. This way, the user can click on a sentence in the list box, then click OK to insert that sentence in the document. Alternatively, the user can double-click on the chosen sentence in the list box.

```
If chosen = - 1 Then 'they clicked OK
        Insert closer$(dlg.listbox1)
End If
```

Putting it all together, our entire dialog box macro looks like the following, and Figure 7-10 shows how the dialog box appears when you run the macro.

The Complete Macro

```
Sub MAIN

Dim closer$(4)

closer$(0) = "We appreciate your comments and will pass them
along."

closer$(1) = "We hope this matter is now resolved."

closer$(2) = "Our president, Jim Nobles, has resigned as a
result of your letter. We assume this closes the issue."

closer$(3) = "Your question has been submitted to Mrs. Murphy of
our customer service department. She will be in contact with you
when she returns to work."

closer$(4) = "Please consider that our final offer."


Begin Dialog UserDialog 984, 282, "Closings to official let-
ters...."
```

```
            ListBox 439, 9, 528, 242, Closer$( ), .ListBox1
            Picture 20, 10, 393, 176, "D:\CLOSING.BMP", 0, .Picture1
            Text 21, 195, 320, 79, "Choose a closing by double-
clicking on it in the list", .Text1
            OKButton 878, 257, 88, 21
            CancelButton 776, 257, 88, 21
    End Dialog

    Dim dlg As UserDialog
    chosen = Dialog(dlg)

    If chosen = - 1 Then'they clicked OK
            Insert closer$(dlg.listbox1)
    End If

    End Sub
```

Now you can test your macro by running it. Click on the dark triangle button, the third button from the left on the Macro toolbar. Or select Tools | Macro, type the name of the macro, and then click on Run. You should see something like Figure 7-9.

If you get a syntax error and your macro won't run, proofread your typing. Or just cut and paste the programming from this book's Companion CD-ROM. (Remember to change the path and name of the .BMP file to one that you have on your hard drive.)

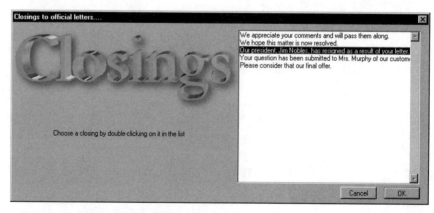

Figure 7-10: The dialog box, ready to type any of these closings.

Modifications

Once you've recorded or written a useful macro, customizing it or adapting it to serve other purposes is easy. Let's make a couple of changes to the closebox dialog box macro that we created above. We'll add additional choices, going from five to seven possible pieces of text. We'll also use a different, descriptive set of labels for the list box rather than merely displaying the actual pieces of text.

Open the macro for editing by clicking on Tools | Macros, and then typing **closebox** in the Macro Name text box or locating closebox in the list box. Click on Edit. Now in the macro editing window, hold down the Ctrl key while clicking in the left margin. This selects the entire macro. Press Ctrl+C to copy the macro to the clipboard. Close the macro window with File | Close. Now, select Tools | Macro again, and this time type **openings** as the Macro Name, then click on the Create button. Click in between Sub Main and End Sub to establish the location of your cursor, and press Ctrl+V to paste the programming from closebox into the new macro named "openings." You'll want to delete the extra Sub Main and End Sub—you can have only one of each of these lines rather than the two you've got after pasting. Now we'll modify how the macro behaves.

We want to insert addresses rather than boilerplate letter closings. And this time, we want to just see brief descriptions in the list box, not the actual text that will be inserted. Doing so is simple: create two arrays, one for the list box display and one for the actual inserted text. First create the array for the actual inserted text. We've decided to provide seven options, so we Dim(6) rather than (4) as before:

Replace:

```
Dim closer$(4)

closer$(0) = "We appreciate your comments and will pass them
along."

closer$(1) = "We hope this matter is now resolved."
```

```
closer$(2) = "Our president, Jim Nobles, has resigned as a
result of your letter. We assume this closes the issue."

closer$(3) = "Your question has been submitted to Mrs. Murphy of
our customer service department. She will be in contact with you
when she returns to work."

closer$(4) = "Please consider that our final offer."
```

with:

```
Dim opener$(6)
opener$(0) = "Dear"

opener$(1) = "Dear Customer,"

opener$(2) = "Dear Valued Customer,"

opener$(3) = "Dear Claxon Corp. Customer,"

opener$(4) = "Dear Valued Claxon Corp. Customer,"

opener$(5) = "Greetings to one of our favorite customers,"

opener$(6) = "Salutations to the best customer we've got,"
```

Then immediately below, type the following to create a separate array for the labels that will appear in the list box:

```
Dim labels$(6)

labels$(0) = "Standard"
labels$(1) = "Standard Extra"
labels$(2) = "Warm"
labels$(3) = "Warmer"
labels$(4) = "Warmest"
labels$(5) = "Very friendly"
labels$(6) = "Ecstatic"
```

To display the second array in the List Box,
Replace:

```
ListBox 439, 9, 528, 242, Closer$( ), .ListBox1
```

with:

```
ListBox 439, 9, 528, 242, labels$( ), .ListBox1
```

To cause the opener$ text to be inserted into the actual document,
Replace:

```
Insert closer$(dlg.listbox1)
```

with:

```
Insert opener$(dlg.listbox1)
```

To change the title and help text on the dialog box,
Replace:

```
Begin Dialog UserDialog 984, 282, "Closings to official let-
ters...."
```

with:

```
Begin Dialog UserDialog 984, 282, "Salutations for business
letters...."
```

and replace:

```
Text 21, 195, 320, 79, "Choose a closing by double-clicking on
it in the list", .Text1
```

with:

```
Text 21, 195, 320, 79, "Choose an opening by double-clicking on
it in the list", .Text1
```

Now when you run the openings macro, you'll select from the
labels as shown in Figure 7-11, but the correct text will be inserted.

Figure 7-11: Using the closebox macro as a template, we've built a new, custom openings macro.

A Little Magic

We also adjusted the size and position of several elements such as the list box and text. You can adjust size and position by editing the horizontal, vertical, width, and height numbers directly in the macro editing window. But it's much easier to use the Dialog Editor, where you can *see* what you're designing and don't have to pay any attention to the numbers.

Can you move the text description of a dialog box (in the macro editing window) back into the Dialog Editor? You bet. To move text from the macro back to visibility in the Dialog Editor, just reverse the process of copying from the picture via the clipboard to the editor. For example, open your macro for editing (using Tools | Macro), then select (drag your mouse over it to highlight it) the dialog box description:

```
Begin Dialog UserDialog 984, 282, "Salutations for business
letters...."
        ListBox 739, 9, 228, 242, labels$( ), .ListBox1
        Picture 20, 10, 393, 176, "D:\OPENING.BMP", 0, .Picture1
        Text 21, 195, 360, 79, "Choose an opening by double-
clicking on it in the list", .Text1
        OKButton 878, 257, 88, 21
        CancelButton 776, 257, 88, 21
End Dialog
```

From Word's Edit menu, choose Copy. Run the Dialog Editor (as described earlier in this chapter in the section "Dialog Boxes & Lists"). Open the Dialog Editor's Edit menu, and then choose Paste. The Dialog Editor displays the dialog box description you pasted as a graphical dialog box, as shown in Figure 7-12.

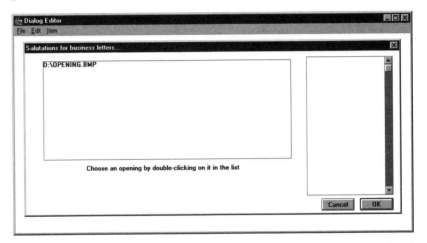

Figure 7-12: You can copy a text description of a dialog box back into the visual Dialog Editor.

We also created a new picture saved as "D:\OPENING.BMP" for our openings dialog box, and therefore replaced "D:\CLOSING .BMP" with "D:\OPENING.BMP." The entire new macro looks like this:

```
Sub MAIN

Dim opener$(6)

opener$(0) = "Dear"

opener$(1) = "Dear Customer,"

opener$(2) = "Dear Valued Customer,"

opener$(3) = "Dear Claxon Corp. Customer,"
```

```
opener$(4) = "Dear Valued Claxon Corp. Customer,"

opener$(5) = "Greetings to one of our favorite customers,"

opener$(6) = "Salutations to the best customer we've got,"


Dim labels$(6)

labels$(0) = "Standard"
labels$(1) = "Standard Extra"
labels$(2) = "Warm"
labels$(3) = "Warmer"
labels$(4) = "Warmest"
labels$(5) = "Very friendly"
labels$(6) = "Ecstatic"


Begin Dialog UserDialog 984, 282, "Salutations for business
letters...."
        ListBox 739, 9, 228, 242, labels$( ), .ListBox1
        Picture 20, 10, 393, 176, "D:\CLOSING.BMP", 0, .Picture1
        Text 21, 195, 360, 79, "Choose an opening by double-
clicking on it in the list", .Text1
        OKButton 878, 257, 88, 21
        CancelButton 776, 257, 88, 21
End Dialog

Dim dlg As UserDialog
chosen = Dialog(dlg)

If chosen = - 1 Then'they clicked OK
        Insert opener$(dlg.listbox1)
End If

End Sub
```

EDITING TOOLBARS

Launching macros from the Macro dialog box or with shortcut keys aren't your only options. Many people find toolbars a useful feature. If you want, it's easy to add a button that triggers a macro to a toolbar. For example, this section explains how to create a toolbar button that will run the opening macro we constructed in the preceding section. In Word, click on the View menu, and select Toolbars. Click on the Customize button. Then in the Categories list, locate Macros. Finally, locate opening in the Macros list, and drag it onto your toolbar.

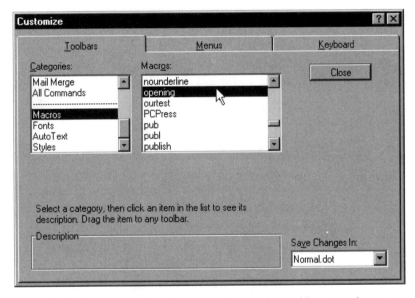

Figure 7-13: You can use the Customize dialog box to add a macro button to a toolbar.

The Custom Button dialog box appears (see Figure 7-14). At this point, the button on the toolbar is blank. In the Custom Button dialog box, you can click on Text Button to create a labeled button (click on the Edit button to create the label). Or you can click on an icon graphic in the Button area to select that icon for your new macro button. If you select an icon, then click on Edit, you'll see the Button Editor dialog box shown in Figure 7-15.

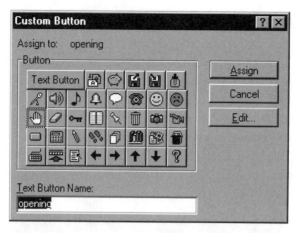

Figure 7-14: You can assign either a label or an icon to your button.

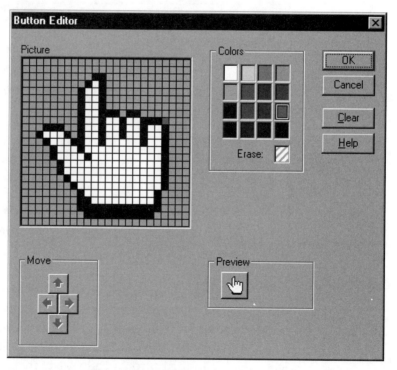

Figure 7-15: Use the tools in this dialog box to redraw the currently selected icon.

Hi-Res Buttons

You can use any .BMP file as an icon in Word 95. It will be automatically resized to fit the default icon size—so if you want it to look good, choose a .BMP that's the same shape (square) as the button. If you have high-resolution video, a good .BMP looks quite attractive on a toolbar and is often more quickly identifiable than an icon. To place a .BMP onto a button, load it into Windows Paint or some other graphics editing application. Then select it, and copy it (from the Edit menu). Now it's on the clipboard. Go back to Word. Right-click on the target icon on the toolbar, and choose Customize. This displays the Customize dialog box, so you can use its Toolbars tab to change any toolbar or its buttons. Select the toolbar with the icon you want to change in the Categories list. Then, in the group of buttons for that toolbar, right-click on the button you want to change, and choose Paste Button Image. The contents of the clipboard will be affixed to this button. Figure 7-16 shows two examples of toolbar buttons with custom high-resolution images.

Figure 7-16: A toolbar with high-resolution images used in place of icons.

The Secret Icon Collection

If you don't find an icon to your liking among the 29 symbols presented to you as default choices (shown in Figure 7-14), you can access hundreds more that are ordinarily hidden. The following steps open the treasure chest of 366 (312 in Word 6.0) secret buttons. In this example, we'll replace one of the existing button symbols with one of these hidden ones to demonstrate the technique. You can thereafter change icons on any toolbar using this technique.

1. First, we'll choose which of the hidden button symbols you want to add to your toolbar. Either pick one from the collection displayed in Figures 7-17 through 7-21, or look up the table of icons in Word Help as described in steps 2 and 3.

2. Click on Word's Help menu (or press F1). Choose Microsoft Word Help Topics, Index, and type **AddButton**. Double-click on AddButton, and then double-click on the hypertext Toolbar Button Images and Numbers entry. (If you're using Word 6.0, choose Contents, and then Programming with Microsoft Word. Click on Toolbar Button Images and Numbers.)

3. Browse around until you find a button that appeals to you (see Figures 7-17 through 7-21). Jot down its number. For our example, we're going to use number 329, which looks like the international symbol for NO!. Close Help.

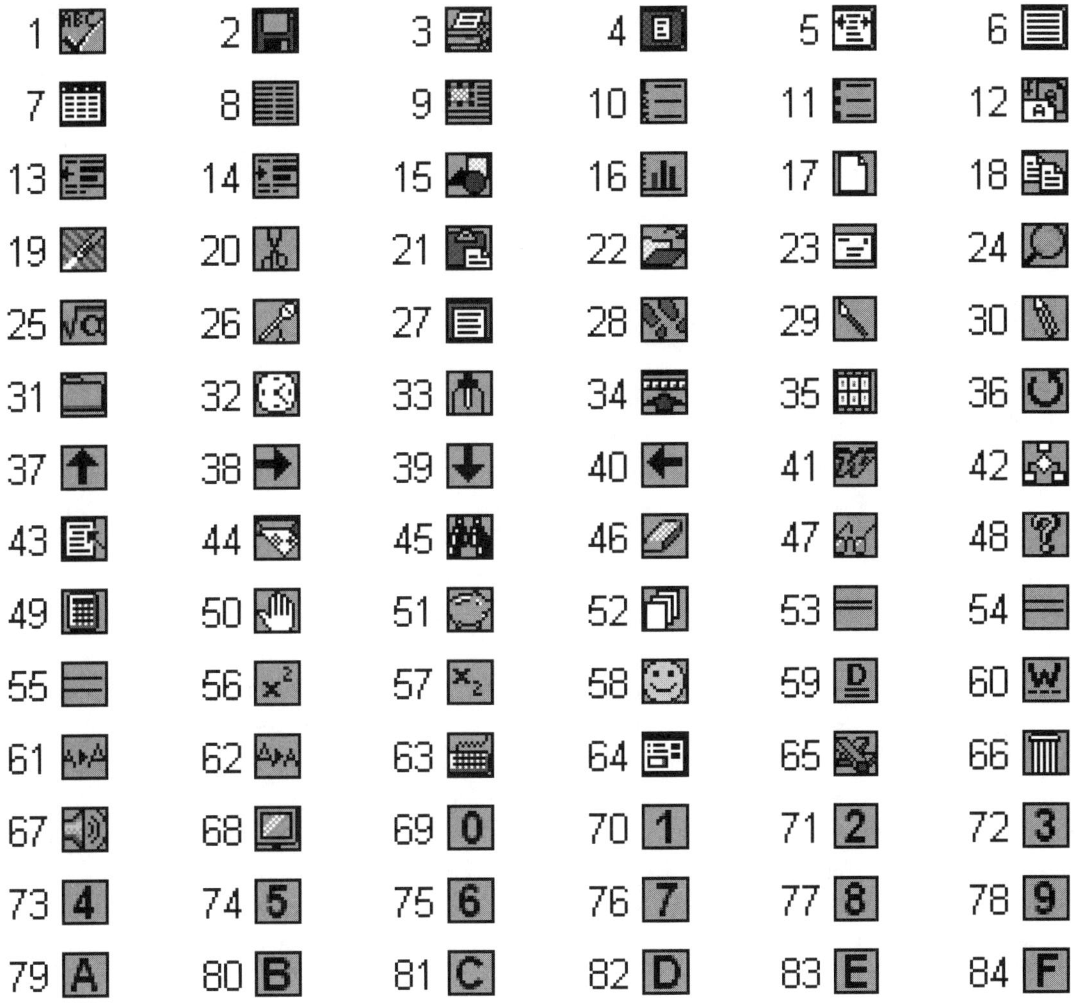

1 ✓ 2 💾 3 🖨 4 ▣ 5 ▤ 6 ▤

7 ▦ 8 ▤ 9 ▤ 10 ▤ 11 ▤ 12 ▤

13 ▤ 14 ▤ 15 ● 16 ▥ 17 ▯ 18 ▤

19 ▨ 20 ✂ 21 ▤ 22 ▤ 23 ▭ 24 ○

25 √α 26 ▨ 27 ▤ 28 ▨ 29 ◸ 30 ◹

31 ▭ 32 ✪ 33 ▣ 34 ▦ 35 ▦ 36 ↻

37 ↑ 38 → 39 ↓ 40 ← 41 W 42 ▨

43 ▤ 44 ▨ 45 ▨ 46 ▱ 47 ▨ 48 ?

49 ▦ 50 ✋ 51 ◉ 52 ▤ 53 ▤ 54 ▤

55 ═ 56 x² 57 x₂ 58 ☺ 59 D 60 W

61 ▨ 62 ▨ 63 ▦ 64 ▤ 65 ▨ 66 ▥

67 ◈ 68 ▢ 69 0 70 1 71 2 72 3

73 4 74 5 75 6 76 7 77 8 78 9

79 A 80 B 81 C 82 D 83 E 84 F

Figure 7-17.

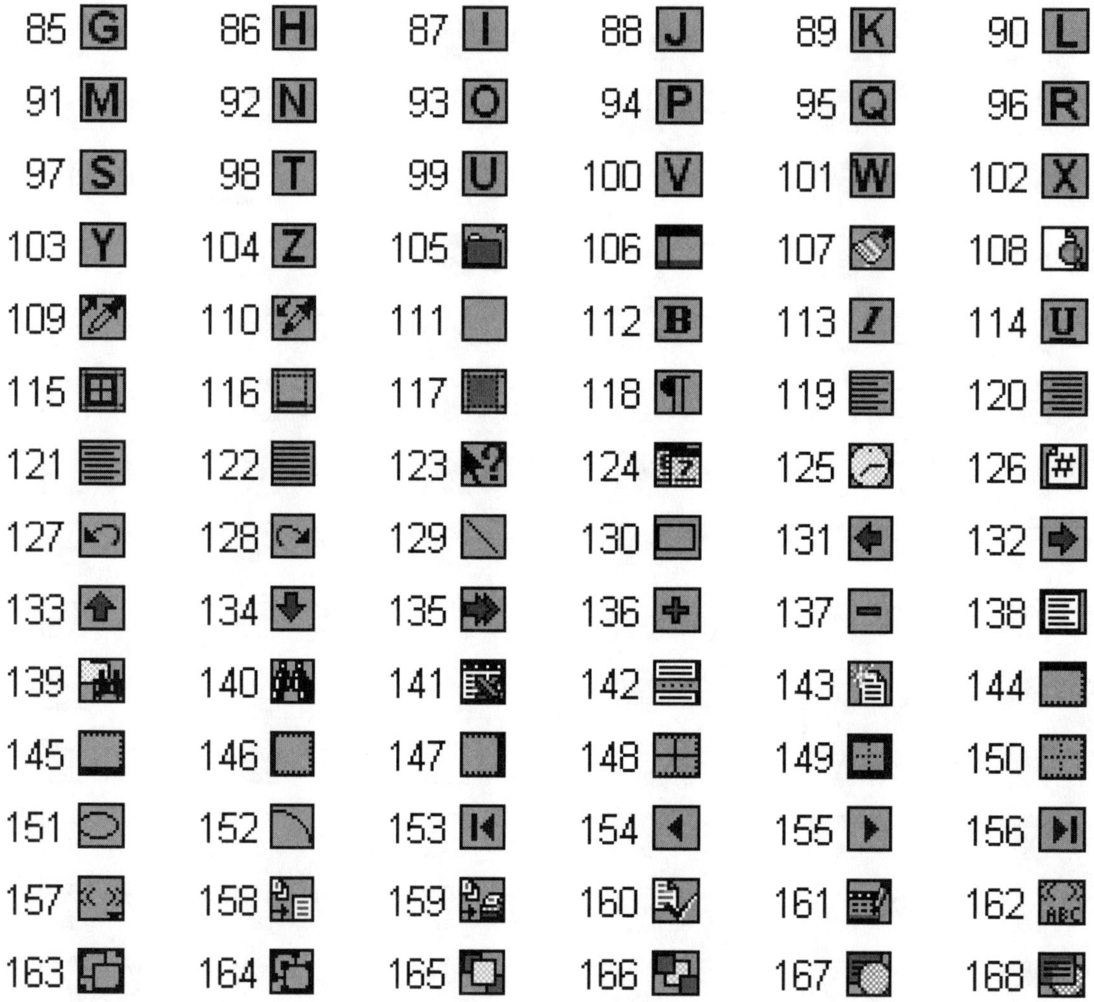

85 G	86 H	87 I	88 J	89 K	90 L
91 M	92 N	93 O	94 P	95 Q	96 R
97 S	98 T	99 U	100 V	101 W	102 X
103 Y	104 Z	105	106	107	108
109	110	111	112 B	113 I	114 U
115	116	117	118 ¶	119	120
121	122	123	124	125	126
127	128	129	130	131	132
133	134	135	136	137	138
139	140	141	142	143	144
145	146	147	148	149	150
151	152	153	154	155	156
157	158	159	160	161	162
163	164	165	166	167	168

Figure 7-18.

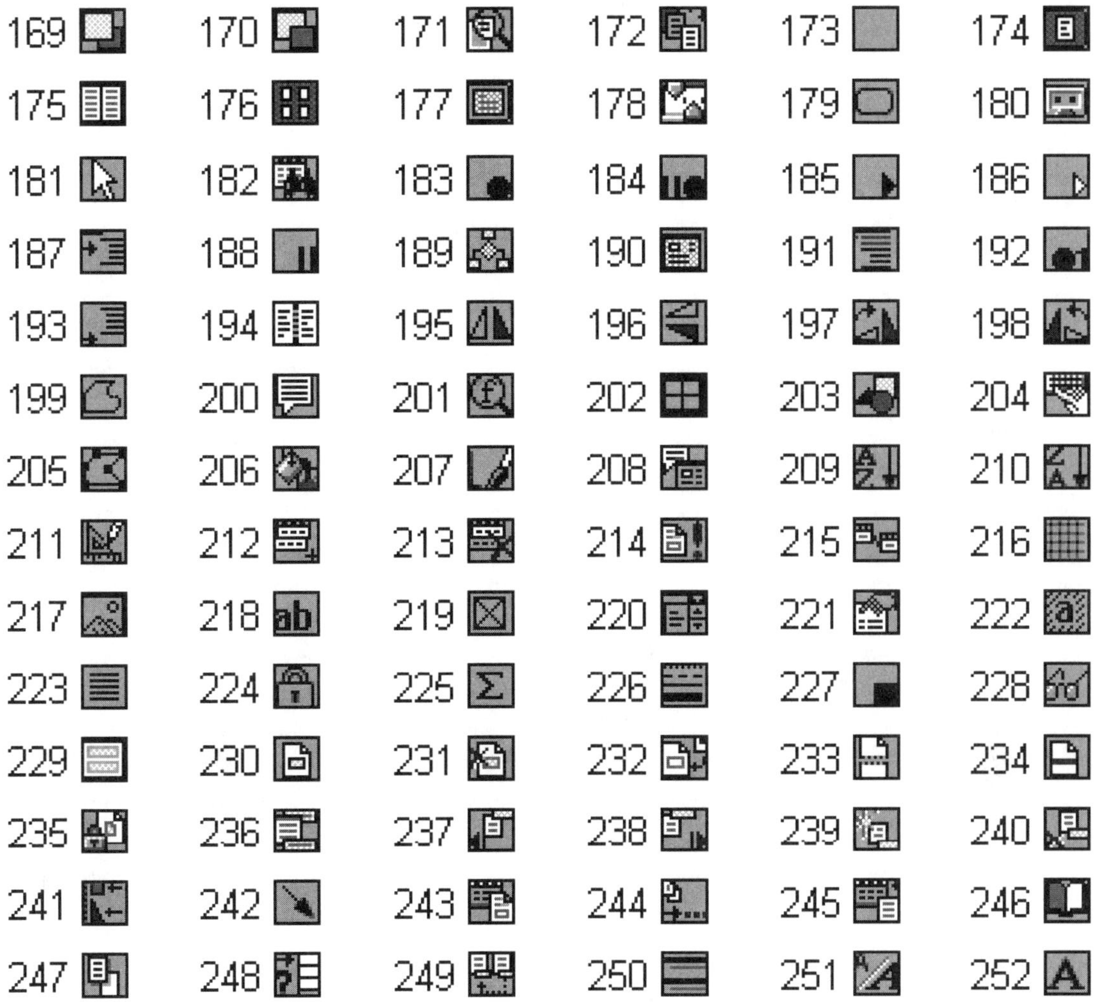

169 ⬛ 170 ⬛ 171 ⬛ 172 ⬛ 173 ⬜ 174 ⬛

175 ⬛ 176 ⬛ 177 ⬛ 178 ⬛ 179 ⬛ 180 ⬛

181 ⬛ 182 ⬛ 183 ⬛ 184 ⬛ 185 ⬛ 186 ⬛

187 ⬛ 188 ⬛ 189 ⬛ 190 ⬛ 191 ⬛ 192 ⬛

193 ⬛ 194 ⬛ 195 ⬛ 196 ⬛ 197 ⬛ 198 ⬛

199 ⬛ 200 ⬛ 201 ⬛ 202 ⬛ 203 ⬛ 204 ⬛

205 ⬛ 206 ⬛ 207 ⬛ 208 ⬛ 209 ⬛ 210 ⬛

211 ⬛ 212 ⬛ 213 ⬛ 214 ⬛ 215 ⬛ 216 ⬛

217 ⬛ 218 ⬛ 219 ⬛ 220 ⬛ 221 ⬛ 222 ⬛

223 ⬛ 224 ⬛ 225 ⬛ 226 ⬛ 227 ⬛ 228 ⬛

229 ⬛ 230 ⬛ 231 ⬛ 232 ⬛ 233 ⬛ 234 ⬛

235 ⬛ 236 ⬛ 237 ⬛ 238 ⬛ 239 ⬛ 240 ⬛

241 ⬛ 242 ⬛ 243 ⬛ 244 ⬛ 245 ⬛ 246 ⬛

247 ⬛ 248 ⬛ 249 ⬛ 250 ⬛ 251 ⬛ 252 ⬛

Figure 7-19.

253 | 254 | 255 | 256 | 257 | 258

259 | 260 | 261 | 262 | 263 | 264

265 | 266 | 267 | 268 | 269 | 270

271 | 272 | 273 | 274 | 275 | 276

277 | 278 | 279 | 280 | 281 | 282

283 | 284 | 285 | 286 | 287 | 288

289 | 290 | 291 | 292 | 293 | 294

295 | 296 | 297 | 298 | 299 | 300

301 | 302 | 303 | 304 | 305 | 306

307 | 308 | 309 | 310 | 311 | 312

313 | 314 | 315 | 316 | 317 | 318

319 | 320 | 321 | 322 | 323 | 324

325 | 326 | 327 | 328 | 329 | 330

Figure 7-20.

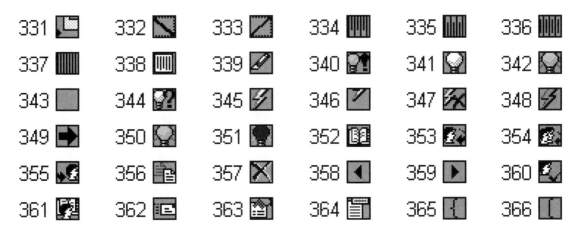

Figure 7-21.

Figures 7-17 through 7-21 contain the hidden collection of icons within Word for Windows 95.

WordBasic is a complete computer language, with hundreds of commands that you can use to make Word jump through hoops, to customize it to your heart's content. We'll use just one of these commands now in a new macro, ChooseButtonImage, which allows you to change an icon on any toolbar. It won't change what that button *does*—just the image on the button.

4. To directly write a WordBasic macro, use the Tools | Macro command, and then type the name of your new macro in the Macro Name text box. Let's name it **changebut,** so type that as the name.

5. Click the Create button in the Macro window (or just press Enter since Create is the default, highlighted button anyway).

6. Let's replace the image on the button that stops a running macro. That image is a simple square, and we're going to replace it with the more memorable international NO! symbol—a circle with a line through it. This is icon 329 in the Word 95 set of hidden icons. So, we'll set the .Face variable to 329 and the .Toolbar variable to Macro. We have to also tell WordBasic which button we want to

489

change. List boxes (the place where it says "changebut") and spaces count, so if you count over from the left of the Macro toolbar, you'll see that our target, the stop button, is button number nine. (See Figure 7-22.)

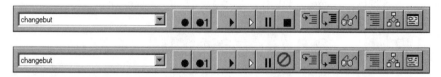

Figure 7-22: We didn't like the stop symbol on the Macro toolbar (top), so we changed it to the more memorable International NO! symbol (bottom).

7. In the macro editing window, type the following between Sub MAIN and End Sub:

```
Sub MAIN

ChooseButtonImage .Face = 329, .Button = 9, .Context =
0, .Toolbar = "Macro"

End Sub
```

(The .Context variable determines whether this change to the button's icon is stored in the Normal.dot template (0) or the currently active template (1)).

If you're using Word 6.0, choose an icon from the collection in Word 6.0, and replace .Face = 329 with the correct number from the icons in Word 6.0. Then type the following between Sub MAIN and End Sub:

```
Sub MAIN

ChooseButtonImage .Face = 180, .Button = 1, .Toolbar =
"Standard"

End Sub
```

8. We need to run this macro only once—the change will persist after you've made it because you've added the macro to the Normal.dot template, which loads each time you start

Word. So let's run the macro now. Click the solid triangle button (start) on the Macro toolbar to run this macro.

You should see your stop button change to the International NO! symbol. If it doesn't or if you get an error message, make sure that you've put a period (dot) in front of each of the variables: .Face, .Button, .Toolbar. Also be sure that you've separated them with commas. In other words, proofread your typing against the text in step 7 above.

9. Close the macro editing window just as you would close any other document window (select Close from the File menu). Word will ask whether you want to save this macro. Click Yes, and your window closes. We want to save this macro because you can use it any time to change any icon on any of your toolbars. Merely change the .Toolbar, .Face, and .Button variables.

Note that there's a .TEXT option in the full specifications for the ChooseButton command (the variables within brackets are optional):

```
ChooseButtonImage [.Face = number,] .Button = number, [.Context
= number,] [.Text = text,] .Toolbar = text
```

■■■

TIP

You can always find the full specifications for any WordBasic command by clicking on Help, then selecting Index, and typing in the name of the command.

■■■

Therefore, a WordBasic macro that dynamically creates a text-style button would look like this:

```
Sub MAIN

ChooseButtonImage .Button = 9, .Toolbar = "Macro", .Text =
"STOP!"

End Sub
```

Restoring Icons to Their Original State

It's easy to restore toolbar buttons to their out-of-the-box state.

If you want to restore the icon that was on any button when Word was first installed on your computer—the default icon chosen by Microsoft—go to the Tools | Customize | Toolbars dialog box, and select the toolbar you're restoring from the Categories list. (For the Macro toolbar that we edited in the last example, choose the Tools category.) Find the button you want—in our preceding example, it was the square symbol for stop—from the group of buttons Word provides. Drag the original icon up onto the toolbar, and drop it next to the one you've modified. Then drag the modified button you no longer need off the toolbar (it will disappear). If necessary, drag the restored button into whatever position on the toolbar that you prefer.

HANDY MACROS

Next we'll look at several Word for Windows macros that we've found useful over the years. These are all written in WordBasic, but their features and the techniques described can easily be adapted to other applications.

Find Toggle

If you frequently use the Edit | Find feature, you might enjoy being able to quickly reverse the direction of a find operation. For example, if you're searching downward, running this macro will start a search upward toward the beginning of the document. If you're going up, triggering the macro will restore the default downward search. This is another one you can't just record; you must type it in. Click on Tools | Macro, and type **findtog** as the Macro Name. Then click on Create, and type this in full:

```
Sub MAIN

Dim dlg As EditFind

GetCurValues dlg
```

```
If dlg.Direction = 0 Then
dlg.Direction = 1
Print "Find set to UP"
Else
dlg.Direction = 0
Print "Find set to DOWN"
End If

EditFind dlg

End Sub
```

(Note: If you try to test this in the macro editing screen, nothing will seem to happen. You must use it with a normal Word document.)

This time, the macro doesn't use Dim dlg to create a new, user-defined dialog box. Instead, it works with one of Word's own dialog boxes, the EditFind dialog box (the input box you see when you click on the Edit | Find menu). The EditFind dialog box won't be displayed because we don't want it to be, but we can use our macro to directly modify the various check boxes, text boxes, option buttons, or whatever else the user could adjust with the mouse or keyboard as if the real dialog box were, in fact, displayed. Most any aspect of Word can, in this way, be directly adjusted from within a macro. Note that these built-in Word dialog boxes are named after the menu and submenu that displays them. For instance, if you wanted to adjust an aspect of the Macro dialog box, you would Dim dlg As ToolsMacro.

If you assign the findtog macro to, say, Ctrl+Up arrow, any time you press that key combination, the direction of your search reverses. This macro uses the Basic decision structure If…Then…Else, which translates: if the Direction element within our EditFind dialog box is currently set to 0 (down) then make it 1 (up). Otherwise make it 0 (down). The macro also uses the Print command to display a message to the user on the status bar at the bottom of the Word window, telling you when you've changed the direction of a search.

Revision Marks Toggle

A similar macro can turn on and off any feature of Word. We often need to toggle revision marks, so here's a macro that does so:

```
Sub MAIN
Dim DR As ToolsRevisions
GetCurValues DR
If DR.MarkRevisions = 0 Then
Print "Revision Marks ON"
ToolsRevisions .MarkRevisions = 1
Else
Print "Revision Marks OFF"
ToolsRevisions .MarkRevisions = 0
EndIf
End Sub
```

Finding Dialog Box Item Names

From the preceding couple of macros, it's probably becoming clear to you that you can pretty much take control of Word through dialog box settings, querying them and adjusting them at will from macros. But how did we know what to call the item that specifies the feature we want to query or change, the .Mark-Revisions or the .Direction in the above examples? To get a list of all the items in a dialog box and their proper names, simply record a temporary macro during which you use the dialog box, and then look at the WordBasic contents of the macro by clicking on its name in the Tools | Macro window and choosing Edit. You'll be able to pick out any items you want to modify, because they're all English words. Here's the process, step-by-step. This example reveals the diction used by the File | Open dialog box:

1. Choose Tools | Macro (or press Alt+T, M), and then type **temp** in the Macro Name text box.
2. Click Record (or press Alt+O, Enter) to start the recording.
3. Click on the File menu, and then click on Open.
4. When the dialog box is displayed, double-click on some filename to actually open that document—it doesn't

matter what document you open (the macro won't record the dialog items unless you actually open a file).

5. Then stop the recording by clicking on the square icon in the macro-recording toolbar or by opening the Tools menu, choosing Macro, then choosing Stop Recording (Alt+T, M, Alt+O, Esc).

6. To see the results, the dialog box items, choose Tools | Macro (Alt+T, M). Highlight temp in the Macro Name list.

7. Click on Edit.

You should see something like this:

```
Sub MAIN

FileOpen .Name = "AUTOEXEC.BAT", .ConfirmConversions = 0,
.ReadOnly = 0, .AddToMru = 0, .PasswordDoc = "", .PasswordDot =
"", .Revert = 0, .WritePasswordDoc = "", .WritePasswordDot = ""

End Sub
```

Recall that in Word-Basic macros (and all versions of Microsoft Basic, including VBA) 1 means "true" or "on" and 0 means "false" or "off."

From this, we can tell that the .Name item describes to FileOpen which file (and default filter) to open.

Toggling Toolbars

Toolbars are useful, but they do take up precious document space on your screen, reducing the amount of text you can read at any one time. One solution is to create a macro that toggles a set of toolbars. When you need the ruler or the set of formatting buttons, it's handy to have them onscreen, but at other times they usually are just a distraction. We'll create a macro to display a set of our favorite toolbars, and hide them when we're done with them.

Our toggle switch knows its status; it remembers what you last did to it.

A true *toggle* knows its current state. Like a light switch, changing it turns something on (if it's currently off), and vice versa. Therefore, our toggle toolbar's macro has to check the current status—deciding whether we want the toolbars to appear or disappear. We don't want the mess of having to use two shortcut keys, one to display, and a different key combination to hide, these toolbars. In older houses, you may still find light switches like that, with a button for on and another separate button for off. Eventually, somebody realized that a light switch could be a single object, with two possible states, like a teeter totter. Here's how to create the toggle toolbars macro:

1. Decide which set of your toolbars you want to toggle. We always leave a single, main toolbar visible but toggle the formatting toolbar, and the Ruler. Use View | Toolbars (Alt+V, T) to find the names of the toolbars you want to toggle.

2. Create the empty macro. Choose Tools | Macro (Alt+T, M), and then type the Macro Name **toggletools**, and click the Create button.

3. Type the following in between Sub MAIN and End Sub. When finished, select Close in the File menu to save the macro.

```
Sub MAIN
On Error Goto Exit
X = ViewRuler( )
If x = - 1 Then
    ViewToolbars .Toolbar = "Formatting", .Hide
    ViewRuler
Else
    ViewToolbars .Toolbar = "Formatting", .Show
    ViewRuler
EndIf
Exit:
End Sub
```

We use The ViewRuler command to test whether the Ruler is currently showing. ViewRuler puts a –1 in the variable x if it's true that the Ruler is visible. If not, it puts a 0 in x. This is how the macro knows whether to .Hide or .Show the Ruler and any other toolbars you want to list within the If...Else...Endif decision-making structure. The On Error Goto Exit command sends us down to the label *Exit:*. (Labels hold a position within the lines of a macro to provide a target for the Goto command. Labels always end in a colon.) The value of On Error Goto Exit command—it's optional really—is that if some error occurs, no message is displayed to the user. Instead, because of the On Error Goto Exit, the macro does nothing at all, merely carries out the End Sub command, which quits the macro.

If you don't want the Ruler among the specified toolbars that drop down, then test for the visibility of one of the toolbars in the group you do want to toggle:

Change this:

```
x = ViewRuler( )
```

to this:

```
x = ToolbarState("Borders")
```

(using one of the toolbar names that you are toggling in place of "Borders"). Note that any custom toolbars you may have created earlier might not have actual names; instead, they might be called Toolbar 1, Toolbar 2, and so on. These names can also be used as the test (x = ToolbarState("Toolbar 4")).

You can now attach this macro to a shortcut key combination like Ctrl+T (for "toggle" or "toolbar") or add it as a button on your main, always visible, toolbar.

TIP

You can customize Word 95 to display both the name and the shortcut key combination, of any buttons on your toolbars that have shortcut keys. To do so, select ViewIToolbars. Then click on both Show ToolTips and With Shortcut Keys.

More GetCurValues

The GetCurValues command is useful for finding out, within a macro, any information that would ordinarily be displayed in a dialog box. Macros can save you time by carrying out tasks that are awkward to access with menus. For example, suppose you frequently need to know how many words are in your document.

Accomplishing this by navigating the menus can be annoying. You have to open the Tools menu and choose Word Count, or you have to remember a weird, unmemorable key combination (Alt+T, W). Also, how do you remember what menu to access? There's nothing intuitive about the location of the Word Count feature. It's in the Tools menu, rather than, perhaps, the View or Edit menus. Plus, Word displays the word count along with other information you may not be interested in, such as statistics about the number of pages, characters, paragraphs, and lines.

Wouldn't Ctrl+W, or a button on your toolbar, be easier to use when you want a word count? Wouldn't you like to see just the word count and not a lot of other unnecessary information?

The solution? Create a macro that displays only the word count. Figures 7-23 and 7-24 illustrate the ordinary Word Count dialog box and our new custom one.

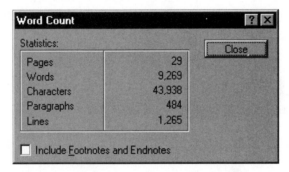

Figure 7-23: BEFORE: The default Word Count Statistics message box contains perhaps too many statistics.

Figure 7-24: AFTER: A custom pop-up message box, crafted by you to display only what you want to see.

The technique illustrated by the macro we'll describe next enables you to capture the information contained in any Word dialog box and do with it what you will. Notice that the actual dialog box *need not be visible* for us to extract information from it. In this case, we want the word count, so we'll extract that information from Word's Tools | Word Count menu command.

*d*lg is an important variable—enabling you to query or change nearly any quality or status within an application.

Sometimes the easiest way to figure out how to *write* a macro is to first *record* something similar to what you want to do—then modify it. Record a macro that displays Word's File | Properties (Statistics) dialog box. Start a new macro recording (name it "words" or some other name you prefer), and then choose Tools | Word Counts to display the Properties dialog box.

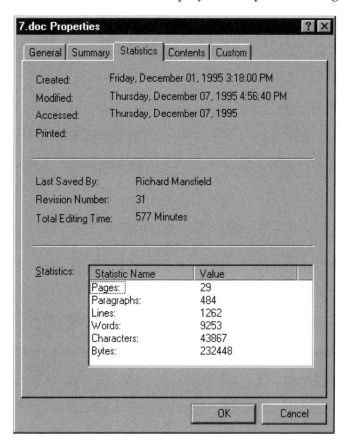

Figure 7-25: To get the proper syntax for modifying it, run this built-in statistical display while recording it.

You'll get something like the following if you look at the macro you recorded in the Macro editing window:

```
Sub MAIN
ToolsWordCount .CountFootnotes = 0, .Pages = "29", .Words =
"9,271", .Characters = "43,963", .Paragraphs = "485", .Lines =
"1,262"
End Sub
```

Or, in Word 6.0:

```
Sub MAIN

FileSummaryInfo .Title = "Chapter 7", .Subject = "", .Author =
"Richard Mansfield", .Keywords = "", .Comments = "", .FileName =
"7.DOC", .Directory = "D:\BOOK", .Template =
"C:\WINWORD\TEMPLATE\NORMAL.DOT", .CreateDate = "05/23/95 7:04
AM", .LastSavedDate = "05/25/95 10:46 AM", .LastSavedBy =
"Richard Mansfield", .RevisionNumber = "34", .EditTime = "210
Minutes", .LastPrintedDate = "", .NumPages = "9", .NumWords =
"2,588", .NumChars = "12,167", .NumParas = "144", .NumLines =
"434", .FileSize = "38,912 Bytes"

End Sub
```

We want to customize this raw WordBasic code—throw away all the useless data about lines, characters, and so on. The only commands we need from within this entire structure are: ToolsWordCount and .Words (in Word 6.0: FileSummaryInfo and .NumWords).

So open a new macro editing document (use Tools | Macro, type **wordcount** as the Macro Name, and then click the Create button).

Then type this in between Sub MAIN and End Sub:

```
Sub MAIN

FileSummaryInfo .Update

Dim dlg As DocumentStatistics

GetCurValues dlg

MsgBox "    " + dlg.Words

End Sub
```

The .Update command forces the statistics to be recalculated, so they will be current and accurate each time this macro runs. The Dim command creates a *dlg* variable that represents Document Statistics. The macro gets the current values in that dialog box and ignores all the various statistics except .Words, which it displays to the user with the MsgBox command.

Cycle Through Windows With a Special Key

If you have more than one Word document open at a time, it's nice to be able to cycle through them, much as pressing Alt+F4 cycles you through currently running Windows applications. We use this particular macro so often that we've given it a place of honor on the keyboard, a most valuable key, the tilde in the upper left next to the number 1 key. In English, the tilde and accent grave symbols (they're on the same key) are rarely used, so this is a key that you can assign a macro to without worrying that you'll ever need to type an accent grave or tilde. You can get to quickly access this key while you're typing, and you don't have to press Ctrl or Alt or any key along with it.

Quite sensibly, Word doesn't allow you to attach macros to ordinary keys, such as the *k* or +. After all, if *k* triggered a macro, how would you type *quick* if, instead of the *k*, the File Open dialog appeared because you'd told Word that k didn't mean k, it meant run a macro you'd assigned to *k* that opened a file?

Writers, like any other workers, want their tools (their keyboards) to be sleek, effective instruments. And, for most of us, a few keys—the square brackets ([ ]), the accent grave ('), and the lowercase tilde (~)—usually aren't needed in our documents. Why not have them trigger something we do often?

The accent grave key in the upper left-hand corner can be used for a shortcut. In spite of Word's refusal (in the Tools I Customize I Keyboard menu) to permit you to assign a single key to a macro, we can manage to do it with a little trick.

If you want to use the accent grave to cycle through all open documents—a good use for it—follow these steps:

1. Create a macro that toggles between open screens. Choose Tools I Macro (Alt+T, M), and then type **nextdoc** as the Macro Name.

2. Click the Create button, and type the following:

```
Sub MAIN

NextWindow

End Sub
```

3. Close the document to save this macro.

4. Now create the macro that assigns the accent grave key to nextdoc. Choose Tools I Macro (Alt+T, M), and type **assignkey** as the Macro Name.

5. Click the Create button, and type the following:

```
Sub MAIN

ToolsCustomizeKeyboard .Category = 1, .Name = "nextdoc",
.KeyCode = 192, .Add

End Sub
```

6. Click on the start symbol in the Macro toolbar (the solid triangle) to run this macro. It assigns the key code 192 (the code for the accent grave key) to our nextdoc macro.

7. Now test the macro. Press the accent grave key a few times, and you'll see Word toggle through all currently open documents.

8. You need to run this assignkey macro only once, but you might as well save it in case you want to assign other keys to other macros. So, close the macro editing window, and click on Yes when asked if you want to keep the changes.

Here is a list of other keys that you might want to consider using as super fast macro triggers:

Key	Key Code
Pause	19
Scroll Lock	145
Semicolon (;)	186
Equal Sign (=)	187
Slash (/)	191
Accent grave (')	192
Left Bracket ([)	219
Backslash (\)	220
Right Bracket (])	221

Removing a Keyboard Macro Assignment

Do you unexpectedly have to translate a Spanish novel? If so, you'll want to get that accent grave key back to its normal state. Should you need to restore a specially assigned key like the accent grave, just create and run the following macro to restore the assigned key:

1. Choose Tools | Macro (Alt+T, M), and type **removekey** as the Macro Name.
2. Click the Create button, and type the following:

```
Sub MAIN

ToolsCustomizeKeyboard .Category = 1, .KeyCode = 192,
.Remove

End Sub
```

3. Click on the start symbol in the Macro toolbar (the solid triangle) to run this macro. It restores the accent grave key so it can be typed into a document. The key no longer triggers a macro.

Delete Word

Deleting individual words is something most writers need to do quite often. Unhappily, the key combinations built into Word for deleting a word are perversely awkward: Ctrl+Del deletes the word to the right, Ctrl+Backspace deletes the word to the left.

There are several problems with this approach. First, on most keyboards, you have to be more than usually dexterous to hit these keys accurately while typing because they're so far apart. Second, there should be only one key combination for word deletion, and it should always delete the word to the right of the cursor (as WordPerfect used to do). Forget deleting the word to the left. Finally, if you're *within* a word, rather than on a space between words, Word again takes a strange approach: only the *characters* to the right or left of the cursor position are deleted, *not the entire word*. Most peculiar indeed. Trying to delete the word *why* with your cursor between the *w* and the *h* leaves the *w* untouched.

Luckily, we can construct our own delete-word macro. It will solve all the problems with Word's built-in word delete feature. We'll also assign it to *two* keys—to both brackets ([ ]). This way we'll have two keys to slam when we want to remove a word. Even the wildest typist will be able to hit one of those keys during a furious bout of writing.

You can vacuum entire paragraphs with our delete-word macro.

Our delete-word macro should combine *both* the Ctrl+Backspace and Ctrl+Del styles of deletion. That way, no matter where your cursor is located within the target word, the entire word is removed. However, if the cursor is located on a space, we want to delete only the word to the right (Ctrl+Del). (Otherwise, we'd delete two words at once.)

So our macro has to test for:

❑ Is the cursor to the left of a space?

❑ To the right of a space?

❑ Within a word?

We want the macro to behave differently in each case—producing a reliable word deletion to the right of the cursor. In effect, repeatedly triggering this macro will make Word appear to *suck words, one by one, into the cursor.* This is highly efficient. You can vacuum entire paragraphs this way once you get used to it.

To create the macro:

1. Choose Tools | Macro (Alt+T, M), and type **killword** as the Macro Name.

2. Click the Create button, and type the following:

```
Sub MAIN

'If cursor is:

'to left of a space...

If Selection$( ) = " " Then

    CharRight( ) : DeleteWord : Goto Exit

EndIf


CharLeft( )
```

```
'in middle of a word..

If Selection$( ) <> " " Then

    CharRight( ) : DeleteWord : DeleteBackWord

    CharRight( ) : Goto Exit

EndIf


'to right of a space

CharRight( ) : DeleteWord


Exit:

End Sub
```

3. Now close the macro editing document, and answer Yes when asked whether you want to keep the changes.

To attach this macro to both square bracket keys:

1. If you created the previously described macro called assignkey, open it for editing, and skip the next steps, steps 2 and 3, in this list. (Choose Tools | Macro, then locate assignkey, and click the Edit button. Go to step 4.)

2. To create the macro that assigns a single key to a macro, choose Tools | Macro (Alt+T, M), and type **assignkey** as the Macro Name. Click the Create button.

3. Type this into the macro:

```
Sub MAIN

ToolsCustomizeKeyboard .Category = 1, .Name =
"killword", .KeyCode = 219, .Add

End Sub
```

4. Click the start symbol (the solid triangle) in the toolbar to run this macro. It assigns the code 219 (the left bracket key) to the killword macro.

5. Edit the macro again, changing the .Keycode to 221:

```
Sub MAIN

ToolsCustomizeKeyboard .Category = 1, .Name =
"killword", .KeyCode = 221, .Add

End Sub
```

6. Again, click on the start symbol in the toolbar to run the macro, assigning the killword macro to the right bracket key this time.

LastFile

This useful macro prompts Word to load the document you were working on when you last exited Word. When the file is loaded, the macro moves your cursor to the precise position where you were last editing the document. This macro is particularly helpful when you spend several days working on a document—you're always taken directly to where you can continue editing. Create a macro named lastfile, and assign it a keyboard shortcut or attach it to a toolbar button. The macro's WordBasic contents should read as follows:

```
Sub MAIN

FileList 1

GoBack

End Sub
```

The FileList 1 command loads the most recent file. It's the same as clicking on the File menu and then clicking on the first filename in the list of recent files. The GoBack command places the cursor at the most recently edited position within the document. (This is the same as pressing Shift+F5, which cycles you through the three most recently edited locations within any document, at any time—a valuable tool.) This macro is a good one to put on your toolbar, as described earlier in this chapter. That way you can fire up Word and, if desired, go directly and automatically to the right place in the right document with a single mouse click.

CUSTOMIZING WORD

Word, of course, has hundreds of internal, previously written behaviors. When you change the formatting to boldface, for example, Word goes to a particular location in its .EXE file and finds the instructions that tell it how to accomplish this job. These previously written behaviors are not, technically speaking, macros (*functions* is the usual official term), but they carry out tasks just as macros do. For every item on a menu, there's a corresponding internal Word function. And you can make adjustments to these functions if you want to. Can you change the way Format | Font works? Can you customize the File | Open behavior? You bet.

More Than .DOC

Many people find it annoying that Word always displays only the
.DOC files when you choose Open from the File menu. Often
enough, you want to look at a .TXT file or some other document
format. It's exasperating to have to click on the little drop-down
list box and locate .TXT or whatever, before you can see a full list
of the files. If you're one of those who want to see all files right off
the bat (similar to using DIR *.* in DOS), this macro is for you.

Note that when you give a macro the same name as a built-in
menu item or other Word behavior, your macro takes precedence.
For example, Word has a behavior it calls FileOpen. If you create a
macro with the name FileOpen, Word follows the instructions in
your macro, not its own built-in instructions, when the user clicks
on the File menu and selects Open. This is one way to modify
built-in Word features.

Personalizing one of Word's internal behaviors couldn't be
easier. Here's an example, step-by-step:

1. Open the Macro dialog box by choosing Tools | Macro
    (Alt+T, M).

2. In the Macros Available In list box, select Word Com-
    mands (see Figure 7-26).

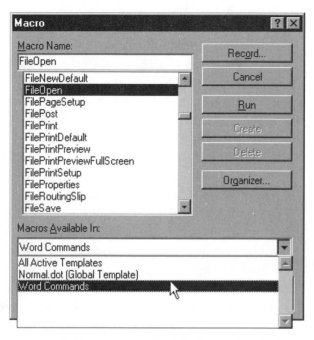

Figure 7-26: You can customize Word's own built-in features by opening this set of functions.

3. The upper list box displays most of the features built in to Word. Select the one named FileOpen. Don't double-click it, or you'll run it. Just single-click so it's highlighted.

4. With FileOpen highlighted in the upper list, go back to the Macros Available In list box at the bottom, and select Normal.dot [Global Template].

5. At this point, you'll see FileOpen listed among your own macros (instead of among the Word commands). Click the Edit button. The usual macro recording window opens, and it is filled with the commands Word uses to perform a File | Open. So here you are, presented with the appropriate commands—all you have to do now is to make a few insertions to customize it to suit yourself.

Word's File | Open behaviors are listed like this:

```
Sub MAIN

Dim dlg As FileOpen

GetCurValues dlg

Dialog dlg

FileOpen dlg

End Sub
```

6. Add three lines to the existing Word lines, so the total listing looks like this:

```
Sub MAIN

Dim dlg As FileOpen

GetCurValues dlg

On Error Goto Exit

dlg.Name = "*.*"

Dialog dlg

FileOpen dlg

Exit:

End Sub
```

7. Close the macro editing document, and answer Yes when Word asks whether you want to keep the changes.

Now try it out. You'll see that all files (not just .DOC files) are displayed in the Open dialog box whenever you select Open from the File menu.

We've now changed an element of Word's own behavior.

Two of the lines we added (On Error Goto Exit and, later, Exit:) react to the possibility that the user might press Esc or Cancel to abort the FileOpen dialog box. Without this exit mechanism, Word would display an error message (harmless, but exasperating) if the user cancels a File | Open operation.

The primary change we made was to tell Word that the .Name property of this dialog box will, henceforth, be *.* so that all files will be displayed. If you frequently work with .TXT files and want to put a button on your toolbar to display only .TXT files, change it to:

```
dlg.Name = "*.TXT"
```

You have complete freedom to make Word display whatever kinds of files (through whatever "filter") you want.

TIP

To find out how we knew to use .Name to change the default file filter, see "Finding Dialog Box Item Names" earlier in this chapter.

What we've done here is to add this customized macro named FileOpen to our personal macros in the Normal.dot template. Recall that when a macro has the same name as a built-in menu item or other Word feature, the macro takes precedence, and Word follows the instructions in your macro, not its own built-in instructions. By storing this modified macro, you are *overriding* Word's built-in FileOpen feature. In other words, when you select Open from the File menu, Word first checks to see whether you have a personal macro by that name. If so, it doesn't look any further; it just carries out whatever instructions your macro contains. Word doesn't look to its interior list of features to find FileOpen.

Restoring Word's Original Behaviors

If you want to revert to Word's native state—that is, to have FileOpen show only .DOC files as it did before we made our changes in the previous example—simply remove your personal FileOpen macro, and Word reverts to its built-in FileOpen feature. Here are the steps to remove the FileOpen macro:

1. Open the Macro window by choosing Tools | Macro (Alt+T, M).

2. Scroll to locate FileOpen in the list of macros in Normal.dot. Highlight FileOpen.

3. Click on the Delete button.

That's it. The FileOpen macro is gone. (If you choose File | Open, you'll still see *.* because Word retains the last filter you've used. But, trust me, .DOC will be the default filter the next time you run Word.)

Temporarily Restoring Word's Defaults

If you want to preserve your macro but temporarily permit Word to behave in its default way, just use the macro Organizer to rename FileOpen to some other name. As long as your macro has some other name, Word's own FileOpen takes effect, not the custom macro. Here's an example illustrating how to use Organizer to rename the custom FileOpen macro:

1. Open the Macro window by choosing Tools | Macro (Alt+T, M).

2. Use the scroll bar to locate FileOpen in the list of macros in Normal.dot so that FileOpen is highlighted.

3. Click the Organizer button.

4. Click on Rename.

5. Change the name from FileOpen to zFileOpen, which keeps the name down at the bottom of your list of personal macros, ready to be renamed once again to FileOpen should you want to customize Word's behavior again.

Text Formatting

File format incompatibility is one of the more annoying aspects of telecommunications, the Internet, bulletin board systems, and all the rest. When you look at a text file, it frequently has carriage returns in all the wrong places. It often looks something like this:

```
A toggle remembers its current state. Like a light switch,
changing it turns something on (if
it's currently off) and vice versa.


Therefore, our toggle toolbars macro has to check the current
status
-deciding whether we want the
toolbars to appear or disappear. We don't want the mess of
having one
key-combination display, and a
different key-combination hide, these toolbars. In older houses,
you
```

Word and other word processors insert a carriage return (a code that starts a new line) only at the end of a *paragraph*. However, documents created in simple text editors often insert a carriage return at the end of every line. This results in uneven lines when you try to read such a document in Word. We can fix this, though, with a macro. A text document usually indicates a paragraph break by inserting two carriage returns. Therefore, our solution to this problem is straightforward: first replace all carriage returns with a marker (some nonsensical text that never appears in a real document but can be replaced later). Then we search for any double markers (indicating a paragraph break) in the text and replace these with a carriage return. Finally, to get rid of the remaining false end-of-line breaks, we'll replace the remaining markers with just a space character.

This macro is a good candidate for recording. Select Tools | Macro, then type **filter** for the Macro Name. Click on Record. Now click on Edit | Replace, and type **^p** into the Find What text box (^p is Word's code for a carriage return). In the Replace With text box, type **xxx**. Then click on Replace All. Next type **xxxxxx** into the Find What text box (this is two of our markers together, indicating a double carriage return). In the Replace

With text box, type **^p**. Click on Replace All. Finally, type **xxx** into the Find What text box. In the Replace With text box, press the spacebar to create a single space. Click on Replace All. Turn off the macro by clicking on the button with a square icon (or clicking on Tools | Macro | Stop Recording).

Let's look at what we've recorded. Select Tools | Macro, and type **filter** in the Macro Name text box. Click on Edit, and you should see this:

```
Sub MAIN

EditReplace .Find = "^p", .Replace = "xxx", .Direction = 0,
.MatchCase = 0, .WholeWord = 0, .PatternMatch = 0, .SoundsLike =
0, .ReplaceAll, .Format = 0, .Wrap = 1, .FindAllWordForms = 0

EditReplace .Find = "xxxxxx", .Replace = "^p", .Direction = 0,
.MatchCase = 0, .WholeWord = 0, .PatternMatch = 0, .SoundsLike =
0, .ReplaceAll, .Format = 0, .Wrap = 1, .FindAllWordForms = 0

EditReplace .Find = "xxx", .Replace = " ", .Direction = 0,
.MatchCase = 0, .WholeWord = 0, .PatternMatch = 0, .SoundsLike =
0, .ReplaceAll, .Format = 0, .Wrap = 1, .FindAllWordForms = 0


End Sub
```

That's it. But recall that we can eliminate many of these variables, the ones that don't affect the behavior of the macro because their default is what we desire. If you prefer a sleeker macro, just delete the unused portion of the macro, resulting in this:

```
Sub MAIN

EditReplace .Find = "^p", .Replace = "xxx", .ReplaceAll, .Wrap =
1

EditReplace .Find = "xxxxxx", .Replace = "^p", .ReplaceAll,
.Wrap = 1

EditReplace .Find = "xxx", .Replace = " ", .ReplaceAll, .Wrap =
1

End Sub
```

TIP

The .Wrap variable, set to 1 (meaning true or yes), tells Word to automatically adjust the entire document, even if the current cursor position isn't at the very top of the document. In other words, to "wrap around" from the bottom if a portion of the top hasn't yet been adjusted. With .Wrap set to yes, we were even able to remove the .Direction variable since it then becomes irrelevant. Paring down a macro like this doesn't significantly increase the speed at which the macro executes, but for those who are typing the macro rather than recording, we thereby provide the essence. Note, too, that because each variable has its own label—.Replace, .Wrap, and so on—you can list them in any order you wish. This order would work: EditReplace .Wrap = 1, .Replace = " ", Find = "xxx", .ReplaceAll.

The Executive Triggers

Generally, the user launches a macro by clicking on the Toolbar button or using a shortcut key, but you can use five built-in triggers to define macros that will go off automatically without user intervention. (For another way to create automatic macros, see "More Than .DOC," earlier in this chapter. You can intervene in Word's behaviors far more deeply than the list that follows would suggest.)

You can give macros five names that will cause Word to automatically execute the macro when Word takes the action specified by the macro name:

Macro Name	Triggered When...
AutoExec	You first start Word.
AutoOpen	Word opens a document file on the disk (File I Open).
AutoNew	You create a new document (File I New).
AutoClose	You close a document (File I Close).
AutoExit	You exit Word (File I Exit).

For example, if you create a macro and name it AutoExec, Word will run that AutoExec macro every time it (Word) starts up. These macros aren't visible in the list of active macros that you see when you click on Tools | Macro. But if you name a macro using one of those five names, Word will carry out your instructions whenever the associated trigger event takes place. In this way, you can customize these common events. Perhaps you'll want to use a MsgBox in the AutoExit macro to remind the user to save a backup copy. Or maybe just automatically save a backup onto drive A:.

We've found that there are a couple of bugs in Word when it first starts up. It doesn't always maximize itself, and it doesn't always put our various toolbars on the same line. In other words, it wastes space by setting one of our short, two-button toolbars on a separate line all of its own (see Figure 7-27). This isn't the way we designed the toolbars, and it isn't what we want. A macro to the rescue.

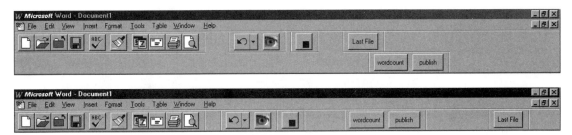

Figure 7-27: We don't want the bloated toolbar (top), so we created a macro to force Word to collapse all toolbars onto a single line.

As is so often the case, the shortest line between a desired behavior and the automation to accomplish that behavior is recording. Click on the button at the top right of your Word window that reduces Word to a "normal" (not maximized) window. Now start recording by clicking on Tools | Macro and typing **autoexec** as the Macro Name. Then click Record. Now click on the button at the top right of your Word window to maximize the window. For the badly set up toolbars, click on View | Toolbars, and click on Customize. Then drag the various toolbars into whatever position you prefer. Now stop the macro recording by clicking on the button with the square icon. Click on Tools | Macro, and then click on Edit. Select the macro named autoexec by clicking on it in the list, then click on Edit. You should see something like this:

517

```
Sub MAIN

AppMaximize
MoveToolbar "Toolbar 18", 1, 616, - 2
MoveToolbar "Toolbar 25", 1, 889, - 2

End Sub
```

The AppMaximize command fills the screen with the application's window; in this case Word is the application.

The exact numbers describing the location of the toolbars and their names depend on your particular toolbar names and where, exactly, you dragged them during the recording. The variables for the MoveToolbar command are:

- ❒ MoveToolbar Toolbar$
- ❒ Dock
- ❒ HorizPos
- ❒ VertPos

These variables describe:

- ❒ **Toolbar$** The toolbar's name (View I Toolbars).
- ❒ **Dock** How to position this toolbar within the Word window. If 0, the toolbar is detached, and "floats" within a document (as does the Macro Recording toolbar while you are recording a macro); if 1 (as in our example macro above), the toolbar is attached to the top of the window; if 2, on the left; if 3, on the right; if 4, on the bottom. We wanted it at the top, and 1 will place it there.
- ❒ **HorizPos, VertPos** The final two location specifications are, as you can see from their names, the horizontal and vertical position where you want the toolbars, measured from the upper left of the Word window and expressed in pixels. (Pixels are the smallest unit of measurement on a video screen. They're the dots you can only just see if you put your eye right up against the monitor.)

VISUAL BASIC FOR APPLICATIONS (VBA)

Until now, each application had a different macro language. Even Microsoft applications—Word, Excel, Access, and others—had languages that were incompatible. There were different commands, syntax, and punctuation. However, in the past couple of years Microsoft has been endeavoring to create a common macro language for all its applications—Visual Basic for applications, or VBA. Now VBA is part of all major Microsoft applications with the exception of Word. And everyone expects the next version of Word to include VBA and join the club. Alas, VBA is not part of applications from software sources other than Microsoft.

VBA is the latest in a long line of computer languages.

To understand VBA, we should first look at its precursors. VBA grew out of the venerable Basic language and its children. Indeed, VBA is a superset of Basic, WordBasic, AccessBasic, and other flavors of Basic. Basic is a tremendously popular and powerful programming language. We've so far been looking at how to utilize the main features of WordBasic, but we've also covered most of the main features of VBA as well. It's not that different.

The First Choice in Languages

Basic was first developed as a way to introduce college students to the techniques of communicating with computers. However, Basic has proven so powerful and understandable—so English-like and sensible—that it endures today as the first choice of many programmers. It is likely that Basic will continue to be the most popular language of many professionals and of most ordinary computer users. Also of major importance to the future vitality of Basic is the fact that Bill Gates strongly supports it as the language of choice for popular computing in Windows and beyond.

Basic has evolved through DOS's QuickBasic, assorted macro Basics, Visual Basic, and now VBA. Along the way Basic has gained efficiency, new capabilities and many new commands. Visual Basic is a stand-alone language (not a macro language built into an application). Visual Basic is designed to make it easy to write programs that work under Windows, independent of any running application. As such, Visual Basic is the child of DOS's QuickBasic and the parent of VBA (Visual Basic for Applications).

With Visual Basic, the Basic language gained additional powers: the ability to display and manage graphics, and to produce Windows programs that have the look and feel of professionally programmed Windows applications. Programs that would take many months to program in C (a computer language that many people consider to be somewhat awkward (but is currently the fashion among academics and professional programmers) can be constructed in mere days or weeks using Visual Basic (VB). And, because VBA is VB's offspring, much of the efficiency you find in VB is also included in VBA.

In VB, sets of intelligent objects (such as text boxes, file list boxes, command buttons, and so on) can simply be dragged from a toolbar, or selected from a list, and placed onto a window that the user will see. These objects are "intelligent" because they contain built-in behaviors (you don't have to write any programming to make them accomplish certain jobs). The text box, for example, automatically wraps words onto the next line as necessary to make the text visible. You don't have to write any programming commands to tell the text box how to display text properly. The box is smart. (See the previous section "Dialog Boxes & Lists" for the WordBasic version of this new kind of elegant, direct programming.)

A file list box is called an *object*. It has qualities (called "properties"), built-in behaviors (called "methods"), and places where it can be made to react (called "events") to mouse clicks, and many other outside actions such as being dragged, the user pressing a key on the keyboard, and so on. All this is quite similar to the elements that make up VBA, as we will see. When you create a File List Box in VB, it automatically displays files in the folder you specify (Figure 7-28).

"Intelligent objects" make programming much easier.

auto32ld.vbp
biblio.ldb
biblio.mdb
bright.dib
ctrlref.cnt
ctrlref.fts
ctrlref.hlp
datamgr.cnt
datamgr.ftg
datamgr.fts
datamgr.gid
datamgr.hlp
datman32.exe
entprise.cnt
entprise.ftg
entprise.fts
entprise.gid
entprise.hlp
module1.bas
pastel.dib
pss.ftg
pss.fts
pss.gid
pss.hlp
rainbow.dib

Figure 7-28: No programming required. VB's File List Box automatically reads and displays files in any folder.

WordBasic and VBA toolbars have similar buttons, similar options.

Full Visual Basic is overkill for many computer users. They don't want or need to create stand-alone, runnable .EXE programs. Instead, they just want do some minor programming, to tell their word processor, for example, that when they press Ctrl+D they want to change the way it displays the date: December 12, 1996 instead of the default 12/12/96. For this, macro languages like Word Basic and, now, VBA do the trick.

The WordBasic macro toolbar that we've been using so far to write and edit macros is similar to the VBA toolbar found in Excel (see Figure 7-29). The buttons on the VBA toolbar are, from left to right, Insert Module (create a blank module you can then use to write a macro), Menu Editor, Object Browser, Run Macro, Step

Macro, Resume Macro, Stop Macro, Record Macro, Toggle Breakpoint, Instant Watch, Step Into, and Step Over. The buttons on the WordBasic toolbar are, from left to right, Record, Record Next Command, Start, Trace, Continue, Stop, Step, Step Subs (same as Step Into), Show Variables, Add/Remove Rem (remarks), Macro (the main Macro window, same as Tools | Macro), and Dialog Editor. A *module* is Excel's equivalent to Word's blank document page that you see when you select Edit from the Tools | Macro menu. In other words, you write or edit Excel macros in a module.

VBA's debugging facilities (tools that help you locate errors in your macro) are more sophisticated than WordBasic's. VBA also includes a menu editor and an Object Browser. We'll look at the Object Browser—the third button from the left in Figure 7-29—later in this chapter.

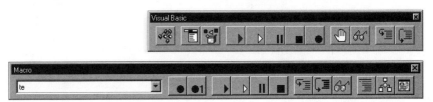

Figure 7-29: The VBA toolbar in Excel (top) is quite similar to WordBasic's toolbar (bottom).

The various macro basics will wither, yielding to VBA.

Even though VBA is now being built into all major Microsoft applications, the older macro languages, such as WordBasic or AccessBasic, are still included in the applications as well, for backward compatibility with macros you may have created to use in earlier software versions. These older macro languages will probably reside side-by-side with VBA in applications for some time to come.

The core commands of VBA are essentially identical in all applications. Adding two numbers is accomplished the same way (1 + 2). However, because the various implementations of VBA each work within varied host programs with varied features, the different flavors of VBA include—in addition to all of Basic's traditional commands—an entire set of application-specific commands. VBA for Word will certainly have a command that can change the way Word handles hyphenation (ToolsHyphenation .AutoHyphenation = 0). Likewise, Excel has a command that can make a legend visible on a chart (Charts(1).HasLegend = True).

A Brief VBA Demonstration

Before we go any further into VBA, it's hard to resist a brief demonstration of *OLE Automation*. OLE Automation is the most sophisticated use of VBA, and we will save an in-depth exploration of it for Chapter 8. But since it's so interesting, let's just try a simple example here.

OLE Automation involves a kind of *linking between applications* (as opposed to the more typical OLE linking, which is between a file and an application). With OLE Automation, you link two or more applications by communicating from VBA directly to the interior of another application. The application that starts the communication (and thereby manipulates the second application) we'll call the *source*. The second application we'll call the *container*. The second application contains objects, like a spell-checker for example, that can be activated and controlled by the source application. During OLE Automation, one application is active, the second application is acted upon. What's really revolutionary is that the source application can take complete control of the container, can make it jump through flaming hoops.

Let's have Excel VBA contact Word, open a new document, type some text, change the text's font size, type some more, then save the resulting file, and close Word. It's like turning a robot loose in the computer.

Start Excel. (You need not start Word; it will be activated by our macro.) Use the Insert | Macro | Module command (press Alt+I, M, M) to insert a fresh macro module sheet in which you can type in our new macro. If this doesn't work, click somewhere in the currently visible worksheet so the macro facilities will be available on the Insert menu.

You can now link applications, not just data.

Now you can type the following commands to build this "robot" or, as it's now often called, an "agent":

```
Sub OLEAUTO( )

Dim WordObj As Object
Set WordObj = CreateObject("Word.Basic")

WordObj.FileNewDefault 'start a blank document
WordObj.StartOfDocument 'move to the top

WordObj.FontSize 12
WordObj.Insert "HELLO WORD!! We've taken control!"
WordObj.InsertPara   'move down two lines
WordObj.InsertPara
WordObj.Insert "Signed,"
WordObj.InsertPara
WordObj.Bold 1
WordObj.FontSize 48
WordObj.Insert "The Excel ROBOT"
WordObj.FileSaveAs "C:\ROBOT.DOC" 'save the file to disk

Set WordObj = Nothing 'release memory/resources
End Sub
```

We can make Excel force Word do whatever Excel wants.

We'll explain the meaning of these commands in Chapter 8, but if you want to see this magic act now, click the Run Macro button on Excel's Visual Basic toolbar, or press F5. If Word is already running but Excel is occupying the full screen, you won't see anything happen. The hard drive will whir briefly, and that will be that. If Excel isn't occupying the full screen, you'll see Word responding to your commands. In any case, look on your disk for the new file called ROBOT.DOC. Its contents should look something like Figure 7-30.

```
HELLO WORD!! We've taken control!

Signed,
```

The Excel ROBOT

Figure 7-30: This Word document was created entirely automatically from within Excel. No human hands touched it.

Pretty amazing. Excel started Word, entered some text, changed the font size and typeface, and then saved the new document to disk. Of course you could also animate Word in many other ways—including sending it data from Excel, opening other files to import data, embedding pictures, and so on. Anything you could do from the keyboard within Word, you can also do via OLE Automation commands from VBA Excel. And you can also do many things you *can't* do from the keyboard. Turn your robot loose, and if you can think it up, the robot can do it. It can even trigger Word macros.

Even better, creating the script for the robot to follow can be simplicity itself. You just turn on macro recording in Word, carry out whatever tasks you want accomplished, then copy the resulting macro, and paste it into an Excel VBA module. You need to make some syntax adjustments before VBA will know what WordBasic was doing, but these adjustments are simplifications.

For example, WordBasic's command:

```
FormatFont .Bold = 1
```

becomes in VBA:

```
WordObj.Bold 1
```

We'll go into all this in detail in the next chapter, but we couldn't resist giving you a sample of this exciting and powerful technique right off the bat. With OLE Automation, you've got virtually unlimited control over any application that "exposes its objects," as the colorful phrase goes. And because OLE 2.0 is now a standard, you'll see most Windows applications migrate to full compliance. Exposed objects will be all over the place soon. With VBA, you can contact and use these objects as you will.

VBA EDITING BASICS

Let's look at some simple macro programming in Excel—some introductory, elementary VBA.

There are three fundamental categories in any Visual Basic language (whether VB or the several VBA macro languages):

❒ Controls (such as list boxes and buttons)—these are also called *objects*.

❒ Properties (such as the color and size of a control)—these are the qualities of an object.

❒ Methods (actions that a control or other entity is capable of, such as the AddItem Method of a list box that inserts a new line of text into the list.)

Properties are the *qualities* of an object, such as color and size.

VBA Excel can display interactive windows to a user. It calls these windows *dialog boxes*. (You also can put buttons or other controls directly on an ordinary Excel worksheet if you prefer that approach.)

Adding & Programming a Control

Here's how to put some programming into a control (to define what your program should do if the control's OnAction event is triggered, in this case). Start Excel, and create a new dialog box (Insert I Macro I Dialog or Alt+I, M, D). Click on the Create Button icon in the Dialog toolbox (the second one on the right). Then drag your mouse across the Dialog window to make the button control appear. Then, follow these steps to edit the VB code, thereby determining what that control will do:

1. Select the button control. To do so, click on it in your Dialog window so it is highlighted.

2. Click on the Edit Code button (second from the bottom on the right) in the Forms toolbar, which appears when you display a Dialog sheet.

3. VB opens a module and provides you with the beginning and ending for a procedure (an "event"): Sub Name ( ) . . . End Sub. You enter programming instructions between these commands.

Try putting the following into your new module. (Figure 7-31 shows this work in progress.)

```
Sub Button4_Click ( )
        ActiveWindow.GridlineColor = RGB(0, 256, 0)
End Sub
```

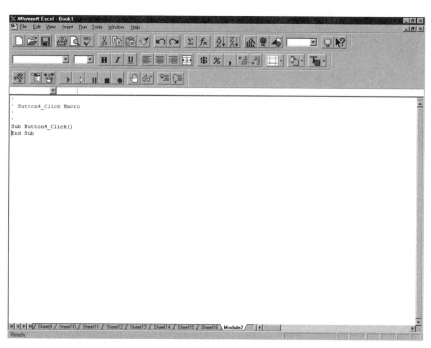

Figure 7-31: Click on the Edit Code button, and VBA opens a new module.

That's it. Now the user of your macro can turn a grid green by clicking on your button. Let's explain what's happening.

A *module* is a VBA container; it holds a macro (or several macros). If you go back to the Dialog window by clicking on the tabs at the bottom of the screen and add an additional control (such as a check box) to your dialog box, a new programming stub will appear just below the Sub Button4_Click ( ) procedure. Click on the Module tab at the bottom of the Excel workbook window to return to the module, and it will look like this:

```
'
' Button4_Click Macro
'
'
Sub Button4_Click( )
ActiveWindow.GridlineColor = RGB(0, 255, 0)
End Sub
'
' OptionButton5_Click Macro
'
'
Sub OptionButton5_Click( )

End Sub
```

By the way, you might find it strange that the first button you add to this dialog box is named "Button4". Shouldn't it be "Button1"? Well, each dialog box automatically has an OK and a Cancel button on it, that's two. By default, the OK button is given the name "Button2", and the Cancel button is given the name "Button3" (Nobody knows what Button1 is....) You just have to live with this oddity until it gets fixed.

Switching Between a Dialog Box & Its Module

You might find that you want to frequently switch back and forth between the dialog box sheet and the module sheet. That's not easy, unfortunately. By default, dialog boxes are entered to the left side of the currently active workbook sheet. Modules, though, are added to the right. You might even have to utilize the "first" and "last" arrows at the lower left corner of the workbook window to switch between the module and the dialog box. The solution is to drag a module's tab to a location more convenient for switching between a dialog box and a module.

Testing a Control's Code

The RGB () function defines what color you want the grid to change to (using the GridlineColor property). RGB stands for Red Green Blue, the combination of colors that can produce any color of the rainbow on a monitor or television screen. Each one can be set from 0 to 255. For Button4, we left red and blue at zero but turned green all the way up.

How can we test our Turn It Green procedure? You could try to run the macro by pressing F5 (or selecting Macro from the Tools menu, and then choosing Run). To run a macro by pressing F5, though, you must be in the module that contains the macro or in the dialog sheet that contains your dialog box.

However, because this particular procedure expects to act upon an active window (that contains a grid it can turn green), you might get an error message: "Unable to set the GridlineColor Property of the window class". That's a fancy way of telling you that the active window (which in this case is the Module window itself) has no grid.

It's easier to test a dialog box from within the dialog box itself. Click on the Dialog 1 tab at the bottom of the Workbook window to redisplay the dialog box. Now click on the Run Dialog button on the Forms toolbar (at bottom right). This starts your dialog box. Click on Button 4, and watch the grid turn green.

What if you want to reverse the effect? Let's assume that we want the Cancel button to change the grid back to black. To edit the Cancel button, click on it to highlight (select) it. Then click on the Edit Code button, and you'll see that VBA has provided another procedure stub (Sub Main...End Sub) for you to fill in. Type this in between the starting and ending points:

```
ActiveWindow.GridlineColor = RGB(0, 0, 0)
```

Use the Run Dialog button for quick tests.

Notice that clicking on the Cancel button automatically closes the dialog box. If you want to restore a black grid (but allow the dialog box to continue appearing onscreen until the user clicks OK), put another button on the dialog box, and label it something like Black Grid. Or, to cause Button4 to *toggle* the color:

```
If ActiveWindow.GridlineColor = RGB(0, 0, 0) Then
ActiveWindow.GridlineColor = RGB(0, 255, 0)
Else
ActiveWindow.GridlineColor = RGB(0, 0, 0)
End If
```

Note that you can query information like this RGB setting just as easily as you can change it. In the line of programming above that begins with *If*, we're asking for the current status of the color of the active window. Based on the answer to this query, we change it either to green or to black.

Adjusting Control Properties

The Control Properties button (second up from bottom, on the left) on the Forms toolbar displays the Format Object dialog box, which allows you to adjust a few of the qualities (properties) of each control. You might be disappointed, though. Very few qualities can be adjusted using the Format Object dialog box. For example, if you put an Option button on a dialog box, and then click the Control Properties button, you'll see that there are only six properties of the Option button that you can adjust in this dialog box. An Option button actually has 28 properties. Fortunately, you can manipulate most VBA control properties, however, by changing them through programming.

To see the 22 properties that don't appear on the Format Object dialog box, click on Excel's Help menu, and use the Index feature to locate Option Buttons. Double-click on that choice, and choose OptionButton Object from the list that is displayed. Excel displays a Help screen.

After you've displayed the Help screen for the OptionButton object, click on Properties at the top, and you'll see the complete list in the Topics Found dialog box (Figure 7-32). For the syntax to use when adjusting one of these properties in one of your macros, click on a property's Name, and you'll see a full description of the property, as shown in Figure 7-33.

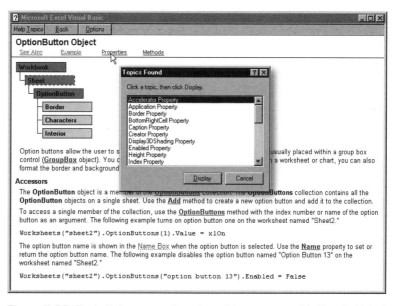

Figure 7-32: Find all the properties of an object or control in Excel's Help feature.

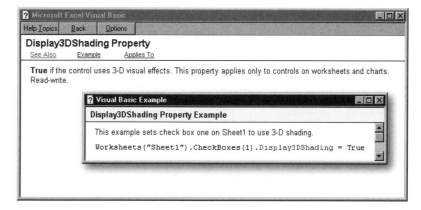

Figure 7-33: When you look at a property in Help, you'll usually find an example showing how to adjust it.

Making VBA Controls React to the User

Many times you'll want a dialog box to be, in fact, a *dialog*. You'll want to get some information from the user. A typical example is having your macro (or VBA) behave one way if the user clicks on one button, and another way if the user clicks on a different button.

Your program can detect which button the user clicks.

For this kind of interaction, you can use the Click event of a button (or any other event that makes sense). *Events* are things that the user can do to a control, such as typing something into an edit box (text box) or clicking. Also, some controls react to the Tab key as the user cycles among them. Other events are triggered when a dialog box or another object is first displayed. The main thing to remember about events is that *something happens*, and you can write programming to react to what happens. With a Click event, you can add programming that responds whenever that object is clicked on with the mouse. What's more, you can always query the contents of a check box, option button, or other control (usually you ask the Value property as in "If Checkbox4.Value = True) to see what the user has done to it or what state it's in. To display a message when the user clicks on the OK button, for instance:

```
Sub Button2_Click()
MsgBox "Thanks!"
End Sub
```

Using the Object Browser

The word *object* is extremely general. Almost anything is an object: a house or a housefly, a stamp album or a single stamp. The only things that are *not* objects are general ideas (like hope) and physical phenomena that have no distinct boundaries (like fog). In VBA, objects are defined as list boxes, command buttons, and so on. You can also create objects of your own. The distinction rests mainly on the fact that an object is not a property (a quality, like color) or an event (something that happens to an object, like the Click event of a command button).

Objects, in VBA, are everywhere. Theoretically, every little item within an application such as Excel or Word is an object. You can make use of these objects for your own purposes. After all, we can display objects we create (such as list boxes)—why not also display or otherwise manipulate the many objects that are built into Excel itself? We've been creating our own dialog boxes, but can we display one of Excel's own dialog boxes? Let's look at a list of Excel's built-in dialog boxes, and then we'll display one in a VBA macro.

You can display
Excel's built-in dialog
boxes.

To see the list of Excel's dialog boxes, first make sure that the Visual Basic toolbar is showing; choose Tools | View (Alt+V, T), click Visual Basic, and click OK. Then click on the Insert Module button on the Visual Basic toolbar (it's the button on the far left). Now that you're in module view, you can access the Object Browser. Click on the Object Browser button on the Visual Basic toolbar (third from left), or simply press F2 to see the Object Browser.

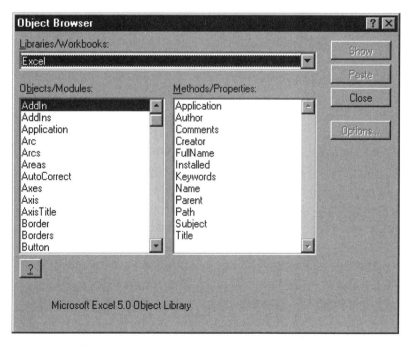

Figure 7-34: The VBA Object Browser lists all currently active objects.

In the Object Browser, pull down the Libraries | Workbooks menu, and select Excel. Then in the Objects | Modules list, choose Constants, and scroll down in the Methods | Properties list until you start seeing the Excel dialog boxes (they all start with *xlDialog*). Click on the particular dialog box we're after: xlDialogFindFile. Then click on Paste, and the proper name (the constant) for the Find File dialog box will be inserted into our module.

Let's create a macro to display this Excel dialog box. Type the following into a module:

```
Sub DisplayFindFile( )
 Sheets("Sheet1").Select
 Application.Dialogs(xlDialogFindFile).Show
End Sub
```

Test this macro by clicking on the Run Macro or Step Into button on the Visual Basic toolbar.

You cannot display the FindFile dialog box when you're viewing a module sheet, so first off, the macro switches to a regular workbook sheet. How did we know the syntax for *that*? Recall from our discussion earlier in this chapter that often the quickest way to write a macro is to *record* a macro; that way, VBA itself "types" the correct commands with the correct punctuation.

To find out how to make a particular sheet active, all we did was click on the red circle (on the Visual Basic toolbar) to start recording, then click on the Sheet1 tab at the bottom of the window. We stopped recording by clicking on the black square button on the Macro toolbar. Switching to Module view, we saw that VBA had thoughtfully typed the following, which is exactly what we need.

```
Sub Macro1( )
 Sheets("Sheet1").Select
End Sub
```

We renamed this macro to DisplayFindFile, just to make it more descriptive and added the second line, which actually shows the FindFile dialog box. The second line means: in the Application

Object (Excel itself), locate Dialogs (a collection, or "array," of all Excel's built-in dialog boxes). Then show the one named xlDialogFindFile. You can, of course, display any of the other dialog boxes listed in the Object Browser in this same way. If one of them fails to display, just check to be sure that you're in the right context. Some won't display unless a chart is visible, some require that at least one cell with some data in it be visible, and so on. It's easy enough to find out the necessary context by trying to display a dialog box with your mouse via menus, then noting what view or context works. To see the Customize Toolbar dialog box, just change the macro above to:

```
Sub DisplayCustom( )
 Sheets("Sheet1").Select
 Application.Dialogs(xlDialogCustomizeToolbar).Show
End Sub
```

MOVING BEYOND THE BASICS

To round out our discussion of basic VBA programming, let's create a variety of examples and test them in real-world situations. We'll write some macros in WordBasic and some in Excel VBA to get a feel for the transition from traditional Basic to VBA. In addition, we'll look at some new programming structures and the way VBA handles variables. In particular, we want to understand the highly useful new variable type called the *variant*.

With...End With

With...End With is new to Basic and quite useful for assigning properties to an object.

With...End With is new to Basic, appearing first in VBA. It is a quick way to format (or assign other properties or actions to) a given object. Let's record a small program, and then see what it looks like. In the process, we'll see an example of how With...End With works. Load the sample Excel worksheet EXCEL\EXAMPLES\BOOK1.XLS, or simply fill a few cells with some numbers. We'll assume that we often want to change the font size and the background color of a group of selected cells. Instead of using the commands each time, we'll *record* the changes, and then we can just run the macro the next time we want to change the format. That, in essence, is the virtue and utility of computer programming: You teach it how once; it follows the instructions forever after.

Make sure that your Visual Basic toolbar is visible: choose View | Toolbars (press Alt+V, T), select the Visual Basic toolbar, and click OK. You should see something similar to Figure 7-35.

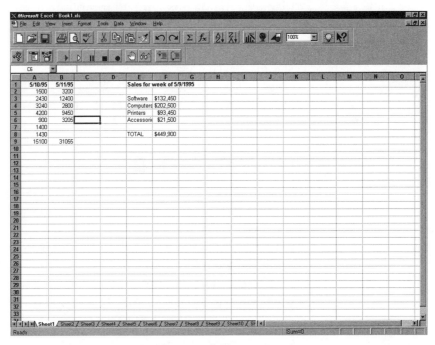

Figure 7-35: Display the Visual Basic toolbar when you want to record steps in Excel.

Click on the button with the red circle in the Visual Basic toolbar to start the recording. In the dialog box that appears, give the macro a name such as UsualFormat, and click on the OK button. A small temporary toolbar appears, containing a single stop button. (We'll click this button when we're ready to stop recording.)

Drag your mouse around the cells to select them (they will reverse to white lettering on a black background). Then right-click on the selected cells to pop up the associated menu, and select Format Cells. Click on the Font options, and change the font size to 12 under the Size list. Then click on the Patterns tab, and choose a light gray pattern. Finally, click on the OK button to close the Format Cells window. Stop recording the macro by clicking on the stop button.

You can look at the VBA macro. Choose Tools | Macro (Alt+T, M), and select the UsualFormat macro (or whatever you called it). Click the Edit button to edit it, and you should see something similar to the following:

```
'
' usualformat Macro
' Macro recorded 1/16/96 by Richard Mansfield
'
'
Sub usualformat( )
 Range("A1:G9").Select
 With Selection.Font
   .Name = "Arial"
   .Size = 12
   .Strikethrough = False
   .Superscript = False
   .Subscript = False
   .OutlineFont = False
   .Shadow = False
   .Underline = xlNone
   .ColorIndex = xlAutomatic
 End With
 With Selection.Interior
   .ColorIndex = 15
   .Pattern = xlSolid
   .PatternColorIndex = xlAutomatic
 End With
End Sub
```

Essentially, in the preceding VBA example, With...End With says: make the following conditions apply to the font in the selection (the cells we selected). Then make the following qualities apply to the interior (the background) of the selected area.

All we did was change the size of the font, but VBA entered the status of all possible other qualities that could apply to the Selection.Font. Likewise, we changed the color but didn't change the pattern—even though VBA specified the pattern as well. The reason for this is that VBA wants to specify the complete set of qualities so those qualities will be reproduced exactly when the macro is run. Assume that you have a Times New Roman font in the selected cells when you run this macro. The Selection.Font .Name quality (property) will be changed to Arial. And so on. If you don't want the macro to change the existing font, remove the line that specifies .Name from the macro.

In fact, if all you want the macro to do is change the font size and background color, you could edit the macro so it looks like this:

```
Sub usualFormat( )

 Range("B4:D8").Select

 With Selection.Font
 .Size = 11
 End With

 With Selection.Interior
 .ColorIndex = 40
 End With

End Sub
```

And if you want it to affect *any selected range of cells*, remove this line:

```
Range("B4:D8").Select
```

You can, of course, edit the macro to suit your own needs and to the extent that you wish. Notice how With…End With differs from some previous versions of the Basic language. Before, you presented a list of items to be adjusted. (Such a list is called an *argument list*, and the individual items are called *arguments* or, sometimes, *parameters*.) In any case, *all* the items, *all* the arguments, had to be there (you couldn't remove some of them, even if you wanted them left as they were). At best, you could leave some out, but you still had to include a series of commas representing the position of any missing items. The arguments were interpreted and identified by the computer language *by their position*. Assuming that you didn't care to change the second and third items in the list, they still had to be represented—even if only as empty commas. If you wanted to specify a value of 27 for the fourth item in the following argument list, you had to insert comma placeholders to establish that it was, in fact, the fourth item in the list:

```
ChangeColor (33,,,27)
```

With VBA, each item in the list of font qualities is independent and has its own *name* (such as SuperScript). This same independence is now true of the latest version of WordBasic as well, though WordBasic isn't yet fully VBA:

```
Font.Size := 11
```

An Additional Note About With…End With

The new With…End With structure can also be used to test expressions (If .Column = 2) as well as to change properties (.Value = 777). The following properties are all assumed to be properties of the ActiveCell object, thanks to With…End With. Notice that within a With…End With structure, property applies to the object named after the With command:

```
Sub TextIt ( )
      With ActiveCell
            If .Row = 4 Then
                  .Value = 23.5
            End If
      End With
End Sub
```

WordBasic Does It Differently

Let's try recording the same kind of formatting macro in Word-Basic to see what WordBasic does differently than VBA. Type some text, and then turn on macro recording. (To turn on macro recording, choose Tools | Macro, type a Macro Name such as ReFormat, and click on the Record button.) You'll see a temporary toolbar similar to the one that Excel displays during macro recording. However, this toolbar has the added advantage of a pause button as well as a stop button. Pressing the Pause button allows you to do some things that aren't recorded, actions that won't appear in the finished macro.

Use the keyboard to select your text (Shift+arrow keys), then choose Format | Font, and change the current format to Times New Roman with 12 for the font size. Then click on the button (with the square) in the Macro Record toolbar to stop the macro recording. To see the macro, press Alt+T, M, select the macro name (ReFormat), and then click on the Edit button. You'll see something similar to this:

WordBasic's properties use = rather than VBA's := punctuation.

```
Sub MAIN
FormatFont .Points = "12", .Underline = 0, .Color = 0,
.Strikethrough = 0, .Superscript = 0, .Subscript = 0, .Hidden =
0, .SmallCaps = 0, .AllCaps = 0, .Spacing = "0 pt", .Position =
"0 pt", .Kerning = 0, .KerningMin = "", .Tab = "0", .Font =
"Times New Roman", .Bold = 0, .Italic = 0, .Outline = 0, .Shadow
= 0
End Sub
```

Notice that this is similar to the Excel VBA macro, but the qualities (properties) are not lined up inside a With...End With structure. That structure is a part of VBA and isn't yet available in WordBasic. However, you can streamline this WordBasic macro by removing all but the only two qualities we are really changing:

```
Sub MAIN

FormatFont .Points = "12", .Font = "Times New Roman"

End Sub
```

Recording Within a VBA Macro

Here's how to edit an existing macro by recording just a *portion* of it—within the extant programming. Using your mouse or the arrow keys, move the cursor (the I-beam symbol) on the VB module sheet to the location within the macro you want to "record within." Then choose Record Macro from the Tools menu, and select Mark Position For Recording. Move to the worksheet where you'll perform the actions you want inserted into your macro. To activate the recording process, again, choose Record Macro from the Tools menu, but this time select Record at Mark. Go ahead and change a font name or perform some other task. When you're finished, click on the Stop toolbar or the stop button (with the square icon) on the Visual Basic toolbar.

Writing Macros & Programs

Of course, you need not record all or part of a macro or program. In VBA you can type in commands and then test the result. This is traditional "programming" because when you're creating a stand-alone application, an .EXE file, there's no surrounding application. So, what could you record? What built-in behaviors or menus could you activate?

However, even if you're writing a macro, you sometimes cannot record. To accomplish some jobs, there is no way at all to "record" (since there is no direct way—or perhaps no way at all—to do what you want to do via the keyboard, a menu, or the mouse). In those situations, you must *write* the program, using the macro language's commands and just typing the program.

For example, the italics feature works rather eccentrically in Word 6.0: if you try to italicize *part* of a word or two words that are temporarily together, Word doesn't italicize only the selected text. It italicizes the whole word. The following macro offers a cure—something you simply cannot do via recording:

```
Sub MAIN

If Italic( ) Then
  Insert " "
  Italic 0
Else
  Italic 1
End If

End Sub
```

MACROS IN ACCESS

Now we'll look briefly at how macros and VBA work in Microsoft Access. Prior to the latest version, Access had a most eccentric macro-writing environment. It all involved a clumsy list box approach. Don't ask.

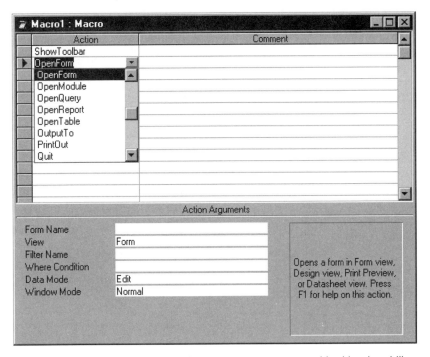

Figure 7-36: Ordinary Access Basic macros are constructed in this wizard-like query screen.

Now, though, Access has joined the VBA bandwagon and you can create macros in a Module, very much the way you create macros in Excel. A primary difference, though, is that Access doesn't include a macro recording facility. Let's try some examples.

With Access running, click on the View | Toolbars menu. Select Visual Basic so that you can work with the VB Toolbar. On the far right of the toolbar you'll see the usual Help button, but just next to that is a "New Object" button. Click on its arrow and choose "New Module" from the drop-down menu.

As you can see in Figure 7-37, a new, blank module is created into which you can type VBA programming commands. By default, two commands are automatically inserted: Option Compare Database and Option Explicit. The compare option is defined by VBA-Access help as: "Option Compare Database can only be used within Microsoft Access. This results in string comparisons based on the sort order that is determined by the locale ID of the database where the string comparisons occur." Loosely translated, this means that if you compare text variables to see which is "greater" (higher in alphabetical order)—the comparison will be based on the technique in effect in whatever database launches the macro. We'll construct a sample VBA Access example shortly.

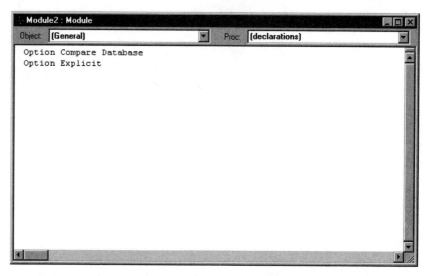

Figure 7-37: You write VBA-Access macros much the same way as VBA-Excel macros—in a Module.

Option Explicit means that you must declare (Dim) all variables:

```
Dim X As String
X = "Sally"
```

You can't just create a variable by using it:

```
X = "Sally"
```

For more on this distinction, see "Creating a Variable via a Formal Declaration" below. However, if you want, you can just erase these two default commands from the Module.

Classic Access Basic

Now let's try creating an Access Basic macro, then we'll create a VBA macro.

To create a traditional Access Basic macro, first open a database so the macro will be "attached" (embedded) in that database. Click on Access's File | Open Database menu. If you don't have a database of your own, use one of the sample databases in the Access folder.

Now click on the Macro tab, then choose "New," as shown in Figure 7-38.

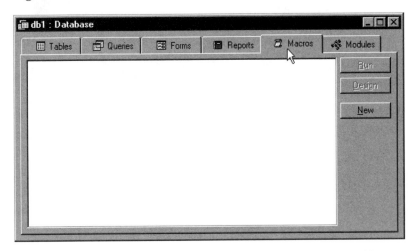

Figure 7-38: You can start a new Access Basic macro by clicking on this "Macro" tab.

Your job now is to choose commands from the list box in the upper left corner of the macro design window. Click on the list box, the arrow symbol under "Action," and choose "MsgBox" as shown in Figure 7-39.

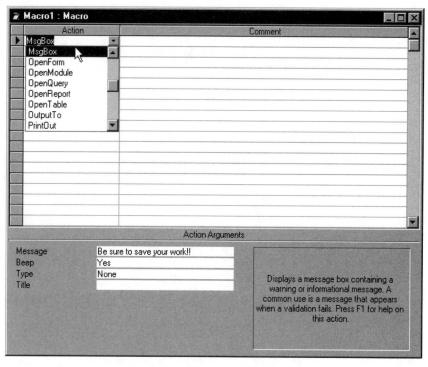

Figure 7-39: The Access Basic commands—all 50 of them—are listed in this list box (VBA, by contrast, has hundreds of commands).

As soon as you click on "MsgBox," you'll see some text entry boxes in the lower left corner. Here's where you can refine the behavior and action of your message box. We added the message "Be sure to save your work!!" If you like, you can put an icon-like symbol on the message box by clicking on the "Type" option, then selecting from the drop-down list you'll see if you click on the arrow symbol that appears.

Now let's test it. Click on the button with the exclamation point symbol on the Macro Toolbar. This is the "Run" command. You'll see the message in Figure 7-40.

You can test Access Basic macros by clicking on the Run button.

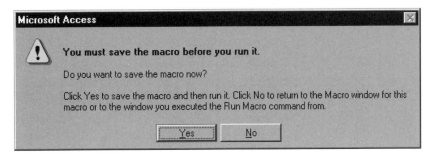

Figure 7-40: You can't test an Access macro until you've first saved it.

So let's go ahead and save this macro. Click on "Yes" in the message window and give this macro the name "Autoexec." After Access saves it, it then runs it to show you how it will look.

We named it "Autoexec" because any macro with that name will be automatically launched whenever this database runs (the database that's currently active and to which this macro is "attached"). Now minimize or close the macro design window and take a look at the property sheet window for your database, as shown in Figure 7-41.

Figure 7-41: Now we've got a macro in this database—right-click on its name to make any changes to it.

If you right-click on a macro's name, you can then rename, delete, edit, and otherwise manage it.

AutoKeys

As you might expect, Access has its own unique way of assigning shortcut key combinations to macros. It's called *AutoKeys*. Let's try assigning it to a shortcut key combination, just to see how it's done.

In the Database property sheet (see Figure 7-41), click the Macros tab. Click on "New" then click on the "Macro Names" button in the Macro toolbar (the button is about in the middle of the toolbar, and has XYZ across the top of it). This reveals a Name field in the Macro design window.

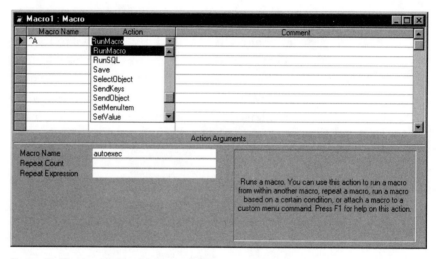

Figure 7-42: Use the RunMacro command to assign a keyboard shortcut to a macro.

In the Macro Name column, type the key or key combination that you want to use to trigger your macro. Use the following conventions:

RIGHT ARROW	{RIGHT}
SCROLL LOCK	{SCROLLLOCK}
TAB	{TAB}
UP ARROW	{UP}
F1	{F1}
F2	{F2}
F3	{F3}
(and so on)	

If you want to use a SHIFT, CTRL, and ALT key along with another key, use one (or more) of these symbols:

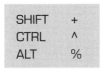

SHIFT	+
CTRL	^
ALT	%

Therefore, ^A would be Ctrl+A, while ^+C would be Ctrl+Shift+C, and so forth. For example, to cause Shift+F3 to trigger your macro, use: +{F3}.

Next, in the "Action" drop-down list, select "RunMacro" and then choose a macro in the drop-down list labeled "Macro Name."

Now close this window and, when asked "do you want to save changes…" click on "Yes" and name it AutoKeys. (You must use the name *AutoKeys*.)

As with shortcut key combinations in Word and other applications, your macros will take precedence over any shortcut key combination that's built into Access.

VBA In Access

You create a VBA macro in Access much the same way as you do in Excel. First open a Module, then type in Sub…End Sub and write your commands within. Let's create an example. First in the Database property sheet (see Figure 7-41), click the Modules tab. Click on "New" and delete the Option Explicit line. (This way you don't have to Dim all your variables.) Type in:

```
Sub DateCalc
```

```
End Sub
```

You'll see the window shown in Figure 7-43:

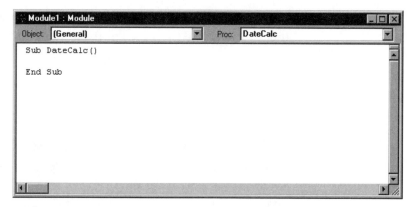

Figure 7-43: You use a Module to write your Access VBA macros.

Now, between the Sub and End Sub structure, type in the following:

```
Dat = InputBox("Enter a date")
MsgBox ("Days from today: " & DateDiff("d", Now, Dat))
```

The first line displays a window to the user, asking for a date (such as 12/14/98). Then, whatever the user types in (held in the variable *Dat*) is fed to a message box. This shows the results to the user. We used the VBA command *DateDiff* to calculate the difference, in days, between what the user typed in (Dat) and "Now," the computer clock's report of the current date.

Testing VBA macros is cumbersome.

Testing a VBA Access macro or procedure is rather roundabout. You must first launch the Debug Window, then type in the name of the procedure that you want to test. Click on the View menu, then select "Debug Window." Into the Debug Window type in the name of our example macro, *DateCalc*, and press Enter to run it:

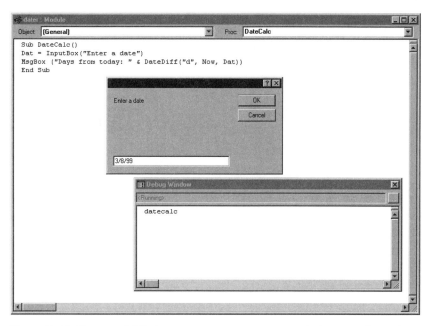

Figure 7-44: To test a VBA Access macro, you must type in its name from the Debug Window.

In general, creating macros in Access is more difficult than it is in either Word or Excel. Access has no recording feature, so you don't have the convenience of seeing and editing samples of programming created automatically by the application. Also, the Access testing and debugging facilities are clumsy. Finally, Access Basic macros are built from lists rather than typed in. For beginners this "Builder" approach is doubtless simpler, but once you get past the elementary level, it becomes cumbersome and restrictive.

At this point, let's look closely at several essential concepts—procedures, variables, arrays, and other key concepts. These are ideas you must understand to become a proficient macro programmer.

UNDERSTANDING VBA PROCEDURES

A *procedure* is one or more lines of programming, contained within a stub.

```
Sub Noise ( )
        Beep
End Sub
```

OR

```
Function Noise ( )
        Beep
End Function
```

The *stub* is the Sub...End Sub (or Function...End Function) that frames the actual programming. The stub serves to label the procedure with a name (in this case Noise). As you've seen earlier, WordBasic and VBA automatically insert a stub if you ask to create a new macro or start recording a macro. Within the stub, you insert the actual programming (in this case the Beep command, which makes a noise).

The most common kind of procedure is a subroutine, hence *Sub*. Technically and traditionally, a sub is a procedure that does not return a value. A function is a procedure that does return a value. But, even this distinction no longer holds. Read on.

Subroutines are small programs.

A subroutine is a little program. In traditional Basic, a sub exists within a larger program—the sub performing some limited useful task (and usually available to be called upon to perform that task from anywhere in the program). The classic structure of an old-style Basic program starts with a series of calls to subroutines, within a main loop. The program might look similar to this:

```
GOSUB GetUserInput
GOSUB ShowResult
End

GetUser:
Input "What screen?"; X
RETURN

ShowResult:
Print Screen(X)
RETURN
```

Creating a subroutine is like teaching your dog to fetch the paper. You first name the trick "paper," and then teach the behaviors that the word *paper* is supposed to elicit. After he learns the trick, you can sit in your rocking chair on the porch, just say *"paper"*, and let him find it in your yard and bring it to you.

A subroutine is:

❑ Available anytime.

❑ Part of a larger structure.

❑ Able to do something limited but useful.

❑ Going to be needed by your program (or if it's a macro, needed by the user while the host application is running) more than one time.

However, VBA uses the Sub...End Sub structure for subroutines. As a result, the GOSUB...RETURN structure has little if any utility in VBA.

Classic Subroutines

V BA uses few traditional GoSub...Return routines.

VBA relies much less on classic subroutines than do older computer languages. It used to be that a Basic program had many subroutines, and you used the GoSub and Return commands often.

But regardless of how they are structured or implemented, the contributions of subroutines are, of course, inherent to programming and will always exist as long as people need to communicate with computers. You use them for the same reason that you buy address labels so you don't have to write your name and address each time you send something in the mail. Subroutines are fundamentally efficient; they extend a computer language in much the same way that abbreviations, labels, and acronyms extend human language.

Just how the concept of the subroutine is implemented in each computer language, though, can differ considerably. VBA's design essentially eliminates the need for traditional subroutines to which you would GoSub and then Return—everything in VBA is a subroutine, so in a way nothing is.

In place of GoSub...Return, VBA coagulates all instructions, all commands into Sub...End Sub structures (or the similar function structure). In VBA, these events are the main location for programming, the place where you put your instructions to the computer.

In VBA, GoSub...Return *can* be used within a given procedure, within a sub or function structure. However, this is rarely done. Among other drawbacks, GoSub...Return requires that you awkwardly leap out of the procedure, using the Exit Sub command:

```
Sub DoSomething ( )
        X = 5
        GoSub addit 'go to subroutine
        Msgbox Num
        Exit Sub 'Don't repeat the subroutine

Addit:  ' subroutine
        X = X + X
        Return ' Return to main routine
End Sub
```

In practice, there is little use for a GoSub...Return structure in VBA. If you are tempted to use the GoSub...Return structure, you might want to consider creating a separate Sub...End Sub, and then call the sub to utilize the services of the stand-alone procedure:

```
Sub DoSomething( )
 X = 5
 Addit 'go to separate procedure
 Msgbox X
End Sub

Sub Addit( )
 X = X + X
End Sub
```

Procedures are "called" instead of "GoSubbed."

Notice that in VBA syntax, you call (in earlier Basics you'd use the GoSub command) a separate procedure *by just using its name* (as we did above with Addit). Also, you cannot pass (or send) variables to a GoSub...Return structure, but you don't need to. Note that a VBA event is a procedure—a Sub...End Sub structure.

The GoSub...Return structure must now reside, in VBA, within a Sub...End Sub or Function...End Function structure. The GoSub...Return structure therefore has access to all the local variables within its host structure. We'll explain the meaning of *local* (and other terms such as *public, private, global,* etc.) later in the discussion of VBA variables.

If you do choose to use the archaic GoSub...Return structure, be careful that your program doesn't "fall through" into the host procedure. A label identifies the start of a subroutine within the Sub...End Sub structure (like our Addit above), but the label does not stop the computer from continuing further and carrying out the commands within the embedded subroutine. Just before the label, you need to put an Exit Sub, Exit Function, End, or GoTo command to prevent the computer from falling through into the embedded subroutine. You want that subroutine to be used only when specifically called by the GoSub command.

Subroutines Enclose All Programming

In VBA you record or write a procedure (or event) inside the Sub...End Sub (or Function...End Function) framework. If some other procedure wants to use this procedure, fine. It can just use the name of the sub, and the sub does its thing. Unfortunately, some confusion has arisen as Microsoft languages pile up on each other—evolving toward an eventual full-service VBA across all Windows applications. The primary problem is that a *subroutine* meant GoSub...Return in classical Basic programming. Now we have the Sub...End Sub structure in contemporary VBA. The trend is to eliminate that old "main loop" that calls a series of subroutines.

The GUI interface encourages user-activated, *modular* programming.

The reason for this shift in style is that Windows is a GUI, a graphical user interface. In classic Basic (or any other older, DOS-bound language), you would ordinarily first present the user with a numbered list, a menu of choices. The user would maybe press the 3 key, which would trigger the third option in your list (and then a subroutine would come to life). The user would then be presented with another menu of choices or behaviors. This step-by-step behavior—controlled by the layout of your program—proceeded in a largely linear fashion: the user couldn't do B until he or she did A.

Today, with GUIs, the user doesn't expect to work with an application in a linear, predetermined way. Instead of riding a train (the tracks inexorably leading to a predefined destination), users now expect to have their own private auto, to decide for themselves where and when they stop, and for how long.

In a graphical interface, things are of course *visual*. But they are also independent—*by clicking on an object, the user hasn't bought a ticket to some unstoppable ride.* In a GUI, there are many icons, menus, submenus, tabs that can be clicked, drop-down menus accessed right-clicking on visual symbols, scroll bars, and all the other visual apparatus. It's more like a cafeteria of choices than the classical step-by-step options that become available only in series and only if you follow the *rules*. In a GUI, the user directs the flow of the program more completely. To the programmer, this means programming becomes atomized into relatively small "objects" or "procedures" that are self-contained and don't depend on the completion of other objects or procedures.

```
Sub ItsName ( )
(Your programming goes here)
End Sub
```

The structure above is by far the most common kind of procedure in VBA. (There are two other kinds of procedures: the function and the eccentric, new property procedure). When you call a sub, the (*your programming goes here*) happens. Then the computer returns to the place where the call took place and continues.

However, as we will see shortly, the previous distinction between function and sub is more or less gone now. They are both just the same thing, *procedures*, and (from the programmer's point of view) there is nothing that distinguishes one from the other.

In previous versions of Basic, a sub did something (maybe it changed the color of a group of Excel cells or started spell-checking in Word). However, a sub didn't return a value. That is, you couldn't use a sub as part of an expression. Returning information is something that you *could* do with a function (the second most common kind of procedure). Now, though, subs and functions are indistinguishable: you can write them into your program using identical punctuation.

In VBA, commands can't appear outside subroutines or functions (or VB's events, which are a kind of subroutine). Subroutines and functions (Sub...End Sub or Function...End Function stubs) must contain all your instructions.

Right:

```
Function Printnumber ( )
Msgbox X
End Function
```

Wrong:

```
Print Msgbox X
```

VBA won't allow you to do this simple Print X; the instruction has no container, no stub, no name. (The fact that you cannot use a free-floating command makes VBA radically different from previous versions of the Basic language.)

Writing an uncontained instruction will cause an error message such as "End Sub or End Function must be last statement" or "Invalid outside procedure." In other words, no commands, virtually no instructions to the computer, can be free-floating without a sub or function to contain them and give them a name. (The only major exception is declarations of types of variables, such as Global z As Integer or Public z$, which can exist outside procedures. We'll get to variable declarations below.)

All commands must be "contained" except for declarations and a few rare ones, such as DefInt, Declare, and Option.

You give functions and subroutines unique names when you create them. We called the example function above Printnumber. This way, other places within your program can refer to and use the procedures. Likewise, you can run a procedure as a macro by merely *naming* the procedure within your programming. VBA comes with over 350 separate commands, such as Msgbox. When you write a subroutine or function, it's as if you are adding a *new* command to the language. And the program can then use this new command just as it would an existing command.

```
Function Printnumber (X)
Msgbox X
End Function
```

Functions: Another Kind of Procedure

Functions illustrate many of the qualities and techniques of procedures, so we'll spend some time exploring Functions. However, you can still use words *Sub* and *Function* if you wish, you can even still use the syntax in your programming—VBA will recognize the old equals sign and parentheses that Functions used to require. *But you must use both* the equals sign and the parentheses if you choose to use either. If you just use parentheses, VBA will think you are "protecting" the variable (the same thing as receiving it using the ByVal command). For more on this, see "Bye Bye ByVal" below. However, as we will see, Subs and Functions are, in VBA, essentially the same. The distinctions between them have now fundamentally evaporated.

Functions are rather like super variables. (If you don't know what a variable is, see "An In-Depth Look at Variables" later in this chapter.) They can behave like variables within a line of programming (within expressions), but they can also perform some action on the information they contain. Ordinary variables cannot adjust the piece of text or number they hold. Ordinary variables merely "contain" a piece of information—some outside agent must be used to change the contained data.

A key distinction between a classic function and a subroutine is that a function returns something to the location in the program that called the function: X$ = Capital( ). The variable *X$* would be given some value from the actions taken by the function named Capital. Sometimes, though, you don't care what the function returns and just ignore it. But this structure (the X= and the parentheses) is always required when using a function—even if you don't care what is returned. However, *neither the X= nor the ( ) are required in VBA—although they are required in all other versions of Basic.*

Here's a typical, traditional function:

```
Sub Changeit ( )
        A$ = "mary morie"
        Z$ = Upper (A$)
        Msgbox Z$
End Sub


Function Upper (n$)
        Upper = UCASE$(n$)
End Function
```

This function results in changing *mary morie* to *MARY MORIE.* The UCASE$ command turns a text variable into uppercase characters. We pass (or send) A$ to the Upper function, the function does its job, and then passes the result back. (As we will soon see, it is no longer necessary to pass something directly back into a waiting variable. The *Z$ =* in *Z$ = Upper (A$)* is not needed in VBA.)

Notice that because our function Upper *is* a function, we can streamline this programming even further by using Upper(a$) as if it were a variable that we wanted to print. We can *call the function in-line with other commands*:

```
Sub Changeit( )
 a$ = "mary morie"
 Msgbox Upper(a$)
End Sub


Function Upper (n$)
        Upper = UCASE$(n$)
End Function
```

This in-line syntax is another way that a function behaves as if it were a special, enhanced kind of variable. X$ = "Hide the Secret" is a typical, *ordinary* variable. *X$* holds the phrase in this ordinary variable, but *X$* cannot, by itself, have any effect on the phrase (or whatever value) it holds. By contrast, this call to a function— Msgbox Upper(a$)—*includes* the function Upper. This will *do something* to the variable. A function can analyze, modify, and report information or take action based on some data.

All other versions of Basic require a variable to hold the value returned by a function when using (calling) a function—even if you don't care what is returned. And, further, a function in other Basics requires that you send a variable (or variables) enclosed within parentheses:

```
X$ = NameofFunct (N$)
```

VBA *does not require a return-value variable* (though you can use one if you wish). Nor does VBA require parentheses around the "sent" value. You can strip those two things off and just write it like this: NameofFunct N$. So how does this syntax differ from calling a sub? It doesn't. If you like, we could just call them all *procedures,* some of which return a value and some of which don't. The VBA programmer can call functions and subs with identical punctuation.

The following example demonstrates the new syntax: calling a function named DoubleIt by merely naming it and then providing a parentheses-free variable: DoubleIt F$:

```
Sub SendString( )
        F$ = "Bingo"
        DoubleIt F$
        MsgBox F$
End Sub

Function DoubleIt(N As String)
        N = N & N
End Function
```

Results in:
BingoBingo

VBA also permits violation of scoping when using procedures.

Notice that this approach also violates scoping rules. In the above example, F$ has not been defined as module-wide in scope (Dim F$), nor as program-wide (Public F$). Therefore, according to scoping rules, the only place where F$ can be modified is within the SendString procedure in which it resides. Yet, thanks to the DoubleIt Function, F$ is indeed changed.

To demonstrate how VBA makes no distinction between functions and subs, here's the same example written using a sub rather than a function:

```
Sub SendString( )
        F$ = "Bingo"
        DoubleIt F$
        MsgBox F$
End Sub

Sub DoubleIt(N As String)
        N = N & N
End Sub
```

There is no longer any meaningful distinction between subs and functions.

The only difference between this sub and the previous example of a function is that we changed the word *function* to *sub*, and the *End Function* to *End Sub*. Therefore, the only remaining distinction between subs and functions in VBA is that functions can have a variable on the left of an equals sign and can enclose any variables sent to the function within parentheses. But these two remaining distinctions in the use of punctuation in a sub and function are preserved only for the purposes of permitting VBA to understand programs written for previous versions of Basic. The bottom line: there are now only procedures. And all procedures can return a variable or can change it outside of the usual scoping rules (so "returning" it is unimportant).

Bear in mind in the discussions that follow the term *function* has lost nearly all its original meaning, its original distinction from the term *sub*. We are, in VBA, merely talking about procedures. For convenience, though, we'll continue to use the terms *function*, *subroutine*, and *sub*—their historical meanings are too strong to abandon just yet.

Built-in Functions

Many functions are built in to VBA, and you can create your own functions, too. InStr is an important built-in function:

```
X$ = "WARNING!! The Martians Have Landed."

If InStr(X$, "Martians") <> 0 Then
        Print "Head for the ocean!"
Else
        Print "No Problem"
End If
```

The InStr function returns (will be equal to) 0 if it doesn't find the word *Martians* inside *X$*. Otherwise, it returns the character position in *X$* in which the word *Martians* begins. Imagine how difficult getting this information would be using the Mid$ command or some other approach.

Notice that we used the function as if it were a variable. It's as if we said, If X <> 0 Then....; but instead, the function did something. It analyzed the *X$* within the If...Then expression.

Functions Versus Subroutines

Functions and subroutines both act as containers (stubs) for an instruction or a series of instructions that you give to the computer so it can accomplish some task when the program runs.

Functions and subroutines are the two basic units of organization when you're programming in VBA. (Recall that a macro is, normally, a single subroutine.) Each subroutine and function has a name, so you can call (refer to) it to activate it.

Subroutines and functions can accept variables "passed" to them when you "call" them by name and put any variable you want to pass following their names. Subroutines and functions can also change the passed variables.

Here's an example of how to pass variables. Create a subroutine in a module, and then tell it that it will be getting a string variable (some text) passed to it. This sub (subroutine) reports the number of letters in any text that's passed to it:

```
Sub CountLetters (X$)
        Msgbox LEN(X$)
End Sub
```

We're using the Msgbox command so you can step through the subroutine, to see how the program proceeds through the various instructions. Msgbox shows the results in the Immediate Window while you are clicking on the Step button on the Visual Basic toolbar. If you are trying this example in WordBasic, make these changes:

```
Sub MAIN
        Send$ = "How many letters?"
        CountLetters Send$
End Sub

Sub CountLetters(X$)
        Print Len(X$)
End Sub
```

(We have to make two minor adjustments so it works in Word-Basic. Each macro in WordBasic is required to start with Sub MAIN and there is no Debug mode, so we'll "print" the result in the status bar at the bottom of the screen.)

Let's define a piece of text that we'll pass to the subroutine. (You can pass variables or literals—see "An In-Depth Look at Variables" later in this chapter for more on this distinction.) We could also pass a variable such as $Y\$$. Note that if you do pass a variable, the passed variable name does not have to match the name of the received variable in the sub or function (the name in the parentheses following the sub's name).

The sub receives an $X\$$ in this example; we've said $X\$$, but you could pass it $Y\$$ or any other variable name. The $X\$$ is for *internal identification* within the sub and has no side effects on variables outside of the sub. The only restriction is that the passed and received variables must be the same type (see "An In-Depth Look at Variables" later in this chapter). In this case, we're passing and receiving a text ("string") variable.

The variable name you use is irrelevant, as long as you're consistent within the procedure.

```
Sub Testit ( )
        Send$ = "How many letters?"
        CountLetters Send$
End Sub
```

Note that you can pass one or more variables to functions by enclosing the variables to be passed inside the parentheses. When you do that, you can decide elsewhere in the program which number will be printed.

In the following example, we pass the variable *Y* to our PrintNumber function. Recall that the function manipulates *X*, but we're passing *Y*. That doesn't matter because as long as the variables are the same type (in this case the default variant type), the function accepts whatever you pass it.

```
Sub Button1_Click ( )
Y = 45
Result = Printnumber (Y)
End Sub
```

Notice also that we could not simply name the function to use it. The following would not work:

```
Printnumber(Y)
```

Traditional functions (unlike subroutines) must be contained within expressions. In other words, they must be part of a larger command, such as X = Functionname( ) or If Functionname( ) = 5 Then. This was the primary distinction between a function and a subroutine in previous versions of Basic. Functions return a value, and there must be somewhere (some variable) to put this value, even if you don't use what is returned. A subroutine, by contrast, returns nothing and can be simply called by giving its name:

```
X = Funct( )
```

(A Function must be part of an expression and must include parentheses—even if the parentheses are empty and you have no use for whatever is returned in the Variable X.)

```
Subrt (A Subroutine can simply be named to be used.)
```

Only functions can
pass data back.

Another way to think of this traditional distinction is that although both subs and functions can manipulate variables, only a function directly *passes back* a variable to the command that called the function. We had to say Result = Printnumber(Y); we had to use the Result = structure, even though the variable *Result* is not used in this case. Nothing is passed back from our Printnumber function, so nothing happens to *Result*. Nonetheless, you always had to call upon a function from within some kind of expression, or you'd get an error message. A lesser distinction between functions and subroutines is that you enclose the passed variables within parentheses when using a function. You usually omit the parentheses around passed variables when calling a subroutine:

Function:

```
X = PrintSomething (Z)
```

```
Subroutine:
PrintSomething Z
```

Generic VBA has many built-in functions:

```
X$ = UCase$("bombs away")
The UCase$ Function changes the characters involved to all
uppercase:
Msgbox X$
```

Results in:

```
BOMBS AWAY
```

Likewise, in addition to general programming functions in VBA, you can also provide Excel worksheet functions to the user. You can view lists of the VBA functions by choosing Insert I Function and looking in the Function wizard (see Figure 7-45). To cause the Function wizard to be displayed to the user within a macro, type the following into an Excel module. Then run it by pressing F5.

```
Sub Main( )
Worksheets("Sheet3").Activate
ActiveCell.FunctionWizard
End Sub
```

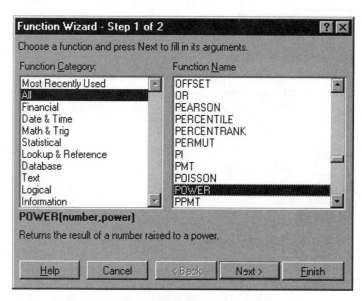

Figure 7-45: Excel has dozens of built-in functions.

Many programs, even some large ones, are written without using any built-in functions or creating any functions of your own.

However, subroutines are convenient when several places in your program have to accomplish the same task, and you want to write the instructions for this task only one time. As with functions, you can pass variables to a subroutine.

Note that no matter how many variables you pass to a procedure, it always *returns* only one variable:

```
X$ = AddStrings$ ("Hit", " The Deck")
Msgbox X$

Function AddStrings$ (A$, B$)
        AddString$ = A$ + B$
End Function
```

Results in:

```
Hit The Deck
```

Here we passed two variables; but, as always with a traditional function, we get only one back, which in this case, is *X$*. Also, the variable *passed back* is the *name* of the function, AddStrings$. X$ equals AddStrings$, and AddStrings$ contains the result of the function's actions. This is another reason we can think of functions as super variables. You can use them as if they were variables, within all the kinds of expressions in which variables are used:

```
Msgbox AddStrings$ ("Hit", " The Deck")
```

Though you can get only one variable back from a function, you can still cause massive effects by using subs or functions. Variables that are passed to the function, no matter how many you pass, can all be changed by the function. When you return, you'll find that any variables changed by the function have indeed become different.

Bye Bye ByVal

The only exception to this (that functions can change variables) is if you specifically *protect* a variable using the ByVal keyword, or if the variable's scope is too limited to permit the function access to it. However, the ByVal command is best avoided in Basic programming. Instead, to protect the contents of a variable in ordinary VBA programming, use parentheses. *P* here is a typical unprotected variable:

```
Dim P As Integer

Sub SendString( )
        P = 4
        Multiply P
        MsgBox P
End Sub

Function Multiply(N As Integer)
        N = N * N
End Function
```

Results in:

16

However, if you change the line *Multiply P* to *Multiply (P)*, the result is 4—the variable has been protected from anything the function might want to do to it.

Also, with VBA's new approach to procedures, you *can* now send more than one variable and expect them both to be manipulated. In this example, we send both *F$* and *Z$* to the DoubleIt function, and both those variables are changed:

```
Sub SendString( )
        F$ = "Bingo"
        Z$ = "Co"
        DoubleIt F$, Z$
        MsgBox F$ & Z$
End Sub


Function DoubleIt(N As String, R As String)
        N = N & N
        R = R & R
End Function
```

Results in:

BingoBingoCoCo

Some Rules About Functions & Variables

You can pass either variables or the literal thing you want changed. Above, we passed the literals "Hit" and "The Deck." Here we pass variables:

```
d$ = "Hit"
y$ = " the Deck"
x$ = AddStrings$(d$, y$)
```

A function must follow the same rules that apply to any variable. (You can't use words already used by VBA itself, such as print; you can't use words you used previously for variables in the same module; etc.)

Functions can have "types," too: Functions, like variables, are types—string (text), integer, long, etc. (for more about variable types, see the section "An In-Depth Look at Variables" later in this chapter). You can declare a function type by:

```
Function Sort$ ( )
```

or

```
Function Sort ( ) As String
```

If you don't add a type symbol—such as the $, which makes that a text-type ("string") function—or the As command, the function will be of the default data type. VBA defaults to the variant variable type (described later in this chapter).

Any of the variables passed to a procedure can be changed by the function. The only exception is if you use the ByVal keyword to protect a variable (or, preferably, parentheses—see "Bye Bye ByVal" above). In that case, the passed variable can be used for information and even changed temporarily while within the procedure. But when you return to the place that called the procedure, a variable passed ByVal will not have been changed. In this example, X will not be changed, no matter what changes might occur to it inside the procedure. Y, however, can be permanently changed by the procedure:

```
Function Newcost (ByVal X, Y)
```

ByVal cannot be used with user-defined variable types (see "User-Defined Variable Types" later in this chapter).

If you're passing an array (see the section "Arrays: Cluster Variables"), use the parentheses ( ) but do not include any dimensions that were declared. Here's how to pass an array:

```
X = SortThem (MyArray( ))
```

VBA allows you to pass fixed-length string arrays to procedures (for a definition of *fixed-length*, see the section "Fixed-Length versus Dynamic Text Variables" later in this chapter).

Here's a sample:

```
Sub FixedOne( )
 ReDim a(1 To 10) As String * 1
<C x = func1(a( ))
 MsgBox a(1)
End Sub

Function func1(a( ) As String * 1)
 a(1) = "3"
End Function
```

Here are two essential points about passing variables to procedures:

❏ The variable type of variable(s) passed to a procedure can be indicated by the As keyword or by attaching a type symbol. Here are the two styles. Both passed variables are text ("string") variables; the $ is the type symbol for a text variable:

```
Function Square (X As String, Text$)
```

❏ All variables within a procedure (except those passed to it) are local to that function or sub. They come into being when the procedure runs; they die when the procedure is finished with its job. The only exceptions are variables declared in at the top of a module and therefore deliberately given wider scope (with such statements as "Global" or "Public." (See "Procedure-Only Variables.") You can use a Static keyword to maintain the value of a local variable when a procedure is finished. We'll describe that in greater detail in the section "Understanding Variable Scope," later in this chapter.

You can use the Exit Function or Exit Sub commands to quit a procedure abruptly, prior to its normal conclusion (at the End Function or End Sub command). Sometimes, based on what happens while your procedure does its tasks, you may want to quit early and not do everything that's listed to do within the procedure.

AN IN-DEPTH LOOK AT VARIABLES

As you've seen in the last several pages, variables are an important tool in computer programming. You create variables for the same reason that you might write "VISA" on a manila envelope and put your most recent Visa statement inside each month. Each time you get a new bill, you replace last month's bill, putting the new bill in the envelope.

The amount you owe varies from month to month, but this particular envelope, called VISA, always "contains" the value (the amount) of the bill. If someone asks to know your current balance you could just hand them the envelope. In other words, the container named VISA holds the information about your credit card account. In this analogy, the *variable* is the manila envelope, its *variable name* is VISA, and its *value* (the contents) varies from month to month. At any given time, you can request the contents. For example, *Msgbox Visa* would display the contents, perhaps $1,200 owed.

You use a variable's name in place of the number it contains:

```
Msgbox "704.12"
```

(Or alternatively, you can use the more contemporary, "typeless" syntax with the Msgbox command. No need to enclose it in quotes anymore.):

```
Msgbox 704.12
```

This printing a *literal* amount of money is the same as putting that amount into a variable, then using the variable name instead of the actual value when, for example, you want to print the amount:

```
CurrentBill = 704.12
```

```
Msgbox CurrentBill
```

Results in:

```
704.12
```

You put the current Visa total each month in your envelope. You can always go to your stack of manila envelopes and look for the one labeled VISA to find out how much you're in debt. Similarly, once you create a variable in a running program, a location in the computer's memory always contains the variable's name and its "contents," the information that this label "holds"—until, or if, the contents are changed by the running program. Note that Object Variables are exceptional—they "point" to an object rather than "contain" any data (other than the description and location of that object).

Except for Object variables, all variable types "hold" information.

How to Create a Variable

You can create a variable in VBA by simply assigning some value to a variable name, in any procedure anywhere in your macro. This act simultaneously creates the variable's name (the label you give it) and assigns some value to it:

```
Donkeys = 15
```

Here you have provided a label (a variable name)—*Donkeys*—and said that the variable "holds" the quantity 15. Your program's user won't ever see this label, Donkeys. You use it when you are programming, and you give it a name that means something to you. Most programmers give Variables names that help them to understand the meaning of the contents. A Variable named *X* is less useful than one named MasterCard when you later read, test, or modify your program. However, when the meaning of a variable is obvious, you can use labels such as *X* or *Y* or *N*.

You can use any label you want when creating a variable, except that the label cannot be a word that VBA uses, like Msgbox or Show or End. VBA tells you if you make this error; it won't allow you to assign a value to one of these "reserved words."

Creating a Variable via a Formal Declaration

Alternatively, you can create a variable by formally "declaring" it with one of the four primary commands in VBA that declare variables—Public (also known as Global), Private, Dim, and Static. This approach has some advantages and is preferred by some programmers. It uses marginally less memory; it is said to make the program run slightly faster; and it can help you locate a particular kind of error (accidentally creating a new variable by mistyping the name of an existing variable you actually intended to use). If you want VBA to remind you to formally declare all your variables, use the Option Explicit statement at the top of each of your modules:

```
Option Explicit


Sub Test ( )
      Dim X As Integer
      X = 5
      Y = 10
      Msgbox X + Y
End Sub
```

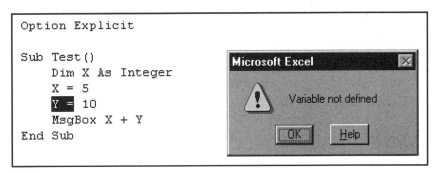

Figure 7-46: The Option Explicit command prevents you from using undeclared variables.

The above code generates an error message ("Variable Not Defined") when you try to run it because the variable *Y* hasn't been declared. There will be no error if you remove the Option Explicit statement. Option Explicit means that all variables used within this module must be formally declared. To cure the problem, type: **Dim Y As Integer**.

Text & Numeric: The Two Basic Kinds of Variables

This section discusses the two fundamental kinds of variables (plus a couple of brand new types, variant and object variables):

❒ *Text variables* (often called *string variables*) can be used in captions, text boxes, and so on. Text variables are made up of the symbols that we call the alphabet. They cannot be divided or used to calculate the amount of linoleum that you would need to redo your kitchen floor. Text is for communication, not calculation.

❒ *Numeric variables* cannot be set into caption or text properties. They are used to make calculations; they are numbers rather than symbols. The *12* stamped on top of a carton of eggs is text, and the number of eggs in that carton is numeric.

How do you change a text variable into a numeric variable, and vice versa? The Str$ and Val commands mediate between the two kinds of numbers. Str$ translates a true number into a text digit, or series of digits, that can be displayed. Val does the opposite: it turns a text digit such as *5* into a real number that you could multiply. Val can turn *1992* into *1,992*. (However, with the new variant variable type, you don't have to worry about this anymore.)

Two Kinds of Text Variables

There are two flavors of text variables—fixed-length and variable-length. Most people are used to the variable-length style; it's by far the most commonly used. The computer just makes room for however much text the variable holds. The variable D$ = "Tommy"is 5 bytes, but if you later stuff it with more (D$ = D$ & "Lasorda"), room is made for the additional 7 bytes. All this takes place dynamically, and the programmer need not worry about text length.

However, in some cases, it is useful to have a fixed-length string. Namely, when you want to employ a user-defined type (see the Type command below). Here is how you would define the two types of text variables:

```
dim varstring as String ' or just dim varstring
```

```
dim fixstring as String * 20 ' a string that always contains
20 characters.
```

Several Kinds of Numeric Variables

There are several types of numeric variables because there are several ways of expressing numbers to a computer. VBA refers to numeric variable types as *data types*, which means the same as *variable types*.

The New Variant Type Goes Both Ways

The variant variable type is new to the Basic language. It is enticing, and it has been made the default variable type in Visual Basic 3.0 and VBA. *Default* means that unless you deliberately specify a variable's type, a variable will be of the variant type.

Are the following variables text or numeric types? If these variables are variants, *the context defines the type*. If your program tries to manipulate them mathematically, they will behave like numbers. If your program tries to print them as text, they will act like text:

V ariants allow you to be ambiguous about the nature of your variables.

```
A = 12
B = 3
Msgbox A
Msgbox A & B
Msgbox A + B
Msgbox A / B
```

Results in:

12
123
15
4

Notice that the first two times we display, we are printing text digits (characters), not actual numbers. Then the variables are used as actual numbers to arrive at arithmetic results: 15 and 4.

The Variant's Special Nature

Traditionally, there are two main types of variables: numeric or text ("string") variables. Text variables cannot be arithmetically divided by each other, for instance, because they are characters— letters of the alphabet or character-digits like *123*. Clearly, it is meaningless to divide Cadillac by marble. If you tried to divide one text variable by another like this:

```
A$ = "12"
B$ = "3"
Print A$ / B$
```

You would get a "Type Mismatch" error message because it makes no sense to try to divide letters of the alphabet or digit symbols mathematically. Text characters are just graphic symbols to the computer—important containers of information to humans; impossible to manipulate for arithmetic purposes to the computer. The Str$ and Val commands in the VBA language translate numeric-to-text and text-to-numeric variables, respectively.

Variant variables shift some of the burden of worrying about variable types from the programmer to VB. Variants *automatically change type* depending on the context in which they are used. They are sensitive to the way you are using them at any given time. For example, if you use the & command, variants will know you intend to combine the variables as if you placed two pieces of text next to each other (123123); but if you use the + command, the same variables behave as if they are numeric, and addition takes place:

```
Sub Form_Click ( )
        a = 123
        Msgbox a & a
        Msgbox a + a
End Sub
```

Results in:

123123
246

Variants are sensitive to numeric types, too.

The chameleon behavior of variants is interesting and valuable (it makes the computer do more of the work that a programmer used to do). And a variant can also sense which of the five numeric variable types should be used, based on which kind of number the variant is given.

For instance, an integer type can hold only whole numbers up to 32,767. We'll test this by assigning a number that is small enough to be an integer and another, bigger, number that must perforce be a long integer type. Then we'll use the VarType command that reports to us how VBA is handling these variables—which type it thinks each is:

```
Sub Test ( )
        a = 15      'This could be an Integer
        b = 123456 'This is too big; must be a Long Integer
        Msgbox VarType(a)
        Msgbox VarType(b)
End Sub
```

Results in:

2
3

The VarTypes

The VarType function tells you what kind of variable is involved:

0	Empty
1	Null
2	Integer
3	Long Integer
4	Single
5	Double
6	Currency
7	Date
8	Text (string)

The important point here is that *you*, the programmer, need not specify that this big number 123456 must be held in a variable type with sufficient room—the *long* integer type. You don't have to define a special variable as long. VB's new variant data type has the brains to understand this need for extra space. It looks at the size of the number it's given—*and makes the adjustment by itself.* Same with fractions—the variant sees a decimal point, it turns into a *floating point type* (as numbers with fractional parts are so colorfully called).

Technically, if you give this to a variant:

```
Z = 3
```

the variant doesn't really *turn into* any particular variable type at that time. It just holds the symbols z=3 in the computer. While your program is running, at some point this variable, Z, might be called upon to produce a piece of text. The & symbol means put these two pieces of text together:

```
MsgBox Z & Z
```

Results in:

```
33
```

Or, if you request this:

```
MsgBox 1 / Z
```

the variant is interpreted by VBA as a floating-point number, and the math takes place:

0.3333333

Notice that the variant knows that it must resort to the floating point (decimal) type. However, it does use the smaller of the two floating point types (the single-precision). If your situation requires greater precision, you have to force the issue by defining the variable as the double-precision type yourself:

```
Dim Z As Double

Sub HowLong ( )
        MsgBox 1 / Z
End Sub
```

Results in:

0.333333333333333

which is as far toward infinity as VBA and the computer are prepared to go.

IsDate, IsEmpty, IsNumeric, IsNull

The IsDate, IsEmpty, IsNumeric, and IsNull commands can tell you the status of a variant variable. To see if you can use a variant type in a mathematical calculation:

```
A = "N123"
B = "456"
If IsNumeric(A) Then MsgBox A + 1
If IsNumeric(B) Then MsgBox B + 1
```

Results in:

457

Here the letter N in N123 prevents this variable from being used as a number, and the IsNumeric function reveals this fact.

Warning—No Free Lunch

Variants use up more memory than any other variable type. They can also slightly retard the speed at which your programs run because VBA has to do extra work to analyze a variant's context. However, since computers get lots more memory and speed every year, as a general rule, you should program as if you were using a Cray.

Notes on Using Variants

❒ The most obvious use for this novel addition to computer languages is to relax and just let variants worry about all the variable types, more or less without you, the programmer, thinking about types at all.

❒ Arrays will also be of the variant type unless you specify otherwise. You can therefore mix text, numbers, and date and time data within the same array. This, too, is new to computer programming and, let's admit, is pretty terrific, in spite of the currently mild memory/speed penalties described earlier.

❒ Variants introduce some new variable data types. (Technically, *NULL* and *Empty* are states, rather than actual data types. The NULL and Empty responses are useful for determining the state of the data contained inside a variant.)

❒ NULL is different from Empty (when you get those responses by using the VarType command to quiz a variable about what type it is). NULL means that the variable is deliberately empty. You've *assigned* nothingness to the variable:

```
X = 0 'for numeric
```
or
```
X = "" 'for text
```

These two examples create a zero number or a text variable with nothing in it. However, an empty variable, by contrast, *has not yet been used* in the program in any fashion (even to fill it with nothingness, nullness). An empty variable has not been declared either implicitly (V = 12) or explicitly (Dim V As Integer).

NULL Is Special

The NULL variable type has another unique quality you need to remember—it always makes an expression false. For example:

```
z = NULL
```

```
If z = Null Then MsgBox "Yes."
```

This doesn't print Yes. NULL more or less infects ("propagates") an otherwise true expression, turning it false.

To find out if a variable is of the NULL type, use the following:

```
If IsNull(z) Then MsgBox "Yes."
```

Note that the other predefined VBA constants True (-1) and False (0) do not "propagate" and can be freely used as if they were normal numbers:

```
z = True
If z = True Then MsgBox "Yes",
If z = -1 Then MsgBox "Yes",
If z Then MsgBox "Yes",
```

Results in:

```
Yes Yes Yes
```

In general, you can let VBA worry about the variants. However, if you try to perform math with variants that hold text (such as "Word") or at least text that can be translated by VBA into a numeric variable ("z12" cannot be translated; "12" can), then you'll generate an error. If you are unsure whether a variant holds text, add this line:

```
If IsNumeric(A) And IsNumeric(B) Then X = A + B
```

DIFFERENCES BETWEEN THE VARIABLE TYPES

Different variable types take up different amounts of space in the computer's memory (and on disk files). Often this is irrelevant. Memory now costs only approximately $50 for a megabyte, and the price is falling.

VBA defaults to the variant type unless you specify otherwise. Variants use more memory than any other variable type and make programs run more slowly. You could use the DefInt command to make integer the default type (many programs run much faster when most variables are integers), but if you want to deal with huge numbers or tiny fractions, you'll need to define those particular variables individually as being of numeric variable types that can accommodate large ranges or highly precise numbers that feature the decimal point.

Division—The Problem Child

If your application can get by with the Integer numeric type, you can make the program run as much as 25 times faster. (At the top of each module, put this: DEFINT A-Z.) This increase in speed applies to 486, 586, and even 100086 microprocessors, because the underlying reasons that integers are so swift have nothing to do with a computer's clock speed or the kind of microprocessor being used.

Fractions, and the act of division that produces them, are difficult for computers to manipulate. They're difficult for the same reasons that fractions and division are hard for humans to learn.

It's much easier, isn't it, to give three friends six cookies than to give three friends seven cookies.

Computers calculate in different ways with different numeric variable types. They can do arithmetic faster with integer types than with floating point types because integers have no decimal point and no bothersome fractions to the right of that decimal point as floating point numbers do.

Why? The simplest explanation is found in the fact that elementary school teachers have to spend much more time teaching division than teaching multiplication. The four kinds of arithmetic—addition, subtraction, multiplication, and division—are not symmetrical: multiplication is pretty easy once you understand the idea of addition. Addition is grasped by anyone who has written a list for Santa or filled a bag on Halloween. Subtraction, too, is clear enough: older brother steals some cookies from the bag.

But division is in a class by itself. It's something that happens less often in real life, except to pies and to the victims of mad killers. And, compared to the other three arithmetic maneuvers, division is inherently inexact, messy.

The problem is that division can cause something to go below unity, below one, into the problematic world of fractions, pieces. Suddenly, two simple digits like 3 and 1 can expand into a list of digits bigger than the universe, .3333333333333333333 infinitely long, if you try to divide 1 by 3.

And there are those remainders, unsettling leftovers that show up after the arithmetic is supposedly finished. Computers have precisely the same problems working with division that people do—there's more to consider and more to manipulate. Just like us, the computer calculates more slowly when working with numeric variable types like "double" or "single" that can have fractions. If you want to speed up your programs, allow the computer to use integers as the variable type. Integers don't produce fractions. If you don't need the precision fractions offer—and most of the time you don't—stick with integers.

Here is a list of the traditional variable types that you can use in VBA—along with their symbols, the range of numbers they can hold, and the amount of space in the computer each requires to store a number of that type:

Computers, too, have trouble with long division.

Name	Symbol	Range	Storage Required
Boolean		True or False (-1 or O)	2 bytes
Integer	%	-32,768 to 32,767	2 bytes
Long Integer	&	-2,147,483,648 to 2,147,483,647	4 bytes
Single-Precision Floating Point	!	-3.402823E38 to 3.402823E38	4 bytes
Double-Precision Floating Point	#	-1.797693134862315D308 to 1.797693134862315D308	8 bytes
Currency	@	-922337203685477.5808 to 922337203685477.5807	8 bytes
Text ("string")	$	0 to 65,535 (bytes, individual characters)*	

*The exact amount of storage required by a given text ("string") variable fluctuates, of course. VBA has to do some extra housekeeping, so the largest text variable—the largest number of text characters—you can store in a single text variable is somewhat less than 65,535 in Windows 3.1x. However, with Windows 95 and later versions, text variables are permitted to contain approximately two billion characters per variable.

Table 7-1: Capacity and Memory Usage of the Variable Types.

There is also a specialized, user-defined variable structure that you define with the Type command explained below. The amount of space a type variable structure takes up depends on the number and types of variables you include.

Special Technical Notes: The E38 as the range of single precision floating point in the table means move the decimal 38 places over; 1E6 equals 1,000,000. E means the same thing as D, except D means the number is stored as double-precision floating point type. 1D6 still equals 1,000,000, but it is in a "double" variable, so further calculations using this number will be more accurate than using the single-precision variable type. E stands for *exponential* and is universally used in the scientific community.

NUMERIC TYPE SYMBOLS & EXAMPLES

X% Integer (This variable type uses no decimal points. It can include only whole numbers between –32,768 and 32,767. It can make mathematical parts of your programs run up to 25 times faster.)

Attaching the percent (%) symbol to a variable name forces the variable to include no digits to the right of the decimal point. In effect, there is no decimal point, and any fraction is stripped off.

X% = 1 / 20 results in X% becoming 0

X = 1 / 20 is .05

X% = 15 / 4 results in X% being 4 (it gets rounded off)

X = 15 / 4 makes X 3.75

X& Long Integer (This variable type also uses no decimal points. It's the same as regular integer but has a larger range. Can range from –2,147,483,648 to 2,147,483,647.) Attaching & to a Variable's name strips off any fractional part, but the Variable is capable of calculating with large numbers.

X! Single-Precision Floating Point (This variable type can include numbers over a huge range.)

X# Double-Precision Floating Point (This variable type is the same as single-precision floating point but its range is even bigger.)

X@ Currency (Ranges from –922,337,203,685,477.5808 to 922,337,203,685,477.5807) This variable type has a fixed point rather than a floating point (although it does have a fractional component of four decimal points). The Currency numeric variable type is superior in its accuracy. (Accuracy is not the same as precision. Someone could give you an incorrect, yet very precise, description of how to go about placing a call to London.)

X Variant This variable type uses no type symbol attached to the variable name; it's the default variable type in VBA. It adjusts itself as appropriate to the data assigned to it. It can also transform itself, its type, based on how it is being used in the program at the time.

Extra memory space and program execution speed penalties extracted by the variant type balance the blessings it offers the programmer in its automatic type adjustment and general versatility. See the section "The Variant Variable Type" later in this chapter.)

FIXED-LENGTH VERSUS DYNAMIC TEXT VARIABLES

A text ("string") variable is, by default, dynamic. VBA makes enough space in computer memory to handle whatever amount of text you the programmer, a disk file, or the user assigns to the variable. However, you can also request that a text variable can be of a specific, predefined size. Fixed-length or dynamic—each text variable type has its advantages and uses.

You create a fixed-length string by describing its length in the process of defining its size. To create a fixed-length string that's 45 characters long:

```
Dim Name As String * 45
```

or

```
A$ = String$(30,"a") is another way to create a fixed-length
string. Here we've filled a string with 30 "a's."
```

If you don't assign a length, a string variable is dynamic by default; it expands and contracts as necessary, depending on the data that is stuffed into it or removed from it while the program is running.

The following two string variables are not given a specific length, so they default to dynamic, variable-length strings:

```
Dim Name$
```

or

```
Dim Name As String
```

If you are going to use a text variable within a single event procedure, subroutine, or function (and you want it to be dynamic—an expandable-length to fit the size of whatever text is assigned to it), you don't need to define, to Dim, the variable. Just assign some text to it, and it's a dynamic string variable:

```
A$ = "Noisome"
```

You might well ask: "If all variables default to the variant type, why do we say that an unDimmed text variable defaults to the dynamic type?" The answer is that a variant is *always* dynamic if the contents are text.

Defining a fixed-length string stabilizes the variable so that it always is the same size. This frozen size is important when working with random-access files that expect predictable lengths for all the data contained within them.

PRACTICAL VARIABLE ADVICE

All variables that you don't specifically define otherwise default to the variant type in VBA (see "The Variant Variable Type" later in this chapter). To define a variable that will not be of this default type, attach a symbol to it: Mynum& makes the variable named *mynum* into a long integer type. Or, define variable types by using the Public, Private, Dim, or Static commands:

```
Public mynum As Integer
Private mynum%
Dim mynum As Double
```

(When you define a variable in this fashion, you can use either the type symbols or the As command to spell out the type.) Unless you want to speed up a program (you often will), you can simply ignore variable types and let them default to variant without worrying about it. If you do need speed, type **DefInt A-Z** at the top of each module.

Mostly, you need not concern yourself with types.

Most programmers type DefInt A-Z at the top of the modules in a program to make the integer the default variable type. Most of the things you'll be working with—unless you're Bill Gates working on his income tax or a rocket scientist plotting a precise trajectory—fall within the range of the integer type (roughly plus or minus 30,000; see Table 7-1 earlier in this chapter).

If, on the other hand, you are calculating big bucks in income tax or gravitational slingshots for interplanetary exploration, you might need to specifically define some of your numeric variables so they have a larger range or greater precision. If all this defining variable types sounds like unnecessary labor (and it is), take advantage of the new simplicity offered by the variant type. Let the computer sort it out. Computers are so much better than we are at clerical jobs.

Understanding Variable Scope

Variables can have different zones of influence in a program.

There are three different ways to declare a variable because variables can have different levels of impact, different ranges of influence in a program. Sometimes called *scope*, this range of influence determines whether a variable can be used or recognized everywhere in the program (Public/Global), only within a particular module (Private/Dim), or only within a particular procedure—a sub, function, or event—(Static or Dim).

Public (Global) Variables

Everything in your program can access a variable if, within a module, you declare the variable with the Public statement:

```
Public Myvariable.
```

or

```
Public Myvariable as Integer
```

Then commands within any procedure or module can get information about what is in *Myvariable*, and any of them can change *Myvariable* as well.

Module-Wide Variables

One step down in scope from Public are variables that you also declare in a module by using the Private or Dim commands. These variables are available to all procedures that are part of that module. However, other modules cannot access private variables.

Procedure-Only Variables

For use in a single sub or function, at the lowest level (the narrowest scope), this kind of variable is like an insect that lives only briefly, does its duty, and then dies. Variables created inside procedures pop into existence only when the program is running within that procedure and disappear again as soon as the program goes on to some other procedure. The next time the procedure is triggered, the variable comes back to life. However, the value it had when it last died is lost. Any value you assign to it within its procedure (A$ = "Norman") is reassigned.

There are three advantages to using locally restricted variables such as these:

❏ You can use the same variable name over and over should you wish (in different procedures), without an untoward effect. Each instance of this variable label is a unique variable, specific to its procedure.

❏ The use of local variables makes for the efficient use of memory. You could create a large array of information, for instance, and then manipulate it. When you're finished, the array collapses, returning the memory space it used to the computer for other uses. (See the section "Arrays: Cluster Variables" later in this chapter.)

❏ Local variables also eliminate one of the most frequent—and hardest to track down—errors in traditional programming: two variables with the same name that are interacting and messing each other up as a program runs. You need not declare variables at the procedure level; you can simply use them. Y = 2346 creates a numeric variable and puts the number 2,346 into that variable.

Static Variables

Variables declared with the Static command are a special type of local variable. Recall that local variables (those intended for use in a single sub or function) cannot retain their contents if the program moves to a different procedure. A static variable does not lose its value (its contents) when the program is not in its procedure. When you come back to its procedure, a static variable still retains whatever was in it when you last left the procedure. How is this different from Y = 9, which always is reassigned that 9 each time the event is triggered?

A static variable can be changed within the event and retain the change. An assigned variable always gets reassigned the same value:

```
Sub Test( )
        Y = 9
        Static Z
        Z = Z + 1
        Msgbox Y, Z
End Sub
```

Results in:

The first time this procedure runs: 9 1. The second time: 9 2, and so on. Static is used when you want a procedure to act as a counter or a toggle. For example:

```
Static Toggle
Toggle = Not Toggle
If Toggle = 0 Then
        Msgbox "It's off, make the text gray."
Else
        Msgbox "It's on, restore the text to black."
End If
```

Using Variables That Interact

Variables can interact, as in the following example:

```
Donkeys = 15
Monkeys = 3
TotalAnimals = Donkeys + Monkeys
```

V ariable names are used to represent the data they hold.

You can use variables' labels (their names) as if they were the same as the contents of the variables. If you say Monkeys = 3, then you have made the variable name, *Monkeys,* equivalent to the variable's value, *3.* You can thereafter use Monkeys just as you would use the number 3:

```
TotalAnimals = Donkeys + Monkeys
```

The preceding line is the same as the following:

```
TotalAnimals = Donkeys + 3
```

VARIABLES VERSUS CONSTANTS

A variable's label, its name, remains the same, but the contents of a variable can vary, which is how a variable differs from a constant.

Constants are not changed while a program runs; they are a known quantity, like the number of donuts in a dozen:

```
Const MONTHSINYEAR = 12
```

Variables vary:

```
MyVisaBillAtThisPoint = 1200.44
```

(but a month later . . .)

```
MyVisaBillAtThisPoint = 1530.78
```

Some programmers love using constants; some never use them at all.

In practice, some programmers make frequent use of constants, and other programmers avoid them. If you look at sample macros that come with programs such as Excel or Word, you'll see that some programmers believe that constants make their programs more readable, more English-like:

```
Font.Color = WHITE
```

The preceding line is preferred by many people to the following line:

```
Font.Color = RGB(255, 255, 255)
```

To see the pre-defined Constants, use the Object Browser.

VBA comes with a large set of built-in constants. In addition, any VBA-capable application also contains a collection of built-in constants applicable to that application. And, of course, you can define your own constants. Use the Object Browser in Excel to view and work with constants.

If you have a VBA module in Excel, switch to the module (click on the tab at the bottom of the window). If you don't have a module, you must create one. The Object Browser won't appear unless you are viewing a module. To create a module, choose Insert | Macro | Module.

To see the Object Browser, choose View Object Browser (or press F2). From the Libraries/Workbooks drop-down list at the top of the dialog box, select VBA or Excel. Then in the Objects/Modules list on the left, select Constants to see the list.

The Case Against Constants

Many programmers argue that constants are known and stable numbers, so why not just use the number itself and forget about defining a constant for it. To calculate your average monthly bank interest, for example, you would use two variables and the number 12:

```
MyAverageMonthlyInterest = MyTotalInterestThisYear / 12
```

rather than:

```
Const MONTHSINYEAR = 12
MyAverageMonthlyInterest = MyTotalInterestThisYear /
MONTHSINYEAR
```

Constants can certainly make programs more readable and can make odd things like &HFF00& (the RGB value for green) more easily understood. Nevertheless, a large contingent of the programming community finds that there's rarely any compelling reason to use constants.

The Case for Constants

Other programmers, though, like to use constants. They argue that in the interest of program maintainability (being able to go back and more efficiently change the program later), it is always better to use constants to define a number that would otherwise not be obvious. This is especially true for programmer-defined values (e.g., CONST NUMBEROFSTATES = 50). That way, if you need to alter the value, you need to change it only in one place in the program, rather than track down every occurrence where 50 refers to the number of states. This can avoid the time wasted when a programmer tries to decipher somebody else's code that had numbers or text variables hard-coded (used literally, like the digit *50* instead of the constant NUMBEROFSTATES). (The general convention is to capitalize the first letter of a variable name and capitalize the entire name of a constant.) Now that we've seen the virtues and uses of variables, let's see how to combine them into an *expression*.

UNDERSTANDING VBA EXPRESSIONS

V BA looks at all the components of an expression and treats them as a single entity.

What is an expression? If someone tells you she has a coupon for $1 off a $15 Tractors CD, you immediately think $14. In the same way, VBA reduces the several items linked into an "expression" into its simplest form.

The phrase "numeric expression" means anything that, in Basic, represents or results in a single number. Strictly speaking, the expression "evaluates" into a single number. When an intelligent entity hears an expression, the entity collapses that expression into its simplest form.

In plain English, if you type 15 – 1 into one of your programs, VBA reduces that group of symbols to 14. VBA simply evaluates what you've said and uses it in the program as the essence of what you are trying to say.

We humans always reduce things, too. Sometimes we call it "putting two and two together." But the result is the essence of a more complicated expression or idea. 5 * 3 is a numeric expression, and, as far as Basic is concerned, 5 * 3 is just another way of expressing 15 (a single number). 5 * 3 collapses into 15 inside the program and is essentially that single number.

There are many kinds of numeric entities that you can combine into expressions:

❏ A numeric variable

❏ A numeric variable in an array

❏ A function that returns a number

❏ A literal number (12 is a literal number, as opposed to a variable)

❏ Print Sqr(12)—literal number vs. Print Sqr(N)—variable

❏ A numeric constant, like Const Pi = 3.14159265358979

❏ A combination of literal and variable numbers:
Print X + 14

Any combination of the preceding examples that can evaluate to a single numeric value is an expression. An expression is made up of two or more of the preceding items connected by one or more operators. The plus symbol in 2 + 2 is an *operator*. Altogether there are 23 operators. (See the section "Arithmetic Operators" later in this chapter.)

When you combine variables with other variables, you create a variable expression. An expression can involve either numeric or text ("string") information. If the variable *Days* has the value 7, and the variable *Hours* has the value 24, the following expression has the value 168:

```
Days * Hours
```

You can assign the preceding expression to another variable:

```
HoursInAWeek = Days * Hours
```

You can also use the expression within a structure, such as If...Then, to test its validity.

Expressions True & False

An expression can be evaluated by VBA as either 0 (false) or not 0 (true). Let's see how this works:

```
BobsAge = 33
BettysAge = 27
If BobsAge > BettysAge Then Msgbox "He's Older"
```

BobsAge > BettysAge is an expression making the assertion that Bob's age is greater than Betty's age. The greater than symbol (>) is one of several relational operators. VBA looks at the variables *BobsAge* and *BettysAge* and at the relational operator that combines them into the expression. VBA then determines whether your expression is true. The If...Then structure bases its actions on the truth or falsity of the expression.

The following are relational comparison operators:

<	Less than
<=	Less than or equal to
>	Greater than
>=	Greater than or equal to
<>	Not equal
=	Equal
Is	(Do two object variables refer to the same object?)
Like	Pattern matching

The relational operators are comparisons, and the result of a comparison is always true or false.

You can use the relational operators with text as well. When used with literal text (or text variables), the operators refer to the alphabetic relationship between the pieces of text, with *Andy* being "less than" *Anne*).

The first six relational operators have been around for a long time—used for sorting items in a list, and so on. However, Is and Like are quite new to Basic. Is compares two object variables to see if they refer to the same object. (If *ThisObj* Is *TheOtherObj* Then...). Like allows you to be sloppy when comparing two pieces of text (two "string" variables). It's something similar to the way you can "pattern match" when asking DOS for a directory. For example, DIR *.EXE lists all files ending in .EXE, and DIR F*.* list all files starting with F.

Using the Like operator, you can compare text Variables, as follows:

```
A$ = "Rudolpho"
If A$ Like "Ru*" Then Msgbox "Close Enough"
```

To compare against a single character in a particular position:

```
X = "Nora" Like "?ora": Msgbox X
```

Results in:

```
-1 (meaning "True")
X = "Nora" Like "F?ora": Msgbox X
```

Results in:

```
0 (meaning false-the first letter in Nora isn't F, the third
letter isn't o, and so on.)
```

or (to compare when you don't care about a match between a series of characters):

```
If "David" Like "*d" Then
        Msgbox "Match"
Else
        Msgbox "No Match"
End If
```

Results in:

```
Match
"D*d" or "**D*d" or "*i*" all match "David".
```

or (to find a match against a single digit, 0–9, but only a digit):

```
If "99 Elide Rd." Like "???###" Then
```

Results in:

```
No Match
"????##" would match, however.
```

To match a single character in the text against a single character or range of characters in the list enclosed by brackets:

```
If "Empire" Like "??[n-q]*" Then
```

Results in:

```
Match
```

You can also use multiple ranges such as: "[n-rt-w]" or (to match if a single character in the text is not in the list):

```
If "Empire" Like "??[!n-q]*" Then
```

Results in:

```
No Match
```

Arithmetic Operators

^	Exponentiation (the number multiplied by itself: 5 ^ 2 is 25 and 5 ^ 3 is 125)
-	Negation (negative numbers, such as –25)
*	Multiplication
/	Division
\	Integer division (division with no remainder, no fraction, no floating point decimal point: 8 \ 6 is 1. Integer division is easier, and the computer performs it faster than regular division.
Mod	Modulo arithmetic*
+	Addition
-	Subtraction
&	String concatenation (This is really not an *arithmetic* operator—it works on text—but there is nowhere else to put it.)

Variant variables can be combined in a similar way to the traditional text variable concatenation:

```
A$ = "This":B$ = "That": Msgbox A$ + B$
```

Results in:

```
ThisThat
```

When you use variants (unless you specify otherwise, VBA defaults to the variant variable type):

```
x = 5:a = "This": Msgbox x & a
```

Results in:

```
5This
```

The Variant Variable Type

The variant data (or variable) type is new to Basic, and it's intriguing. Variants are in an indeterminate state, like Schroedinger's Cat, until they are used. Also, when you use the & operator, VBA converts a numeric variable into a variant. If both variables used with & are text variables, the result is a text string variable. Otherwise, the result will be a variant type.

We'll have more to say about variants shortly.

Logical Operators

Not	Logical Negation
And	And
Or	Inclusive OR
XOR	(Either but not both)
Eqv	(Equivalent)
Imp	(Implication—first item false or second item true)

In practice, you'll probably need to use only Not, And, XOR, and Or logical operators. These four operators work pretty much the way they do in ordinary English:

```
If 5 + 2 = 4 Or 6 + 6 = 12 Then Msgbox "One of them is true."
' (one of these expressions is True, so the comment will be
printed. Only one OR the other needs to be True.)
```

```
If 5 + 2 = 4 And 6 + 6 = 12 Then Msgbox "Both of them are true."
' (this is False, so nothing is printed. Both expressions, the
first AND the second, must be True for the Printing to take
place.)
```

Use the XOR operator to change an individual bit within a number, without affecting the other bits. See the example under GetAttr for the way to use XOR.

*Special Note on Mod: The Modulo (Mod) operator gives you any remainder after a division—but not the results of the division itself. This operation is useful when you want to know if some number divides evenly into another number. Using this operator, you can do things at intervals. If you wanted to print the page number in bold on every fifth page, for example, you could enter the following:

```
If PageNumber Mod 5 = 0 Then
        FontBold = -1
Else
        FontBold = 0
End IF
```

15 Mod 5 results in 0.
16 Mod 5 results in 1.
17 Mod 5 results in 2.
20 Mod 5 results in 0 again.

The Text Operator

The ampersand (&) adds pieces of text in an expression:

```
N$ = "Joan"
N1$ = "Rivers"
J$ = N$ & " " & N1$
```

```
Msgbox J$
```

Results in:

```
Joan Rivers
```

(You can also use the relational operators to compare the alphabetical relationship between two pieces of text.)

Operator Precedence

When you use more than one operator in an expression, which operator should be evaluated first:

```
Msgbox 3 * 10 + 5
```

Does this mean first multiply 3 times 10, getting 30? And then add 5 to the result? Should VBA print 35? Or does it mean add 10 to 5, getting 15? And then multiply the result by 3? This would result in 45.

Expressions are not necessarily evaluated by the computer from left to right. Left to right evaluation would result in 35 because 3 would be multiplied by 10 before the 5 was added to that result.

Instead an "order of precedence," a hierarchy, specifies how the various relationships are resolved between numbers in an expression. For instance, multiplication is carried out before addition. To

Expressions are resolved in a particular order.

make sure that you get the results you intend when using more than one operator, use parentheses to enclose the items you want evaluated first. If you intend to multiply 3 by 10 and then add 5, use the parentheses as shown below:

```
Msgbox (3 * 10) + 5
```

By enclosing something in parentheses, you tell VBA that you want the enclosed items to be considered a single value and to be evaluated before anything else happens. If you intend to add 10 and 5 and then multiply by 3, use the parentheses as shown in the following example:

```
Msgbox 3 * (10 + 5)
```

In complicated expressions, you can even nest parentheses to make clear which items are to be calculated in which order:

```
Msgbox 3 * ((9 + 1) + 5)
```

If you work with numbers a great deal, you might want to memorize the following table. Although most people just use parentheses and forget about this problem, here's the order in which VBA evaluates an expression, from first evaluated to last:

Arithmetic Operators in Order of Precedence

^	Exponents (6 ^ 2 is 36. The number is multiplied by itself *x* number of times.)
-	Negation (Negative numbers such as –33)
* /	Multiplication and division
\	Integer division (division with no remainder, no fraction, no floating point decimal point. 8 \ 6 is 1)
Mod	Modulo arithmetic (any remainder after division. 23 Mod 12 is 11. See "Mod.")
+ -	Addition and subtraction
	Relational operators
	Logical operators

Given that multiplication has precedence over addition, our ambiguous example would be evaluated in the following way:

```
Msgbox 3 * 10 + 5
```

Results in:

```
35
```

Expressions Combined into Larger Expressions

You can put expressions together, building a larger entity that, itself, is an expression:

```
Z$ = "Tom"
R$ = Right$(Z$,2)
L$ = "om"
N = 3
M = 4
O = 5
P = 6
If N + M + O + P = 18 AND Z$ = "Tom" OR R$ = L$ Then Msgbox
"Yes."
```

You can include literals as well as variables when creating an expression. Z$ is a variable, but Tom is a literal. *M* is a variable in the preceding example, and 4 is a literal. You can mix and match. You could also create the preceding example with some literal numbers mixed in:

```
If 3 + M + 5 + P = 18 And Z$ = "Tom" Then Msgbox "Yes."
```

Expressions Can Include Functions

When you create an expression, you can include a function within it. Here, for example, the Val function (built into VBA) tests the value of a text expression. In other words, Val(A$) here will be the number 44 when this program runs. So, another way to view the following example is: If 44 <> 55 (if 44 doesn't equal 55):

```
A$ = "44 Rue Madeline"

If Val(A$) <> 55 Then Msgbox "The text Variable doesn't start
with the digits 55."
```

ARRAYS—CLUSTER VARIABLES

Arrays, unlike constants, are universally regarded as extremely useful. Arrays are variables that have been clustered together into a structure, and they enable you to manipulate the items in the cluster by using loops.

By giving a group of variables the same name, distinguished only by an index number, you can manipulate the group by referring to the index number. This approach might look like a small savings of effort, but imagine that your program will probably have to use these variables in many situations. And eventually you'll have to save them to disk.

Here's an example of an array, used earlier in this chapter to illustrate some points about WordBasic :

```
Sub MAIN

Dim closer$(4)

closer$(0) = "We appreciate your comments and will pass them
along."

closer$(1) = "We hope this matter is now resolved."

closer$(2) = "Our president, Jim Nobles, has resigned as a
result of your letter. We assume this closes the issue."

closer$(3) = "Your question has been submitted to Mrs. Murphy of
our customer service department. She will be in contact with you
when she returns to work."

closer$(4) = "Please consider that our final offer."
```

```
Begin Dialog UserDialog 984, 282, "Closings to official let-
ters...."
        ListBox 439, 9, 528, 242, Closer$( ), .ListBox1
        Picture 20, 10, 393, 176, "D:\CLOSING.BMP", 0, .Picture1
        Text 21, 195, 320, 79, "Choose a closing by double-
clicking on it in the list", .Text1
        OKButton 878, 257, 88, 21
        CancelButton 776, 257, 88, 21
End Dialog

Dim dlg As UserDialog
chosen = Dialog(dlg)

If chosen = - 1 Then'they clicked OK
        Insert closer$(dlg.listbox1)
End If

End Sub
```

When creating an array, you must first use the Dim command (for *dimension*) to tell Basic the number of items in your array. In the above example, we used Dim closer$(4), which means: create an array named *"closer$"* that can contain five items. Even though it says 4, you have to remember that arrays start counting up from zero, so the first element is the zero element: closer$(0). Then we fill this array with data, with the contents we want to assign to each of the array elements 0 through 4. This example provides the array to the ListBox by including the array name—closer$( )—in the list of parameters following the ListBox. However, it's also quite common in programming to manipulate an array within a loop—a structure that repeatedly carries out some action. You could use a loop, for instance, to fill cells in a spreadsheet or print a list of items to a printer:

```
For I = 0 To 4
        Print Closer$( I )
Next I
```

This would print each element in the *closer$* array in turn. Note that in a loop, the value of the variable *I* changes each time through the loop—incrementing from 0 to 4 in this example. The Next I command VBA to go back up and print the next item. VBA will stay in this loop, printing over and over, until it reaches the upper limit we've established in the For statement (4).

USER-DEFINED VARIABLE TYPES

You generally use the Type statement to create a customized cluster of variables for use with the random-access file technique.

A random access file stores pieces of information of fixed sizes, within records of a fixed size (and records are themselves subdivided into fields of fixed sizes). You decide what amount of information these subdivisions contain—how many characters in each piece of text, for example. However, you must then make all the records and fields that same size.

Ordinarily, you cluster the variables used with a random access file into a group of related information:

❏ Name

❏ Address

❏ Telephone Number

When used with a random access file, the smallest unit of data (each variable)—the name, the address, or the phone number—is called a *field*. Together, they are called a *record*. The easiest way to manipulate these records is to put the fields together into a user-defined variable with the Type command.

Because text variables ("strings") by default can be of varying length, you can fix their length by using the * N technique. (Using Dim Mytext As String * 30 is one approach. The Type command can also create fixed-length strings.)

You can use the Type command only in a module, not within a procedure. In other words, you can't put it between a Sub . . . End Sub stub.

You can freeze the length of string variables.

In a sense, the Type command enables you to create a special kind of array. A normal array is a collection of variables, but they must all be the same kind of variable. (The new variant variable type—see the section "The Variant Variable Type" earlier in this chapter—allows you to get around this rule.) You can make an array of text variables or an array of a particular type of numeric variable, such as integers, etc., but you cannot make an array with mixed variable types (except for variants). However, using the Type command you can create a custom grouping of mixed variables, called a *user-defined data type*.

You can now even place object variables within a user-defined type:

```
Type oType
 object1 As Object
End Type

Sub foo( )
 Dim x%
 Dim g As oType
 Set g.object1 = ActiveSheet
 MsgBox g.object1.Name
End Sub
```

Results in:

```
Module1
```

(or whatever the name of the module is in which you typed this example.)

To create a more typical user-defined type (with ordinary variables rather than objects), type the following at the top of a module (where you usually put declarations such as Public and other kinds of definitions):

```
Type AddressBook
        Nam As String * 50
        Address As String * 200
        Phone As String * 12
        Age As Integer
End Type
```

Three Things You Must Do to Create a Type Structure

Creating and using a type variable structure requires that you follow three steps:

1. Define the general type structure in a module as illustrated above.

2. Create a particular variable of that type, for example:

   ```
   Dim NewVar As AddressBook
   ```

3. Manipulate this new variable as if it were an ordinary variable (add, change, or examine the data). The only difference between this "type-variable" and ordinary variables is that the variable *NewVar* we created has four interior variables. You manipulate them by using the name *NewVar* separated by a period (.) from the name of one of the interior variables: NewVar.Nam = "Rusty Wheels" or Print NewVar.Age.

Let's define a particular variable as being of the AddressBook type. Once the general type has been defined, you must then give a name to a particular variable that will be of that type. You can use four variable-defining commands to make a particular variable a type: Public, Private, Dim, or Static.

Using any of these declaration commands creates a variable and defines its structure as being of the custom type. In other words, this new variable has the interior variables of the defined type: Nam, Address, Phone, and Age.

You must first declare the variable.

Only after you have declared this new variable can you then use the custom structure. You cannot use the name of the type (AddressBook) directly within commands that save, retrieve, print, or otherwise manipulate data. The type is a structure that you define; and then later you can define other variables as being of that type. The word *AddressBook* is used only when you are defining a new variable to be of the AddressBook type.

In other words, you establish a type by describing the kinds of variables it contains, and the order in which they reside within the structure. You define a structure in a module:

```
Type AddressBook
        Nam As String * 50
        Address As String * 200
        Phone As String * 12
        Age As Integer
End Type
```

Then you announce that a variable is of that already-defined structural type.

To complete this example, we'll announce that a variable called *PersonnelRecords* is to be constructed like the AddressBook structure we have already defined as containing Name, Address, Phone, and Age. PersonnelRecords will be a structure with four interior variables of an already described variable type and length:

```
Dim PersonnelRecords As AddressBook
```

PersonnelRecords has now become a variable structure. How do you manipulate the interior variables in this structure? PersonnelRecords can now be used in the following fashion: (To put literal information into the structure):

```
PersonnelRecords.Nam = "Alice Dragonnette"
PersonnelRecords.Address = "2455 West Circle Drive"
PersonnelRecords.Phone = "929-4549-9090"
PersonnelRecords.Age = 45
```

or (to use variables to put information in the structure):

```
PersonnelRecords.Nam = N$
```

or (to get information from the structure):

```
Telephone$ = PersonnelRecords.Phone
```

or (if you are really attracted to Type variables as a concept, you could make a more complex structure—an array of a user-defined Type variable):

```
Dim PersonnelRecords(1 To 30) As AddressBook
```

Now you have an array of structures, with all the usual benefits of arrays.

```
PersonnelRecords(12).Age = 45
```

or (you can put arrays inside a Type structure. In a module, define the type):

```
Type CDCollection
        Jazz (300) As String
        Classical (1 to 600) as Variant
        Rock (400,400) As String
End Type
```

```
Dim cds As CDCollection
```

Then, to use one of the internal arrays:

```
Sub Tryit ( )
        cds.jazz(3) = "Miles Davis"
End Sub
```

Notice that an item in an internal array within a Type structure is referenced by putting the index in parentheses after the internal name of the array: cds.jazz(3). By contrast, if you're using an array of Type structure, you put the parentheses after the structure name but before the interior variable name: PersonnelRecords(12). Age = 45.

One significant advantage of a Type variable structure is that you can manipulate the *entire structure* with one command. You can copy or save a structure as a total entity, without having to specify each of its internal variables. For instance, if you are storing the following structure into a random access file, you don't go through and store each separate element of the structure:

```
Put #1, PersonnelRecords.Nam
Put #1, PersonnelRecords.Address
Put #1, PersonnelRecords.Phone
Put #1, PersonnelRecords.Age
```

Instead, you simply save the entire structure as a single item:

```
Put #1, PersonnelRecords
```

M**ass structure manipulation is possible with the Type variable.**

Likewise, you can copy this cluster variable *PersonnelRecords* into another variable of the same type. (You must have previously defined some other variable as being of the *AddressBook* type—Dim Backup As AddressBook, for example.) Then to copy all the information stored in the interior variables of PersonnelRecords into the parallel structure of the variable Backup, you use the LSet command:

```
LSet Backup = PersonnelRecords
```

Some programmers like to use Type variable structures in other ways. Random access files aren't the only way to use this handy technique. If you like to organize your data in this quasi-array fashion, you might use the Type command often. If you want to define custom groupings of variables for some special purpose, use Type. However, ordinary variables and arrays are usually simpler to manipulate. The structures of variables created by the Type command are similar to the records used in the Pascal programming language or to structures in C.

Type structures can also pass a group of variables to a subroutine.

You can create Type structures that include variable-length text ("string") variables (just leave off the * 25 in Newname As String * 25). However, you cannot then use such a structure with random access files.

You can build complicated structures by using one Type structure as a variable within another:

```
Type Directions
        North As String * 10
        South As String * 10
        East As String * 10
        West As String * 10
End Type
Type Mileage
        Car As Integer
        Bus As Integer
        Trailer As Integer
        Distance As Directions 'this is a Type structure
End Type
```

This type-within-type technique, however, could get too complex to be easily visualized and become a source of programming errors.

MOVING ON

In the next chapter, "Customizing Applications," we'll explore numerous step-by-step examples to learn how to personalize your applications. These examples are based on real-world situations, so you'll not only learn programming, but also can benefit from using the example programs in your everyday work. If you've ever been curious about computer programming, Chapter 7 is a good place to start exploring.

Chapter 8

Compound Documents & OLE

This last chapter of the book is about interapplication communications. You'll find out how to make Windows applications work together, how to create compound documents with Word, and finally how to automate tasks that involve multiple applications. We'll show you how to process worksheets and images and how to incorporate sound and video in Word documents. You'll learn how to move data between applications and how to control one application from within another one. For example, you'll see how to retrieve selected data from a database to further process the information in Excel or make it part of a Word document. Finally, if you perform similar operations frequently, you'll find some useful techniques for automating the exchange of data between applications.

This chapter is not about programming. It's a collection of a few interesting, useful techniques, which you can extend on your own. Using OLE operations is the simplest form of "programming" in the Windows environment, and for all intents and purposes, it can be considered an extension to macro and VBA programming, which we have explored in the previous chapter. However, there's a lot you can accomplish without programming, just by mastering the OLE techniques described in the first half of this chapter.

NO APPLICATION IS AN ISLAND

Since the early days of personal computing, there have been attempts to create all-in-one applications that do just about everything—word processing, spreadsheet calculations, database management, communications, and possibly more. (WindowWorks, Microsoft Works, and WordPerfect Works are programs in this genre that linger in the software market today.) The motivation behind this idea was that the user need become familiar only with a single user interface and not have to learn several different programs. Moreover, the individual applications within the integrated package had built-in mechanisms for data exchange, and they were easier to integrate. The spreadsheet application, for example, was able to save its data in a format that the word processing application could understand. The database management application could import data from both the word processor and the spreadsheet applications. Considering that in the days of DOS there wasn't even a rudimentary form of data exchange, such as the clipboard, the idea of integrated suites of applications wasn't a bad one.

These products never caught up, though, because users didn't want to give up their favorite applications. Uniformity is not part of the human nature. Besides, no single integrated application could satisfy the requirements of all users. Exchanging data between applications in the DOS environment has been a sore point—and has never been resolved in a satisfactory way.

Data exchange capabilities were built into Windows since its very early versions.

Programmers knew that data exchange between applications would become a reality only if it were part of the operating system. Individual applications would still be able to provide unique features and operate independently of each other, yet communicate with each other. And this is one of the much-sought-after features that Windows brought to PC users. Microsoft managed to create a more or less uniform user interface with Windows. Not only that, it offered a way to integrate applications without sacrificing the individual character of each application.

The clipboard was the first step in providing data exchange capabilities between applications. Then DDE (dynamic data exchange) came along. DDE is a mechanism for applications to exchange data, and it uses a small number of commands that both applications should understand. Exchange capabilities were greatly improved under Windows 95 with the introduction of scraps, which were explained in Chapter 3. Finally, for real integration, Windows offers OLE.

Object Linking and Embedding

OLE stands for Object Linking and Embedding. In short, OLE is the capability to copy a piece of information from one document and paste it into another. This sounds just like a copy and paste operation, but through OLE you can move around more than isolated pieces of information. You can actually copy and paste objects.

The key word in OLE is *object*. Windows 95 is an object-oriented operating system and will become more so with future releases. (For a discussion of the object-oriented nature of Windows, see Chapter 3.) Objects have built-in intelligence, and they are more or less independent entities. A worksheet object, for example, may exist outside Excel. It may well become part of a Word document—not as a table of numbers but as a full-blown worksheet, with calculated fields that change every time a number is changed. And that's the very nature of objects.

Objects can be incorporated into documents in two ways: they can be *embedded* or *linked*. Embedded objects exist only in the document in which they were embedded and can't be modified outside the document. An embedded object may come from another file (a segment of an existing worksheet, or an Access table, for example) or be created entirely within the application. When you link an object to a document, though, no copies are created. In this case, the object is linked to the original document. The linked documents remain synchronized; updating the original updates the linked copy. The only place where you can edit the linked document is within the application that created it.

Objects can be either embedded or linked in a document.

Figures 8-1 and 8-2 demonstrate the difference between embedding and linking. The image was created with Picture Publisher and then inserted twice into a Word document, once as an embedded object and once as a linked object. Any changes you make to the original image file in Picture Publisher do not affect the embedded image in the Word document. Yet, you can edit the embedded image from within Word. The linked picture, on the other hand, is tied to the original and is updated automatically (see Figure 8-2). Any changes you make to the original from within Picture Publisher affect the linked picture as well. Moreover, you can't edit the linked image from within Word. You can edit it only from within the source application (Picture Publisher).

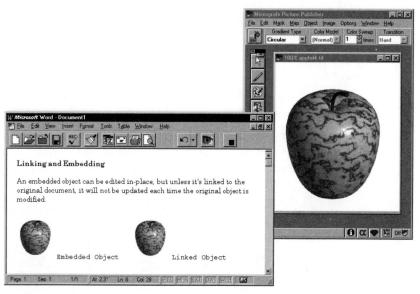

Figure 8-1: After being prepared in Picture Publisher, the picture was copied into a Word document twice: once as an embedded object and once as a linked object.

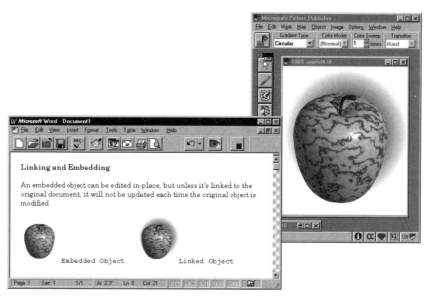

Figure 8-2: After modifying the picture in the image processing application (adding a shadow behind it), only the linked picture in Word is updated.

OLE is a major step in turning Windows 95 into a docucentric operating system.

OLE is more than a mechanism for sharing information. It is a major step in building a docucentric environment, in which you can concentrate on working with documents, not with applications. With OLE, you don't have to create a text document in Word, then switch to Excel to process numbers and paste the results back to Word. You can work with a single application and create a single document. If you need some of Excel's capabilities, you can have them right in Word's environment. In short, OLE makes it possible for one application to borrow the functionality of other applications and use them in creating compound documents. When you embed an image or a worksheet in a compound document, you don't just transfer pixels, or numbers. You transfer an object, which carries with it a lot of the functionality of the application in which it was created. The most important aspect of OLE is that it allows the user to focus on the document he or she wants to create, not the application(s) involved.

Note: If you have used OLE in the past, you know very well that a worksheet can exist in a Word document only if Excel has been installed on the system. The intelligence, therefore, is not within the object; it's in the application. Think of the applications as part of the operating system. If they cooperate with the operating system in providing solutions, they are extensions to the operating system. Eventually, all basic applications will become part of the operating system, and the application intelligence will be hidden somewhere among the objects themselves and the operating system.

For the examples in this chapter we are going to use the Microsoft Office applications (Word, Excel, and Access). There are other applications that support OLE, from Microsoft and other manufacturers, but the Microsoft Office suite of applications are the most popular ones. We expect that most of our readers have one or more of them installed on their systems. Every application written for Windows 95 is OLE-capable so all the techniques discussed in this chapter can be used with any Windows 95 application.

THE COMPOUND DOCUMENT

The kind of document that combines tools from multiple applications is called a *compound document*, or *container*. It contains all types of objects, not just the objects Word (or the application being used to create the document) can handle on its own (see Figure 8-3). If you add more OLE-capable applications to your system, you will have more objects at your disposal.

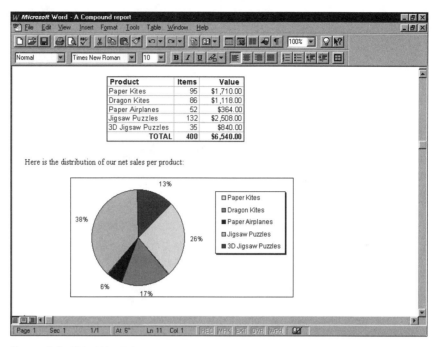

Figure 8-3: This Word document contains much more than text—it's a compound document.

A compound document contains several types of objects and manipulates them by borrowing the appropriate tools from other applications.

In Figure 8-3 you see a Word document that contains a line of text, a table, and a chart. All the elements are contained in the Word file. Word can handle all three elements of the document: text, tables, and graphics. If you look at the document carefully, though, you'll see that the table is not a simple Word table. Some of its elements are calculated (they are the sums of the columns), and they should change every time an entry changes value. Figure 8-4 shows what happens when you edit the table. This is not a Word table; it's a worksheet embedded in the document. Change the first number, and the sum is recalculated instantly. (Actually, it's simpler to create a table that calculates the sum of a certain column in Word and press F9 to recalculate the sums of its columns, but for more complicated calculations, you'll have to switch to Excel.) The embedded worksheet looks a lot like a miniature version of Excel, blended in Word's environment.

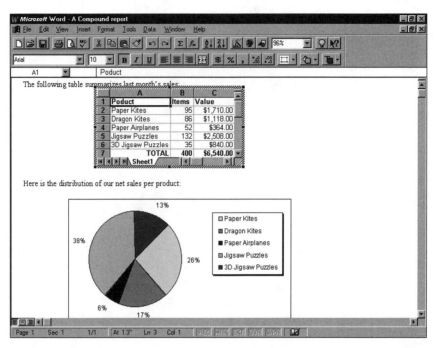

Figure 8-4: The table in the document shown in Figure 8-3 is actually an object (an Excel spreadsheet), embedded within the document.

Embedded objects can be edited within the compound document with a process called *in-place editing*.

Most of Excel's menu options are now displayed in place of Word's menus, and Word's toolbars have been replaced by Excel's toolbars. This is known as *in-place editing*: there's no need to switch applications to edit the worksheet. The appropriate tools appear right where you need them. That's exactly what we meant when we said that one application "can borrow the functionality of another application." Word doesn't know how to handle worksheets, but Excel does. If Excel is installed on your computer, Word contacts it and borrows the tools needed to process the embedded worksheet. Word itself moves quietly to the background, letting Excel do what it knows best. Word simply waits until the user clicks on the text outside the object to take control again.

In the examples noted so far, we used Word to create compound documents, because Word handles text (what most people still use computers to manage) better than Excel or Access. However, you are not limited to Word when creating compound documents. If you are preparing a presentation, you may use PowerPoint as your primary application and link worksheets, graphs, and images into the compound document, which is a presentation. If you have to, you can embed an entire Word document in an Excel cell. A compound document can be created with any application, but Word is often the most natural choice.

The chart shown in Figure 8-4 wasn't created with Word's tools either. Figure 8-5 shows what happens when you edit the chart. Clearly, the editing tools you see on the window are not Word's tools. They belong to a data-charting application called Microsoft Graph. The charting tools appear whenever you need to edit the chart, right where you need them.

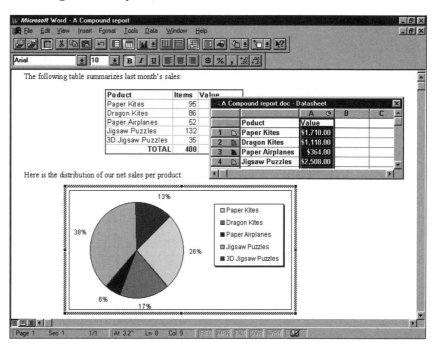

Figure 8-5: To edit the embedded chart, Word must borrow the tools of another application, Microsoft Graph.

Note: In a previous note we discussed the intelligence of the objects and whether this intelligence is built into the object, or the application. Having seen the examples of Figures 8-4 and 8-5, one could argue that if the objects can carry the necessary toolbars with them wherever they go, then they have built-in intelligence. But that's not the case. Even though the tools are not incorporated into the objects, the objects themselves simply know which tools they need and where to get them. The application still must be available to provide the tools the objects must carry with them. (It is also a way for companies to make sure users buy their applications to use them. If you distribute this compound document, other users will see both the table and the image, but they will not be able to edit them unless they have the necessary applications installed on their systems.)

Creating Compound Documents

Creating compound documents in Word is quite simple, as long as you have all the applications that can handle the components of the compound document: Excel for worksheets, Graph for data graphs, Paint for images, and so on. Of course, you have to know a little about their operation, too, but don't let that stop you from creating compound documents. It's easy to create a worksheet that performs a few calculations on the rows and columns of a table with Excel. The tools make it almost intuitive. The same applies for image processing, retrieving data from databases, and so on.

Embedding a Worksheet Object

Let's follow the steps used to create the compound document shown in Figure 8-3. It's the basis of a sales report with a sales summary in table format and the corresponding graph.

Open a new document in Word, and type the lead-in text as usual, leaving space for the objects you can't create with Word. Position the insertion point where you want to insert the first object. Then open the Insert menu, and select Object. The Object dialog box appears and displays the kinds of objects in the Object

Type list, as shown in Figure 8-6. The list's length depends on the number of OLE-compliant applications you have installed on your computer and the objects they provide. Select Microsoft Excel Worksheet, click OK, and an empty worksheet is inserted in your document at the insertion point. As soon as the object is inserted in your document, you'll see the Excel menus and toolbar on Word's window, and you can perform any Excel operation you need to build the worksheet, such as entering and formatting cell contents, from within Word.

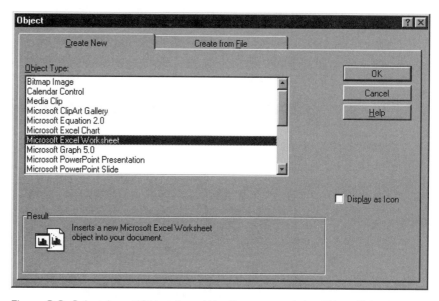

Figure 8-6: Select Insert|Object from Word's menu, and the Object dialog box lists the available objects on your system.

To embed objects, applications provide an Object command in their Insert menu.

If you click somewhere else in your document, the worksheet is displayed as a table, and Excel's menu and toolbars disappear, replaced by the original Word menu and toolbars. To get the Excel tools back, double-click on the worksheet object. When you're working in Word, the worksheet numbers are displayed as a table, because a table is the best structure Word can provide for storing data in a worksheet arrangement.

Activate the worksheet object by double-clicking it, and enter the monthly sales figures. Type a few product names in the first column and their sales figures in the second column. Don't enter their total value. Let's have the worksheet calculate this cell so that it will be always correct. Select the cell that should contain the total value, and then click on the button with the Σ symbol (the AutoSum button) on the data entry toolbar above the window. This button inserts a sum formula in the current cell. Now you must specify the values to be summed. Use the mouse to select the cells above the same column (excluding the one where you're inserting the formula, of course). As you select the cells, a sum expression that includes all selected cells is displayed in the data entry box of the toolbar. When you're finished, click on the green check box on the same toolbar, and the sum of the values is displayed in the last cell of the column. If you change a value in the worksheet now, the sum adjusts automatically.

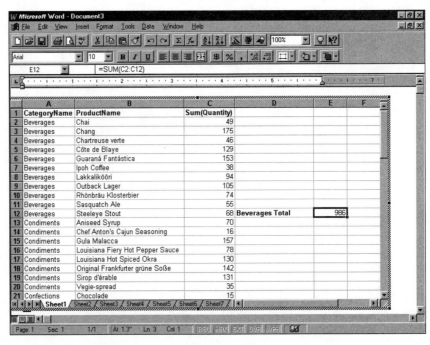

Figure 8-7: In-place editing provides you with Excel's editing tools, even though the window's title says Microsoft Word.

Now you can format the contents of the worksheet, adjust the width of its columns, format the text in the cells bold or italic, and in general make it look the way you want. Click somewhere outside the worksheet, and you're back in Word's environment. The worksheet now looks like a table. Select it by clicking it once (don't double-click), and click on Word's Align Center button to center the object on the page. You can manipulate it to some extent with Word's own tools. But it's not an editable table, because you can't edit individual entries. To change a value, or its appearance, you must double-click on it. The Excel menu and toolbar appear again, and now you can change the object values or its format.

Embedded objects do not live in external files; they are part of the compound document.

This worksheet doesn't live anywhere else outside the document it belongs to. It was obviously created by Excel, but there's no .XLS file for this worksheet. It's an embedded object. In the section "Embedding Existing Documents," you'll see how you can embed an existing worksheet in a Word document.

Embedding a Graph Object

Let's add a graphical representation of the worksheet's data. Place the pointer somewhere below the table, and insert a new object by choosing Insert|Object. This time select Microsoft Graph 5.0 from the list of available objects. A graph object is similar to an Excel graph, but you don't need Excel to create it. As soon as you insert the object in your document, you'll see a sample graph and a datasheet (a small worksheet arrangement with the data that correspond to the sample graph). Obviously, we must replace the sample data with the actual data from the worksheet. Double-click on the worksheet to edit it, select the range you want to plot, and from the Edit menu, choose the Copy command (or click the Copy icon on the toolbar). Then switch to the graph (double-click on it). If you don't see the datasheet with the graph's data, select Datasheet from the View menu.

To paste the actual data in the graph's datasheet, select the first datasheet cell, and choose the Paste Link command from the Edit menu. Notice that this isn't Word's menu, it is the MS Graph menu. The Paste Link command replaces the existing data in the datasheet with the data you copied from the worksheet and also links it to the original data, so that as you change the numbers in the worksheet, the datasheet's contents are updated, too. This in turn updates the graph. Now you can use the MS Graph menus to change just about any parameter of the graph: its type, the legends and titles, the colors and/or patterns, and so on.

You can link data within the same documents.

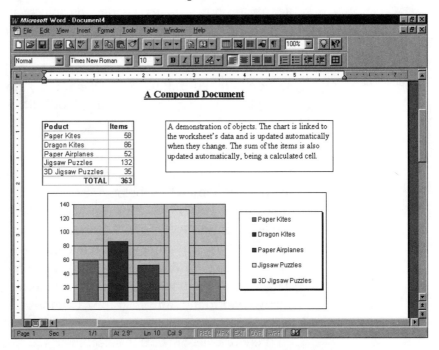

Figure 8-8: The worksheet and the graph are not only embedded in a Word document, they are also linked within the same document.

If you switch to the Excel worksheet and change any values, both the Datasheet and the graph are updated automatically. Well, not quite automatically—you still have to double-click on the chart for the changes to take effect. In general, linked objects are updated automatically, but MS Graph seems to be an exception.

The graph is an embedded document, because it doesn't live outside Word. It is also linked to some information in the same Word document. Although there are simpler examples of linking documents (which we will explore in the following sections), you've seen the epitome of linking: links within the same document! This should tell you something about the objects, too. The various objects are truly independent of each other, and they are not linked to each other through the application. They are linked by the operating system itself.

More Objects

A compound document may also contain audio and visual information.

Worksheets and charts are two very basic objects, but they are not the only components you can use to create a compound document. You can bring other components into a compound document. Practically, every object Windows can handle can become part of a compound document. Let's say you are preparing a document for the company's shareholders. It will include some tables and the corresponding graphs, but how about adding the president's message to the shareholders? You can append it as text, but it is also possible to embed the message as a sound file, even a video file. A document's ultimate destination is not always the printer. If transmitted electronically, it may contain any type of information computers can produce and store.

Open a new document in Word, type some text, and then insert a video clip. (Select Object from the Insert menu, and from the Object Type list, select Video Clip.) Word's menu, with the exception of the File menu, disappears altogether, and you'll see the Media Player's menu. (Media Player comes with Windows 95 and enables you to play video and animation files, CD audio, and more.) From the Insert Clip menu, select Video for Windows, and you'll be presented with a File Open dialog box, in which you can select the appropriate .AVI file. After selecting the filename, you're returned to Word's environment, and the video clip's first frame is displayed in the document, as shown in Figure 8-9. Double-click on this picture to play the clip.

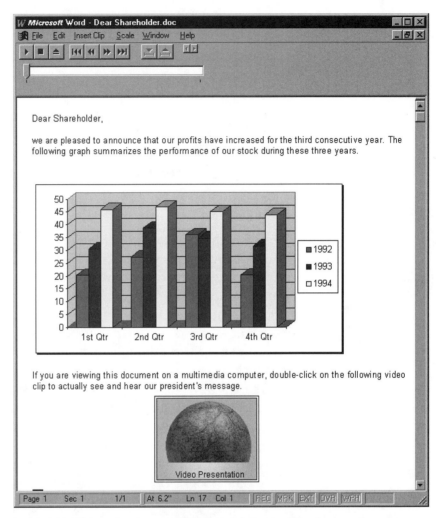

Figure 8-9: Notice what happened to what used to be Word's menu bar when inserting a video clip in a Word document.

Embedding Existing Documents

In the previous section, you saw how to create a compound document from within Word. All the objects were created by their corresponding applications, but they "lived" in the Word document. In most practical situations, however, the objects you want to embed in a compound document exist in other documents already.

An embedded object may come from an existing file, but it won't be connected to its source any longer.

To embed existing objects, you must use the Edit menu, instead of the Insert menu. Open an existing worksheet in Excel, and select a range of cells. Then copy them to the clipboard, and open a new document in Word. Place the insertion point in the location where you want the Excel data to appear in the Word document, and select Paste Special from the Edit menu. A Paste Special dialog box similar to the one shown in Figure 8-11 with various settings will appear on the screen. This dialog box is explained in the next section, but for now, just select Microsoft Excel Worksheet Object, and leave the check boxes unchecked. Then click on the OK button to paste the information in the document.

The selected range has now become an object in the current Word document. You can either double-click on it to edit the object in-place with Excel's tools or convert it to a table with the Convert Text To Table command on the Table menu. The selected range of the worksheet is embedded within the Word document. You can double-click it to edit it as we explained previously, but it's not connected to the source of the information in any way.

It is also possible to embed an existing document from the Insert menu's File tab. This tab lets you select a document and embed it into another one. In most practical situations, you don't need the entire document but only part of it. For example, in composing a sales report, we only need summary data and not all the details of the entire worksheet. Similarly, you rarely need all the sales figures from a database, just a few totals.

Linking Objects

Linked objects follow the changes in the source document.

Creating a compound document is fairly simple, but there's more to OLE than that. What if you modified the original version of the Excel worksheet you just embedded a selection from? Someone could change one of the numbers on the original worksheet, and this change could very well affect the formulas contained in the selected range that you used to create the embedded object. How would you know to change the numbers in the Word document to match the numbers in the original worksheet file? Isn't there a better way?

There is a better way, indeed. What you need is a *link* between the two applications, similar to the link between the two objects of the same document presented in the earlier section "Embedding a Graph Object." You would like Word to be aware that some of the document's contents were imported from another application, and every time they are changed in the original document, the changes should be reflected in the compound document as well. That's what the *L* in OLE is all about. It's about *linking* documents.

We have already seen an example of linking data within the same document. The worksheet's data in Figure 8-8 was linked to the chart so that the chart would always be up-to-date. The same principle applies to different documents as well. This time we'll link data from an Excel file to a Word document, so that every time you (or someone else) change the data in the Excel file, the changes will become immediately available in the Word document as well. The document that provides the object you embed into another document is called the *source document*, and the corresponding application is called the *source application*. The document that accepts the object is called the *client document*, and the corresponding application is called the *client application*.

Let's say you maintain sales data in an Excel worksheet. Every month you must extract some data from the sales worksheet and use it to build a report in Word. You must create another compound document as we did in the previous example, only this time you'll extract the numbers you need from their source: an Excel worksheet.

First start Excel, and select the range of the cells you want to extract. Figure 8-10 shows a worksheet with the total sales figures for a given time period. The selected cells must form a solid range. Although it is possible to select nonadjacent cells for other operations, you cannot link a disjoint range to another application. The cells you are about to link must belong to a contiguous range. Select Edit|Copy to copy the selected cells to the clipboard from where they'll be read into the Word document. So far, it's all as simple as copying and pasting in the same document.

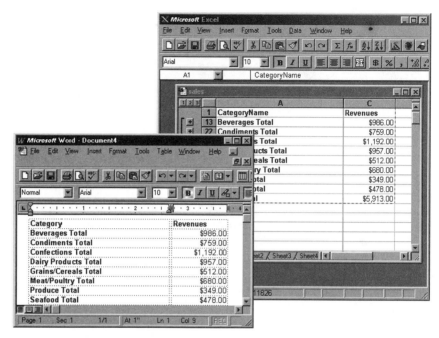

Figure 8-10: The sales figures originate in an Excel spreadsheet. Select the range of cells you need for your report, copy them, and link them to a worksheet in the Word document. As you modify the data in Excel, the linked data changes as well.

Open a Word document in which you want to insert the data, and place the insertion point at the position where the cells must be inserted. Select Paste Special from the Edit menu. Paste Special is just like the Paste command, except Paste Special offers more options, which are displayed in the dialog box shown in Figure 8-11.

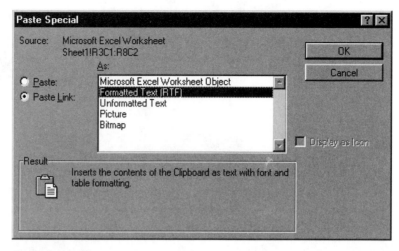

Figure 8-11: Word pastes the selected data as a linked object if you select the Paste Link option button.

The number and type of objects in the As list of the Paste Special dialog box depends on the contents of the clipboard. They specify how the selected cells appear in the compound document. You can import them as plain text (not the most useful option), formatted text, and, of course, a worksheet. Select the Microsoft Excel Worksheet Object option to bring the data into the Word document as an embedded worksheet object.

Even more important are the two option buttons, Paste and Paste Link. The Paste option is just like the Paste command. It simply pastes the clipboard's contents in the current document, creating an embedded object. The Paste Link option, however, not only pastes the clipboard's contents in the current document, but it also links them to the original application. If the original data changes, the linked data changes as well. Check the Paste Link option, and then click on the OK button. A worksheet will be embedded at the current location in the document, only this time it won't be empty. It will contain the values of the cells you previously selected and copied in the Excel document.

To verify that the new object in the compound document is linked to the original worksheet, switch to the Excel worksheet now, and change the values of some of the cells. When you return to the Word document you'll see that the changes have also

You can use the Paste Special command from the Edit menu to link inserted objects.

affected the document. You can actually keep both documents visible on the screen and watch how the changes you make in Excel affect the Word document.

What you have in your document now is a table. Or is it? It's not a table, because the Convert Text to Table command in the Table menu is enabled. Then it has to be formatted text, right? Wrong again. Try to select a word in this text. You can't. If you double-click anywhere on the pasted text, you'll be switched to Excel.

This is another very characteristic difference between embedding and linking an object: an embedded object can be edited within the application in which it was embedded (the container application). The process, which we discussed earlier in this chapter, is called in-place editing. A linked object must be edited by the original application. The reason for this behavior is the very essence of linked objects: they should be modified in a single place only. If you want to get some data out of Excel and then modify it in your application, you don't need to (and you shouldn't) link the data to the original worksheet. A paste operation would be simpler.

Mail & OLE

Most Windows 95 applications support OLE. Ideally, every application should support OLE so that it could be integrated with the rest of the applications and the operating system. Microsoft Exchange, which was covered in Chapter 6, is OLE-capable. If you were thinking that electronic mail is just a way to exchange text files, and maybe attach other documents (such as images), you'll probably be surprised to find out that you can link documents even to mail messages.

Suppose you know that by Friday afternoon you must send a message to your boss in the company's headquarters about the weekly sales figures. And you also know that Friday afternoon things get a little hectic around the office. You can prepare the message whenever it's convenient for you (even on Mondays, if you can't do any better), embed the sales figures as a linked object in the body of the message (see Figure 8-12), and don't send it. Wait until all the data is collected and updated in the original Excel worksheet, and then send the message. (Once you've discovered the trick, you can go all the way and send the message even later, to make the boss think you were slaving away on a Friday evening.)

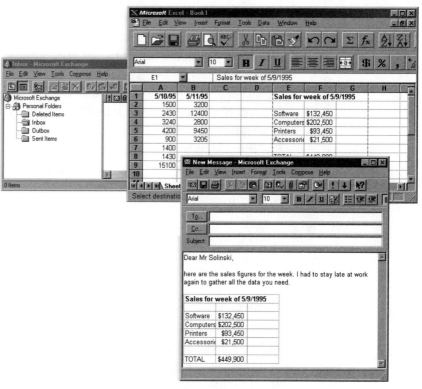

Figure 8-12: Link data to a mail message to make sure the recipient of the message receives the most recent data.

Link objects in your mail messages to ensure that they contain the most up-to-date information when they are sent.

The message your boss receives contains the latest data, from right up until the moment it was delivered. If more up-to-date data arrives during the weekend, it isn't reflected in the message on Monday morning. The only way to get around this problem is to place a shortcut to the actual file into the message itself.

More Options for Pasted Objects

The dialog box in Figure 8-11 offers a number of options for pasting and linking information. Let's bring the Excel data you've been working with into a document as formatted text (an .RTF file). In this case, the individual entries of the table will maintain their original formats (font sizes, bold, italic, and so on). Moreover, this time the data can be changed within the Word document. Not only can you change the entries' appearance, you also can change the actual values entered. This feature is of dubious value when you link objects, though, because if the original entries are changed for some reason in Excel, they will overwrite any changes you made to the table within Excel.

Two options for pasting and linking data available from the Paste Special dialog box are Picture and Bitmap. These choices apply not only to images but to text as well. Why represent text as an image? There's hardly any reason to do that, but because the clipboard can convert text to the equivalent bitmap, this option is available. The only reason for pasting alphanumeric data as a bitmap is if the application in which the data originated couldn't provide any better alternative—and in this case, you probably shouldn't be using this application, anyway.

Breaking a Link

If a linked object need not be updated any longer, break its link to the source document.

We've mentioned already that all Windows 95 applications should be OLE-compliant so that they can communicate flawlessly with each other. As a user, you must be OLE-aware too! Say you've prepared a sales report, your data has changed several dozen times over the course of preparing the report (you can blame the accounting department for that), and finally the report went out. At this point, would it make sense to update the report, should the original data change? Not only does it not make sense, it may actually do some harm. If the accounting department is really slow, the next time you open the report, it may contain the most up-to-date information, but it sure won't be the information you sent out. Therefore, you should be able to break links too.

Here's how you can break a link. Start Word or the application you used to create the compound document. Open the document with the linked objects, and from the Edit menu, select Links. You'll see a list of all links in the document, similar to the one shown in the Links dialog box in Figure 8-13. Select the link you want to break. (If you don't know the linked file's name, select the linked object in the document before issuing the Edit|Links command, and the filename will be automatically highlighted for you.) Click on the Break Link button. It's that simple.

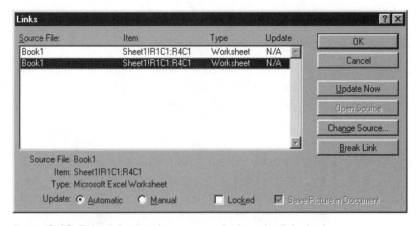

Figure 8-13: This dialog box lets you manipulate the links in the current document.

The linked objects aren't removed from your document. They remain in the document as tables (or text, graphics, whatever), and you can move them, or delete them altogether, but you cannot edit them or update them with the source applications. Some objects, when their links to the source are broken, are converted to static pictures. If Word can't handle them any better, it converts them to pictures.

In such a case, a better approach would be to convert the linked objects to some kind of object Word can handle, such as a table, before breaking the links. If you ever want to change the data, it's much easier to edit a table than the image of a table.

The Links command on the Edit menu lets you manipulate links in many ways, even change their source.

Links Are Quite Flexible

The Links dialog box in Figure 8-13 offers an array of possibilities, as you can see. Let's review them briefly. A link can be updated either automatically or manually. If a document contains many links, automatic updates may take a while, especially every time you open the document. If you don't really want to have up-to-date information as you work (you only want to be sure that the document will be up-to-date when printed), select the Update Manual option button in the Links dialog box. It's up to you now to remember that you have to update the links manually. To manually update a link, just open the Links dialog box, and click on the Update Now button.

The Locked check box prevents the system from updating a link, either automatically or manually. If you check this box, the Update Now button is disabled. You should use this button to temporarily disable the updates of lost links. For example, if one of the objects is linked to a file on a server that has gone down, click the Locked check box to prevent the system from displaying error messages or converting the linked object to some other type of object because it thinks the source document doesn't exist anymore.

The Open Source button starts the application that can handle the objects of the selected link. If for any reason Word (or the application used to create the compound document) can't start it, or the in-place menus aren't adequate for the type of processing you want to perform on the object, start the application with this button.

Finally, you can change the source of a link. If the document contains a link to a file that was moved to another disk, or subfolder, you can change the file of the link yourself. If you attempt to edit a linked object and the application can't locate the source of the link, use the Links dialog box to fix the problem yourself—unless, of course, the source file was deleted, in which case there isn't much you can do about it.

Links should update on their own (just as shortcuts do), even if you move the files around or rename them. But you shouldn't count on that in a networked environment, in which disk names may change or in which disks may simply not be mounted when you open the document. When the container file can't find the source file to a link, Word (or any other container application) won't let you edit the corresponding object. Say you've created a document that contains an Excel Worksheet object linked to an .XLS file. If the .XLS file is deleted, Word won't let you edit the object, not even as an embedded worksheet (which would be the most reasonable alternative). Instead, Word converts the information to a bitmap, and you can only edit it as an image within Word.

Links Within the Same Document

You can also link two objects within the same document, and you've seen an example of this in the section "Embedding a Graph Object." In this section we'll show you how to link the contents of the worksheet to the document's text, so that you can use the embedded worksheet as a calculator and see the results right in your text, formatted in any way you like. Here's how to create a document like the one in Figure 8-14. Create a document with an embedded worksheet, select some cells, and copy them to the clipboard. Switch to Word's environment by clicking somewhere on the document outside the worksheet, and select Paste Special from the Edit menu. In the Paste Special dialog box, check the Paste Link option button, and from the list of available format types, select Formatted Text (RTF). Now your document contains a table, which is linked to the worksheet's contents. Change the value of a single cell, and the text is modified automatically. What good is this for you? Plenty good, especially if you plan to distribute this document. You can use the worksheet as a temporary working area, and when you're finished, delete the worksheet and keep the table. You could create an elaborately formatted table (see Figure 8-14) and yet be able to watch the changes as you process the data. Once the table has been formatted, you can change the data in the worksheet and have the operating system update your table, while maintaining its format.

It is possible to link different objects to each other, within the same compound document.

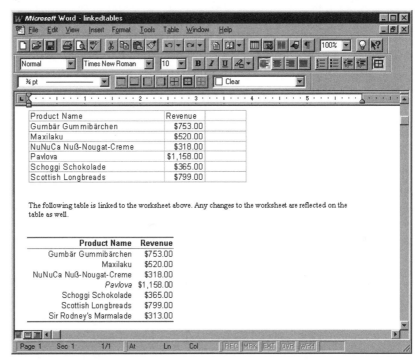

Figure 8-14: The worksheet in this document is used as an advanced calculator to help you prepare the actual table. Once the table is ready, you can get rid of the worksheet. The linked table maintains both the data and its format.

When Not to Link

As convenient as OLE sounds, it's not trouble free. Embedded objects can significantly increase the size of the compound document. If the file is going to be transmitted electronically, you should convert embedded objects to the equivalent data structures (usually tables). The only reason not to convert objects to other types of data is, of course, if the recipient of the message may have to edit it. You must also keep in mind that compound documents can't be modified unless the machine on which they are viewed has the corresponding applications installed.

Linking poses two additional problems. First, links take up resources. If you have many linked items in a document, you'll suffer a performance penalty. Also, if you plan to distribute a document with links, you should keep a few things in mind. The links in a given document are not established magically. If your Word document contains a link to the file C:\DATA\SALES1995.XLS, this link cannot be reconstructed unless there is a C:\DATA subdirectory containing a file named SALES1995.XLS. If you send the document to a coworker, chances are the links will be broken because the system can't access the locations they point to. If you work in a networked environment, you should make links to files residing on the servers or other disks that are available to everyone. If you just copy the document to a disk and pass it to a friend, it's almost certain that he or she won't be able to reconstruct the links on a different computer.

If you plan to distribute compound documents, you must also include the corresponding source documents.

One solution to this problem is to provide all the files with the links and instruct the other party as to where to copy the files on his or her hard disk. Ideally, you should place the container (or client) document and the source document(s) in the same folder. This is anticlimactic, though, since it takes away all the magic of OLE. The information is duplicated and can be modified in multiple locations. What's the point of supplying a document with links, when you can change the source of the information and nothing will change in the linked document. The best way to distribute documents with links is to convert all links into static information. Then the document will be self-contained and can be easily distributed.

OLE AUTOMATION

We have seen how to create compound documents by embedding objects in them, how to link information between documents so that it is always up to date, and even how to break the links when they're not needed any longer. It's now time to explore some techniques for linking data in ways that wouldn't be possible with simple copy and paste operations. Our next topic is OLE Automation. If certain OLE tasks are repeated frequently, then it pays to automate them. Automating OLE operations requires some extra effort the first time we perform a task, but it pays off later when we repeat the same task with a simple mouse click. We are not going to get into programming techniques yet. Office 95 applications have built-in OLE Automation features, making it easy for you to use automation in situations like the examples of the following sections. This time we'll use another Microsoft Office application, Access. We'll use an Access database to extract names and addresses to build form letters in Word, as well as numeric data into an Excel worksheet.

Form Letters & Mailing Lists

Creating a form letter in Word is an automated OLE process.

Here's a typical example of using database records in a Word document. We will create a form letter with *merge fields* (names and addresses), which will be replaced later with actual values taken from a database. This is a simple mailing list example, but you can follow the same steps to automate other similar tasks, such as issuing invoices or payment receipts. This example does demonstrate some of the OLE Automation capabilities built into MS Office.

Create a new document in Word, and from the Tools menu, select Mail Merge. The Mail Merge Helper window will appear on your screen (shown in Figure 8-15). You must complete three steps at this point: create the document (form letter), specify the source of the data, and merge the form letter with the data. The steps are explained in detail in the rest of this section. Some of the buttons on the Mail Merge Helper dialog box will not be visible the first time you open it. For example, the Edit button will appear after you have specified the Main Document with the Create button.

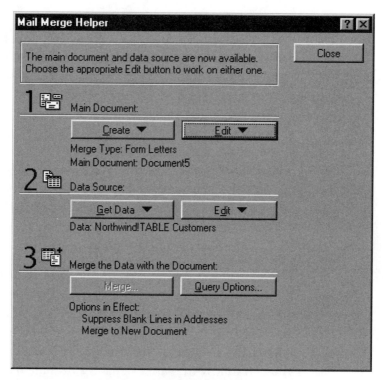

Figure 8-15: The Mail Merge Helper dialog box.

1. Create the form letter (Main Document).

    If you click the Create button, you'll see a list with the following options: Form Letters, Mailing Labels, Envelopes, and Catalog. In this case, you want to create a form letter. After you merge the form letters with the addresses, you will also print the corresponding labels or envelopes.

    Select Form Letters, and you will be prompted as to whether you want to use the current document for form letters or create a new one. As soon as you make your choice, another option, Edit, is added to the dialog box. Don't edit the document yet. It will be much easier to do so after you select the source of the data.

2. Specify the mailing list.

Now click on the Get Data button, and you'll be presented with the following options: Create Data Source, Open Data Source, Use Address Book, and Header Options. Because we are going to retrieve data from an existing database, select Create Data Source. (If you don't have Access installed on your computer, you can either open another database or create your own. The data need not come from an Access database; you can use names and addresses stored in an Excel worksheet or Word table, too.) Click on Open Data Source, and Word displays a list of database types to choose from. Select Access Database, and then from the File Open dialog box that appears, select the Northwind database. (You must first select Access Database from the of File Type box.) This is a sample database that comes with Access. (If you don't have Access installed on your computer, you must use another source for mailing labels or create a new one within the Mail Merge Helper program.) Access will start in the background, and you'll be presented with the list of all of the tables in the database, as shown in Figure 8-16.

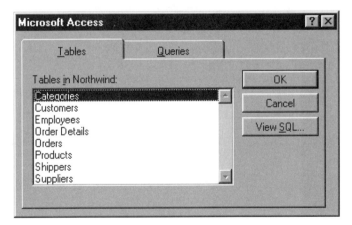

Figure 8-16: Select the Access table whose fields you want to merge with the form letter from this dialog box.

You can retrieve data from databases based on complicated criteria with SQL commands.

Select Customers, and click on the OK button. (The Queries Tab on the dialog box lets you view predefined queries, based on various selection criteria, such as all the customers from Germany or all customers whose annual purchases exceed $10,000, and so on. We will show how to use SQL to select the records you want later in this chapter.)

Because Word can't find any information about creating the form letters in the current document, it prompts you with the message "Word found no merge fields in the main document. Choose the Edit Main Document button to insert merge fields into your main document." Click on the Edit button, and the Merge Helper window disappears so that you can create the form letter. You're ready to add merge fields similar to the ones shown in Figure 8-17.

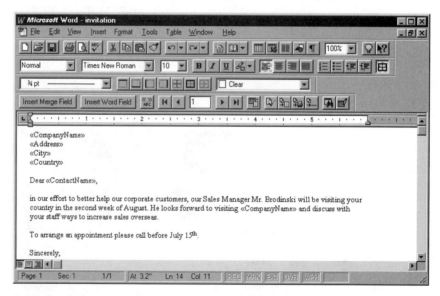

Figure 8-17: Creating a form letter. Notice the Mail Merge toolbar on the Word window (it is the last one).

You'll be brought back to Word's screen, only this time it will contain an additional toolbar: the Mail Merge toolbar, as shown in Figure 8-17. Start composing your form letter, and every time you would ordinarily type a name, address, or any other entry that changes from letter to letter, use a merge field instead. Click on the Insert Merge Field button on the new toolbar, and a list of field names will be displayed, as shown in Figure 8-18. Select the field name you want to use, and it will be inserted in your document enclosed in double angle brackets, as in <<Company Name>> or <<Contact Name>>. These strings are "placeholders," and they will be replaced later with actual field values from the database.

Figure 8-18: A form letter contains the text that doesn't change and the merge fields that are unique for each letter.

When you've finished adding the merge fields into your document, click on the third button of the Mail Merge toolbar. It is the View Merged Data button with <<>>ABC on it. The merge fields onscreen will be replaced with the actual values of the first customer record. Click on the buttons with the arrows to see what the form letter will look like when it's merged with the other records (see Figure 8-19).

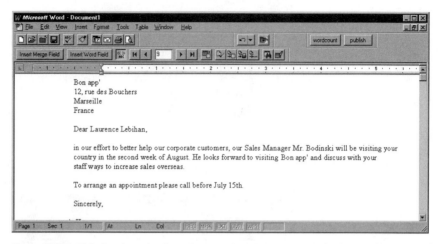

Figure 8-19: This is what the form letter will look like after the Merge Fields are replaced with actual field values.

Another field button, called Insert Word Field, inserts a Word field and will come in handy by adding flexibility to your form letter. One of the Word fields you can insert in the form letter is the If ... Then ... Else item of the drop-down list you'll see if you click on the Word Field button. This field lets you enter conditional text, based on the value of a certain field in the current record. The Customers Table has a blank Country field if the address is in the United States. If you were to use this database overseas, you should include the country name for all addresses. Instead of adding the string "USA" in the records themselves, you can use a Word field to properly address the customers.

Click on the Insert Word Field button, and from the list, select If ... Then ... Else. The dialog box shown in Figure 8-20 will be displayed. Enter **Country** in the Field Name text box, **Equal to** in the Comparison box, and leave the Compare To text box empty. The Insert this Text box holds the text you want to insert when the condition is met (the Country field is empty). Enter **USA** in this box, and leave the other one (which is the text to be used if the condition isn't met) empty.

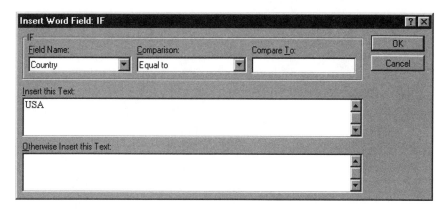

Figure 8-20: Your form letter can also contain conditional strings, based on the value of certain fields.

3. Merge the form letters with the merge fields.

After you have created the form letter and tested it with the actual values of the fields, you can either print the form letters directly or create a new document with all individual letters. To merge the form letter with the actual addresses, you can use one of the following buttons in the Mail Merge Toolbar: Merge to New Document, Merge to Printer, and Mail Merge. This operation is carried out by Word itself, which creates a separate form letter for each address. If you choose to create a new document, make sure there is a page break at the end of the form letter so that every merged letter is printed on a separate page. Printing the labels is not any more complicated. Just select Mailing Labels from the Create Letters list, and follow a similar process to print them on mailing labels or envelopes.

Making Database Queries

So far we've used simple examples in Word and Excel. In the example in the last section, we extracted data from an Access database, namely, all the names and addresses of the company's customers, from within Excel. A more common situation is to extract selected records, based on a number of criteria. This is called a *query* and is the most common operation in working with databases. Queries are designed using a special language called SQL (Structured Query Language, pronounced "sequel").

Using queries can help in many common situations in business computing. Sales and other corporate data is usually maintained in a database. On the other hand, many users prefer to work with spreadsheets (well, at least managers do). For one thing, databases aren't very good at handling numbers. Moreover, it can be a good idea to avoid working with the actual data, especially if you are going to use the data in a way that requires you to make changes.

Let's assume the data you're interested in live in an Access database, and you want to analyze monthly sales figures. Once the data you need (itemized sales for a given month, for example) is in an Excel worksheet, you can do whatever you wish with it. You needn't fear destroying actual data. In the following examples, we are going to use the Northwind database, which comes with Access.

Databases are great for storing data, but you may prefer to process the data with Excel.

- -

TIP

Did you wonder why there are no two-way links? For example, why can't you bring data from Access into Excel, change it, and see the changes take effect in Access as well? If you start examining various scenarios by changing the numbers, you would ruin the original database. The original data should be changed only in a single place, be it an Excel worksheet or an Access database. Two-way links would be useful in a single-user environment. It's your data, and why not change it anywhere you can find it? But two-way links could prove disastrous in a business environment, in which a new user whose responsibility is to prepare the weekly reports could ruin the company database.

- -

Your first concern in this case is how to get the data you want out of the database. You don't need an entire table, just the sales figures for a single period. Moreover, the data you need to extract from a database does not usually reside in a single table. You can get the customers table from the database, but how about the invoices? The Invoices table contains the ID (which is a number) for each customer, and an ID for each item sold. You must use these numbers to look up the customer's name in the customers table and the products' names in the Products table. To get the data you need you must combine multiple tables, based on a number of criteria. You probably know that this is usually done through SQL statements. It's fairly easy for Access programmers, or anyone who knows about SQL. For the average user, though, Microsoft Office provides an alternative: a wizard (MSQuery) that will help you sort out the data you need.

Let's say you want to know how many items of each product were sold in a given time period. Figure 8-21 is an Excel worksheet that contains exactly the information you need. The data came from the Northwind database in Access (a sample database you can install from the Microsoft Access CD).

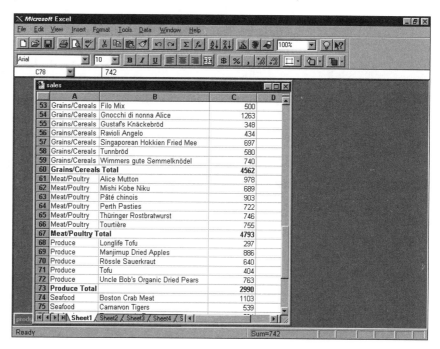

Figure 8-21: Sales figures from the Northwind database displayed in an Excel worksheet.

Open a new worksheet in Excel, and from the Data menu, select Get External Data. Excel will start MSQuery, a utility for creating database queries. If Excel can't start MSQuery (in other words, you don't see the Get External Data command in Excel's Data menu), it means you haven't installed it on your computer. To install it, run Setup from the Office for Windows 95 CD, and click on the Add|Remove button. You will see a list of options to install or remove. Select the Converters, Filters and Data Access option, and click on the Change Options button. Now you'll see a list of options that apply to your previous choice (Converters, Filters and Data Access). Select the option Data Access, and click on the Change Options button again. This time you'll see another list of options, from which you must select the first one, Microsoft Query. Check the box in front of it, and then click on the OK button several times, until you are back to the initial screen. Click on Continue to install the Microsoft Query component.

MSQuery starts by displaying a dialog box listing the data sources it understands (see Figure 8-22). Select MS Access 7.0 Database. If this option isn't available on the window on your screen, click on Other, and a complete list of all database types MSQuery can access will be displayed. From this list select MS Access 7.0 Database. This list contains other database types as well. If you have dBase files and would like to use them from within Excel, this is the place to specify the proper ODBC driver.

MSQuery lets you retrieve database data with point and click operations.

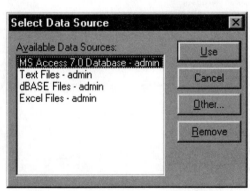

Figure 8-22: From the Select Data Source dialog box, select the type of database you want to open.

Once you've selected the source, the Select Database dialog box lets you select the name of an Access database, as shown in Figure 8-23. Locate the Northwind database (Northwind.mdb, which is most likely in the MSOffice\Access\Samples subdirectory), and open it by clicking on the OK button. You'll see the Add Tables dialog box, with a list of all tables in the database, as shown in Figure 8-24. These are the tables making up the Northwind database, and you can select any table you need to build your query.

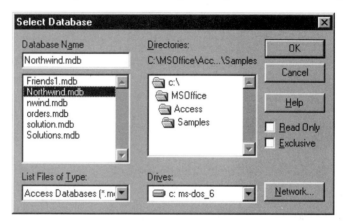

Figure 8-23: From the Select Database dialog box, select the database you want to query.

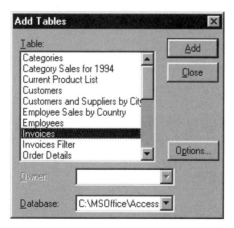

Figure 8-24: The Add Tables dialog box contains a list of all the tables in the current database.

Select the tables you want to work with. In this example query, we are primarily interested in a single table, the Invoices table. However, the structure of the database forces us to use additional tables. The individual products are stored in the Invoices table by their ID numbers. We would rather see actual product names in our list and not just IDs. To link the product IDs to actual product names, we must use the Products table. We will also use the Categories table, which contains a description of each category.

TIP

MSQuery will help you extract the data you need from a database, but you must know the basic structure of the databases you work with. If you can't figure out how to get the information you need on your own, you must consult the database administrator or the programmer who set up the database.

Select the names of the tables you need in the query one at a time, and click on Add. (To extract the data shown in Figure 8-21, we need the following tables: Invoices, Categories, and Products. The actual information (sales figures) is stored in the Invoices table. The other two files, as explained earlier, are needed so that we can view actual category and product names, instead of IDs.) Then click on Close to close the Add Tables dialog box. All the tables will appear in the upper half of the MSQuery window. The names of the fields in each table are displayed in a List Box, as shown in Figure 8-25. Also notice the lines connecting certain fields in different tables. They represent *relations*. The field ProductID in the Invoices table is linked to the field ProductID in the Products table. The Invoices table contains the IDs of the products. To look up the name of the product, you must follow this link to the Products table and find the record that contains the corresponding product name. These relations have been set up for you by the person who designed the database and the database itself will furnish the proper product names in the reports.

Relations between fields are displayed in the MSQuery window as lines between the tables.

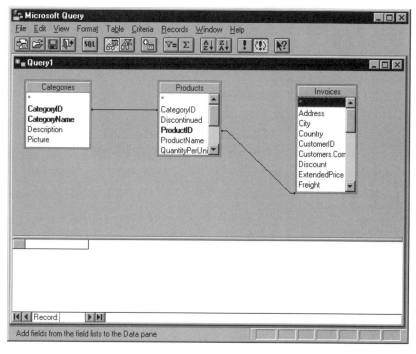

Figure 8-25: This is how the selected tables appear in the MSQuery window.

The lower half of the MSQuery window contains a small frame on the left side. If you move the focus to this frame, an arrow appears, indicating that the frame is a drop-down list. Open the list, and select the field Category.CategoryName, which is the actual name of each category (it is the field CategoryName of the Category table). Then move to the new drop-down list next to it, and select the field Products.ProductName (which is the field ProductName of the Products table). Finally, for the third row, select the field Invoices.Quantity. You may also want to adjust the size of the columns to see all field names. What you see in the lower half of the MSQuery window is a list of all quantities sold to various customers, along with their actual product names and the categories they belong to (see Figure 8-26).

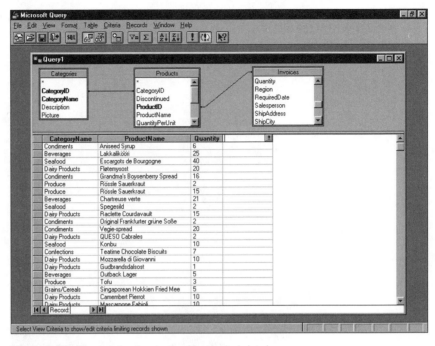

Figure 8-26: The total sales in the Northwind database.

Next we'll apply a restriction to this table. We are rarely interested in the entire contents of a database. Instead, we need the count of items sold in a given period, such as the first quarter of 1994 or a specific month only. Open the Criteria menu, and select Add Criteria. The Add Criteria dialog box will appear on your screen. Select the field on which the criteria will be based (Invoices. Order-Date) in the Field box. Then select "is between" in the Operator box, and in the Value box, enter the following:

01/01/1994, 31/03/1994

This criterion says that you want to retrieve only the invoices that were ordered during the first quarter of 1994 (see Figure 8-27). To specify a different period, adjust the two dates accordingly.

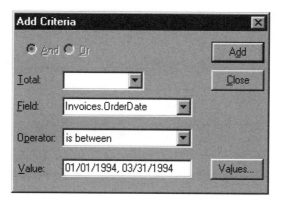

Figure 8-27: Specifying selection criteria for a query with the Add Criteria dialog box.

The Add Criteria dialog box simplifies the specification of selection criteria on the records you wish to retrieve.

As soon as you click on the Close button of the Add Criteria dialog box, a new table appears between the tables in the upper half of the window and the query results below. This table (see Figure 8-28) contains the criteria. Review the definition of the criteria you just entered to see how they are stored and how you can modify them. The Criteria Field box contains a field (or combination of fields) whose values will be checked against the contents of the Value box. In our case, the value of the field OrderDate will be compared against the two dates, and if it falls between them, the corresponding record will appear in the query. If not, the record will be ignored. You can modify the existing criteria, or add new ones, either directly in the table with the criteria or with the help of the Add Criteria command.

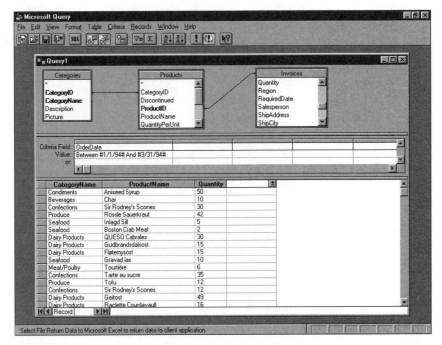

Figure 8-28: The definition of our query includes the tables, selected fields, and criteria.

On your screen you have a catalog of all products sold in the first quarter of 1994, along with the category they belong to. Let's improve the appearance of the results by sorting them according to category and by product name within each category. Select the first two columns (CategoryName and ProductName) by clicking on their gray title buttons while holding down the Shift key. All elements in the first two columns will be selected. Then click on the Sort Ascending button (the one with the letters *A* and *Z* and the arrow pointing down).

The rearranged query looks much better, but it contains many more lines than we need. All we wanted was the total sales for each product, not a complete list of each quantity sold. Select the last column by clicking on its title button. We want to calculate the totals for each product. Locate the Cycle through Totals button on the toolbar (it is the one with the Σ symbol), and click on it. The totals will be calculated, and your query should look like the one in Figure 8-29.

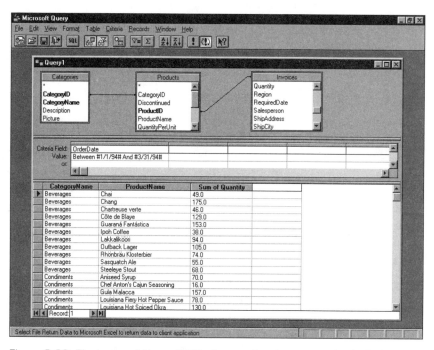

Figure 8-29: The query of Figure 8-26 after sorting the rows and calculating the totals for each product.

That's more like the data we're after. Yet, we would like to see the totals per category and the grand total. And then figure out the percentage of beverages in the company's total revenues. Or see what would happen if certain prices were raised or lowered. That's the kind of thing Excel does best, so let's get the data back to Excel.

Before returning the data to Excel let's save the query, so that we can use it again in the future. Open the File menu, and save the definition of your query with the Save As command. Enter any filename you wish. (Its default extension is .QRY.) You don't have to save the query here because Excel remembers it. Save it before you return to Excel, however, because we will use it later in the section "Point & Click Programming."

Once you've designed a query graphically, you can store it and use it again in the future.

Open the File menu again, and this time select Return Data to Microsoft Excel. You don't need to copy the data to the clipboard and then paste it on the worksheet. MSQuery will return the selected data to Excel automatically. You will be returned to Excel, and a dialog box will appear, asking you whether you want to keep the query definition (so that you can use it later), whether to include the field names, and a few more options. Just click on the OK button, and watch your data being pasted on the worksheet.

Now you can change the data in any way you wish. Change the titles of the columns, make them bold to stand out, adjust the width of the columns, and in general, change the appearance of the worksheet to suit your needs. Once the data is in place and you're satisfied with the way it looks, you can go ahead with more meaningful types of processing. One thing you might like to do with the data shown in Figure 8-29 is to create subtotals and totals per category.

Select Subtotals from the Data menu, and you'll see the dialog box shown in Figure 8-30. Use this dialog box to define how the subtotals should be calculated. Excel did a fairly good job at guessing what you want to do, so all you have to do in this case is click on the OK button.

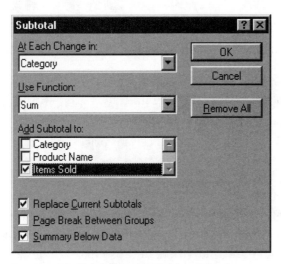

Figure 8-30: The Subtotal definition dialog box.

Excel calculates the subtotals from top to bottom, starting to calculate a new subtotal every time it finds a new category (see Figure 8-31). The values used in calculating the totals are the values of the Items Sold column. When it runs out of categories, it sums the subtotals to create a total for all entries.

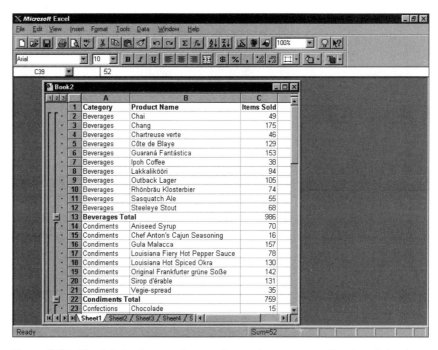

Figure 8-31: The total sales per item and per category, as an Excel worksheet.

Figure 8-31 shows how the subtotals are displayed on the worksheet. Click on the buttons labeled 1, 2, and 3 on the upper left corner of the worksheet to see the various subtotals: the totals per product, the totals per category, and the grand total. Now you can easily add new cells, with the percentage of each product in its category or the percentage of each category, and in general perform all the operations you'd use Excel for.

OLE Is Not Magic

To get a better feeling for what OLE can do for you, start Access, and change an invoice or two. Find an invoice that contains the item Mishi Kobe Niku, and change the quantity to a very large value. One invoice containing this item is invoice #809, as you can see in Figure 8-32. (To change this invoice, start Access, open the North-wind database, and select the Forms tab. Double-click on the name of the Orders Form and use the navigational keys to move to record #809.) Change the quantity of the Mishi Kobe Niku item from 6 to 600, and then move to the previous or next order to commit the change to the database. Return to your worksheet, and look up the row with the total sales for Mishi Kobe Niku. Nothing has changed. The linked data haven't been updated automatically. To refresh the worksheet's data, you must issue the Refresh Data command from the Data menu. Do so and examine your worksheet again.

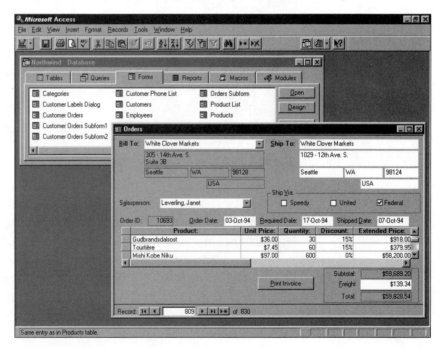

Figure 8-32: Change the quantity of an existing invoice in Access to see how it affects the query results.

Something has gone awry. You have the new data in the worksheet, but Access has placed the new values over the existing ones, without taking into account the rows that correspond to the subtotals you added. What is actually linked to the database is a range of cells. And when you refreshed the linked data, they were moved to their original position. OLE is not as intelligent as you would expect it, or as you would like it, to be. To update the linked data after changing it at its source, you must select the Refresh Data from Excel's Data menu. Moreover, you must not change the original arrangement of the linked data, or else any new cells you've created will be overwritten.

Data retrieved from databases are linked to the source but are not automatically updated.

Point & Click Programming

Do you know what you've been doing so far with all these point and click operations in the MSQuery application? You've just built a SQL statement, a command that instructs Access to retrieve the data you want from the database. We'll discuss SQL statements later in this chapter in the section "Understanding SQL Statements," but it's interesting to see how MSQuery converted your point and click operations into a small program. To see the SQL command MSQuery created to carry out your request, switch to MSQuery, and from the File menu, select Open Query. Select the filename in which you saved the query of the last example, and you will get back the query definition window (see Figure 8-28). Now click on the SQL button on MSQuery's toolbar. A window with the following text will be displayed:

```
SELECT Categories.CategoryName, Products.ProductName,
Invoices.Quantity
FROM C:\MSOffice\Access\Samples\Northwind.Categories Categories,
C:\MSOffice\Access\Samples\Northwind.Invoices Invoices,
C:\MSOffice\Access\Samples\Northwind.Products Products
WHERE Products.ProductID = Invoices.ProductID AND
Products.CategoryID = Categories.CategoryID AND
((Invoices.OrderDate Between {ts '1994-01-01 00:00:00'} And {ts
'1994-03-31 00:00:00'}))
```

This is a fairly simple SQL statement, yet quite a lengthy one. It represents all the actions we performed in the query example. If you read the SQL statement carefully, you'll understand what it does, even if you haven't used SQL statements before. It SELECTs three fields (CategoryName, ProductName, and Quantity) FROM three different tables (Categories, Products, and Invoices). The WHERE keyword specifies the restrictions. The ProductID field of the Invoices table must match the ProductID field of the Products table, so that we can view the product's name instead of its ID. The second restriction is that the CategoryID field in the Products and Categories tables should also match, so that we can view the actual category name instead of its ID. Finally, the OrderDate field of the Invoices table must fall between the two dates.

You may find SQL statements intimidating, but you needn't worry. You can specify them with simple point and click operations, as we just did. We will return shortly to the topic of SQL commands, but for now keep in mind that if you don't know how to write a SQL statement on your own, you can use MSQuery to do it for you.

M SQuery translates your point and click operations into small programs.

The Future of OLE

It's interesting to see where OLE will eventually lead. Let's use a before-and-after analogy. Before, the application was the starting and ending point. Each document had to be created and processed by the same application. The first versions of Excel were self-contained. They could handle worksheets and nothing else. Not only that, but the documents they created could not be handled by other applications either. (Sure, Lotus could read Excel worksheets—or spreadsheets, as they were called then—but this was just a conversion process.) You weren't thinking in terms of the document and what you could do with it. You were thinking in terms of the application that could create the document.

W indows 95 makes you think in terms of documents, rather than in terms of applications.

OLE is slowly forming the "after" picture. Now you don't think as much in terms of the application. Instead you shift your focus from the application to the document. When you see an icon called Neat Pictures on your desktop, you don't look for an application that can process images, start it, and then open the Neat pictures document. You just double-click on the icon, and expect the operating system to figure out what to do with the pictures. The document may not even contain pictures at all. It may be a text file describing how to shoot great pictures. No matter what it is, you will find out within seconds, once you double-click on the icon.

When creating a report that includes numbers and charts, you don't think of switching to Excel to prepare them and then import them to the document. You start a new document in Word and embed, or link, the appropriate objects as you go along. These objects may be new, or may reside in existing documents. You don't limit yourself to tables because that's all Word can handle. You use all the objects your computer (that is, the operating system and the installed applications) can handle. Whether Word handles the numbers and graphs, or it relies on another application, isn't your business. You just want to get the job done, and the job is to create a new document.

Applications aren't the center of the universe any more. They are just tools. They become less and less important, until they reach a point where they are indistinguishable from the operating system. They will be little pieces of intelligence, floating around in the operating system, waiting to provide their services when asked. A typical example of this situation is spell-checking. There used to be stand-alone spell checkers. Then they were incorporated into applications. Now they are part of the operating system. Did you notice that all Microsoft applications use the same spell checking engine? Is it part of a specific application, or part of the operating system? An even better example is the Sound Recorder. You no longer need to start the Sound Recorder to record a sound and then insert it in a document. You just insert the sound in your document and when you want to hear it, you borrow the Sound Recorder's functionality from within any document.

This trend will continue. We'll reach a point when individual applications will be merely extensions to the operating system, and we'll not think much of them. The applications will complement the operating system more or less the same way application extensions complement other applications today.

A_t some point applications will be blended with the operating system to provide the tools we need to manage documents.

In Figure 8-33 you see Picture Publisher, an image-editing application and some special effects it can perform on images. Yet, the special effects did not come with Picture Publisher, neither were they developed by the same company. They are specialized tools that help you process images in ways that were not possible with the original application. You can think of the Picture Publisher application as the "operating system for images" and its filters as the little pieces of intelligence that are available when you need them. They are not built into the application, and you can use them only if you have them installed on your computer. However, you don't think of them as applications. They are there where you need them, and for all you care, they could be part of the operating system.

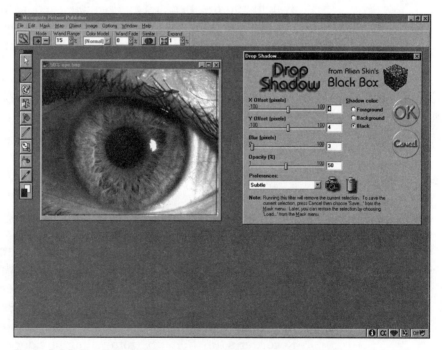

Figure 8-33: The Drop Shadow dialog box provides additional features (special effects) to the Picture Publisher application, similar to the way OLE-capable applications can lend their functionality to other applications.

PROGRAMMING OLE AUTOMATION

So far, we've explored the no-programming approach to OLE. Even this approach can get complicated, as the last example demonstrated. You can use OLE to help you coordinate your applications and make them work together without any programming requirements on your part. As a power user, however, you will eventually look for programmatic ways to automate different OLE processes. Automating OLE operations requires a little programming, but it will save you a lot of trivial steps, which you would have to perform manually otherwise. Fortunately, programming OLE actions isn't as complicated as programming in other computer languages. Much of what you want to do is already built into the applications, and all you must do is put the built-in functionality to work for you. The example in the section "Making Database Queries" was an example of OLE Automation, except MSQuery took care of the programming. It created a SQL statement, which it used later to refresh the data.

The Mechanics of OLE

To better understand how to automate OLE operations, you must first understand how it is possible for an application to use the menus and toolbars of another application. OLE is an object-based technology. Applications include their own objects. Some of them let you control the application, similar to the way you use certain objects (such as the steering wheel) to drive a car. Other objects are internal to the applications, similar to the objects in your car's engine, and you can't access them. An application "exposes" some of its objects to another application, so that the external application can control the objects. Excel, for example, can expose various objects: a single cell, a range of cells, even an entire workbook. The external application can use commands that Excel understands and can manipulate the exposed object. For example, a program could add new columns to a worksheet, increase the values of a range of cells by 10 percent, and then read the results.

B y exposing some of their objects, applications can lend their functionality to other applications.

In order to use OLE Automation, therefore, you must know the objects exposed by each application and the commands each object understands. Mastering the objects isn't difficult because they are the basic objects you use when you work with an application. How about the commands, though? Different applications use different commands, because they accomplish different tasks. Excel, for example, has commands for manipulating the values of individual cells. These commands wouldn't be of much use in Word. Similarly, Word provides commands for manipulating and formatting text. These commands would be of little use to Access, which has its own commands for manipulating databases.

The Role of VBA

The lack of a common programming language is indeed a sore point in OLE Automation. To simplify matters, Microsoft has been building a standard language for OLE Automation. It's based on the extremely successful Visual Basic language, and it's called Visual Basic for Applications (or VBA for short). VBA is easy to learn—you may be using Visual Basic already. Excel, for example, uses VBA as its internal programming language. The same is true for Access. If only Word would use it! Unfortunately, Word doesn't use VBA. Its programming language is called WordBasic, and although it bears some resemblance to VBA, it's not VBA. So many users use Word macros on a daily basis, and Microsoft can't abandon them. The plans of the company, however, are to make VBA the "glue" behind its Office applications. VBA will be a universal language for Windows, which will allow programmers and power users to customize their applications and integrate them as they wish.

VBA is not a common language for all Office applications. It is a foundation, which provides a few common mechanisms and every individual application adds its own commands (or extensions) to the language. Some of the most basic VBA commands and mechanisms were covered in the previous chapter. In this chapter we will offer a few useful examples, which demonstrate many aspects of OLE Automation and will explain the commands we are going to use. One way to learn VBA and use it to automate OLE operations is to get a feeling for the language and then look up the help files of each application and the examples. VBA is sometimes referred to as the "glue" among OLE-capable applications. You can also think of VBA as the Windows batch language. It's not nearly as simple as the DOS batch language, but Windows is a much more powerful environment than DOS.

VBA is the "glue" that makes all Office applications work in harmony.

The Origins of OLE Automation

Microsoft's first attempt to make applications talk to each other was a mechanism called DDE, for dynamic data exchange. It was a simple mechanism that allowed two running applications to exchange commands and data. DDE was rather short-lived. OLE Automation made it almost obsolete; not completely obsolete, because not all Office applications can be OLE automated. Word, for example, can't control other applications by any other means beyond DDE. A short introduction to DDE will not only help you automate certain tasks from within Word, it will also help you appreciate the role of VBA in the operating system.

Exchanging Data With DDE

DDE is a simple mechanism, based on a few commands. Before we present the commands, let's explain briefly the basic mechanism of dynamic data exchange. Two applications can exchange data and commands by engaging in a DDE conversation. In a DDE conversation, one application controls the conversation, and it is called the *client*. When Word asks Excel to carry out some calculations or provide the values of certain cells, Word is the *client* application (the one that sends the commands or "orders" the other application). Excel is the *server* (the application that serves the client). The DDE conversation is initiated by the client application. It is also the client application's responsibility to terminate the conversation.

In a DDE conversation, one application makes the requests, and the other one provides the data.

Let's take a look at the steps involved, and the corresponding DDE commands.

The command to initiate a conversation is appropriately named DDEInitiate, and its syntax is:

```
channel = DDEInitiate(application, topic)
```

Application is the name of the server application, and *topic* is usually the name of a file the server application can handle. The topics are the names of the server application files open at the time. To initiate a DDE conversation with Excel and request data that reside in the file SALES.XLS, you should issue the command:

```
channel = DDEInitiate("Microsoft Excel","C:\DATA\SALES.XLS")
```

(You replace the pathname of the SALES.XLS file with that of the Excel file on your disk.) The conversation will be established only if the server application is running at the time. Here's a typical sequence of commands for initiating a DDE conversation and opening the server application:

```
If AppIsRunning("Microsoft Excel") = 0 Then Shell
"c:\msoffice\excel\excel.exe c:\msoffice\excel\sales"
channel = DDEInitiate("Excel", "sheet2")
```

Make sure the server application is running before you attempt to establish a DDE conversation.

The AppIsRunning function returns zero if the application isn't running. In this case, you can start the server application with the Shell command. Notice that you can also specify the name of the workbook, or worksheet, you want to work with in the Shell command. In the DDEInitiate command, we specified the worksheet we want to work with.

If communication is established, the DDEInitiate command returns a channel number, a special number that must be used in all subsequent commands. (Multiple DDE conversations can be going on at the same time, and each one has a different channel number.)

Once the commands have been issued to open the DDE conversation, Word can send data and commands to Excel, or it can receive data. It must use the channel number returned by the DDEInitiate command, and all commands will operate on the workbook or worksheet specified in the DDEInitiate command.

The most common operation is for Word to request a range of cells, which is accomplished with the DDERequest command. DDERequest is a function that accepts two arguments: the channel number of a DDE conversation and a topic. The topic is the specification of the information to be retrieved. For Excel, the topic would be a range of cells. The following command requests the values in the range from A1 to C19 from the Sheet2 worksheet of the Sales workbook. Notice that the DDERequest command doesn't recognize named ranges or other forms of range specifications. You must use the Row Column convention to reference ranges in Excel.

Once you've established communication between two applications, use the DDERequest command to make requests.

```
s$ = DDERequest$(channel, "R1C1:R19C6")
```

The specified range contains a summary of sales figures, as shown in Figure 8-34.

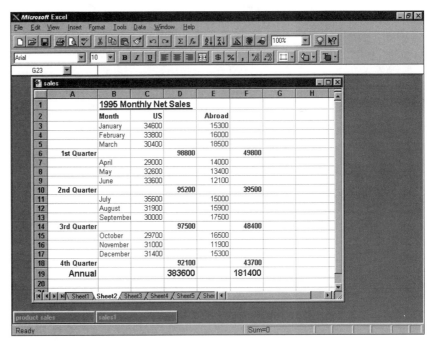

Figure 8-34: The sales figures used in this example are in an Excel workbook.

The requested data are stored in the *s$* variable, and from there, it can be inserted into the document with the Insert command. Here is complete WordBasic macro that requests the previous range of data from Excel:

```
Sub MAIN
If AppIsRunning("Microsoft Excel") = 0 Then
Shell "c:\msoffice\excel\excel.exe c:\msoffice\excel\sales"
EndIf
channel = DDEInitiate("Excel", "sheet2")
s$ = DDERequest$(channel, "R1C1:R19C6")
Insert s$
DDETerminate channel
End Sub
```

As explained in the previous chapter, create this new macro in Word, name it GetExcelData, and run it. Once the data is inserted into the current document, you can edit it, convert it to a table, and Autoformat it with the Table|Autoformat command. The process of requesting the data from Excel and formatting it in Word is demonstrated in Figures 8-35 and 8-36. Notice the last command in the macro: the DDETerminate command ends a DDE conversation and returns the resources to the system. If you don't terminate a DDE conversation explicitly, it remains active until you exit Word.

Always terminate a DDE conversation with the DDETerminate command.

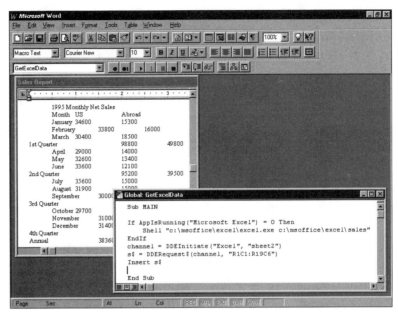

Figure 8-35: Run the GetExcelData macro to automatically start Excel, open the Sales workbook, and get the sales figures.

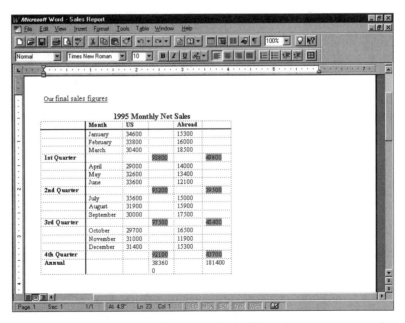

Figure 8-36: Once the sales figures are in the Word document, you can format them as text, or convert them to a table and Autoformat the table.

Controlling Word From Excel With VBA

In the earlier examples, you saw how to link Excel data to a Word document to create a report. We've also shown you how to request Excel data from within Word. This time we'll use a short Excel macro to send data to Word, format it, and finally save the document under a filename. Given the inefficiencies of DDE, this is the preferred way to automate the two applications—from within Excel.

One of the major advantages of VBA is its ability to send commands directly to Word. While Word is limited to DDE commands only, Excel can send any WordBasic command to Word, which in turn will execute it. Let's see how this is done.

One of the objects exposed by Word is WordBasic itself. Once Excel can see the WordBasic object, it can send any command WordBasic understands and automate many OLE tasks. This is an excellent demonstration of the benefits of working with objects. By exposing a single object, Word makes itself available to any other application that supports VBA.

By exposing its programming language, Word allows other applications to control it.

Let's say that one of your tasks is to prepare a Word report about the monthly sales figures, similar to the report in Figure 8-37. The data used to prepare this report originates in an Excel worksheet, as shown in Figure 38-8.

Let's follow the steps of automating this task, without even opening Word. We'll write a VBA macro to automate this process within Excel's environment.

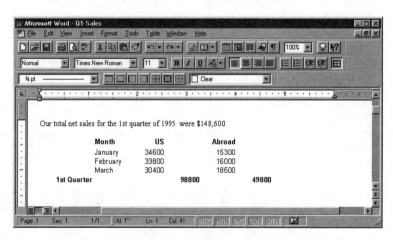

Figure 8-37: This Word document was prepared entirely from within Excel.

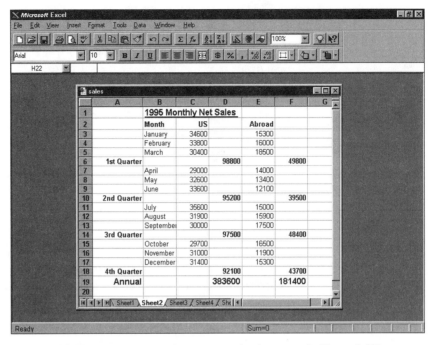

Figure 8-38: This data was used to prepare the document in Figure 8-37.

To create a new macro in Excel, add a macro module sheet to the current workbook (if there isn't one already) as explained in Chapter 7. Then create a new macro with the Macro command of the Tools menu. The first step is to establish communication with Word, by gaining access to the WordBasic object. This is done with the CreateObject command:

```
Set WordObj = CreateObject("Word.Basic")
```

You can automate Word through its WordBasic object.

CreateObject is a VBA function that establishes a link with an object of another application. One of objects Word can expose is its built-in language. After establishing a link to WordBasic, you can manipulate Word from within Excel, by sending any command to it.

As soon as we gain access to the WordBasic object, we create a new document and then save it under a filename. By doing so immediately, we don't have to worry about assigning a filename later on. We can simply save the file when we're finished with it.

The WordBasic command to create a new file is (what else) FileNew. And as you probably guessed, the commands to save it are FileSave and FileSaveAs. Here's the VBA code that accesses WordBasic and creates a new Word file:

```
Set WordObj = CreateObject("Word.Basic")
WordObj.FileNew
WordObj.FileSaveAs ("Sales for Q1 1995")
{more commands}
WordObj.FileSave
WordObj.Exit
Set WordObj = Nothing
```

The preceding example is a skeleton for creating macros to control Word. The last command tells VBA that we no longer need the link between Excel and Word. In other words, it disposes of the WordObj object, and any resources allocated to this link are returned to the system.

TIP

Be careful with the filenames you choose. If the filename used to save the new file exists, Word overwrites it without confirmation.

Let's insert some commands in this macro. We'll create commands that add a line of text and then the data for the Word report. The WordBasic command to do this as you recall from the previous chapter, is Insert. First, we are going to calculate the total, format it, and then pass it as an argument to the Insert command:

```
TotalQuarter = Worksheets(2).Range("D6").Value +
Worksheets(2).Range("F6").Value
 txt$ = "Our total net sales for the 1st quarter of 1995 "
 txt$ = txt$ + " were " + Format$(TotalQuarter, "$###,###")
 WordObj.Insert txt$
 WordObj.InsertPara
```

The total sales are the sum of the cells D6 and F6 (sum of domestic and overseas sales). Then we format the result as a dollar amount with the Format$() function and form the sentence we want to insert in the document. The Format$() function accepts a numeric argument (148600) and returns the same number as a string ($148,600).

Next we are going to copy a range from the worksheet and paste it into the Word document. Instead of specifying a range by address, you can assign a name to the range. Switch back to the worksheet tab that holds the data, and select the range of cells you want to name. Then open the Insert menu, select Name, and from its submenu, select Define. You will see a dialog box similar to the one in Figure 8-39.

It is possible to refer to a cell or range by name, rather than its address.

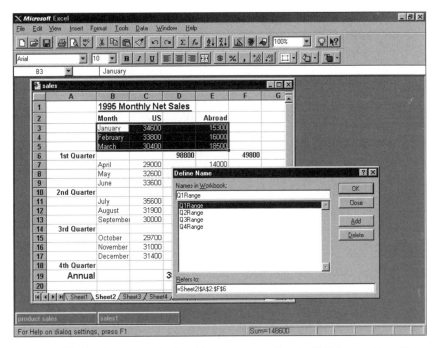

Figure 8-39: Naming ranges in Excel is most convenient in OLE Automation. Not only do you not have to remember cell addresses, you can even change the size of the range without affecting the operation of the macro.

Type the name by which you want to refer to the selected cells ("Q1Range" for this example). From now on, you can address all selected cells with the construct Range ("Q1Range"). Switch back to the macro module tab, and continue writing the macro. To copy the cells to the clipboard, use the method Copy:

```
Range("Q1Range").Copy
```

Finally, once the named range is on the clipboard, you can send the EditPasteSpecial command to WordBasic to paste the data in the current document and link it to the original worksheet. Once the Excel data is pasted in the document, you can save the document and close it. The WordBasic commands you need are properly named FileSave and Close. Here is the complete code for creating the document shown in Figure 8-38 from within Excel, as a subroutine:

```
Sub MakeQuarterReport()
 Set WordObj = CreateObject("Word.Basic")
 WordObj.FileNew
 WordObj.FileSaveAs ("Q1 Sales")
 TotalQuarter = Worksheets(2).Range("D6").Value +
Worksheets(2).Range("F6").Value
 txt$ = "Our total net sales for the 1st quarter of 1995 "
 txt$ = txt$ + " were " + Format$(TotalQuarter, "$###,###")
 WordObj.Insert txt$
 WordObj.InsertPara
 WordObj.InsertPara
 Worksheets(2).Range("Q1Range").Copy
 WordObj.EditPasteSpecial
 WordObj.InsertPara
 WordObj.InsertPara

 WordObj.FileSave
 WordObj.FileClose

 Set WordObj = Nothing

End Sub
```

Insert these lines in a macro, and every time you want to create this report, just run it. To create a new document with the figures of the second quarter, you must change a few references in this macro. The "Q1Range" range must be replaced with "Q2Range", and the references to the cells D6 and F6 must also be modified.

With some extra effort you can further automate this process by using named ranges for all four quarters. Then you can prompt the user for the quarter he or she wants to create a report. In the following macro, we use the InputBox function to get user input. The InputBox function displays a box like the one in Figure 8-40, in which the user can type the number of the quarter for which he or she wants to generate a report. Then the program examines the value returned by the InputBox function and proceeds accordingly. If the value is an empty string, it means the user has clicked on the Cancel button and the program quit. If the value is outside the range 1 to 4, the program displays a message and quits.

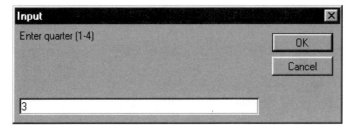

Figure 8-40: The Input dialog box prompts the user to enter the quarter for which he or she wants to generate a report.

Once the program verifies that the user has entered a valid value, it creates the appropriate references (file name, address of partial totals, range to be copied) and uses them to send the appropriate commands to Word. Here is the complete code of the MakeReport subroutine:

```
Sub MakeReport()
 quarter = InputBox("Enter quarter (1-4)")
 If quarter = "" Then Exit Sub
 If quarter < 1 Or quarter > 4 Then
 MsgBox "Invalid quarter value!"
 Exit Sub
 End If
 FileName$ = "Q" + Format$(quarter, "#") + " Sales"
 CellRange = "Q" + Format$(quarter, "3") + "Range"
 Total1Cell = "D" + Format$(2 + 4 * quarter)
 Total2Cell = "F" + Format$(2 + 4 * quarter)
 Set WordObj = CreateObject("Word.Basic")
 WordObj.FileNew
 WordObj.FileSaveAs (FileName$)
 TotalQuarter = Worksheets(2).Range(Total1Cell).Value +
Worksheets(2).Range(Total2Cell).Value
 txt$ = "Our total net sales for the "
 If quarter = 1 Then q$ = "1st"
 If quarter = 2 Then q$ = "2nd"
 If quarter = 3 Then q$ = "3rd"
 If quarter = 4 Then q$ = "4th"
 txt$ = txt$ + q$ + " quarter of 1995 "
 txt$ = txt$ + " were " + Format$(TotalQuarter, "$###,###")
 WordObj.Insert txt$
 WordObj.InsertPara
 WordObj.InsertPara
 Range(CellRange).Copy
 WordObj.EditPasteSpecial
 WordObj.InsertPara
 WordObj.InsertPara

 WordObj.FileSave
 WordObj.FileClose

 Set WordObj = Nothing

End Sub
```

This example was pretty simple, but it is intended to demonstrate the basic mechanism of OLE Automation between Excel and Word. No matter how complicated the worksheet is, or how many cells it contains, all you need is the value of a few cells to create a report. The rest of the commands add the appropriate text and format it. They are WordBasic commands, which you don't even have to type yourself. Record a macro in Word, and use it from within Excel by prefixing every Word command with WordObj, or whatever you have named the Word.Obj object with the CreateObject command.

Controlling Access From Excel

An earlier example in this chapter dealt with controlling Access from within Excel. As you saw in the section "Making Database Queries," when you use the command Get External Data, to retrieve Access data, Excel (actually MSQuery) builds a SQL expression. It is possible to build a SQL statement yourself and pass it to Access with the help of VBA. Building SQL statements is not always as simple as in the examples of that section. They can get quite complicated. However, you can automate many useful tasks with simple SQL statements, and we'll show you a few in the examples in this section. You can pick up a lot about SQL statements by building them with MSQuery, or Access, and examining their definitions. If your daily work calls for extensive use of SQL statements, you'll eventually have to buy a more specific book.

Access Objects

You can program Access databases through the Data Access Object.

To use VBA commands to control Access, you must know a little about the Data Access Object (DAO). The main object in DAO is the Database object. A database is made up of tables, which contain fields and records. You can find out what tables make up a database by opening the database in Access and examining the tables and their relationships. If someone else has designed the database, you should ask for help or, even better, have the database administrator provide the SQL statements you need.

Every time you retrieve information from Access, a temporary storage area, called *Recordset*, is created. A Recordset is a set of records from one or more tables, selected according to user-specified criteria. The list of customers from Germany, France, and Switzerland form a Recordset. They all come from a single table, and the criteria are the countries of origin. The sales figures we used in another example come from multiple tables, and they also meet certain criteria (they were sold within a given time period). The Recordset was placed on the Excel worksheet for you automatically. It is also possible to manipulate it with VBA commands. Let's see how you can create and manipulate Recordsets.

The Database Object

At first, you must tell Excel that you'll be using the Data Access Object, or DAO. DAO is similar to the WordBasic object, which gave you access to Word's programming language. This object gives you access to Access's objects and programming language. From Excel's Tools menu, select References, and you'll see a list of objects Excel understands, as in Figure 8-41. Check the item Microsoft DAO 3.0 Object Library, and click on the OK button. From now on, you can manipulate Access and its databases through the Data Access Object.

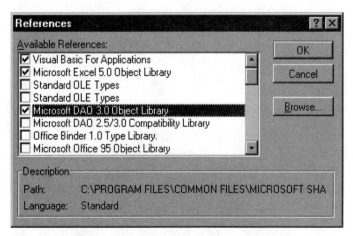

Figure 8-41: By exposing the DAO, Access lets other applications control its databases.

You can automate Access through the Data Access Object.

Before presenting an actual macro to automate Access, we'll look at the commands we're going to need, explain a few basic concepts, and explore SQL statements. We'll cover a few simple commands for opening a database and creating Recordsets, which you'll need in just about every macro that controls Access. Then we'll put these commands together to create an Excel macro.

In order to access databases, you must first create a Database object. Unlike other objects, the Database object can't be placed on a form, or document. You must open them with the OpenDatabase command and then manipulate it through the Recordset object, which is explained next. The OpenDatabase command, in its simplest form, has the following syntax:

```
MyDB = OpenDatabase(DBName)
```

DBName is the name of the database you want to open. The OpenDatabase command accepts a few more optional arguments, such as whether you want to open it as read-only, whether you'll allow other users to access the database while you work on it, and so on. Consult the documentation or online help for more information on the various arguments of the OpenDatabase command. *MyDB* is a database variable, which will be used later in every command that makes use of the database. The MyDB variable can be declared as:

```
Dim MyDB As Database
```

but this declaration is optional. VBA knows it is a database variable once you assign a database to it with the OpenDatabase command. To open the Northwind database, use the command:

```
MyDB = OpenDatabase("C:\MSOFFICE\ACCESS\SAMPLES\NORTHWIND")
```

The remaining parameters have their default values and need not be included in the statement.

Once the Database variable (which holds a Database object) has been created, you can perform a number of actions on it. The Database object provides numerous commands for examining, or modifying, its contents. In the following paragraphs we will explain only a few basic commands that we will need for our examples.

The way to access the records of a database is through Recordsets. A recordset is a collection of records. It can be an entire table, such as all the customers; or part of a table, such as all customers overseas; or combined records from multiple tables, such as all customers whose orders have exceeded a certain amount. The method to create a Recordset is called OpenRecordset, and it applies to the Database object. Its syntax is:

```
OpenRecordset(Select Criteria)
```

where *Select Criteria* is a table name or a valid SQL statement. The command:

```
CustomerSet = OpenRecordset("Customers")
```

retrieves all the rows of the Customers table and stores them in the *CustomerSet* variable. You will see shortly how Recordsets are handled, but first we must talk about SQL statements, since you can't do much without them.

Understanding SQL Statements

SQL is a language for manipulating databases, and a rather old one. Unlike most programming and macro languages, SQL is a nonprocedural language. In other words, there are no procedures (subroutines or functions), and it operates at a much higher level than other languages. A nonprocedural language is one that is told what to do, but not how to do it. For example, you can issue a SQL command to ask for all invoices issued to certain customers in the first quarter of 1995. How the computer does it is not your concern. The mechanism that performs the query and reports the results is complicated, but fortunately SQL hides from you.

Use SQL statements to specify the data you want to retrieve from a database.

SQL provides many commands, for all types of operations you'd want to perform on a database. Covering the entire range of SQL commands is beyond the scope of this book. We'll show you only a few basic SQL commands for retrieving data from databases, because this is mostly what you'll need them for. They are called *select statements* (as opposed to *action statements*, which allow you to actually manipulate the database).

SQL statements begin with a verb that indicates the kind of action to be performed on the database. For example, the SELECT verb indicates that certain records must be selected. The UPDATE verb updates certain records in the database, while the DELETE verb deletes records. In this chapter, we'll explore the SELECT verb only, which lets you retrieve data from the database and put it into a Recordset.

The SELECT verb is followed by the names of the fields on which the verb acts and by the keyword FROM, which specifies the table from which the records will be read. Here's a statement that extracts all customer names along with the company names:

```
SELECT CustomerName, CompanyName FROM Customers
```

The corresponding OpenRecordset method looks like this:

```
CustomerSet = OpenRecordset("SELECT CustomerName, CompanyName
FROM Customers")
```

where *CustomerSet* is a Recordset variable, declared as:

```
Dim CustomerSet As Recordset
```

The result of a SQL query is stored in a Recordset object.

(You don't have to declare the variable. VBA automatically creates a Recordset variable as soon as you assign a Recordset to it.)

Notice that the SQL statement is enclosed in a pair of parentheses. Alternatively, you may assign it to a string variable and use the variable in the SQL statement:

```
SQL$ = "SELECT CustomerName, CompanyName FROM Customers"
CustomerSet = OpenRecordset(SQL$)
```

This technique is used with long SQL statements to make the code easier to read.

You can also apply restrictions to the records to be extracted, with the WHERE keyword. To retrieve the names of German customers only, use the following SQL statement:

```
SELECT CustomerName, CompanyName FROM Customers
WHERE Country = "Germany"
```

And the corresponding OpenRecordset method:

```
SQL$ = "SELECT CustomerName, CompanyName FROM Customers"
SQL$ = SQL$ + "WHERE Country = 'Germany' "
GermanCustomerSet = OpenRecordset(SQL$)
```

Notice that strings within SQL statements are enclosed in single quotes. Double quotes delimit the SQL statement itself.

Manipulating Recordsets

Now that we've created a Recordset, what can we do with it? Recordsets have properties, which make it possible to manipulate them programmatically. The RecordCount property, for example, returns the number of records in the Recordset:

```
Recs = CustomerSet.RecordCount
```

The *Recs* variable holds the number of records you've retrieved from the Customers table.

Our goal is to place the Recordset in an Excel worksheet. To do so, we'll use VBA's CopyFromRecordset method in the Excel macro we're building. The command:

```
Worksheet(1).Cells(1, 1).CopyFromRecordset(CustomerSet)
```

copies all the records of the Recordset on the worksheet, starting at cell (1, 1) and moving down and to the right.

You can send SQL statements to Access from within any application, as long as it has access to the DAO.

Putting the Macro Together

Let's put the previous commands together to create an Excel macro. Start Excel with a new workbook or select a new worksheet, add a module sheet, and start a new macro. Then type the following commands:

```
Sub GetCustomers()
 Set DB = OpenDatabase("C:\MSOFFICE\ACCESS\SAMPLES\NORTHWIND")
 SQL$ = "SELECT CustomerID, CompanyName FROM Customers"
 Set CustomerSet = DB.OpenRecordset(SQL$)
 Set DataRange = Worksheets(1)
 DataRange.Cells(2, 2).CopyFromRecordset (CustomerSet)
End Sub
```

All records in the Customers table will be copied to the worksheet, starting at the cell (2, 2), or any other cell you may have specified in the macro. The CopyFromRecordset method performs a simple copy; it doesn't link the data to the database, but neither does Excel. Data retrieved from databases must be refreshed manually. In the example in the section "Making Database Queries," you used Excel's Refresh Data command. Now you must run the GetCustomers macro again to refresh the data.

More SQL Statements

Let's move to a more complicated queries that involve numeric calculations, too. This time we'll ask Access to calculate the total net sales made by Northwind Corporation. Detailed sales data reside in the Order Details table of the Northwind database. The total net is the sum of all quantities times the price minus the corresponding discount. The SQL statement that calculates the sum is:

```
SELECT SUM(Quantity*UnitPrice*(1-Discount)) FROM [Order Details]
```

We multiply each item's quantity by its price (minus the discount percentage), and we add it to the sum. (SUM is a built-in function that calculates the sum of its argument for all records.) The macro GetTotalSales retrieves the total net sales from the database and stores it in the first cell of the second worksheet:

```
Sub GetSalesTotal()

Set SalesDB = OpenDatabase("C:\MSOFFICE\ACCESS\SAMPLES\NORTHWIND")
SQL$ = "SELECT SUM(Quantity*UnitPrice*(1-Discount))"
SQL$ = SQL$ + " FROM [Order Details]"
Set RecSet = SalesDB.OpenRecordset(SQL$)
Set DataRange = Worksheets(2)
DataRange.Cells(1, 1).CopyFromRecordset (RecSet)

End Sub
```

This total value isn't very helpful, since it includes all sales recorded in the database. A more meaningful number would be the sales figure for a given month or quarter. All we have to do is add a restriction to the query, namely, that it should look up records within a given time period.

This restriction introduces an additional complication. The Order Details table doesn't contain dates. The dates are stored in the Orders table. We must somehow combine the two tables to get the results we want. The main restriction is that the date the invoice was issued must fall within two dates. Every time Access finds an invoice that matches the previous criteria (was issued between the two dates), it should look up the details in the Order Details table whose ID matches the ID of the invoice. The statement that retrieves all the invoices issued in the first quarter of 1994 is:

You can combine records from multiple tables with the proper restrictions in a SQL statement.

```
SELECT SUM(Quantity*UnitPrice*(1-Discount)) FROM [Order Details]
WHERE [Order Details].OrderID = Orders.OrderID AND
(Orders.ShippedDate Between #1/1/94# AND #3/31/94#)
```

The following subroutine retrieves the total sales for the first quarter from the Northwind database and stores the result in the cell (3, 3). It is very similar to the GetSalesTotal subroutine, except this one extracts the sales figures for the first quarter of 1994.

```
Sub Q1Sales()
Dim SalesDB As Database

 Set SalesDB =
OpenDatabase("C:\MSOFFICE\ACCESS\SAMPLES\NORTHWIND")
 SQL$ = "SELECT SUM(Quantity*UnitPrice*(1-Discount)) "
 SQL$ = SQL$ + " FROM [Order Details] WHERE [Order
Details].OrderID = Orders.OrderID"
 SQL$ = SQL$ + " AND (Orders.ShippedDate Between #1/1/94# AND
#3/31/94#)"
 Set SalesSet = SalesDB.OpenRecordset(SQL$)
 Set DataRange = Worksheets(4)
 DataRange.Cells(3, 3).CopyFromRecordset (SalesSet)
End Sub
```

This SQL statement is quite lengthy but very similar to the previous one. Let's start with the restriction, which follows the WHERE keyword. The construct:

```
WHERE [Order Details].OrderID = Orders.OrderID
```

tells Access to combine the Order Details and Orders tables based on the value of the OrderID, which must be common to both. Our next restriction is that the invoice's shipping date is between 1/1/1994 and 3/31/1994 and is expressed as:

```
WHERE Orders.ShippedDate Between #1/1/94# AND #3/31/94#
```

The ShippedDate field of the Orders table is the invoice's shipping date. The two restrictions are combined with the AND operator (we are interested only in records that meet both restrictions).

Based on the last example, you can easily write a macro that retrieves the total net sales per quarter and displays it in a worksheet. Below is the code that produced the result of Figure 8-42. The YearSales subroutine is very similar to Q1Sales, but it contains code for all four quarters and formats the result.

```
Sub YearSales()
Dim SalesDB As Database

Set SalesDB = OpenDatabase("C:\MSOFFICE\ACCESS\SAMPLES\NORTHWIND")
SQL$ = "SELECT SUM(Quantity*UnitPrice*(1-Discount)) "
SQL$ = SQL$ + " FROM [Order Details], Orders "
SQL$ = SQL$ + " WHERE [Order Details].OrderID = Orders.OrderID AND "
SQL$ = SQL$ + "Orders.ShippedDate Between #1/1/94# AND #3/31/94#"
Set SalesSet = SalesDB.OpenRecordset(SQL$)
Set DataRange = Worksheets(4)
With DataRange
.Cells(3, 4) = "1st Quarter"
.Cells(3, 4).Font.Bold = True
.Cells(4, 4).NumberFormat = "$#,##0.00"
.Cells(4, 4).CopyFromRecordset (SalesSet)
End With

SQL$ = "SELECT SUM(Quantity*UnitPrice*(1-Discount)) "
SQL$ = SQL$ + " FROM [Order Details], Orders"
SQL$ = SQL$ + " WHERE [Order Details].OrderID = Orders.OrderID AND "
SQL$ = SQL$ + "Orders.ShippedDate Between #4/1/94# AND #6/30/94#"
Set SalesSet = SalesDB.OpenRecordset(SQL$)
With DataRange
.Cells(3, 5) = "2nd Quarter"
.Cells(3, 5).Font.Bold = True
.Cells(4, 5).NumberFormat = "$#,##0.00"
.Cells(4, 5).CopyFromRecordset (SalesSet)
End With

SQL$ = "SELECT SUM(Quantity*UnitPrice*(1-Discount)) "
SQL$ = SQL$ + " FROM [Order Details], Orders "
SQL$ = SQL$ + " WHERE [Order Details].OrderID = Orders.OrderID AND "
SQL$ = SQL$ + "Orders.ShippedDate Between #7/1/94# AND #10/31/94#"
Set SalesSet = SalesDB.OpenRecordset(SQL$)
Set DataRange = Worksheets(4)
With DataRange
.Cells(3, 6) = "3rd Quarter"
.Cells(3, 6).Font.Bold = True
.Cells(4, 6).NumberFormat = "$#,##0.00"
.Cells(4, 6).CopyFromRecordset (SalesSet)
End With
```

```
SQL$ = "SELECT SUM(Quantity*UnitPrice*(1-Discount)) "
SQL$ = SQL$ + " FROM [Order Details], Orders "
SQL$ = SQL$ + " WHERE [Order Details].OrderID = Orders.OrderID AND "
SQL$ = SQL$ + "Orders.ShippedDate Between #10/1/94# AND #12/31/94#"
Set SalesSet = SalesDB.OpenRecordset(SQL$)
With DataRange
.Cells(3, 7) = "4th Quarter"
.Cells(3, 7).Font.Bold = True
.Cells(4, 7).NumberFormat = "$#,##0.00"
.Cells(4, 7).CopyFromRecordset (SalesSet)
End With

DataRange.Cells(1, 4).Value = "Northwind Corp. Sales Report"
DataRange.Cells(2, 4).Value = "Net Sales Per Quarter for 1994"
DataRange.Cells(1, 4).Font.ColorIndex = 3
DataRange.Cells(2, 4).Font.Size = 12
End Sub
```

Notice the use of the With structure, which eliminates unnecessary typing. Without it, you would have to type "DataRange" in front of each line between the With/End With statements. The code for this macro could easily be shorter if we used a loop to go through each quarter, since only the address of the cell that accepts the result and the date changes. However, we assumed that most readers are not as familiar with VBA and would prefer a lengthier, but easier to read, code.

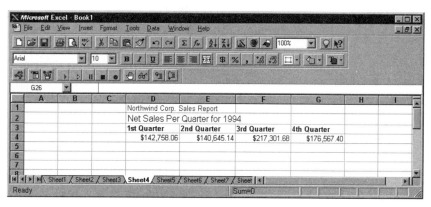

Figure 8-42: Total net sales per quarter, calculated by SQL statements directly on the Northwind database.

NOT THE END

With the discussion of Windows 95's OLE and OLE automation techniques, this book comes to an end. As we mentioned in the Introduction, this book was intended to address advanced topics for the average Windows 95 user. The discussion of the Registry, the collection of customization tips in Chapter 3, the optimization techniques presented in Chapter 4, the networking techniques covered in Chapters 5 and 6, and finally our introduction to Windows 95 programming and automation techniques in the last two chapters were the topics we thought were not adequately covered in most of the other books on the market. We didn't set ourselves to write the ultimate Windows 95 book, or attempt to cover every secret and shortcut of the new operating system. We included just what we thought would help you, the average or power user of Windows 95, make the most of your new operating system.

In this effort, we may have missed a few topics that are important to you. We are also sure we'll discover new interesting and useful tips as we continue to work with Windows 95. We will incorporate them into future versions of this book. In the mean time, we will post them in the *Windows 95 Power Toolkit Online Companion*. Drop in from time to time to see what's new, or leave us messages with suggestions, corrections, tips, and techniques you come across them. Our address on the World Wide Web is http://www.vmedia.com/win95.html. See Appendix A for more information on the *Windows 95 Power Toolkit Online Companion*.

About the Online Companion

The *Windows 95 Power Toolkit Online Companion* is an informative tool as well as an annotated software library. It aids in your exploration of Windows 95 features while at the same time offering you the online support you need to get up to speed with this new operating system. The *Windows 95 Power Toolkit Online Companion* hyperlinks you to Windows 95 Internet resources: newsgroups, archives, and sites pertaining to Microsoft's new operating system. So you can just click on the reference name and jump directly to the resources you are interested in.

Perhaps one of the most valuable features of the *Windows 95 Power Toolkit Online Companion* is its Software Archive. Here, you'll find and be able to download the latest versions of all the software mentioned in *The Windows 95 Power Toolkit* that are freely available on the Internet. Available applications range from simple icon-editing programs to powerful compression utilities, and everything in-between. Also with Ventana Online's helpful description of the software you'll know exactly what you're getting and why. So you won't download the software just to find you have no use for it.

The *Windows 95 Power Toolkit Online Companion* also links you to the Ventana Library where you will find useful press and jacket information on a variety of Ventana Press offerings. Plus, you have access to a wide selection of exciting new releases and coming attractions. In addition, Ventana's Online Library allows you to order the books you want.

The *Windows 95 Power Toolkit Online Companion* represents Ventana Online's ongoing commitment to offering the most dynamic and exciting products possible. And soon Ventana Online will be adding more services, including more multimedia supplements, searchable indexes, and sections of the book reproduced and hyperlinked to the Internet resources they reference.

To access, connect via the World Wide Web to http://www.vmedia.com/win95.html

About the Companion CD-ROM

The CD-ROM included with your copy of the *Windows 95 Power Toolkit* contains a wealth of valuable software as well as the entire contents of the book in ASCII form. In short, this CD offers virtually everything you'll need to become a Windows 95 expert today.

Loading the CD-ROM is simple. With Windows 95 running insert the CD in the CD-ROM drive; the viewer program will autostart. A welcome screen will pop up that introduces the CD. Should you exit the viewer and wish to reactivate, double-click on the My Computer icon, double-click on the win95CD icon, then double-click on the Viewer icon.

Your choices for navigating the CD appear at the bottom of this screen. You can Exit from the CD; get Help on navigating; view, run, or install the included software; browse the entire contents of the book in ASCII form; learn more about Ventana; or view the Hot Picks.

If you click the CD Contents button, you will see a graphical representation of the contents of the CD. As you pass the mouse over the folders that contain the software, notice that the directory structure expands to show the folder's contents. Pass the mouse over the additional folders. You will see a picture or logo and a description of the program. The buttons beneath the description enable you to read more about the program, play a small demo, install the program to your hard drive, or run the program. Notice that only the enabled operations are highlighted. In order to run a program from the CD-ROM (without installing it to your hard drive), you will need the full 16MB of RAM recommended for Windows 95.

After you finish, you can return to the main screen by clicking Menu. If you click on the Ventana button, you can learn more about the products and services that Ventana offers. Simply move the mouse over the icons to learn more about Ventana's books, software, and online products. Return to the main screen by clicking Menu.

By clicking the Hot Picks button, you'll see a bookshelf that displays other Ventana titles. Click on a specific book to learn about other Ventana books or software that may be of interest to you. In all, this CD is very user-friendly, and you can always get help no matter where you are within the CD.

Below is a list of the contents of the *Windows 95 Power Toolkit Companion CD-ROM*.

Contents	Description
ACDSee	One of the fastest, easiest-to-use image viewers available for Windows. It supports all the common image formats, has full-color image previews, and features a slide show presentation.
ANIMATED CURSORS & CURSOR-CLIPS FOR WIN95/NT	A collection of 32 beautifully animated cursors and cursor-clips to replace the standard cursors of Win95/NT.
Astronomy Lab 2	Produces 7 movies that simulate a host of astronomical phenomena, 15 graphs that illustrate many fundamental concepts of astronomy, and 14 printed reports that contain predictions of the most important astronomical events.
Backdrop	Creates wallpaper with multiple bitmaps, uses tiled and single bitmaps in one wallpaper, has a point-and-click interface, and drags bitmaps into place.
BMP Wizard & Earth example	A Basic-like language to manipulate BMP images.
ClipFile	A Shell extension that copies the paths of selected files and folders to the clipboard.
COMt: the Telnet Modem	Allows you to use your favorite Windows communications program to communicate over TCP/IP.
DAUB	A calligraphic Windows program offering ease of use and high quality output at a fraction of the cost of other vector-based graphics programs.

Contents

Description

Drag And File — Streamlines and simplifies the work of managing files.

Easy Icons 95 — A complete icon management system.

EcopadNT — A Windows Notepad replacement that compresses pages.

FaxMail — A faxmail management system integrating FaxModem technologies into computer documentation generation.

Green Screen Savers — Screen savers that display an animated picture (with optional sound) on your screen for a user-selected period of time. The screen then goes completely blank so that Energy Star monitors can enter a power saving mode.

HyperTerminal Private Edition — A more powerful version of the Hilgraeves HyperTerminal communications program that is bundled in Windows 95.

IconScout — A powerful alternative to the Change Icon feature.

Insecta — Allows you to choose and drag wings and legs onto one of eight insects to bring them to life.

Instant File Access — Enables Windows 3.11 applications to use long filenames created by Windows 95 applications, and vice versa.

Kaleidoscope 95 — Generates stunningly beautiful geometric patterns that can be controlled by music if you have a sound card.

Ladybug — A software implementation of MPEG-1 decoder without audio associated.

Launchpad 95 — Lets you launch applications with the click of a button.

LViewPro — An image viewer/editor that is popular on the Internet.

Mbar — A menu bar that holds 30 icons and takes up less than 1/10 of the screen.

Middle Mouse Button — An application that intercepts the middle mouse button of a three-button mouse and converts a single middle button click into a default button (normally the left button) double-click.

NetNote 1 — An application that uses a "PostIt" note format to create graphical reminders.

PEM EdTex — A 32-bit text editor.

PSA Cards for Windows — A personal information manager.

PrintSwitch — A utility that makes changing your default Windows printer or its settings as easy as two clicks or a HotKey press.

Printscreen 95 — A Print screen program that places a screen print button on your desktop that will "float" on top of all of your Windows applications.

RTVReco — Redials a connection that was lost due to the line disconnection.

Contents / Description

Contents	Description
Screen Saver Activate for Windows 95	Allows for convenient activation of the currently selected screen saver by a single mouse click or by a configurable hotkey.
Seven Animated Cursors	A collection of seven sample cursors.
Shutdown	Makes shutdown a shortcut on the desktop.
SmartSurf Online Usage Monitor	A free Windows online time and usage monitoring system.
SNAPSHOT/32	Automatically captures Windows 95 screens.
Somar ACTS	Allows you to set the internal clock of your computer with accuracy of about a second.
System Monitor 32	Monitors the performance of your computer in real time.
TextPad	Provides the power and functionality to satisfy your most demanding text editing requirements.
The Raven	A text management utility.
ThunderByte Anti-Virus	Delivers the ultimate approach in anti-virus protection.
TrayIcon	Provides one-click access to applications.
Tray Exit	Allows you to easily shut down Windows.
TTC Time Client Application	Allows you to retrieve the Greenwich Mean Time from any supporting Internet host.
VidRes	Enables you to quickly switch the display resolution of your machine without making the change permanent.
WebForms	A World Wide Web forms generator that automatically creates HTML forms and reads their responses.
WEB Wizard: The Duke of URL	A program designed to help you create home pages for the World Wide Web.
WinBatch and DLL101	A Windows Batch Language that you can use to write real Windows batch files.
WinGO for Windows 95	Adds an icon to the system tray which, when clicked, brings up a menu containing shortcuts to the directories you use most often.
WinImage	A disk image management utility.
WinPack	A compression utility.
WinShade	A desktop utility that makes it easy to switch between programs.
WinZip 95	Brings the convenience of Windows to the use of ZIP files.
WWPlus	A wallpaper manager and screen saver.

Index

O

P

S

Internet Resources

The Windows Internet Tour Guide, Second Edition
The Macintosh Internet Tour Guide, Second Edition

$29.95, 424 pages, illustrated
Windows part #: 174-0, Macintosh part #: 173-2

This runaway bestseller has been updated to include
Ventana Mosaic™, the hot new Web reader, along with
graphical software for e-mail, file downloading, newsreading
and more. Noted for its down-to-earth documentation, the
new edition features expanded listings and a look at Net
developments. Includes three companion disks.

Walking the World Wide Web, Second Edition

$39.95, 800 pages, illustrated, part #: 298-4

A listing that never goes out of date! This groundbreaking
bestseller includes a CD-ROM enhanced with Ventana's
WebWalker™ technology, and updated online components
that make it the richest resource available for Web travelers.

HTML Publishing on the Internet for Windows
HTML Publishing on the Internet for Macintosh

$49.95, 512 pages, illustrated
Windows part #: 229-1, Macintosh part #: 228-3

Successful publishing for the Internet requires an understanding
of "nonlinear" presentation as well as specialized software.
Both are here. Learn how HTML builds the hot links that let
readers choose their own paths—and how to use effective
design to drive your message for them. The enclosed CD-ROM
includes Netscape Navigator, HoTMetaL LITE, graphic viewer,
templates conversion software and more!

Bestseller

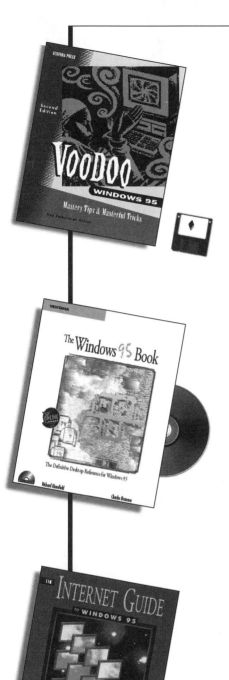

Voodoo Windows 95

$24.95, 504 pages, illustrated, part #: 145-7

Users will need voodoo to make the move to Windows 95! Nelson is back with more secrets, shortcuts and spells than ever. Scores of tips—many never before published—on installing, customizing, editing, printing, virtual memory, Internet connections and much more. Organized by task for easy reference. The companion disk contains shareware utilities, fonts and magic!

The Windows 95 Book

$39.95, 1232 pages, illustrated, part #: 154-6

The anxiously awaited revamp of Windows is finally here— which means new working styles for PC users.
This new handbook offers an insider's look at the all-new interface—arming users with tips and techniques for file management, desktop design, optimizing and much more. A must-have for a prosperous '95! The companion CD-ROM features tutorials, demos, previews and online help plus utilities, screen savers, wallpaper and sounds.

Internet Guide for Windows 95

$24.95, 552 pages, illustrated, part #: 260-7

The *Internet Guide for Windows 95* shows how to use Windows 95's built-in communications tools to access and navigate the Net. Whether you're using The Microsoft Network or an independent Internet provider and Microsoft *Plus!*, this easy-to-read guide helps you started quickly and easily. Learn how to e-mail, download files, and navigate the World Wide Web and take a tour of top sites. An *Online Companion* on Ventana Online features hypertext links to top sites listed in the book.

Books marked with this logo include a free Internet *Online Companion*™, featuring archives of free utilities plus a software archive and links to other Internet resources.

It's Official.

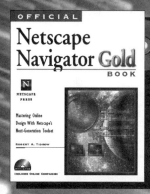
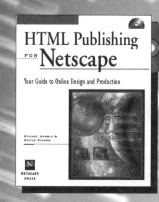

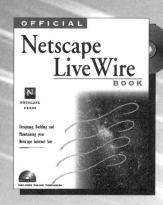
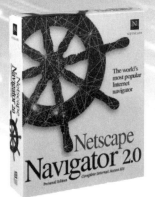

To order any Ventana title, complete this order form and mail or fax it to us, with payment, for quick shipment.

TITLE	PART #	QTY	PRICE	TOTAL

SHIPPING

For all standard orders, please ADD $4.50/first book, $1.35/each additional.
For *Internet Publishing Kit* orders, ADD $6.50/first kit, $2.00/each additional.
For "two-day air," ADD $8.25/first book, $2.25/each additional.
For "two-day air" on the kits, ADD $10.50/first kit, $4.00/each additional.
For orders to Canada, ADD $6.50/book.
For orders sent C.O.D., ADD $4.50 to your shipping rate.
North Carolina residents must ADD 6% sales tax.
International orders require additional shipping charges.

SUBTOTAL = $ _____
SHIPPING = $ _____
TOTAL   = $ _____

Name _____ Daytime telephone _____
Company _____
Address (No PO Box) _____
City _____ State _____ Zip _____
Payment enclosed ___VISA ___MC ___ Acc't # _____ Exp. date _____
Signature _____ Exact name on card _____

Mail to: Ventana • PO Box 13964 • Research Triangle Park, NC 27709-3964 ☎ 800/743-5369 • Fax 919/544-9472

Check your local bookstore or software retailer for these and other bestselling titles, or call toll free: **800/743-5369**